U.S. Leadership in Wartime

U.S. Leadership in Wartime

Clashes, Controversy, and Compromise

VOLUME 2

Dr. Spencer C. Tucker
Volume Editor

Dr. Paul G. Pierpaoli Jr.
Associate Editor

A B C ⬛ C L I O

Santa Barbara, California
Denver, Colorado
Oxford, England

Copyright 2009 by ABC-CLIO, LLC

Library of Congress Cataloging-in-Publication Data

U.S. leadership in wartime : clashes, controversy, and compromise/Spencer C. Tucker, editor.
     p. cm.
  Includes bibliographical references and index.
  ISBN 978-1-59884-172-5 (hard copy : acid-free paper)—ISBN 978-1-59884-173-2 (e-book)
  1. United States—History, Military.   2. Civil-military relations—United States—History.
3. Politics and war—United States—History.   4. Civil supremacy over the military—
United States.   5. Political leadership—United States—Case studies.   6. Command of troops—
Case studies.   7. Generals—United States—Biography.   8. Statesmen—United States—
Biography. I. Tucker, Spencer, 1937–   II. Title: United States leadership in wartime.
  E181.U825   2009
  355.00973—dc22

                                    2009010010

12 11 10 09 1 2 3 4 5

This book is also available on the World Wide Web as an eBook.
Visit www.abc-clio.com for details.

ABC-CLIO, LLC
130 Cremona Drive, P.O. Box 1911
Santa Barbara, California 93116–1911

This book is printed on acid-free paper ∞

Manufactured in the United States of America

For Becky Snyder, president of ABC-CLIO,
recognized leader in academic publishing,
staunch advocate for the study of military history,
and dear friend.

About the Editor

Spencer C. Tucker, PhD, graduated from the Virginia Military Institute in 1959, studied at the University of Bordeaux, France, on a Fulbright Fellowship, and earned his master's and doctorate in modern European history at the University of North Carolina at Chapel Hill. He then served two years of active duty as an army captain in the Office of the Assistant Chief of Staff for Intelligence.

Dr. Tucker taught for 30 years at Texas Christian University in Fort Worth, including one year as a Research Fellow at the Smithsonian Institution. He then held the John Biggs Chair in Military History at the Virginia Military Institute for six years prior to his retirement from teaching in July 2003. Dr. Tucker is currently senior fellow in military history for ABC-CLIO Publishing.

Dr. Tucker has written or edited 30 books and encyclopedias treating military or naval history, as well as numerous book chapters and articles. He has been honored with a number of writing awards, including two John Lyman awards from the North American Society for Oceanic History. His biography *Stephen Decatur: A Life Most Bold and Daring* won the Theodore Roosevelt and Franklin Roosevelt Prize for best book in naval history in 2004. His encyclopedias have also won numerous awards, including the Society for Military History Best Reference Book award in 2008 for the five-volume *The Encyclopedia of the Cold War*.

Editorial Advisory Board by Chapter

ABC-CLIO Military History Advisory Board

Contents

WORLD WAR I

Leadership in World War I

Few wars in history have been more misunderstood than World War I. It is, however, one of the true major turning points in modern history. Although popularly seen as four years of mindless bloodshed and carnage that accomplished nothing, changed nothing, and only led to World War II 21 years later, a closer examination of what was then called the Great War reveals a far more complex picture. World War I changed forever the way the world had worked for the previous 100 years, completely overturning the international system set in place by the Congress of Vienna in 1815 following the defeat of Napoleon I. In his 2001 book, *Forgotten Victory: The First World War, Myths and Realities*, Gary Sheffield correctly called the Great War "the key event of the twentieth century, from which everything else flowed."

At the start of 1914, a large portion of the world was under the control of four great continental European and Eurasian empires. By the end of 1918, four of those empires—the German Hohenzollern, the Russian Romanov, the Austro-Hungarian Habsburg, and the Ottoman Empire—were gone. World War I fostered colonial unrest throughout the world, marking the beginning of the end of colonialism. It is hard to conceive of the Bolsheviks coming to power in Russia without the war, and it marked a definite shift in power toward the United States, which by the end of the war was the world's financial center and largest producer of manufactured goods. World War I also helped to set up World War II. Many historians now regard the two world wars as essentially two phases of the same global conflagration. The Paris peace settlement of 1919 helped bring that about. As Marshal Ferdinand Foch so clairvoyantly noted at the time, "This is not a peace treaty, this is a 20-year cease-fire."

World War II, the second phase, proved to be even more cataclysmic, but in a somewhat different way—more modern and seemingly more relevant. When World War II ended, it was clear that it was over. Rather than both sides stopping from sheer exhaustion and ending in armistice, as happened in 1918, World War II ended in the decisive defeat of one side by the other and the loser's unconditional surrender. The period of global conflict from 1939 to 1945, then, completely overshadowed that from 1914 to 1918 in both the popular and scholarly minds. World War I seemed completely irrelevant and it became something of a forgotten war until only recently. Just within the last 25 years has a completely new body of World War I scholarship begun to overturn the rigid and dogmatic interpretations of that war that had solidified by about the end of the 1920s.

During the mid- to late 1930s, the professional soldiers of most nations were starting to integrate fully into their military systems the battlefield lessons of World War I, but by then the storm clouds of World War II were about to overwhelm the world. When that war ended in 1945, any of the military lessons from the Great War seemed overshadowed and irrelevant, especially when compared with the mass bomber wings, the airborne divisions, and the fast-moving tank formations of World War II. The Great War appeared to have nothing to teach the modern soldier. It was, after all, four years of endless stagnation and trench warfare. The reason for the mindless slaughter clearly seemed to rest squarely with the incompetence and even criminal stupidity of the senior officer corps of all the armies involved. It was not worth the effort to study the war. Thus the "Mud and Blood" and "Lions Led by Donkeys" schools of military history went largely unchallenged until the 1980s.

The battlefield reality of World War I was far more complex and actually far more dynamic than appears to be the case. In the years leading up to 1914, a number of ground-breaking advances in the technologies of warfare would all converge on the battlefields of Europe to produce two of the most revolutionary paradigm shifts in the history of warfare. There has never been such a radical and rapid transformation in how wars were fought. The change in the way armies operated on the battlefield between 1914 and 1918 was far greater than any similar change that took place during the 1939–1945 period. With the exception of radar and nuclear weapons, almost all of the other technologies we associate with warfare in World War II made their battlefield debuts during World War I or in the years just immediately preceding it. These include the internal combustion engine; the tank; the submarine; sonar; the aircraft carrier; radio; electronic warfare; chemical warfare; rapid-firing artillery; indirect artillery fire; bomber, fighter, and ground-attack aircraft; and machine guns and other automatic small arms. Writing in a 1996 monograph published by the British Combat and Strategic Studies Institute, Colonel (later Major General) Jonathan Bailey argued that World War I was "a military revolution which was the most significant development in the history of warfare to date, *and remains so.*"

The first of the two great paradigm shifts centered on mechanization. This was, however, a change that did not occur evenly across the spectrum of war-fighting technologies. The two principal elements of combat power are firepower and maneuver. Since the dawn of warfare these two elements have been in a constant tug-of-war with each other as technology evolved, with neither element gaining the upper hand over the other for very long. But by 1914, firepower mechanization had gotten far ahead of maneuver or mobility mechanization. Innovations such as breech-loading artillery with stable recoil systems, magazine-fed rifles, and the machine gun dramatically increased the volume and lethality of firepower.

Maneuver—defined as battlefield movement to gain positional advantage—was still largely limited to human and animal muscle power at the start of the war. By the end of the war, however, the battlefield applications of the internal combustion engine were finally beginning to mature. The horse had dominated warfare for thousands of years, but between 1914 and 1918 it almost completely disappeared from the battlefield. Armies would continue to use horses through World War II, but by then the storied war steed of history had been reduced to little more than a painfully slow auxiliary source of transport power. The result of the long period of imbalance between firepower and maneuver was trench warfare, and ever since the names of battles like Ver-

Artillerymen and their 37mm gun in the 32nd Division during fighting in Alsace. (National Archives/U.S. Army Signal Corps)

dun, the Somme, and Passchandeale have been the bywords for mindless slaughter and the worst horrors of modern warfare.

The second radical paradigm shift was the change from two-dimensional to three-dimensional warfare. Up until World War I, battles had always been fought and decided at the line of contact between the two armies. The introduction of military aviation took war-fighting into its third dimension. The long-held military concept of dominating the high ground assumed an entirely new meaning. Longer-range artillery and the perfection of the techniques of indirect fire—the ability to engage and hit targets far beyond the visual range of the gun crew—added the element of depth to the battlefield and vastly increased the space over which battle was prosecuted. The battle zone expanded far beyond the line of contact. Armies for the first time had the capability to strike deep into their opponent's rear and base areas, and even to attack directly the enemy's homeland and industrial base. That in turn made World War I the first total war, in the modern sense. The respective armies of nations were no longer at war with each other; entire nations and all their resources and populations were now involved.

Is it any wonder, then, that the military leaders of all nations in World War I had such difficulty coming to grips with the radical new realities of modern warfare? Although present-day soldiers now routinely think in such terms, soldiers in 1914 had never encountered such challenges. Military planners did not have a frame of reference or even the basic intellectual tools necessary to solve the new problems immediately.

Eddie Rickenbacker, the leading American ace of World War I, shown with other aviators of his 94th Aero Pursuit "Hat in the Ring" Squadron in France, 1917. (Bettmann/Corbis)

The initial result was tactical and operational gridlock on a massive scale. By 1918, however, most armies were starting to come to terms with the radical changes and the tactical problems of the modern battlefield were close to being solved. The war, however, ended in mutual strategic exhaustion before either side could bring together all the disparate elements necessary to achieve decisive victory.

Why was World War I misunderstood for so long? Much of the long-held image of World War I was based on the vivid descriptions of contemporary poets and popular writers who had directly experienced the horrors of the Great War. The dramatic poems of Wilfred Owen ("Anthem for Doomed Youth"), Rupert Brooke ("The Dead"), Siegfried Sassoon ("I Stood with the Dead"), and Robert Service ("On the Wire") and the searing novels of Erich Maria Remarque (*All Quiet on the Western Front*), Robert Graves (*Good-bye to All That*), Siegfried Sassoon (*Memoirs of an Infantry Officer*), Vera Brittain (*Testament of Youth*), and C. S. Forester (*The General*) left a lasting imprint on the popular mind and for many years influenced the scholarly mind as well. With few exceptions, the most notable being Germany's Ernst Jünger (*Storm of Steel*), World War I writers and poets cast their own experiences in a largely antiheroic light, which profoundly influenced the way people looked at war in general for the remainder of the 20th century. There can be little doubt that these important literary works made vital contributions to understanding the realities of modern warfare and their effects on individual human beings. But as Brian Bond pointed out in his book, *The Unquiet Western Front*, the literary writers either ignored, or failed to address convincingly, the larger historical, political, and strategic questions of the war. What was the war about and why was it fought? Not that the historians and military theorists of the same period did any better job addressing those questions.

World War I marked the emergence of America as a major power on the global stage. Although the United States sat out almost the first three years of the war, the large-scale insertion of U.S. military units starting in early to mid-1918 proved to be the weight that tipped the strategic scales against Germany and the Central Powers. By the end of 1917, all of the European powers were exhausted and almost out of manpower. The Bolsheviks had come to power in Russia and had taken that nation out of the war. With its enemy in the east eliminated, Germany shifted large numbers of troops to the Western Front to mass there sufficient combat power for a last-ditch attempt to force a militarily decisive solution before American troops could arrive in large numbers. The Germans launched five massive offensives between March and July 1918. These failed, though not by much. American troops, some already in the line, now arrived in France in large numbers and the Allies went over on the offensive, not to lose it the rest of the war.

U.S. president Woodrow Wilson had tried to stay out of the war, and, on its outbreak in 1914, he called on Americans to be neutral in "thought" as well as in action. The United States entered the war because of a mistaken German strategic decision. On January 31, 1917, Germany announced that it would be resuming unrestricted submarine warfare, gambling that, while the United States would no doubt enter the war as a result, Britain, which had to import a majority of its food and raw materials, could be starved into submission before U.S. military strength could be brought to bear in any meaningful way. The U.S. government had repeatedly warned the German government that the sinking of American merchantmen and loss of American lives would bring war. Had Germany not made this decision, Russia still would have dropped out and the United States would not have entered the war, and no doubt the Germans would have won it. Soon the sinking of U.S. merchant ships, coupled with the revelation of the Zimmerman Telegram (a diplomatic effort by the German government to get Mexico to declare war on the United States should Germany and the United States go to war) and revelations of German sabotage in the United States, propelled the nation into the war, on April 6, 1917.

By 1917, Wilson hoped to refashion the international order along the lines of what has come to be known as Wilsonian internationalism. This would best be embodied by his Fourteen Points, enunciated in January 1918, the capstone of which was the creation of a League of Nations to help maintain the new world order. Wilson knew that the United States had to enter the war in order to preside over the peace settlement and to implement these Wilsonian ideals. True to form, Wilson himself headed the American delegation to the Paris Peace Conference in 1919, against the advice of many who claimed that such wrangling was best left to seasoned diplomats rather than idealistic politicians. Once the United States entered the war, President Wilson, who knew nothing of the conduct of war, became a sort of cheerleader for the war effort. In two fundamental ways, Wilson erred. First, he styled the war as a conflict to "make the world safe for democracy" and, second, as "the war to end all wars." It was neither, and such positions contributed to the profound American disillusionment with its participation after the war, leading to isolationism.

To lead the American war effort in France, Wilson selected General John J. Pershing as commander of the American Expeditionary Forces (AEF). Wilson left the conduct of the war up to him and his subordinate commanders. He did make clear, however, that the United States was an "associated," and not "allied" power (simply fighting the same enemy, Germany), in order to disassociate the United States from the secret Allied partition treaties being published by the Bolshevik government. He and Pershing also insisted that the American forces be held together and fight as a single army. This proved impossible in the crisis of the spring of 1918, but, once that had passed, Pershing did command a separate American army in the field.

When the United States entered the war, the U.S. Army consisted of a mere 130,000 regular soldiers and some 70,000 National Guardsmen. Over the course of the next 20 months, America raised an army of more than 4 million men and managed to send about half that number across the Atlantic. In May 1917, the Americans had only 1,308 troops in Europe and the German High Command estimated that based on the British experience, the U.S. Army would need 10 months or more to organize, equip, and train any major units. By the time the Germans launched their first major offensive in March 1918, there were only 245,378 American troops and seven divisions in France, and only one of those divisions was even close to being ready for combat. But then the numbers started to increase almost exponentially. Within 2 months that number more than doubled to 667,100, and by July 1918 there were 1.2 million American soldiers in Europe. By the end of the war that November, the number had grown to just a little more than 2 million.

The navy was ready for the war and soon destroyers were operating with the British Navy. The army was not prepared, however. The rapid expansion, training, equipping, fielding, and deploying of the U.S. Army in World War I was a masterpiece of organization, management, and above all, leadership. Much of this was owing to the hard work of Secretary of War Newton Baker. It also proved a good rehearsal for the even larger and more rapid expansion the American military would have to undergo at the start of World War II. Nonetheless, it is important to understand that the United States tipped the balance in World War I more through the sheer weight of numbers than through combat skill and war-fighting virtuosity. When the Americans finally got into the war, they too came with a mostly pre-1914 mindset as to how wars should be fought. Many American officers were disdainful of the almost complete loss of basic marksmanship skills in all the European armies. They believed that traditional American straight shooting would soon set matters right. They learned very quickly, however, and at a high price, that they were in a war like no other before in all recorded history.

The first American units did not enter combat until late March 1918 and the U.S. Army did not fight its first divisional-level battle until Cantigny on May 28. By the time the war ended that November, American losses were 53,402 killed in action, 63,114 dead from disease or non-battle injuries, and 204,002 wounded. To put those losses in perspective, the 116,516 American soldiers who died in World War I were twice the total and in one-tenth of the time of the number who died in Vietnam.

Another major problem the Americans faced was a complete lack of officers with experience commanding anything much larger than a battalion. The U.S. Army had brigades, divisions, and corps during the Civil War, but they were not permanent organizations and all were disbanded immediately after the war's end in 1865. Eche-

Mules hauling ammunition to American forces near St. Baussant, France, on September 13, 1918. (National Archives)

lons above the regimental level were again established April 1898 at the start of the Spanish-American War, but the war ended that August and within two months the brigades, divisions, and corps were again disbanded. In the immediate years leading up to World War I, the U.S. Army conducted various experiments with echelons above the regimental level, but those units existed for the most part on paper only. The U.S. Army's first permanently organized division, today's 1st Infantry Division, was not established until May 24, 1917.

Along with a lack of experienced higher-level commanders, the army also suffered from a dire shortage of trained staff officers. Large-unit operations require highly skilled and specialized staffs to plan and coordinate all the complex and interlocking components of a modern battle. Staff skills and knowledge had atrophied during the years following the Civil War. It was not until wide-ranging reforms introduced in 1903 under Secretary of War Elihu Root that the U.S. Army had a general staff or even a systematic program of continuing professional education for officers. When America entered World War I, the U.S. Army and its staff systems were very much a work in progress. In 1917, AEF commander General Pershing considered both the French and the British staff systems. He adopted the simpler and more straightforward four-bureau French model for the AEF, consisting of Personnel and Administration; Intelligence; Operations and Training; and Logistics and Supply. Pershing also established a staff college at Langres, France, to provide crash training for the 500 general staff officers the AEF needed to operate.

When Pershing became the chief of staff of the U.S. Army in 1921, he put his former AEF chief of staff Major General James Harbord in charge of a staff reorganization board. Harbord's board adopted the French-inspired AEF model as the standard staff structure for the whole U.S. Army. With only minor changes, that system remains in place to this day. When the North Atlantic Treaty Organization (NATO) was established following World War II, the American/French system of staff organization became the model for the staffs of NATO's combined military commands. All of NATO's members eventually changed their own staff systems to mirror the American/French system, which has since been adopted by almost all major Western armies.

Despite America's key role in the final if indecisive defeat of the Central Powers, the United States emerged from the war with an ambivalent attitude toward its new status as a world power. By November 1918, the German Army clearly was no longer capable of achieving the decisive military victory it had sought for four years, but it was far from a defeated force. The Germans still had not been pushed back to their home territory, and were the most tenacious and technically skillful defenders in modern military history. Had they chosen to continue fighting on the strategic and operational defensive, the war most certainly would have dragged on for much longer than it did. But it would not have changed the outcome. Germany was completely exhausted and slowly strangling under the weight of the Allied naval blockade. The new German chancellor, Prince Max of Baden, attempted to secure a peace settlement based on President

U.S. general of the armies John J. Pershing leads a parade through the Arc de Triomphe and along the Champs-Élysées in Paris on Bastille Day, July 14, 1919. (Library of Congress)

Woodrow Wilson's Fourteen Points. It was not to be. An armistice was concluded on November 11, 1918, with Germany agreeing to evacuate occupied territory and to surrender most of its navy and much of its war-making capacity. Peace terms were to be drafted at a subsequent conference, but it was clear that it would not be a negotiated peace, but a dictated settlement, as the Germans had dictated peace to France in 1871 following the Franco-Prussian War.

When the Allies assembled at Paris to draft the peace settlement after the war, the French had ambitious plans to ensure that Germany did not again invade France. Premier Georges Clemenceau sought to separate the Rhineland from Germany and form it into one or more states that would then be permanently garrisoned by an Allied force. It was not to be. The ensuing Treaty of Versailles, while harsh on Germany, was basically written not by the French, but by the British and the Americans, who favored a lenient peace. As it turned out, it did not matter what type of peace settlement was hammered out, for it was never enforced. Britain and the United States retreated into isolation, leaving France, a power inferior in population and resources to Germany, to enforce the settlement alone. Wilson got his cherished League of Nations, but it lacked the policing power the French wanted, and too many people came to place a misguided trust in an organization, the strongest weapon of which was economic sanctions. In effect, Germany was left to police itself and to decide whether it would live up to the peace terms. Given what had happened in World War I, that was too much to ask. The growth of nationalism and militarism in Germany, coupled with chronic inflation and the Great Depression, brought Adolf Hitler to power, and he was determined to resume World War I and reverse its verdict.

In recent years the generation of American soldiers, sailors, airmen, and marines who fought in World War II has come to be called "The Greatest Generation." But it is important to recognize that the then-young GIs who carried the major individual burdens of combat in that war were not of the same generation as their senior leaders, the ones who carried the burdens of the planning, organization, coordination, and the strategic direction of the war. There were really two greatest generations of Americans in World War II. Most of the members of the senior of those two generations had learned their professions and honed their leadership skills in World War I. Key American leaders, such as George C. Marshall, William O. Donovan, Courtney Hodges, Douglas MacArthur, George S. Patton, Harry S. Truman, and many others served in relatively junior positions on World War I battlefields and would play key senior leadership roles in World War II. President Franklin D. Roosevelt served in World War I as a highly effective assistant secretary of the navy. Their World War I experiences are integral to understanding their roles in World War II. The brief but incredibly violent apprenticeship Americans served in World War I went a long way in reducing the slope of the steep learning curve they would have to climb again 21 years later.

David T. Zabecki

References

Bailey, J.B.A. *The First World War and the Birth of Modern Style of Warfare,* "The Occasional, Number 22." Camberley, England: British Staff College, 1996.

Sheffield, Gary. *Forgotten Victory: The First World War Myths and Realities.* London: Headline Book Publishing, 2001.

About the Author

General David T. Zabecki, PhD, retired from the Army of the United States in 2007. He began his military career in 1966, serving in Vietnam as an infantry rifleman. After receiving his commission as a field artillery officer, he commanded as a captain, lieutenant colonel, colonel, brigadier general, and major general. In 1995 and 1996, he served in the Balkans. From 2000 to 2002, he was assigned to the Pentagon as the deputy chief of the Army Reserve. In 2003, he served in Israel as the senior security adviser on the U.S. Coordinating and Monitoring Mission, responsible for advancing the Roadmap to Peace in the Middle East initiative. In 2004 and 2005, he was the Department of Defense executive director for all World War II 60th anniversary observances in Europe. In 2005 and 2006, he commanded the U.S. Southern European Task Force Rear and served as the senior U.S. Army commander south of the Alps.

General Zabecki is a graduate of the U.S. Army Command and General Staff College, the U.S. Army War College, and the John F. Kennedy School of Government Executive Program for Russian and American General Officers, and he holds a PhD in military history from the Royal Military College of Science, Cranfield University. General Zabecki is the author or editor of eight books on military history. He also has been an assistant editor of several ABC-CLIO encyclopedias. From 2000 to 2008 he was the editor of *Vietnam* magazine, and he is currently the senior historian for the Weider History Group, the world's largest publisher of history magazines.

World War I Battles

Cantigny, Battle of
(May 28–31, 1918)

First offensive action involving American Expeditionary Forces (AEF) in the Picardy region of France. In response to an appeal by the Allies in March 1918, AEF commander General John J. Pershing agreed to send American troops to Picardy to help halt the German spring, or Ludendorff, offensives. The U.S. 1st Division, which had at the time nearly completed its training in northeastern France, was the most immediately available combat force.

As the 1st Division assembled in Picardy, Pershing viewed their training and, according to George C. Marshall, then a lieutenant colonel, told them: "You are about to enter this great battle of the greatest war in history, and in that battle you will represent the mightiest nation engaged. . . . Our people today are hanging expectant upon your deeds. The future is hanging upon your action in this conflict."

The 1st Division closed on the Cantigny sector near Montdidier on April 26 between the French 45th and 162nd Colonial Divisions, which shifted left and right on the line to make way for it. 1st Division commander Major General Robert Lee Bullard had fallen ill just prior to the deployment from eastern France, but his chief of staff, Colonel Campbell King, oversaw the movement.

Initially, the front near Cantigny had no completed trenches or barbed wire entanglements to separate the contending forces, but these appurtenances of war soon appeared. Meanwhile, German mortar and artillery fire from the north nibbled away daily at the division's strength. General Bullard termed Cantigny the "gateway toward the British Army," the separation of which from the French was the chief object of the Ludendorff offensives.

Colonel Hanson E. Ely's 28th Infantry Regiment was selected to make the assault and fell back to the rear to rehearse. Pershing and representatives of the Allied governments observed the attack, which began at 6:45 a.m. on May 28, following a one-hour artillery preparation. Thirty-five minutes later the 28th Infantry had secured the objective to the north and east of the small farming village of Cantigny. True to German doctrine, they counterattacked immediately. Major Theodore Roosevelt Jr.'s 1st Battalion, 26th Infantry, reinforced a threatened point of the line. Three-quarters of the division's losses of more than 1,000 men killed, wounded, missing, or captured in the battle came during the May 28–31 defense of the swiftly secured objective.

Cantigny was a regimental-sized action conducted by a division, but Pershing was determined that this first offensive action

U.S. troops firing machine guns against the Germans during the Battle of Cantigny. This battle of May 28–31, 1918, was the first major offensive action for the American Expeditionary Forces in World War I. (Duncan-Clark, S. J. and W. R. Plewman, *Pictorial History of the Great War, with Canada in the Great War,* 1919)

of his AEF would succeed and serve as a demonstration to the other Allied Powers that the Americans could hold their own in combat. The 1st Division met that challenge, but ahead lay more hard fighting and many more casualties.

John F. Votaw

References

Bullard, Robert Lee. *American Soldiers Also Fought.* New York: Maurice H. Louis, 1939.

———. *Personalities and Reminiscences of the War.* Garden City, NY: Doubleday, Page, 1925.

Coffman, Edward M. *The War to End All Wars: The American Military Experience in World War I.* Lexington: University Press of Kentucky, 1998.

Marshall, George C. *Memoirs of My Services in the World War, 1917–1918.* Boston: Houghton Mifflin, 1976.

Château-Thierry (May 31–June 5, 1918)

During the period March 21 to July 18, the German Army mounted five major operations on the Western Front. These were known as the spring, or Ludendorff, offensives for their chief architect, 1st Quartermaster General of the German Army *General der Infanterie* Erich Ludendorff. The offensives were made possible by the defeat of the Russians on the Eastern Front, which allowed the Germans to transfer resources to the West in an effort to achieve victory before large numbers of Americans could arrive. It is clear in retrospect that the Germans erred in retaining too many men in the East initially.

Although they resulted in the German capture of considerable terrain and large numbers of Allied troops, the first two German offensives, michael (the St. Quentin Offensive) and georgette (the Lys Offensive), failed to achieve any decisive results. Following a brief period of consolidation, Ludendorff on May 27 launched his third drive, Operation blücher. Ludendorff hoped that a diversionary thrust toward Paris would cause the French to transfer all their reserves and American Expeditionary Forces (AEF) divisions to defend the French capital. The German plan called for the men of Prince Wilhelm's Army Group to advance only about 12 miles and halt after crossing the Vesle River and taking the high ground to the south. Ludendorff then would initiate a rapid shift north to execute Operation hagen against the British by Crown Prince Rupprecht's Army Group.

Operation blücher was launched in the area south of St. Quentin and west of Reims, with the Chemin des Dames ridge as the initial objective and the Vesle River as the final objective. The German Seventh Army would make the main effort, attacking from north to south with 29 divisions along a 25-mile front. Two smaller supporting attacks would be conducted by the German First Army on the left (Operation georz) and the Eighteenth Army on the right (Operation yorck).

This sector was perhaps the weakest of the Western Front. The French Sixth Army had 11 front line and 5 reserve divisions, including the British IX Corps, which had been transferred here from Flanders to reconstitute in what was supposed to be a quiet sector of the front. For the attack, the Germans massed 5,263 artillery pieces against 1,422 French and British guns in the highest artillery superiority achieved by the Germans during any Western Front battles of the war. The fire plan was worked out by the brilliant artillerist

Colonel Georg Bruchmüller. The German guns opened up at 2:00 a.m. on May 27 and caught the Allies almost completely by surprise. The carnage was all the worse because French Sixth Army commander General Denis Duchêsne, reluctant to yield an inch of French soil to the Germans, ignored French Army commander General Henri Philippe Pétain's orders to adopt a defense-in-depth with a thinly held front line. Instead, he packed his forces into the front lines, where they were easy targets for the German guns, which fired 3 million rounds on the first day alone.

The German infantry moved forward at 4:40 a.m. and within two hours had captured the eastern end of the Chemin des Dames ridge. By 10:00 a.m., the first German units were across the Aisne River, three miles to the rear. Employing the infiltration tactics perfected earlier, the attackers moved so swiftly that the French were unable to withdraw their artillery from the north side of the Aisne, and the Germans captured some 650 French guns.

By the end of the first day, the German lead elements had crossed the Vesle and had advanced 13 miles, exceeding the objective for the entire operation. It was the largest single-day advance on the Western Front during World War I. On the evening of the second day, the German penetration was 15 miles deep and 42 miles wide at its base. Ludendorff had accomplished his geographic objective far more quickly than he thought possible, but there were as yet no signs that the Allied reserve units were starting to move out of Flanders. Rather than following through with his own plan, Ludendorff once more allowed himself to be diverted by his own tactical success. He ordered the Seventh Army to continue pushing toward Paris, and he committed and redirected the reserves he had been husbanding for

Operation hagen. At no point, however, was Paris an actual German objective. The German Army did not have anywhere near the mobility or logistical capabilities to sustain such a drive, even if that had been the intent. Ludendorff, then, essentially squandered precious resources in order to reinforce an already failed diversion.

For the next several days the German steamroller surged forward. French front line resistance disintegrated. Pétain committed his 16 reserve divisions with little apparent effect. Then, doing exactly what Ludendorff had originally wanted, Pétain requested the immediate transfer of the Allied theater reserves from Flanders to his control. But Allied commander General Ferdinand Foch recognized that unlike michael or georgette, blücher was advancing into the Allied depth and would almost certainly reach its culminating point and become an operational dead end for the Germans. Foch clearly possessed a better appreciation of the strategic situation than Ludendorff at that point.

Initially Foch refused to send Pétain any additional support; but then he finally began slowly feeding reinforcements into the sector. On May 30, AEF commander General John J. Pershing received an urgent request from Pétain for assistance. He had available only two divisions, the 2nd under Major General Omar Bundy and the 3rd commanded by Major General Joseph T. Dickman. The 3rd Division was rushed by motor and rail to Château-Thierry on the Marne.

The first Americans to arrive were two companies of the 7th Machine Gun Battalion of the 3rd Division. Traveling 110 miles in trucks for 22 hours, they arrived at the front on the afternoon of May 31 and took up position to protect bridges over the Marne at Château-Thierry. That evening the infantry regiments began to arrive. The 2nd Division received its orders to move on May 30 and did not trail the 3rd by much. The 2nd Division, composed of regular army troops and one

The road where U.S. forces first encountered the Germans in the key Battle of Château-Thierry, during which the Americans halted the German advance on Paris, May 31–June 5, 1918. (Forbes, Edgar Allen, ed. *Leslie's Photographic Review of the Great War,* 1920)

marine brigade, took up position along a line running east and north of Château-Thierry. In the ensuing heavy combat beginning on June 1, the 17,000-man 3rd Infantry Division helped to stop the German advance, earning the nickname it still carries, "The Rock of the Marne."

During June 1–4, the Americans repulsed all German attempts to cross the river. On June 6, the 2nd Division's attack at Belleau Wood, although it became a symbol for heroism, was badly handled and the 4th Marine Brigade suffered heavy casualties for minimal gains. Nonetheless, both divisions had fought well, and the Germans' worst nightmare had come to pass. The U.S. Army had finally arrived on the battlefield in force and had more than proved its mettle against battle-hardened German units.

On June 6, Ludendorff ordered Operation blücher ended. The Germans were less than 42 miles from Paris, but they were in no position to exploit their advantage. In 11 days of fighting, the Allies had suffered approximately 127,000 casualties; the Germans, who were now far less able to replace their losses, had sustained 105,000 casualties and now had a large salient that they would have to defend. German lines of communication into the blücher salient were poor and completely incapable of supporting the logistics flow necessary to support the position. Worse still, Ludendorff had squandered much of the resources he needed for hagen. At that point he was still clinging to the totally unrealistic belief that hagen was yet possible.

David T. Zabecki
and Spencer C. Tucker

References

Eisenhower, John S. D. *Yanks: The Epic Story of the American Army in World War I.* New York: The Free Press, 2001.

Holmes, Richard. *The Western Front.* London: BBC Books, 1999.

Paschall, Rod. *The Defeat of Imperial Germany, 1917–1918.* Chapel Hill, NC: Algonquin Books, 1990.

Pitt, Barrie. *1918: The Last Act.* New York: Ballantine Books, 1963.

Zabecki, David T. *Steel Wind: Colonel Georg Bruchmüller and the Birth of Modern Artillery.* Bridgeport, CT: Praeger, 1994.

———. *The German 1918 Offensives: A Case Study in the Operational Level of War.* London: Routledge, 2006.

Belleau Wood, Battle of (June 6–26, 1918)

Land battle that pitted U.S. forces against the German Army, brought on when the French High Command ordered the U.S. 2nd Division to secure the Bois de Belleau (Belleau Wood). The wood, about a mile in length and half a mile at its widest point, was located five miles northwest of the town of Château-Thierry on the Marne River. The German 1,200-man 461st Regiment of the 237th Division had taken the three-square-mile wooded area during the Chemin des Dames Offensive (Operation blücher), one of the five separate Ludendorff offensives of the spring of 1918, and had turned it into a defensive bastion.

On May 31, 1918, the 2nd Division, now under French operational control, received orders to replace French forces at the front. On June 6, without benefit of any reconnaissance of the German positions, the 4th Marine Brigade of the U.S. 2nd Division was ordered to occupy the woods, declared by the French to be free of Germans. After the 5th Marine Regiment captured Hill 142, west of the woods, the 5th and 6th Marine Regiments made frontal assaults on the south

U.S. troops advance against entrenched German positions in the Battle of Belleau Wood in June 1918. (National Archives)

and west ends of the woods. By the end of the first day of fighting, the 6th Marines were able to take the village of Bouresches. The marines had gained a foothold, but at a cost of 1,087 casualties. After four days of small raids, American forces on June 9 directed heavy artillery fire on the woods. The next day, the marines began an assault that lasted four days. In the drive, they were able to capture two-thirds of the woods but again at the cost of heavy casualties.

On June 13, the Germans counterattacked and almost recaptured Bouresches, but the offensive stalled on the concentrated rifle fire of U.S. forces. With both sides entrenched, the positions remained static until the 24th, when the marines resumed the offensive. Two days later, the marines declared the woods secured. In

the battle, U.S. forces sustained 1,062 killed and 3,615 wounded—55 percent of the marine force engaged. With the exception of 300 prisoners, most German defenders were killed in the 20 days of fighting.

The merits of the marine victory at Belleau Wood have been much debated. Many French believed that the marines halted the German drive on Paris. Since the Germans were only conducting a large-scale feint in the first place, never had any intention of taking Paris, and did not have the capability even if they had wanted to, the "saving Paris" myth is completely unfounded. Some critics saw the battle as having little value, pointing out that much of the slaughter could have been avoided through better tactics. The battle, however, endeared the marines to

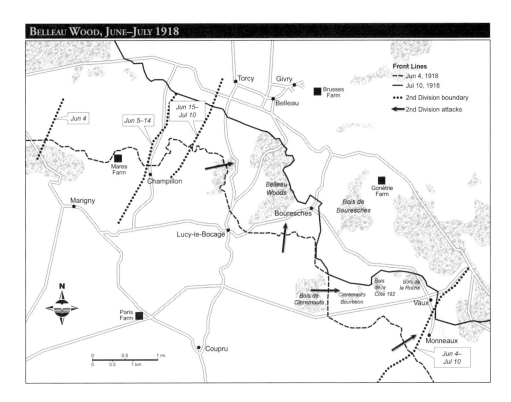

BELLEAU WOOD, JUNE–JULY 1918

the American public and secured continuation of the Corps, the existence of which had been questioned by many American policymakers before the war. Some hold that from this battle the German soldiers called the marines *Teufelhunde* (Devil Dogs). In any case, the French awarded the 4th Brigade the *Ordre de l'Armée* and renamed the woods Bois de la Brigade Marine.

T. Jason Soderstrum

References

Asprey, Robert B. *At Belleau Wood.* New York: Putnam, 1965.

Rice, Earle. *The Battle of Belleau Wood.* Chicago: Lucent, 1996.

Suskind, Richard. *The Battle of Belleau Wood: The Marines Stand Fast.* New York: Macmillan, 1969.

Zabecki, David T. *The German 1918 Offensives: A Case Study in the Operational Level of War.* London: Routledge, 2006.

Marne Counteroffensive (July 18–August 6, 1918)

Allied campaign to reduce the salient between the Aisne-Vesle and Marne rivers that had been created as the result of the three German offensives of May–July 1918 on the Western Front. Following the successful American combat actions at Cantigny (May 28–31, 1918) and Belleau Wood (June 1–26), the Allied High Command resolved to take advantage of the dangerously overextended and inadequately supplied German salient. In 1914, during the opening campaign of the war, German forces had reached the banks of the Marne River and were driven back. The concerted effort of Allied (French, American, British, and Italian) combat power would be needed to contain and then push the Germans back again.

The salient extended about 38 miles from Soissons in the west to Reims in the east and about 25 miles from the Aisne and Vesle rivers in the north to the Marne River in the south. The Germans occupied the salient with 22 divisions of the Seventh Army, totaling some 280,000 troops. The German Ninth and First armies occupied the sectors of the German line west and east, respectively, of the shoulders of the salient. Ringing the salient, the French Tenth Army, with two attached U.S. divisions, was west of Soissons; the French Sixth Army, with four attached U.S. divisions, held the nose of the salient west of Château-Thierry; the French Ninth Army, with two attached U.S. divisions, held the nose east of Château-Thierry; and the French Fifth Army occupied the line on the east side south of Reims. With the typical American division being more than twice as large as the standard French divisions, the Americans at the start of the battle contributed some 230,000 troops to the total Allied force of 700,000.

Allied supreme commander General Ferdinand Foch issued the orders for the attack on July 12, with a scheduled jump-off date of July 18. The plan called for General Charles Mangin's Tenth Army to spearhead the attack toward the key rail center at Soissons with his XX Corps, which consisted of five divisions, including Major General Charles P. Summerall's U.S. 1st Division, Major General James G. Harbord's 2nd Division, and General Daugan's 1st Moroccan Division. The Sixth Army attack on the right of the Tenth Army was to follow immediately behind, with the French Fifth and Ninth armies to attack against the east side of the salient a few days later.

Before the Allies could strike, however, the Germans on July 15 launched Operation MARNESCHUTZ-REIMS, the so-called *Friedensturm* (Peace Offensive). This fifth of the Ludendorff offensives was not intended as another feint toward Paris, rather it was a desperate attempt to capture Reims on the east shoulder of the salient in order to open critically needed rail lines into the German perimeter. The main German effort, therefore, was in the sector opposite to the one where the French intended to initiate their own counteroffensive. Ludendorff, who had lost all touch with reality by this point, still believed he would somehow be able to launch his much delayed Operation hagen against the British in the north.

Allied intelligence had largely anticipated the German attack, and the Allies therefore were not caught completely by surprise. The Germans for the first time in 1918 ran into a well-prepared defense, and their last great offensive of the war ground to a complete halt by July 17. On the first day of the German attack, however, the initial reaction of commander in chief of the French Army, General Henri Pétain, was to postpone Mangin's attack. Foch overruled Pétain, clearly seeing that the German attack would fail and only overextend the Germans all the more.

The Tenth Army attacked behind a creeping barrage but without an artillery preparation at 5:35 a.m. on July 18. General Pierre Berdoulet's XX Corps had the two U.S. divisions, with the Moroccan division between them in the first echelon. The main effort was against the west shoulder of the salient just south of Soissons. The approach march to the line of departure was arduous, much of it in the rain and mud. Several of the attacking regiments barely reached the line of departure on time. The U.S. 1st and 2nd Divisions, the American Expeditionary Forces' (AEF) most experienced, were still learn-

Medical Corps personnel removing the wounded in the course of fighting at Vaux, France, on July 22, 1918. (National Archives)

ing the value of firm command and control and the absolute necessity for close coordination with the supporting artillery.

The French Sixth Army launched its attack shortly thereafter, but following a 90-minute artillery preparation. The four U.S. divisions under the operational control of the Sixth Army for the attack included Major General Joseph T. Dickman's 3rd Division, Major General George H. Cameron's 4th Division, Major General Charles H. Muir's 28th Division, and Major General Charles T. Menoher's 42nd Division.

On July 20, the French Fifth and Ninth Armies joined the Allied counterattack, hitting on the eastern side of the Marne salient. The Ninth Army had operational control of Major General Clarence R. Edward's U.S. 26th Division and Major General William G. Haan's 32nd Division.

Foch's intent was to cut off the salient at its base and trap as many German divisions as possible. With so many Allied divisions advancing on converging lines, the challenge for the Allied senior commanders was the coordination of fire and the squeezing of friendly units out of the line at the critical moment to prevent unwanted meeting engagements.

For the Americans it also was their first real test of army corps organization in a large operation. Major General Hunter Liggett's I Corps, which controlled the 4th and 42nd Divisions, was the first American corps headquarters in combat. On August 4, Major General Robert Lee Bullard's III Corps assumed operational control of the 28th and 32nd Divisions, and by the next day the French Sixth Army's entire front line was held by the two American corps.

Throughout the hard fighting, the Allies cut the railway between Soissons, Château-Thierry, and Paris. As the Germans continued to be driven back to the Vesle River, General Erich Ludendorff was forced to accept the reality that the Germans would never launch their scheduled Flanders offensive against the British.

By August 6, the Allies had largely eliminated the German Marne salient, although they failed to cut off and destroy any significant German forces. Ludendorff called the forced withdrawal a "great setback" and a "turning point in the history of the World War." The Germans suffered approximately 110,000 casualties, while the Allies sustained about 160,000. Although the German Army was on the ropes by that point in the war, the Germans were still skillful and tenacious defenders, and they did not yield ground easily. Of the 310,000 Americans who eventually participated in the offensive, about 67,000 were casualties, approximately 22 percent of the force.

Foch had promised the Americans that they would be assigned their own sector of the front once the German drives had been blunted. On July 24, the U.S. First Army was officially established, and on August 10 General John J. Pershing assumed personal command. The Americans would apply lessons learned in the reduction of the Marne salient in July–August 1918 to their own action at Saint-Mihiel.

When the U.S. Army later established criteria for granting campaign participation credit to units and individual soldiers, the defensive action during the German attack of July 5–18 was designated the Champagne-Marne Campaign, and the offensive action of July 18 to August 6 was designated the Aisne-Marne Campaign.

John F. Votaw
and David T. Zabecki

References

Greenwood, Paul. *The Second Battle of the Marne, 1918.* Shrewsbury, UK: Airlife Publishing, 1998.

Johnson, Douglas V., II, and Rolfe L. Hillman Jr. *Soissons, 1918.* College Station: Texas A&M University Press, 1999.

Neiberg, Michael S. *The Second Battle of the Marne.* Bloomington: Indiana University Press, 2008.

Patch, Joseph Dorst. *A Soldier's War: The First Infantry Division, A.E.F. (1917–1918).* Corpus Christi, TX: Mission Press, 1966.

Wise, Jennings C. *The Turn of the Tide: American Operations at Cantigny, Château Thierry, and the Second Battle of the Marne.* New York: Holt, 1920.

Zabecki, David T. *The German 1918 Offensives: A Case Study in the Operational Level of War.* London: Routledge, 2006.

Saint-Mihiel Offensive (September 12–16, 1918)

First major action of World War I planned and carried out by an independent U.S. force. Saint-Mihiel is a small town located in northeastern France along the banks of the Meuse River. The U.S. First Army was formed in August 1918 under the command of General John J. Pershing. Prior to this time, U.S. divisions had fought under Allied command. Establishment of the First Army put most of those divisions under direct U.S. control, although three U.S. divisions on the Vesle remained under French command. Facing the new U.S.

SAINT-MIHIEL OFFENSIVE, SEPTEMBER 12–16, 1918

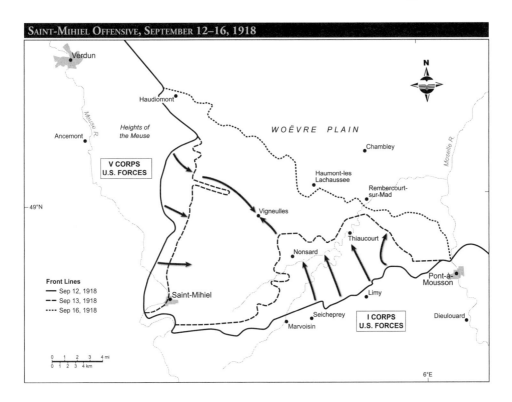

First Army were several German armies defending in depth from trenches that ran from an area southeast of Verdun and then east to Pont-au-Mousson.

For some time Pershing had sought permission from Allied commander in chief Marshal Ferdinand Foch for an independent American offensive. After sometimes sharp debate, Foch finally agreed to Pershing's plan to eliminate the German salient in the Lorraine region that had stood for four years and took its name from the town of Saint-Mihiel at its tip. For over a year Pershing had hoped for the chance to pinch out this salient that jutted into Allied lines south of Verdun and threatened the Paris-Nancy railroad line. The salient was also the entrance to the important Briey basin that supplied Germany with much of its iron ore.

The initial plan called for a push beyond Saint-Mihiel to seize Metz, or at least to cut the highway running from Metz to Antwerp, the main German line of lateral communications. However, Foch changed the plan so as to better support his planned subsequent offensive in the Meuse-Argonne sector. Foch directed that once the Saint-Mihiel salient was eliminated, the U.S. objective would be changed from Metz to Mezières along the French-Belgian frontier northeast of Reims. This attack would serve to cut the German railroad lines and converge with an ongoing British attack.

To assist U.S. forces in the Saint-Mihiel operation, Foch assigned five French divisions to the U.S. First Army. Under Pershing's plan, the II French Colonial Corps was to press the tip of the salient while Major General George H. Cameron's V Corps, in its first combat action, hit the western flank. Meanwhile, Major General Hunter Liggett's I Corps and Major General Joseph T. Dickman's IV Corps, also new in the line, would attack the southern flank. Pershing wanted to envelop the salient by joining the two U.S. pincers in the center of the salient at the town of Vigneulles. The French and British provided the bulk of the artillery support for the attack, a total of 3,000 guns, while the only tanks available were 267 light French Renaults of the 304th Tank Brigade, commanded by Lieutenant Colonel George Patton. The Allied air element was controlled by Colonel William Mitchell and numbered almost 1,500 planes (600 piloted by Americans), the largest concentration of aircraft yet assembled for a single operation.

On September 12, 1918, before daylight and following a four-hour artillery bombardment, the 16 American and French divisions began their advance. Most of the tanks fell victim to mechanical failure or mud, but were not needed initially. Resistance was from the first surprisingly moderate, particularly on the southern flank, where the Germans had already thinned their forward troops as a step in what would prove to be a general withdrawal. By nightfall on the first day, a gap of only 10 miles separated the two converging U.S. forces.

When Pershing learned that roads leading from the salient were filled with withdrawing Germans, he urged a con-

German prisoners at Ansauville, France. The Germans had been captured by American forces during the first day of the Saint-Mihiel Offensive, September 12–16, 1918. (National Archives)

tinued attack through the night to block all escape routes. A regiment of the 26th Division pushed swiftly from the west to enter Vigneulles two hours after midnight, there to be joined after dawn by a regiment of the 1st Division. By September 16, the entire Saint-Mihiel salient was under Allied control.

During the course of the battle, Patton employed his tanks in an unsupported cavalry-style attack outside the town of Jonville. On September 13, Patton aggressively committed his tanks to a fluid situation that help turned the tide at that particular point on the battlefield. As the U.S. forces consolidated their gains, Colonel Douglas MacArthur, then a brigade commander, went forward through German lines with his adjutant to conduct a reconnaissance. He determined with binoculars that the city of Metz was apparently poorly defended and at once proposed to his superiors that the attack be continued in order to take Metz. MacArthur was supported in this view by First Army operations officer Colonel George C. Marshall, but Foch rejected the U.S. proposal because he did not want a premature attack to distract from what was to be a new general offensive. Thus, a great opportunity was lost.

Despite the failure of Foch to exploit this first victory of the war by a U.S. Army force, the Saint-Mihiel Offensive netted 15,000 German prisoners and 257 guns at a cost of 7,000 U.S. casualties. Following this campaign, U.S. forces shifted to a new front to participate in the Meuse-Argonne Offensive, which forced a German retreat and continued until the end of the war.

James H. Willbanks

References

Coffman, Edward M. *The War to End All Wars: The American Military Experience in World War I.* Lexington: University Press of Kentucky, 1998.

Hallas, James H. *Squandered Victory: The American First Army at St. Mihiel.* New York: Praeger, 1995.

Pitt, Barrie. *1918: The Last Act.* New York: Ballantine, 1963.

Meuse-Argonne Offensive (September 26– November 11, 1918)

Allied campaign planned by Allied supreme commander Marshal Ferdinand Foch to cut the German lines of communication between their armies on the Western Front and bases to Metz and the east. As a preliminary to the Meuse-Argonne Offensive, Foch had agreed to allow American Expeditionary Forces (AEF) commander General John J. Pershing and his U.S. First Army to mount an attack on the Saint-Mihiel salient. Foch gave Pershing a time limit and told him that his army would have to be available for the attack in the Meuse Valley toward Sedan. Pershing hoped to reduce the Saint-Mihiel salient, then continue to attack northeast directly toward Metz, but Foch would not permit that divergence of forces from the main effort. The attack at Saint-Mihiel went very quickly and was concluded in only four days, partly due to the withdrawal of German forces in the salient just as the attack began on September 12.

Foch designed his great offensive as a huge two-pronged pincer movement with the final objectives being Aulnoye and Mézières, which were the two key rail junctions in the logistical network behind the German front lines. Foch's intent was to deprive the Germans of their vital rail communications to the east through Metz. The loss of either Aulnoye or Mézières would seriously restrict any German efforts to withdraw, and the critical lines of communications were only within 35 miles of the front line in the Meuse River valley.

On September 3, Foch assigned the northern objective to the British, while the AEF would execute the main pincer move in the south. Those attacks would be supported by a combined French-British-Belgian attack in the far north toward Ghent, while another all-French force in the center would continue to exert pressure on the Germans all along their line. Foch was most concerned to set boundaries between the national armies and insisted on adequate lateral liaison to prevent any German exploitation of gaps in the line.

Masters of defensive warfare, the Germans had prepared their positions with great depth opposite the American sector. The German defenses consisted of three well-prepared successive defensive lines, backed by a fourth that was less well constructed. The Germans also had excellent observation of the battle zone from the fortified heights at Montfaucon and other hills. It was those tough, reinforced positions that the U.S. First Army would attack on September 26. The terrain in front of the U.S. sector also was quite rugged, with many east-west ridges and the Argonne Forest on the left flank of the zone.

Before the campaign could start, all of the attacking units had to move to their jumping-off positions. In what was a masterpiece of staff work, Colonel George C. Marshall, the First Army's assistant chief of staff for operations (G–3), planned and coordinated the movement of both the combat forces and the extensive logistical support from the Saint-Mihiel sector to the Meuse-Argonne sector. During the 10 days prior to the jump-off date of September 26, some 600,000 American troops with all their supporting artillery, engineers, and trains were shifted into their assembly areas, while 220,000 French troops and their support were shifted out.

Pershing deployed his U.S. First Army with three corps of three divisions each on line and one corps in reserve. Most of the American divisions in the first echelon of the initial attack were inexperienced. Major General George H. Cameron's V Corps in the center was designated to make the main effort, with the 91st, 37th, and 79th Divisions on line from west to east, and the 32nd Division in reserve. On the left, Major General Hunter Liggett's I Corps had the 77th, 28th, and 35th Divisions in line west to east with the 92nd and the French 5th Cavalry Divisions in corps reserve. On the right, Major General Robert L. Bullard's III Corps had the 4th, 80th, and 33rd Divisions in the line from west to east, and the 3rd Division in reserve. Just to the east of Verdun and on the east bank of the Meuse, where the front line turned south, the American front extended some 60 more miles, held by the U.S. IV Corps and two French corps under American operational control.

The first phase of the campaign lasted from September 26 to October 3. The attack began in thick fog on the morning of the 26th. The high ground of Montfaucon at the eastern edge of the V Corps boundary dominated the zone of the main attack. The 79th Division had the mission of taking that position. Cameron planned to penetrate the German defenses and drive on the heights at Romagne, with I Corps on his left and III Corps on his right providing artillery support. The U.S. troops were generally successful all along the line except at Montfaucon, which held out until the 27th and gave the Germans time to reinforce their sub-

U.S. troops in French-built Renault tanks advancing on the Western Front on September 26, 1918, in the Meuse-Argonne Offensive. (National Archives)

sequent defensive positions, including their fourth line.

On the extreme right of I Corps Major General Robert Alexander deployed the 77th Division in standard attack formation with all four infantry regiments on line. By October 2, nearly five miles deep in the forest, six companies from two battalions of the 308th Infantry Regiment found themselves isolated and surrounded by the Germans. The so-called Lost Battalion, consisting of 670 men, was commanded by Major Charles Whittlesey, who later received the Medal of Honor for his heroic leadership. By the time the isolated force was relieved on October 7, it was down to fewer than 200 men.

By the time the first phase of the campaign ended, the U.S. First Army had penetrated the first two German defensive lines but stalled in front of the third.

After experienced divisions replaced some of the less experienced divisions in the line, the second phase of the campaign, October 4–31, resumed the slow grind through the German third line.

During the night of October 6–7, I Corps received most of the 82nd Division from First Army reserve and Liggett committed the unit against the German eastern flank in the Argonne Forest. During this attack, Corporal Alvin C. York of the 328th Infantry Regiment performed the acts for which he later received the Medal of Honor.

On October 12, the AEF established the Second U.S. Army. Pershing relinquished direct command of the First Army, which passed to Liggett. Bullard assumed command of the Second Army. Major General Charles P. Summerall replaced Cameron at V Corps, while

Major General Joseph Dickman took over I Corps and Major General John Hines replaced Bullard at III Corps. Pershing retained command of the AEF, which now functioned as an army group.

The second phase of the campaign ended with the Americans finally breaking through the German third line of defense. The third phase started on November 1, with the Americans pushing through the now-strengthened German fourth line toward Mézières and Sedan on the Meuse River. The results were rapid and spectacular, with the V Corps advancing almost six miles the first day. But V Corps also mishandled the 1st Division's advance across the front of the divisions of I Corps. On November 4, III Corps crossed the Meuse and advanced to the northeast, toward Montmédy.

By November 7, V Corps units reached the high ground south of Sedan, effectively interdicting the Sedan-Mézières rail line and accomplishing the U.S. First Army's primary mission in the campaign. Foch at that point shifted the First Army's boundary to the east, placing Sedan in the sector of the French Fourth Army, so that the French city captured by the Prussians in 1870 could be retaken by a French force. Pershing had personally directed the final push to Sedan, hoping to capture it before the French could. George Marshall called it a "typical American 'grandstand finish,'" words he considered a compli-

ment, not a criticism. The offensive ended with the final push and the armistice on November 11, 1918.

A total of 22 American divisions participated in the 47-day campaign, the largest American military operation up to that time. The American units decisively defeated 47 separate German divisions, which was almost one-quarter of the entire German Army on the Western Front. The 1.2 million U.S. troops engaged suffered about 117,000 casualties (some 10 percent of the force). German casualties totaled some 100,000 men with 847 cannon and 3,000 machine guns captured. Although many Americans did not fully comprehend the details of the recently concluded campaign, all recognized that their country's forces had won a significant victory.

John F. Votaw
and David T. Zabecki

References

Braim, Paul F. *The Test of Battle: The American Expeditionary Forces in the Meuse-Argonne Campaign.* Shippensburg, PA: White Mane, 1998.

Coffman, Edward M. *The War to End All Wars: The American Military Experience in World War I.* Lexington: University Press of Kentucky, 1998.

Marshall, George C. *Memoirs of My Services in the World War, 1917–1918.* Boston: Houghton Mifflin, 1976.

McHenry, Herbert L. *As a Private Saw It: My Memories of the First Division, World War I.* Indiana, PA: A. G. Halldin, 1988.

World War I Leaders

Baker, Newton Diehl
(1871–1937)

Democratic Party politician and U.S. secretary of war (1916–1921). Born in Martinsburg, West Virginia, on December 3, 1871, Newton Baker attended Johns Hopkins University, graduating in 1892. Two years later, he received a law degree from Washington and Lee College School of Law. He returned to Martinsburg that same year and began practicing law but soon became active in Democratic Party politics. After a short stint as secretary to the U.S. postmaster general, Baker relocated to Cleveland, Ohio, where he served as the city's solicitor from 1902 to 1912. In 1913, he ran successfully for mayor on a Progressive, reformist ticket.

In March 1916, President Woodrow Wilson appointed Baker secretary of war. He replaced the forceful Lindley M. Garrison, who had resigned over differences with the president as to how best to enhance national preparedness to meet the threat of a potential European war. Baker, known for his pacifist leanings, effectively had no defense or military experience, facilitating his acquiescence in both presidential direction and the National Defense Act of 1916. That legislation expanded both the regular army and the National Guard but rejected the army's proposed large federal volunteer reserve force.

Newton D. Baker. As secretary of war during 1916–1921, Baker played a highly important role in the successful U.S. military effort in World War I. (Library of Congress)

When the United States entered World War I in April 1917, its army was small and still largely unready for the conflict. Baker oversaw its expansion from 95,000 to some 4 million men, instituting a program of national conscription that his well-known antimilitarist tendencies made somewhat more palatable to American liberals. Baker's antiracist and pro–civil libertarian tendencies also helped to restrain

479

some of the worst excesses of wartime hyperpatriotism, although abuses still occurred.

In early 1918, the tardiness of the Wilson administration's initial preparations for war had generated a U.S. Senate investigation and heavy congressional criticism. Baker responded by recruiting several able, energetic, and well-qualified civilians to the War Department to organize industrial mobilization, concentrating procurement in the general staff. Included in the setup was a reorganized and much more efficient War Industries Board (WIB), which mobilized the U.S. economy for war and facilitated defense production. He shrewdly tapped New York financier and able organizer Bernard M. Baruch to run the WIB. Baker asserted the general staff's authority over the War Department's various bureaus, although the National Defense Act of 1920 reversed this development.

When the American Expeditionary Forces (AEF) arrived in Europe, Baker loyally supported the president and AEF commander General John J. Pershing in maintaining the army's integrity rather than amalgamating its troops into more experienced Allied units. On two visits to Europe, he negotiated agreements that determined the American contingent's strength and provided it with shipping.

Baker deplored but publicly supported Wilson's 1918 decision to contribute U.S. troops to the Allies' Russian intervention effort. In autumn 1918, when Pershing attempted to undercut Wilson's efforts to negotiate an armistice with Germany, Baker asserted civilian control by threatening to fire the recalcitrant commander. Baker was an effective rather than great secretary of war. Often handicapped by his department's entrenched structural deficiencies, Baker responded adequately

and conscientiously to the challenges presented by a major mobilization program.

Upon leaving office in 1921, Baker returned to the law and his practice flourished. He remained active in national politics, however, and became a strong supporter of U.S. membership in the League of Nations and the World Court. He was a founder of the Council on Foreign Relations and a leading Democratic internationalist, ardently representing those principles set forth by Wilson. Baker died in Cleveland on December 25, 1937.

Priscilla Roberts

References
Baker, Newton D. *Why We Went to War.* New York: Harper, 1936.
Beaver, Daniel R. *Newton D. Baker and the American War Effort, 1917–1919.* Lincoln: University of Nebraska Press, 1966.
Cramer, C. H. *Newton D. Baker: A Biography.* Cleveland, OH: World Publishing, 1961.

Benson, William Shepherd (1855–1932)

U.S. Navy admiral and first chief of naval operations (CNO), from 1915 to 1919. Born in Macon, Georgia, on September 25, 1855, William S. Benson graduated from the United States Naval Academy, Annapolis, in 1877. He served on the *Hartford,* on the *Constitution,* and then on the *Yantic* during U.S. Army lieutenant Adolphus Greely's Arctic expedition of 1882–1883 and on the *Dolphin* in a circumnavigation of the globe in 1888–1889. Benson was an instructor at the Naval Academy from 1890 until 1893, when he was promoted to lieutenant. During the Spanish-American War of 1898, he served aboard the cruiser *Chicago.* He was pro-

U.S. Navy admiral William Shepherd Benson. An advocate of reform, Benson served as the first chief of naval operations during 1915–1919. He is shown here in dress uniform. (Naval Historical Center)

moted to lieutenant commander in 1900 and commander in 1905.

Following a year as commandant of midshipmen at the Naval Academy, Benson was promoted to captain in 1909 and assigned as chief of staff, Pacific Fleet, simultaneously commanding the cruiser *Albany*. In 1911, he assumed command of the new battleship *Utah*, which at the time was the largest warship in the world. He had charge of the Philadelphia Navy Yard from 1913 to 1915. In May 1915, Benson was appointed the U.S. Navy's first CNO, a position long advocated by naval reformers, with the rank of rear admiral until August 1916, when Congress authorized the rank of full admiral. Benson was charged with reorganizing the navy hierarchy and coordinating the resulting changes with policies set by his civilian superiors, including Secretary of the Navy Josephus Daniel and Assistant Secretary of the Navy Franklin D. Roosevelt.

Secretary Daniels asked Benson to create a staff system for the U.S. Navy similar to those adopted by the world's armies, including the U.S. Army's general staff. He also had to prepare the American fleet for possible deployment in World War I. In this role he was active in developing the navy's submarine and air arms. Benson served abroad in 1917 and 1918 as the navy's liaison to the Allied war councils, and in 1919 he served as the naval adviser to the U.S. delegation to the Paris Peace Conference.

Benson was forced to retire from the U.S. Navy in September 1919, having reached the maximum service age of 64. He received less credit than is his due in the naval history of the war. During his tenure as CNO, he effected significant improvements in the Navy Department administration and oversaw a significant buildup in U.S. Navy strength, such that the United States achieved naval parity with Britain by war's end. Benson remained active in naval affairs until his death on May 20, 1932, in Washington, D.C.

Curtis Nieboer

References

Coletta, Paolo E. *A Survey of U.S. Naval Affairs, 1865–1917.* Lanham, MD: University Press of America, 1987.

Klachko, Mary, with David F. Trask. *Admiral William Shepherd Benson, First Chief of Naval Operations.* Annapolis, MD: Naval Institute Press, 1987.

Trask, David F. *Captains and Cabinets: Anglo-American Naval Relations, 1917–1918.* Columbia: University of Missouri Press, 1972.

———. "William Shepherd Benson." In *The Chiefs of Naval Operations.* Pp. 3–20. Edited by Robert W. Love Jr. Annapolis, MD: Naval Institute Press, 1980.

Bliss, Tasker Howard (1853–1930)

U.S. Army general and army chief of staff. Born in Lewisburg, Pennsylvania, on December 31, 1853, Tasker Bliss attended Lewisburg University (now Bucknell) but transferred in his second year to the United States Military Academy, West Point, from which he graduated in 1875. Commissioned in the artillery, Bliss early won recognition for being both cerebral and a linguist. He was an instructor at West Point (1876–1880) and at the Naval War College (1885–1888). He was also a special assistant to the secretary of war, and during 1897–1898 was military attaché in Madrid, serving as chief adviser to U.S. minister Stewart L. Woodford. In this position, Bliss counseled moderation and sought to prevent a war with Spain.

On the eve of the Spanish-American War, Bliss was recalled to the United States and promoted to lieutenant colonel. He subsequently went to Puerto Rico as chief of staff of the 1st Division, commanded by Major General James H. Wilson. His fluency in Spanish proved invaluable, and Bliss personally carried news of the August 12 armistice protocol to Spanish forces.

Promoted to colonel on August 12, 1898, Bliss then served in Cuba. That December he was appointed collector of customs in Cuba. He held this post until May 1902 and was able to root out a great deal of corruption.

Promoted to brigadier general in April 1901, Bliss served as adviser to Secretary of War Elihu Root on army reorganization, to include the formation of the general staff. Bliss became the first president of the Army War College in 1903. Ordered to the Philippines, he commanded the Department of Luzon in the Philippines during

General Tasker Bliss held the key position of chief of staff of the army when the United States entered World War I. (Library of Congress)

1905–1906, and then headed the Department of Mindanao, where he managed to keep the peace between the fractious rival Moro leaders. He also helped establish a progressive educational program on the island. During 1908–1909, he commanded the Philippine Division. Upon his return to the United States in 1909, Bliss was interim president of the War College, briefly assistant chief of staff, and then successively commanded the Departments of California (1910–1911), the East (1911–1913), and the South (1913–1915). In February 1915, Bliss became assistant chief of staff of the army.

Promoted to major general in November 1915, Bliss became acting chief of staff of the army in May 1917 and chief of staff of the army in September. In October 1917, he was promoted to general. As chief of staff when the United States entered World War I in April 1917, Bliss supervised the rapid mobilization and expansion of the U.S. Army. Although Bliss reached the mandatory retirement age of 64 in December, President Woodrow Wilson ordered him continued on active duty and he remained chief of staff until May 1918.

In October 1917, Wilson named Bliss military representative for the U.S. mission to Europe headed by "Colonel" Edward M. House. Following the formation the next month of the Supreme War Council, charged with coordinating Allied military strategy, Bliss became its U.S. representative. He opposed the splitting up of U.S. units to serve with British and French forces and under their command, but in the crisis of the Ludendorff offensives in the spring of 1918, he supported limited amalgamation. His relations with American Expeditionary Forces (AEF) commander General John J. Pershing were correct but not cordial. Early in 1918 Bliss favored Allied military intervention in Russia against the Bolsheviks, but he turned against it as the year wore on.

Bliss shared Wilson's views regarding the peace and was named a member of the U.S. delegation to the Paris Peace Conference in 1919. He advocated the admission of Germany and Russia to the League of Nations and postwar disarmament. Following his return to the United States, Bliss actively promoted the League of Nations and international disarmament in a series of speeches and articles. In 1920, he was appointed governor of the Soldiers' Home in Washington, D.C., and served in that capacity until 1927. Bliss died in Washington, D.C., on November 9, 1930.

Spencer C. Tucker

References

Palmer, Frederick. *Bliss, Peacemaker: The Life and Letters of General Tasker Howard Bliss*. Reprint ed. Freeport, NY: Books for Libraries Press, 1970, first pub. New York: Dodd, Mead, 1934.

Roberts, Priscilla. "Tasker H. Bliss and the Evolution of Allied Unified Command, 1918: A Note on Old Battles Revisited." *Journal of Military History* 65, no. 3 (July 2001): 671–695.

Trask, David F. *The AEF and Coalition Warmaking, 1917–1918*. Lawrence: University Press of Kansas, 1993.

Wainwright, John D. "Root versus Bliss: The Shaping of the Army War College." *Parameters* 4, no. 1 (March 1974): 52–65.

Bullard, Robert Lee (1861–1947)

U.S. Army general. Born in Yongesborough near Opelika, Alabama, on January 5, 1861, William Robert Bullard as a youngster persuaded his parents to rename him Robert Lee Bullard to connect him with the famed Civil War commander of the Army of Northern Virginia. Lee, as he was known to his family, graduated from the United States Military Academy, West Point, in 1885. Commissioned in the infantry, Bullard served at posts in the American West with the 10th Infantry Regiment in New Mexico, Oklahoma, Texas, and Kansas. In 1898, in order to secure promotion to captain, Bullard requested transfer to the Quartermaster Corps. Before this could be approved, however, the Spanish-American War began. Bullard served in the United States during the war, as a major in the African American 3rd Alabama Volunteer Infantry Regiment. The unit did not see action, but Bullard won recognition for his training methods. He did see action in the Philippines during the Philippine-American War, as colonel of the 39th U.S. Volunteer Infantry Regiment, especially in Mindanao. In 1901, he was promoted to major in the regular army.

Bullard participated in the Cuban intervention of 1906–1909, was a National Guard Instructor, and attended the Army War College in 1912. He commanded the 26th Infantry Regiment on the Mexican-American border during heightened tensions with Mexico during 1915–1916, earning praise for his organizational skills.

On U.S. entry into World War I, Bullard, a protégé of both generals Leonard Wood and John J. Pershing, was advanced to brigadier general, and in June 1917 he deployed to France with the 1st Expeditionary Division as commander of its 2nd Brigade. In September, the American Expeditionary Forces (AEF) commander, General Pershing, reassigned him to AEF headquarters to command the Infantry Officers' School. Promoted to major general that same month, Bullard held that post until he replaced Major General William Sibert as commanding general of the U.S. 1st Division in mid-December 1917. Bullard commanded the 1st Division during the Battle of Cantigny on May 28, 1918, the first independent American attack of the war that captured the town of Cantigny, which the Germans had been using as an advance observation point. In mid-July, following the Château-Thierry operation, he received command of the newly established U.S. III Corps, which was attached to the French Tenth Army. Bullard commanded the 1st Division under Charles P. Summerall and the 2nd Division under General James G. Haarbord in the Soissons attack, although III Corps headquarters played only a minor role. Bullard then took part in both the Aisne-Marne and Meuse-Argonne offensives. Pershing was well aware of Bullard's fitness for higher command.

With the AEF continuing to grow, in October Bullard received command of the U.S. Second Army of some 190,000 men and promotion to temporary lieutenant general. Fluent in French, Bullard also proved to be an effective diplomat, coordinating planning and operations with French senior commanders.

Following the armistice and the demobilization, Bullard served on classification boards and commanded several army departments and administrative headquarters until his retirement in January 1925. He wrote several books, most notably *Personalities and Reminiscences of the War*. His criticism of the entire AEF, but most notably the entire African American 92nd Division, created considerable controversy. In June 1930, Bullard was advanced to the rank of lieutenant general on the retired list. In his last decades, he also served as president of the National Security Board, an organization dedicated to maintaining adequate U.S. military defenses. Bullard died at Fort Jay, New York, on September 11, 1947.

John F. Votaw

References

Bullard, Robert L. *Personalities and Reminiscences of the War.* Garden City, NY: Doubleday, Page, 1925.

Marshall, George C. *Memoirs of My Services in the World War, 1917–1918.* Boston: Houghton Mifflin, 1976.

Millett, Allan R. *The General: Robert L. Bullard and Officership in the United States Army, 1881–1925.* Westport, CT: Greenwood, 1975.

Butler, Smedley Darlington (1881–1940)

U.S. Marine Corps officer. Smedley Darlington Butler was born into a prominent went on leave for nine months; he eventually returned to the Marine Corps.

Butler earned two Medals of Honor as a major: the first during the U.S. occupation of Veracruz, Mexico, in 1914 and the second for the capture of Fort Rivière, Haiti, in 1915. He was the only Marine Corps officer ever to earn the Marine Corps Brevet Medal and two Medals of Honor. From 1909 to 1912, he was stationed in Nicaragua. Appointed to command the *Gendarmerie d'Haiti* in December 1915, he was given the rank of Haitian major general and threw himself into the project with enthusiasm, creating by the time of his departure in 1918 a force of 120 American officers and 2,600 Haitian enlisted men.

Much to his disappointment, Butler did not see combat during World War I. Advanced to temporary brigadier general in 1918, he commanded the debarkation depot of Camp Pontanezen, Brest, France, from October 1918 to July 1919. He was appointed permanent brigadier general on March 5, 1921. As commander of the Marine Corps Barracks, Quantico, Virginia, from 1919 to 1924, Butler was an enthusiastic advocate of enlisted education.

During January 1924–December 1925, Butler was on temporary leave of absence from the Marine Corps to serve as director of the Department of Safety in Philadelphia, Pennsylvania, where he achieved considerable success in a full-scale assault on crime in the city. From 1927 to 1929, Butler commanded the Marine Expeditionary Force in China. He returned from China to be promoted to major general on July 5, 1929, and resumed command of Quantico, which he made the showplace of the Marine Corps.

Many expected Butler, as the senior marine general, to be named commandant

Marine Corps major general Smedley D. Butler was one of the most decorated marines in history and one of a handful of individuals to be awarded the Medal of Honor twice. (Library of Congress)

Quaker family in West Chester, Pennsylvania, on July 30, 1881. His father, Thomas Stalker Butler, was a lawyer and for 31 years a U.S. congressman. The younger Butler attended the Haverford School, but dropped out on the occasion of the war with Spain, joining the Marine Corps on April 8, 1898, while still 16. His first assignment was to the Philippines and in 1900 he participated in the expedition to Peking (Beijing) to crush the Boxer Rebellion, during which he was wounded twice. For a singular act of heroism helping wounded comrades during the campaign, Butler received the Marine Corps Brevet Medal, which until 1914 was the highest decoration for Marine Corps officers. In 1908, he was diagnosed with a nervous condition and of the Marine Corps in 1930, but he failed to receive the appointment and retired from the Marine Corps at his own request on October 1, 1931. In his later years he became an outspoken opponent of U.S. interventions abroad. Butler was one of the first to write about the military-industrial complex (*War is a Racket*, 1935). A frequent speaker at meetings organized by pacifists and church groups, Butler spoke out against war profiteering and what he regarded as the growth of fascism in the United States. For a time in the mid-1930s he acted as a spokesman of the American League Against War and Fascism. Butler ran unsuccessfully as a candidate for the Republican nomination for the U.S. Senate from Pennsylvania in 1932. In 1934, he claimed that a group of wealthy industrialists planned to overthrow the U.S. government and the administration of President Franklin D. Roosevelt. Butler died in the Naval Hospital, Philadelphia, Pennsylvania, on June 21, 1940.

Spencer C. Tucker

References

Heinl, Robert Debs, Jr. *Soldiers of the Sea: The United States Marine Corps, 1775–1962*. Baltimore: The Nautical & Aviation Publishing Company of America, 1991.

Millett, Allan R. *Semper Fidelis: The History of the United States Marine Corps*. New York: The Free Press, 1982.

Schmidt, Hans. *Maverick Marine: General Smedley D. Butler and the Contradictions of American Military History*. Lexington: University Press of Kentucky, 1987.

Venzon, Anne Ciprion. *General Smedley Darling Butler: The Letters of a Leatherneck, 1898–1931*. New York: Praeger, 1992.

Conner, Fox (1874–1951)

U.S. Army officer and chief of army operations of the American Expeditionary Forces (AEF) in France during and after World War I. Fox Conner was born in Slate Spring, Calhoun County, Mississippi, on November 2, 1874. Entering the United States Military Academy, West Point, in 1894, he graduated in 1898 as a 2nd lieutenant of artillery and was sent to Cuba in 1899 as part of the American occupation forces there following the brief Spanish-American War. Following garrison duty in the United States, Conner commanded a company of the newly organized Coast Artillery.

A close student of military history and doctrine, Conner rose steadily through the ranks. He graduated from the Army School of the Line and Staff at Fort Leavenworth, Kansas, in 1906. His posts included time on the army general staff in Washington, D.C., during 1907–1911 and an instructorship at the Army War College at Carlisle Barracks, Pennsylvania. In 1911, he served for a time with a French artillery regiment, improving his knowledge of French.

In 1916, Conner returned to France as an observer on the Western Front. His knowledge of French stood him in good stead and he helped coordinate French Army general Joseph Joffre's visit to the United States. When the United States started deploying the AEF to Europe in 1917, Colonel Conner accompanied Major General John J. Pershing to France as a member of his staff. During much of the war, Conner performed effectively as Pershing's chief of operations at the rank of brigadier general, with Colonel John McAuley Palmer and Lieutenant Colonel George C. Marshall as his two principal subordinates.

Conner, who had an uncanny eye for extraordinary talent, was quickly taken by Marshall's keen mind and dogged determination, and he subsequently became one of Marshall's chief mentors and advocates. Besides Marshall, Conner assembled an impressive team of staff officers who aided him in developing the AEF's operational plans and coordinating their execution. Conner also accurately forecasted German attempts to mount a counteroffensive in the Meuse-Argonne. Throughout the final 10 months of the war, Connor's operations section planned and coordinated all aspects of the AEF's operations.

After the end of the war, Conner supervised the preparation of the meticulously detailed after-action report of AEF operations in France. The report recommended changes and improvements in army organization, many of which were incorporated in the National Defense Act of 1920 that essentially established the organizational structure of the army until 1941.

In 1919, Conner first met a young Major Dwight Eisenhower, while the latter was serving as an instructor at the Infantry Tank School at Fort Meade, Maryland. When Conner assumed command of the 20th Infantry Brigade in Panama in 1921, he arranged to have Eisenhower assigned to his staff.

Like George Marshall, Conner became Eisenhower's close mentor and staunch advocate. Conner stressed repeatedly to Eisenhower the importance of organization and the need for strong joint commands and the ability to interact with other Allied armed forces. These lessons served Eisenhower—and Marshall—well during World War II.

When he returned from Panama in 1925, Conner was promoted to major general and became deputy chief of staff of the U.S. Army in Washington, D.C. He went on to command the Hawaiian Department during 1928–1930 and then I Corps Area from 1930 until his retirement in 1938, after nearly 41 years of service.

Conner stated that his greatest career disappointment was not having led troops in combat. But the influence he had on future general officers was immense, and his visionary thinking had a profound influence on the American senior military leaders of World War II and beyond. Eisenhower stated that Conner was the best soldier he had ever known. Historians credit Conner for having had a great influence on Eisenhower and his career. Conner died on October 13, 1951.

Paul G. Pierpaoli Jr.

References

Ambrose, Stephen E. *Eisenhower: Soldier, General of the Army, President-Elect, 1890–1952.* New York: Simon & Schuster, 1983.

Smith, Gene A. *Until the Last Trumpet Sounds: The Life of General of the Armies John J. Pershing.* Somerset, NJ: John Wiley & Sons, 1998.

Cushing, Harvey Williams (1869–1939)

Doctor, widely recognized as the father of neurological surgery and also credited as being the first endocrinologist. Harvey Williams Cushing was born on April 8, 1869, in Cleveland, Ohio, to a family descended from a long line of New England physicians. He finished secondary school in Ohio before going to Yale University with instructions from his Calvinist father to avoid smoking, drinking, and college ball clubs.

After graduating from Yale, Cushing went to Harvard Medical School, from which he graduated in 1895. In the late 19th century, it was customary for

American neurosurgeon Harvey Cushing developed the basic techniques for operating on the brain, which saved many American lives during World War I. He is regarded as the first endocrinologist. (National Library of Medicine)

medical students to administer ether during surgery, and Cushing had the misfortune of losing a patient from an overdose of anesthetic gas. This incident led him to begin charting pulse and respirations—the first use of the graphic anesthetic record that remains standard practice. Cushing's interest in intraoperative monitoring also led to his introduction of the Riva-Rocca blood pressure measuring apparatus to the operating room in 1901.

In 1897, Cushing went to the new Johns Hopkins Medical School to work with William Halsted and to become the first American surgeon to devote his entire energies to brain surgery. Indeed, at the time the mortality rate for intracranial surgery was so great that Halsted warned Cushing he would be unable to earn a living if that was all he did. In

1900, Cushing traveled to Europe, where he worked with Charles Sherrington, Sir Victor Horsley, and Theodor Kocher.

While in Kocher's laboratory, Cushing studied the elevation in blood pressure and decrease in pulse rate that accompany increased pressure on the brain. He published his findings without crediting Kocher, leading on the one hand to having the famous reflex named for him and, on the other, to being expelled from the Swiss laboratory.

On returning to Hopkins, Cushing helped form the Hunterian Laboratory, which became a world-renowned center of surgical and physiological research. Cushing's interest in pituitary tumors led to his development of techniques to reach the gland through the nose and to the development of endocrinology as a specialty. In 1912, Cushing moved to the Peter Bent Brigham Hospital in Boston as Harvard's Moseley Professor of Surgery.

Cushing was a committed Francophile and, in 1915, took the Harvard Ambulance Hospital to France to work with the American Hospital of Paris in treating wounded French soldiers. When the United States entered World War I on the Allied side in April 1917, Cushing returned to France as director of Base Hospital 5 and senior consultant in neurosurgery to the American Expeditionary Force. His monograph on neurosurgery (which had been initially published as a section of W. W. Keen's *Surgery*) was reprinted by the surgeon general of the U.S. Army and became the standard neurosurgery reference for American military surgeons. Cushing's meticulous technique and concentration on hemostasis were credited with halving the mortality rate of intracranial surgery during the war. Cushing also introduced innovative methods of using X-rays to localize metallic foreign bodies and magnets to remove them from the brain.

Cushing was a notoriously slow surgeon who was fanatical about hemostasis. In 1911, he invented a silver clip that replaced the painstaking technique of individually tying off even very small severed blood vessels. In 1926, in cooperation with engineer Frank Bovie, he popularized the use of electrical currents to coagulate bleeding vessels, thus reintroducing heat cauterization to surgery.

Besides being a magnificent surgeon and teacher, Cushing was an accomplished artist who regularly augmented his written operative notes with elegant sketches. He was also an elegant writer and received the Pulitzer Prize for his biography of Sir William Osler.

Cushing took a position as professor of medical history at Yale after his retirement from Harvard—an involuntary termination occasioned by Cushing's own rule that no surgeon could operate past age 62. Cushing finished his career at the New Haven, Connecticut, school and left one of the world's finest collections of antique medical books to the Sterling Library following his death on October 7, 1939.

Jack McCallum

References

Fulton, John. *Harvey Cushing: A Biography*. Springfield, IL: Charles C. Thomas, 1946.

Sweet, William. "Harvey Cushing: Author, Investigator, Neurologist, Neurosurgeon." *Journal of Neurosurgery* 50 (January 1979): 5–12.

Thomson, Elizabeth. *Harvey Cushing: Surgeon, Author, Artist*. New York: Schuman's, 1950.

Walker, A. Earl. *A History of Neurological Surgery*. Baltimore: Williams & Wilkins Co., 1951.

Daniels, Josephus (1862–1948)

Politician, journalist, and U.S. secretary of the navy (1913–1921). Born in Washington, North Carolina, on May 18, 1862, Josephus Daniels entered the newspaper field at age 16 and within 2 years was the local editor of a paper serving 3 North Carolina counties. He studied at the Wilson Collegiate Institute and attended the law school of the University of North Carolina at Chapel Hill. Although admitted to the bar, he never practiced law. In 1892–1895, during the Grover Cleveland administration, Daniels, an ardent southern Democrat, served in the Department of the Interior but soon returned to North Carolina to become editor of the *Raleigh News & Observer*. He was an early supporter of Woodrow Wilson's candidacy

Josephus Daniels was secretary of the navy during 1913–1921. Adroit in public relations, he also understood governmental processes and was a valuable link between the Wilson administration and Congress. (Library of Congress)

for the presidency in 1912 and later became a key figure in the Wilson presidential campaign.

As a reward for his support, when Wilson won the presidency in the November 1912 election he appointed Daniels as secretary of the navy. Skilled in public relations, Daniels became a valuable liaison between the administration and Congress. He understood congressional processes and reportedly got on well with both conservatives and Progressives.

Daniels picked young (32-year-old) Franklin D. Roosevelt to serve as his assistant secretary, a post Roosevelt held until 1920. The two men instituted a series of controversial and Progressive reforms of the navy's personnel and its officer and cadet education system. These included efforts to improve the lot of sailors, while reducing prerogatives of officers. They also sought to improve the quality of programs at both the United States Naval Academy and the Naval War College. In addition, Daniels established the position of chief of naval operations (CNO) and oversaw a comprehensive shipbuilding program in 1915 designed to give the U.S. Navy parity with Britain by 1921. By the end of fiscal year 1917, the U.S. Navy had 745 ships in commission. Daniels was also a staunch supporter of naval aviation. Although some of his programs and reforms attracted postwar criticism, especially from Admiral William Sims, the navy's strong wartime performance undercut much censure, and Daniels enjoyed the reputation as an innovative and effective administrator.

Following the war, Daniels returned to his newspaper career, all the while remaining in contact with Roosevelt. After his election to the U.S. presidency in 1932, Roosevelt appointed Daniels ambassador to Mexico, an appointment that initially disappointed Daniels, who had hoped for a reprise of his earlier navy role or another cabinet-level position. Daniels served in Mexico until 1941. Although without diplomatic experience and unable to speak Spanish, Daniels performed superbly. He deftly defused a potentially explosive crisis in 1938 when Mexican president Lazaro Cardenas expropriated foreign oil holdings, and he rightfully deserved the lion's share of the credit for preventing a break in Mexican-American relations as the United States contemplated the coming of a new world war. Thanks in large part to Daniels, Roosevelt would, unlike Wilson, fight a world war with a friendly and cooperative Mexico on his country's southern flank. During his retirement, Daniels wrote a two-volume study of the Wilson presidency. Daniels died in Raleigh, North Carolina, on January 15, 1948.

Charles F. Brower IV

Reference

Coletta, Paolo E. "Josephus Daniels." In *American Secretaries of the Navy.* 2 vols. Edited by Paolo E. Coletta. Annapolis, MD: Naval Institute Press, 1989. II:525–582.

Drum, Hugh Aloysius (1879–1951)

U.S. Army general. Born on September 19, 1879, at Fort Brady, Michigan, Hugh Aloysius Drum was the son of U.S. Army captain John Drum, who was killed in the Spanish-American War in 1898. Hugh Drum was then attending Boston College, but President William McKinley offered him a regular army commission as a 2nd lieutenant in tribute to his father, and Drum left school to accept it just before his 19th birthday.

Marked by great ambition, Drum advanced swiftly in the army. He served with the 12th Infantry Regiment in the Philippines and fought in the Philippine-American War. He then served with the 15th Infantry and saw action against the Moros in the southern Philippines, winning a brevet to captain as well as the Silver Star. Drum graduated from the Army School of the Line and Staff, Fort Leavenworth, Kansas, in 1912, and then participated in the U.S. expedition to Veracruz, Mexico, and served on the Mexican border.

Following U.S. entry into World War I, in May 1917 Drum accompanied American Expeditionary Forces (AEF) commander General John J. Pershing to France as one of six general staff officers. He assisted in logistical planning and troop organization and deployment and was promoted to lieutenant colonel in August 1917. Drum played a major role in the organization of the large U.S. "square divisions," which were twice the strength of British or French infantry divisions.

In July 1918, Drum was promoted to colonel and named chief of staff of the newly activated U.S. First Army, helping to plan the Saint-Mihiel and the Meuse-Argonne offensives. His outstanding performance brought advancement to temporary brigadier general in October 1918. In April 1919, Drum was named assistant to the chief of staff of the Service of Supply of the AEF and oversaw the redeployment home of AEF troops from France.

Upon his return to the United States, Drum reverted to his regular grade of major. In 1922, he was again promoted to brigadier general and commanded first an infantry brigade and then the 1st Division (1927–1930). He served as inspector general of the army during 1930–1931 and was promoted to major general in December 1931. Drum then commanded the First Army (1931–1933), was deputy chief of staff of the army (1933–1935), and commanded both the Hawaiian Department (1935–1937) and the Second Army (1937–1938). He then resumed command of the First Army headquartered on Governors Island, New York, and was advanced to lieutenant general in August 1939.

As the peacetime army's highest-ranking officer, Drum expected to have field command of the army if the United States entered World War II. Offered the post of adviser to the Nationalist government of China, which ultimately went to Lieutenant General Joseph Stilwell, he declined. This action and his criticism of his superiors, notably Generals George Marshall and Lesley J. McNair, led to Drum remaining on Governors Island and to his retirement from the army in October 1943.

Drum commanded the New York National Guard until 1948. He was also president of the Empire State Corporation, which owned and operated the Empire State Building. He was military adviser to Thomas E. Dewey during the latter's unsuccessful 1944 Republican presidential campaign. Drum died in New York City on October 3, 1951.

Spencer C. Tucker

References

Dawes, Charles G. *A Journal of the Great War.* 2 vols. Boston: Houghton Mifflin, 1921.

Marshall, George C. *Memoirs of My Service in the World War, 1917–1918.* Boston: Houghton Mifflin, 1976.

Pershing, John J. *My Experiences in the World War.* 2 vols. New York: Frederick A. Stokes, 1931.

Vandiver, Frank E. *Black Jack: The Life and Times of John J. Pershing.* 2 vols. College Station: Texas A&M University Press, 1977.

Fiske, Bradley Allen (1854–1942)

U.S. naval officer, reformer, and inventor. Bradley A. Fiske was born in Lyons, New York, on June 13, 1854. Growing up in New York and the Midwest, Fiske displayed a knack for invention. Inspired by an uncle who was a naval officer, he entered the United States Naval Academy, Annapolis, and graduated in 1875. Afterward, he alternated between posts onshore and at sea. In these years, Fiske became one of the navy's so-called Young Turks, progressive-minded officers who sought to reform and modernize the fleet, the ships of which had deteriorated markedly during the 1870s. Fiske produced an electric rangefinder as early as 1889 and two years later he patented a naval telescopic sight. Mounted on a sleeve around the gun barrel, the sight did not recoil when the gun was fired.

Fiske's inventions brought him to the attention of the navy's Bureau of Ordnance, to which he was twice assigned. In that capacity, he supervised the installation of ordnance on the cruiser USS *Atlanta,* one of the navy's first steel warships, and he later oversaw the installation of electric lighting and other electrical systems on other warships of the rapidly modernizing American navy. Fiske became one of the navy's premier experts on electricity, and in 1887 authored a well-regarded textbook on the subject, *Electricity in Theory and Practice.* On the eve of the Spanish-American War in 1898, many U.S. cruisers and battleships carried Fiske rangefinders. Fiske personally used one of these, the stadimeter, to direct the gunboat *Petrel*'s fire in the Battle of Manila Bay on May 1, 1898.

Fiske's inventions and wartime service earned him promotion to lieutenant commander in 1899. He attained the rank of captain and assumed his first command, the cruiser USS *Minneapolis,* in 1907. Following his promotion to rear admiral in August 1911, Fiske rotated through the command of three different divisions of the Atlantic Fleet and briefly served as deputy commander of the fleet. In February 1913, Secretary of the Navy Josephus Daniels appointed him aide for operations. The previous secretary of the navy, George von Lengerke Meyer, had established four aides to assist him. The aide for operations was the senior of these, and Fiske and other naval reformers hoped that the office would develop more authority and evolve into the nucleus of a naval general staff. In his new capacity, Fiske argued forcefully for the creation of that general staff, which he hoped to lead. He clashed routinely with Daniels over this issue and also his regular condemnation of the Woodrow Wilson administration's refusal to prepare for hostilities following the outbreak of World War I in Europe in August 1914.

Daniels accepted the need for a larger and better organized naval staff and a chief of naval operations to lead it, but he worried about maintaining civilian control of the navy. In 1915, he created a naval general staff, but it lacked the full authority naval reformers advocated. To lead it, he promoted the relatively unknown Captain William S. Benson over Fiske and several dozen other officers to become the first chief of naval operations. That same year, 1915, he appointed Fiske president of the Naval War College at Newport, Rhode Island. Fiske retired the following year, having reached the mandatory retirement age of 62. He continued to write on naval affairs and served as president of the U.S. Naval Institute, the naval officers' professional organization, from 1921 to 1923. Over the course of his life, Fiske wrote 6 books and 60 articles and patented 60 inventions. Fiske died on April 6, 1942, in New York City.

Stephen K. Stein

References

Coletta, Paolo E. *Admiral Bradley A. Fiske and the American Navy.* Lawrence: Regents Press of Kansas, 1979.

Cooling, Benjamin Franklin. "Bradley Allen Fiske: Inventor and Reformer in Uniform." Pp. 120–145. In *Admirals of the New Steel Navy: Makers of the American Naval Tradition, 1880–1930.* Edited by James R. Bradford. Annapolis, MD: Naval Institute Press, 1990.

Fiske, Bradley A. *From Midshipman to Rear Admiral.* New York: Century, 1919.

Ford, Henry (1863–1947)

Prominent American industrialist and automaker. Born on July 30, 1863, in Greenfield Township, Wayne County, Michigan, the son of Irish immigrants, Henry Ford left the family farm at age 16 and found work in a machine shop in Detroit. Here he learned about the internal combustion engine. Returning to the farm, he worked part-time for the Westinghouse Engine Company but also set up a small machine shop at the farm and began working with engines.

In 1891, Ford returned to Detroit as an engineer with the Edison Illuminating Company. He continued his mechanical experiments, and in 1896 he completed his first powered vehicle, which he dubbed the "Quadricycle." He continued to develop passenger vehicles, and he also built racing cars and drove them himself. In 1903, Ford produced a vehicle for the commercial market, forming the Ford Motor Company with financial backing from Detroit citizens. In 1908, he introduced his famous Model T, which

he was able to market successfully because of advanced production techniques. In 1912, Ford introduced at his Highland Park, Michigan, plant the first modern assembly line, which dramatically reduced both production time and unit cost for automobiles. Ford also instituted the $5 for eight hours of work a day minimum wage, which he claimed increased worker productivity. At the time, the $5 per day wage was considered a radical concept, but Ford's bet paid off handsomely in worker loyalty and increased productivity. Ford liked to say that his workers should earn a wage high enough to allow each one to purchase a Ford Model T automobile.

When World War I began, Ford, an outspoken pacifist, refused to allow the

Henry Ford, founder of the Ford Motor Company, revolutionized the automobile industry, life in the United States, and possibly Western culture with the Model T automobile and assembly-line production method. A great many Model Ts saw service in France during World War I. (Ford Motor Company)

export of any Ford Motor products to the belligerent powers. He also agreed in 1915 to finance an unofficial peace conference in Stockholm and to provide a ship, the *Oskar II,* to transport the American delegation there.

Despite Ford's efforts, the British government obtained Ford automobiles through other suppliers and used them as ambulances in France. When the United States entered the war in 1917, Ford reversed his position, devoting his full attention to the war effort and claiming, "Everything I've got is for the government and not one cent of profit." By the end of the war, the Ford Motor Company had produced more than 7,000 farm tractors to assist British agriculture. Some 39,000 of his Model Ts saw service in France and Belgium, and the company manufactured 415,377 cylinders for the famed Liberty aircraft engine as well as 3,940 complete engines. Ford even built 60 subchaser Eagle Boats, which, however, came too late to see service in the war. The War Department also contracted with Ford to build 15,015 2-man, 3-ton tanks powered by 2 Model T engines hooked up in tandem, but only 15 were completed by the November 11, 1918, armistice.

In 1918, Ford ran unsuccessfully for the U.S. Senate. Although his son Edsel was named president of Ford Motor Company the following year, the elder Ford remained very much in charge. Ford introduced the Model A in 1927 and the first Ford V-8 in 1932. Ford strongly resisted unionization. In the 1930s, Ford workers went on strike, resulting in bitter clashes between labor and management and prompting Ford to order a lockout of striking employees. Not until 1941 did his company sign its first contract with the United Automobile Workers. In 1945, Ford relinquished control to his grandson Henry Ford II. Henry Ford died at his home, Fair Lane, in Dearborn, Michigan, on April 7, 1947.

T. Jason Soderstrum
and Spencer C. Tucker

References

Gelderman, Carol. *Henry Ford: The Wayward Capitalist.* New York: Dial, 1981.

Kraft, Barbara S. *The Peace Ship: Henry Ford's Pacific Adventure in the First World War.* New York: Macmillan, 1978.

Lacey, Robert. *Ford: The Men and the Machine.* New York: Ballantine, 1986.

Nevins, Allan, and Frank E. Hill. *Ford: Expansion and Challenge, 1915–1933.* New York: Scribner, 1957.

Nye, David E. *Henry Ford: Ignorant Idealist.* Port Washington, NY: Kennikat, 1979.

Gerard, James Watson (1867–1951)

Attorney, jurist, U.S. diplomat, and U.S. ambassador to Germany (1913–1917). Born in Geneseo, New York, on August 25, 1867, James Watson Gerard graduated from Columbia University in 1890 and then studied law at New York University. He entered the law firm founded by his grandfather, married a wealthy heiress, and became active in Democratic Party politics in New York. For years he served as chairman of the Democratic Campaign Committee of New York County, which included New York City. Gerard also served in the New York National Guard, rising to the rank of major. In 1908, he was appointed to the New York State Supreme Court, which position he held until 1911. He also contributed substantially in 1912 to Woodrow Wilson's successful presidential campaign.

Gerard's reward for his dedicated service to the Democratic Party came in 1913 with his appointment, despite hav-

James Watson Gerard was U.S. ambassador to Germany during 1913–1917. He is shown here at his desk in the American embassy in 1915. (Library of Congress)

ing no previous diplomatic experience, as ambassador to Germany, which post he held until early 1917, when the two countries severed relations prior to declaring war on each other. Gerard disliked the imperial pomp and circumstance and militarist atmosphere of Kaiser Wilhelm II's court, and he presented himself as a forthright democrat and civilian.

Gerard's relations with imperial German officials were never satisfactory because the latter demonstrated their support for Mexican dictator General Victoriano Huerta, whom the Wilson administration openly opposed. In addition, the German government declared that it would not be bound by the 1823 Monroe Doctrine. When World War I

began in 1914, Wilson soon came to believe that Gerard's unabashed anti-Germanism and forthright style were liabilities rather than assets, which compromised his effectiveness. Gerard protested bluntly against German submarine attacks on ships carrying American civilians, notably after the May 1915 sinking of the British passenger liner *Lusitania* and the March 1916 attack on the Channel steamer *Sussex*. He firmly rebuffed suggestions by German officials that, should their two countries go to war, the U.S. government would be toppled by resentful German-American protests. Gerard attempted to cultivate influential German politicians, but his contacts had little impact on the course of diplomatic relations.

In Berlin, Gerard had the thankless task of representing the interests of several Allied nations, including Great Britain, Japan, Serbia, and Romania, which had broken relations with Germany, and relaying complaints between their governments and German officials. He became heavily involved in efforts to improve conditions in prisoner-of-war camps and to assist relief activities in Belgium and Poland. Before departing Germany in 1917, Gerard refused German requests to sign documents altering the texts of American treaties with Prussia so as to provide greater wartime protection for German citizens and property in the United States. Although Wilson administration officials tended to denigrate him, on his return the American public gave Gerard a hero's welcome.

Gerard remained prominent in Democratic Party politics at the state and national levels until after World War II and took up the practice of law in New York City. He supported U.S. membership in the League of Nations, vigorously opposed German dictator Adolf Hitler, and campaigned strongly for American intervention in World War II and for Lend-Lease aid to Britain. He also wrote two well-received books about his experiences in Germany and his take on Kaiserism in Germany. A third book was a memoir of his life. Shortly before Gerard's death, President Harry S. Truman appointed him to a committee to supervise Point Four economic assistance to underdeveloped countries. Gerard died on September 6, 1951, at Southampton, Long Island, New York.

Priscilla Roberts

References

Devlin, Patrick. *Too Proud to Fight: Woodrow Wilson's Neutrality.* New York: Oxford University Press, 1975.

Gerard, James Watson. *My Four Years in Germany.* New York: Doran, 1917.

———. *Face to Face with Kaiserism.* New York: Doran, 1918.

———. *My First Eighty-Three Years in America.* Garden City, NY: Doubleday, 1951.

Harbord, James Guthrie (1866–1947)

U.S. Army general. Born on March 21, 1866, at Bloomington, Indiana, James Guthrie Harbord graduated from Kansas State Agricultural College in 1886. He failed to secure an appointment to the United States Military Academy at West Point, and taught in the public schools and at Kansas State University before enlisting in the army as a private in 1889. He became a 2nd lieutenant by competitive examination in July 1891 and was assigned to the cavalry. Harbord graduated from the Infantry and Cavalry School at Fort Leavenworth, Kansas, in 1895, the same year he earned a master's degree from Kansas State. During the 1898 Spanish-American War, he served briefly in Cuba. Harbord and Captain of Volunteers John J. Pershing shared a tent for several weeks while Harbord served as quartermaster with the 10th Cavalry in 1899.

Harbord served in the Philippine Constabulary as its assistant chief with the constabulary rank of colonel from 1903 to 1914. During this time, he became close friends with Pershing. On his return to the United States, Harbord was promoted to captain and assigned to the 1st Cavalry. When the United States declared war on Germany in April 1917, he was a student at the Army War College. The next month, Pershing selected Harbord as chief of staff of the American Expeditionary Forces (AEF).

Harbord played an important role in the establishment and organization of the AEF, and he shared Pershing's concern that it be kept independent. In August 1917, Harbord was promoted to brigadier general. In May 1918, he took command of the 4th Brigade (5th and 6th Marines) of the 2nd Division, leading his brigade in the bloody Battle of Belleau Wood during June 6–26, 1918. In June, Harbord was promoted to temporary major general, and in July he took command of the 2nd Division, participating in the early days of the Aisne-Marne Offensive (July 18–August 6).

Only two weeks later, at the end of July, Pershing requested that Harbord relinquish his divisional command and take over the Services of Supply (SOS). Harbord had hoped to retain his combat command, but loyally agreed to Pershing's request, which was in large part motivated by Pershing's desire to block the intention of Secretary of War Newton Baker and army chief of staff General Peyton C. March to send Major General George W. Goethals to France to head up the supply effort. Harbord then managed effectively the massive supply service for the AEF.

Harbord continued as head of the SOS until May 1919, and then was again briefly Pershing's chief of staff. Promoted to major general in 1919, he briefly commanded the 2nd Division in Texas. In July 1921, he became deputy chief of staff of the army. His most significant contribution in that position was chairing a reorganization board that adopted the AEF's French-inspired staff system as the model for the army general staff and all subordinate echelons.

Harbord retired from the army in December 1922 and subsequently joined private industry, serving as president of the Radio Corporation of America (RCA) during 1923–1930 and chairman of the board from 1930 to 1947. Promoted to lieutenant general on the retired list in July 1942, Harbord died in Rye, New York, on August 20, 1947.

Claude R. Sasso
and Spencer C. Tucker

References

Coffman, Edward M. *The War to End All Wars: The American Military Experience in World War I.* Lexington: University Press of Kentucky, 1998.

Cooke, James J. *Pershing and His Generals: Command and Staff in the AEF.* Westport, CT: Praeger, 1997.

Gerard, James Watson. *Leaves from a War Diary.* New York: Dodd, Mead, 1931.

Harbord, James G. *The American Army in France, 1917–1919.* Boston: Little, Brown, 1936.

Pershing, John J. *My Experiences in the World War.* 2 vols. New York: Frederick A. Stokes, 1931.

Hoover, Herbert Clark (1874–1964)

U.S. political leader and president of the United States (1929–1933). Born in West Branch, Iowa, on August 10, 1874, Herbert Clark Hoover graduated from Stanford University in 1895 with an engineering degree. He was then a highly successful mining entrepreneur around the world, and his work in China during the Boxer Rebellion influenced his views on war relief. Although from fairly humble origins, Hoover became a self-made millionaire as a young man.

From 1902, Hoover was based in London. After World War I started in 1914, Hoover began urging U.S. ambassador to Great Britain Walter Hines Page to call on him to form an American Relief Commission to assist Americans living or

Herbert Hoover established the Commission for Relief in Belgium early in World War I. After the United States entered the conflict in 1917, the immensely popular and highly effective Hoover headed the U.S. Food Administration (USFA). (Library of Congress)

traveling abroad in returning to the United States. With the backing of American and other neutral diplomats, Hoover also established the Commission for Relief in Belgium (CRB). It did splendid service, ultimately handling $1 billion in assistance and distributing 5 million tons of food and supplies to that country during a four-year period.

In May 1917, after the United States had joined the war, President Woodrow Wilson named Hoover head of the U.S. Food Administration (USFA). The immensely popular Hoover focused on making both production and distribution more efficient. He encouraged American farmers to increase their yields and urged U.S. consumers to decrease consumption and waste. Hoover also sought to keep food prices down. People willingly

"Hooverized," and food surpluses soon accumulated.

Hoover was one of the major American figures to emerge from the war, viewed as a highly efficient administrator and a humanitarian. Hoover and Wilson recognized the need for relief efforts in Europe when the war ended, and in November 1918 the USFA became the American Relief Administration (ARA). Hoover traveled to Europe, cut through mountains of red tape, and secured in February 1919 an initial $100 million congressional appropriation for the ARA. Hoover's main goal was to alleviate food shortages. Within two years, he had overseen the distribution of food and clothing to more than 200 million Europeans. The ARA also aided Russian famine victims in the early 1920s. Disappointed in 1919 by the failure of the Treaty of Versailles to support the Wilsonian war aims, almost four decades later Hoover published *The Ordeal of Woodrow Wilson* (1958), a book sympathetic to the president in the dilemmas he faced at the Paris Peace Conference.

Hoover's experiences distributing food to hungry Europeans during World War I benefited his relief work as secretary of commerce (1921–1928), especially during the devastating 1927 Mississippi River flood. Hoover visited flood-damaged areas to consult with local relief committees, and the media lauded him as a hero for securing funds and supplies for flood victims.

Hoover won the 1928 presidential election as a Republican, but had the extreme misfortune of leading the country at the start of the Great Depression. Hoover tried diligently to jump-start the U.S. economy, but could not do so, and his unwillingness to experiment with more radical economic prescriptions led many to blame him—unfairly—for the economic morass. Defeated for reelection in 1932 by Democrat Franklin D. Roosevelt, after World War II Hoover made an international trip for the Harry S. Truman administration to evaluate potential famine conditions and the world food situation. He wrote a four-volume study, *An American Epic* (1959–1961), about his international relief service. Hoover also devoted himself to the study of 20th-century politics, establishing the Hoover Institution on War, Revolution, and Peace at Stanford University. Hoover died in New York City on October 20, 1964.

Elizabeth D. Schafer

References

Burner, David. *Herbert Hoover: A Public Life.* New York: Alfred A. Knopf, 1979.

Gelfand, Lawrence E., ed. *Herbert Hoover: The Great War and Its Aftermath, 1914–23.* Iowa City: University of Iowa Press, 1979.

Mullendore, William C. *History of the United States Food Administration, 1917–1919.* Stanford, CA: Stanford University Press, 1941.

Nash, George H. *The Life of Herbert Hoover.* 3 vols. New York: Norton, 1983–1996.

A close adviser and friend to President Woodrow Wilson, Edward House played an important role in shaping American foreign policy before and during World War I. After the war, he was one of the U.S. commissioners to the Paris Peace Conference. (Library of Congress)

House, Edward Mandell (1858–1938)

U.S. politician, diplomat, and close adviser and confidant of President Woodrow Wilson. Born into a wealthy Houston, Texas, family on July 26, 1858, Edward Mandell House lost his mother when he was 12 years old. In 1877 he enrolled at Cornell University, but in 1879 left Cornell to care for his ailing father, who died the following year. After a decade of managing his substantial inheritance, House sold off his family's vast cotton plantations, invested in banking and financial institutions, and then turned to politics. In 1892, he managed the successful Texas gubernatorial campaign of James S. Hogg. House subsequently became Hogg's personal adviser and was given the title of lieutenant colonel. From that time on, the media referred to him as "Colonel House."

House thrived in Texas politics as one who could relate well to diverse constituencies, and he helped three other men win the governorship between 1894 and 1902. He served as an adviser to all of them. Drawn into national politics for the Democratic Party, in November 1911, House met then–New Jersey governor Woodrow Wilson. They soon formed an abiding friendship, and House proved vital to Wilson's nomination for the presidency in 1912, garnering key Texas votes and the support of three-time Democratic Party presidential candidate William Jennings Bryan. He also helped manage Wilson's presidential election victory of November 1912.

Following Wilson's inauguration, House refused official appointment but soon became the president's trusted adviser and confidant, especially in matters relating to foreign affairs. Wilson sent House to meet with European leaders in the summer of 1914, in March 1915, and in late 1916. Once the United States entered the war in April 1917, House led U.S. diplomatic efforts, especially those with the Allied powers, helping to formulate Wilson's Fourteen Points and the Covenant of the League of Nations. In October 1918, when the Germans sought a peace based on Wilson's Fourteen Points, the president dispatched House to work out the details of an armistice and peace with the Allies.

Following the war, House became one of the five U.S. peace commissioners at the Paris Peace Conference, where he acted as Wilson's chief deputy. After the signing of the Treaty of Versailles on June 28, 1919, Wilson appointed House his personal representative in London to draft the provisions of the mandate system created by the peace conference and the League of Nations. Wilson disagreed with some of House's compromises, and relations between the two men grew strained. As Wilson became increasingly exhausted and ill health plagued him, he began to grow distant from his advisers, including House, whom he had largely cast aside by the end of 1919.

During the Senate fight to secure ratification of the Treaty of Versailles, Wilson's doctrinaire tactics ran counter to House's pragmatic counsel, which urged compromise and accommodation with Sen. Henry Cabot Lodge and the so-called reservationists. Following Wilson's debilitating stroke in September 1919, the two men drifted further apart, and in 1920 House left Washington. A year later, he and Charles Seymour published a memoir of the Paris Peace Conference, *What Really Happened at Paris.*

Between 1926 and 1928, House and Seymour completed the four-volume *The Intimate Papers of Colonel House.* House took interest in Franklin D. Roosevelt's 1932 Democratic nomination effort, but he never again served as a political manager or presidential adviser. He died in New York City on March 28, 1938.

William Head

References

Floto, Inga. *Colonel House in Paris: A Study of American Policy at the Paris Peace Conference, 1919.* Princeton, NJ: Princeton University Press, 1980.

George, Alexander L., and Juliette L. George. *Woodrow Wilson and Colonel House.* New York: Dover, 1956.

Williams, Joyce Grigsby. *Colonel House and Sir Edward Grey: A Study in Anglo-American Diplomacy.* Lanham, MD: University Press of America, 1984.

Lansing, Robert (1864–1928)

U.S. lawyer, diplomat, and secretary of state (1915–1920). Born the son of a judge in Watertown, New York, on October 17, 1864, Robert Lansing graduated from Amherst College in 1886. He then read law in his father's office. Admitted to the New York bar in 1889, Lansing became a junior partner in the newly formed law firm Lansing & Lansing with his father, remaining with the firm until his father's death in 1907.

In 1890, Lansing married Eleanor Foster, daughter of John Foster, a distinguished international lawyer and diplomat who exerted considerable influence on Lansing's future career and who was soon thereafter secretary of state. Lansing now turned to international law. Beginning in 1892, he became a U.S. associate counsel assisting on international arbitration cases, including the Bering Sea Fur Seal Arbitration case. In 1906 he helped organize the American Society for International Law, and in 1907 he contributed to the establishment of the *American Journal of International Law.* In March 1914, President Woodrow Wilson appointed Lansing, a Democrat, as counselor at the State Department. When William Jennings Bryan resigned as secretary of state in the spring of 1915 after a disagreement with Wilson's policies, the president elevated Lansing to that post.

Lansing seemed an ideal choice, as Wilson was determined to direct his own foreign policy and was a firm believer in the efficacy of international law, which Lansing had championed. As German ambassador to the United States Johann von Bernstorff put it, "Since Wilson decides *everything,* any interview with Lansing is a matter of form." Lansing believed in a legalistic, pragmatic approach to foreign policy, however, and he and Wilson frequently disagreed. Lansing believed that the United States should assume a dominant role in the Western Hemisphere but follow a conciliatory path in relations with Japan in East Asia and the Pacific. He also believed that

Germany must not be allowed to dominate the European continent and that the United States would eventually have to intervene in World War I. Lansing did, however, have some influence with the president. For example, Wilson accepted his position that American citizens and bankers should be allowed to arrange loans for the Allied Powers. Wilson also agreed to Lansing's strategy of arming U.S. merchant vessels in early 1917.

When the United States entered World War I in April 1917, Lansing paid much attention to containing Japanese expansionist policies toward China. His efforts culminated in the Lansing-Ishii Agreement of November 1917, which recognized Japan's "special interest" in Manchuria and Inner Mongolia while also embracing the U.S. notion of the "open-door" for investment in China as well as maintaining that nation's territorial integrity. The wording of this agreement was so ambiguous that both Japan and the United States could interpret it as they liked. In the short run the careful phrasing of the agreement reduced tensions between the two powers, but over the long run its ambiguity helped lead to the confrontation that culminated in World War II.

Lansing went to Paris with Wilson after the war as one of five U.S. commissioners to the Paris Peace Conference, but Wilson paid little attention to his advice, especially on the League of Nations, which the president regarded as key to any comprehensive peace settlement. Lansing also found much to criticize in Wilson's idealism. During the subsequent and contentious U.S. Senate hearings on the Treaty of Versailles held in the summer of 1919, William C. Bullitt, another member of the U.S. delegation to the Paris Peace Conference, revealed Lansing's serious objections to Wilson's approach. This and the fact that Lansing had convened cabinet meetings after Wilson suffered a paralyzing stroke in October 1919 led Wilson to demand Lansing's resignation, which he tendered on February 13, 1920. Lansing then returned to his law practice. After his retirement in 1925, he served as a trustee and later vice president of the Carnegie Endowment for International Peace. Lansing died in Washington, D.C., on October 20, 1928.

Sugita Yoneyuki

References

Hartig, Thomas H. *Robert Lansing: An Interpretive Biography.* New York: Arno Press, 1982.

Lansing, Robert. *The Peace Negotiations: A Personal Narrative.* Boston: Houghton Mifflin, 1921.

Smith, Daniel M. *Robert Lansing and American Neutrality, 1914–1917.* New York: Da Capo, 1972.

Lieutenant General John A. Lejeune was the first U.S. Marine Corps officer to lead an army division in battle. He emerged from the war as one of the most respected U.S. commanders. (Library of Congress)

Lejeune, John Archer (1867–1942)

U.S. Marine Corps general. Born on January 10, 1867, in Pointe Coupée Parish, Louisiana, John Archer Lejeune entered Louisiana State University in 1881 but transferred to the United States Naval Academy, Annapolis, in 1884, graduating as a midshipman in 1888. He was then assigned to the cruiser *Vandalia,* which sank in a typhoon off Samoa in March 1889. When he learned that he was to become a naval engineer because of his high grades, Lejeune appealed to the secretary of the navy and won his case, instead being commissioned in the Marine Corps in July 1890.

Lejeune served a series of ship assignments and commanded the marine detachment on board the cruiser *Cincinnati* during the Spanish-American War. He was promoted to captain in 1899 and to major in 1903, when he took command of the Floating Battalion of the Atlantic Fleet. He served in Panama, and from 1907 to 1909 commanded the Marine Brigade in the Philippines.

Promoted to lieutenant colonel in 1908, Lejeune became the first marine officer to graduate from the Army War College (in 1910). He commanded the Advanced Base Brigade during 1913–1914 and was promoted to colonel in 1914. Lejeune then took part in the 1914 occupation of Veracruz, Mexico, where he organized the marines' first motorized unit and also conducted the first Marine Corps air operations.

Appointed assistant to the commandant of the Marine Corps in 1915, in November 1916 Lejeune was promoted to brigadier general. He lobbied both for increases in marine personnel and for deployment of marines to France following U.S. entry into the war in April 1917. That September, Lejeune took command of the Marine Barracks at Quantico, Virginia.

Lejeune deployed to France in June 1918. As the senior marine in France, he requested American Expeditionary Forces commander General John J. Pershing to create a marine division. Pershing refused. Nevertheless, Lejeune went on to prove himself as an effective commander of a National Guard Brigade and then the 4th Marine Brigade in the 2nd Division in July 1918. Only three days after Lejeune assumed the latter command, Pershing reassigned the 2nd Division commander, Major General James C. Harbord, as director of Services of Supply, and on July 29, Lejeune took over from Harbord and became the first marine to command a U.S. Army division in combat. The 2nd Division was considered one of the army's best. Lejeune was promoted to major general in August 1918. His division distinguished itself in the Saint-Mihiel Offensive in September; in the battle for Blanc Mont Ridge in October, where it breached the Hindenburg Line and took more than 3,300 prisoners and 121 guns; and in the Meuse-Argonne Offensive. Lejeune emerged from World War I as one of the most decorated U.S. officers. After the armistice, the 2nd Division moved into southern Belgium and then crossed into Germany, assuming occupation duties at Coblenz until its redeployment to the United States in July 1919.

Lejeune then resumed command of the Marine Corps Base at Quantico. In June 1920, he was appointed commandant of the U.S. Marine Corps. During three terms as commandant until March 1929, Lejeune emphasized education and modernization, established professional military schools for all ranks, adopted modern amphibious tactics, and strengthened the aviation sector of the U.S. Marine Corps. Many regard him as the architect of the modern Marine Corps.

Lejeune retired in November 1929 to become superintendent of the Virginia Military Institute in Lexington, Virginia. He held this post until 1937. In February 1942, he was promoted to lieutenant general on the retired list. Lejeune died in Baltimore, Maryland, on November 20, 1942. Camp Lejeune, North Carolina, is named in his honor.

Derek W. Frisby
and Spencer C. Tucker

References

Bartlett, Merrill L. *Lejeune: A Marine's Life, 1867–1942.* Columbia: University of South Carolina Press, 1991.

Lejeune, John A. *The Reminiscences of a Marine.* Quantico, VA: Dorrance, 1930.

Lewis, Charles Lee. *Famous American Marines.* Boston: L. C. Page, 1950.

Millett, Allan R. *Semper Fidelis: The History of the United States Marine Corps.* Rev. and expanded ed. New York: Free Press, 1991.

Liggett, Hunter (1857–1935)

U.S. Army general. Born on March 21, 1857, in Reading, Pennsylvania, Hunter Liggett graduated from the United States Military Academy, West Point, in 1879 and was commissioned a 2nd lieutenant in the infantry. He then served on the Northern Great Plains, taking part in various Indian campaigns, and on the Mexican border against Geronimo, leader of the Chiricahua Apaches. He was promoted to captain in 1897. During the 1898 Spanish-American War, Liggett served as a major of volunteers and was involved in training duties. He went to Cuba in 1899

U.S. Army general Hunter Liggett. The widely admired and respected Liggett commanded I Corps in the Second Battle of the Marne and Saint-Mihiel Offensive and First Army in the Meuse-Argonne Offensive. (Library of Congress)

and was then stationed in the Philippines until 1902, seeing action in the 1899–1902 Philippine-American War.

Promoted to major in the regular army, Liggett was then adjutant general of the Department of the Lakes at Chicago. In 1907, he took command of an infantry battalion at Fort Leavenworth, Kansas. During 1909–1910, Liggett attended the Army War College, remaining there as a director of instruction, and serving concurrently as a member of the army general staff overseeing war planning.

In 1913, Liggett was promoted to brigadier general, and during 1913–1914 he was the president of the Army War College, where he instituted reforms in the curriculum that helped prepare the army for modern warfare. By now,

Liggett enjoyed a reputation as a capable and innovative military planner. Liggett commanded a brigade during the Mexican border crisis of 1914, and in 1916 he was named commander of the Department of the Philippines. He was promoted to major general in March 1917.

After the United States entered World War I in April 1917, Liggett took command of the 41st ("Sunset") Division, composed of National Guard units from the western states. In October, he took the division to France with the American Expeditionary Forces (AEF). Although Liggett's great girth and his advanced age seemed to work against him as a combat commander, he nevertheless had the support of AEF commander General John J. Pershing. Liggett liked to remark that fat above the collar was more serious than fat below it.

In January 1918, Liggett took command of I Corps, ably leading it in the Second Battle of the Marne, in the Saint-Mihiel Offensive, and, until mid-October, in the Meuse-Argonne Offensive, when Pershing named him to command the First Army. Liggett spent the remainder of October 1918 reorganizing his command. He managed to hold off Pershing, who was trying to get him to attack before he was ready, resuming the offensive only on November 1. Widely admired and respected, Liggett drove the First Army forward with great skill until the armistice on November 11.

In April 1919, Liggett took command of the U.S. Army of Occupation in Germany. Lieutenant General Liggett retired in 1921 and died in San Francisco on December 30, 1935.

Claude R. Sasso

References

Coffman, Edward M. *The War to End All Wars: The American Military Experience in World War I.* Lexington: University Press of Kentucky, 1998.

Cooke, James J. *Pershing and His Generals: Command and Staff in the AEF.* Westport, CT: Praeger, 1997.

Liddell Hart, Basil H. *Reputations: Ten Years After.* Boston: Little, Brown, 1928.

Smythe, Donald. *Pershing: General of the Armies.* Bloomington: Indiana University Press, 1986.

Lippmann, Walter (1889–1974)

American journalist, intellectual, and influential adviser to key U.S. policy makers, especially in matters of foreign policy. Walter Lippmann was born in New York City on September 23, 1889. He attended Harvard University, where he studied under the influential writer/philosopher George Santayana and became a socialist. He graduated in 1909. Always attuned to politics and international affairs, Lippmann soon became interested in journalism. In 1911, he was hired by the renowned muckraking journalist Lincoln Steffens, for whom he worked as an assistant. When Steffens wrote publicly in support of former president Theodore Roosevelt's third-party bid as a Progressive reformer in the 1912 election, Lippmann also strongly supported the Bull Moose Party candidate. The young Lippmann published a well-received book entitled *A Preface to Politics* (1913), in which he analyzed popular prejudices in the United States and how they affected the political process. The book garnered much attention. In 1913, the journalist Herbert Croly personally recruited Lippmann as one of the founding editors of the new, liberal weekly publication *The New Republic.*

Lippmann's cogent essays and articles in *The New Republic* caught the eye of President Woodrow Wilson, who himself was a student and scholar of politics and history. By 1916, Lippmann had cast off his earlier flights with socialism and became a firm and vocal supporter of Woodrow Wilson's 1916 reelection bid. The following year, after the United States entered World War I, Wilson tapped Lippmann to be Secretary of War Newton Baker's primary assistant. Eager and full of ideas, Lippmann soon ingratiated himself with the White House. Indeed, Lippmann helped President Wilson craft his Fourteen Points and was influential in the conception of the League of Nations, which was near and dear to Wilson's heart and became the linchpin of his postwar peace settlement. By the time the war ended in November 1918, Lippmann had become an indispensable part of Wilson's diplomatic team and accompanied the president to the postwar Paris Peace Conference in 1919. There Lippmann continued to offer advice to Wilson. More important, however, was Lippmann's firsthand view of international power politics and the insights he gained into the personalities of the leaders involved in the talks. This "education" informed Lippmann's worldview for the next 50 years.

After the war, Lippmann expanded his writing to include columns and articles in the *New York World* and *New York Herald Tribune.* He also became a critic of modern American journalism, arguing that many journalists, contrary to their stated goal of unbiased reporting, often wrote news articles that were based on preconceived notions of people and situations. Journalism was not, he opined, the best way to educate or inform the public. Readers, on the other hand, he asserted, were often too self-absorbed and myopic to understand the nuances of national or international policy. Having lost faith in

Americans' capability of taking an active role in democracy, Lippmann came to believe that the United States had to, by necessity, be governed by a class of bureaucratic, intellectual elites who were specially trained to understand and overcome the biases and complexities of the modern, industrialized world.

In 1931, when the *New York World* closed its doors, Lippmann moved to the *New York Herald Tribune*. Besides his editing responsibilities there, he also authored a nationally syndicated column called "Today and Tomorrow," which was carried in more than 250 newspapers. The column ran for 30 years. Lippmann also contributed regularly to *Newsweek* magazine and the *Washington Post* and won two Pulitzer Prizes. Lippmann was not doctrinaire politically, and in fact took a very pragmatic, realist approach to politics and foreign policy.

In the aftermath of World War II, Lippmann wrote a book entitled *The Cold War*, and is generally credited with having coined the phrase. In it, he recognized the state of belligerency between the United States and Soviet Union, but recommended that Western economic and political integration would be better defenses against the Soviet threat than military power alone. Although considered a foreign policy realist, Lippmann did not support the containment policy, believing it to be an overreaction to the Soviet threat. He asserted that the United States should not support regimes that were either unpredictable or undemocratic just because they claimed to be anticommunist.

Not surprisingly, Lippmann strongly opposed American military intervention in Vietnam, claiming that the Republic of Vietnam was an unsustainable, dictatorial regime that had little chance of attracting support from its own people. Retiring in 1967, Lippmann continued to write op-ed pieces for *Newsweek* and grant interviews. He died in New York City on December 14, 1974.

Paul G. Pierpaoli Jr.

References

Blum, D. Steven. *Walter Lippmann: Cosmopolitanism in the Century of Total War.* Ithaca, NY: Cornell University Press, 1984.

Steel, Ronald. *Walter Lippmann and the American Century.* Boston: Little, Brown & Company, 1980.

Lodge, Henry Cabot (1850–1924)

U.S. senator and highly influential in the formation of U.S. foreign policy. Born in Boston, Massachusetts, on May 12, 1850, to a prominent and wealthy family, Henry Cabot Lodge was educated at Harvard College, where he received an undergraduate degree in 1871, a law degree in 1874, and, in 1876, one of the first doctorates in history and government granted by that institution. He entered the legal profession in 1876 after admission to the bar the previous year. Lodge lectured on American history at Harvard from 1876 to 1879 while he continued to practice law and write history.

Lodge entered the political arena in 1880, when he was elected to the Massachusetts state legislature. He won election to the U.S. House of Representatives in 1887 and served there until 1893, when he was appointed to the U.S. Senate, serving there until his death in 1924.

Lodge, a Republican, became a close friend and confidant of Theodore Roosevelt. Both men held similar views regarding foreign affairs, both were historians, and both wrote works about men who inspired their leadership. As an admirer of Roosevelt's foreign policy, Lodge was highly critical of the foreign policy of Roosevelt's two successors as president, William Howard Taft and Woodrow Wilson. Lodge advocated a strong international role for the United States, including early entry into World War I on the Allied side. He also pushed for U.S. military preparedness.

As Senate majority leader following the November 1918 elections and chairman of the Senate Committee on Foreign Relations beginning in 1919, Lodge held a pivotal position in the fight against Woodrow Wilson's cherished League of Nations, which became a key issue shortly after the November 1918 elections and continued into March 1920. President Wilson failed to consult or take with him any leading Republicans when he went to the Paris Peace Conference in 1919, nor did he consult them regarding his proposed League of Nations, which Wilson saw as an absolute key to achieving an effective peace settlement.

The Senate was divided into three groups on the issue of League ratification: Wilson's Democratic supporters, who favored immediate ratification; Lodge's Republican moderates, who favored participation in the League but with reservations that would preserve U.S. interests and freedom of action; and the so-called irreconcilables who opposed the League completely, such as senators Hiram Johnson, William Borah, and Robert La Follette.

On November 6, 1919, Lodge advanced a resolution of ratification of the League of Nations with 14 reservations that, while somewhat circumventing U.S. obligations under the Covenant, did not seriously impair the League. Wilson, unwilling to compromise, urged its

defeat, and Democrats joined with the irreconcilable Republicans on November 19 to vote down the resolution 53 to 38. Had the Democrats voted for the Lodge resolution, the treaty would have been carried by a very large margin. Lodge refused to modify his original reservations, while Wilson remained defiant that the Senate must not modify the treaty in any way. After suffering a debilitating stroke, Wilson dug in his heels even more, which all but assured that the League of Nations would not be adopted by the United States.

On March 19, 1920, 21 Democrats deserted Wilson to join the reservationists, and the Senate voted down the Treaty of Versailles, which contained the League of Nations Covenant. Not until July 1921, under Wilson's Republican successor Warren G. Harding, did Congress, by joint resolution, formally terminate war with Germany and Austria-Hungary. Although Lodge is sometimes blamed for the failure of the United States to join the League of Nations, most historians argue that this distinction more properly belongs with President Wilson and his refusal to compromise.

Lodge was also a noted author, and he continued to write throughout his life and years in the Senate. In addition to many essays and articles, Lodge published biographies of Daniel Webster and George Washington. Lodge died in Cambridge, Massachusetts, on November 9, 1924.

Pamela Lee Gray

References

Garraty, John A. *Henry Cabot Lodge: A Biography.* New York: Alfred A. Knopf, 1953.

Lodge, Henry Cabot. *The Senate of the United States and Other Essays and Addresses Historical and Literary.* New York: Scribner, 1925.

Widenor, William C. *Henry Cabot Lodge and the Search for an American Foreign*

Policy. Berkeley: University of California Press, 1980.

Zimmermann, Warren. *First Great Triumph: How Five Americans Made Their Country a World Power.* New York: Farrar Straus and Giroux, 2002.

March, Peyton Conway (1864–1955)

U.S. Army officer and chief of staff during World War I. Born at Easton, Pennsylvania, on December 27, 1864, Peyton Conway March attended Lafayette College, where he graduated with honors in classics in 1884. Four years later, he graduated from the U.S. Military Academy at West Point. He commanded an artillery battery in the Spanish-American War in 1898, participating in the campaign leading to the capture of Manila. After serving briefly as aide-de-camp to Major General Arthur MacArthur, March took part in several campaigns during the Philippine-American War and served as a provincial governor. At the conclusion of hostilities, he returned to Washington in 1903 to serve on the new War Department General Staff and as a military observer of the Russo-Japanese War in 1904.

In 1916–1917, Colonel March commanded the 8th Field Artillery Regiment along the tense Mexican border, after which he was promoted to brigadier general and placed in command of the 1st Field Artillery Brigade, 1st Division, American Expeditionary Forces (AEF), and deployed to Europe. Following promotion to major general in August 1917, March became chief of AEF artillery, a duty he held until his return to Washington in March 1918 to serve as acting chief of staff of the U.S. Army as part of an overhaul of the War Department by Secretary of War Newton D. Baker.

Baker handpicked March to supervise the mobilization, training, equipping, and deployment of U.S. forces sent to Europe; to establish the organization, control, and effectiveness of its supply; and to ensure the base of support and cooperation upon which the success of General John J. Pershing and the AEF depended. In this role as the first modern U.S. military manager, March performed brilliantly, and he established the primacy of the chief of staff in the army hierarchy. During his tenure, significant numbers of U.S. forces were trained and transported to France. March also oversaw the establishment of several new branches, including the U.S. Air Service, Tank Corps, Chemical Warfare Service, and Motor Transport Service.

Under March's leadership, the War Department became an efficient and powerful agency, and its general staff functioned as the brain of the army. At war's end, March supervised the AEF's return to the United States, the demobilization and discharge of the bulk of U.S. forces, and the integration of the AEF regulars into the peacetime army. The army released more than 3 million men in the 10 months following the armistice, an accomplishment March viewed with justifiable pride.

March's plan for demobilization created friction between him and Pershing and with a U.S. Congress eager to reassert itself after the war. This friction worsened when March's plans for a strong general staff, a 500,000-man postwar army, and a 3-month universal training program clashed with congressional preferences for a stronger role for the National Guard and more robust universal military training. Pershing's opposition to the March proposal in testimony to Congress in 1920 proved its death knell.

March retired as a major general in November 1921, but in 1930 he was advanced to general on the retired list. He published a memoir of his wartime service in 1932. Brutally frank, *The Nation at War* harshly criticized Pershing and engendered a strong counterattack from the latter's followers. Ironically, March was respected by two later chiefs of staff who were both Pershing men: Douglas MacArthur and George C. Marshall. March followed closely the course of World War II and the Korean War and in 1953 was recognized by a concurrent congressional resolution for his "selfless and patriotic interest in the U.S. Army since his retirement." March died in Washington, D.C., on April 13, 1955.

Charles F. Brower IV

References

Coffman, Edward M. *The Hilt of the Sword: The Career of Peyton C. March.* Madison: University of Wisconsin Press, 1966.

March, Peyton C. *The Nation at War.* Garden City, NY: Doubleday, 1932.

Palmer, Frederick. *Newton D. Baker: America at War.* 2 vols. New York: Dodd, Mead, 1931.

Vandiver, Frank E. *Black Jack: The Life and Times of John J. Pershing.* 2 vols. College Station: Texas A & M University Press, 1977.

Marshall, George Catlett (1880–1959)

U.S. Army general, chief of staff of the army, secretary of state, and secretary of defense. Born in Uniontown, Pennsylvania, on December 31, 1880, Marshall graduated from the Virginia Military Institute in 1901. Commissioned in the infantry in 1902, he then held a variety of assignments, including in the Philippines. He attended the Infantry and Cavalry School, Fort Leavenworth, Kansas, in 1906 and was an instructor in the Army School of the Line and Staff during 1907–1908. Marshall returned to the Philippines during 1913–1916. It was in the Philippines that he established his reputation as a superlative planner. He was promoted to captain in 1916.

Following the U.S. entrance into World War I in April 1917, Marshall went to France in June 1917 with the American Expeditionary Forces (AEF) as training officer to the 1st Division. During a visit by AEF commander John J. Pershing to 1st Division headquarters, Marshall astonished everyone by admonishing Pershing for his highly critical comments of the division. It was the

U.S. Army lieutenant colonel George C. Marshall. An extraordinarily capable administrator, Marshall first made his mark by developing the plan for the U.S. attack at Cantigny in May 1918. He was chief of staff of the army during World War II. (Library of Congress)

beginning of a close association between the two men.

Promoted to lieutenant colonel in 1918, Marshall made his mark as a superlative planner in developing the orders for the highly successful attack by the U.S. 1st Division at Cantigny on May 28, 1918. Assigned to Pershing's headquarters on July 13, Marshall was the principal planner of the highly successful U.S. and French Saint-Mihiel Offensive on September 12–16, 1918. He then earned widespread admiration for his logistical skills in directing the repositioning of more than 400,000 men and more than 2,700 guns across the rear of the attacking army so that they could be in position for the commencement of the Meuse-Argonne Offensive from September 26 to November 11. Marshall learned much from his wartime planning experiences, especially the need for thorough training in both small- and large-unit operations. He also came away from the war with an understanding of the need for unity of command in Allied operations. The changes he later instituted based on his World War I experiences would have profound impact on the army.

After working on occupation plans for Germany, Marshall reverted to his permanent rank of captain and served as aide to General John J. Pershing from 1919 to 1924, who then became chief of staff of the army in 1921, serving until 1924. Marshall was promoted to major in 1920 and lieutenant colonel in 1923.

Marshall served in Tianjin (Tientsin), China, during 1924–1927 and then was assistant commandant in charge of instruction at the Infantry School, Fort Benning, Georgia, from 1927 to 1932. Promoted to colonel in 1932, he held assorted command posts in the continental United States, including instructor with the Illinois National Guard from 1933 to 1936. He advanced to brigadier general in 1936.

Marshall became head of the War Plans Division in Washington with promotion to major general in July 1938, and was reassigned as deputy chief of staff that October. President Franklin D. Roosevelt advanced him over many more senior officers to appoint him chief of staff of the army with the rank of temporary general on September 1, 1939. As war began in Europe, Marshall worked to revitalize the American defense establishment and to coordinate efforts with America's allies. Marshall stressed firepower and maneuver and, by war's end, the U.S. Army had grown to more than 8 million men and women and was the most mechanized and motorized combat force in the world. Marshall also strongly supported the Army Air Forces. For his great accomplishments in the war, Marshall became known as the "Organizer of Victory."

Marshall was a strong supporter of opening a second front in Europe, a campaign ultimately deferred until June 1944. Between 1941 and 1945, Marshall attended all the major wartime strategic conferences. He was the first to be promoted to the newly authorized five-star rank of general of the army in December 1944.

On the urging of President Harry S. Truman, Marshall agreed to serve as special envoy to China during 1945–1947. He became secretary of state in 1947 and advanced the Marshall Plan to rebuild Europe that same year. From 1949 to 1950, he was president of the American Red Cross. He returned to government service as secretary of defense in September 1950. He opposed General Douglas MacArthur's efforts for a widened war with China and supported Truman in his decisions to fight a "limited war" and to remove MacArthur as commander of United Nations forces.

Marshall resigned in September 1951, ending 50 years of dedicated government service. Awarded the 1953 Nobel Prize for Peace for the Marshall Plan, he was the first soldier so honored. Marshall died in Washington, D.C., on October 16, 1959. If not America's greatest soldier, Marshall was one of the nation's most capable military leaders and statesmen and certainly one of the most influential figures of the 20th century.

Spencer C. Tucker

References

Cray, Ed. *General of the Army: George C. Marshall, Soldier and Statesman.* New York: W. W. Norton, 1990.

Marshall, George C. *Memoirs of My Services in the World War, 1917–1918.* Boston: Houghton Mifflin Company, 1976.

Pogue, Forrest C. *George C. Marshall.* 4 vols. New York: Viking, 1963–1987.

Stoler, Mark A. *George C. Marshall: Soldier-Statesman of the American Century.* Boston: Twayne, 1989.

Mayo, Henry Thomas
(1856–1937)

U.S. Navy officer and commander of the Atlantic Fleet during World War I. Born on December 8, 1856, in Burlington, Vermont, Henry Thomas Mayo was commissioned in the navy on graduation from the United States Naval Academy, Annapolis, in 1876. His initial assignment was to the Asiatic Squadron of the Pacific Fleet. In 1883, he participated in the Greely Relief Expedition in the Arctic.

During the 1898 Spanish-American War, Mayo served aboard the gunboat *Bennington*, which operated off the West Coast of the United States. Promoted to commander in 1905, two years later Mayo assumed his first sea command, the cruiser *Albany*, off South America. Promoted to captain in 1908, Mayo took command of the cruiser *California*. He was promoted to rear admiral in 1913 and was assigned as aide to Secretary of the Navy Josephus Daniels.

In 1913, Mayo took command of the 4th Division of the Atlantic Fleet in the Caribbean. In April 1914, Mexican authorities at Tampico arrested some of Mayo's sailors on shore leave. Mayo demanded their immediate release as well as a public apology, causing a brief international crisis that almost led to war between the United States and Mexico. The incident made Mayo a public hero and helped bring his promotion to vice admiral in June 1914 and to full admiral and commander of the Atlantic Fleet in June 1916.

After the United States entered World War I in April 1917, Mayo commanded all U.S. warships in the Atlantic and European waters. Mayo represented the United States at a naval conference in London, where he pushed for more aggressive action. He also endorsed construction of a large antisubmarine force and recommended such measures as a mine barrage from Scotland to Norway.

Mayo commanded the redesignated U.S. Fleet after the war and kept that position until June 1919, when he reverted to his permanent rank of rear admiral. Following service on the General Board, during which he argued forcefully for the development of naval aviation assets, Mayo retired in December 1920. During

1924–1928, he was governor of the Philadelphia Naval Home. In 1930, he was advanced to the rank of admiral on the retired list. Mayo died at Portsmouth, New Hampshire, on February 23, 1937.

Christopher J. Richman

References

Jones, Jerry W. *U.S. Battleship Operations in World War I.* Annapolis, MD: Naval Institute Press, 1998.

Lewis, Charles Lee. *Famous American Naval Officers.* Boston: L. C. Page, 1948.

McAdoo, William Gibbs (1863–1941)

Attorney, railroad executive, politician, and U.S. secretary of the treasury (1913–1918). Born on October 31, 1863, into poverty in Marietta, Georgia, William Gibbs McAdoo had an irregular education before entering the University of Tennessee at Knoxville. He abandoned his studies in 1882 to accept a position as deputy clerk of the U.S. Circuit Court. Admitted to the Tennessee bar in 1885, he established a law practice at Chattanooga and served as a railroad attorney.

McAdoo eventually became president of an electrified railway, steering the company into bankruptcy by 1892. Starting anew in New York City in 1897, McAdoo sold railroad bonds and spearheaded an effort to improve rail service by building additional lines in and out of the city. In 1901, the construction of twin rail tunnels under the Hudson River made McAdoo into one of New York City's leading figures. As president of the Hudson and Manhattan Railway Company, he soon gained a reputation as a Progressive manager and an excellent financial steward.

In 1910, McAdoo met Woodrow Wilson for the first time and was impressed

Born into poverty, William McAdoo served as U.S. secretary of the treasury during 1913–1918. During this time period, the economic power of the federal government expanded exponentially. (Library of Congress)

with his integrity and Progressive vision. That same year, he supported Wilson's New Jersey gubernatorial campaign and, in 1912, he briefly led Wilson's presidential bid. After Wilson won the November 1920 election, McAdoo was rewarded with a cabinet position in 1913 as secretary of the treasury.

McAdoo presided over a dramatic increase in the economic power of the federal government as treasury secretary. McAdoo became even more closely tied to Wilson when, following his own wife's death in 1912, McAdoo married Wilson's daughter Eleanor in 1914. McAdoo played a prominent role in the passage of the December 1913 Federal Reserve Act, which helped to systematize the nation's banking system, stabilized the currency and interest and bond rates, and most notably created a permanent Federal Reserve Board of Governors, over which McAdoo presided as its first chairman.

On the beginning of World War I in 1914, McAdoo opposed sending U.S. troops, preferring to employ economic rather than military power to advance U.S. interests and support America's allies. McAdoo believed that to prevent the collapse of the U.S. economy and the failure of the Allied war effort, the United States had to lend the European powers the money they needed to continue purchasing supplies in U.S. markets. To this end, he coordinated massive loans to the Allied powers and mandated that the Europeans could spend federal money only in the United States. He also helped establish the War Risk Insurance Bureau in 1914 to issue insurance on ships and cargoes that had been refused reasonable rates by private companies and also helped establish the U.S. Shipping Board to maintain transatlantic traffic.

McAdoo also created and promoted the enormously successful Liberty Loan campaigns, which raised almost $17 billion from the American public in less than two years. The funds went to support the war effort. When the American rail system almost collapsed because of the crush of war shipments, Wilson ordered a temporary government takeover and appointed McAdoo as director of the United States Railroad Administration in early 1918. The move was controversial at the time, as the setup seemed quasi-socialistic to some Americans, but it was nevertheless a badly needed prescription to the bottlenecks in the railroad sector that were hampering mobilization. As a former railroad executive, McAdoo was a natural for the position. Indeed, he coordinated rail lines, eliminated the backlog of shipments, and,

true to his Progressive roots, intervened on behalf of railway employees to increase wages and improve working conditions.

Personal financial obligations forced McAdoo to tender his resignation three days after the signing of the armistice in 1918, having fulfilled his promise to stay until the war was over. Returning to his law practice, he moved to California and made an unsuccessful run for the 1924 Democratic presidential nomination. Unfortunately, McAdoo became embroiled in the Teapot Dome oil scandal and saw his political hopes dashed. In 1932, he won a U.S. Senate seat from California, riding the wave of Democratic triumph that ushered out the Republicans and gave birth to President Franklin D. Roosevelt's New Deal. Defeated for reelection in 1938, McAdoo died in Washington, D.C., on February 1, 1941.

Caryn E. Neumann

References
Broesamle, John J. *William Gibbs McAdoo: A Passion for Change, 1863–1917.* Port Washington, NY: Kennikat, 1973.
McAdoo, William Gibbs. *Crowded Years: The Reminiscences of William G. McAdoo.* Boston: Houghton Mifflin, 1931.
Shook, Dale N. *William G. McAdoo and the Development of National Economic Policy, 1913–1918.* New York: Garland, 1987.

Mitchell, William (1879–1936)

U.S. Army Air Corps general, considered by many to be the father of the U.S. Air Force. Born to American parents in Nice, France, on December 29, 1879, William "Billy" Mitchell grew up on his family's estate outside Milwaukee, Wisconsin, and attended Columbian College (today a division of George Washington University). In 1898 during the Spanish-American War,

An important early exponent of air power, Brigadier General William Mitchell had operational command of the U.S. Army Air Service in World War I. He is shown here at Château Chamarande, France, in September 1917. (Library of Congress)

he left school and enlisted in the 1st Wisconsin Volunteer Infantry.

Receiving a commission in the Signal Corps, Mitchell subsequently served in Cuba, the Philippines, and Alaska. In 1903, Mitchell joined an observation balloon unit and, later, the Signal Corps Aeronautics and Flying Section. In 1909 he graduated from the Army School of the Line and Staff and during 1912–1916 he served on the general staff.

Major Mitchell learned to fly and briefly directed army aviation. He participated with the 1st Aero Squadron in the 1916–1917 Punitive Expedition into Mexico under Brigadier General John J. Pershing and then went to France as an observer, arriving there a few days after the United States entered World War I in

1917. In France, Mitchell was deeply influenced by air power visionaries such as Major General Hugh Trenchard, commander of the Royal Flying Corps (RFC), a staunch proponent of a separate air arm and the employment of airplanes as offensive weapons in warfare.

In early 1918, commander of the American Expeditionary Forces (AEF) General Pershing placed Brigadier General Mason Patrick in overall command of the American Air Service in France, but he gave now Colonel Mitchell operational air command. In September 1918, Mitchell planned the air support for the Saint-Mihiel Offensive, sending aloft 1,481 aircraft against German air and ground targets with great success. Mitchell pioneered mass, large-scale bombing raids. An enthusiastic and intrepid leader, he alienated many of his superiors because of his flamboyant and sometimes seemingly reckless behavior. Nevertheless, by the end of the war Mitchell had become a brigadier general.

Following the war, Mitchell was assistant chief of the Air Service and campaigned in the press and with Congress for an independent air force modeled after the newly established Royal Air Force. He also published the books *Our Air Force* (1921) and *Winged Defense* (1925), both designed to sway public opinion in support of an independent air arm. Mitchell demonstrated the potential of air power in a mock attack on New York City and the sinking of the German prize battleship *Ostfriesland.* Mitchell's abrasive approach continued to win him many enemies in the navy and army, including those who supported his views regarding the future of air power. When Congress refused to establish a separate air force and left aviation underfunded in the early 1920s, Mitchell became more outspoken in his public criticism. Reduced in rank to colonel in 1925, Mitchell was transferred to a minor assignment at San Antonio, Texas.

Mitchell refused to curb his public campaign, however. Following the 1925 crash of the navy airship *Shenandoah,* Mitchell accused the national defense establishment of "incompetency, criminal negligence, and almost treasonable administration of the national defense." Court-martialed for his comments, Mitchell was convicted of conduct "prejudicial to good order and military discipline" and suspended from duty without pay for five years. He resigned his commission in January 1926. In retirement Mitchell continued to write and publicize his views. He died in New York City on February 19, 1936.

World War II clearly revealed the accuracy of Mitchell's predictions. The noted medium bomber, the North American B-25, was named in his honor. His cherished independent air force became a reality in 1947. That July, the U.S. Congress granted Mitchell a posthumous promotion to major general and awarded him a special Medal of Honor.

William Head

References

Cooke, James J. *Billy Mitchell.* Boulder, CO: Rienner, 2002.

Davis, Burke. *The Billy Mitchell Affair.* New York: Random House, 1967.

Flogel, Raymond R. *United States Air Power Doctrine and the Influence of William Mitchell and Giulio Douhet at the Air Corps Tactical School, 1921–1935.* Norman: University of Oklahoma Press, 1966.

Head, William P. *Every Inch a Soldier: Augustine Warner Robins and the Building of U.S. Air Power.* College Station: Texas A & M University Press, 1995.

Morgan, John Pierpont (1837–1913)

Influential U.S. financier and industrialist whose activities facilitated the American industrial revolution, which in turn gave impetus to U.S. overseas economic and territorial expansion at the end of the 19th century. Born in Hartford, Connecticut, on April 17, 1837, John Pierpont Morgan was the son of Julius Morgan, a wealthy financier. After attending the University of Göttingen in Germany, Morgan worked as an accountant for Duncan, Sherman, and Company, a New York City banking firm, from 1857 to 1861. At the outbreak of the Civil War in 1861, he avoided military service by paying for a substitute soldier to take his place, a practice that was legal at the time and not unusual for men in his position. During the war, he first worked for George Peabody and Company, then moved to Dabney, Morgan, and Company, working there from 1864 to 1871. He joined the Philadelphia firm of Drexel, Morgan, and Company as a partner in 1871. After the death of the firm's founder, Anthony J. Drexel, in 1893, Morgan became the senior partner of the firm. The firm, which subsequently became J. P. Morgan and Company, grew to be one of the most powerful banking houses in the world.

Morgan bought, consolidated, or restructured many U.S. railroads during the last two decades of the 19th century. By 1900, he controlled more than 5,000 miles of rail lines. Morgan also implemented regulations and standards that the federal government was either unwilling or unable to enact. His vast holdings in the railroad industry included the New York Central, the New Haven and Hartford, as well as the Pennsylvania, the

Reading, and the Chesapeake and Ohio networks. Given the vast quantities of steel that railroads required, Morgan also began to look into acquiring interests in the steel industry.

In 1892, Morgan financed the formation of General Electric, by merging Edison General Electric and the Thomson-Houston Electric Company. In 1896, General Electric was one of the first companies listed on the newly formed Dow Jones Industrial Average. In 1893, Morgan supplied the U.S. government with $62 million in gold to issue government bonds, which restored a surplus to the U.S. Treasury. This financial coup helped to return the nation to economic prosperity following the devastating economic depression of 1893–1897.

In 1901, Morgan financed the creation of the U.S. Steel Corporation by purchasing the interests of steel magnate Andrew Carnegie and other steel-producing industrialists. At the time of its creation, the U.S. Steel Corporation, which became the world's first billion-dollar corporation, was the largest steel producer in the world and accounted for two-thirds of all U.S. steel production. Federal antitrust legislation unsuccessfully attempted to break up U.S. Steel in 1911. Increased steel production greatly facilitated the role of the United States as a great power during and in the aftermath of the Spanish-American War. It also allowed the United States to continue building a first-class, all-steel navy that would soon become the envy of the world.

In 1902, Morgan facilitated the creation of the International Mercantile Marine Company by financing the purchase of the Leyland Line and other British steamship companies operating in the Atlantic Ocean. Among the companies purchased was the White Star Line, which built and operated the ill-fated ocean liner *Titanic*. Indeed, Morgan was to have been a passenger on the ship's maiden voyage, but business activities in Europe kept him from departing on the doomed ship in 1912.

Morgan also made substantial contributions to numerous charities, churches, hospitals, and schools during his lifetime. He died in Rome, Italy, on March 31, 1913, at which time Morgan's son, J. P. Morgan Jr., inherited his father's financial empire. Morgan's mighty financial, industrial, and transportation empires helped turn the United States into an economic powerhouse second to none by the eve of World War I. This allowed the United States to aid the Allies (Entente Powers) with all sorts of war matériel and to provide them with vast sums of money in the form of war loans. Indeed, because of Morgan's financial consolidation and the ascendant power of Wall Street, New York had surpassed London as the world's financial capital by 1917.

Michael R. Hall

References

Chernow, Ron. *The House of Morgan: An American Banking Dynasty and the Rise of Modern Finance.* New York: Grove Press, 2001.

Morris, Charles R. *The Tycoons: How Andrew Carnegie, John D. Rockefeller and J. P. Morgan Invented the American Supereconomy.* New York: Times Books, 2005.

Pershing, John Joseph (1860–1948)

General of the Armies of the United States and commander of the American Expeditionary Forces (AEF). Born in Laclede, Missouri, on September 13, 1860, John Joseph Pershing received an appointment to the United States Mili-

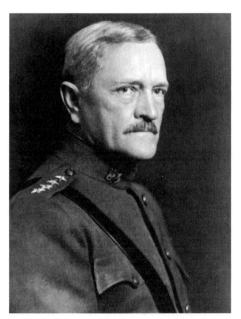

General of the Armies of the United States John J. Pershing commanded the American Expeditionary Forces in France during 1917–1918. (Library of Congress)

tary Academy, West Point, in 1882. Commissioned a 2nd lieutenant on graduation in 1886, he joined the 6th Cavalry Regiment in New Mexico, where he saw limited action in the final subjugation of the Apaches.

In 1891, Pershing became professor of military science at the University of Nebraska, where he also studied law. He completed a law degree in 1893 and, frustrated by the lack of military advancement, considered a legal career. In 1895, he returned to the field with the African American 10th Cavalry and in 1897 became an instructor of tactics at West Point. Here, cadets unhappy with his dark demeanor and rigid style labeled him "Black Jack," a derogatory reference to Pershing's 10th Cavalry posting.

During the 1898 Spanish-American War, Pershing rejoined the 10th Cavalry for the Cuba Campaign. There the black soldiers under him performed admirably during the Battle of San Juan Heights, and Pershing drew praise for his coolness under fire. Returning to the United States, he was promoted to major of volunteers and assigned to the Office of the Assistant Secretary of War, where he organized the War Department's new Bureau of Insular Affairs. Pershing's experience and legal training prepared him well for the changing role of the U.S. military establishment and the challenges of colonial administration, which he first encountered in 1899 in the Philippines. In 1901, after finally receiving promotion to captain in the regular army, he campaigned successfully against the Moros, attracting further recognition.

In 1905, as a military attaché to Japan, Pershing was a military observer of the Russo-Japanese War. Having earned the confidence of President Roosevelt for his handling of Philippine affairs and his reports on the Russo-Japanese War, in September 1906, Roosevelt advanced Pershing from captain to brigadier general over 862 more senior-ranking officers—a rare occurrence. Pershing spent most of the next eight years in the Philippines. In 1914, he was sent to Fort Bliss near El Paso, Texas, to confront problems associated with the Mexican Revolution.

In March 1916, Mexican revolutionary leader Francisco "Pancho" Villa led a raid on the small border town in New Mexico that prompted a massive response by the United States. Pershing took charge of the Punitive Expedition into Mexico, with orders to capture or kill Villa and his followers while avoiding conflict with Mexico. The expedition of more than 10,000 men was carried out in a politically charged and hostile environment. It lasted almost a year, cut deep into northern Mexico, and threatened to trigger an all-out war between the United States and Mexico. Although Villa escaped, Pershing used the expedition to test some of the new technologies of war, including machine guns, aircraft, motorized transport, and radio.

In May 1917, following the U.S. declaration of war, President Woodrow Wilson named Pershing, only recently promoted to major general, to command the AEF, which was to fight in Europe as a distinctive American force. Once more, Pershing faced a delicate situation, as he was forced to maintain U.S. autonomy amid persistent pressure from his European allies for U.S. divisions to fill holes in their deteriorating ranks. Pershing, promoted to full general in October 1917, stubbornly refused to have his forces fed piecemeal into the trenches, and he labored to avoid subjecting his men to the failed practices that had made the war so horrible. But during the crisis occasioned by Germany's 1918 Ludendorff offensives, Pershing offered individual U.S. divisions as reinforcements to the Allied command, and the U.S. troops quickly proved their worth in the heavy fighting that followed.

Pershing continued to ready his fighting force—the U.S. First Army—for the long-desired independent action, which supreme Allied commander Marshal Ferdinand Foch finally authorized. In September 1918, the largest U.S. military operation since the Civil War struck and reduced the German-held Saint-Mihiel salient. Pershing hoped to follow up this victory with a drive on Metz and beyond, but Foch refused. At the insistence of Foch, Pershing instead redirected U.S. efforts to participate in the massive Meuse-Argonne Offensive that began on September 26 and lasted until the armistice in

November. Pershing's attention to logistics and his emphasis on mobility complemented his soldiers' tenacity in battle and allowed the United States to play the decisive role in the final months of the war. After overseeing the demobilization of U.S. forces, in 1919 Pershing returned to the United States a hero.

In September 1919, Congress confirmed Pershing's status as a four-star general with the rank of general of the armies (which did not include a fifth star as would the later general of the army rank established in December 1944). He was appointed army chief of staff in 1921 and retired from active service in 1924. While still serving as chief of staff in 1923, he also became chairman of the American Battle Monuments Commission, the organization responsible for the administration of all American military cemeteries outside the United States. He continued serving in that capacity until 1948.

Active in public life, he also excelled as an author, receiving the Pulitzer Prize for his book, *My Experiences in the World War* (1931). Something of a mentor to future leaders like George C. Marshall, Dwight D. Eisenhower, and Douglas MacArthur, Pershing, although confined to bed for many years, lived to see the men he influenced triumph in World War II. As a soldier, he served in an army that had evolved from a frontier constabulary to an international police force and finally to world power, and he played a large role in fostering that evolution. Pershing died in Washington, D.C., on July 15, 1948.

David Coffey

References

Cooke, James J. *Pershing and His Generals: Command and Staff in the AEF.* Westport, CT: Praeger, 1997.

Smith, Gene. *Until the Last Trumpet Sounds: The Life of General of the Armies John J. Pershing.* New York: Wiley, 1999.

Smythe, Donald. *Pershing: General of the Armies.* Bloomington: Indiana University Press, 1986.

Read, George Windle (1860–1934)

U.S. Army general. Born in Indianola, Iowa, on November 19, 1860, George Windle Read attended the United States Military Academy, West Point, where he was 1st captain of the Corps of Cadets. He was commissioned a 2nd lieutenant of infantry on his graduation in 1883. Read's first assignment was with the 16th Infantry Regiment in the American West. Within a few months he transferred to the 5th Cavalry, continuing his service in the West until 1889. During 1889–1893, he was professor of military science and tactics at the University of Iowa. He then served in Texas. During the Spanish-American War, he was in Cuba with an ordnance unit until 1899. Promoted to captain, he then served in New Mexico. During 1901–1902, he was in the Philippines during the Philippine-American War. He then served in California and Hawaii and was assigned to the general staff during 1905–1909. He subsequently saw service in Cuba, Puerto Rico, and, following promotion to major, again in the Philippines during 1910–1912. Read graduated from the Army War College in 1914. He was then promoted to lieutenant colonel. During 1914–1915 in a period of heightened tensions with Mexico, he served along the border in both Arizona and Texas. He was again with the general staff in Washington in 1915–1917.

Following U.S. entry into World War I in April 1917, Colonel Read had charge of army recruiting. Promoted to brigadier general in August 1917, Read took command of a brigade at Camp Upton, Long Island, New York. Advanced to temporary major general, that December he took command of a cavalry division at El Paso, Texas. In April 1918, he became commander of the 30th ("Old Hickory") Division, which he immediately led to France. In June, American Expeditionary Forces commander General John J. Pershing selected Read to command II Corps, which consisted of five U.S. divisions, all serving in the British sector of the Western Front. When three of his divisions were transferred to participate in the Saint-Mihiel Offensive, the remainder operated as a corps under the British Fourth Army in the Ypres area, where they occupied a sector of the line just south of Ypres and participated in offensive operations in August and September 1918 that pierced the Hindenburg Line. Read held this command until demobilization of II Corps in February 1919. He then commanded the American Embarkation Center at Le Mans, France, for two months.

In May 1919, Read took command of V Corps at Camp Jackson, South Carolina. He was promoted to major general on March 8, 1921. In October 1922, Read assumed command of the Philippine Department, serving in that position until his retirement from the army on November 19, 1924. Read died in Washington, D.C., on November 6, 1934.

Spencer C. Tucker

References

Coffman, Edward M. *The War to End All Wars.* Lexington: University Press of Kentucky, 1998.

Pershing, John J. *My Experiences in the World War.* 2 vols. New York: Stokes, 1931.

Roosevelt, Franklin Delano (1882–1945)

U.S. political leader and president (1933–1945). Born at the family Hyde Park estate in Dutchess County, New York, on January 30, 1882, Franklin Roosevelt was educated at home until age 14. He then attended Groton Preparatory School, Harvard University, and Columbia University Law School. In 1905, Roosevelt married his distant cousin Eleanor Roosevelt, President Theodore Roosevelt's niece.

Upon passing the bar examination, Roosevelt joined the law firm of Carter, Ledyard, and Milburn. Elected to the New York Senate in 1910, he advocated progressive reform and was active in Democratic Party politics. A strong supporter of Woodrow Wilson for the presidency in the election of 1912, Roosevelt was awarded by President Wilson with the post of assistant secretary of the navy under Secretary of the Navy Josephus Daniels in 1913.

In his new position, Roosevelt showed excellent administrative skills and worked tirelessly to promote the navy, expand its size, and prepare it for war. Roosevelt's early advocacy of U.S. intervention on the Allied side, however, found him at odds with Wilson, Daniels, and a majority of the cabinet. A strong internationalist, Roosevelt also supported U.S. intervention in Haiti.

Roosevelt reorganized the navy's administrative system and introduced more effective management techniques. When the United States entered the war in April 1917, he oversaw a vast naval expansion program. He was a strong advocate of the extensive British and U.S. mining of the North Sea and he traveled to the war zone twice to inspect U.S. bases. He was also a supporter of the new League of Nations.

Assistant Secretary of the Navy Franklin Delano Roosevelt rendered important service in preparing the U.S. Navy for World War I. He was president of the United States during 1933–1945. (Library of Congress)

Roosevelt left the Navy Department in 1920 to run unsuccessfully for vice president of the United States on the Democratic Party ticket headed by James M. Cox. Stricken with polio in 1921, he was permanently disabled but retained his intense interest in politics. Serving as governor of New York from 1929 to 1933, he worked effectively to alleviate suffering caused by the Great Depression, which began in 1929.

Winning election to the presidency in November 1932 over incumbent Herbert Hoover, Roosevelt rallied the American people and promised a "New Deal." His early legislative successes included banking reform, the Agricultural Adjustment Act (AAA), and the National Industrial

Recovery Act (NIRA). The National Recovery Administration (NRA) set minimum wages and limited hours for employees. The Civilian Conservation Corps (CCC) employed thousands of men to replant forests and work on flood control projects. Roosevelt also established the Securities and Exchange Commission (SEC), while the Works Progress Administration (WPA) extended employment to millions of workers in construction projects. Social Security legislation provided for the aged and disabled. The American people reelected Roosevelt in 1936, 1940, and 1944, making him the only U.S. president elected to four terms.

With the beginning of World War II in Europe in September 1939, Roosevelt increasingly turned to foreign affairs and military preparedness. He gradually moved the United States from isolation, concluding arrangements with Britain. Roosevelt also initiated a major rearmament program and secured passage of the Selective Service Act, the first peacetime draft in the nation's history. On his urging, Congress passed the Lend-Lease Act in March 1941, which extended U.S. aid to countries fighting the Axis.

Roosevelt pressed Japan to withdraw from China, and when Japanese troops occupied southern Indochina in spring 1941 he embargoed scrap metal and oil to Japan. Roosevelt also ordered the Pacific Fleet to move its headquarters from San Diego to Honolulu, Hawaii, in order to increase pressure on Japan, but the embargo led that nation's leaders to opt for war with the United States and order an attack on the Pacific Fleet at Pearl Harbor on December 7, 1941.

Roosevelt guided the United States through the war. During the course of the conflict, the United States not only fielded a navy larger than all the other navies of the world combined, but the largest air force and the most mobile, most heavily mechanized, and best-armed army in world history. It also provided the machines of war, raw materials, and food that enabled other nations to continue fighting the Axis. In these circumstances, full economic recovery occurred.

Roosevelt met frequently with British and Soviet leaders in an effort to secure a stable postwar world. Although criticized for making unnecessary concessions to the Soviet Union at the Yalta Conference (February 4–11, 1945), Roosevelt really had little choice, as the Red Army already occupied much of Eastern Europe and the United States military wished to induce the Soviet Union to enter the war against Japan.

Roosevelt died at his summer home in Warm Springs, Georgia, of a massive cerebral hemorrhage on April 12, 1945. A highly effective communicator and one of the best-loved presidents in U.S. history, Roosevelt led the nation through two of its greatest trials, the Great Depression and World War II.

Spencer C. Tucker

References

Davis, Kenneth S. *FDR: The Beckoning of Destiny, 1882–1928*. New York: Putnam, 1972.

Freidel, Frank. *Roosevelt: A Rendezvous with Destiny*. New York: Little, Brown and Co., 1990.

Marolda, Edward J., ed. *FDR and the U.S. Navy*. New York: St. Martin's Press, 1998.

Sims, William Sowden (1858–1936)

U.S. Navy admiral. Born in Port Hope, Ontario, Canada, on October 15, 1858, William Sowden Sims was the son of an American father and Canadian mother.

Admiral William S. Sims commanded U.S. Navy forces in European waters during World War I. (Library of Congress)

His family moved to Pennsylvania when he was 10, and Sims graduated from the United States Naval Academy, Annapolis, in 1880. The transformation of the U.S. Navy in this period to new steel ships and breech-loading guns marked the beginning of his lifelong interest in the development of naval equipment, technology, and doctrine.

Intelligence reports that Sims sent the Office of Naval Intelligence during the 1895 Sino-Japanese War carefully analyzed the performance of the various vessels involved and drew lessons as to how the effectiveness of the U.S. fleet might be improved. From 1897 to 1900, Sims was U.S. naval attaché to France and Russia, and information on European naval innovations that he provided as well as extensive intelligence gathering

he conducted against Spain during the Spanish-American War favorably impressed Assistant Secretary of the Navy Theodore Roosevelt, who became president in 1901. In 1901, Sims served on the staff of the commander of the U.S. Asiatic Fleet and there became friends with British captain Percy Scott, learning from him the new techniques of gunnery developed by the Royal Navy. Sims's efforts to interest the U.S. Navy in these were not successful, leading him to write directly to President Roosevelt, technically an act of insubordination. Recalled to Washington in 1902 and appointed as inspector of target practice, Sims during 1902–1909 achieved significant success in U.S. naval ordnance reform, reducing the firing time for large-caliber guns from 5 minutes to 30 seconds, while at the same time improving accuracy. Sims served as an observer during the 1904–1905 Russo-Japanese War.

Promoted to captain in 1911, Sims was an instructor at the Naval War College during 1911–1912. He then commanded the Atlantic Torpedo Flotilla. Promoted to rear admiral in 1916, the following year he returned to the Naval War College as its president.

With war between the United States and Germany looming, Sims was dispatched to Britain to discuss naval cooperation with the Allied Powers. The United States declared war on Germany on April 6, 1917, before his arrival. Promoted to temporary vice admiral in May and made commander of U.S. naval forces in European waters, Sims bombarded Washington with recommendations on convoying, antisubmarine warfare, intelligence gathering, and strategic planning. He urged the immediate implementation of convoys, which gained the support of British prime minister David Lloyd George, and he also urged that U.S. battleships be assigned primarily to escort duties convoying supplies and men for the Allies, ventures that brought drastic reductions in Allied shipping losses but generally involved resigning overall control of U.S. naval operations in Europe to British admirals.

Sims's can-do attitude and his excellent relations with his British counterparts led Washington officials, including Secretary of the Navy Josephus Daniels and Chief of Naval Operations William Shepherd Benson, to consider him too much of an Anglophile. For his part, Sims ascribed the navy's initially somewhat disappointing wartime performance to his superiors' failure to adopt some of his suggestions and what he viewed as their earlier reluctance to prepare the navy for a major conflict, charges he aired to Congress during a 1920 investigation that he largely precipitated and that provoked bitter feuding within the navy.

By November 1917, Sims and his staff were supervising the operations of 350 ships and 75,000 men. Promoted to temporary admiral in December 1918, Sims returned to the United States and reverted to his permanent rank of rear admiral. He headed the Naval War College from April 1919 until his retirement in October 1922. He continued to speak out on naval and defense issues, publishing his wartime memoirs, *The Victory at Sea* (1920), which won the Pulitzer Prize for History. He also forcefully urged the development of naval aviation. A dynamic and energetic reformer and proponent of naval expansion, in later life Sims's unfortunate tendency to demonize those who opposed him vitiated his numerous concrete achievements. Sims died in Boston, Massachusetts, on September 25, 1936.

Priscilla Roberts

References

Hagan, Kenneth J. "William S. Sims: Naval Insurgent and Coalition Warrior." Pp. 187–203. In *The Human Tradition in the Gilded Age and Progressive Era.* Edited by Ballard C. Campbell. Wilmington, DE: Scholarly Resources, 2000.

Morison, Elting E. *Admiral Sims and the Modern American Navy.* Boston: Houghton Mifflin, 1942.

Sims, William S. *The Victory at Sea.* Garden City, NY: Doubleday, 1920; reprint, Annapolis, MD: Naval Institute Press, 1984.

Trask, David F. *Captains and Cabinets: Anglo-American Naval Relations, 1917–1918.* Columbia: University of Missouri Press, 1972.

Summerall, Charles Pelot (1867–1955)

U.S. Army general. Born in Blounts Ferry, Florida, on March 4, 1867, Charles Pelot Summerall graduated from secondary school and briefly taught at a school in Florida until he was appointed to the United States Military Academy at West Point in 1888. He graduated in 1892 and was commissioned in the infantry but transferred to the artillery the following year. Summerall saw service in the 1898 Spanish-American War as an aide-de-camp to two generals, after which he served in a succession of artillery units, including in the Philippine-American War from 1899 to 1900 and during the relief expedition to Peking (Beijing) during the Boxer Rebellion. In September 1914, as a major, he was assigned to the War Department.

Summerall worked in the Militia Bureau with the field artillery of the National Guard then in the summer of 1917 with the Baker Board, which was a military mission to Europe. He was promoted to lieutenant colonel in July 1916 and, following U.S. entry into World War I, to colonel in May 1917.

Advanced to brigadier general in August 1917, two months later Summerall departed for France in command of the 67th Field Artillery Brigade of the 42nd (Rainbow) Division, but he was transferred to command of the 1st Field Artillery Brigade of the 1st Division in December, when Major General Robert Lee Bullard took command of the division. Bullard had known Summerall from service in the Philippines. In June 1918, Summerall was promoted to major general, and the next month he assumed command of the 1st Division when Bullard was promoted to command III Corps. Summerall's leadership and toughness helped his division weather the bloody Soissons battle. Following the Saint-Mihiel Offensive, in October 1918 Summerall was assigned command of V Corps during the Meuse-Argonne Campaign. As the U.S. First Army closed in on Sedan, Summerall achieved some notoriety as he launched his old command, the 1st Division, now commanded by Brigadier General Frank Parker, across the front of several divisions of Major General Joseph Dickman's I Corps to take Sedan in advance of the French Fourth Army. In fairness to Summerall, American Expeditionary Forces (AEF) commander General John J. Pershing had told both his corps commanders that he wanted them to "take Sedan," so Summerall was merely following the orders of his commanding officer.

Following the armistice in November 1918, Summerall served on the American Peace Commission in 1919 and commanded several corps and departments before his appointment as chief of staff of the army in 1926 at the rank of lieutenant general. Three years later, he was advanced to full (four-star) general. After a brief retirement in Florida in 1930–1931, he accepted appointment as president of the Military College of South Carolina, the Citadel, in September 1931. He held that post until 1953. Summerall died in Washington, D.C., on May 14, 1955.

John F. Votaw

References

Bullard, Robert Lee. *Personalities and Reminiscences of the War.* Garden City, NY: Doubleday Page & Company, 1925.

Coffman, Edward M. *The War to End All Wars: The American Military Experience in World War I.* Lexington: University Press of Kentucky, 1998.

Cooke, James J. *Pershing and His Generals: Command and Staff in the AEF.* Westport, CT: Praeger, 1997.

Wilson, Thomas Woodrow (1856–1924)

Democratic Party politician and president of the United States (1913–1921). Born on December 28, 1856, in Staunton, Virginia, Thomas Woodrow Wilson grew up in Augusta, Georgia, and South Carolina. The son of a Presbyterian minister and seminary professor, he was raised in a strict religious and academic environment. Wilson studied history and politics at Princeton University, graduating in 1879. He then studied law at the University of Virginia for a year and passed the Georgia bar examination in 1882. He practiced law for a time in Atlanta, but abandoned it to earn a doctorate in constitutional and political history at Johns Hopkins University in 1886. By then he had joined the faculty at Bryn Mawr College. In 1890, Wilson returned to Princeton, first as a professor and then as president of the university in 1902.

Woodrow Wilson was president of the United States during 1913–1921. He sought to pursue a foreign policy based on morality and hoped to avoid involvement in World War I. The ensuing League of Nations was primarily his work. (Library of Congress)

A Progressive reformer, Wilson turned to politics and won election as governor of New Jersey in 1910. His success in bringing about Progressive legislation led him to become the Democratic Party nominee in the 1912 presidential election. Wilson won the election after the Republican Party split, because former president Theodore Roosevelt attempted to return to the White House at the head of the newly formed Bull Moose Party.

As president, Wilson was preoccupied with domestic policy and his belief that government should encourage free and competitive markets. On his initiative, Congress passed the Federal Reserve Act of 1913 that created 12 regional Federal Reserve banks, supervised by a Federal Reserve Board of Governors. Its primary duty was to regulate the volume of money in circulation to ensure a healthy economy. In 1914, Wilson signed into law the Clayton Anti-Trust Act, which prevented interlocking directorates and declared illegal certain monopolistic business practices.

Wilson was not as successful in his foreign policy, where he sought to implement diplomacy based on morality. Wilson pledged that the United States would forgo territorial conquests, and he and his first secretary of state, William Jennings Bryan, worked to establish a new relationship between the United States and Latin America.

Despite Wilson's best intentions to avoid conflict with U.S. neighbors, his distaste for political upheaval in Mexico led him to send forces to occupy Veracruz in April 1914. Incidents along the border caused him two years later to mobilize the National Guard and dispatch a regular army force into northern Mexico in a vain attempt to capture Mexican revolutionary Pancho Villa.

Wilson proclaimed U.S. neutrality when World War I began in August 1914. Germany's submarine warfare brought the nation to the brink of war, however. The sinking of the passenger liner *Lusitania* in May 1915, which killed 128 American passengers, led Wilson to issue a series of threatening notes that compelled Germany to halt unrestricted submarine warfare.

Although Wilson won reelection in 1916, primarily on the platform of having kept the United States out of the war, he had also secured congressional approval that year of the National Defense Act, which greatly enlarged the peacetime army and National Guard. German acts of sabotage against the United States and publication of the Zimmermann Telegram, in which the German government proposed an alliance with Mexico, alienated American opinion. But the great blow to Wilson's efforts to keep the United States neutral came on February 1, 1917, when Germany resumed unrestricted submarine warfare. The sinking of U.S. merchant ships and the loss of American lives led Wilson to request a declaration of war, which Congress approved on April 6.

To avoid entangling alliances, Wilson made it clear that the country was merely an "associated power," fighting the same enemy. With no military experience of his own, Wilson deferred to his military advisers. Wilson instructed American Expeditionary Forces (AEF) commander General John J. Pershing to cooperate with the forces of other countries fighting Germany, but to keep U.S. forces distinct and separate from those of the Allies. Wilson supported Pershing in his refusal to allow the Allies to commit AEF units piecemeal, but when General Ferdinand Foch became supreme Allied commander in the crisis of the spring of 1918, Wilson made it clear that Pershing was subordinate to him.

Wilson's platform was to "make the world safe for democracy." He also unwisely referred to the conflict as "the war to end all wars." But Wilson was determined to keep the United States free of territorial commitments, and in January 1918 he announced his Fourteen Points as a basis of peace. These included "Open covenants openly arrived at"; freedom of the seas; international disarmament; return of territory captured by the Central Powers, as well as the return to France of Alsace-Lorraine; an independent Poland with access to the sea;

and a League of Nations. Meanwhile, the United States tipped the balance of the scales in favor of the Allies, and Wilson played this to full advantage.

Following the armistice of November 11, 1918, Wilson unwisely decided to head the U.S. delegation to the Paris Peace Conference. Wilson knew little of European affairs, and was convinced that the peoples of Europe wanted him to be the arbiter of the peace and that they favored a settlement based on "right" rather than on narrow national self-interest. Although Secretary of State Robert Lansing accompanied Wilson to Paris, the president largely ignored him and other advisers. He also failed to include in the delegation any key Republicans.

At Paris, Wilson developed a close working relationship with British prime minister David Lloyd George. The two men stood together on most key issues against French premier Georges Clemenceau. The League of Nations was based on an Anglo-American draft. The resulting Treaty of Versailles with Germany and general peace settlement was essentially Wilson's work.

By the time Wilson returned to the United States in July 1919, popular sentiment had moved toward isolationism. The Republicans, led by Sen. Henry Cabot Lodge, insisted upon restricting the power of the League of Nations. Even some Democrats wanted amendments. Wilson embarked on a grueling cross-country speaking tour in an effort to sway public opinion, but he suffered a stroke on October 2, 1919, that left him virtually incapacitated. When he insisted that Democrats in the U.S. Senate reject any compromises in the agreements, the Senate refused twice to ratify either the Treaty of Versailles or to enter the

League of Nations. Wilson died in Washington on February 3, 1924.

Sugita Yoneyuki
and Spencer C. Tucker

References

Ambrosius, Lloyd E. *Wilsonian Statecraft: Theory and Practice of Liberal Internationalism during World War I.* Wilmington, DE: Scholarly Resources, 1991.

Esposito, David M. *The Legacy of Woodrow Wilson: American War Aims in World War I.* Westport, CT: Praeger, 1996.

Link, Arthur S. *Wilson.* 5 vols. Princeton, NJ: Princeton University Press, 1947–1965.

Nordholt, John Willem Schulte. *Woodrow Wilson: A Life for World Peace.* Berkeley: University of California Press, 1991.

Thompson, John A. *Woodrow Wilson.* New York: Longman, 2002.

Major General Leonard Wood became chief of staff of the army in 1910, but trained the 10th and 89th Infantry Divisions during World War I. Wood advocated a program of universal military training and wartime conscription known as the Preparedness Movement. (National Archives)

Wood, Leonard (1860–1927)

U.S. Army general. Born on October 9, 1860, in Winchester, New Hampshire, Leonard Wood received a medical degree from Harvard College in 1884. He joined the army as a contract surgeon in 1885 and participated in the Geronimo Campaign, for which he ultimately received the Medal of Honor. In 1890, he married Louise Conditt-Smith, a favorite niece of U.S. Supreme Court Justice Stephen Field, whose political influence proved to be important in Wood's later career.

In 1895, Wood was assigned to Washington, D.C., where he became personal physician to the families of Presidents Grover Cleveland and William McKinley and Assistant Secretary of the Navy Theodore Roosevelt. When the Spanish-American War began in 1898, he was given command of the 1st Volunteer Cavalry Regiment (the Rough Riders) with Roosevelt as his second-in-command.

Wood commanded the Rough Riders at the Battle of Las Guásimas, after which he was promoted to brigadier general, and then commanded the 2nd Cavalry Brigade in the Battle of San Juan Hill. Shortly after the Spanish surrendered Santiago de Cuba, Wood was made first military governor of the city and then of the province. He used his medical training to bring disease and starvation under control and proved an exceptional administrator. Wood's success, coupled with his political ties and penchant for political machinations, led to him being named military governor of Cuba in December 1899. As governor he made notable strides in education, public health, and prison reform and established a fiscally responsible republican government. Perhaps his greatest accomplishment was his sponsorship of Walter Reed's yellow fever experiments in Cuba. Although he had attained the rank of major general of volunteers, Wood was still a captain in the medical corps until 1901 when, in a controversial move, he was promoted to brigadier general in the regular army with the help of now-president Roosevelt, over 509 more senior officers.

Wood turned the government of Cuba over to an elected government in 1902 and was named commander of the Department of Mindanao, Philippines, where he fought to control Islamic insurgents. He was promoted to major general in the regular army in 1904 and named commander of the Division of the Philippines in 1906. In 1908, he assumed command of the Department of the East. He served as chief of staff of the army from 1910 to 1914. As chief of staff he introduced techniques of scientific management and worked to professionalize the officer corps.

From 1914 to 1917, Wood served in the Department of the East as its commander. Convinced as early as 1910 that the United States would eventually participate in a European war, he was a vocal advocate of military preparedness and led the Preparedness Movement, designed to train civilians who could serve as officers in such a war. He also advocated universal military training and was an outspoken opponent of President Woodrow Wilson's pacifism. In 1916, Wood, who repeatedly crossed the traditional line separating military officers from politics, was briefly considered as a Republican candidate for president.

When the United States entered World War I in April 1917, Wood was passed over for command of the American Expeditionary Forces in favor of his former subordinate, General John J. Pershing. Wood was relegated to training the 89th Division at Camp Funston, near Manhattan, Kansas, and when that unit was sent to Europe in May 1918 Wood was (at Pershing's specific request) relieved and reassigned to train the 10th Division. In January 1918, while on an inspection tour of the Western Front, Wood received a minor injury from a mortar shell. In spite of the fact that he never was formally assigned a combat role, he was the most senior U.S. officer actually wounded by hostile fire in the war.

When Theodore Roosevelt died unexpectedly in 1919, Wood became his political heir and narrowly missed receiving the Republican nomination for president in 1920, even though he was still a general officer on active duty. From 1919 until 1921 he commanded the Central Division, and then served on a special mission to the Philippines. He retired from active service in late 1921 and then returned to the Philippines, serving as governor-general until 1927. Wood died in Boston on August 7, 1927, during surgery to remove a benign brain tumor.

Jack McCallum

References

Hagedorn, Hermann. *Leonard Wood: A Biography.* New York: Harper, 1931.

Lane, Jack. *Armed Progressive: General Leonard Wood.* San Rafael, CA: Presidio, 1978.

McCallum, Jack. *Leonard Wood: A Biography.* New York: New York University Press, 2005.

Further Reading in World War I

American Battle Monuments Commission. *American Armies and Battlefields in Europe: A History, Guide, and Reference Book.* Washington, DC: U.S. Government Printing Office, 1938.

Asprey, Robert B. *At Belleau Wood.* New York: Putnam, 1965.

———. *The German High Command at War: Hindenburg and Ludendorff Conduct World War I.* New York: William Morrow, 1991.

Bailey, J. B. A. *Field Artillery and Firepower.* Annapolis, MD: Naval Institute Press, 2004.

———. *The First World War and the Birth of the Modern Style of Warfare*, "The Occasional, Number 22." Camberley, England: British Staff College, 1996.

Baker, Newton D. *Why We Went to War.* New York: Harper, 1936.

Barnett, Correlli. *The Swordbearers; Supreme Command in the First World War.* Bloomington: Indiana University Press, 1964.

Bartlett, Merrill I. *Lejeune: A Marine's Life, 1867–1942.* Columbia: University of South Carolina Press, 1991.

Beaver, Daniel R. *Newton D. Baker and the American War Effort, 1917–1919.* Lincoln: University of Nebraska Press, 1936.

Braim, Paul F. *The Test of Battle: The AEF in the Meuse-Argonne Campaign.* Newark: University of Delaware Press, 1983.

Broesamle, John J. *William Gibbs McAdoo: A Passion for Change, 1863–1917.* Port Washington, NY: Kennikat, 1973.

Brose, Eric Dorn. *The Kaiser's Army: The Politics of Military Technology in Germany during the Machine Age, 1907–1918.* New York: Oxford University Press, 2001.

Bullard, Robert L. *American Soldiers Also Fought.* New York: Maurice H. Louis, 1939.

———. *Personalities and Reminiscences of the War.* Garden City, NY: Doubleday, 1925.

Butler, Smedley D. *War is a Racket.* New York: Round Table Press, 1935.

Calhoun, Frederick S. *Power and Principle: Armed Intervention in Wilsonian Foreign Policy.* Kent, OH: Kent State University Press, 1986.

Chasseaud, Peter. *Topography of Armageddon: A British Trench Map Atlas of the Western Front, 1914–1918.* Lewes, East Sussex, England: Mapbooks, 1991.

Coffman, Edward M. *The Hilt of the Sword: The Career of Peyton C. March.* Madison: University of Wisconsin Press, 1966.

———. *The War to End All Wars: The American Military Experience in*

World War I. Lexington: University Press of Kentucky, 1998.

Coletta, Paolo E. *Admiral Bradley A. Fiske and the American Navy.* Lawrence: Regents Press of Kansas, 1979.

Cooke, James J. *Billy Mitchell.* Boulder, CO: Rienner, 2002.

———. *Pershing and His Generals: Command and Staff in the AEF.* Westport, CT: Praeger, 1997.

———. *The Rainbow Division in the Great War, 1917–1919.* Westport, CT: Praeger, 1994.

Coombs, Rose E. B. *Before Endeavours Fade: A Guide to the Battlefields of the First World War.* 7th ed. London: Battle of Britain Prints International, 1994.

Cooper, John M., Jr. *Breaking the Heart of the World: Woodrow Wilson and the Fight for the League of Nations.* New York: Cambridge University Press, 2001.

Cronon, E. David, ed. *The Cabinet Diaries of Josephus Daniels, 1913–1921.* Lincoln: University of Nebraska Press, 1963.

Cushing, Harvey. *From a Surgeon's Journal, 1915–1918.* Boston: Little, Brown, and Company, 1936.

Davis, Kenneth S. *FDR: The Beckoning of Destiny 1882–1928.* New York: Putnam, 1972.

Department of the Army. *United States Army in the World War, 1917–1919.* 17 vols. (reprints). Washington, DC: Center of Military History, 1988–1991.

Ellis. John. *Eye-Deep in Hell: Trench Warfare in World War I.* Baltimore: Johns Hopkins University Press, 1976.

Esposito, David M. *The Legacy of Woodrow Wilson: American War Aims in the World War.* Westport, CT: Praeger, 1996.

Essame, Hubert. *The Battle for Europe 1918.* London: Batsford, 1972.

Falls, Cyril. *The Great War.* New York: Putnam, 1959.

Ferrell, Robert. *Woodrow Wilson and World War I, 1917–1921.* New York: Harper and Row, 1985.

Floto, Inga. *Colonel House in Paris: A Study of American Policy at the Paris Peace Conference, 1919.* Princeton, NJ: Princeton University Press, 1980.

Foch, Ferdinand. *The Memoirs of Marshal Foch.* New York: Doubleday, 1931.

Fulton, John F. *Harvey Cushing: A Biography.* Springfield, IL: Charles C. Thomas Publishers, 1947.

Fussell, Paul. *The Great War in Modern Memory.* Oxford: Oxford University Press, 1975.

Gelderman, Carol. *Henry Ford: The Wayward Capitalist.* New York: Dial, 1981.

Gelfand, Lawrence E., ed. *Herbert Hoover: The Great War and its Aftermath, 1914–23.* Iowa City: University of Iowa Press, 1979.

George, Alexander L., and Juliette L. George. *Woodrow Wilson and Colonel House.* New York: Dover, 1956.

Gerard, James W. *Face to Face with Kaiserism.* New York: Doran, 1918.

———. *My Four Years in Germany.* New York: Doran, 1917.

Gilbert, Martin. *The First World War: A Complete History.* New York: Henry Holt, 1994.

Gregory, Barry. *Argonne 1918: The AEF in France.* New York: Ballantine Books, 1972.

Gudmundsson, Bruce I. *Stormtroop Tactics: Innovation in the German Army, 1914–1918.* Westport, CT: Praeger, 1989.

Hallas, James H. *Squandered Victory: The American First Army at St. Mihiel.* Westport, CT: Praeger, 1995.

Hagood, Johnson. *The Services of Supply: A Memoir of the Great War.* Boston: Houghton Mifflin, 1927.

Harbord, James G. *The American Army in France, 1917–1919.* Boston: Little, Brown and Company, 1936.

Herwig, Holger H. *The First World War: Germany and Austria-Hungary, 1914–1918.* London: Arnold, 1997.

Hindenburg, Paul von. *Out of My Life.* New York: Harper and Brothers, 1921.

Hoffmann, Max. *The War of Lost Opportunities.* Reprint, Nashville: Battery Press, 1999.

Hogg, Ian V. *Gas.* New York: Ballantine Books, 1975.

———. *The Guns 1914–1918.* New York: Ballantine Books, 1971.

Holmes, Richard. *The Western Front.* London: BBC Books, 1999.

Hoyt, Edwin P. *The House of Morgan.* New York: Dodd, Mead and Co., 1966.

Hurley, Alfred F. *Billy Mitchell: Crusader for Air Power.* Bloomington: Indiana University Press, 1975.

Jünger, Ernst. *The Storm of Steel: From the Diary of a German Storm-Troop Officer on the Western Front.* New York: Zimmermann and Zimmermann, 1985.

Klachko, Mary, and David E. Trask. *Admiral William Shepherd Benson: First Chief of Naval Operations.* Annapolis, MD: Naval Institute Press, 1987.

Kraft, Barbra S. *The Peace Ship: Henry Ford's Pacific Adventure in the First World War.* New York: Macmillan, 1978.

Lane, Jack. *Armed Progressive: General Leonard Wood.* San Rafael, CA: Presidio, 1978.

Lansing, Robert. *The Peace Negotiations: A Personal Narrative.* Boston: Houghton Mifflin, 1921.

Lawson, Eric, and Jane Lawson. *The First Air Campaign: August 1914–November 1918.* Norwalk, CT: MBI, Inc., 1996.

Lejeune, John A. *The Reminiscences of a Marine.* Quantico, VA: Dorrance, 1930.

Liddell Hart, Basil H. *The Real War 1914–1918.* Boston: Little, Brown and Company, 1930.

Liggett, Hunter. *Commanding an American Army: Recollections of the World War.* Boston: Houghton Mifflin, 1925.

Lincoln, W. Bruce. *Passage Through Armageddon: The Russians in War & Revolution, 1914–1919.* New York: Simon and Schuster, 1986.

Lippmann, Walter. *Early Writings.* New York: Liveright, 1970.

Lodge, Henry Cabot. *The Senate of the United States and Other Essays and Addresses Historical and Literary.* New York: Scribner, 1925.

Ludendorff, Erich. *My War Memories.* 2 vols. London: Hutchinson, 1919.

MacDonald, Lyn. *To the Last Man: Spring 1918.* London: Penguin Books, 1999.

MacMillan, Margaret. *Paris, 1919: Six Months that Changed the World.* New York: Random House, 2002.

March, Peyton C. *The Nation at War.* New York: Doubleday, 1932.

Marolda, Edward J., ed. *FDR and the U.S. Navy.* New York: St. Martin's, 1998.

Marshall, George C. *Memoirs of My Services in the World War, 1917–1918.* Boston: Houghton Mifflin, 1976.

McAdoo, William G. *Crowded Years: The Reminiscences of William G. McAdoo.* Boston: Houghton Mifflin, 1931.

McCallum, Jack. *Leonard Wood: A Biography.* New York: New York University Press, 2005.

Middlebrook, Martin. *The Kaiser's Battle*. London: Allen Lane, 1978.

Millet, Alan R. *The General: Robert L. Bullard and Officership in the United States Army, 1881–1925*. Westport, CT: Greenwood, 1975.

Millet, Alan R., and Williamson Murray, eds. *Military Effectiveness*. Vol. 1, *The First World War*. Boston: Unwin Hyman, 1988.

Morison, Elting E. *Admiral Sims and the Modern American Navy*. Boston: Houghton Mifflin, 1942.

Nash, George H. *The Life of Herbert Hoover*. 3 vols. New York: Norton, 1988–1996.

Neiberg, Michael S. *The Second Battle of the Marne*. Bloomington: Indiana University Press, 2008.

O'Brien, Francis W., ed. *The Hoover–Wilson Wartime Correspondence, September 24, 1914 to November 11, 1918*. Ames: Iowa State University Press, 1974.

Palmer, Frederick. *Bliss, Peacemaker: The Life and Letters of General Tasker Howard Bliss*. New York: Dodd, Mead, 1934.

———. *Newton D. Baker: America at War*. 2 vols. New York: Dodd Mead, 1931.

Paschall, Rod. *The Defeat of Imperial Germany, 1917–1918*. Chapel Hill, NC: Algonquin Books, 1990.

Pershing, John J. *My Experiences in the World War*. 2 vols. New York: Frederick A. Stokes Company, 1931.

Pitt, Barrie. *1918: The Last Act*. New York: Ballantine Books, 1963.

Pogue, Forrest C. *George C. Marshall*. Vol. I, *Education of a General 1880–1939*. New York: Viking, 1963.

Rice, Earle. *The Battle of Belleau Wood*. Chicago: Lucent, 1996.

Roberts, Frank E. *The American Foreign Legion: Black Soldiers of the 93rd in World War I*. Annapolis, MD: Naval Institute Press, 2004.

Schmidt, Hans. *Maverick Marine: General Smedley D. Butler and the Contradictions of American Military History*. Lexington: University Press of Kentucky, 1998.

Seymour, Charles, ed. *The Intimate Papers of Colonel House*. Boston: Houghton Mifflin, 1926.

Sheffield, Gary. *Forgotten Victory: The First World War Myths and Realities*. London: Headline Book Publishing, 2001.

Sims, William S. *The Victory at Sea*. Garden City, NY: Doubleday, 1920.

Smith, Daniel M. *Robert Lansing and American Neutrality, 1914–1917*. Berkeley: University of California Press, 1958.

Smythe, Donald. *Pershing: General of the Armies*. Bloomington: Indiana University Press, 1986.

Steel, Ronald. *Walter Lippmann and the American Century*. New York: Random House, 1980.

Strachan, Hew. *The First World War*. Vol. I, *To Arms*. New York: Oxford University Press, 2001.

Sulzbach, Herbert. *With the German Guns: Four Years on the Western Front, 1914–1918*. Hamden, CT: Archon Books, 1981.

Terraine, John. *White Heat: The New Warfare 1914–18*. London: Sidgwick & Jackson, 1982.

Toland, John. *No Man's Land: 1918, The Last Year of the Great War*. Gansevoort, NY: Corner House Publishers, 1980.

Trask, David E. *The AEF and Coalition Warmaking, 1917–1918*. Lawrence: University of Kansas Press, 1993.

———. *Captains and Cabinets: Anglo-American Naval Relations, 1917–1918*. Columbia: University of Missouri Press, 1972.

Tucker, Spencer C., ed. *The Encyclopedia of World War I: A Political, Social, and Military History*, 5 vols. Santa Barbara, CA: ABC-Clio, 2005.

———, ed. *The Great War, 1914–1918*. Bloomington: Indiana University Press, 1998.

Vandiver, Frank E. *Black Jack: The Life and Times of John J. Pershing*. 2 vols. College Station: Texas A&M University Press, 1977.

Venzon, Anne Cipriano, ed. *General Smedley Darlington Butler: The Letters of a Leatherneck, 1898–1931*. Westport, CT: Praeger, 1992.

Widenor, William C. *Henry Cabot Lodge and the Search for an American Foreign Policy*. Berkeley: University of California Press, 1980.

Wynne, Graeme. *If Germany Attacks: The Battle in Depth in the West*. London: Faber and Faber, 1940.

Zabecki, David T. *Steel Wind: Colonel Georg Bruchmüller and the Birth of Modern Artillery*. Westport, CT: Praeger, 1994.

———. *The German 1918 Offensives: A Case Study in the Operational Level of War*. London: Routledge, 2006.

———, ed. *Chief of Staff: The Principal Officers Behind History's Great Commanders*. Vol. I, *Napoleonic Wars Through World War I*. Annapolis, MD. Naval Institute Press, 2008.

Zimmermann, Warren. *First Great Triumph: How Five Americans Made Their Country a World Power*. New York: Farrar Straus and Giroux, 2002.

WORLD WAR II

Leadership in World War II

Some historians regard World War II as the second stage of a modern 30 years' war, a global conflagration that started in 1914, passed through a 21-year ceasefire phase, and then exploded again in 1939. Still other historians look at World Wars I and II as the hot eruptions in a longer chain of events that ended when the collapse of the Soviet Union and the Warsaw Pact brought the Cold War to a close in the late 1980s. British historian Eric Hobsbawm advanced this latter model with what he called the "Long 19th Century" and the "Short 20th Century." Looking at modern history's sharp turning points and the logical progression of events between them, rather than at arbitrary dates on a calendar, Hobsbawm argued that the Long 19th Century started with the French Revolution in 1789 and ended with the outbreak of World War I.

The Short 20th Century lasted only from 1914 to 1989. Certainly, it was the most violent and bloody 75-year period in all human history. And in a strictly legalistic sense, World War II did not officially end until September 8, 1994, when the last troops of the U.S. occupation forces left Berlin, exactly eight days after the last Russian occupation troops left the city. Up until that date, Berlin was technically an occupied city from World War II, and U.S. soldiers stationed there still received the American World War II Army of Occupation Medal.

The vast majority of the "firsts" in modern warfare actually occurred during World War I, but there were many uniquely significant aspects to World War II as well. Although World War I is officially called a world war, almost all of the military actions of what was then called the Great War took place in Europe, the Atlantic, or in the Middle East around the Mediterranean periphery. The few exceptions included one major land battle on the Chinese mainland and some naval actions around the German colonies in the Pacific. World War II was truly a global conflict, with major battles in Europe, Asia, Africa, the Middle East, the Atlantic, the Pacific, the Mediterranean, the Artic waters, and the skies above all those areas. Smaller-level attacks also were launched against the mainland and coastal waters of North America and Australia.

Most of the new war-fighting technologies of the 20th century first appeared during World War I, but did not mature significantly until long after 1918. World War II was, therefore, history's first "high-tech" war in the modern sense of the term. Electronic warfare especially emerged as a potent force to be reckoned with, and the resulting "Battle of the Beams" often had a decisive influence on the outcome of the battles fought with kinetic energy weapons. Firepower weapons themselves became increasingly sophisticated and more lethal, and at the very end of World War II the introduction of nuclear weapons changed forever the calculus of warfare.

Perhaps most relevant to the main theme of this volume, which is leadership, World War II was fought with the largest, and arguably the most successful, coalition in all history. World War I had been fought between two opposing alliances, but neither was an effective coalition. Neither the Central Powers nor the Entente ever had a unified military command until as late as March 26, 1918, when General Ferdinand Foch was appointed the supreme Allied generalissimo in a desperate attempt to forge a coordinated response to the seemingly overwhelming onslaught of Operation MICHAEL, launched by the Germans five days earlier. The appointment of Foch worked, and the Allies did not forget that lesson 20 years later.

During World War II, the members of the Axis still had not learned the lessons of coalition warfare. The haphazard alliance that officially bound together Germany, Italy, and Japan was in no way synchronized or coordinated. There was no overarching strategy, no integrated military command. The three major partners more often than not pulled in opposite directions and blindsided each other throughout the war.

The Allies, on the other hand, assembled and sustained the largest and most successful military coalition in history to that time. The center of gravity of the Allied coalition was the Anglo-American Grand Alliance, under which U.S. president Franklin D. Roosevelt and British prime minister Winston Churchill fashioned a global strategic vision, and their immediate military subordinates established the Combined Chiefs of Staff of the two nations. It was a significant leap forward for America in particular, which up until that time did not even have its own Joint Chiefs of Staff to coordinate all the actions of the different military services.

The British and the Americans designated single unified commanders for each theater of operations and established integrated military staffs at the theater level. Other countries from what came to be called the United Nations contributed forces to the respective theater commands, placing them under the operational control of the theater commanders. When Britain and America first established their Grand Alliance, Britain was the senior partner. That changed relatively quickly, as the U.S. military expanded exponentially and American force levels surpassed those of Britain and its empire combined. Although the British military had far more experience fighting the Germans—and fought them far longer than anyone else in World War II—by February 1943 the relatively untested General Dwight D. Eisenhower was the commander of all Allied forces in northwest Africa, and less than a year later he assumed command of all the forces preparing for the invasion of northwest Europe. The "Special Relationship" that Britain and America formed during the war remains to this day, especially between the military and intelligence establishments of the two countries.

The Soviet Union, which did not even declare war on Japan until the final days of the war, was never a formal member of the coalition's integrated military command. Roosevelt and Churchill did coordinate overall strategy with Soviet premier Joseph Stalin through the series of wartime conferences that concluded with the Potsdam Conference in July 1945. Two pillars of the post-1945 international system, the United Nations and the North Atlantic Treaty Organization, are the direct descendants of the political and military alliances respectively that formed against the Axis during World War II.

U.S. president Franklin D. Roosevelt and British prime minister Winston L. S. Churchill meet aboard the British battleship *Prince of Wales* on August 10, 1941. Their meeting led to the proclamation of the Atlantic Charter. (Library of Congress)

As in World War I, the United States entered World War II only well after the start of the conflict. The war started when Germany invaded Poland on September 1, 1939. America remained officially neutral until the Japanese attacked Pearl Harbor on December 7, 1941. Even then, it was almost another year before the U.S. Army entered large-scale ground combat operations. By that point, World War II had been raging for slightly more than half of the 2,194 days it would eventually run.

The U.S. Army of the 1930s was little more than a border constabulary force, rather than a true national army. By 1938, the British had the world's first completely motorized army, while the U.S. Army was still a force built primarily around cavalry and artillery horses, and infantry pack mules. At the start of 1939, the U.S. Army had only 190,000 soldiers, which included the Army Air Corps. The ground combat forces were organized into 9 infantry and 2 cavalry divisions. Both of the cavalry divisions were some 1,200 troops below their authorized strengths, and 6 of the 9 infantry divisions were 10,000 troops short of their authorized strengths of 14,000. By the time of the Pearl Harbor attack, the army's ranks had swelled to 1.6 million troops organized into 36 full-strength divisions. At the end of 1942, the army's strength was 5.4 million, including 700,000 black Americans, most of whom served in segregated support units. The U.S. Army reached its peak strength of 8,291,336 troops on May 31, 1945, which included 2,314,201 in the Army Air Forces. The U.S. Navy had only 126,000 officers and men in 1939 and in June 1941 it had 384 warships and 715 other vessels in service. When the war ended in late August 1945, it had 3,408,347 personnel, 1,557 warships, 1,780 auxiliary ships, 1,915 patrol ships and craft, and more than 9,000 landing ships and landing craft of all types. The U.S. Navy at that point was larger than all of the navies of the rest of the world combined.

The number of U.S. Army divisions peaked in August 1943 with 90 divisions. The U.S. Marine Corps fielded an additional 6 divisions. By contrast, the Germans fielded some 300 divisions during the war, the Soviets 400, and even the Japanese fielded 100. Although the total number of American combat units was relatively small in comparison to the country's population base, virtually the entire remainder of the available American manpower was channeled into the country's war industry.

American battlefield, strategic, and political leadership were critical factors in winning World War II, but those elements alone were not enough. America's industrial base retooled and rapidly expanded, not only to arm and equip a military force that had grown by a factor of more than 40, but also to provide substantial supplies to the Allies. Between 1940 and 1945, America produced 88,276 tanks, 257,390 artillery pieces of all types, and 2,679,840 machine guns. American industry also produced 324,750 military aircraft, which accounted for 51 percent of all military aircraft pro-

Women working in Douglas Aircraft's Long Beach, California, assembly plant during World War II complete final inspection of nose cones for A-20 attack bombers. (National Archives)

duced by the Allies; 2,382,311 military trucks (78 percent of the Allied total); and 1,247 warships (48 percent of the Allied total). Included in the warships were 141 aircraft carriers of all types, accounting for an incredible 91 percent of all carriers produced by the Allies. In addition to the warships, American shipyards also produced just less than 34 million gross registered tons of merchant shipping, 79 percent of the Allied total. The term "Arsenal of Democracy" was no idle propaganda slogan, and industrial leaders like Henry Kaiser and William Knudsen were in the forefront of those who made it happen.

The cohort of Americans who for many years following World War II had been called simply the "G.I. Generation," was rechristened the "Greatest Generation" with the 1998 publication of Tom Brokaw's book of the same name. All of the 52 people profiled by Brokaw were relatively young men and women in the first half of the 1940s. Many served in lower leadership positions during the war, and several, including Robert Dole, Daniel Inouye, Casper Weinberger, and George Schultz, became respected civilian leaders on the national stage many years later.

All of the people profiled in this encyclopedia are from an earlier generation, the "Other Greatest Generation" of World War II. With few exceptions, their experience in World War I was the defining moment in their lives. It shaped their characters and gave them the opportunities to develop their leadership skills and to acquire the practical experience what would prove so valuable slightly more than 20 years later. Even though Eisenhower never left the continental United States and spent World War I training tank crews at Camp Colt in Pennsylvania, the experience left him with a profound understanding of this new but still primitive weapons system that would dominate the European battlefields during World War II.

There is another common thread that connects the American military leaders profiled in this volume. Almost all of them endured the almost two decades of public apathy and abject neglect of the American military that characterized almost the entire period between the two world wars. When the "war to end all wars" finally ended and America quickly retreated into its traditional cocoon of isolationism, the U.S. military immediately shrank back to less than 5 percent of its 1918 peak strength of more than 4 million. Funds dried up for equipment, for training, and even for adequate pay. America would never have to fight a major war again, and didn't really need an army—although the need for a robust navy to secure both coasts was still generally recognized. Anyone could see that there was no future in a military career. Many career officers left the service for the lure of the world of big business, which was starting to boom in the early 1920s.

Some professional soldiers, however, elected to remain in uniform. Many stayed because soldiering was their chosen profession, and they were dedicated to it. Others stayed because they could see clearly that the international conditions at the end of the Great War were inherently unstable and the eruption of another global conflagration was only a matter of time. For all too many of their fellow American citizens, however, those who remained in the military were just simply the losers. Everyone knew you couldn't make any real money in the army.

Thus, the George Marshalls, and the Dwight Eisenhowers, and the George Pattons, and the Omar Bradleys and countless other professional soldiers whose names are now only recorded in footnotes or passing sentences of obscure unit histories—if they are recorded at all—stuck out the long, dismal period between the wars, honing their technical and tactical skills, while their troops trained with bizarre mockups to simulate modern weapons. Throughout most of that period America had little more than the army of a third-rate power. When Germany rolled over and crushed the Low Countries in 1940, the United States replaced Holland as the number 10 military power in the world.

It wasn't easy for those who stuck it out. Promotion was glacially slow. Carl Spaatz, who would become the first chief of staff of the newly independent U.S. Air Force following World War II, spent 15 years as a major. Yet, when the time came and the war clouds in the late 1930s were gathering so dark and ominous that even the most ardent isolationists and pacifists could see that another global war was looming on the horizon, America was fortunate to have an incredibly talented military leadership cadre as a foundation upon which to build the explosive expansion that was to come.

That is not to say that the American military of the late 1930s was stacked with leadership talent from top to bottom. There was, in fact, an incredible amount of deadwood at the top. No one was more painfully aware of that situation than the commander in chief, President Franklin D. Roosevelt. In late 1939, Roosevelt reached down over the heads of 33 more senior general officers to appoint Brigadier General George C. Marshall the chief of staff of the army. Marshall was promoted to major general and then almost immediately vaulted to full general. He was sworn into office on September 1, 1939, the day Germany invaded Poland and started World War II.

Marshall, too, understood the ossification in the ranks of the senior generals. After only a month in office he confided off the record to the well known military journalist George Elliot Fielding; "The present general officers of the line are for the most part too old to command troops in battle under the terrific pressures of modern war. Many of them have their minds set in outmoded patterns, and can't change to meet the new conditions that they face if we become involved in the war that's started in Europe. . . . They'll have their chance to prove what they can do. But I doubt many of them will come through satisfactorily. Those that don't will be eliminated" (Larrabee1987).

Marshall meant what he said. Of all the army's senior generals at the time he assumed office, only Walter Krueger commanded troops in combat during World War II. Marshall ruthlessly purged those general officers incapable of meeting his tough standards, and many senior colonels as well. Many had been his longtime personal friends, but Marshall understood he had to get his army ready for a war of national survival. In place of those he eliminated Marshall started moving up the talented and dedicated cohort of mid-ranking officers.

"I'm going to put these men to the severest tests which I can devise in time of peace," Marshall told Fielding. "I'm going to start shifting them into jobs of greater responsibility than those they hold now. I'm going to change them, suddenly, without warning, to jobs even more burdensome and difficult. . . . I'm going to allow them plenty of room to think that I'm treating them arbitrarily, even unreasonably, that I'm asking more than human beings should be required to deliver. . . . Those who stand up under the punishment will be pushed ahead. Those who fail are out at the first sign of faltering" (Larrabee 1987).

General George C. Marshall is pictured with members of his staff in his office at the War Department. Marshall is seated, fifth from the left. (Bettmann/Corbis)

More than one-third of the subjects profiled in this volume are those who rose to the top of George C. Marshall's brutal but effective grooming and selection system—Marshall's "Leadership Factory." Matthew B. Ridgway, who finished the war as a lieutenant general, was only promoted to lieutenant colonel in July 1940. James Gavin was still a captain in August 1941. By October 1944, he was a major general, and at age 37, the youngest division commander in the U.S. Army. Eisenhower himself was promoted to colonel only in March 1941—one month after Omar Bradley was promoted to brigadier general. Three years and nine months later Eisenhower was wearing five stars. Even at the lower levels, some noncommissioned officers who were company 1st sergeants in late 1941 ended up commanding battalions by 1945. Some even commanded regiments.

The nature and the quality of military leadership during any given war are not isolated or static phenomena. The junior leaders of the younger generations constantly learn from the leaders of the older generations—sometimes by negative example—and carry those lessons forward into the future. Just as the foundations of American leadership in World War II were laid in World War I, many of those senior leaders of World War II continued to exert a profound leadership influence on the American wars that followed. Those profiled in this volume who later were significant figures during Korea, the Cold War, and even Vietnam include Eisenhower, Harry S. Truman, Marshall, Douglas MacArthur,

Bradley, Gavin, Maxwell D. Taylor, Ridgway, and Curtis LeMay. Likewise many lower-level military leaders not included in this volume, but who first learned their professions in World War II, became the senior leaders of the subsequent wars, some exerting significant influence well into the post-Vietnam years. They include Joseph L. Collins, Lyman Lemnitzer, Harold K. Johnson, William C. Westmoreland, Creighton W. Abrams, Frederick C. Weyand, Walter T. Kerwin, and Donn A. Starry.

Wars play out on multiple levels, and in order to persevere and to win a nation and its military must have leaders capable of functioning at all those echelons. Warfare itself is generally divided into three primary levels, the tactical, the operational, and the strategic. Each requires its own body of knowledge and its own set of war-fighting tools and leadership skills. The objective of tactics is to win battles. The objective of strategy is to win wars. The objective of operational art is to win the campaigns, which are based upon battles and which in turn contribute to strategic victory. The three levels of war-fighting are different, but they tend to overlap. During World War II, Marshall, Ernest King, and Henry Arnold operated almost exclusively on the strategic level of war, while leaders up to the rank of major general, such as James Gavin, Norman Cota, and William T. Frederick, operated almost exclusively on the tactical level. Theater commanders, like Eisenhower and Chester Nimitz, often functioned with one foot in the strategic arena and the other in the operational, while their immediate subordinates, such as George Patton and Raymond Spruance, straddled the operational and the tactical levels.

The skills, techniques, and overall philosophical approach that result in effective leadership at one level of warfare do not necessarily translate to the next level. One size does not fit all. Nor are experience and success as a leader at one level necessarily a prerequisite for success as a leader at the next higher level. Would Eisenhower have been as effective a corps or army commander as Patton? Probably not. Could Patton have ever succeeded as a combined theater commander? Not in a million years. For a wide number of reasons, many of which can be traced directly back to George Marshall, these two military leaders were for most of the war at exactly the right levels respectively that capitalized on their strengths and minimized their weaknesses. They were the right leaders in the right places at the right times.

Military prowess and leadership and even economic and industrial might by themselves are not sufficient to win wars. If they were, Germany almost certainly would have won World War I, and America would have won decisively in Vietnam by no later than 1967. As Carl von Clausewitz noted almost 200 years ago, "War is not a mere act of policy but a true political instrument, a continuation of political activity by other means." Thus, the political sphere must complement and support the actual war-fighting, which Clausewitz also discussed with his concept of the "Remarkable Trinity" of the people, the army, and the government. "A theory that ignores any one of them or seeks to fix an arbitrary relationship between them would conflict with reality to such an extent that for this reason alone it would be totally useless" (Clausewitz 1976).

America arguably was more united during World War II than at any other time in its history. Socially, politically, and economically there were very few gaps between the people, the military, and the government. Fault lines were there, to be sure, but by almost universal consensus America "closed ranks" for the duration of the war. There were multiple reasons for this phenomenon, not the least of which was the incredible

Victory gardeners show off their vegetables. During World War II, Americans planted more than 20 million victory gardens in backyards, schools, and city parks across the United States to increase the production of food. (Library of Congress)

political leadership skills of the man most responsible for the political level, President Franklin D. Roosevelt. Aided by other skilled political leaders, including Henry Stimpson, Cordell Hull, and James Byrnes, the administration ensured that the government and the people—and as a consequence the economy—gave the military everything it needed to prosecute the war.

The leaders at the very top of the political level in democracies also have the final responsibility for the strategic direction of the war. As president, only Harry S. Truman had the authority to order the use of nuclear weapons against Japan in August 1945. Through their series of wartime conferences, Roosevelt and Churchill set and controlled the highest level of strategy—the grand strategy—of what started out as the American-British Grand Alliance and evolved into the United Nations. Their first conference, the Atlantic Conference held aboard the British battleship HMS *Prince of Wales* anchored in Placentia Bay, Newfoundland, was conducted in early August 1941, four months before America was even in the war. The resulting Atlantic Charter established the "common principles in the national policies of their respective countries on which they would base their hopes for a better future of the world" (Green 1999).

Churchill had a tendency to be a micro manager, and throughout the war General Sir Alan Brooke, the chief of the British Imperial General Staff, had to struggle constantly to keep the prime minister from interfering with the theater and battlefield commanders. Marshall had no such problem with Roosevelt. The president was perfectly comfortable letting his generals and admirals fight the war, so long as they stayed within the parameters he and Churchill laid down. Roosevelt's strategic war management stands in sharp contrast to some of his successors in the White House. Compared to Lyndon B. Johnson having a terrain model of the Khe Sanh fire base in Vietnam, complete with individual foxhole locations, installed in the White House situation room, consider the simple and broad task statement that Roosevelt and Churchill issued to Eisenhower for the Operation OVERLORD landings in Normandy: "2. *Task.* You will enter the continent of Europe and, in conjunction with the other United Nations, undertake operations aimed at the heart of Germany and the destruction of her armed forces. The date for entering the Continent is the month of May, 1944. After adequate channel ports have been secured, exploitation will be directed towards securing an area that will facilitate both ground and air operations against the enemy" (Harrison 1951).

Making decisions is one of the most important functions of leadership, and all decisions carry an element of risk. Virtually every major decision made in warfare is a controversial one at the time it is made. In the almost 20/20 vision that hindsight offers, most of those controversial decisions can be seen well after the fact as having been clearly good ones or bad ones—but not all. More than 60 years after the end of World War II some of the war's most controversial decisions are still being debated.

Was Mark Clark right when he ordered the bombing of the Monte Casino monastery, or did the resulting rubble give the Germans a better position from which to defend? Did Clark commit a huge operational blunder after the breakout from Anzio when he ordered the Fifth Army to turn north toward Rome, instead of heading east to cut off the escape of the German Tenth Army? Was Eisenhower right to pursue the Broad Front Strategy, or did that prolong the war in Europe? Did his decision to minimize American and British casualties by not trying to beat the Soviets to Berlin doom Germany to remain divided throughout the Cold War? Was daylight, so-called precision bombing and the entire Combined Bomber Offensive, as so forcefully advocated by Henry Arnold, Carl Spaatz, James Doolittle, and Curtis LeMay, the key to Allied victory? Or was it a waste of resources and manpower that did almost nothing to undercut the wartime economy of the Third Reich? Did Roosevelt exceed his constitutional authority and blatantly violate American neutrality by pursuing an undeclared naval war against the Germans in the Atlantic? Was his executive order to imprison the Nisei a necessary and prudent security precaution in time of war, or was it an overtly racist policy that did not necessarily fly in the face of the flawed civil rights standards of the times? And perhaps the most controversial and raw of the lingering questions, was Truman's decision to drop the atomic bomb on Japan a blatant war crime that murdered thousands of civilians, or was it the war-ending *coup de main* that prevented the deaths of thousands of soldiers and civilians on both sides? Many of these decisions will still be the subject of debate for years to come.

David T. Zabecki

References

Clausewitz, Carl von. *On War.* Translated and edited by Michael Howard and Peter Paret. Princeton, NJ: Princeton University Press, 1976.

Green, Philip. "Conferences, Allied." In *World War II: An Encyclopedia.* Edited by David T. Zabecki. New York: Garland Publishing Company, 1999.

Harrison, Gordon A. *Cross-Channel Attack: United States Army in World War II.* Washington, DC: U.S. Center of Military History, 1951.

Larrabee, Eric. *Commander in Chief: Franklin Delano Roosevelt, His Lieutenants, and Their War.* New York: Simon and Schuster, 1987.

About the Author

General David T. Zabecki, PhD, retired from the Army of the United States in 2007. He began his military career in 1966, serving in Vietnam as an infantry rifleman. After receiving his commission as a field artillery officer, he commanded as a captain, lieutenant colonel, colonel, brigadier general, and major general. In 1995 and 1996, he served in the Balkans. From 2000 to 2002, he was assigned to the Pentagon as the deputy chief of the Army Reserve. In 2003, he served in Israel as the senior security adviser on the U.S. Coordinating and Monitoring Mission, responsible for advancing the Roadmap to Peace in the Middle East initiative. In 2004 and 2005, he was the Department of Defense executive director for all World War II 60th Anniversary observances in Europe. In 2005 and 2006, he commanded the U.S. Southern European Task Force Rear and served as the senior U.S. Army commander south of the Alps.

General Zabecki is a graduate of the U.S. Army Command and General Staff College, the U.S. Army War College, and the John F. Kennedy School of Government Executive Program for Russian and American General Officers, and holds a PhD in military history from the Royal Military College of Science, Cranfield University. General Zabecki is the author or editor of eight books on military history. He also has been an assistant editor of several ABC-CLIO encyclopedias. From 2000 to 2008, he was the editor of *Vietnam* magazine, and he is currently the senior historian for the Weider History Group, the world's largest publisher of history magazines.

World War II Battles

Atlantic, Battle of the (September 1939–May 1945)

The Battle of the Atlantic was the longest campaign of World War II. In it, the German Navy tried to sever the Allied sea lines of communication along which supplies necessary to fight the war were sent to Great Britain. To carry out the battle, the Germans employed a few surface raiders, but principally they used U-boats.

At the beginning of the war, the German Navy possessed not the 300 U-boats deemed necessary by Kommodore (commodore) Karl Dönitz (he was promoted to rear admiral in October 1939), but just 57 boats, of which only 27 were of types that could reach the Atlantic from their home bases. Although an extensive building program was immediately begun, only in the second half of 1941 did U-boat numbers begin to rise.

On the Allied side, British Navy leaders were at first confident that their ASDIC (Allied Submarine Detection Investigating Committee) location device (later redesignated Sonar) would enable their escort vessels to defend the supply convoys against the submerged attackers, so that shipping losses might be limited until the building of new merchant ships by Britain, Canada, and the United States might settle the balance. However, Dönitz planned to concentrate groups of U-boats (called "wolf packs" by the Allies)

against the convoys and to attack them jointly on the surface at night. It took time, however, before the battles of the convoys really began. The Battle of the Atlantic became a running match between numbers of German U-boats and the development of their weapons against the Allied merchant ships, their sea and air escorts (with improving detection equipment), and new antisubmarine warfare (ASW) weapons.

The Battle of the Atlantic may be subdivided into eight phases. During the first, from September 1939 to June 1940, a small number of U-boats, seldom more than 10 at a time, conducted individual sorties west of the British Isles and into the Bay of Biscay to intercept Allied merchant ships. Generally, these operated independently because the convoy system, which the British Admiralty had planned before the war, was only slowly put into effect. Thus, the U-boats found targets, attacking at first according to the prize rules of international law by notifying the ship before the attack and providing for the safety of its crew. However, when Britain armed its merchant ships, increasingly the German submarines struck without warning. Dönitz's plan to counter the convoy with group, or "pack," operations of U-boats—also developed and tested before the war—was tested in October and November 1939 and in

BATTLE OF THE ATLANTIC, 1939–1945

February 1940. The results confirmed the feasibility of vectoring a group of U-boats to a convoy by radio signals from whichever U-boat first sighted the convoy. However, at this time, the insufficient number of U-boats available and frequent torpedo failures prevented real successes.

The German conquest of Norway and western France provided the U-boats with new bases much closer to the main operational area off the Western Approaches and marked the start of the second phase of the campaign, which lasted from July 1940 to May 1941. In this phase, the U-boats operated in wolf packs and were directed by radio signals from the shore against the convoys, in which was now concentrated most of the maritime traffic to and from Great Britain. Even if the number of U-boats in the operational area still did not rise to more than 10 at a time, a peak of effectiveness was achieved in terms of the ratio between tonnage sunk and U-boat days at sea. This was made possible partly by the weakness of the convoy escort groups—a result of the Royal Navy's holding back destroyers to defend against an expected German invasion of Britain. British merchant shipping losses also greatly increased during this phase because of the operations of German surface warships in the north and central Atlantic; because of armed merchant raiders in the Atlantic, Pacific, and Indian oceans; because of the attacks of German long-range land-based bombers against the Western Approaches; and because of heavy German air attacks against British harbors. The Germans were also supported by Italian submarines based at Bordeaux and deployed into the Atlantic, the numbers of which in early 1941 actually surpassed the number of German U-boats.

In late 1940 and spring 1941, when the danger of an invasion of Britain had receded, London released destroyers for antisubmarine operations and redeployed Royal Air Force (RAF) Coastal Command aircraft to support the convoys off the Western Approaches. Thus, in the third phase of the Battle of the Atlantic, from May to December 1941, the U-boats were forced to operate at greater distances from shore. Long lines of U-

boats patrolled across the convoy routes in an effort to intercept supply ships. This in turn forced the British in June to begin escorting their convoys along the entire route from Newfoundland to the Western Approaches and—when the U-boats began to cruise off West Africa—the route from Freetown to Gibraltar and the United Kingdom as well.

In March 1941, the Allies captured cipher materials from a German patrol vessel. Then, on May 7, 1941, the Royal Navy succeeded in capturing the German Arctic meteorological vessel *München* and seizing its Enigma machine intact. Settings secured from this encoding machine enabled the Royal Navy to read June U-boat radio traffic almost concurrently. On May 9, during a convoy battle, the British destroyer *Bulldog* captured the German submarine *U-110* and secured the settings for the high-grade officer-only German naval signals. The capture on June 28 of a second German weather ship, *Lauenburg,* enabled British decryption operations at Bletchley Park (BP) to read July German home-waters radio traffic concurrently. This led to interception of German supply ships and the termination of German surface ship operations in the Atlantic. Beginning in August 1941, BP analysts could decrypt signals between the commander of U-boats and his units at sea. The Allies were thus able to reroute convoys and save perhaps 1.5 million gross tons of shipping.

During this third phase, the U.S. Atlantic Fleet first entered the battle. In what essentially became an undeclared naval war, U.S. destroyers started operating with the Royal Navy in the Atlantic on September 9, 1940. In April 1941, the United States assumed responsibility for the defense of Iceland, relieving the British of that task. On April 10, the U.S.

Navy destroyer *Niblack* fired the first American shot of World War II when it dropped a depth charge on a U-boat. Eight days later Admiral Ernest King ordered U.S. ships in the Atlantic to attack any Axis ship within 25 miles of the Western Hemisphere. On July 19, 1941, the U.S. Navy assumed the mission of convoy escort of all non-Axis shipping to and from Iceland, further reducing the Royal Navy's operational burden. German U-boats attacked an American warship for the first time on September 4, when the U.S. Navy destroyer *Greer* was fired on while helping a British patrol bomber track submarine movements. President Franklin D. Roosevelt responded by giving the U.S. Navy "shoot on sight" authority to attack the U-boats. During the cat-and-mouse maneuverings that followed, the *U-568* on October 17 hit the U.S. destroyer *Kearny* with 2 torpedoes, killing 11 and wounding 20 American sailors. On October 31, 1941, the U.S. destroyer *Reuben James*, which was escorting a convoy bound for Britain, was torpedoed and sank, killing 115 members of its 160-man crew.

The entry of the United States into the war after the Japanese attack on Pearl Harbor ushered in the fourth phase of the campaign, presenting the U-boats with a second golden opportunity from January to July 1942, called Operation DRUM-BEAT. Attacking unescorted individual ships off the U.S. East Coast, in the Gulf of Mexico, and in the Caribbean, German U-boats sank greater tonnages than during any other period of the war.

But sightings and sinkings off the U.S. East Coast dropped off sharply after the introduction of the interlocking convoy system there, and Dönitz found operations by individual U-boats in such distant waters were now ineffective. Thus, in July 1942, he shifted the U-boats back to the North Atlantic convoy route. This began the fifth phase, which lasted until May 1943. Now came the decisive period of the conflict between the U-boat groups and the convoys with their sea and air escorts. Increasingly, the course of the battle turned on technical innovations, most significantly, the efforts of both sides in the field of signals intelligence.

On February 1, 1942, the Germans introduced their new M-4 cipher machine, resulting in a blackout in Allied decryption that lasted until the end of December 1942. That, however, was of limited influence during the fourth phase, because the German U-boats now operated individually according to their given orders, and there was relatively little signal traffic in the operational areas. And when the convoy battles began again, the Germans could at first decrypt Allied convoy signals.

When Bletchley Park was able to reestablish decryption of the German signals, the rerouting of the convoys again became possible, although this was at first limited by rising numbers of German U-boats in patrol lines. In March 1943, the U-boats achieved their greatest successes against the convoys, and the entire convoy system—the backbone of the Allied strategy against "Fortress Europe"—seemed in jeopardy. Now Allied decryption allowed the commitment of additional surface and air escorts to support threatened convoys. Perhaps the most significant was the introduction of the U.S.-built escort carriers after March. Essentially cargo ships fitted with a flight deck and carrying only 15 to 20 aircraft, the escort carriers were critical in providing air cover for the convoys in the 600-mile stretch of the mid-Atlantic that lay beyond the range of

Crewmen of the U.S. Coast Guard cutter *Spencer* observing the explosion of a depth charge that resulted in the sinking of German submarine *U-175*, on April 17, 1943. (National Archives)

land-based aircraft at the time. This development, in connection with the introduction of new weapons and high-frequency direction finding, including centimetric radar equipment for the sea and air escorts, led to the collapse of the U-boat offensive against the convoys only eight weeks later, in May 1943.

The collapse came as a surprise to Dönitz. In a sixth (intermediate) phase from June to August 1943, the U-boats were deployed to distant areas where the antisubmarine forces were weak, while the Allied air forces tried to block the U-boat transit routes across the Bay of Biscay.

The change to a new Allied convoy cipher in June, which the German decryption service could not break, made it more difficult for the U-boats to locate the convoys in what was the seventh phase from September 1943 to June 1944. During this time, the German U-boat command tried to deploy new weapons (acoustic torpedoes and increased antiaircraft armament) and new equipment (radar warning sets) in another attempt to force a decision with the convoys, first in the North Atlantic and then on the Gibraltar routes. After short-lived success, these operations failed and tapered off as the Germans tried to pin down Allied forces until new, revolutionary U-boat types became available for operational deployment.

The final, or eighth, phase of the Battle of the Atlantic, from June 1944 to May 1945, began with the Allied invasion of

Normandy. The U-boats, now equipped with "snorkel" breathing masts, attempted to carry out attacks against individual supply ships in the shallow waters of the English Channel and in British and Canadian coastal waters. The U-boats' mission was to pin down Allied supply traffic and antisubmarine forces to prevent the deployment of warships in offensive roles against German-occupied areas. But construction of the new U-boats (of which the Allies received information by decrypting reports sent to Tokyo by the Japanese embassy in Berlin) was delayed by the Allied bombing offensive, and the German land defenses collapsed before sufficient numbers of these boats were ready.

The Battle of the Atlantic lasted without interruption for 69 months, during which time German U-boats sank 2,850 Allied and neutral merchant ships, 2,520 of them in the Atlantic and Indian oceans. The U-boats also sank many warships, from aircraft carriers to destroyers, frigates, corvettes, and other antisubmarine vessels. The Germans lost in turn 1 large battleship, 1 pocket battleship, some armed merchant raiders, and 650 U-boats, 522 of them in the Atlantic and Indian oceans.

The Allied victory in the Battle of the Atlantic resulted from the vastly superior resources on the Allied side in shipbuilding and aircraft production (the ability to replace lost ships and aircraft) and from superior antisubmarine detection equipment, weapons, and tactics. Allied signals intelligence was also critical to the victory.

Although the Atlantic was a secondary theater for the U.S. Navy, the American contribution to the campaign was significant, if not even decisive. But as early as September 3, 1940, the Destroyers for Bases Deal provided Britain with 50 additional warships at a time when the Royal Navy was hard pressed. In addition to easing the operational burden on the Royal Navy during the period immediately before America was officially in the war, U.S. warships also operated as escorts on the convoys to Murmansk and Arkhangelsk, bringing essential Lend-Lease supplies to the Soviets. Finally, American shipyards produced merchant and warships—most significantly the escort carriers—at numbers never before thought possible, literally producing shipping faster than the Germans could sink it.

Jürgen Rohwer

References

Blair, Clay. *Hitler's U-Boat War.* Vol. 1, *The Hunters, 1939–1942*; vol. 2, *The Hunted, 1942–1945.* New York: Random House, 1996, 1998.

Gardner, W. J. R. *Decoding History: The Battle of the Atlantic and Ultra.* Annapolis, MD: Naval Institute Press, 1999.

Rohwer, Jürgen. *The Critical Convoy Battles of March 1943.* Annapolis, MD: Naval Institute Press, 1977.

———. *Axis Submarine Successes of World War Two: German, Italian and Japanese Submarine Successes, 1939–1945.* London: Greenhill Books, 1999.

Runyan, Timothy J., and Jan M. Copes, eds. *To Die Gallantly: The Battle of the Atlantic.* Boulder, CO: Westview Press, 1994.

Pearl Harbor, Attack on (December 7, 1941)

Japanese military action against the U.S. naval base at Pearl Harbor, the Hawaiian Islands, that caused the United States to enter World War II. By early 1941, tensions between Japan and the United States had reached the breaking point. Japan's invasion of China beginning in 1937 and its occupation of French

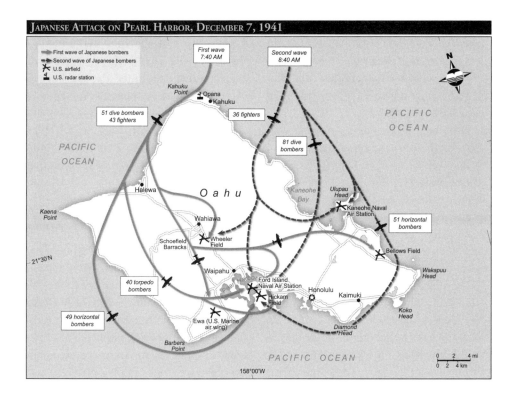

JAPANESE ATTACK ON PEARL HARBOR, DECEMBER 7, 1941

Indochina in 1940 and 1941 had led President Franklin D. Roosevelt to embargo scrap metal and oil and to freeze Japanese assets in the United States. The Japanese particularly resented the embargo on oil, characterizing it as "an unfriendly act." Japan had no oil resources of its own and had limited stockpiles. Without oil, the Japanese might have to withdraw from China. An army-dominated government in Tokyo now sought to take advantage of British, French, and Dutch weakness in Asia to push its own plans to secure hegemony and resources in East Asia. Japan was determined to seize this opportunity, even if that meant war with the United States. The United States misread Tokyo's resolve, believing that it could force Japan to back down without military confrontation.

Both sides visualized the same scenario for war in the Pacific. The Japanese would seize U.S. and European possessions in the Far East, forcing the U.S. Navy to fight its way across the Pacific to relieve them. Somewhere in the Far East, a great naval battle would occur to decide Pacific hegemony. In March 1940, commander of the Combined Fleet Admiral Yamamoto Isoroku scrapped the original plan—which called for using submarines and cruisers and destroyers with the Long Lance torpedo and savaging the U.S. battle fleet as it worked its way west—in favor of a pre-emptive strike against the U.S. fleet, which Roosevelt had shifted from San Diego to Pearl Harbor on the island of Oahu. Yamamoto believed that such an attack, destroying the U.S. carriers and battleships, would buy time for Japan to build its defensive ring. However, Yamamoto misread American psychology when he believed that such an attack might demoralize the American people and force Washington to negotiate a settlement that would give Japan hegemony in the western Pacific.

With both sides edging toward war, U.S. Pacific Fleet commander Admiral Husband E. Kimmel and army lieutenant general Walter C. Short made their dispositions for the defense of Oahu. Both men requested additional resources from Washington, but the United States was only then rearming, and little additional assistance was forthcoming.

The Japanese, meanwhile, trained extensively for the Pearl Harbor attack. The successful attack by the British on the Italian fleet anchorage of Taranto in November 1940 proved a useful study for Japanese planning. They fitted their torpedoes with fins so that they could be dropped from aircraft in the shallow water of Pearl Harbor, and they also planned to use large armor-piercing shells to be dropped as bombs from high-flying aircraft. No deck armor would be able to withstand them.

Following the expiration of a self-imposed deadline for securing an agreement with the United States, Tokyo ordered the attack to go forward. On November 16, 1941, Japanese submarines departed for Pearl Harbor, and 10 days later the First Air Fleet, commanded by Vice Admiral Nagumo Choichi, sortied. This attack force was centered on six aircraft carriers: the *Akagi, Hiryu, Kaga, Shokaku, Soryu,* and *Zuikaku.* They carried 423 aircraft, 360 of which were to participate in the attack. Accompanying the carriers were 2 battleships, 3 cruisers, 9 destroyers, and 2 tankers.

Surprise was essential if the attack was to be successful. The Japanese main-tained radio silence, and Washington knew only that the fleet had sailed. A "war warning" had been issued to military commanders in the Pacific, but few American leaders thought the Japanese would dare attack Pearl Harbor. Nagumo planned to approach from the northwest and move in as close as possible before launching his aircraft, and then recover them farther out, compelling any U.S. air reaction force to fly two long legs.

Nagumo ordered the planes to launch beginning at 6:00 a.m. on December 7 at a point about 275 miles from Pearl Harbor. Two events should have made a difference to the Americans but did not. Before the launch, American picket ships off the harbor entrance detected a Japanese midget submarine. Then they sank another. There were five Japanese midget submarines in the operation. Carried to the area by mother submarines, they were to enter the harbor and then wait for the air attack. Probably only one succeeded.

A U.S. radar station also detected the Japanese aircraft approaching but it was assumed that this was a flight of B-17s from the mainland, which arrived during the attack. The detected aircraft were, however, coming from the wrong direction and in far greater numbers. The report was thought to be the result of operator error with the new radar system.

At 7:50 a.m., the first wave of Japanese aircraft began its attack on the ships at Pearl Harbor and air stations at Ewa, Ford Island, Hickam, Kaneohe, and Wheeler. Most U.S. planes were destroyed on the ground. They were easy targets as Short, to avoid sabotage by the many Japanese on the island, had ordered the planes bunched together and ammunition stored separately. The attack achieved great success. Over some 140 minutes, the Japan-

Aftermath of the Japanese attack on Pearl Harbor, December 7, 1941. The Battleship *West Virginia* is in the background. (Library of Congress)

ese sank 4 of the 8 U.S. battleships in the Pacific and badly damaged the rest. Seven smaller ships were also sunk, and 4 were badly damaged. A total of 188 U.S. aircraft were destroyed, and 63 were badly damaged. The attack also killed 2,280 people and wounded 1,109. The attack cost the Japanese only 29 aircraft and fewer than 100 aircrew dead.

The chief drawbacks in the attack from the Japanese point of view were that the U.S. carriers were away from Pearl Harbor on maneuvers and could not be struck. The Japanese failed to hit the oil tank storage areas, without which the fleet could not remain at Pearl. Nor had they targeted the dockyard repair facilities. Nagumo had won a smashing victory but was unwilling to risk his ships in any attempt to exploit that victory. The task force recovered its aircraft and departed.

Yamamoto's preemptive strike was a brilliant tactical success. The Japanese could carry out their plans in the South Pacific without fear of significant U.S. naval intervention. However, the Pearl Harbor attack also solidly united American opinion behind a war that ultimately led to Japan's defeat.

T. Jason Soderstrum
and Spencer C. Tucker

References

Clausen, Henry C. *Pearl Harbor: Final Judgment.* New York: Crown, 1992.

Prange, Gordon W., with Donald M. Goldstein and Katherine V. Dillon. *At Dawn*

We Slept: The Untold Story of Pearl Harbor. New York: Harper and Row, 1975.

Russell, Henry Dozier. *Pearl Harbor Story.* Macon, GA: Mercer University Press, 2001.

Satterfield, Archie. *The Day the War Began.* New York: Praeger, 1992.

Weintraub, Stanley. *Long Day's Journey into War: December 7, 1941.* New York: Dutton, 1991.

Midway, Battle of (June 3–6, 1942)

Decisive naval engagement of World War II that turned the tide of the war in the Pacific. Beginning in January 1942, the Japanese had attempted to extend their defensive perimeter by seizing bases in Papua and New Guinea and in the Solomon Islands, which would be used to support future operations against New Caledonia, Fiji, and Samoa. By early March, they had taken the entire north coast of Papua and New Guinea and begun preparations for an amphibious invasion of Port Moresby.

On May 7–8, these events resulted in the Battle of the Coral Sea when the Japanese invasion force encountered an American carrier force. In the first naval battle in which neither fleet sighted the other, the aircraft carrier *Lexington* was sunk and the carrier *Yorktown* was heavily damaged. However, the Japanese had their light carrier *Shoho* sunk, and the loss of its air cover caused the invasion force to turn back. At the same time, the Americans damaged the carrier *Shokaku*. The Americans were able to repair the *Yorktown* in time for the next battle, whereas the *Shokaku* could not be readied for that second and decisive fight. The second carrier, *Zuikaku*, also did not participate because of an aircraft short-

age. Thus, on balance, the Battle of the Coral Sea was a strategic U.S. victory.

A second battle soon developed after the Japanese turned their focus on the strategic island of Midway. Despite the setback at Coral Sea, the Japanese continued with their plans to seize Midway Island and bases in the Aleutians. Admiral Yamamoto Isoroku, commander in chief of the Combined Fleet, convinced the imperial general staff that the capture of Midway would allow Japan to pursue its Asian policies behind an impregnable eastern shield of defenses in the Central Pacific. The capture of Midway would serve as a forceful response to the April 1942 U.S. air raid on Tokyo. It would also deprive the United States of a forward base for submarines, and it would be a stepping stone for the capture of Hawaii. Perhaps most important, it would draw out the U.S. aircraft carriers, giving the Japanese the opportunity to destroy them.

Admiral Yamamoto deployed the bulk of the Japanese fleet. For the operation, he would commit some 200 ships—almost the entire Japanese Navy—including 8 carriers, 11 battleships, 22 cruisers, 65 destroyers, 21 submarines, and more than 600 aircraft. His plan called for diversionary attacks on the Aleutian Islands to both decoy the Americans from Midway and place them in a position where the Japanese could crush the U.S. reaction force between their forces to the north and at Midway. The Aleutian operation would also secure the islands of Attu and Kiska, placing forces astride a possible U.S. invasion route to Japan.

Yamamoto correctly assumed that U.S. Pacific Fleet commander Admiral Chester W. Nimitz would have to respond to a landing on Midway. When the Pacific Fleet arrived in the area, Japanese carrier

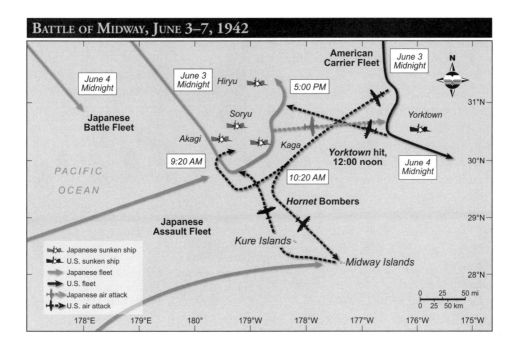

BATTLE OF MIDWAY, JUNE 3–7, 1942

and battleship task forces, waiting unseen to the west of the Midway strike force, would fall on and destroy the unsuspecting Americans. Yamamoto assumed that the *Yorktown* had been sunk in the Coral Sea fight and that the *Enterprise* and *Hornet* were not likely to be in the Midway area when the strike force attacked the island. He was not correct. This miscalculation resulted from one of several breakdowns in Japanese intelligence and communications that contributed to the eventual American victory.

For the Aleutians, Yamamoto committed an invasion force of 2,400 men in 3 escorted transports, a support group of 2 heavy cruisers and 2 light carriers, and a covering force of 4 older battleships. The battle began in the Aleutians with air strikes on June 3, followed by landings three days later. The Aleutian phase of the operation went well for the Japanese. Carrier aircraft inflicted heavy damage on the U.S. base at Dutch Harbor, and the

Japanese then made unopposed landings on Kiska and Attu. They kept this toehold on continental U.S. territory until mid-1943.

Despite the Japanese success in the Aleutians, the action there proved insignificant to the coming battle at Midway. U.S. intelligence had broken the Japanese naval code, putting the basic outlines of the Midway plan into American hands and thus allowing the Americans to disregard the attacks on the Aleutians in favor of concentrating on Midway. The Pacific Fleet was ready with three fleet aircraft carriers, including the *Yorktown*. It had been hastily repaired at Pearl Harbor and made operational in only 2 days instead of an initial estimate of 90 and was sent back to sea with an air group formed of planes from other carriers. The *Yorktown* sailed just in advance of the establishment of a picket line of Japanese submarines that Yamamoto hoped would intercept American ships departing Pearl.

The U.S. ships concentrated in an ambush position some 350 miles northeast of Midway, awaiting the westward advance of Yamamoto's armada.

On June 3, American naval reconnaissance planes sighted, at a distance of 600 miles, the Japanese fleet of some 185 ships advancing on Midway. The battle began when Boeing B-17 Flying Fortress bombers from Midway Island struck without effect at the Japanese carrier strike force, about 220 miles southwest of the U.S. fleet. That same night, four Consolidated PBY patrol bombers from Midway staged a torpedo attack and damaged an oiler, which was able to regain its place in the formation.

Early on June 4, Japanese First Air Fleet commander Nagumo Choichi sent 108 Japanese planes from the strike force to attack and bomb Midway, while the Japanese carriers again escaped damage from U.S. land-based planes. However, as the morning progressed, the Japanese carriers were soon overwhelmed by the logistics of almost simultaneously sending a second wave of bombers to finish off the Midway runways, zigzagging to avoid the bombs of attacking aircraft, and rearming to launch planes to sink the now sighted U.S. naval forces. American fighters and bombers, sent from Midway airfields, and aircraft from three U.S. carriers attacked the Japanese fleet. But three successive waves of U.S. torpedo-bombers were virtually wiped out during their attacks on the carriers from 9:30 to 10:24 a.m.: Japanese fighters and antiaircraft guns shot down 47 of 51 planes. The Japanese now believed that they had won the battle.

Nagumo had ordered planes returning from strikes on Midway to rearm with torpedoes to strike the American ships. But as this effort was in progress at about

Scene on board the U.S. aircraft carrier *Yorktown* (CV-5), shortly after it was struck by three Japanese bombs on June 4, 1942. (Naval Historical Center)

10:30 a.m. 37 dive-bombers from the carrier *Enterprise* at last located the Japanese carriers in their most vulnerable state, while their decks were cluttered with armed aircraft, ordnance, and fuel. The Japanese fighters in the air were also operating at low altitudes, having dealt with the torpedo-bomber attacks. Within the span of a few minutes, three of the four Japanese carriers—the *Soryu*, *Kaga*, and *Akagi*—were in flames and sinking. Planes from the only still operational Japanese carrier, the *Hiryu*, struck back, heavily damaging the *Yorktown*. In the late afternoon, the *Hiryu* was also hit and badly damaged. The Japanese abandoned the ship the following day.

During the battle between the U.S. and Japanese naval forces, the two fleets neither saw each other nor exchanged gunfire; all contact was made by Japanese carrier-based planes and American land- and carrier-based aircraft. Yamamoto's first reaction on learning of the loss of three of his carriers was to bring up his battleships and recall the two light carriers from the Aleutians in hopes of fighting a more conventional sea battle. But the loss of the *Hiryu* and Nagumo's gloomy reports led him to call off the attack on Midway.

Yamamoto still hoped to trap the Americans by drawing them westward into his heavy ships, but the U.S. task force commander, Rear Admiral Raymond Spruance, refused to take the bait and reported to Nimitz that he was unwilling to risk a night encounter with superior Japanese forces. By the night of June 6, the Battle of Midway was over. It had been costly for Japan. In the battle itself, the Japanese lost 4 fleet aircraft carriers and 332 aircraft, most of which went down with the carriers. The Japanese also lost a heavy cruiser sunk and another badly damaged. Three destroyers and a fleet oiler were damaged as well, and a battleship was slightly damaged. The Americans lost the aircraft carrier *Yorktown*, 1 destroyer, and 147 aircraft, 38 of which were land-based.

The Japanese Navy was still a formidable fighting force, but once it had lost the four fleet carriers and its well-trained aircrews and maintenance personnel, the continued Japanese force ratio superiority in battleships and cruisers counted for little. The subsequent Japanese defeat in the protracted fight for Guadalcanal was caused by a loss of air superiority. It can be reasonably stated that the Battle of Midway was indeed the turning point of the long struggle in the Pacific Theater.

James H. Willbanks

References

Fuchida, Mitsuo, and Okumiya Masatake. *Midway: The Battle That Doomed Japan—The Japanese Navy's Story.* Annapolis, MD: Naval Institute Press, 1955.

Lord, Walter. *Incredible Victory.* New York: Harper and Row, 1967.

Morison, Samuel Eliot. *History of United States Naval Operations in World War II.* Vol. 4, *Coral Sea, Midway, and Submarine Actions, May 1942–August 1942.* Boston: Little, Brown, 1949.

Prange, Gordon W. *Miracle at Midway.* New York: McGraw-Hill, 1982.

Combined Bomber Offensive (June 10, 1943–April 1945)

Sustained strategic bombing campaign of Germany conducted by the British Royal Air Force (RAF) and the United States Army Air Forces (USAAF). At the Casablanca Conference in French Morocco, North Africa, during January 14–24, 1943, British prime minister Winston Churchill, U.S. president Franklin D. Roosevelt, and the British-American Combined Chiefs of Staff (CCS) met to plan and decide overall strategy for continuing the war against Nazi Germany. Having decided that an invasion of the European continent through France was not feasible in 1943, they worked to find another means by which to engage the Germans actively. The Allied senior leadership ultimately decided to support U.S. major general Ira C. Eaker's plan to begin a "combined" bomber offensive against Germany, with the Americans bombing principally during the day and the British bombing at night.

Chief of the RAF Air Staff marshal Sir Charles Portal was assigned the mission of coordinating the operation. On January 21, the CCS issued the Casablanca Directive, which established the objective of the Combined Bomber Offensive (CBO) as "the progressive destruction and dislocation of the German military, industrial, and economic system, and the undermining of the morale of the German people to a point where their capacity for armed resistance is fatally weakened." A supplemental document called the Directive for the Bomber Offensive required the Allies to "take every opportunity to attack Germany by day, to destroy objectives that are unsuitable for night attack . . . to impose heavy losses on the German day fighter force, and to contain German fighter strength away from the Russian and Mediterranean theatres of war."

The CBO concept was actually a compromise between the two opposing doctrines of the RAF and the USAAF. The American commanders believed that their heavily armed and supposedly "self-defending" long-range B-17 and B-24 bombers would be able to defend themselves sufficiently well without fighter escort to reach and attack the designated target while sustaining only minimal losses. Because the American bombers were equipped with the Norden bombsight, strategic precision bombing operations could be conducted from high altitudes, above the ceiling of ground-based antiaircraft artillery. American aircraft would therefore be able to bomb in daylight with minimal loss and strike specific military and industrial targets with only limited collateral damage.

The RAF, which began the war in 1939 with a similar doctrine, quickly discovered that its lightly armed and armored bombers could not operate during the day without suffering crippling losses. In response, the British switched to nighttime area bombing. Although the CBO joined together the two operational concepts, both sets of doctrine were seriously flawed.

Although planned out in four phases between April 1943 and April 1944, the CBO did not actually begin until the Pointblank Directive was adopted by the CCS in June 1943. According to that document, continuous aerial warfare would effectively engage and disperse the German *Luftwaffe* through a war of attrition, particularly through maintaining regular Allied fighter intrusion by day. Putting further pressure on the German fighter defenses, aircraft factories were designated as primary bombing targets. Both the Casablanca and the Pointblank directives were based on the establishment of Allied air supremacy as a condition for the success of the Allied invasion of France. A follow-on Allied conference in August 1943 at Quebec, code named "Quadrant," confirmed the previously established set of priorities, but rejected bombing attacks specifically to break German civilian morale as a means to achieve the strategic goal.

The missions resulting from the Pointblank Directive included the large-scale attacks against Berlin, Hamburg, the Ruhr industrial area, and the ball-bearing manufacturing plants at Schweinfurt. The August 17, 1943, raid on Schweinfurt in particular was a failure because of the devastatingly high losses of U.S. Eighth Air Force bombers and air crew. Attacking in 2 waves of 300 bombers without fighter cover, the U.S. aircraft were subjected to relentless attack by German fighters for some 6 hours. The USAAF lost 60 bombers shot down and 130 damaged. Every bomber lost also meant the loss of 10 highly trained air crew members.

The Schweinfurt fiasco produced a crisis of confidence in the effectiveness and sustainability of CBO operations. The Americans suspended raids deep into Germany until the P-51 Mustang became operational in significant numbers. The new, long-range fighter had the operational radius necessary to escort the

A B-17 Flying Fortress of the U.S. Eighth Air Force bombing a fighter aircraft assembly plant in Marienburg, Germany, 1943. (National Archives)

bombers all the way to the target and back. Since dense cloud clover severely limited the effectiveness of the Norden bombsight, the Americans also postponed their attacks to wait for better weather. By February 1944, the Americans were ready to resume bombing operations.

The final decision for the Operation OVERLORD plan (the cross-Channel invasion of France) did much to refocus the conflicting priorities of the early CBO strategy. The Allied air forces were now given specific and limited operational target sets specifically designed to reduce the German ability to reinforce against the Allied invasion force ashore, rather than the earlier and more ambiguous military and economic strategic targets.

The shift produced a rapid effect. In February 1944, the first six days of the renewed offensive, designated "Big Week," undercut an already weakened and demoralized *Luftwaffe*, and deep interdiction missions effectively disrupted German rail communications in Western Europe. By June 1944, when Operation OVERLORD started, the *Luftwaffe* was virtually incapable of mounting any significant attacks against the invasion force.

Despite the CBO, the production of German fighters actually increased, and continued to do so until September 1944. But while the Germans were not quite running out of fighter aircraft, they were running out of fuel and adequately-trained pilots. The resumed bombing raids with complete fighter cover cost the *Luftwaffe* heavily in both aircraft and pilots, but one trained pilot took far longer to replace than one fighter. On D-Day (June 6, 1944), therefore, the Allies were able to commit 12,387 aircraft, including 5,400 fighters. German *Luftflotte* 3 could launch only 329 aircraft in response. The virtual elimination of the *Luftwaffe* and the establishment of Allied air supremacy was one clear-cut success of the CBO.

At the end of the war the CBO was generally considered to have been an overall but costly success. The U.S. Eighth Air Force alone lost 2,400 bombers and RAF Bomber Command lost more than 8,000. The casualty rate for aircrew was significantly higher than for infantrymen. The postwar U.S. Strategic Bombing Survey, however, concluded that the CBO largely failed to achieve its broader objective of inflicting significant damage on German strategic targets. Despite the large-scale destruction inflicted on German cities and the casualties to the civilian population, there was no evidence that the German "will to fight" had been measurably reduced. High-level "precision" bombing, especially in and near population centers in close proximity to the industrial and military targets, had killed more than 600,000 civilians. The outcome, therefore, continues to be questioned by historians on both moral and operational effectiveness grounds.

Lee W. Eysturlid

References

Crane, Conrad. *Bombs, Cities and Civilians: American Airpower Strategy in World War II*. Lawrence: University Press of Kansas, 1993.

Davis, Richard C. *Bombing the European Axis Powers: A Historical Digest of the Combined Bomber Offensive, 1939–1945*. Maxwell AFB, AL: Air University Press, 2006.

Hansell, Haywood S., Jr. *The Air Plan that Defeated Hitler*. New York: Arno Press, 1980.

Verrier, Anthony. *The Bomber Offensive*. New York: Macmillan, 1969.

Tarawa, Battle of (November 20–24, 1943)

One of the bloodiest amphibious assaults in military history that pitted American troops against Japanese defenders on the small atoll of Tarawa in the Gilbert Islands. In December 1941, a Japanese task force seized Tarawa—part of the Gilbert Islands—which stretch some 500 miles along the equator in the central Pacific Ocean. Tarawa is a hook-shaped atoll with a lagoon formed by a coral reef just beneath the ocean surface. The barb in the hook is formed by 2-mile-long, triangular-shaped Betio Island, less than 300 acres of nondescript coral sand and coconut palms rising no more than 15 feet above sea level.

The Japanese constructed an airfield there, and by November 1943, they had turned Betio into a fortress. Rear Admiral Shibasaki Keiji commanded 5,000 naval infantry troops who manned reinforced concrete blockhouses, coconut-log bunkers, and gun pits, all connected by a network of tunnels and trenches. Heavy guns in hardened revetments commanded virtually every approach to the island, prompting Shibasaki to remark that Betio could not be taken by a million men in a hundred years.

The Central Pacific commander, U.S. admiral Chester W. Nimitz, decided to seize the Gilberts in a joint assault by the army and the marines as the first test of offensive amphibious operations. V Amphibious Corps, commanded by U.S. Marines major general Holland M.

Smith, was responsible for the landing, code named Operation GALVANIC. The 2nd Marine Division, led by Major General Julian C. Smith, would seize Tarawa, while the army's 27th Infantry Division, commanded by Major General Ralph C. Smith, landed at nearby Makin.

V Amphibious Corps staffers decided the portion of Betio that faced the lagoon was the least heavily defended terrain, and they designated landing areas there as Red Beaches 1, 2, and 3. A disadvantage to those sites was the precise navigation required for the landing craft to pass into the lagoon and then maintain formation as they approached the beaches. Amphibious doctrine called for landings at high tide so

the landing craft could clear defensive obstacles. The planners did not have reliable tide charts, and when Holland Smith designated November 20, 1943, as D-Day, the tides would not be favorable to the marines. By then, U.S. aircraft had flown hundreds of sorties against Betio, saturating the island with bombs as ships of the U.S. Fifth Fleet pounded the island's defenses one last time. Faulty U.S. reconnaissance reports indicated that nothing was left alive on Betio.

At 9:00 a.m., almost two hours after the last bombardment began, Colonel David M. Shoup led three reinforced battalions of his 2nd Marine Regiment toward Red Beaches 1, 2, and 3. Japanese

U.S. marines take cover behind a sea wall during the fighting for Tarawa, November 20–24, 1943, one of the most costly amphibious assaults in history. (National Archives)

heavy guns then opened up, unleashing a deadly hail of fire into the tightly packed amphibious tractors (amtracs) as they neared the reef, paused briefly to climb over it, and then landed on the beaches. However, the shallow-draft Higgins boats that followed could not get over the reef. A nightmare for the marines began when they were forced to debark into the water about 600 yards from the shore. Withering Japanese machine-gun fire met the marines, who were unable to return fire as they slowly waded toward shore laden with equipment. A small sea-wall afforded little cover from Japanese small-arms fire as navy corpsmen set up aid stations.

By afternoon, the marines had penetrated no more than a few hundred feet in many places. Shoup, who was wounded, still directed the fight and requested that reserves be committed in a message that emphasized the precariousness of the situation, stating, "Issue in doubt." Of the 5,000 marines who landed that day, almost 1,500 became casualties. During the night, the Japanese threatened with counterattacks, snipers, and infiltrators. Many marines had drained their canteens and emptied their cartridge belts. The wounded suffered and could only wait for evacuation in the morning.

The morning saw little improvement. Stiff resistance compelled the attackers to destroy each Japanese strong point at a heavy price as U.S. Navy destroyers provided fire support at dangerously close ranges. The day of November 21 ended with more of Betio in marine hands, but the island was not yet secure. At mid-morning on November 22, the marines began their final assault on the Japanese command post, where they poured gasoline down air vents and then ignited it, killing those inside, including Shibasaki.

Many Japanese committed suicide as the marines cleared the western portion of the island and pushed the remaining defenders into a narrow tail of land in the east.

Making their final stand, the Japanese launched a series of nighttime banzai attacks, in which mobs of enemy soldiers charged marine positions with drawn swords and bayonets. They were cut down by artillery and machine-gun fire from the exhausted marines. Commanders declared the battle over on the morning of November 23, after 76 hours of horrendous fighting. The Japanese lost 4,690 men killed; only 17 prisoners were taken, along with 129 Korean laborers. The desperate Japanese defense of the island cost the marines and the navy 1,027 dead, 88 missing, and 2,292 wounded. The casualties shocked an American public that viewed the fight on Tarawa as evidence there would be no cheap victories as the battles were carried to the Japanese homeland. The Battle of Tarawa brought many changes, including improved naval fire support and significant increases in firepower ashore, to include more automatic weapons, tanks, explosive charges, and flamethrowers.

Steven J. Rauch

References

Alexander, Joseph H. *Utmost Savagery: The Three Days of Tarawa.* Annapolis, MD: Naval Institute Press, 1995.

Russ, Martin. *Line of Departure: Tarawa.* New York: Doubleday, 1975.

Normandy Invasion (June 6–July 31, 1944)

The Allied cross-Channel invasion of France. U.S. officials, principally army chief of staff General George C. Marshall, had long sought the earliest possible invasion of France as the way to win the war in the shortest possible time. They supported both GYMNAST, a British cross-Channel invasion contingency plan for late 1942, and ROUNDUP, a 48-division invasion of France projected to occur by April 1943. The failure of the Allied raid on Dieppe, France (Operation JUBILEE), on August 19, 1942, however, led the Americans to concede to the British position that a cross-Channel invasion was many months, if not years, in the future. Prime Minister Winston L. S. Churchill and British planners, meanwhile, sought to interest the United States in a supposedly more opportunistic approach that would include operations in the Mediterranean Theater, and the Americans reluctantly went along.

This led to Operation TORCH, the Allied invasion of North Africa, and to subsequent British and U.S. landings in Sicily and Italy. The United States insisted, however, that the Italy Campaign would be a secondary effort. At the Tehran Conference in November 1943, Soviet leader Joseph Stalin had pressed President Franklin D. Roosevelt and Churchill for the cross-Channel invasion. Stalin agreed to mount a major offensive by the Soviets on the Eastern Front to coincide with the landing. He also pressed Roosevelt to name the commander of the invasion force, and shortly after the conference Roosevelt appointed General Dwight D. Eisenhower to the post of supreme commander, Allied Expeditionary Forces.

Fortress Europe and its coasts of Holland, Belgium, and France bristled with all manner of German fortifications and booby traps. Organization Todt, the German construction organization, had begun building defenses there in mid-1942. Over the next 2 years, the Germans used some 17.3 million cubic yards of concrete and 1.2 million tons of steel in thousands of fortifications. Field Marshal Erwin Rommel, who had command of Army Group B and the coastal defenses, disagreed with German commander in chief West Field Marshal Gerd von Rundstedt. Rommel, well aware from the campaign in North Africa what complete Allied domination of the air would mean, believed that, if it was to be stopped at all, the invasion had to be defeated on the beaches. Rundstedt and German dictator Adolf Hitler placed their hopes in a large mobile reserve that would defeat the Allied forces once they were ashore. Indeed, Hitler seems to have welcomed the invasion as a chance to engage and destroy the British and U.S. forces. In Britain, the Allied armies could not be touched; in France, they could be destroyed. Hitler was convinced that the Allied effort would result in another Dieppe. "Let them come," he said. "They will get the thrashing of their lives."

Rommel did what he could, supervising the construction of elaborate defenses, the placement of a half million foreshore obstacles, and the laying of some 4 million mines. Rommel had operational command of the Fifteenth Army in northern France and the Seventh Army in Normandy, with a total force of 25 static coastal divisions, 16 infantry and parachute divisions, 11 armored and mechanized divisions, and 7 reserve divisions. The Germans were weak in the air and on the water, however. The Third Air Fleet in France deployed only 329 aircraft on D-Day and the German naval forces in sector had only 4 destroyers and 39 E-boats. Germany also deployed several dozen U-boats, most from French ports, during the campaign.

Compounding the problem for the Germans, theater commander Rundstedt did not have operational control over the Ger-

NORMANDY INVASION, JUNE 6–JULY 31, 1944

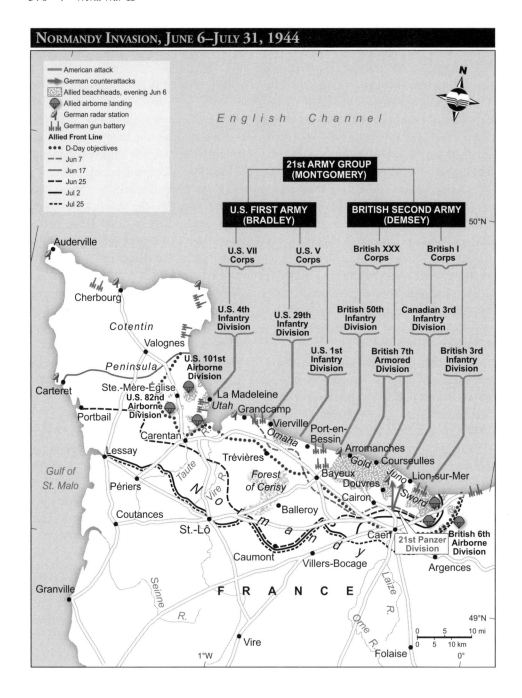

man air and naval forces in his sector, while his Allied counterpart, Eisenhower, had overall command of all Allied forces. Rundstedt and his subordinate field army commanders did not even have operational control of the Panzer divisions in their sector. The Panzers could only be committed upon specific orders from Berlin.

Prior to the landings, U.S. and British air forces worked to soften the German defenses and isolate the beachheads. Between April 1 and June 5, 1944, Allied aircraft flew 200,000 sorties in support of the coming invasion and dropped 195,000 tons of bombs. The Allies lost 2,000 of their own aircraft in the process, but by D-Day they had largely isolated the landing areas and they had achieved virtual air supremacy.

The Germans also greatly strengthened the Channel port defenses, which Hitler had ordered turned into fortresses. All of this was for naught because, as German minister of armaments Albert Speer noted, the Allies came over the beaches and "brought their own port with them. . . . Our whole plan of defense had proved irrelevant." In one of the greatest military engineering achievements in history, thousands of men labored in Britain for months to build two large artificial harbors known as "Mulberries." Plans called for two to be established after the initial Allied landings, to be hauled across the Channel from Britain and sunk in place directly offshore from the American and British landing sectors. Their importance to the Allied cause may be seen in that, by the end of October, 25 percent of stores, 20 percent of personnel, and 15 percent of vehicles had passed through Mulberry B.

The Allies worked out precise and elaborate plans for the mammoth cross-Channel invasion, code named OVER-LORD, to land on the Cotentin Peninsula in Normandy. Directly under Eisenhower's command, British admiral Bertram H. Ramsay had overall command of the naval operation, code named NEPTUNE. British air chief marshal Trafford Leigh-Mallory commanded the combined air forces, and British general Bernard Montgomery exercised overall command of the land forces. The objec-

tive of the operation was simply to secure a bridgehead from which further offensive operations could be mounted.

The landing itself would be preceded by a night drop of paratroops. General Marshall, an enthusiastic supporter of airborne forces, urged the use of five airborne divisions, but Eisenhower had his doubts, and as it transpired, only three were used: the British 6th and the U.S. 82nd and 101st. The lightly armed paratroopers, operating in conjunction with the French Resistance, had the vital task of securing the flanks of the lodgment and destroying key transportation choke points to prevent the Germans from reinforcing their beach defenses. The German 21st Panzer and 12th SS Panzer Divisions were stationed just outside Caen. If they were permitted to reach the beaches, they could strike the amphibious forces from the flank and roll them up.

The amphibious assault would occur early in the morning after the airborne assault with 5 infantry divisions wading ashore along the 50-mile stretch of coast, divided into 5 sectors. The designated beaches were, from west to east, the U.S. 4th Infantry Division (Utah), the U.S. 1st Infantry Division and elements of the 29th Infantry Division (Omaha), the British 50th Infantry Division (Gold), the Canadian 3rd Infantry Division (Juno), and the British 3rd Infantry Division (Sword).

Operation OVERLORD proved a vast undertaking. The airborne forces alone required 1,340 C-47 transports and 2,500 gliders. Ten thousand aircraft secured the skies. Naval support for the invasion came from 1,213 warships; 4,126 transport vessels, including landing ships and landing craft; 736 ancillary craft; and 864 merchant vessels.

Invasion commander General Eisenhower faced a difficult decision, given terrible weather in the days preceding the planned landing. Informed by his chief meteorologist that a brief break in the weather would most probably occur early on June 6, Eisenhower decided to proceed. This decision worked to the Allies' advantage, for the Germans did not expect a landing in such poor weather. The French Resistance was informed by radio code, and the airborne forces took off.

The airborne operation involving 23,400 U.S. and British paratroops dropped on schedule on the night of June 5–6, but thick cloud banks over Normandy caused pilots to veer off course to avoid midair collisions. German antiaircraft fire, jumpy flight crews, and Pathfinders who were immediately engaged in firefights on the ground and unable to set up their beacons led to premature drops and to paratroopers being scattered all over the peninsula. Some were even dropped into the English Channel, where they were dragged down by their heavy equipment. Gliders crashed into obstacles, and they and the paratroopers came down in fields that had been deliberately flooded by the Germans as a defensive measure. Much equipment was thus lost. Nonetheless, the wide scattering of forces caused confusion among the defenders as to the precise Allied intent. Officers and noncommissioned officers collected as many men as they could, and improvised units were soon moving on the objectives, most of which were secured.

Success was likely if the Allies could establish a bridgehead large enough to allow them to build up their strength and overcome the German defenders. Once they broke out, the Allies would have the whole of France for maneuver, because their armies were fully motorized or mechanized and the bulk of the defending German forces were not. The only possibility of German success was for the defenders rapidly to introduce Panzer reserves, but this step was fatally delayed by two factors. The first was Allied naval gunfire support and air superiority of 30:1 over Normandy itself (there were large numbers of ground-support aircraft, especially the P-47 Thunderbolt and the P-51 Mustang). Any German armored units operating too close to the beachhead would become instant targets for the overwhelmingly superior Allied naval and air fires. The second factor was Hitler's failure to release operational control of the Panzer divisions to the local commanders. Hitler was convinced that the invasion at Normandy was merely a feint and that the main thrust would come in the Pas de Calais sector. Prior to the landings, Allied counterintelligence and deception operations played a key role reinforcing this fatally flawed German assessment.

The British "Doublecross" system worked to perfection. Every German agent in Britain was either dead, jailed, or working for British intelligence. The British actually controlled the entire German spy network in the United Kingdom and used it to feed disinformation to the Germans. Operations FORTITUDE NORTH and FORTITUDE SOUTH also deceived Hitler. FORTITUDE NORTH led him to assume that the Allies intended to invade Norway from Scotland, resulting in the Germans leaving and even reinforcing a substantial German force there. FORTITUDE SOUTH led Hitler to assume that any Allied main effort in France would be a landing north of Normandy in the Pas de Calais area, the narrowest point of the English Channel. Any landing in Normandy would only be a feint. Supporting the deception plan the Allies established the phantom "First U.S. Army Group" under Lieutenant General George S. Patton, who was still without an operational command following an incident in which he had slapped soldiers suffering from combat fatigue in Sicily. The Germans assumed the aggressive Patton would command any Allied invasion of the Continent. First U.S. Army Group, a notional formation of 18 divisions and 4 corps headquarters and the appropriately huge amount of bogus communications traffic, contributed significantly to the success of OVERLORD by deceiving the Germans until well after the Normandy bridgehead had been established and consolidated.

Not until late July did Hitler authorize the deployment of the Panzer divisions of the Fifteenth Army from the Pas de Calais to Normandy. In effect, the deception totally immobilized 19 German divisions east of the Seine. Although units of the Fifteenth Army were moved west to Normandy before that date, this was done piecemeal and hence they were much easier for the Allies to defeat.

In the days immediately prior to the Allied landings some 2,700 vessels manned by 195,000 men were on the move. They transported 130,000 troops, 2,000 tanks, 12,000 other vehicles, and 10,000 tons of supplies. At about 5:30 a.m. on June 6, 1944, the warships opened up against the 50-mile-long invasion front, engaging the German shore batteries. The first U.S. assault troops landed 30

U.S. soldiers landing on the Normandy coast of France under heavy German machine-gun fire, D-Day, June 6, 1944. (National Archives)

to 40 minutes later, and the British landing craft were ashore 2 hours later.

The landing was in jeopardy only on Omaha Beach, where, because of rough seas, only 5 of 32 amphibious duplex-drive tanks reached the shore. Support artillery was also lost when DUKW amphibious trucks were swamped by the waves. Some landing craft were hit and destroyed, and those troops of the 1st Infantry Division who reached the beach were immediately pinned down by a withering German fire. U.S. First Army commander Lieutenant General Omar N. Bradley even considered withdrawal from Omaha. At 9:50 a.m., the warships opened fire against the first line German defensive positions.

Allied destroyers repeatedly risked running aground to provide close-in fire support to the troops ashore; indeed, several destroyers actually scraped bottom. It was nearly noon before the German defenders began to give way. The 1st Infantry Division overcame German opposition with sheer determination reinforced by the knowledge that there was no place to retreat.

Landings on the other beaches were relatively less difficult. Overall, for the first day, the Allies sustained some 10,300 casualties—4,300 British and Canadian and 6,000 U.S. A recent study suggests that a nighttime landing would have produced fewer casualties. The Allies had used nighttime landings with limited success in the Mediterranean, but Montgomery believed that overwhelming Allied air and naval power would make a daytime landing preferable. Still, the losses were comparatively light.

Unfortunately for the Allies, a force 6–7 storm blew out of the northwest during June 19–20 and severely damaged Mulberry A in the American sector. The storm also sank more than 100 small craft and drove many more ashore, bringing to a halt the discharge of supplies. Vital ammunition stocks had to be flown in. Mulberry A was abandoned, but a reinforced Mulberry B just off Arromanches provided supplies to both armies until July 1945.

The Allies put ashore 75,215 British and Canadian troops and 57,500 U.S. forces on D-Day and 1 million men within a month. Eventually, the United States committed 60 divisions to the battle for the European continent. The British and Canadians never had more than 20, and as the disparity grew, so too did U.S. influence over military and political strategy. Churchill was understandably insistent that Montgomery exercise prudence and not sacrifice his men needlessly, which would reduce British influence even further.

The Allied ground offensive, meanwhile, proceeded more slowly than expected. Hitler ordered his armies to fight for every inch of ground rather than withdraw along phase lines as his generals wanted. This decision by Hitler at first delayed the Allied timetable. However, it also greatly accelerated the ultimate defeat and ensured that it would be costly. Complete Allied air superiority devastated the Germans by day and forced them to move largely at night. The French Resistance also played an important role, providing the invading Allied forces with intelligence information and impeding German resupply efforts through sabotage and the destruction of rolling stock and bridges.

The Normandy countryside proved ideal defensive terrain. Over the centuries, the dividing lines between individual fields had been allowed to grow up into tangled hedgerows. This bocage resisted passage and slowed the Allied advance to a crawl. On June 17 and 18, the Germans blocked Montgomery's efforts to take the city of Caen. Major General J. Lawton Collins's U.S. VII Corps had more success on the Allied right, gradually pushing across the base of the Cotentin Peninsula. On June 18, it turned north to liberate the important port of Cherbourg, while the remainder of Bradley's army maintained an aggressive defense. Cherbourg fell on June 27, but its German defenders destroyed the harbor facilities, and it would take U.S. engineers under Major General Lucius Clay six weeks to get the harbor facilities back in operation.

Not until Operation COBRA on July 25–31 were the Allies able to break out. Bradley's U.S. First Army forced the German line west of Saint-Lô, and Collins's VII Corps made the main effort. All northern France was open for the highly mechanized Allied units to maneuver. On August 15, Allied forces also came ashore on the French Mediterranean coast in Operation DRAGOON. The German defenders were now in full retreat, but it remained to be seen if the Allies could maintain their fast-lengthening supply lines and end the war in the west before the Germans had a chance to recover.

Spencer C. Tucker

References

Ambrose, Stephen E. *D-Day: June 6, 1944: The Climactic Battle of World War II.* New York: Simon and Schuster, 1994.

D'Este, Carlo. *Decision in Normandy.* New York: E. P. Dutton, 1983.

Hastings, Max. *Overlord: D-Day, June 6, 1944.* New York: Simon and Schuster, 1984.

Lewis, Adrian R. *Omaha Beach: A Flawed Victory.* Chapel Hill: University of North Carolina Press, 2001.

Hürtgen Forest Campaign (September 12– December 16, 1944)

Although it is little remembered today, the battle for the Hürtgen Forest was one of the worst defeats ever suffered by the U.S. Army. In three months of combat operations, the Americans sustained almost 33,000 casualties but accomplished almost nothing tactically or operationally in the process.

By late August 1944, the apparently defeated German Army had been pushed out of France and back to the borders of the Third Reich. Many GIs began to believe that the war would be over by Christmas. But the situation changed as the Allies reached German territory and the defenses of the German West Wall (called the Siegfried Line by the Americans but never by the Germans). In the central sector of the West Wall defensive line lay the dark and almost impenetrable Hürtgen Forest.

At that point in the war, the Allied logistics system was stretched to the breaking point, and the advancing armies were on the verge of running out of ammunition and fuel. Allied military planners were faced with the two strategic options of attacking Germany—on a broad front or on a narrow front. Lieutenant General George S. Patton Jr. and Field Marshal Sir Bernard Montgomery were the two leading advocates of the narrow-front approach, but each general thought his forces should execute the "dagger thrust" into the heart of the Reich.

Pressed hard by Montgomery, supreme commander, Allied Expeditionary Forces General Dwight D. Eisenhower agreed in September 1944 to support the British plan for a combined ground and airborne thrust into Holland and then across the Rhine River at Arnhem. Launched on September

17, Operation MARKET-GARDEN soon failed. With supplies starting to dwindle to a trickle, the western Allies had no real choice other than to revert to the broad-front strategy of applying even pressure against the Germans all along the line.

Just prior to the start of MARKET-GARDEN, the U.S. First Army, commanded by Lieutenant General Courtney H. Hodges, breached the West Wall in two places and attacked the city of Aachen immediately north of the Hürtgen Forest. Hodges's 250,000-man force consisted of eight veteran divisions in the U.S. VII, V, and VIII Corps. After taking Aachen, Hodges planned to attack around the north end of the Hürtgen Forest across the flat open Rhine plain toward the city of Köln (Cologne). But Hodges also believed that he had to first secure the Hürtgen Forest to avoid dangerously exposing his southern flank.

The Hürtgen Forest is a classic piece of defender's terrain. It is an interlaced network of bald, exposed ridgelines and deeply wooded ravines, and the Roer River runs through the middle of the forest and then out across the Rhine plain. The small river itself was not a significant military obstacle, but a series of dams high in the forest had created a huge artificial lake holding millions of gallons of water. By releasing that water at the right moment, the Germans could flood the Rhine plain, which would slow, disrupt, and channelize Allied military movement for weeks. Those dams, in the vicinity of the town of Schmidt, were the one significant military operational objective in the Hürtgen Forest; but ironically, neither side appeared to recognize that significance until the battle was almost over.

Although the German Army had a reputation as the master of mobile, offensive warfare, it also was tenacious and resourceful in the defense. The German Army group commander in that sector, Field Marshal Walter Model, was a master defensive tactician.

The Hürtgen Forest Campaign started on September 12, 1944, when the veteran 9th Infantry Division attacked the southern end of the forest in an attempt to move through a passage known as the Monschau Corridor. The 9th Infantry Division took the town of Lammersdorf in the south, but it was stopped just short of Germeter in the center of the forest. In late October, the 9th Infantry Division was withdrawn from the line after suffering 4,500 casualties. The 28th Infantry Division replaced it.

The U.S. First Army planned another attack, this time with VII Corps, commanded by Major General J. Lawton Collins. It was to move through the northern passage called the Stolberg Corridor. As a diversionary effort to draw off German forces, Major General Leonard Gerow's V Corps to the south would attack with one division against Schmidt on the far side of the Kall River gorge. The supporting attack was scheduled for November 2, and the main attack was to follow on November 5. However, VII Corps could not get ready in time, and the main attack was postponed—first until November 10 and then until November 16. For some reason, the timing for the supporting attack never changed.

The 28th Infantry Division launched the attack toward Schmidt with all three of its infantry regiments attacking in diverging directions, which dissipated rather than concentrated its combat power. The most notable feature of that battle was the near-epic struggle to get a handful of M-4 tanks and M-10 tank

U.S. infantrymen push through the Hürtgen Forest. In three months of fighting during September–December 1944, the Americans sustained almost 33,000 casualties and accomplished little operationally. (Library of Congress)

destroyers down the steep and narrow forest trail into the Kall River gorge and back up the other side to the open ground near the towns of Kommerscheidt and Schmidt. The 112th Infantry Regiment took Schmidt on November 3. The Germans counterattacked immediately, supported by PzKpfw-V Panther tanks.

Despite the gallant fight against superior odds, in which antitank platoon leader Lieutenant Turney Leonard earned a posthumous Medal of Honor, all American armor east of the Kall River was destroyed. By November 8, the 28th Infantry Division was pushed back almost to its starting positions, having sustained 6,184 casualties in only 7 days of fighting. Major General Norman Cota, the 28th Infantry Division commander, was widely criticized for the tactically

stupid offensive scheme, a plan that actually had been imposed on him by V Corps. Cota had tried to protest it.

The 28th Infantry Division was relieved in the line by the 8th Infantry Division on November 13. Three days later, the Americans launched the postponed main assault, with VII Corps' 104th, 1st, and 4th Infantry Divisions attacking through the north of the forest. South of VII Corps and just to the north of where the 28th Infantry Division had been mauled, V Corps' 8th Infantry Division launched a supporting attack. Once again, the Americans ran into a determined and skillful German defense. The attackers suffered heavy casualties in exchange for mere yards of ground. The GIs fought under terrible conditions of snow, rain, mud, cold, and almost impenetrable woods in fierce infantry combat reminiscent of World War I.

The Americans were still trying to punch their way through the Hürtgen Forest and making almost no progress when, on December 16, the Germans launched their Ardennes Offensive to the south. The almost complete tactical and operational surprise the Germans achieved brought the Hürtgen Forest campaign to a halt, as all Allied forces focused on containing the Germans in the Ardennes Offensive (Battle of the Bulge). Even after the major German offensive was turned back, the Americans did not take Schmidt and the Roer River dams until early February 1945. Just before the Germans withdrew, they managed to blow up the valves controlling the spillway of the Schwammenauel Dam, the major dam in the system.

The Hürtgen Forest Campaign was a brilliantly executed economy-of-force operation by the Germans. Most of the German records from that period did not survive, but Germany probably suffered more casualties than did the United States. Nonetheless, the Germans held the vastly better supplied and better equipped attackers to a dead standstill for three months, while just a few miles to the south, three German field armies assembled in almost complete secrecy for the Ardennes Offensive.

David T. Zabecki

References

MacDonald, Charles B. *United States Army in World War II: Special Studies: Three Battles: Arnaville, Altuzzo, and Schmidt.* Washington, DC: Department of the Army, U.S. Center of Military History, 1952.

———. *The Battle of the Huertgen Forest.* New York: Jove, 1983.

Miller, Edward G. *A Dark and Bloody Ground: The Hürtgen Forest and the Roer River Dams, 1944–1945.* College Station: Texas A&M University Press, 1995.

Ardennes Offensive (Battle of the Bulge, December 16, 1944–January 16, 1945)

Largest land battle on the Western Front during World War II and the largest engagement ever fought by the U.S. Army. In early December 1944, supreme Allied commander General Dwight D. Eisenhower planned major offensives in the northern and southern sectors of the Western Front. To ensure sufficient power for these offensives, he left his 80-mile-wide central sector in the Ardennes lightly defended by Major General Troy Middleton's VIII Corps of the 4th, 28th, and 106th Infantry Divisions; the 9th Armored Division (less Combat Command B); and the 2-squadron 14th Cavalry Group. The Allies used this area for new commands to gain experience and to train replacements. The rugged Ardennes terrain and presumed light German force gave Eisenhower reason to deploy fewer troops there. Further, the Allies saw no tactical or strategic objectives in the area.

Neither the 9th Armored nor the 106th had experienced combat, and the 28th and 4th were absorbing thousands of replacements after suffering massive casualties in fighting in the Hürtgen Forest. From south to north on the Corps front were the 4th and part of the 9th Armored, the 28th on a 25-mile front, and the 106th holding 1 of almost 16 miles. The 14th Cavalry screened a 5-mile sector between Major General J. Lawton Collins's VII Corps to the south and Major General Leonard T. Gerow's V Corps to the north.

With the Eastern Front largely static and with the Allies gaining ground in the west, German leader Adolf Hitler ordered a massive counteroffensive into this lightly defended area to retake the port of Antwerp. He hoped thereby to

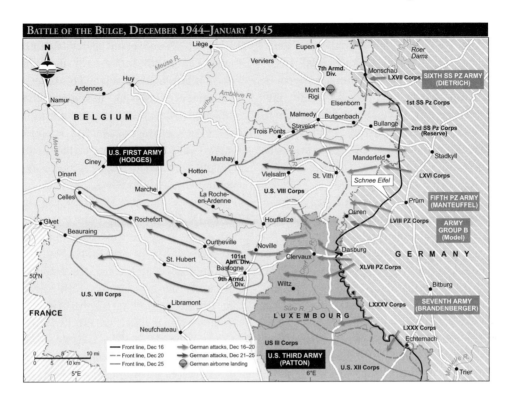

BATTLE OF THE BULGE, DECEMBER 1944–JANUARY 1945

purchase three or four additional months to deal with the advancing Soviets. Field Marshal Gerd von Rundstedt, German commander in the West, thought Hitler's plan too ambitious and tried to dissuade him from it, as did other high-ranking officers, to no avail.

Preparations for the offensive began in September 1944 with strict security and no radio communication. As a consequence, Allied code-breaking did not learn of the German plans. Other information that might have given Allied commanders pause was ignored.

Early on the morning of December 16, Field Marshal Walther Model's Army Group B mounted the attack. Bad weather prevented Allied air intervention. Attacking German forces included *General der Panzertruppen* (U.S. equivalent lieutenant general) Hosso-Eccard von Manteufel's

Fifth Panzer Army; SS *Oberstgruppenführer* (U.S. equivalent full general) Josef "Sepp" Dietrich's Sixth SS Army; and *General der Panzertruppen* Erich Brandenburger's Seventh Army. Army Group B numbered 250,000 men, 1,900 artillery pieces, and 970 tanks and assault guns and was supported by 2,000 aircraft.

In the north, the 99th Division of V Corps stopped the 12th, 277th, and 326th *Volksgrenadier* Divisions (VGD). But the 14th Cavalry was forced back, and elements of the 3rd Parachute Division (Sixth SS Army and 18th VGD [Fifth Panzer Army]) made headway against the 106th Division. The 28th's northern regiment, the 112th, held against elements of the 116th Panzer Division and 560th VGD (Fifth Panzer Army). The 110th Infantry Regiment in the center—hit by the Panzer Lehr Division, elements of the 116th Panzer Division, and the 26th VGD (Seventh Army)—was decimated. Small, isolated fragments of U.S. forces were surrounded and destroyed. In the south, the hard-pressed 109th held back the 352nd VGD and 5th Parachute Division (Seventh Army). Elements of the 9th Armored and 4th Divisions south of the 28th stopped the 276th and 282nd VGD (Seventh Army).

German forces soon created a bulge in the Allied lines, which gave the battle its name. Ultimately, the salient was 50 miles wide and 70 miles deep. Eisenhower correctly assessed the offensive as a major German effort and immediately ordered the 82nd and 101st Airborne Divisions up from rest areas in France. Traveling by cattle truck, the 101st arrived in the vicinity of the key road hub of Bastogne, Belgium, at midnight on December 18.

December 19 was pivotal. Eisenhower also sent the 7th and 10th Armored Divisions to support VII Corps. Combat Command R (CCR), 9th Armored Division; Combat Command B (CCB), 10th Armored Division; the 755th Armored Field Artillery Battalion; 705th Tank Destroyer Battalion; and remnants of the 28th Infantry Division joined the 101st. Major General Maxwell D. Taylor, commanding the 101st, was not with the division, which was then commanded by divisional artillery commander Brigadier General Anthony C. McAuliffe.

Both the 28th and 106th had been destroyed by December 19, but these two U.S. divisions had irretrievably set back the German timetable. The Germans surrounded and forced the surrender of the 106th's 422nd and 423rd Infantry Regiments, but the 424th extricated itself and withdrew west of the Our River. CCB, 9th Armored Division and the 7th Armored

Division under Brigadier General Robert W. Hasbrouk came in on the 424th's north flank. The 112th Infantry of the 28th Division bolstered its south. This diverse force under Hasbrouk defended Saint Vith until December 21 and then withdrew to new positions, which it defended for two more days before withdrawing through elements of the 82nd Airborne and 3rd Armored Divisions.

Also on December 19, Field Marshal Bernard L. Montgomery, commanding the 21st Army group, on his own initiative deployed his XXX Corps (43rd, 51st, and 53rd Infantry and the Guards Armored Divisions) into positions between Namur and Brussels, blocking further German advances. Meanwhile, the 1st SS Panzer Division, spearheaded by a battle group under SS *Oberststurmbannführer* (lieutenant colonel) Joachim Peiper was slowed, then halted by U.S. troops. Peiper's mission, absolutely critical to the success of the German operation, had been to penetrate deeply and rapidly into American lines to seize and hold the crossings over the Meuse River by the end of the first day of the battle. Almost every step of the way, however, Peiper was thwarted and blocked by fierce resistance, most especially by U.S. engineer units that continually blew up the key intermediate bridges along Peiper's axis of advance before he could reach them.

From December 19 until it was relieved on December 26, the 101st, supported by armor, artillery, and other miscellaneous units, defended Bastogne against determined attacks by the Panzer Lehr, 26th VGD, and elements of the 15th Panzer Grenadier Division. The U.S. stands at Saint Vith and Bastogne ended any possibility that the Germans could recover their operational plan, which had been fatally disrupted by the tenaciously

U.S. soldiers of the 289th Infantry Regiment on their way to cut off the Saint Vith–Houffalize road in Belgium in January 1945. The Battle of the Bulge in the Ardennes Forest was the largest battle on the Western Front in World War II and the largest engagement ever involving U.S. troops. (National Archives)

unexpected American defense on the North Shoulder. From December 18 on, German rear areas had been chaotic. The road network, inadequate to support the German offensive, was jammed with traffic, denying the front badly needed reinforcements, supplies, and ammunition.

On December 22, Major General John Milliken's U.S. III Corps of the 26th and 80th Infantry and 4th Armored Divisions (from Lieutenant General George S. Patton's Third Army) attacked to the north to relieve Bastogne. That same day, too, a thaw set in, slowing tank movements. By December 22, the Sixth SS Army was bogged down in mud and rain, the Fifth Panzer Army was hampered by fog and snow, and supply lines were assailed by continuous snow. Clearing weather permitted Allied aircraft to inflict heavy losses (especially on German armor) and to further snarl German traffic and resupply efforts throughout the Bulge. Fighting continued until late January, when the Germans were finally forced back to their original positions.

For the Allies, the Ardennes Offensive was a classic example of a tactical defeat but a strategic victory. Although severely mauled in the process, the fierce resistance put up by the U.S. 99th and 28th Infantry Divisions on the North Shoulder completely disrupted the German timetable and unhinged their entire operational plan. The U.S. stands at Saint Vith and Bastogne only sealed the German defeat. This allowed the Allies to reallocate and realign troops to contain and then destroy the German salient. Both sides sustained heavy casualties in the battle: for the Germans some 100,000 men (almost one-third of those engaged), 700 tanks, and 1,600 aircraft; for the Allies (mostly American, of whom 700,000 were ultimately engaged) 90,000 men, 300 tanks, and 300 aircraft. The difference was that the United States could replace its losses, but Germany could not. Hitler's gamble was an irretrievable disaster. It delayed Eisenhower's campaign by five weeks, but it also devoured already slim German reserves of personnel, tanks, guns, fuel, and ammunition. Germany surrendered four months later.

Uzal W. Ent

References

Eisenhower, John S. D. *The Bitter Woods.* New York: G. P. Putnam's Sons, 1969.

Forty, George. *The Reich's Last Gamble: The Ardennes Offensive: December 1944.* London: Cassell, 2000.

Giles, Janice Holt. *The Damned Engineers.* Boston: Houghton Mifflin Company, 1970.

MacDonald, Charles B. *A Time for Trumpets: The Untold Story of the Battle of the Bulge.* New York: William Morrow, 1985.

Morelock, Jerry D. *Generals of the Ardennes: American Leadership in the Battle of the Bulge.* Washington: National Defense University Press, 1994.

World War II Leaders

Andrews, Frank Maxwell
(1884–1943)

U.S. Army Air Forces general. Born in Nashville, Tennessee, on February 3, 1884, Frank Andrews graduated from the United States Military Academy, West Point, in 1906 and was commissioned in the cavalry. He then held routine assignments in the American West, Hawaii, and the Philippines. When the United States entered World War I in 1917, Andrews transferred to the Signal Corps, and in 1918 he qualified as a military aviator, although too late to see active service in France. In mid-1920, Andrews succeeded Brigadier General William Mitchell as the air service officer of the American Army of Occupation in Germany.

Returning to the United States in 1923, Andrews then commanded the 1st Pursuit Group. He established several speed and altitude records until transferred to staff assignments. In March 1935, Andrews was promoted to temporary brigadier general and assigned to command General Headquarters (GHQ), Air Force. The new organization placed for the first time all the U.S. Army's airstrike elements under a single commander. He became a strong advocate of the four-engine strategic bomber that became the Boeing B-17 Flying Fortress, and he was certainly one of the leading architects of American military air power

in the years before World War II. Andrews molded GHQ, Air Force, into the offensive combat arm that became the model for the U.S. Army Air Forces in World War II. GHQ, Air Force, was also the model of the Air Force's post–Cold War Air Combat Command.

In 1937, Andrews clashed seriously with elements in the army general staff when he forcefully advocated an air force as an independent service during testimony before the House Military Affairs Committee. In 1939, he was reassigned to an insignificant staff position at Fort Sam Houston, Texas, and reduced from his temporary rank of major general to his permanent rank of colonel. But just a few months later, General George C. Marshall became chief of staff of the U.S. Army; Marshall brought Andrews back to Washington and made him assistant chief of staff of the army for training and operations. Andrews was the first aviator to hold that key general staff position.

In 1941, Andrews took over the Caribbean Defense Command, becoming the first American air officer to command a theater. In November 1942, he assumed command of U.S. forces in the Middle East. On February 5, 1943, Andrews became the supreme commander of U.S. forces in the European Theater of Operations (ETO). Three months later, on May 3, 1943, Lieutenant General Andrews died at the controls of a B-24 bomber while attempting a landing at Kaldadarnes, Iceland, during poor weather.

Andrews's appointment to command the ETO was a tacit recognition that the majority of American forces in Europe at the time were air rather than ground units. However, many contemporary observers at the time of his death considered him rather than Dwight Eisenhower the leading candidate for supreme Allied commander of the invasion of the Continent. Andrews had the total confidence of General Marshall and he possessed an almost ideal balance of intellect, character, courage, and military skill. Andrews Air Force Base in Maryland was later named for him.

David T. Zabecki

References

Copp, DeWitt. *A Few Great Captains: The Men and Events that Shaped the Development of U.S. Air Power.* New York: Doubleday, 1980.

Frisbee, John L., ed. *Makers of the United States Air Force.* Washington, DC: Air Force History and Museums Program, 1987.

McClendon, R. Earl. *The Question of Autonomy for the U.S. Air Arm.* Maxwell Air Force Base, AL: Air University Press, 1950.

Arnold, Henry Harley (1886–1950)

U.S. Army Air Forces (USAAF) general who led the USAAF and its predecessor, the Army Air Corps, throughout World War II. Born on June 25, 1886, in Gladwyne, Pennsylvania, Henry Harley "Hap" Arnold graduated from the United States Military Academy, West Point, in 1907 and was commissioned in the infantry. He transferred into the aeronautical division

of the Signal Corps in 1911 and received his pilot's certificate after training with the pioneer aviator Orville Wright. In 1912, Arnold set a world altitude record and won the first Mackay Trophy for aviation.

During World War I, Arnold served on the army staff in Washington, rising to the rank of colonel and overseeing all aviation training. After the war, Arnold reverted to his permanent rank of captain. During the 1920s, he held a variety of assignments. He supported Colonel William Mitchell at the latter's court-martial, although this was not well received by his superiors. Arnold wrote or cowrote five books on aviation, won a second Mackay Trophy, and continued to rise in the army air corps. He became its assistant chief as a brigadier general in 1935. Three years later he became chief

General Henry Harley "Hap" Arnold, who commanded the U.S. Army Air Forces in World War II and was the only airman to be awarded five-star rank during World War II. (Library of Congress)

of the army air corps as a major general after the death of Major General Oscar Westover in a plane crash.

Arnold proved particularly adept at improving the readiness of his service and expanding its resources, even with tight interwar budgets. Promoted to lieutenant general in December 1941, he was designated commanding general of the U.S. Army Air Forces in the March 1942 War Department reorganization plan, which raised the air arm to equal status with the Army Ground Forces and Army Service Forces. Because the British had a chief of air staff, Arnold was included on the British-American Combined Chiefs of Staff as well as the U.S. Joint Chiefs of Staff. Although he was not a major player in their decisions, he was a loyal supporter of U.S. Army chief of staff George C. Marshall, who repaid Arnold during the war as a staunch advocate of the U.S. Army Air Forces and after the war by supporting the establishment of an independent U.S. Air Force. Arnold was promoted to general in March 1943 and became one of four five-star generals of the army in December 1944.

During the war, Arnold built an organization that reached a peak of approximately 2.5 million personnel and more than 63,000 aircraft. He was a fine judge of people and selected only the best men as his advisers, staff, and field commanders. Arnold also established an emphasis on technological research and development that the U.S. Air Force retains today. Although Arnold was not really involved in day-to-day combat operations, his authority to relieve the field commanders who really did run the war gave him leverage to influence their actions. Poor health limited his effectiveness late in the war, especially after a fourth heart attack in January 1945.

Arnold was a proponent of precision bombing, but his pressure for more raids despite bad weather led to increased use of less accurate radar-directed bombardments in Europe, and his demand for increased efficiency in Japan inspired the fire raids there. His main goals were to make the largest possible contribution to winning the war and to ensure that the USAAF received credit for the win through proper publicity.

Although Arnold retired in June 1946, his goal of an independent U.S. air service was realized the following year by his successor, General Carl Spaatz. In May 1949, Arnold's five-star rank was changed to designate him the first and so far only general of the air force. Arnold truly deserves the title "Father of the U.S. Air Force." He died in Sonoma, California, on January 15, 1950.

Conrad C. Crane

References

Arnold, Henry H. *Global Mission*. New York: Harper, 1949.

Crane, Conrad C. *Bombs, Cities, and Civilians: American Airpower Strategy in World War II*. Lawrence: University Press of Kansas, 1993.

Coffey, Thomas M. *Hap: The Story of the U.S. Air Force and the Man Who Built It*. New York: Viking, 1982.

Daso, Dik Alan. *Hap Arnold and the Evolution of American Airpower*. Washington, DC: Smithsonian Institution, 2000.

Bradley, Omar Nelson (1893–1981)

U.S. Army general and commander of 12th Army Group. Born in Clark, Missouri, on February 12, 1893, Omar Nelson Bradley graduated from the United States Military Academy, West Point, in 1915, a member of what would become

General Omar Bradley commanded 12th Army Group in Europe, the largest army deployed by the United States in World War II. He later served as chief of staff of the army and then first chairman of the Joint Chiefs of Staff, when he was advanced to general of the armies. (Library of Congress)

known as the "class the stars fell on," and was commissioned a 2nd lieutenant of infantry.

Assigned to the 14th Infantry Regiment in Spokane, Washington, Bradley saw service along the Mexican border during the 1916 crisis that followed Pancho Villa's raid on Columbus, New Mexico. Like his classmate Dwight D. Eisenhower, Bradley missed combat in World War I. During the interwar period, his career followed a familiar pattern, with a number of troop commands interspersed with assignments at various military schools, including West Point. His most significant assignment was as chief of the Weapons Section during Colonel George C. Marshall's tenure as deputy

commandant at the Infantry School at Fort Benning, Georgia.

Bradley graduated from the Army War College in 1934. Following service in General Marshall's secretariat of the general staff between 1939 and 1941, he was promoted to brigadier general in February 1941 and assigned command of the Infantry School. Promotion to major general followed in February 1942, and Bradley successively commanded the 82nd Infantry Division and the 28th National Guard Division. In February 1943, Marshall dispatched him to North Africa, where General Eisenhower assigned him as deputy commander of Lieutenant General George S. Patton's II Corps in the wake of the Kasserine Pass debacle. When Patton assumed command of Seventh Army, Bradley took command of II Corps and led it with great distinction both in Tunisia and in Sicily.

In October 1943, Bradley assumed command of First Army and transferred to England to prepare for the cross-Channel invasion. He commanded U.S. ground forces on D-Day in Operation OVERLORD in June 1944 and during the ensuing Normandy Campaign. On July 26, First Army broke the German lines outside Saint-Lô in Operation COBRA, Bradley's operational masterpiece. On August 1, 1944, he assumed command of 12th Army Group, which then encompassed General Courtney Hodges's First Army and General George Patton's Third Army.

During the subsequent drive across France, Bradley performed well but not spectacularly. His failure to close the Falaise-Argentan gap reflected poorly on his ability as a strategist and undoubtedly extended the war in the west. When Germany launched the Ardennes Offensive (Battle of the Bulge), Bradley was slow to react, but in the subsequent campaign, he renewed Marshall's and Eisenhower's confidence by carefully orchestrating the advance of the American armies on British field marshal Bernard L. Montgomery's right flank. By war's end, Bradley had clearly emerged as Eisenhower's most trusted military adviser. As 12th Army Group grew to include four separate armies, the largest purely American military force in history, Bradley was promoted to full general in March 1945, on the eve of Germany's capitulation.

Following the war, Bradley headed the Veterans' Administration, and in February 1948 he succeeded Eisenhower as army chief of staff. In this post, he championed the continued unification of the nation's armed forces. In 1949, he became the first chairman of the Joint Chiefs of Staff (JCS) and was subsequently promoted to the five-star rank of general of the army in September 1950, in the midst of the Korean War. During that war, Bradley supported President Harry S. Truman's April 1951 relief of General Douglas MacArthur and opposed expansion of the war into China, famously testifying to Congress that a war with China would be the "wrong war, at the wrong place, at the wrong time, and with the wrong enemy." Bradley retired from active military service in August 1953 to become chairman of the board of the Bulova Watch Corporation. During the Vietnam War, he served as an adviser to President Lyndon B. Johnson. Bradley died on April 8, 1981, in Washington, D.C.

Cole C. Kingseed

References

Bradley, Omar N. *A Soldier's Story.* New York: Henry Holt, 1951.

Bradley, Omar N., and Clay Blair. *A General's Life.* New York: Simon and Schuster, 1983.

Weigley, Russell F. *Eisenhower's Lieutenants.* Bloomington: Indiana University Press, 1981.

Byrnes, James Francis (1879–1972)

U.S. politician, jurist, wartime "assistant president" to Franklin D. Roosevelt, and secretary of state from 1945 to 1947. During World War II, Byrnes headed up the Office of Economic Stabilization and the Office of War Mobilization and was given unprecedented power to mobilize the U.S. economy for war.

Born on May 2, 1879, in Charleston, South Carolina, the son of Irish immigrants, James Byrnes studied law. After qualifying as a lawyer, he won election to Congress in 1910. In 1930, he became a U.S. senator for South Carolina. In the meantime, Byrnes, who had a keen intellect, invested his money well and became wealthy. He often attributed his financial success to New York financier Bernard Baruch, with whom he became fast friends. Baruch, who headed up the World War I mobilization effort, would also advise Byrnes on mobilization issues during World War II.

A longtime friend of President Roosevelt, Byrnes used his considerable negotiating talents to steer New Deal legislation through Congress from 1933 on. In 1941, Roosevelt appointed him to the U.S. Supreme Court as an associate justice. Sixteen months later, in 1942, Byrnes left the bench to head the new Office of Economic Stabilization (OES). The OES helped set tax policies, a vital function in raising adequate revenue for war supplies, and also set price and wage controls to help stem inflation and avoid shortages of critical war matériel.

The following year, Byrnes became director of the Office of War Mobilization (from 1944, the Office of War Mobilization and Reconversion). In domestic policy, Byrnes, often called the "assistant president," exercised powers second only to those of Roosevelt himself. Responsible for coordinating all domestic war agencies and federal government departments, he worked closely with both Congress and the Washington bureaucracy to devise the most efficient arrangements to implement the war effort. Under his purview also came rationing programs and the coordination of industrial production.

Passed over as Roosevelt's vice presidential running mate in 1944, Byrnes, already considered a hard-liner toward the Soviet Union, attended the February 1945 Yalta Conference of the "Big Three" Allied leaders. Returning to Washington, he successfully lobbied Congress to support the outcome of Yalta, deliberately glossing over outstanding contentious issues dividing the Soviet Union and its allies. Still disappointed over the 1944 election, he resigned his post in March 1945.

Upon Roosevelt's death one month later, Vice President Harry S. Truman became president. Truman immediately appointed Byrnes as head of a top-secret committee on the employment of atomic weapons, then in their final stage of development, whose existence Byrnes recommended be kept secret even from U.S. allies until their first use in combat. He believed U.S. possession of the bomb would make Soviet behavior more malleable.

In June 1945, Truman appointed Byrnes his secretary of state. Attending the July 1945 Potsdam Conference, Byrnes hoped the speedy employment of atomic weapons against Japan would prevent the Soviet Union from entering the Pacific war and enhancing its influence in Asia. He also helped to reach a compromise agreement on German reparations. Returning to Washington, he took part in drafting the Japanese surrender agreement in August 1945, implicitly agreeing to retain the emperor. As Soviet-U.S. relations became more strained after the war, Byrnes sought for several months to negotiate compromise solutions, traveling extensively to meet with other foreign ministers outside the United States. In early 1946, political complaints that he was too conciliatory led Byrnes to assume a harsher rhetorical stance toward the Soviets. Even so, at the end of the year, Truman—increasingly irked by Byrnes's policies, his secretive diplomacy, and his condescending attitude—appointed George C. Marshall secretary in his stead.

Byrnes resigned in January 1947, returned to South Carolina, and wrote his memoirs. In 1948, he broke with Truman over the issue of civil rights; subsequently, he served two terms, from 1951 to 1955, as governor of South Carolina, defending segregationist policies. Byrnes died in Columbia, South Carolina, on April 9, 1972.

Priscilla Roberts

References

Byrnes, James F. *Speaking Frankly.* New York: Harper, 1947.

———. *All in One Lifetime.* New York: Harper, 1958.

Messer, Robert F. *The End of an Alliance: James F. Byrnes, Roosevelt, Truman, and the Origins of the Cold War.* Chapel Hill: University of North Carolina Press, 1982.

Morgan, Curtis F. *James F. Byrnes, Lucius Clay, and American Policy in Germany, 1945–1947.* Lewiston, NY: Edwin Mellen Press, 2002.

Robertson, David. *Sly and Able: A Political Biography of James F. Byrnes.* New York: Norton, 1994.

Walker, Richard, and George Curry. *The American Secretaries of State and Their Diplomacy.* Vol. 14, *E. R. Stettinius, Jr., and James F. Byrnes.* New York: Cooper Square, 1965.

Chennault, Claire Lee (1893–1958)

U.S. Army Air Forces general and leader of the American Volunteer Group (AVG, "Flying Tigers"). Born in Commerce, Texas, on September 6, 1893, Claire Lee Chennault was raised in rural Louisiana. He taught English and business at a number of southern colleges until August 1917, when he became a 2nd lieutenant in the army reserve. He remained in the United States during World War I, transferring to the Signal Corps and completing pilot training in 1920.

An accomplished airman, Chennault then held a number of assignments, among them command of the 19th Pursuit Squadron in Hawaii between 1923 and 1926. He developed into an outspoken advocate of fighter aircraft in a period when prevailing military thought subscribed to the doctrines espoused by Italian airpower theorist Giulio Douhet and the underlying assumption that "the bomber will always get through." While serving as an instructor at the Air Corps Tactical School in 1935, Chennault wrote *The Role of Defensive Pursuit,* an important but controversial book at the time because it made a strong case for the efficacy of fighter aircraft. In 1937, the army removed him from flying status because of a serious hearing loss and forced him into medical retirement as a captain.

In May 1937, Chennault went to China as aviation adviser to the Nationalist government of Chiang Kai-shek (Jiang Jieshi). When the Japanese attacked China that September, he became a colonel in the Chinese Air Force and began testing his tactical theories. In late 1940, Chennault was allowed to recruit American military pilots for service in China, despite the strong opposition of the State, War, and Navy departments. His American Volun-

U.S. Army Air Forces lieutenant general Claire Chennault, a brilliant and controversial aerial tactician, commanded at the beginning of the war the American Volunteer Group in China, popularly known as the Flying Tigers. (National Archives)

teer Group, popularly known as the Flying Tigers, consisted of some 200 ground crew and 100 pilots flying semi-obsolete Curtiss P-40B fighters. The AVG entered combat for the first time on December 20, 1941. By the time the unit disbanded in July 1942, it had claimed 296 Japanese aircraft shot down, with only 12 of its own planes and 4 of its pilots lost.

In April 1942, Chennault was recalled to active duty with the U.S. Army as a colonel. A few months later, he was promoted to brigadier general and put in command of the newly formed China Air Task Force (CATF), a subordinate command of the U.S. Tenth Air Force in India. In March 1943, the CATF became the Fourteenth Air Force, with Chennault promoted to major general.

The CATF and later the Fourteenth Air Force were economy-of-force organizations in a tertiary theater and therefore always operated on a shoestring. Applying Chennault's theories, however, both organizations achieved combat effectiveness far out of proportion to their size and resources. By 1945, the Fourteenth Air Force had destroyed some 2,600 Japanese aircraft and thousands of tons of supplies.

During his time in China, Chennault conducted a long-running and public feud with Lieutenant General Joseph Stilwell, the equally stubborn and irascible U.S. commander of the China-Burma-India Theater. Chennault engineered Chiang's demand for Stilwell's recall, but Chennault himself was removed from command and forced into retirement for a second time on August 1, 1945.

Following the war, Chennault remained in China. He established and operated the Civil Air Transport (CAT) airline, which supported Chiang's Nationalist government in its civil war with Mao Zedong and his communist forces. In 1950, Chennault sold his interest in CAT to the Central Intelligence Agency, but he remained the chairman of the airline's board until 1955. He died at Walter Reed Army Hospital in Washington, D.C., on July 27, 1958. Only days before his death, Chennault was promoted to lieutenant general.

David T. Zabecki

References

Byrd, Martha. *Chennault: Giving Wings to the Tiger.* Tuscaloosa: University of Alabama Press, 1987.

Chennault, Claire Lee. *Way of a Fighter.* New York: G. P. Putnam, 1949.

Ford, Daniel. *Flying Tigers: Claire Chennault and the American Volunteer Group.* Washington, DC: Smithsonian Institution Press, 1991.

Samson, Jack. *Chennault.* New York: Doubleday, 1987.

Clark, Mark Wayne (1896–1984)

U.S. Army general. Born at Madison Barracks, New York, on May 1, 1896, Mark Wayne Clark graduated from the United States Military Academy, West Point, in 1917 and was wounded during action in France in 1918. He graduated from the Infantry School in 1925, the Command and General Staff School in 1935, and the Army War College in 1937.

Advanced to brigadier general in August 1941, Clark was working on army expansion programs when the Japanese bombing of Pearl Harbor on December 7, 1941, brought the United States into World War II. Clark was appointed major general and made chief of staff of Army Ground Forces in April 1942. He rose to lieutenant general in November 1942 and was named deputy supreme commander for the Allied invasion of North Africa, Operation TORCH, under Lieutenant General Dwight D. Eisenhower. In October 1942, Clark met secretly with Vichy French officials prior to the Allied invasion to seek their cooperation, and he negotiated a cease-fire with the French authorities two days after the landings in Algeria in November 1942.

Assigned command of Fifth Army, Clark led the invading U.S. troops at Salerno, Italy, in September 1943. However, Fifth Army's slow advance up the western side of the Italian peninsula led to harsh criticism of Clark's abilities. His troops suffered heavy casualties in the attempt to penetrate the German Gustav Line, and the bombing of the monastery at Monte Cassino plagued his reputation; heavy casualties during the Rapido River crossing in January 1944 prompted a Senate investigation. The Anzio landings in January 1944 did little to speed up Fifth

General Mark Clark commanded the Fifth U.S. Army and later the Allied 15th Army Group in Italy. He was much criticized for several decisions, especially that of electing to capture Rome instead of attempting to trap the fleeing German Tenth Army. (Library of Congress)

Army's advance, and the assault failed to lead, as was hoped, to a quick capture of Rome. Fifth Army finally liberated Rome on June 4, 1944, but Clark was roundly criticized for his determination that U.S. troops be the first to liberate the Eternal City, which allowed the German Tenth Army to escape encirclement and reach the Gothic Line to the north.

As the cross-Channel invasion of France (Operation OVERLORD) became the chief focus of Allied efforts in Europe, Italy became a secondary theater. In December 1944, Clark succeeded Sir Harold Alexander as commander of the multinational 15th Army Group, and in March 1945 he became the U.S. Army's youngest full general. He led the Allied offensive that breached the Gothic

Line, crossed the Po River, and entered Austria just as the war in Europe was ending in early May 1945. On May 4, 1945, Clark personally received the surrender of all German forces in Italy.

Following the war, Clark commanded U.S. occupation forces in Austria (1946–1947), Sixth Army (1947–1949), and Army Field Forces (1949–1952). He succeeded General Matthew Ridgway as commander of U.S. forces in the Far East and of United Nations Forces in Korea (May 1952–October 1953) and chafed repeatedly at restrictions placed on his command. Clark wrote two memoirs, *Calculated Risk* (1950) and *From the Danube to the Yalu* (1954). On his retirement from the army in 1954, he served as president of The Citadel, in Charleston, South Carolina, from 1954 to 1960. Clark died in Charleston, South Carolina, on April 17, 1984.

Thomas D. Veve

References

Blumenson, Martin. *United States Army in World War II: The Mediterranean Theater of Operations—Salerno to Cassino.* Washington, DC: Office of the Chief of Military History, U.S. Army, 1969.

———. *Mark Clark.* New York: Congdon and Weed, 1984.

Clark, Mark W. *Calculated Risk.* New York: Harper, 1950.

Cota, Norman Daniel (1893–1971)

U.S. Army general. Born in Chelsea, Massachusetts, on May 30, 1893, Norman Daniel "Dutch" Cota graduated from the United States Military Academy, West Point, in 1917 and was commissioned a 2nd lieutenant of infantry and assigned to the 22nd Infantry Regiment. He was an instructor at West Point between 1918 and 1920.

Cota transferred to the Finance Department in 1920 and was the finance officer of West Point until 1924, when he transferred back to the infantry. He graduated from the Infantry School, Fort Benning, Georgia, in 1925 and served in the Hawaiian Department. He graduated from the Command and General Staff School in 1931, was an instructor at the Infantry School in 1932 and 1933, graduated from the Army War College in 1936, and was an instructor at the Command and General Staff School from 1938 to 1940.

Cota was the deputy chief of staff for operations and training (G-3) of the 1st Infantry Division from March 1941; he was its chief of staff from 1942 to February 1943, taking part in the capture of Oran during Operation TORCH, the invasion of French North Africa in November 1942. Promoted to brigadier general in February 1943, he became U.S. adviser to the Combined Operations branch of the European Theater of Operations. Later that year, he was assistant commander of the 29th Infantry Division.

On June 6, 1944, Cota landed with his division on Omaha Beach, Normandy, France. Several of the men in his LCVP (landing craft vehicle and personnel) were killed by German fire as soon as the ramp went down, and Cota was the only general officer on Omaha Beach that day. With American forces almost pushed back into the sea, he was an inspiring presence. Realizing that the men were doomed if they remained on the beach, he exposed himself to German fire as he repeatedly led small parties forward. Many historians credit him with almost single-handedly preventing a disaster on Omaha that day. Cota later received the Distinguished Service Cross for his actions. Wounded in

fighting at Saint-Lô, he spent two weeks in the division hospital.

On August 13, 1944, Cota took command of the 28th Infantry Division, which he led through Paris in a liberation parade in August 1944, part of a show of force in support of General Charles de Gaulle to prevent a possible communist takeover. Cota was promoted to major general in September 1944.

On November 2, 1944, the 28th Infantry Division began an attack to capture the town of Schmidt in the heart of the Hürtgen Forest, as part of the Siegfried Line Campaign. The plan of attack was a recipe for disaster, with all three regiments of the division attacking in diverging directions. The plan had been imposed on the division by staff officers at V Corps. Cota protested his orders to both V Corps commander Major General Leonard Gerow and First Army commander Lieutenant General Courtney Hodges but was ordered to execute the plan. Over the next 9 days, the 28th Infantry Division suffered more than 6,000 casualties. Near the end of the battle, Cota himself collapsed under the pressure of what was happening to his division.

If not for his performance on Omaha Beach, Cota almost certainly would have been relieved of his command after this debacle; as it was, the Schmidt fiasco cast a long shadow over him. The 28th Infantry Division was pulled out of the line and sent south to a quiet sector in Belgium to reconstitute. On December 16, it was manning the sector of the line known as Skyline Drive when the Germans launched the Ardennes Offensive. Although Cota's already weak division was mauled during the German attack, it did not break. Rather, it conducted a tenacious and effective fighting withdrawal that contributed in no small part to disrupting the German timetable for the offensive.

Cota returned to the United States in August 1945 to prepare for the invasion of Japan, which proved unnecessary. He retired from the army as a major general in 1946. Cota died in Wichita, Kansas, on October 4, 1971.

David T. Zabecki

References

Ambrose, Stephen E. *D-Day, June 6, 1944: The Climactic Battle of World War II.* New York: Simon and Schuster, 1994.

MacDonald, Charles B. *A Time for Trumpets: The Untold Story of the Battle of the Bulge.* New York: William Morrow, 1985.

Miller, Robert A. *Division Commander: A Biography of Major General Norman D. Cota.* Spartanburg, SC: Reprint Publishers, 1989.

Brigadier General Benjamin O. Davis Sr. in France on August 8, 1944. Davis became the first African American general in the U.S. military in October 1940. (National Archives)

Davis, Benjamin Oliver, Sr. (1877–1970)

U.S. Army officer and the first African American general officer in the U.S. military. Born on July 1, 1877, in Washington, D.C., Benjamin O. Davis enrolled at Howard University in 1897 but left school the next year to join the 8th U.S. Volunteer Regiment during the Spanish-American War. As a lieutenant he saw no action, but in June 1899 he enlisted as a private in the regular army in the 9th U.S. Cavalry Regiment, one of the original Buffalo Soldier regiments created in 1866. He went on to serve from corporal to sergeant major before being commissioned a 2nd lieutenant in the 10th U.S. Cavalry in 1901. Davis was military attaché to Liberia (1909–1911), professor of military science at Wilberforce University (1906–1911, 1915–1917, 1929–1930, and 1937–1938), supply officer for the 9th Cavalry in the Philippines (1917–1920), instructor with the Ohio National Guard (1924–1928), and professor of military science at Tuskegee Institute (1921–1924 and 1931–1937).

Davis's race presented him with many obstacles, despite his sharp intellect and strong work ethic. At the beginning of World War II in 1939, Davis was one of only two African American officers in the combat arms branches of the U.S. Army. The other was his son, Benjamin O. Davis Jr., who led the famed Tuskegee Airmen in World War II and later became the first African American general officer in the U.S. Air Force. In October 1940, on the recommendation of President Franklin D. Roosevelt, Davis was promoted to brigadier general. He was the first African American to achieve flag rank.

Davis retired from the army in 1941 but was recalled to active duty as an assistant to the Inspector General of the Army, serving in the European Theater of Operations as an adviser on race relations. At the same time, he fought to end segregation and discrimination within the armed forces. Davis remained in the Inspector General's office until his final retirement in 1948. He continued to speak in favor of desegregation in the U.S. military, which was achieved when President Harry S. Truman, by executive order in January 1948, mandated the full integration of the U.S. armed forces.

In the years following his retirement from the military, Davis served on numerous civilian boards and the American Battle Monuments Commission. He died in Chicago on November 26, 1970.

Nicholas W. Barcheski

References

Astor, Gerald. *The Right to Fight: A History of African-Americans in the Military.* Navato, CA: Presidio Press, 1998.

Fletcher, Marvin. *America's First Black General: Benjamin O. Davis, Sr.* Lawrence: University Press of Kansas, 1989.

Devers, Jacob Loucks (1887–1979)

U.S. Army general. Born on September 8, 1887, in York, Pennsylvania, Jacob Loucks Devers graduated from the United States Military Academy, West Point, in 1909 and was commissioned a 2nd lieutenant of artillery. In 1912, he returned to West Point as an instructor.

During World War I, Devers was at Fort Sill, Oklahoma. In 1919, he served in the occupation of Germany and attended the French Artillery School at Treves before again teaching at West Point. Devers graduated from the Command and General Staff School (1925) and the Army War College (1933). From 1925 to 1928,

he was the director of the Gunnery Department at the Field Artillery School, where he pioneered many of the fire-direction control innovations that provided American artillery with its marked qualitative superiority during World War II. From 1936 to 1939, he was at West Point, where he was advanced to colonel.

After World War II began in Europe in 1939, Army chief of staff General George C. Marshall ordered Devers as chief of staff of the Panama Canal Department to place the Canal Zone on a wartime footing. The following year, Devers was promoted to brigadier general. Following staff duty in Washington, he commanded the 9th Infantry Division at Fort Bragg, North Carolina. Supervising the rapid expansion of this base, he earned promotion to major general.

Known for his ability to train troops, Devers in July 1941 took command of the Armored Force at Fort Knox, Kentucky, and there he supervised the rapid expansion of U.S. armored forces. He soon became an enthusiastic advocate of mobile combined-arms warfare, but he and Army Ground Forces commander, Lieutenant General Lesely J. McNair, disagreed vehemently over the exact role of tanks in combat.

Devers was promoted to lieutenant general in September 1942. In May 1943, Devers took command of the European Theater of Operations, while General Dwight D. Eisenhower was in North Africa. Devers supervised the rapid U.S. buildup in Britain and hoped to lead the cross-Channel invasion. Instead, he was sent at the end of 1943 to the Mediterranean as deputy supreme Allied commander and commander of all U.S. forces in that theater. Devers planned and commanded Operation DRAGOON, the invasion of southern France from the Mediterranean, in August 1944.

As Devers's invasion force moved north into France, it merged with Eisenhower's force moving east from the Atlantic coast on September 15, 1944. Devers's force became subordinate to Supreme Headquarters, Allied Expeditionary Force, as the 6th Army Group of 23 divisions, consisting of Lieutenant General Alexander Patch's Seventh Army and General Jean de Lattre de Tassigny's French First Army.

In March 1945, Devers was promoted to general. That same month his 6th Army Group crossed the Rhine and drove into southern Germany and Austria, where he accepted the surrender of German forces on May 6.

Devers commanded U.S. Army Ground Forces from 1945 to 1949 and retired in September 1949. He died in Washington, D.C., on October 15, 1979.

Brent B. Barth Jr.

References

Devers, Jacob L. *Report of Activities: Army Ground Forces.* Washington, DC: U.S. Army, 1946.

Perret, Geoffrey. *There's a War to Be Won: The United States Army in World War II.* New York: Random House, 1991.

Weigley, Russell F. *Eisenhower's Lieutenants: The Campaigns of France and Germany, 1944–1945.* Bloomington: Indiana University Press, 1981.

Wilt, Alan F. *The French Riviera Campaign of August 1944.* Carbondale: Southern Illinois University Press, 1981.

Donovan, William Joseph
(1883–1959)

Attorney, army officer, intelligence expert, and head of the U.S. Office of Strategic Services (OSS), the precursor of the Central Intelligence Agency (CIA). Born on January 1, 1883, in Buffalo, New York, William Donovan attended St. Joseph's Collegiate Institute and Niagara University before going to Columbia University, where he graduated in 1905. He played football while at Columbia, earning the sobriquet "Wild Bill" for his intrepid playing. In 1907, he earned a law degree, also from Columbia, and afterward practiced law in Buffalo. He also served as a captain in the New York National Guard. Donovan was stationed along the Mexican border in 1916 when the Guard was called up to assist as the army sought to capture notorious Mexican bandit and revolutionary leader Pancho Villa.

After the United States entered World War I in 1917, Donovan was sent to Europe with the American Expeditionary Forces (AEF). As a major, he commanded the 1st Battalion, 165th Infantry Regiment (the federal designation of the famed New York 69th Infantry Regiment), in the 42nd Division. In July 1918, he received the Distinguished Service Cross for leading his battalion during the Marne Counteroffensive. He also commanded his battalion during the Saint-Mihiel Offensive in September and the Meuse-Argonne Campaign in October. He was wounded a total of three times, and received the Medal of Honor when he was wounded severely while personally leading an attack in October, but refused evacuation and remained in command of his unit.

Following the war, Donovan returned to Buffalo to practice law. From 1924 to 1929, he was an assistant U.S. attorney general. He ran unsuccessfully for state political office in New York State and in 1929 moved to New York City. Greatly interested in international affairs, Donovan undertook several overseas missions for the Rockefeller Foundation and the Franklin D. Roosevelt administration during the 1930s.

After the start of World War II in Europe in September 1939, President Roosevelt attempted to ready the nation for war, no easy task given the prevalence of isolationist sentiment. On the specific recommendation of Secretary of the Navy Frank Knox, Roosevelt tapped Donovan to perform a number of increasingly critical tasks in an attempt to place the United States on a war footing and to aid the Allies in their fight against Axis aggression. Donovan and Roosevelt by now enjoyed a close personal relationship, despite the fact that Roosevelt was a Democrat and Donovan a Republican. In late 1940 and into 1941, Donovan acted as Roosevelt's personal emissary to Britain and other European countries that were still free of German or Italian occupation. In answer to the two questions of were the British serious about the war and if they were worth supporting, Donovan reported "definitely yes."

Donovan recommended strongly to Roosevelt that the United States needed a centralized, strategic intelligence-gathering organization similar to Britain's MI-6. Subsequently Donovan in July 1941 was designated as the head of the newly established Office of Coordinator of Information, which in June 1942 became the Office of Strategic Services (OSS).

Operating directly under the Joint Chiefs of Staff, the mission of the OSS was to gather and analyze intelligence; prepare intelligence estimates; conduct guerrilla and sabotage operations; assist and advise partisans; conduct counterintelligence operations; and coordinate the disparate intelligence operations that had heretofore been fragmented among army and navy intelligence arms, the U.S. State Department, the Federal Bureau of Investigation (FBI), and other government agencies.

Upon the establishment of the OSS, Donovan was recalled to active duty at the rank of colonel and by the end of the war was a major general. Donovan supervised all U.S. intelligence and covert direct action activities in Europe and parts of Asia. FBI director J. Edgar Hoover, however, retained control of intelligence operations in South America. Donovan was also shut out of the Philippines, mainly because of General Douglas MacArthur's distrust of the OSS.

After World War II, Donovan advised President Harry S Truman to set up a permanent intelligence organization. Truman initially rejected the concept, but the coming of the Cold War led in 1947 to the establishment of the Central Intelligence Agency (CIA), modeled directly on the OSS. Although considered the "father of the CIA" Donovan never actually led that organization. He briefly returned to government service as ambassador to Thailand during 1953–1954. Donovan died on February 8, 1959, at Walter Reed Army Medical Center in Washington, D.C.

Graham Carssow
and Paul G. Pierpaoli Jr.

References

Cave Brown, Anthony. *The Last Hero: Wild Bill Donovan.* New York: Times Books, 1982.

Dunlop, Richard. *Donovan, America's Master Spy.* Chicago: Rand McNally, 1982.

Troy, Thomas F. *Wild Bill and Intrepid: Donovan, Stephenson, and the Origin of CIA.* New Haven, CT: Yale University Press, 1996.

Doolittle, James Harold (1896–1993)

U.S. Army Air Forces (later Air Force) general. Born on December 14, 1896, in Alameda, California, James Harold Doolittle grew up in Nome, Alaska. He attended Los Angeles Community College and the University of California, but he left school following the entry of the United States into World War I in 1917 and enlisted as a flying cadet in the Signal Corps Reserve. He attended flight school, became a pilot, and was commissioned a 2nd lieutenant. He then served as a flight-gunner instructor at Rockwell Field in San Diego, California. His request for assignment to France was denied because of the armistice of November 11, 1918.

In 1920, Doolittle secured a regular army commission, and on September 4, 1922, he became the first pilot to make a transcontinental flight in less than 24 hours. He then studied at the Massachusetts Institute of Technology, where he received both master's and doctorate degrees in aeronautical engineering. A leader in advances in both military and civilian aviation, Doolittle helped develop horizontal and directional gyroscopes and pioneered instrument flying, personally making history's first successful blind, instrument-controlled landing.

Doolittle also gained prominence through stunt flying, racing, and demonstrating aircraft. In 1930, he left active duty but retained a reserve commission. He became the aviation manager for Shell Oil, where he helped develop new high-octane aviation fuels that greatly benefited the United States in World War II. He won the Harmon (1930) and Bendix (1931) trophies, and in 1932 he broke the world airspeed record.

In July 1940, Doolittle returned to active duty as a major. In January 1942, he was promoted to lieutenant colonel. On April 18, 1942, Doolittle commanded the first U.S. air strike on the Japanese mainland, which has since come to be known as the Doolittle Raid. Flying 16

Lieutenant Colonel James Doolittle led the audacious April 1942 bombing raid on Japan that bears his name. As a general, he subsequently commanded several Army Air Forces in North Africa, Europe, and the Pacific. (Library of Congress)

B-25 medium-range bombers launched from the American aircraft carrier *Hornet*, Doolittle's force struck targets in Tokyo, Kobe, Osaka, and Nagoya. The raid resulted in little damage to Japanese facilities, but it was both a great boost for U.S. morale and a terrific public relations boon for Washington. For the raid Doolittle was awarded the Medal of Honor and promoted to brigadier general.

In July 1942, Doolittle took command of the Twelfth Air Force in England, which he commanded during the Operation TORCH invasion of North Africa. In November 1943, he assumed command of the Fifteenth Air Force in the Mediterranean Theater, directing raids against German-held Europe. In January 1944,

Doolittle assumed command of the Eighth Air Force in the European Theater, and that March he was promoted to temporary lieutenant general. On Germany's surrender in May 1945, Doolittle moved with the Eighth Air Force to Okinawa, although the Eighth arrived in the Pacific Theater too late to see much action.

Leading the daylight bombing campaign against Germany, Doolittle's command consisted of 200,000 men at its peak. Doolittle was influential in modifying the bombing mission tactics that initially required fighter escorts to fly at all times in close support of the bombers. Freed to maneuver and to strafe German airfields and bases during the return legs of the missions, the fighters eventually ground down the *Luftwaffe* and established Allied air supremacy in the skies over Europe.

In May 1946, Doolittle returned to the civilian sector as a vice president for Shell Oil, and later he became its director. He also served on the National Advisory Committee for Aeronautics, the Air Force Science Advisory Board, and the President's Science Advisory Committee. In June 1985, by act of Congress, Doolittle was promoted to general on the retired list. He died on September 27, 1993, in Pebble Beach, California.

Sean K. Duggan

References

Doolittle, James H., with Carroll V. Glines. *I Could Never Be So Lucky Again: An Autobiography by General James H. "Jimmy" Doolittle.* Atglen, PA: Schiffer, 1991.

Glines, Carroll V. *Doolittle's Tokyo Raiders.* Salem, NH: Ayer, 1964.

Merrill, James M. *Target Tokyo: The Halsey–Doolittle Raid.* New York: Rand McNally, 1964.

Thomas, Lowell, and Edward Jablonski. *Doolittle: A Biography.* Garden City, NY: Doubleday, 1976.

Eberstadt, Ferdinand (1890–1969)

Wall Street financier, influential adviser to several U.S. presidents, and the motivating force behind the United States' World War II industrial mobilization effort. Born in New York City on June 19, 1890, Ferdinand Eberstadt graduated from Princeton University in 1913 and served in the U.S. Army during World War I. In 1923, he began what would become a legendary career in investment banking by joining Wall Street's most prestigious investment firm of Dillon, Read & Company. Indeed, Eberstadt's uncanny savvy made him a fortune as a Wall Street analyst and speculator.

In 1928, Eberstadt earned high praise for his role in the Chrysler Corporation's buyout of the rival Dodge Brothers Automobile Company. In 1929, he served as assistant to Owen D. Young on the World War I War Reparations Committee meeting in Paris. Eberstadt continued his investment work during the Great Depression, garnering acclaim for his attempts to keep smaller businesses afloat. Indeed, in 1931, he founded his own finance company with the express purpose of dealing in the securities of smaller business enterprises. He is credited with having established one of the first successful Wall Street investment funds, the precursor to today's wildly popular mutual funds. During his many years on Wall Street, Eberstadt came to know future high-level government officials such as Paul Nitze and James Forrestal. He remained a close and lifelong friend of Forrestal.

An uncanny problem solver, Eberstadt joined the World War II mobilization effort in September 1942. He held the dual—and critically important—positions of chairman of the Army and Navy Munitions Board and vice chairman of the War Production Board (WPB). Although he was subordinate to Donald M. Nelson, chairman of the WPB, Eberstadt was in fact the organizational genius behind the war mobilization effort, and many have since asserted that his insight may have helped shorten the war by as much as a year. Eberstadt excelled in these positions and devised the ingenious Controlled Materials Plan (CMP), a highly successful scheme whereby military production could be prioritized according to need and then simultaneously synchronized with the needs of civilian industry. The basis of the CMP was the control of the three primary raw materials necessary to industrial production: steel, aluminum, and copper. The plan was a vertical control program that was pyramidal in form and managerially decentralized. The CMP was employed for all industrial consumers and producers, both military and civilian. It essentially worked as both an allocator of the controlled materials and as a system for industrial prioritization. The CMP was so successful that the Harry S. Truman administration resurrected it in 1951 for the Korean War mobilization program. It is no exaggeration to say that Eberstadt's organizational and managerial genius was the engine behind the United States' extraordinary industrial output between 1942 and 1945.

As World War II drew to a close, Secretary of the Navy James Forrestal urged Eberstadt to draft a memorandum for the president that outlined the many deficiencies in U.S. intelligence and military operations. Eberstadt correctly understood that the lack of a centralized intelligence agency was a significant detriment to U.S. defensive capabilities. Thus, he proposed a single agency to coordinate military intelligence with domestic intelligence and State Department directives. He also suggested that the military services be better coordinated and supervised. The resulting 1945 report provided the framework for the 1947 National Security Act, which incorporated many of Eberstadt's suggestions, including the establishment of the Central Intelligence Agency (CIA).

In 1946, Eberstadt served as Bernard Baruch's assistant on the United Nations Atomic Energy Commission, and in 1948 he authored another influential report on the deficiencies of the National Security Resources Board, an arm of the National Security Council. His recommendations fostered revisions to the agency within months. That same year he became chairman of the Commission on National Security Organization, part of the Hoover Commission. Thereafter, he continued to work on an ad hoc basis for subsequent administrations and remained one of the nation's most respected financiers. Eberstadt died in Washington, D.C., on November 11, 1969.

Paul G. Pierpaoli Jr.

References

Dorwart, Jeffery M. *Eberstadt and Forrestal: A National Security Partnership, 1909–1949.* College Station, TX: Texas A&M University Press, 1991.

Perez, Robert C., and Edward F. Willet. *Will to Win: A Biography of Ferdinand Eberstadt.* Westport, CT: Greenwood Press, 1989.

Eichelberger, Robert Lawrence (1886–1961)

U.S. Army general and commander of the Eighth Army in the Pacific Theater. Born on March 9, 1886, in Urbana, Ohio, Robert Lawrence Eichelberger attended Ohio State University for two years before

Lieutenant General Robert Eichelberger distinguished himself in fighting in New Guinea and later commanded the Eighth Army, which he led to victory in the Philippines. He subsequently had charge of U.S. occupation forces in Japan. (Library of Congress)

entering the United States Military Academy, West Point, where he graduated in 1909. He served in a variety of assignments before becoming assistant chief of staff of the Siberian Expeditionary Force (1918–1919), where he was promoted to temporary lieutenant colonel.

Eichelberger served in the Philippines and in China and then on the War Department General Staff (1921–1924), mostly as an intelligence officer. He graduated from the Command and General Staff School (1926) and the Army War College (1930). Eichelberger then served at West Point (1931–1935), where he was promoted to lieutenant colonel (1934). He served as secretary of the general staff (1935–1938). In 1938, he was promoted to colonel and assumed command of the 30th Infantry Regiment. Promoted to

brigadier general, he was appointed superintendent of West Point (1940).

In March 1942, Eichelberger became a temporary major general and took command of the 77th Infantry Division. He commanded XI Corps and then I Corps, in Australia. He led I Corps in New Guinea in September 1942. Promoted to temporary lieutenant general the next month, he commanded the costly attack to take the port of Buna (November 1942–January 1943) and then operations in New Guinea and New Britain (January 1943–July 1944).

Eichelberger took command of Eighth Army in September 1944 and led it to Leyte Island in the Philippines that December. He directed operations on Luzon (January–April 1945), including the liberation of Manila, and his forces also liberated the southern Philippine Islands, including Mindanao. He was entrusted with command of all Philippine operations in July 1945. His Eighth Army carried out 14 major and 24 smaller landings.

Between 1945 and 1948, Eichelberger commanded Eighth Army in Japan. He returned to the United States in September 1948 and retired from the army. Two years later, he published a book entitled *Our Jungle Road to Tokyo*. During the 1950–1953 Korean War, he was briefly a special adviser in the Far East. In July 1954, he was promoted to full general on the retired list. He died in Asheville, North Carolina, on September 26, 1961.

Alexander D. Samms

References

Eichelberger, Emma G., and Robert L. Eichelberger. *Dear Miss Em: General Eichelberger's War in the Pacific, 1942–45.* Edited by Jay Luvaas. Westport, CT: Greenwood Press, 1972.

Eichelberger, Robert L. *Our Jungle Road to Tokyo.* New York: Viking, 1950.

Shortal, John F. *Forged by Fire: General Robert L. Eichelberger and the Pacific War.* Columbia: University of South Carolina Press, 1987.

Eisenhower, Dwight David (1890–1969)

U.S. Army general, supreme commander, Allied Expeditionary Forces, European Theater of Operations during World War II, first supreme Allied commander, Europe (1951–1952), and president of the United States (1953–1961). Born in Denison, Texas, on October 14, 1890, Dwight David "Ike" Eisenhower grew up in Abilene, Kansas. Graduating from the United States Military Academy, West Point, he was a member of the Class of 1915, the "class the stars fell on." Commissioned a 2nd lieutenant of infantry, his first posting was Fort Sam Houston, Texas.

Eisenhower commanded the fledgling tank corps training center at Camp Colt outside Gettysburg, Pennsylvania, during World War I. Following service in Panama, he graduated first in his class at the Command and General Staff School, Fort Leavenworth, Kansas, in 1926. He also graduated from the Army War College in 1928. During the interwar period, Eisenhower served under a number of the army's finest officers, including generals Fox Conner, John J. Pershing, and Douglas A. MacArthur. Following his return from the Philippines in 1939, he served successively as chief of staff of the 3rd Infantry Division, IX Corps, and Third Army, where he was promoted to temporary brigadier general in October 1941 and captured army chief of staff General George C. Marshall's attention for his contributions to Third Army's "victory" in the Texas–Louisiana war maneuvers of 1941.

General of the Armies Dwight D. Eisenhower proved to be an excellent coalition leader as supreme commander of the Allied Expeditionary Forces, European Theater of Operations. He was subsequently the first commander of North Atlantic Treaty Organization forces, then president of the United States. (National Archives)

Summoned to the War Department in the aftermath of the Japanese attack on Pearl Harbor, Eisenhower headed the War Plans Division and then the Operations Division of the general staff before being promoted to major general in April 1942. Marshall then appointed Eisenhower commanding general of the European Theater of Operations, in June 1942. Promotion to lieutenant general followed in July 1942. His appointment was met with great skepticism from senior British military officers because of his lack of command experience.

Eisenhower commanded Allied forces in Operation TORCH (the invasion of northwest Africa) in November 1942 and in Operation HUSKY (the invasion of Sicily) in July 1943. In the interim Eisenhower was promoted to full general in February 1943. The efficient operation of his headquarters, Allied Forces Headquarters, became a model of Allied harmony and led to increased responsibilities in the Mediterranean Theater of Operations. In September 1943, his forces invaded the Italian mainland. Eisenhower's generalship during this phase of the war has long been subject to controversy, but his adept management of diverse personalities and his emphasis on Allied harmony led to his appointment as supreme commander, Allied Expeditionary Force, for the invasion of Northwest Europe.

As commander of Operation OVER-LORD, the invasion of Normandy on June 6, 1944, Eisenhower headed the largest Allied force in history. Following the expansion of the lodgment area, Eisenhower took direct command of the land battle on September 1, 1944. As the Allied forces advanced along a broad front toward the German border, Eisenhower frequently encountered opposition from senior Allied generals over command arrangements and logistical support. Eisenhower displayed increasing brilliance as a coalition commander, but his operational decisions remained controversial. His support of British field marshal Bernard L. Montgomery's abortive Operation MARKET-GARDEN is evidence of his unflinching emphasis on Allied harmony in the campaign of Northwest Europe. In mid-December 1944, Eisenhower was promoted to general of the army as his forces stood poised to strike into the heartland of Germany.

When German dictator Adolf Hitler launched the Ardennes Offensive (Battle of the Bulge) on December 16, 1944, it was Eisenhower, among senior Allied commanders, who first recognized the scope and intensity of Germany's attack, and he immediately saw the opportunity the Allies had to deal the Wehrmacht a severe blow. Marshaling forces to stem the German advance, he defeated Hitler's last major offensive in the west. By March 1945, his armies had crossed the Rhine River and had encircled the Ruhr industrial area of Germany. As Soviet armies stood on the outskirts of Berlin, Eisenhower decided to seek the destruction of Germany's armed forces throughout southern Germany and not to launch a direct attack toward the German capital. On May 7, 1945, the mission of the Allied Expeditionary Forces was accomplished as he accepted the unconditional surrender of Germany's armed forces.

Following the war, Eisenhower succeeded General Marshall as army chief of staff. In February 1948, Eisenhower retired from the military and assumed the presidency of Columbia University, before being recalled to active field duty by President Harry S. Truman in December 1950 to become supreme Allied commander, Europe (SACEUR), for the recently formed North Atlantic Treaty Organization (NATO). Eisenhower's appointment came amidst the devastating reverses associated with the Chinese intervention in the Korean War, which had raised the prospect of a wider war, perhaps even with the Soviets, who were then in a position to launch a major offensive into Western Europe. In 1952, Eisenhower again resigned from active military service and accepted the Republican Party's nomination for president.

Elected by a wide majority in 1952 and again in 1956, Eisenhower stressed reduced military spending and nuclear over conventional forces, and warned of the dangers of a military-industrial complex. He also ended the Korean War in

July 1953, which had been his principal campaign promise in 1952. He left office in 1961 as one of this nation's most popular chief executives, his two administrations marked by peace and relative prosperity. In 1961, Eisenhower retired to his farm in Gettysburg, Pennsylvania. He died in Washington, D.C., on March 28, 1969.

Cole C. Kingseed

References

Ambrose, Stephen E. *Eisenhower: Soldier, General of the Army, President-Elect.* New York: Simon and Schuster, 1983.

D'Este, Carlo. *Eisenhower: A Soldier's Life.* New York: Henry Holt, 2002.

Eisenhower, David. *Eisenhower at War, 1943–1945.* New York: Random House, 1986.

Eisenhower, Dwight D. *Crusade in Europe.* New York: Doubleday, 1948.

Fletcher, Frank Jack (1885–1973)

U.S. Navy admiral. Born in Marshalltown, Iowa, on April 29, 1885, the son of Rear Admiral Thomas Jack Fletcher, Frank Jack Fletcher graduated from the United States Naval Academy at Annapolis in 1906. Commissioned an ensign in 1908, Fletcher commanded the destroyer *Dale* in the Asiatic Torpedo Flotilla in 1910. Fletcher saw action in the 1914 U.S. intervention at Veracruz, Mexico. For his bravery in moving more than 350 refugees to safety, he earned the Medal of Honor. Lieutenant Fletcher then served in the Atlantic Fleet.

Following U.S. entry into World War I in 1917, he was promoted to lieutenant commander and commanded the destroyer *Benham* on convoy escort and patrol operations. Fletcher's postwar commands included submarine tenders, destroyers, and a submarine base in the Philippines, where he helped suppress an insurrection in 1924. Fletcher attended both the U.S. Naval War College (1929–1930) and U.S. Army War College (1930–1931).

From 1933 to 1936, Fletcher served as aide to the secretary of the navy. During 1936–1938, he commanded the battleship *New Mexico* and then served in the navy's Bureau of Personnel. Following his promotion to rear admiral, Fletcher commanded Cruiser Division 3 in the Atlantic Fleet.

On December 15, 1941, Fletcher took command of the Wake Island relief force centered on the carrier *Saratoga*, but he moved cautiously, and the island fell on December 23 before he could arrive. In January 1942, Fletcher received command of Task Force 17, which was centered on the carrier *Yorktown*. He participated in carrier raids on the Marshall and Gilbert Islands and joined Task Force 11 in attacks on Japanese shipping in the Solomon Islands. Fletcher commanded U.S. forces in the May 1942 Battle of the Coral Sea. Following his return to Pearl Harbor for hasty repairs to the *Yorktown,* Fletcher raced back with the vessel to join the U.S. force near Midway, where he helped orchestrate the dramatic U.S. victory on June 3–6, 1942, in which four Japanese carriers were lost in exchange for the *Yorktown.*

Fletcher then commanded the three-carrier task force supporting 1st Marine Division assaults on Tulagi and Guadalcanal (Operation WATCHTOWER). Unwilling to risk his carriers, Fletcher made the controversial decision to withdraw them before the transports had completed unloading supplies to the marines, forcing the transports to depart as well. He then committed his forces against the Japanese counterattack toward Guadalcanal, resulting in the Battle of the Eastern Solomons.

Fletcher was wounded when his flagship, the carrier *Saratoga*, was torpedoed, and he returned to the United States.

Following his recovery, Fletcher commanded the 13th Naval District and the Northwestern Sea Frontier. Fletcher's reputation for caution led Chief of Naval Operations Admiral Ernest J. King in 1943 to assign him to command the North Pacific area. Following Japan's surrender in August 1945, Fletcher oversaw the occupation of northern Honshu and Hokkaido.

In 1945, Fletcher joined the navy's General Board, which advised the secretary of the navy; he served as its chairman from May 1946 until May 1947, when he was promoted to full admiral and retired. Fletcher died in Bethesda, Maryland, on April 25, 1973.

Stephen Patrick Ward

References

Hammel, Erich. *Carrier Clash: The Invasion of Guadalcanal and the Battle of the Eastern Solomons, August 1942*. Pacifica, CA: Pacifica Press, 1997.

Regan, Stephen. *In Bitter Tempest: The Biography of Frank Jack Fletcher*. Ames: Iowa State Press, 1994.

Frederick, Robert Tryon (1907–1970)

U.S. Army general. Born in San Francisco, California, on March 14, 1907, Robert Tryon Frederick graduated from the United States Military Academy, West Point, in 1928 and was commissioned in the Coast Artillery Corps. Prewar postings included stints in the Panama Canal Zone and Hawaii and study at the Coast Artillery School. Frederick graduated from the Command and General Staff School in 1939.

Promoted to colonel in 1941, Frederick was assigned to the War Plans Division of the War Department. In 1942, he was appointed to prepare and lead the 1st Special Service Force (SSF), an elite unit composed of specially selected U.S. and Canadian soldiers trained for mountain, amphibious, and airborne operations. Later dubbed "the Devil's Brigade" by its German adversaries (and made legendary as the subject of the 1967 Hollywood motion picture by the same name, starring William Holden as Frederick), the 1st Special Service Force became the direct predecessor organization to the U.S. Army's Special Forces.

The initial 1st SSF assignment, after it had received intensive training in often harsh conditions, came during the 1943 Aleutian Islands Campaign. Transferred to the Italian Front, the brigade participated in a series of impressive mountain engagements, which demonstrated its special capabilities and resulted in Frederick's promotion to brigadier general in January 1944. Early that same year, the brigade reinforced the beachhead at Anzio, Italy, again earning recognition for its performance in an otherwise disappointing operation.

In July 1944, Frederick took charge of the 1st Airborne Task Force, which was committed to Operation DRAGOON, the August 15, 1944, invasion of southeastern France. Advanced to major general that same month, in December, at age 37, Frederick assumed command of the 45th Infantry Division, which he led into Germany and remained with until the end of the war. In addition to being one of the youngest division commanders in the U.S. Army, Frederick was also the most frequently wounded of any American general officer of the war, receiving eight Purple Hearts, along with two Distinguished Service Crosses and the British Distinguished Service Order. Throughout the war, Frederick's commands were never defeated.

During the postwar years, Frederick commanded occupation forces in Europe and later the 4th and 6th Infantry Divisions. In 1951, he led U.S. support efforts in Greece, retiring because of disability in March 1952. Frederick died at Palo Alto, California, on November 30, 1970.

David Coffey

References

Adleman, Robert H., and George Walton. *The Devil's Brigade.* Philadelphia: Chilton, 1966.

Ross, Robert T. *The Supercommandos: First Special Service Force, 1942–1945, An Illustrated History.* Atglen, PA: Schiffer, 2000.

Whitlock, Flint. *The Rock of Anzio: From Sicily to Dachau, A History of the 45th Infantry Division.* Boulder, CO: Westview Press, 1998.

Gavin, James Maurice
(1907–1990)

U.S. Army general, airborne pioneer, author, and diplomat. Born on March 22, 1907, at Brooklyn, New York, James Maurice Gavin was abandoned by his biological mother and subsequently adopted. At age 16, he enlisted in the army and eventually earned an appointment to the United States Military Academy, West Point. Graduating in 1929, he was commissioned in the infantry.

Gavin attended the Infantry School at Fort Benning, Georgia, served in the Philippines, and then was an instructor at West Point. He transferred to duty with parachute troops and, promoted to colonel in July 1942, rose to command the 505th Parachute Infantry Regiment,

which eventually became part of the 82nd Airborne Division. In 1943, Gavin's 505th jumped into Sicily, where Gavin personally led a portion of his regiment during a fight on Biazza Ridge and stopped elements of the Hermann Göring Panzer Division from breaking through to the invasion beaches. After Sicily, Gavin led the 505th in another combat jump into Salerno on September 14, 1943. Promoted to brigadier general in October, he was appointed assistant division commander.

Gavin left Italy for Britain in November 1943. There he headed the airborne planning effort for Operation OVERLORD, the June 1944 cross-Channel invasion of France. He then rejoined the 82nd Airborne Division and made his third combat

U.S. Army major general James Gavin commanded the 82nd Airborne Division during World War II. In line to be chief of staff of the army as a full general, he criticized U.S. defense policy and chose to retire in 1958 as a lieutenant general. (MPI/Getty Images)

jump into Normandy on June 6, 1944, as commander of Task Force A.

In August 1944, Gavin assumed command of the 82nd Airborne Division at age 37. He led the division in its fourth combat jump in September into Nijmegen, Holland, during Operation MARKET-GARDEN. Advanced to major general in October, he continued in command of the 82nd for the remainder of the war, fighting through the Ardennes Offensive (Battle of the Bulge) and the subsequent drive into Germany. Gavin was only an observer in Operation VARSITY, the March 1945 airborne assault by the British 6th Airborne Division and U.S. 17th Airborne Division to secure British field marshal Bernard Montgomery's bridgehead across the Rhine. However, by the end of the war, Gavin had made more combat jumps than any other general in history. At the end of the war, Gavin accepted the surrender of an entire German army. His combat valor awards included two Distinguished Service Crosses and two Silver Stars.

Gavin continued to command the 82nd Airborne Division until March 1948. He was then, in succession, chief of staff of Fifth Army; chief of staff, Allied Forces South; commander of VII Corps; and army deputy chief of staff for research and development. Promoted to lieutenant general in March 1955, Gavin was in line for promotion to general when he retired in 1958 because of differences with the defense policies of the Dwight D. Eisenhower administration. Specifically, he did not agree on the reliance of nuclear forces alone to defend against a potential Soviet offensive. Gavin returned to public life during the John F. Kennedy administration, serving as ambassador to France in 1960 and 1961. During the early years of the Vietnam War Gavin advocated a limited U.S. strategy of securing a limited number of key bases, such as Da Nang and Cam Ranh Bay—the so-called enclave strategy. He died in Baltimore, Maryland, on February 23, 1990.

Guy A. Lofaro

References

Blair, Clay. *Ridgway's Paratroopers: The American Airborne in World War II.* New York: Simon and Schuster, 1985.

Booth, T. Michael, and Duncan Spencer. *Paratrooper: The Life of General James M. Gavin.* New York: Simon and Schuster, 1994.

Gavin, James M. *Airborne Warfare.* Washington, DC: Infantry Journal Press, 1947.

———. *On to Berlin: Battles of an Airborne Commander.* New York: Viking, 1978.

Groves, Leslie Richard (1896–1970)

U.S. Army general who oversaw the Manhattan Project that developed the atomic bomb. Born in Albany, New York, on August 17, 1896, Leslie Richard "Dick" Groves attended the University of Washington and the Massachusetts Institute of Technology. He secured an appointment to the United States Military Academy, West Point, from which he graduated in 1918. He then entered the Army Corps of Engineers.

After initial training at the Engineer School at Fort Humphreys (later Fort Belvoir), Virginia, Groves served in Hawaii, Texas, Nicaragua (where he was awarded the Nicaraguan Medal of Merit for restoring water to Managua following an earthquake), Washington, D.C., and Missouri. He completed the Command and General Staff School in 1936 and the Army War College in 1939. Assigned to the War Department in 1940, Groves served as deputy chief of the Construction Division, and oversaw the vast

Having supervised construction of the Pentagon, Colonel Leslie Groves was advanced to brigadier general and assumed control of the Manhattan Project in 1942. In this position, he oversaw the development of the first atomic bomb. (National Archives)

Following the war, Groves advocated international control over atomic energy. He also organized the Army Forces Special Weapons Project to study military uses of atomic energy. He remained in command of the Manhattan Project until the establishment of the U.S. Atomic Energy Commission in 1946. Promoted to lieutenant general in January 1948, Groves retired from the army that same month and became vice president for research of the Rand Corporation. He retired altogether in 1961. Groves died in Washington, D.C., on July 13, 1970.

Ryan E. Doltz

References

Gosling, F. G. *The Manhattan Project: Science in the Second World War.* Washington, DC: U.S. Department of Energy, 1990.

Groves, Leslie R. *Now It Can Be Told: The Story of the Manhattan Project.* New York: Harper and Brothers, 1962.

Lawren, William. *The General and the Bomb.* New York: Dodd, Mead and Co., 1988.

Norris, Robert S. *Racing for the Bomb: General Leslie R. Groves, The Manhattan Project's Indispensable Man.* South Royalton, VT: Steerforth Press, 2002.

expansion of military camps and training facilities across the United States. He also supervised construction of the Pentagon, the world's largest office building.

His success in a variety of large and complex engineering projects led to Groves's promotion to brigadier general and assignment in September 1942 to head the Manhattan Project, charged with the development and construction of an atomic bomb. Groves controlled 129,000 personnel and a $2 billion budget. Groves was promoted to major general in March 1944. The Manhattan Project finally produced the detonation of the world's first atomic weapon at Alamogordo, New Mexico, on July 16, 1945. Groves advised President Harry S. Truman to use the bomb and assisted in the selection of Japanese target cities.

Halsey, William Frederick, Jr. (1882–1959)

U.S. Navy admiral. Born in Elizabeth, New Jersey, on October 30, 1882, William Frederick Halsey Jr. was a naval officer's son. He graduated from the United States Naval Academy, Annapolis, in 1904 and was commissioned an ensign in 1906. Halsey served in the Great White Fleet that circumnavigated the globe during 1907–1909 and was then in torpedo boats. When the United States entered World War I in April 1917, Halsey was a lieutenant commander and

An aggressive proponent of naval aviation, Admiral William Halsey epitomized the spirit of the U.S. Navy. He was also widely criticized for several important decisions, for which he eschewed responsibility. (Naval Historical Center)

captain of a destroyer. He then commanded destroyers operating from Queenstown, Ireland.

Following World War I, Halsey's service was mostly in destroyers, although he also held an assignment in naval intelligence and was a naval attaché in Berlin. Promoted to captain in 1927, he commanded the *Reina Mercedes*, the Naval Academy training ship, and became fascinated by naval aviation. Halsey attended both the Naval War College and Army War College, and in 1935, despite his age, he completed naval flight training and took command of the aircraft carrier *Saratoga*. Promoted to rear admiral in 1937, Halsey assumed command of

Carrier Division 2, consisting of the *Enterprise* and the *Yorktown*. He was promoted to vice admiral in 1940.

Halsey was at sea on December 7, 1941, when Japanese aircraft attacked Pearl Harbor. In early 1942, Halsey's carriers raided Japanese central Pacific installations and launched Colonel James Doolittle's raid on Tokyo in April. Acute skin disorders requiring hospitalization prevented his participation in the Battle of Midway in June 1942.

In October 1942, Halsey replaced Admiral Robert Ghormley as commander of the South Pacific Area and South Pacific Force. He was promoted to admiral in November. Despite severe tactical losses, Halsey retained strategic control of the waters around Guadalcanal in late 1942, and during 1943 he supported operations in the Solomon Islands and into the Bismarck Archipelago. Halsey came to be known as "Bull" for his pugnacious nature. In March 1943, Halsey took command of the Third Fleet, while simultaneously retaining command of the South Pacific Area until June 1944.

In the Battle of Leyte Gulf, the Japanese battle plan and the flawed American command system combined with Halsey's aggressiveness to shape one of the more controversial episodes of the war. On October 24–25, a Japanese force centered on four fleet aircraft carriers that were largely bereft of aircraft under Vice Admiral Ozawa Jisaburo decoyed Halsey and his entire Task Force 38 away from the U.S. landing sites, leaving the sites vulnerable to a powerful Japanese surface force under Vice Admiral Kurita Takeo. Although Halsey destroyed most of Ozawa's force in the Battle of Cape Engaño, disaster for the support ships off Leyte was only narrowly averted when Kurita lost his nerve. Widely criticized for not coordinating his movements with Vice Admiral Thomas Kinkaid, who had charge of the invasion force of Seventh Fleet, Halsey never admitted responsibility. He instead blamed the system of divided command.

Halsey received further criticism when he took the Third Fleet into damaging typhoons in December 1944 and June 1945. At the end of the war his flagship, the *Missouri*, was the site of the formal Japanese surrender in Tokyo Bay on September 2, 1945. Promoted to admiral of the fleet in December 1945, Halsey retired in April 1947. He then served on the boards of several large corporations. Halsey died at Fisher's Island, New York, on August 16, 1959.

John A. Hutcheson Jr.
and Spencer C. Tucker

References

Cutler, Thomas J. *The Battle for Leyte Gulf, 23–26 October 1944.* New York: Harper-Collins, 1994.

Halsey, William Frederick, Jr. *Admiral Halsey's Story.* New York: McGraw Hill, 1947.

Potter, E. B. *Bull Halsey.* Annapolis, MD: Naval Institute Press, 1985.

Reynolds, Clark G. *The Fast Carriers: The Forging of an Air Navy.* New York: McGraw-Hill, 1968.

Hodges, Courtney Hicks (1887–1966)

U.S. Army general and commander of the First Army. Born in Perry, Georgia, on January 5, 1887, Courtney Hicks Hodges attended the United States Military Academy at West Point for one year, but he dropped out for academic reasons and enlisted in the army. In 1909, Hodges earned a commission. He then served in the Philippines and in the 1916 U.S. Punitive Expedition into Mexico. During World War I, he fought in France in the Saint-Mihiel and Meuse-Argonne offensives, ending the war as a temporary lieutenant colonel.

Hodges attended the Field Artillery School in 1920 and then served as an instructor at West Point. He graduated from the Command and General Staff School in 1925, taught at the Infantry School, and then graduated from the Army War College. In 1938, he was appointed assistant commandant of the Infantry School at Fort Benning, Georgia. Promoted to brigadier general in April 1940 and to major general in May 1941, Hodges was assigned as chief of infantry. He assumed command of X Corps in May 1942. In February 1943, he was promoted to lieutenant general and took over the Southern Defense Command and Third Army. In January 1944, Hodges joined the First Army in Britain, then preparing for the Normandy Invasion, as deputy commander under Lieutenant General Omar Bradley.

In August 1944, Hodges succeeded to command of the First Army when Bradley moved up to head the 12th Army Group. The First Army then defeated the German counterattack at Mortain, reduced the Falaise-Argentan pocket, supported the August 1944 liberation of Paris, penetrated the Siegfried Line, captured Aachen, and suffered heavy casualties in the battle for the Hürtgen Forest.

In December 1944, the First Army bore the brunt of the German Ardennes Offensive (Battle of the Bulge). Responding to the Ardennes crisis, General Dwight D. Eisenhower temporarily reorganized his command structure and placed all but the southernmost corps of First Army—and Hodges—under British field marshal Bernard Montgomery, who thought Hodges was at his breaking point. Eisenhower refused any suggestion that Hodges be relieved, and Hodges's performance in the Battle of the Bulge vindicated Eisenhower's view. Indeed, the First Army rallied to hold the northern shoulder of the Bulge and then played an important role in the successful counterattack. First Army soldiers crossed the Rhine at Remagen, joined in the closing of the Ruhr pocket, and, at the end of the war, linked up with Soviet forces on the Elbe River.

In April 1945, Hodges was promoted to full general. Following May V-E Day, he and the First Army were under orders for the Pacific Theater to lead the invasion of Honshu when the Japanese surrendered. After the war, Hodges remained in command of the First Army until his retirement in 1949. He died in San Antonio, Texas, on January 16, 1966.

Thomas D. Veve

References

Cole, Hugh M. *United States Army in World War II: The European Theater of Operations: The Ardennes: Battle of the Bulge.* Washington, DC: Office of the Chief of Military History, 1965.

Weigley, Russell F. *Eisenhower's Lieutenants.* Bloomington: Indiana University Press, 1981.

Hull, Cordell (1871–1955)

Politician and U.S. secretary of state (1933–1944). Born in Star Point, Pickett County, Tennessee, on October 2, 1871, Cordell Hull studied law at National Normal University in Lebanon, Ohio, and the Cumberland Law School in Lebanon, Tennessee. In 1892, he entered Tennessee state politics as a Democrat. During the Spanish-American War, Hull volunteered and spent several months in the army. He was elected to Congress in 1903, and in 1930 became senator for Tennessee. He resigned that position in 1933 when President Franklin D. Roosevelt appointed him secretary of state.

An old-fashioned Jeffersonian Democrat and Progressive, Hull greatly admired President Woodrow Wilson; Hull had supported U.S. membership in the League of Nations following World War I. As secretary of state, he favored free trade, peace agreements, international conferences, and reliance on legal principles. During the 1930s, Hull negotiated numerous reciprocal trade agreements with other nations. He also devoted particular attention to revitalizing U.S. relations with Latin America through the "Good Neighbor" policy, under which the United States renounced

Cordell Hull served as U.S. secretary of state under President Franklin D. Roosevelt from 1933 to 1944. He was awarded the Nobel Peace Prize in 1945. (Library of Congress)

the right to intervene in Latin America, and through the conclusion of related hemispheric security agreements.

President Roosevelt, who preferred to retain personal control of American foreign policy, frequently bypassed Hull. This tendency became more pronounced as World War II approached, and Hull found it both irritating and frustrating. Even so, because the two men fundamentally shared the same perspective on international affairs, Hull chose not to resign. Hull believed that European dictators posed a dangerous threat to all free nations and, believing that arms embargoes were ineffective, he opposed the various neutrality acts passed by Congress between 1935 and 1939. He was inclined to be slightly less conciliatory than Roosevelt and was unenthusiastic about Roosevelt's 1938–1939 peace messages to European powers.

Once World War II began, Hull staunchly supported Great Britain and France against Germany and Italy. However, he was virtually excluded from the Anglo-American Destroyers-for-Bases Deal of summer 1940 and the drafting of Lend-Lease legislation some months later. Nor did he attend the Anglo-American military staff conferences held in Washington early in 1941 or the mid-August 1941 Argentina Conference that drafted the Atlantic Charter. Roosevelt, preoccupied with European affairs from April to December 1941, delegated to Hull responsibility for protracted American negotiations with Japan. The objective of the negotiations was to reach a modus vivendi in Asia, where Japan had been at war with China since 1937. Despite the expressed concern of American military leaders that the United States was unprepared for a Pacific war, by late November 1941 Hull—who was privy to intercepted Japanese cable traffic—believed that war was inevitable, and he refused to contemplate further American concessions to Japanese demands.

Following the Japanese attack on Pearl Harbor, Hull was often excluded from key meetings, including the 1942 Casablanca Conference, the 1943 Cairo and Tehran conferences, and the 1944 Quebec Conference. Hull opposed Roosevelt's decision, announced at Casablanca, to demand the unconditional surrender of the Axis nations, believing such a policy would only encourage them to continue the war. Hull also opposed the 1944 Morgenthau Plan to partition a defeated Germany and eradicate its industrial capacity, and with the support of Secretary of War Henry L. Stimson, he succeeded in torpedoing the scheme.

Hull put great effort into establishing the 1942 United Nations alliance of anti-Axis nations. Following his Wilsonian instincts, he then concentrated on planning for the postwar United Nations, an international security organization that would replace the defunct League of Nations. Under Hull's guidance, the State Department drafted the proposals for the United Nations Charter accepted at the 1944 Dumbarton Oaks Conference and adroitly marshaled bipartisan congressional support. Addressing Congress in late 1943, Hull overoptimistically stated that the projected new organization would eliminate spheres of influence and international alliances and rivalries. He shared Roosevelt's anticolonial outlook and his belief that the United States should treat China as a great power and thereby encourage it to become one.

Increasingly poor health led Hull to resign after the November 1944 presidential election. Consulted on the terms of the July 1945 Potsdam Declaration urging Japan to surrender, Hull insisted that it include no promise to retain the emperor. Hull was awarded the Nobel Peace Prize in 1945. He lived quietly in retirement, producing lengthy memoirs. Suffering from strokes and heart problems, he died in Bethesda, Maryland, on July 23, 1955.

Priscilla Roberts

References

Gellman, Irwin F. *Secret Affairs: Franklin Roosevelt, Cordell Hull, and Sumner Welles.* Baltimore: Johns Hopkins University Press, 1995.

Hull, Cordell. *Memoirs of Cordell Hull.* 2 vols. New York: Macmillan, 1948.

Pratt, Julius W. *Cordell Hull, 1933–44.* 2 vols. New York: Cooper Square, 1964.

Kaiser, Henry John (1882–1967)

American industrialist whose shipbuilding prowess was vital to the U.S. war effort. Born in Sprout Brook, New York, on May 9, 1882, Henry J. Kaiser left school at age 13 and worked at various jobs, including in the photography and hardware businesses. He then turned to wholesale hardware and construction. Now in Vancouver, British Columbia, he established his own road construction company in 1914 and built roads in Canada, the United States, and abroad. Soon, his company had offices in Spokane and Skagit in Washington State. Before long, Kaiser's reputation for delivering high quality work on time, and often under budget, caught the attention of government contractors in Washington, D.C. He was subsequently involved in the construction of the Hoover, Shasta, Bonneville, and Grand Coulee dams as well as levees on the Mississippi River. Gradually, Kaiser vertically integrated his company, and before long his factories produced the steel, cement, and aluminum that went into his construction projects.

With the great demand for cargo and merchant ships in World War II, Kaiser turned to shipbuilding, beginning with a British contract to construct 30 merchant vessels. During the war, he came to own seven shipyards in California and Oregon that constructed both cargo/merchant vessels and warships. He helped to revolutionize shipbuilding by introducing assembly-line practices that drastically cut ship construction time. By the end of 1942, Kaiser's shipyards were turning out one 14.25-ton, 441-foot-long cargo ship (known as a Liberty Ship) every 30 days. In November 1942, his Richmond, California, shipyard set a record by launching the 10.5-ton Liberty Ship *Robert E. Peary* in only 111.5 hours. In World War II, Kaiser's shipyards produced 1,490 vessels, including 50 small (escort) aircraft carriers. One of the most strategically important weapons systems of World War II, the escort carriers were based on the Liberty Ship hull and carried only a small number of aircraft. Assigned to the Atlantic convoys, they provided constant air cover against German submarines, which produced the tipping point against the Germans in the Battle of the Atlantic. Kaiser's shipyards also turned out almost one-third of all the merchant/cargo ships built in the United States during the war years.

Kaiser's other wartime construction projects included aircraft, vehicles, and munitions. Kaiser also established the Kaiser Permanente Foundation, which provided hospital and healthcare facilities to all workers in his industrial empire. Revolutionary for the time, Kaiser Permanente went on to become a model for other large corporations. By 1967, the Kaiser Permanente Health Plan was the largest health maintenance organization (HMO) in the United States and remains to this day one of the nation's largest HMOs, operating in nine states as well as Washington, D.C.

Following the war, Kaiser remained in shipbuilding and repair but also expanded into housing and automobiles. Until 1955, his car company Kaiser Motors produced Kaiser and Frazer automobiles, which were generally quite well received. But the industrialist found it difficult to compete with auto giants like General Motors, Ford, and Chrysler. In 1953, Kaiser purchased Willys-Overland, builder of Jeep utility vehicles. Ten years later he renamed the company Kaiser-Jeep, which was sold to American Motors in 1970. The Jeep remains an iconic car in the sports utility market to this very day, and many credit Kaiser for having kept it alive after World War II. Kaiser died on August 24, 1967, in Honolulu, Hawaii. Many of his companies and business practices survive today.

Nicholas W. Barcheski
and Paul G. Pierpaoli Jr.

References
Foster, Mark S. *Henry J. Kaiser: Builder in the Modern American West.* Austin: University of Texas Press, 1989.
Jaffee, Walter W. *The Last Liberty: The Biography of the SS "Jeremiah O'Brien."* Palo Alto, CA: Glencannon Press, 1993.
Sawyer, L. A., and W. W. Mitchell. *The Liberty Ships.* London: Lloyd's of London Press, 1985.

Kenney, George Churchill (1889–1977)

Engineer and U.S. Army general. Born on August 6, 1889, in Yarmouth, Nova Scotia, George Churchill Kenney studied at the Massachusetts Institute of Technol-

ogy and worked as an engineer for several years. Following the U.S. entry into World War I, he joined the Aviation Section of the Army Signal Corps, becoming a fighter pilot in the World War I American Expeditionary Forces Air Service and flying 75 combat missions. After the war, Kenney continued in what became the Army Air Corps in 1926. In 1938, Major General Henry Harley Arnold, the new air corps chief, appointed Kenney as chief of the Production Engineering Sections of the Matériel Division. In January 1941, Kenney, advanced to brigadier general, became head of the Air Corps Experimental Depot. He then briefly commanded the Fourth Air Force, headquartered on the West Coast.

From July 1942, Kenney commanded Allied Air Forces, Southwest Pacific Area; later that year, he was promoted to lieutenant general. In June 1944, he also took command of the new U.S. Far East Air Force, and he became a full general in March 1945. Kenney's boldness and his efficiency and drive in introducing innovative aircraft, equipment, and tactics and inspiring his subordinates helped transform U.S. air power in the Pacific. Kenney oversaw the transformation of the U.S. air service from a primarily defensive arm of the military to a powerful offensive force that wrested control of the skies from the Japanese. Between 1942 and 1945, his U.S. Fifth Air Force provided invaluable strategic and tactical air support to Southwest Pacific Theater commander General Douglas MacArthur's operations, transporting troops and supplies, destroying enemy shipping, and supporting 56 amphibious operations by Australian and U.S. ground forces. Kenney was the Pacific Theater's most distinguished air commander.

Following the war, Kenney headed, in succession, the Pacific Air Command, the Strategic Air Command, and the Air University before retiring in 1951. He wrote four books on the war in the Southwest Pacific. Kenney died in Bay Harbor Islands, Florida, on August 9, 1977.

Priscilla Roberts

References

Griffith, Thomas E., Jr. *MacArthur's Airman: General George C. Kenney and the War in the South Pacific*. Lawrence: University Press of Kansas, 1998.

Kenney, George C. *General Kenney Reports: A Personal History of the Pacific War*. New York: Duell, Sloan and Pearce, 1949.

Wolk, Herman S. "George C. Kenney: The Great Innovator." In *Makers of the United States Air Force*. Pp. 127–150. Edited by John L. Frisbee. Washington, DC: Office of Air Force History, U.S. Air Force, 1987.

———. "George C. Kenney: MacArthur's Premier Airman." In *We Shall Return: MacArthur's Commanders and the Defeat of Japan, 1942–1945*. Pp. 88–114. Edited by William M. Leary. Lexington: University of Kentucky Press, 1988.

Gruff and outspoken, Admiral Ernest J. King was chief of naval operations and one of the major architects of U.S. military strategy during World War II. He was advanced to admiral of the fleet in 1944. (Library of Congress)

King, Ernest Joseph (1878–1956)

U.S. Navy fleet admiral and chief of naval operations during World War II. Born in Lorain, Ohio, on November 23, 1878, Ernest Joseph King graduated from the United States Naval Academy at Annapolis in 1901. He subsequently served in a variety of assignments on cruisers, on battleships, and at the Naval Academy, where he was an instructor of ordnance and gunnery from 1906 to 1908. King commanded a destroyer in 1914. Between 1916 and 1919, he served on the staff of the commander of the Atlantic Fleet.

In 1919, Captain King headed the Naval Postgraduate School. During the next seven years, the ambitious, harddriving, and forceful King specialized in submarines. In 1926, he took command of an aircraft tender and was senior aide to the commander of Air Squadrons, Atlantic Fleet. In 1927, King underwent flight training, and the next year, he became assistant chief of the Bureau of Aeronautics. In 1929, he commanded the Norfolk Naval Air Station, and from 1930 to 1932 he commanded the aircraft carrier *Lexington*.

King then graduated from the Naval War College and, promoted to rear admiral, served as chief of the Bureau of Aeronautics from 1933 to 1936. He spent the next five years in senior naval aviation assignments, including a tour as commander of the Aircraft Base Force. In 1938, he was promoted to vice admiral. Appointed to the Navy General Board in 1939, King criticized the lack of war preparations, recommending that should the United States go to war with Japan, it had to pursue an offensive Pacific naval strategy. He also proposed measures for the better integration of aircraft, submarines, and small fast ships with battleships and aircraft carriers.

In February 1941, King was promoted to admiral and appointed commander of the Atlantic Fleet. On December 30, 1941, following the Japanese attack on Pearl Harbor, he became commander in chief of the U.S. Fleet. The following March, President Franklin D. Roosevelt appointed King as chief of naval operations, making him the only U.S. Navy officer ever to hold both positions concurrently.

As a member of the Joint Chiefs of Staff, King was a major architect of wartime strategy. He vigorously prosecuted a two-front war in both the Atlantic and the Pacific but consistently gave higher priority to operations based primarily on naval forces. He was therefore more committed to extensive Pacific operations, which relied heavily on naval power, than was his colleague General George C. Marshall, the army chief of staff, who generally followed a Europe-first strategy. King forcefully advocated a strategy of aggressive advance against Japan through the Central Pacific, later modified to include a second, southwestern offensive by way of the Philippines and Taiwan. King was often a difficult colleague. Despite feuds over authority with Secretary of the Navy Frank Knox and his successor, James V. Forrestal, King successfully built up American naval forces, introduced tactical and technological innovations, and contributed significantly to the Allied victory in the Pacific. In December 1944, he was promoted to five-star rank, admiral of the fleet.

In October 1945, King abolished the position of commander in chief of the U.S. Fleet and merged its responsibilities with those of the chief of naval operations. King retired in December 1945 and was succeeded as chief of naval operations by Admiral Chester W. Nimitz. Over the next decade, he served as a special adviser to the secretary of the navy and also headed the Naval Historical Foundation. King was one of the few, perhaps the only, American admirals qualified in all three of the U.S. Navy's primary warfighting communities, surface warfare, submarines, and aviation. King died in Portsmouth, New Hampshire, on June 25, 1956.

Priscilla Roberts
and Spencer C. Tucker

References

Buell, Thomas. *Master of Seapower: A Biography of Fleet Admiral Ernest J. King.* Boston: Little, Brown, 1980.

Hayes, Grace Person. *The History of the Joint Chiefs of Staff in World War II: The War against Japan.* Annapolis, MD: Naval Institute Press, 1982.

Love, Robert William, Jr. "Fleet Admiral Ernest J. King." Pp. 75–107. In *Men of War: Great Naval Leaders of World War II.* Edited by Stephen Howarth. London: Weidenfeld and Nicolson, 1992.

Stoler, Mark A. *Allies and Adversaries: The Joint Chiefs of Staff, the Grand Alliance, and U.S. Strategy in World War II.* Chapel Hill: University of North Carolina Press, 2000.

Knudsen, William S. (1879–1948)

American industrialist, mass production expert, automotive executive, and war production manager. Born in Copenhagen, Denmark, on March 25, 1879, Signius Wilhelm Poul Knudsen was

William S. Knudsen was an expert in mass production techniques and president of General Motors when in May 1940 he agreed to serve as chairman of the National Defense Advisory Commission. In this position he made a vital contribution to the war effort, converting U.S. industry to armaments production. (Library of Congress)

educated in Denmark and worked as a merchant's clerk and bicycle assembler. At the age of 21 he immigrated to the United States, Americanized his name to William Knudsen, and found work in a succession of manufacturing industries, thereby learning modern industrial production techniques and scientific management.

While working at the John R. Keim Mills in Buffalo, New York, Knudsen introduced many innovations to the manufacturing of bicycle and automobile parts. The Keim firm was bought out by auto magnate Henry Ford in 1913, and Knudsen then ran assembly lines for the Ford Motor Company from 1913 to 1921. Following a dispute with Ford, he was hired by the Chevrolet Division of

General Motors in 1922, and by 1927 Chevrolet had outpaced Ford in sales. Knudsen advanced steadily through the corporate ranks to become president of General Motors in 1937 and achieve international renown as a mass-production manager. By the time he took over the presidency of General Motors, it was one of the largest companies in the world and the world's largest automaker.

In May 1940, Knudsen resigned his position at General Motors to serve as chairman of the National Defense Advisory Commission, appointed by President Franklin D. Roosevelt to help ready the nation for a potential war. In this capacity, Knudsen was instrumental in convincing American automobile manufacturers to take up the wartime manufacture of military aircraft. By the fall of 1940, Knudsen's work had earned him a cover feature in *Time* magazine. On January 7, 1941, he became director general for production in the newly created Office of Production Management and was involved in expediting U.S. war manufacturing efforts.

By presidential executive order of January 16, 1942, the War Production Board (WPB) headed by Donald M. Nelson superseded the Office of Production Management, and on January 28, 1942, Knudsen accepted a wartime commission as a lieutenant general in the U.S. Army; he served as director of production for the War Department until June 1945. As such, he settled labor disputes, prioritized and expedited the manufacture of war matériel, especially aircraft, and became known as a master troubleshooter. Knudsen was twice awarded the Distinguished Service Medal for his contributions to the war effort. After the war, Knudsen served for a time on the General Motors board of directors and also worked for the Hupp Corporation. He died in Detroit, Michigan, on April 27, 1948.

Charles R. Shrader

References

Beasley, Norman. *Knudsen: A Biography.* New York: McGraw Hill, 1947.

Nelson, Donald M. *Arsenal of Democracy: The Story of American War Production.* New York: Harcourt, Brace, 1946.

Krueger, Walter (1881–1967)

U.S. Army general who commanded Sixth Army in the Pacific Theater. Born in Flatow, West Prussia, on January 26, 1881, Walter Krueger emigrated to the United States in 1889. He enlisted in the army during the 1898 Spanish-American War and saw action in Cuba and in the Philippine-American War, earning a commission in 1901. He graduated from the Infantry and Cavalry School in 1906 and the Command and General Staff School in 1907. He was a faculty member at the army's School of the Line and Staff College between 1909 and 1912. Captain Krueger participated in the 1916–1917 U.S. Punitive Expedition into Mexico. Sent to France during World War I, he rose to be chief of staff of the Tank Corps of the American Expeditionary Forces as a temporary colonel. He was then chief of staff for VI Corps in France and IV Corps in Germany.

Krueger graduated from the Army War College in 1921 and the Naval War College in 1926 and later taught at both schools before serving with the War Plans Division for three years. He was promoted to colonel in 1932 and brigadier general in 1936 and then headed the War Plans Division from 1936 to 1938. He next commanded a brigade and was pro-moted to major general in February 1939, thereafter taking command of the 2nd Division at Fort Sam Houston, Texas. He went on to command VIII Corps, and in May 1941, he took command of Third Army as a temporary lieutenant general. Krueger's Third Army "won" the 1941 Louisiana training maneuvers.

When the United States entered World War II, there seemed little chance that Krueger would receive a battlefield command because of his advanced age and his skill as a trainer of soldiers. In January 1943, however, General Douglas MacArthur personally requested Krueger and the Third Army for deployment to the southwest Pacific. Instead, the War Department transferred Krueger and some of his staff to Australia to activate Sixth Army. Krueger commanded Sixth Army in a series of widespread combat operations across the southwest Pacific until the end of the Pacific War, beginning with the occupation of Kiriwina and Woodlark islands in June 1943. He commanded operations against New Britain, the Admiralty Islands, New Guinea, Biak, and Morotai. By midsummer 1944, New Guinea was in Allied hands, and MacArthur was ready to return to the Philippines.

Krueger led the landings at Leyte and the Lingayen Gulf. In the ensuing campaign, Sixth Army captured Manila and cleared most of Luzon Island. Promoted to general in March 1945, Krueger was scheduled to lead the invasion of Kyushu Island when Japan surrendered in August.

Critics thought Krueger too slow and methodical, but very few have complained about his low casualty rates relative to his successes. Although MacArthur may have been displeased at Krueger's slowness on Luzon, he still selected him to lead the planned invasion of Japan.

Rarely seeking the limelight, Krueger enjoyed MacArthur's full confidence. After the war, Krueger remained with Sixth Army during the occupation of Japan. He retired in July 1946 and died on August 20, 1967, at Valley Forge, Pennsylvania.

Thomas D. Veve

References

Brown, John T. "Steady Ascension: A Biography of General Walter Krueger." Master's thesis, Georgia Southern University, 2002.

Krueger, Walter. *From Down Under to Nippon: The Story of Sixth Army in World War II.* Washington, DC: Combat Forces Press, 1953.

Leary, William M. "Walter Krueger: MacArthur's Fighting General." Pp. 60–87. In *We Shall Return! MacArthur's Commanders and the Defeat of Japan, 1942–1945.* Edited by William M. Leary. Lexington: University Press of Kentucky, 1988.

Admiral of the Fleet William D. Leahy was the unofficial chairman of the U.S. Joint Chiefs of Staff during World War II and a trusted adviser of presidents Franklin D. Roosevelt and Harry S. Truman. (Library of Congress)

Leahy, William Daniel (1875–1959)

U.S. Navy admiral of the fleet and adviser to presidents Franklin D. Roosevelt and Harry S. Truman. Born in Hampton, Iowa, on May 6, 1875, William Daniel Leahy graduated from the United States Naval Academy, Annapolis, in 1897. He first served aboard the battleship *Oregon*, taking part in the Spanish-American War and the Boxer Rebellion. From 1899 to 1907, Ensign Leahy served in the Pacific, including the Philippines, and in Panama. During World War I, he formed a friendship with Roosevelt, then assistant secretary of the navy. In 1918, Leahy was promoted to captain.

Leahy served at sea and also held important posts ashore. Advanced to rear admiral in 1927, he headed the Bureau of Ordnance (1927–1931) and then the Bureau of Navigation (1933–1935). He was promoted to vice admiral in 1935. In January 1937, Leahy advanced to the rank of admiral and was appointed by President Roosevelt as chief of naval operations (CNO). As CNO, he argued forcefully for naval expansion. After retiring from the navy in August 1939, he served as governor of Puerto Rico (September 1939–November 1940). Roosevelt next named Leahy U.S. ambassador to Vichy, France.

In May 1942, Roosevelt recalled Leahy to active duty and made him his chief of staff and unofficial chairman of the Joint Chiefs of Staff (JCS). Leahy also presided over the Combined Chiefs of Staff meetings when the United States was the host. Throughout the war years, he was an adviser and confidant to Roosevelt, especially during meetings with Allied heads of state at places such as

Casablanca, Cairo, Tehran, and Yalta. A strong nationalist, Leahy did not place much credence in Roosevelt's cherished United Nations. In December 1944, he was promoted to admiral of the fleet, becoming the first naval officer to hold that rank, as well as the first American officer of any service to wear five stars.

When Roosevelt died on April 12, 1945, Leahy became one of President Truman's closest advisers, playing an important role at the Potsdam Conference of July and August 1945. He opposed dropping the atomic bomb on Japan, urging Truman to continue conventional bombing and to tighten the naval blockade in the belief that Japan was ready to sue for peace. He also feared that the atomic bomb might not work.

Following the war, Leahy played a major part in the formulation of the National Security Act of 1947. His advice helped lead to the subsequent establishment of the National Military Establishment (NME), later known as the Department of Defense, and the Central Intelligence Group, later known as the Central Intelligence Agency (CIA). He continued to play vital roles in the formation and expansion of the National Security Council (NSC), the JCS, and the North Atlantic Treaty Organization (NATO).

Leahy was an ardent anticommunist who shared Truman's abiding distrust of the Soviet Union. He retired from government service in March 1949 but continued to act as a key adviser to the secretary of the navy. He also helped establish the Naval Historical Foundation and served as its first president. In 1950, Leahy published his autobiography, *I Was There.* He died on July 20, 1959, in Bethesda, Maryland.

William Head

References

Adams, Henry H. *Witness to Power: The Life of Fleet Admiral William D. Leahy.* Annapolis, MD: Naval Institute Press, 1985.

Larrabee, Eric. *Commander in Chief: Franklin D. Roosevelt, His Lieutenants, and Their War.* New York: Harper and Row, 1987.

Leahy, William D. *I Was There: The Personal Story of the Chief of Staff to Presidents Roosevelt and Truman, Based on His Notes and Diaries Made at the Time.* New York: McGraw Hill, 1950.

LeMay, Curtis Emerson (1906–1990)

U.S. Army Air Forces (later, U.S. Air Force) general who commanded the Twentieth Air Force by the close of World War II. Born on November 15, 1906, in Columbus, Ohio, Curtis LeMay graduated from Ohio State University in 1928 with an engineering degree. Completing pilot training at Kelly Field, Texas, he secured a commission in October 1929 as a 2nd lieutenant in the U.S. Army Air Corps Reserve and a regular commission in January 1930.

LeMay spent four years with the 27th Pursuit Squadron and then served with other fighter squadrons before being assigned to the 49th Bombardment Squadron in 1937.

In June 1942, LeMay assumed command of the 305th Bomb Group, flying the B-17 Flying Fortress. That unit's fourth commanding officer within four months, LeMay became known as "Iron Ass" for the relentless pressure he placed on his men. In May 1943, he took command of the 3rd Bombardment Division and was promoted to temporary brigadier general that September. On August 17, 1943, LeMay piloted the lead bomber in

U.S. Army Air Forces major general Curtis LeMay oversaw the massive strategic bombing campaign against Japan at the end of World War II. Later he was the first head of the Strategic Air Command and, during 1961–1965 as a full general, the chief of staff of the U.S. Air Force. (Library of Congress)

the 3rd Air Division's bombing raid on Regensburg, Germany. That day, the 3rd lost 24 of 127 planes, but the raid inflicted heavy damage on the aircraft factory that produced nearly 30 percent of Germany's Messerschmitt Bf-109 fighter aircraft.

Promoted to temporary major general in March 1944, LeMay at age 38 was the youngest two-star general in the U.S. Army Air Force. In August 1944, he assumed command of the 20th Bomber Command in China. In January 1945, he took over the 21st Bomber Command in Guam in the Mariana Islands. LeMay stressed extensive training and instituted new tactics that included low-level night attacks and reduced defensive armament

in the firebombing of Japanese cities. On the night of March 9–10, 1945, his B-29s struck Tokyo in what was the single most destructive bombing raid in history. That July, LeMay assumed command of the Twentieth Air Force, composed of 20th and 21st Bomber Commands.

From 1945 to 1947, LeMay was Air Force deputy chief of staff for research and development. In September 1947, when the air force became a separate military branch, LeMay, a temporary lieutenant general, took command of U.S. Air Forces in Europe (USAFE) and helped organize the 1948–1949 Berlin Airlift.

In October 1948, LeMay became head of the newly established Strategic Air Command (SAC). He was promoted to general in October 1951. At age 44 he was the youngest American full general since Ulysses S. Grant. LeMay commanded SAC until July 1957, when he was appointed air force vice chief of staff. In May 1961, LeMay became chief of staff of the air force, remaining in that post until his retirement in February 1965. His tenure was not without its controversy, as he clashed openly with President John F. Kennedy during the October 1962 Cuban Missile Crisis. Contemptuous of the naval quarantine of Cuba, LeMay argued that the United States should bomb Cuba's nuclear missile sites, a course of action that might have triggered World War III. Even after the crisis had subsided and the Soviets withdrew their missiles from the island, LeMay advocated an American invasion of Cuba to remove Fidel Castro from power.

LeMay published his autobiography in 1965 and was chairman of the board of Network Electronics from 1965 to 1968. In October 1968, he entered politics as Alabama governor George Wallace's vice presidential running mate on the

American Independent Party ticket. The independent bid was defeated in the November 1968 general election that brought former vice president Richard M. Nixon to the White House. LeMay was an outspoken proponent of the bombing of North Vietnam, and his campaign generated a firestorm of controversy. LeMay died on October 1, 1990, at March Air Force Base, California.

Arthur A. Matthews

References

Coffey, Thomas M. *Iron Eagle: The Turbulent Life of General Curtis LeMay.* New York: Crown Publishers, 1986.

LeMay, Curtis E., and MacKinlay Kantor. *Mission with LeMay: My Story.* Garden City, NY: Doubleday, 1965.

Morrison, Wilbur H. *Fortress without a Roof: The Allied Bombing of the Third Reich.* New York: St. Martin's Press, 1982.

MacArthur, Douglas (1880–1964)

U.S. Army general and, during World War II, supreme commander of Allied forces in the Southwest Pacific. Born on January 26, 1880, in Little Rock, Arkansas, the son of Lieutenant General Arthur MacArthur, Douglas MacArthur graduated from the United States Military Academy, West Point, in 1903 with highest honors. Following service in the Philippines and Japan, he became an aide to President Theodore Roosevelt (1906–1907). He took part in the 1914 occupation of Veracruz, Mexico, and served on the general staff (1913–1917).

Following United States entrance into World War I in April 1917, MacArthur went to France as chief of staff of the 42nd Division. Promoted to temporary brigadier general, he fought with the division in the Second Battle of the Marne. MacArthur then led the 8th Infantry Brigade in the Saint-Mihiel and Meuse-Argonne offensives. He commanded the 42nd Division at the end of the war.

Following occupation duty in Germany, MacArthur returned to the United States as superintendent of West Point (1919–1922), where he carried out much-needed reforms. He again served in the Philippines and claimed that his extensive service there gave him special insight into the "Oriental mind." MacArthur was then chief of staff of the army (1930–1935). In 1935, MacArthur returned to the Philippines as adviser to the Philippine government, helping it in establishing an army

General Douglas MacArthur commanded U.S. forces in the Philippines when the United States entered World War II. He subsequently had charge of Allied forces in the Southwest Pacific, and then headed the Allied occupation of Japan. He commanded United Nations forces during the Korean War until he was dismissed by President Harry S. Truman. (Library of Congress)

capable of resisting a Japanese invasion. He retired from the U.S. Army in 1937 and became field marshal of Philippine forces.

Recalled to active service with the U.S. Army as a major general in July 1941, MacArthur received command of all U.S. forces in the Philippines. He was quickly elevated to lieutenant general and then general. Believing his forces could defend the islands, he scrapped the original, sound plan to withdraw into the Bataan Peninsula. Following MacArthur's refusal to allow Major General Lewis Brereton to launch an immediate retaliatory air strike against the Japanese on Formosa in response to the attack on Pearl Harbor, half of the American bombers and one-third of the fighters in the Philippines were caught and destroyed on the ground by the Japanese on December 8.

Although the Japanese force invading the Philippines was composed of only 57,000 men, half that of MacArthur's own numbers, many of the general's men were poorly trained (some were recent inductees), and they were thinly spread. The Japanese had little difficulty taking Manila and much of the island of Luzon. MacArthur then ordered his forces to follow the original plan for withdrawing into the Bataan Peninsula. Unfortunately, the bases there were not ready, and the retreating troops had to abandon precious stocks of supplies and ammunition in the process. Over the next three months, MacArthur spent most of his time on Corregidor Island. Rather than see him become a prisoner of the Japanese, on February 22, 1942, President Franklin D. Roosevelt ordered MacArthur to Australia, where he became supreme commander of Allied forces in the Southwest Pacific. MacArthur also was awarded the Medal of Honor, an

award that many defenders of Bataan and Corregidor believed was undeserved. Officials in Washington were also angered by MacArthur's acceptance of a $500,000 payment from his friend Manuel Quezon, the Philippine president.

From Australia, MacArthur initially developed a deliberate strategy to return to the Philippines. The slow pace of the Allied advance led Washington to insist on a leap-frogging approach that would bypass strongly held Japanese islands and positions, such as Rabaul on New Britain Island and Truk. In the spring of 1944, MacArthur's troops invaded New Guinea and isolated Rabaul. By September, they had taken Morotai and the rest of New Guinea.

In a meeting with Roosevelt in Hawaii in July 1944, Admiral Chester Nimitz, who commanded forces in the Central Pacific, proposed moving against Formosa, whereas MacArthur sought to retake the Philippines. The goal of both approaches was to deny Japanese forces access to supplies in the south. The decision was that Roosevelt agreed MacArthur would be allowed to retake the Philippines, and Nimitz shifted his resources against Okinawa.

In October 1944, U.S. forces under MacArthur's command landed on Leyte. They secured Luzon between January and March 1945, followed by the southern Philippines. The invasion of Japan proved unnecessary when Japan surrendered unconditionally following two atomic bomb attacks. Promoted to the new rank of general of the army in December 1944 and appointed Allied supreme commander in early 1945, MacArthur presided over the formal Japanese surrender ceremony on the battleship *Missouri* in Tokyo Bay on September 2.

President Harry S. Truman appointed MacArthur commander of Allied occupation forces in Japan. He governed Japan as a benevolent despot, presiding over the institution of a new democratic constitution and domestic reforms. On the beginning of the Korean War in June 1950, Truman appointed MacArthur commander of the United Nations forces sent there to defend against the North Korean invasion. As the outnumbered United Nations and South Korean forces were pushed south down the peninsula into what came to be called the Pusan Perimeter, MacArthur husbanded his resources. In September 1950, he launched a brilliant (but also lucky) amphibious landing at Inchon that cut North Korean lines of communication to the south. After the United Nations forces broke out of the Pusan Perimeter, moved north, and linked up with the Inchon landing force, MacArthur then directed the United Nations Command (UNC) invasion of North Korea. MacArthur's faulty troop dispositions and his complete disregard of the potential for a Chinese intervention nearly led to disaster. His increasingly public disagreement with Truman over the course of the war—which the administration in Washington sought to limit and MacArthur wanted to widen by attacking China proper—led to his relief from command in April 1951.

MacArthur returned to the United States as a national hero. He retired from the military, accepting the position of chairman of the board of Remington Rand Corporation. His attempt to run for the presidency as a Republican in 1952 quickly collapsed, and the nomination and office went to another general, whom MacArthur held in great disdain, his own one-time aide-de-camp Dwight D. Eisen-

hower. MacArthur died in Washington, D.C., on April 5, 1964.

T. Jason Soderstrum
and Spencer C. Tucker

References

James, D. Clayton. *The Years of MacArthur.* 3 vols. Boston: Houghton Mifflin, 1970–1985.

Manchester, William Raymond. *American Caesar: Douglas MacArthur, 1880–1964.* Boston: Little, Brown, 1978.

Perret, Geoffrey. *Old Soldiers Never Die: The Life of Douglas MacArthur.* Holbrook, MA: Adams Media, 1996.

Marshall, George Catlett (1880–1959)

U.S. Army general, chief of staff of the army, secretary of state, and secretary of defense. Born in Uniontown, Pennsylvania, on December 31, 1880, George Marshall graduated from the Virginia Military Institute in 1901. Commissioned in the infantry in 1902, he then served in a variety of assignments, including in the Philippines. He attended the Infantry and Cavalry School, Fort Leavenworth, in 1906 and was an instructor in the Army Service Schools during 1907–1908.

After the United States entered World War I, Marshall went to France with the American Expeditionary Forces as operations and training officer of the 1st Division in June 1917. Promoted to lieutenant colonel in 1918, he became deputy chief of staff for operations of the U.S. First Army in August and was the principal planner of the Saint-Mihiel Offensive (September 12–16). He earned admiration for his logistical skills in directing the repositioning of hundreds of thousands of men quickly across the battlefront after the success of the Meuse-Argonne

General George C. Marshall was chief of staff of the U.S. Army during World War II. Known as the "Organizer of Victory" and promoted to general of the armies in 1944, Marshall oversaw the creation and successful employment of the largest military force in U.S. history. After the war as secretary of state, he helped develop what became known as the Marshall Plan for the reconstruction of Europe, and for which he was awarded the Nobel Prize for Peace. During 1950–1951, he served as secretary of defense. (Library of Congress)

Offensive (September 26–November 11). After working on occupation plans for Germany, Marshall reverted to his permanent rank of captain and served as aide to General John J. Pershing from 1919 to 1924, who served as chief of staff of the army from 1921 to 1924. Marshall was promoted to major in 1920 and lieutenant colonel in 1923.

Marshall served in Tianjin (Tientsin), China, with the 15th Infantry Regiment during 1924–1927. He was assistant commandant in charge of instruction at the Infantry School, Fort Benning, Georgia (1927–1932), where he helped to train many officers who would serve as generals during World War II. Promoted to colonel in 1932, he served in various assignments in the continental United States, including instructor with the Illinois National Guard from 1933 to 1936. He advanced to brigadier general in 1936 and assumed command of the 5th Infantry Brigade.

Marshall became head of the War Plans Division in Washington in July 1938, then deputy chief of staff of the army that October. President Franklin D. Roosevelt advanced Marshall over many more senior officers to appoint him chief of staff of the army on September 1, 1939, the day that German armies invaded Poland. He was promoted to major general and simultaneously to temporary general the same day he became chief of staff.

As war began in Europe, Marshall worked to revitalize the American defense establishment. Supported by pro-Allied civilian senior leaders, such as Secretary of War Henry L. Stimson, Marshall instituted and lobbied for programs to recruit and train new troops; expedite munitions production; assist Great Britain, China, and the Soviet Union in resisting the Axis powers; and coordinate British and American strategy. After the United States entered the war on December 7, 1941, Marshall presided over an increase in U.S. Army strength from a mere 200,000 troops to a wartime maximum of 8.1 million men and women. Marshall stressed the tactical basics of firepower and maneuver and he supported mechanization and the most modern military technology. By the war's end the U.S. Army was the most mechanized and motorized combat force in the world. Marshall also strongly supported the army air forces. For his great accomplishments in the war, Marshall became known as the "Organizer of Victory."

Marshall was a strong supporter of opening a second front in Europe as early as possible, a campaign that was deferred by strategic necessity until June 1944. Between 1941 and 1945, he attended all the major Allied wartime strategic conferences, including those at Placentia Bay, Washington, Quebec, Cairo, Tehran, Malta, Yalta, and Potsdam. Marshall was the first general promoted to the newly authorized rank of general of the army in December 1944, and the second American officer, one day after Admiral William Leahy, to wear five stars. Perhaps Marshall's greatest personal disappointment was that he did not hold field command during World War II, especially command of the European invasion forces. Roosevelt and the other wartime chiefs wanted him to remain in Washington and Marshall bowed to their wishes. Marshall advocated employment of the atomic bomb against Japan in August 1945.

On the urging of President Harry S. Truman, Marshall agreed to serve as special envoy to China during 1945–1947. He retired from active duty in early 1947 and then served as secretary of state from 1947 to 1949. He was the architect of the Marshall Plan to rebuild Europe, and president of the American Red Cross from 1949 to 1950. Truman persuaded Marshall to return to government service as secretary of defense in September 1950. Marshall worked to repair relations with the other agencies of government that had become frayed under his predecessor and to build up the U.S. military to meet the needs of the Korean War (1950–1953) and commitments in Europe, while at the same time maintaining an adequate reserve. Marshall opposed General Douglas MacArthur's efforts for a widened war with China and

supported Truman in his decisions to fight a "limited war" and to remove MacArthur as commander of United Nations Forces.

Marshall resigned in September 1951, ending 50 years of dedicated government service. Awarded the 1953 Nobel Prize for Peace for the Marshall Plan, he was the first soldier so honored. Marshall died in Washington, D.C., on October 16, 1959. If not America's greatest soldier, Marshall was one of the nation's most capable military leaders and statesmen and certainly one of the most influential figures of the 20th century.

Spencer C. Tucker

References

Cray, Ed. *General of the Army: George C. Marshall, Soldier and Statesman.* New York: W. W. Norton, 1990.

Pogue, Forrest C. *George C. Marshall.* 4 vols. New York: Viking, 1963–1987.

Stoler, Mark A. *George C. Marshall: Soldier-Statesman of the American Century.* Boston: Twayne, 1989.

McNair, Lesley James (1883–1944)

U.S. Army general responsible for training American ground forces in the war. Born in Verndale, Minnesota, on May 25, 1883, Lesley James McNair graduated from the United States Military Academy, West Point, in 1904 and was commissioned in the artillery. He served as an observer with French artillery in 1913. In 1914, he participated in the occupation of Veracruz, Mexico, and in 1916 he served in the U.S. Punitive Expedition into Mexico. He deployed to France with the 1st Division as a temporary lieutenant colonel in June 1917. That August, McNair transferred to the training section of the American Expeditionary Forces (AEF) general staff at Chaumont, where he was promoted first to colonel in June 1918 and then to brigadier general in October 1918 as the AEF's chief artillery trainer. At the age of 35 he was the youngest general officer in the U.S. Army at the time.

Reverting to his permanent rank of major after the war, McNair held a succession of routine assignments and graduated from the Army War College in 1929. From 1929 to 1933, he served as the assistant commandant of the Field Artillery School at Fort Sill, Oklahoma, where he oversaw a series of major advances in the technical and tactical control of artillery fire. He also played a pioneering role in the development of antitank guns. He was again promoted to colonel in May 1935 and to brigadier general in March 1937, commanding a field artillery brigade. In 1939, he became commandant of the Command and General Staff School at Fort Leavenworth, Kansas, where he completely reorganized the course of instruction to emphasize mobile warfare, speed, simplicity, and flexibility.

When George C. Marshall became chief of staff of the U.S. Army in September 1939, his old friend McNair had long established his reputation as one of the army's most talented organizers and trainers of soldiers. In June 1940, Marshall assigned McNair as chief of staff of the newly established General Headquarters, and put him in charge of organizing and training all of the army's ground forces in World War II. McNair was promoted to major general in September 1940 and lieutenant general in June 1941. He became the commander of Army Ground Forces in March 1942.

As the architect and chief trainer of the U.S. Army of World War II, McNair was responsible for all training, organi-

zation structure, and operational doctrine. He insisted on rigorous and realistic training, and he set high standards for officers. Marshall also relied heavily on his advice in the selection and assignments of the senior commanders.

McNair often went into the field to observe personally the results of his training programs. During one such inspection trip to the 1st Infantry Division in Tunisia in the spring of 1943, McNair was wounded. In July 1944, he relinquished command of Army Ground Forces and went to Europe, where he assumed command of the fictitious U.S. 1st Army Group in the United Kingdom from Lieutenant General George C. Patton Jr. He was killed in Normandy, France, on July 25, 1944, by bombs that fell short near Saint-Lô during the carpet bombing of the German front lines prior to the U.S. breakout in Operation COBRA. He was the first U.S. Army lieutenant general to be killed in action. Fort Lesley McNair in Washington, D.C., was renamed in his honor in 1948, and he was promoted to full general posthumously in July 1954.

John F. Votaw

References

Kahn, E. J., Jr. *McNair: Educator of an Army.* Washington, DC: Infantry Journal, 1945.

Perret, Geoffrey. *There's a War to Be Won: The United States Army in World War II.* New York: Random House, 1991.

Nimitz, Chester William (1885–1966)

U.S. Navy admiral of the fleet and commander of the Pacific Fleet during World War II. Born far from the sea in Fredericksburg, Texas, on February 24, 1885, Chester William Nimitz graduated from the United States Naval Academy,

Admiral of the Fleet Chester W. Nimitz, commander of the U.S. Pacific Fleet in World War II, shown here in 1944. Although the defeat of Germany was the top Allied priority, Nimitz early on pursued an aggressive strategy vis-à-vis Japan. (Naval Historical Society)

Annapolis, in 1905. He then served with the U.S. Asiatic Fleet, steadily advancing in rank and position. Promoted to lieutenant in 1910, he assumed command of the submarine *Skipjack* in 1912. He then studied diesel engine construction in Europe and supervised construction of the U.S. Navy's first diesel ship engine.

On United States entry into World War I in April 1917, Lieutenant Commander Nimitz served as chief of staff to the commander of submarines in the Atlantic Fleet (1917–1919).

Following the war, Nimitz was appointed to the Navy Department staff in Washington, and in 1920 he transferred to Pearl Harbor, Hawaii, to over-

see construction of a new submarine base there. Over the next 20 years, he served in a wide variety of submarine billets as well as aboard battleships and destroyers. He also spent several tours in Washington, D.C., and helped establish the first Naval Reserve Officer Training Corps programs in American universities. He was promoted to rear admiral in 1938.

When Japan attacked Pearl Harbor in December 1941, Nimitz was chief of the Bureau of Navigation. On December 31, 1941, on the recommendation of Secretary of the Navy Frank Knox, President Franklin D. Roosevelt promoted Nimitz to full admiral and appointed him commander of the U.S. Pacific Fleet, replacing Admiral Husband E. Kimmel at Pearl Harbor. Although a single U.S. command in the Pacific would have been far more advantageous, General Douglas MacArthur would not agree to serve under a naval officer. As a result, two commands emerged. As commander in chief, Pacific Ocean Area, Nimitz directed all U.S. military forces in the Central Pacific and provided support to MacArthur and his Southwest Pacific forces.

Although the Allies made the war against Japan secondary to their Europe First strategy, Nimitz did not delay his plans to halt Japanese expansion, retake Japan's gains, and push the war to the Japanese homeland. Using information provided by American code breakers about Japanese plans, Nimitz halted the Japanese invasion of Port Moresby in the Battle of the Coral Sea in May 1942 and the Japanese effort to take Midway Island that June. The latter battle transferred the initiative of the Pacific War to the Americans. Nimitz and MacArthur cooperated in a series of island-hopping campaigns that progressed closer and closer to the Japanese mainland. Nimitz's forces took the Gilbert Islands in November 1943, the Marshall Islands in February 1944, and the Mariana Islands in August 1944. In October, he joined MacArthur's forces to retake the Philippines. Nimitz's accomplishments were recognized in December 1944 by his promotion to the newly established five-star rank of admiral of the fleet.

In early 1945, Nimitz directed the offensives against Guam, Iwo Jima, and Okinawa. His forces were preparing to invade Japan when the Japanese surrendered. On September 2, 1945, Nimitz signed the formal Japanese surrender aboard the battleship *Missouri* in Tokyo Bay.

Nimitz returned to Washington in October and assumed the post of chief of naval operations. For the next two years, he supervised the postwar demobilization of men and ships and provided input into the development of nuclear-powered submarines. Nimitz retired in December 1947. In the following years, he briefly served as adviser to the secretary of the navy and for two years he was the United Nations commissioner for Kashmir. Nimitz died on February 20, 1966, near San Francisco, California.

James H. Willbanks

References

Brink, Randall. *Nimitz: The Man and His Wars.* New York: Penguin, 2000.

Driskell, Frank A., and Dede W. Casad. *Chester W. Nimitz, Admiral of the Hills.* Austin, TX: Eakin Press, 1983.

Hoyt, Edwin P. *How They Won the War in the Pacific: Nimitz and His Admirals.* New York: Weybright and Talley, 1970.

Potter, Elmer B. *Nimitz.* Annapolis, MD: Naval Institute Press, 1976.

———. "Fleet Admiral Chester William Nimitz." Pp. 129–157. In *Men of War: Great Naval Leaders of World War II.* Edited by Stephen Howarth. New York: St. Martin's Press, 1992.

Patton, George Smith, Jr. (1885–1945)

U.S. Army general and commander of the Third Army in the European Theater of Operations. Born on November 11, 1885, in San Gabriel, California, George Smith Patton Jr. attended the Virginia Military Institute for a year before graduating from the United States Military Academy, West Point, in 1909. An accomplished horseman, he competed in the 1912 Stockholm Olympic Games. He also participated in the U.S. Army's 1916–1917 Punitive Expedition into Mexico.

When the United States entered World War I, Patton deployed to France as an aide to American Expeditionary Forces (AEF) commander General John J. Pershing, but he transferred to the Tank Corps and, as a temporary major, commanded the first U.S. Army tank school at Langres, France. He then commanded the 304th Tank Brigade as a temporary lieutenant colonel. Wounded in the Saint-Mihiel Offensive, he was promoted to temporary colonel and took part in the Meuse-Argonne Offensive.

After the war, Patton remained an ardent champion of tank warfare. He graduated from the Cavalry School in 1923, the Command and General Staff School in 1924, and the Army War College in 1932. Returning to armor, Patton was promoted to temporary brigadier general in October 1940 and to temporary major general in April 1941, when he took command of the newly formed 2nd Armored Division. Popularly known as "Old Blood and Guts" for his colorful speeches to inspire his men, Patton commanded I Corps and the Desert Training Center, where he prepared U.S. forces for the invasion of North Africa.

In November 1942, Patton commanded the Western Task Force in the

General George S. Patton commanded the U.S. Third Army in Europe. His drive across France in the summer of 1944 remains one of the most brilliant operations in U.S. military history. By the end of the war, his army had covered more ground and liberated more territory than any other Allied force. (Library of Congress)

landing at Casablanca, Morocco, part of Operation TORCH. Following the U.S. defeat in the Battle of the Kasserine Pass, in March 1943 he was promoted to lieutenant general and assumed command of II Corps. He quickly restored order and morale and took the offensive against the Axis forces.

In April, Patton received command of the Seventh Army for the invasion of Sicily in July 1943. He used a series of costly flanking maneuvers along the northern coast of the island to reach Messina ahead of the British Eighth Army on the eastern side. Patton, however, ran afoul of the press and his superiors when he struck two soldiers who were suffering from battle fatigue.

Relieved of his command, Patton was then used as a Trojan horse to disguise the location of the attack of Operation OVERLORD, the 1944 cross-Channel invasion of France. The Germans assumed that Patton would command any such invasion, but he actually remained in Britain in command of the fictional U.S. 1st Army Group, in a successful ruse to deceive the Germans into believing the invasion would occur in the Pas de Calais area. Simultaneously, he commanded and trained the U.S. Third Army, scheduled to land in France after the initial invasion had established the beachhead.

Third Army became operational on August 1. Following the breakout at Saint-Lô, Patton's forces poured through the gap and then turned west to clear the Brittany Peninsula. Third Army then swung back to the east toward Le Mans and Orleans. During the drive across France Patton was frustrated by the refusal of General Omar Bradley and supreme commander General Dwight D. Eisenhower to recognize the importance of sealing the Falaise-Argentan Gap. Patton's forces crossed the Meuse River in late August to confront German defenses at Metz, where the Germans held the Americans until December. During the German Ardennes Offensive (Battle of the Bulge), Patton executed a brilliant 90 degree turn and counterattack into the German southern flank, to relieve the hard-pressed American forces defending Bastogne.

By the end of January 1945, Patton began another offensive, piercing the Siegfried Line between Saarlautern and Saint Vith. On March 22, the Third Army crossed the Rhine River into Germany at Oppenheim. Patton continued his drive into Germany and eventually crossed into Czechoslovakia. By the end of the war, his men had covered more ground

(600 miles) and liberated more territory (nearly 82,000 square miles) than any other Allied force.

Promoted to temporary general, Patton became military governor of Bavaria. He soon found himself again in trouble for remarks in which he criticized the de-Nazification program and argued that the Soviet Union was the real enemy. Relieved of command of the Third Army, he assumed command of the Fifteenth Army, a headquarters that existed mostly on paper with the mission of writing the official U.S. Army history of the war. Patton suffered a broken neck in an automobile accident near Mannheim and died at Heidelberg, Germany, on December 21, 1945. Although he was not a wartime casualty, he was buried in the American Military Cemetery at Ham, Luxembourg.

T. Jason Soderstrum
and Spencer C. Tucker

References

Blumenson, Martin. *Patton: The Man behind the Legend, 1885–1945*. New York: William Morrow, 1985.

D'Este, Carlo. *Patton: A Genius for War*. New York: HarperCollins, 1995.

Hirshson, Stanley P. *General Patton: A Soldier's Life*. New York: HarperCollins, 2002.

Randolph, Asa Philip
(1889–1979)

U.S. labor and civil rights leader who worked to end racial discrimination in the defense industry during World War II. Born in Crescent City, Florida, on April 15, 1889, Asa Philip Randolph (officially known as A. Philip Randolph) was raised in Jacksonville, Florida. After graduating from the Cookman Institute in Jacksonville, he moved to Harlem, New York, where he continued his studies at the City College of New York. Following the U.S. entry into World War I in 1917, Randolph and a partner founded a magazine, *The Messenger*, a socialist-leaning periodical that demanded more positions in the war industry and armed forces for African Americans. He ran unsuccessfully for elective offices on the Socialist ticket in the 1920s.

In 1925, Randolph began organizing the Pullman porters in the railroad industry into the Brotherhood of Sleeping Car Porters and succeeded in gaining that union's admission into the American Federation of Labor (AFL), which was no small feat. Later, to protest the AFL's racially discriminatory policies, he withdrew the Brotherhood from the AFL and took it into the Congress of Industrial Organizations (CIO), the main rival of the AFL.

By the eve of the U.S. entry into World War II, Randolph had become the preeminent spokesperson for civil rights for African Americans. With the tremendous increase in defense contracts just prior to the U.S. involvement in World War II, Randolph protested racial discrimination in the defense industry's hiring practices. Indeed, many defense suppliers simply refused to hire blacks, no matter their experience or qualifications. In 1941, Randolph and two other civil rights proponents warned President Franklin D. Roosevelt that they were prepared to lead thousands of African Americans on a march to Washington, D.C., to protest discriminatory hiring practices. In response, the president issued Executive Order Number 8802 on June 25, 1941, which barred racial discrimination in the defense industry and created the Fair Employment Practices Committee (FEPC) to ensure compliance with the new law. Randolph then cancelled the proposed march.

Approximately 2 million African Americans obtained work in the war industries by war's end. There were some, however, who criticized Randolph for having caved in to Roosevelt too quickly, arguing that he should have held out for an end to racial segregation in the armed services. That did not occur until 1948. Nevertheless, Randolph had obtained a milestone concession, and it was unlikely given the situation that he could have forced an end to discrimination in the military.

Following World War II, Randolph founded the League for Nonviolent Civil Disobedience against Military Segregation. The organization successfully pressured President Harry S. Truman to issue Executive Order Number 9981, which formally ended segregation in the U.S. military. In 1950, Randolph and Roy Wilkins, head of the National Association for the Advancement of Colored People (NAACP), formed the Leadership Council on Civil Rights, which soon became one of the nation's most respected civil rights advocacy groups. It was involved in almost every major piece of civil rights legislation since 1957. Randolph spent the remainder of his life fighting against workplace discrimination and for civil rights, and was a director of the August 1963 March on Washington for Jobs and Freedom, during which civil rights leader Dr. Martin Luther King Jr. delivered his famous "I Have a Dream" speech. Randolph died in New York City on May 16, 1979.

Minoa Uffelman

References

Anderson, Jevis. *A. Philip Randolph: A Biographical Portrait.* New York: Harcourt Brace Jovanovich, 1973.

Pfeffer, Paula A. *A. Philip Randolph: Pioneer of the Civil Rights Movement.* Baton Rouge: Louisiana State University Press, 1990.

Ridgway, Matthew Bunker (1895–1993)

U.S. Army general and commander of the 82nd Airborne Division and the XVIII Airborne Corps. Born on March 3, 1895, in Fort Monroe, Virginia, Matthew Bunker Ridgway graduated from the United States Military Academy, West Point, in 1917 and was commissioned in the infantry. He was sent to a border post at Eagle Pass, Texas, and rose to captain.

Ridgway returned to West Point and served as an instructor there from 1918 to 1924. In 1925, he graduated from the Infantry School, Fort Benning, Georgia. He then held a variety of overseas assignments in China, Nicaragua, the Panama Canal Zone, and the Philippines. In 1932, he was promoted to major.

Ridgway graduated from the Command and General Staff School, Fort Leavenworth, Kansas, in 1935 and from the Army War College in 1937. Between 1939 and 1942, he was in the War Plans Division of the War Department's general staff. A protégé of army chief of staff General George C. Marshall, he was promoted to lieutenant colonel in July 1940, colonel in December 1941, and temporary brigadier general in January 1942. He was then assigned as assistant division commander of the 82nd Infantry Division assembling at Camp Claiborne, Louisiana, under Major General Omar N. Bradley. In June 1942, Ridgway assumed command of the 82nd, reorganizing it in August into an airborne division when he was promoted to temporary major general.

Ridgway commanded the 82nd Airborne in Sicily in July and August 1943 and in Italy from September to November 1943, during which time the unit captured Naples and fought in the drive to the Volturno River before redeploying to England to prepare for the June 1944

Normandy Invasion. He made his only combat jump with his division on D-Day, June 6, 1944, and he fought with it throughout the Normandy Campaign. In August 1944, he turned over command of the 82nd Airborne to Major General James Gavin and subsequently took command of the newly formed XVIII Airborne Corps, leading it in Operation MARKET-GARDEN, the Ardennes Offensive counterattack (Battle of the Bulge), and throughout the drive into Germany.

Promoted to lieutenant general in June 1945, Ridgway briefly commanded the Mediterranean Theater. From 1946 to 1948 he was U.S. representative to the United Nations (UN) Military Staff Committee, and from 1948 to 1949 he headed the Caribbean Defense Command. Appointed deputy chief of staff of the army for administration in August 1949, Ridgway took command of Eighth Army in Korea on the death of Lieutenant General Walton Walker. In Korea Ridgway halted the Chinese counteroffensive, restored the Eighth Army's morale, and returned to offensive operations. Ridgway subsequently succeeded General of the Army Douglas MacArthur as commander of United Nations Forces, in April 1951. In May 1952, he was promoted to full general and succeeded General of the Army Dwight D. Eisenhower as North Atlantic Treaty Organization (NATO) supreme Allied commander. In August 1953, he was appointed army chief of staff.

Declining to serve his full four-year term because of his disagreement with President Dwight D. Eisenhower's defense polices that placed heavy reliance on nuclear weapons, Ridgway retired in June 1955. He then wrote his memoirs and served on various corporate boards.

He died in Fox Chapel, Pennsylvania, on July 26, 1993.

Guy A. Lofaro

References

Blair, Clay. *Ridgway's Paratroopers: The American Airborne in World War II.* New York: Simon and Schuster, 1985.

Ridgway, Matthew B. *Soldier: The Memoirs of Matthew B. Ridgway, as Told to Harold H. Martin.* New York: Harper, 1996.

Soffer, Jonathan N. *General Matthew B. Ridgway: From Progressivism to Reaganism, 1895–1993.* Westport, CT: Praeger, 1998.

Roosevelt, Franklin Delano (1882–1945)

U.S. political leader and president (1933–1945). Born at the family Hyde Park estate in Dutchess County, New York, on January 30, 1882, Franklin Roosevelt was educated at home until age 14. He then attended Groton Preparatory School, Harvard University, and Columbia University Law School. In 1905, Roosevelt married his distant cousin Eleanor Roosevelt, President Theodore Roosevelt's niece.

Upon passing the bar examination, Roosevelt joined the law firm of Carter, Ledyard and Milburn. Elected to the New York Senate in 1910, he advocated Progressive reform. As assistant secretary of the navy from 1913 to 1920, he proved a highly effective administrator and worked to ready the navy for participation on the Allied side in World War I, which he advocated.

In 1920, Roosevelt ran unsuccessfully for vice president of the United States on the Democratic Party on the ticket headed by James M. Cox. Stricken with polio in 1921, he was permanently dis-

Franklin D. Roosevelt was the nation's longest serving president (1932–1945). He directed national affairs during two of the greatest crises in American history: the Great Depression and World War II. (Library of Congress)

abled but retained his intense interest in politics. As governor of New York from 1929 to 1933, he worked effectively to alleviate suffering caused by the Great Depression, which began in 1929.

Winning election to the presidency in November 1932 over incumbent Herbert Hoover, Roosevelt rallied the American people and promised a "New Deal." His early legislative successes included banking reform, the Agricultural Adjustment Act (AAA), and the National Industrial Recovery Act (NIRA). The National Recovery Administration (NRA) set minimum wages and limited hours for employees. The Civilian Conservation Corps (CCC) employed thousands of men to replant forests and work on flood control projects. Roosevelt also estab-

lished the Securities and Exchange Commission (SEC) to oversee stock trading. Later, the Works Progress Administration (WPA) extended employment to millions of workers in construction projects. Social Security legislation provided for the aged and disabled. The American people reelected him in 1936, 1940, and 1944, making Roosevelt the only U.S. president elected to four terms.

With the beginning of World War II in Europe in September 1939, Roosevelt increasingly turned to foreign affairs and military preparedness. He gradually moved the United States from isolation, securing amendments in the Neutrality Act that allowed the Allies to purchase arms in the United States on a cash-and-carry basis. Following the defeat of France in June 1940, he concluded an agreement with Britain for the delivery to that country of 50 World War I–vintage destroyers in return for granting the United States rights to bases in British territory in the Western Hemisphere in September. He initiated a major rearmament program and secured passage of the Selective Service Act, the first peacetime draft in the nation's history. Roosevelt ordered U.S. destroyers to escort the North Atlantic convoys bound for Britain as far as Iceland in the spring of 1941. On his urging, in March 1941, Congress passed the Lend-Lease Act that extended U.S. aid to countries fighting the Axis.

Roosevelt pressed Japan to withdraw from China, and when Japanese troops occupied southern Indochina in spring 1941 he embargoed scrap metal and oil to Japan. Roosevelt also ordered the Pacific Fleet to move its headquarters from San Diego to Honolulu, Hawaii, in order to increase pressure on Japan, but the embargo led that nation's leaders to opt for war with the United States and ordered an attack on the Pacific Fleet at Pearl Harbor on December 7, 1941.

Roosevelt then guided the United States through the war. During the course of the conflict, the United States not only fielded a navy larger than all the other navies of the world combined, but the largest air force and the most mobile, most heavily mechanized, and best-armed army in world history. It also provided the machines of war, raw materials, and food that enabled other nations to continue fighting the Axis. In these circumstances, full economic recovery occurred.

Roosevelt met frequently with British prime minister Winston Churchill and several times with Soviet dictator Joseph Stalin in an effort to secure a stable postwar world. Roosevelt gambled that he could convince Stalin that he had nothing to fear from the United States, and that Britain, the Soviet Union, China, and the United States could work together to secure a peaceful postwar world. Although criticized for making unnecessary concessions to the Soviet Union at the Yalta Conference of February 4–11, 1945, Roosevelt really had little choice, as the Red Army already occupied much of Eastern Europe and the United States military wished to induce the Soviet Union to enter the war against Japan.

By early 1945, Roosevelt was ill, and that spring he sought rest at his summer home in Warm Springs, Georgia. He died there of a massive cerebral hemorrhage on April 12, 1945. A highly effective communicator and one of the best-loved presidents in U.S. history, Roosevelt led the nation through two of its greatest trials, the Great Depression and World War II.

Spencer C. Tucker

References

Freidel, Frank. *Roosevelt: A Rendezvous with Destiny.* New York: Little, Brown and Co. 1990.

Hanby, Alonzo L. *For the Survival of Democracy: Franklin Roosevelt and the World Crisis of the 1930s.* New York: Simon and Schuster, 2004.

Larrabee, Eric. *Commander in Chief: Franklin Delano Roosevelt: His Lieutenants and Their War.* New York: Simon and Schuster, 1987.

Roosevelt, Theodore, Jr. (1887–1944)

U.S. Army general who was the only general officer to land on Utah Beach during the June 1944 Normandy Invasion. Born in Oyster Bay, New York, on September 13, 1887, Theodore Roosevelt Jr. was the son of President Theodore Roosevelt. He graduated from Harvard University in 1908 and worked with his father in the preparedness campaign prior to World War I. In that conflict, following U.S. entry into the war he was wounded in action and received the Distinguished Service Cross while serving as a major in the 26th Infantry Regiment of the 1st Division during the Saint-Mihiel Offensive.

Following the war, Roosevelt transferred to the reserves as a colonel. He was one of the founders of the American Legion and was elected to the New York legislature. Roosevelt was assistant secretary of the navy from 1921, a post his father had once held, and he ran unsuccessfully for governor of New York State in 1924. That same year, he became the chairman of American Express. Roosevelt served as governor of Puerto Rico from 1929 to 1932 and governor-general of the Philippines from 1932 to 1933. He became an editor at Doubleday, Doran and Company in 1935 and wrote or co-authored eight books.

Roosevelt returned to active duty in April 1941, this time as commander of the 26th Infantry Regiment of the 1st Infantry Division. Following United States entry into the war, he served in North Africa and in Sicily, becoming assistant division commander of the 1st Infantry Division, the "Big Red One," under Major General Terry de la Mesa Allen. In Sicily, II Corps commander Major General Omar Bradley relieved both Allen and Roosevelt due to the division's sluggish advance across central Sicily and the undisciplined conduct of many of its soldiers.

Roosevelt then served as a liaison officer for the U.S. Fifth Army. In 1944, he was assigned as assistant division commander of the 4th Infantry Division for the Normandy landings. On several occasions, he requested permission to go ashore with the first assault wave, but Major General Raymond O. Barton, the division commander, repeatedly refused because Roosevelt, who had a severe case of arthritis, limped and walked with a cane. Roosevelt finally prevailed when he threatened to put his request in writing and send it up the chain of command.

Not only was Roosevelt the only general officer to land on Utah Beach on D-Day (June 6, 1944), he was also the only general officer on any beach to land in the first wave. At age 57, he was one of the oldest soldiers there. His son Quentin II also landed on one of the beaches that day, making them the only father and son pair to have landed on that same day. Drifting tides caused the Utah Beach assault force to land in the wrong place, however, which proved fortunate for the Americans because the spot where they did land was far less well defended. Once on the beach, Roosevelt made the tactically correct decision not to try to shift to the planned landing point but rather to direct the follow-on waves to the new landing points. He is said to have stated, "We'll start the war from right here."

Roosevelt repeatedly led small groups across the beach and established them inland, and he was under constant enemy fire the entire day. General Bradley later said that Roosevelt's conduct on Utah Beach was the bravest act he had seen in more than 40 years of military service. Roosevelt died in Roosevelt's sleep of a heart attack on July 12, 1944, most probably brought on in no small measure by the combat stress of D-Day. At the time, he had been selected for command of the 90th Infantry Division and promotion to major general.

Roosevelt was awarded the Medal of Honor posthumously and was later buried at the World War II American Cemetery at Colleville-sur-Mer, Normandy. The remains of his younger brother, Quentin, who had been killed in World War I and buried at the Château-Thierry Cemetery, were moved to Normandy and interred next to him. With the award of the Medal of Honor to Theodore Roosevelt Sr. in January 2001 for his own actions in Cuba in 1898, the Roosevelts became only the second father and son pair to be Medal of Honor recipients, after Arthur and Douglas MacArthur.

David T. Zabecki

References

Ambrose, Stephen. *D-Day, June 6, 1944: The Climactic Battle of World War II.* New York: Simon and Schuster, 1994.

Jeffers, H. Paul. *Theodore Roosevelt, Jr.: The Life of a War Hero.* Novato, CA: Presidio Press, 2002.

Renehan, Edward J. *The Lion's Pride: Theodore Roosevelt and His Family in Peace and War.* New York: Oxford University Press, 1998.

Smith, Holland McTyeire (1882–1967)

U.S. Marine Corps general. Born in Hatchachubbee, Alabama, on April 20, 1882, Holland Smith graduated from the Alabama Polytechnic Institute (Auburn University) in 1901 and then earned a law degree at the University of Alabama in 1903. More interested in military service than law, Smith received a commission as a 2nd lieutenant in the Marine Corps in 1905.

During the next decade, Smith held a variety of land and sea assignments. He also earned the nickname "Howlin' Mad" for his frequent explosions of temper. In Santo Domingo in 1916, Smith undertook experiments with amphibious landings. Following U.S. entry into World War I, Smith fought in France with the 5th Marine Regiment and then served as adjutant to the 4th Marine Brigade. Following postwar occupation duty in Germany, he returned to the United States in 1919.

Smith graduated from the Naval War College in 1921. An enthusiastic advocate and pioneer of amphibious warfare, in 1937 Colonel Smith became director of operations and training at Marine Corps Headquarters in Washington, D.C., where he worked to develop new tactics, landing craft, and amphibious tractors. Smith believed that amphibious warfare would be an essential element of any U.S. Pacific military strategy. Smith especially emphasized the development of efficient amphibian landing craft, and he worked closely with Andrew J. Higgins on new designs. In September 1939, Smith took command of the 1st Marine Brigade. He was promoted to major general and deployed his brigade to Cuba to practice amphibious landing techniques. Doubled in size, his brigade became the 1st Marine Division. In June 1941, Smith assumed command of what became the Amphibious Force, Atlantic Fleet.

Smith then headed marine amphibious training on the west coast of the United States until June 1943, when he assumed command of the joint army-marine V Amphibious Corps in the Central Pacific. Smith's troops executed his amphibious tactics to seize Japanese-held islands. In November 1943, Smith's forces took the Gilbert Island atolls of Makin and Tarawa. Based on lessons learned at Tarawa, Smith urged the deployment of additional amphibious tractors and the development of more effective landing-support techniques.

In 1944, Smith's forces seized the Marshall Islands and the Mariana Islands, capturing Kwajalein and Eniwetok in the Marshalls in January and Saipan, Tinian, and Guam between June and August. On Saipan, however, Smith relieved U.S. Army 27th Infantry Division commander Major General Ralph K. Smith for failure to operate with sufficient aggressiveness. This action led to sharp marine-army recriminations but did not block Holland Smith's promotion to lieutenant general that August, when he took command of the new Fleet Marine Force, Pacific. In 1945, Smith directed the assault on Iwo Jima.

In July 1945, Smith assumed command of the Marine Training and Replacement Command at Camp Pendleton, California. Smith retired from the marines in July 1946 with promotion to full general, only the third marine in history to reach that rank. He died in San Diego, California, on January 12, 1967.

Elizabeth D. Schafer
and Spencer C. Tucker

References

Cooper, Norman V. *A Fighting General: The Biography of General Holland M.*

"Howlin' Mad" Smith. Quantico, VA: Marine Corps Association, 1987.

Gailey, Harry A. *Howlin' Mad vs. the Army: Conflict in Command, Saipan 1944.* Novato, CA: Presidio, 1986.

Smith, Holland M. *The Development of Amphibious Tactics in the U.S. Navy.* Washington, DC: History and Museums Division, Headquarters, U.S. Marine Corps, 1992.

Smith, Holland M., and Perry Finch. *Coral and Brass.* New York: Charles Scribner's Sons, 1949.

Smith, Walter Bedell
(1895–1961)

U.S. Army general. Born in Indianapolis, Indiana, on October 5, 1895, Walter Bedell Smith was nicknamed "Beetle" as a youth. He joined the Indiana National Guard in 1910 and briefly attended Butler University. He then earned a commission in the National Guard and served with the 39th Infantry in France during World War I. He was wounded in the Aisne-Marne Offensive in August 1918 and sent home.

Smith remained in the U.S. Army after the war and proved to be a capable administrator. Assignments included the Bureau of Military Intelligence, the Bureau of the Budget, and the Federal Liquidation Board. He also served as a student or instructor at the Infantry School at Fort Benning, Georgia; the Command and General Staff School at Fort Leavenworth, Kansas; and the Army War College. His abilities were noted by General George C. Marshall, who became army chief of staff in September 1939. The following month, Marshall named Smith assistant secretary of the general staff and, in August 1941, secretary of the general staff.

After the United States entered World War II in December 1941, Smith became the U.S. secretary to the Combined Chiefs of Staff in February 1942. Following heavy lobbying from European theater commander Lieutenant General Dwight D. Eisenhower, Marshall reluctantly ordered Smith to Europe in September 1942 to assume his most recognizable assignment as Eisenhower's chief of staff. Smith had Eisenhower's complete trust to handle staff planning and administration, thus allowing his commander to spend more time on operational matters. In a post far less glamorous than combat command, Smith often made decisions beyond the scope of staff direction, often issuing orders to field commanders in Eisenhower's name.

Eisenhower rejected any suggestion that Smith should be assigned anywhere but as his chief of staff. Entrusted by Eisenhower with the job of negotiating with Italian emissaries, Smith, through a combination of bluster and intimidation, accepted the Italian surrender on September 3, 1943. As planning for Operation OVERLORD began in earnest, Smith became chief of staff, Supreme Headquarters, Allied Expeditionary Forces. His staff direction established the core of the Operation OVERLORD plan, taking over and building on the solid base already developed by British major general Frederick Morgan. On June 5, 1944, when Eisenhower turned to Smith for advice on whether he should launch the Normandy landings, Smith urged that the attack proceed, calling it, "the best possible gamble." When Germany collapsed, Eisenhower authorized Smith to accept the German surrender at Rheims on May 7, 1945.

In January 1946, Smith returned to Washington to be chief of the Operations and Planning Division of the Joint Chiefs of Staff. In March, President Harry S. Truman appointed him ambassador to the Soviet Union, where he remained until 1949. Smith was convinced that the United States should take a strong stand against Soviet expansionist policies and that the Soviet Union would back down if confronted by American power. From 1950 to 1953, Smith served as the second director of the Central Intelligence Agency (CIA). He was advanced to full general in July 1951. Smith also served as undersecretary of state in the Eisenhower administration.

Smith retired from government service in October 1954. He was embittered that he never received either the fifth star or assignment as chief of staff of the army, which he believed he deserved. He then entered private business. Smith died in Washington, D.C., on August 9, 1961.

Thomas D. Veve

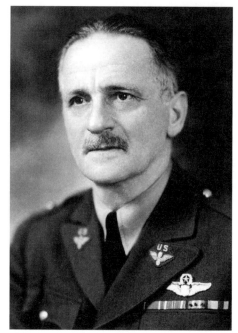

U.S. Army Air Forces general Carl A. Spaatz commanded U.S. Strategic Air Forces in Europe during World War II and directed the air campaign against Germany. In July 1945 he assumed the same position in the Pacific Theater. After the war he was the last commander of the Army Air Forces, and he was the first chief of staff of the U.S. Air Force following its creation in 1947. (Library of Congress)

References

Crosswell, D. K. R. *The Chief of Staff: The Military Career of General Walter Bedell Smith*. New York: Greenwood Press, 1991.

Montague, Ludwell Lee. *General Walter Bedell Smith as Director of Central Intelligence, October 1950–February 1953*. University Park: Pennsylvania State University Press, 1992.

Smith, Walter Bedell. *My Three Years in Moscow*. Philadelphia: Lippincott, 1949.

Spaatz, Carl Andrew (1891–1974)

General in the U.S. Army Air Forces and later the U.S. Air Force. Born on June 28, 1891, in Boyertown, Pennsylvania, Carl Andrew Spaatz (originally Spatz; he added the "a" in 1937) graduated from the United States Military Academy, West Point, in June 1914 and began his military career as an infantry 2nd lieutenant at Schofield Barracks, Hawaii. In October 1915, he was detailed to the Aviation School at San Diego, California, where he received his wings in May 1916. In June, he joined the 3rd Aero Squadron in the U.S. Punitive Expedition into Mexico.

Following U.S. entry into World War I, Captain Spaatz served in France, first as commander of the 31st Aero Squadron and then as an instructor at the American Aviation School. In September 1918, he joined the 13th Squadron, 2nd Pursuit Group, and was credited with downing three German planes.

Following the war, Major Spaatz commanded the 1st Pursuit Group (1921–1924), graduated from the Air Corps Tactical School in June 1925, and spent three years in the Office of the Chief of the Air Corps (OCAC), in Washington, D.C. During January 1–7, 1929, Spaatz commanded an army aircraft, the famous *Question Mark*, in a record endurance flight of nearly 151 hours aloft and established the efficacy of air-to-air refueling. From 1929 to 1935, he commanded the 7th Bombardment Group and 1st Bombardment Wing in California, subsequently returning to the OCAC. In June 1936, he graduated from the Command and General Staff School at Fort Leavenworth, Kansas, and was promoted to lieutenant colonel. He then served at Langley Field, Virginia, and had a third tour with the OCAC. In 1940, during the Battle of Britain, Spaatz spent several weeks in Britain as a military observer. By July 1941, he had risen to the rank of temporary brigadier general, serving as chief of the air staff for the newly established U.S. Army Air Forces (AAF).

Following U.S. entry into World War II, Major General Spaatz deployed to England in July 1942 to command the U.S. Eighth Air Force. That December, Spaatz transferred to command the Twelfth Air Force in North Africa. Promoted to lieutenant general in March 1943, he assumed command of Allied Northwest Africa Air Forces. During the last six months of 1943, Spaatz served as deputy commander of the Mediterranean Allied Air Forces.

Spaatz returned to England in January 1944 to command U.S. Strategic Air Forces in Europe, consisting of the Eighth Air Force in Britain and the Fifteenth Air Force in Italy. These forces proved vital in preparation for, and then support of, the Allies' June 1944 Normandy Invasion.

Promoted to temporary general in March 1945, Spaatz returned to AAF headquarters in June only to be assigned to command U.S. Strategic Air Forces, Pacific, in July. He supervised the final air campaign against Japan. Spaatz remained certain of the efficacy of the strategic bombing of industrial and economic targets, and he believed that still heavier bombing might have obviated the need for the Normandy Invasion. In October 1945, he recommended that atomic weapons should form the backbone of U.S. defense strategy.

In late 1945, President Harry S. Truman nominated Spaatz for the permanent rank of major general, and in February 1946, he made Spaatz commander of the AAF, a post held previously by General of the Army Henry H. "Hap" Arnold. Spaatz played a leading role in the creation of the separate U.S. Air Force, serving as the last commander of the AAF and first chief of staff of the U.S. Air Force in September 1947. Spaatz retired in June 1948. Later, he served as the head of the Civil Air Patrol and wrote a column for *Newsweek* magazine. Spaatz died in Washington, D.C., on July 14, 1974.

William Head

References

Davis, Richard G. *Carl A. Spaatz and the Air War in Europe, 1940–1945.* Washington, DC: Office of Air Force History, 1993.

Mets, David R. *Master of Air Power, General Carl A. Spaatz.* Novato, CA: Presidio Press, 1988.

Spruance, Raymond Ames (1886–1969)

U.S. Navy admiral. Born on July 3, 1886, in Baltimore, Maryland, Raymond Ames

Spruance graduated from the United States Naval Academy, Annapolis, in September 1906. His early assignments included service in the battleship *Minnesota* during the 1907–1909 around-the-world cruise of the Great White Fleet. His first command was the destroyer *Bainbridge* in 1913. During World War I, Spruance rose to the rank of commander and commanded a troop ship. He then commanded destroyers, attended the Naval War College, served in the Office of Naval Intelligence, taught at the Naval War College, and commanded the battleship *Mississippi*.

Spruance was promoted to captain in 1932 and to rear admiral in 1939. In July 1941, he took command of Cruiser Division 5 at Pearl Harbor, Hawaii. As surface screen commander for Vice Admiral William F. Halsey's carriers, he participated in raids on the Gilberts, Marshalls, Wake, and Marcus islands, and in the launch of the Doolittle Raid on Tokyo in April 1942. When Halsey was confined to the hospital with a severe skin allergy, Pacific Fleet commander Admiral Chester Nimitz, on Halsey's recommendation, appointed Spruance to replace him as Task Force 16 commander. Spruance brilliantly handled the air and naval assets available to him and his forces won the Battle of Midway, which is considered the turning point in the Pacific War. Nimitz then named Spruance his chief of staff.

In May 1943, Spruance was promoted to vice admiral and assigned as deputy commander of the Pacific Fleet. In August, he took command of the Pacific Ocean Area, later designated the Fifth Fleet. Promoted to admiral in February 1944, he led campaigns against Japanese naval forces and island strongholds from the Gilberts and Marshalls through the Battle of the Philippine Sea and the invasions of Iwo Jima and Okinawa.

Spruance took command of the Pacific Fleet from Nimitz in November 1945. Although he was recommended for promotion to fleet admiral on multiple occasions, the promotion repeatedly was blocked by Congressman Carl Vinson, who was a staunch supporter of Admiral William Halsey. When the fifth star finally went to Halsey, Congress passed an unprecedented act that directed the navy to retain Spruance on full admiral's pay for the remainder of his life, the same recognition accorded to the five-star generals and admirals in 1949.

In February 1946, Spruance became the president of the Naval War College. He retired from active duty in July 1948, and later served as ambassador to the Philippines during 1952–1955. Spruance died on December 13, 1969, in Pebble Beach, California. The Spruance-class of destroyers is named for him.

William Head

References

Buell, Thomas B. *The Quiet Warrior: A Biography of Admiral Raymond Spruance.* Boston: Little, Brown, 1974.

Forrestel, Emmet P. *Admiral Raymond A. Spruance, USN: A Study in Command.* Washington, DC: U.S. Government Printing Office, 1966.

Stilwell, Joseph Warren (1883–1946)

U.S. Army general. Born on March 19, 1883, near Palatka, Florida, Joseph Stilwell was commissioned a 2nd lieutenant of infantry on graduation from the United States Military Academy in 1904. Promoted to temporary major in August

1917, Stilwell served with British and French forces before his assignment to the U.S. Army IV Corps of the American Expeditionary Forces in France during World War I. Following the war, he studied Chinese and spent several years in China, serving with American units stationed there and as military attaché to China and Siam (Thailand). He was promoted to colonel in August 1935. Stilwell earned his nickname "Vinegar Joe" as a result of his direct and critical manner while an instructor at the Infantry School at Fort Benning, Georgia. Promoted to temporary major general in October 1940, by July 1941 Stilwell was commanding III Corps at Monterey, California.

In February 1942, Stilwell, promoted to temporary lieutenant general, received command of all U.S. Army forces in the China-Burma-India Theater, while simultaneously assigned as chief of staff to Kuomintang (KMT, Nationalist) Chinese leader Generalissimo Chiang Kaishek (Jiang Jieshi). Charged with coordinating the efforts of Britain, China, and the United States against Japan, Stilwell was also responsible for preparing China for the planned Allied invasion of the Japanese home islands. When the Japanese captured Burma in the spring of 1942, Stilwell personally led an Allied column on a 140-mile march through the Burmese jungle to avoid capture. To prevent the collapse of China, Stilwell continued to resupply Chiang's forces, but the loss of the Burma Road forced the Americans to fly the needed matériel over the Himalayas, known as "the Hump."

Stilwell's belief that China's best hope for recapturing its territory from the Japanese was through the employment of Western-trained and -equipped Chinese Army forces brought him into direct conflict with both Chiang and Major General Claire Chennault, former commander of the American Volunteer Group (Flying Tigers). As commander of the China Air Task Force and later the Fourteenth Air Force and a firm proponent of airpower, Chennault believed his air force capable of defeating the Japanese without the assistance of significant ground forces; he continually argued that he should receive the bulk of supplies coming over the Himalayas. Chiang, worried that any forces used against the Japanese would not be available for his anticipated postwar conflict with the Chinese Communists, was more than willing to support Chennault's position. Throughout 1943 and 1944, tensions among Stilwell, Chennault, and Chiang mounted. Despite the demonstration of the potential of Chinese forces against the Japanese and the gains in Burma, demonstrated by the capture of Myitkyina in August 1944, Stilwell was unable to convince Chiang to reform his army. When President Franklin D. Roosevelt urged Chiang to place Stilwell (who had been promoted to temporary general in August 1944) in command of all Chinese forces, Chiang refused and then demanded Stilwell's relief. Unwilling to alienate Chiang, Roosevelt ordered Stilwell's return. On October 18, 1944, Lieutenant General Daniel Sultan replaced him.

Following his relief, Stilwell received command of the Tenth Army, a command slated for the planned invasion of Japan. With Japan's surrender and the inactivation of the Tenth Army, Stilwell returned to the United States and took command of the Sixth Army. Suffering from advanced stomach cancer, Stilwell died at the Presidio in San Francisco, California, on October 12, 1946.

David M. Toczek

References

Prefer, Nathan. *Vinegar Joe's War: Stilwell's Campaigns for Burma.* Novato, CA: Presidio Press, 2000.

Stilwell, Joseph. *Stilwell's Personal File: China, Burma, India, 1942–1944.* Edited by Riley Sunderland and Charles F. Romanus. Wilmington, DE: Scholarly Resources, 1976.

Tuchman, Barbara. *Stilwell and the American Experience in China, 1911–1945.* New York: Macmillan, 1971.

Stimson, Henry Lewis (1867–1950)

U.S. secretary of war (1911–1913, 1940–1945). Henry Lewis Stimson was born in New York City on September 21, 1867, into a family whose ancestry dated back to the 17th-century Puritans and whose long tradition of service he himself would embody. He was educated at Phillips Andover Academy, Yale University, and Harvard Law School. In 1891, he entered the law firm of Root and Clarke. Its leading partner, Elihu Root, a future secretary of war and secretary of state, became one of Stimson's two lifelong role models, the other being future president Theodore Roosevelt.

Like Roosevelt, Stimson found public service more satisfying than the pursuit of a career in the law, and he soon became active in New York Republican Party politics. Appointed secretary of war by President William H. Taft in 1911, Stimson followed in Root's footsteps in attempting to modernize the army and improve troop training and the efficiency of the general staff, although congressional opposition blocked his contemplated consolidation and rationalization of army posts around the country. He resigned his post in 1913 when Democratic president Woodrow Wilson succeeded Taft.

When World War I began in Europe in 1914, the staunchly interventionist and pro-Allied Stimson campaigned ardently for "preparedness" in the form of massive increases in American military budgets in anticipation of war with Germany. After Congress declared war on Germany in April 1917, Stimson volunteered, serving in France as a lieutenant colonel of artillery. He returned from the war convinced that the United States must assume a far greater international role.

As governor-general of the Philippines in 1928, Stimson ruled in the spirit of benevolent paternalism. Appointed secretary of state in 1929 by President Herbert C. Hoover, he played a prominent role in negotiating the London Naval Treaty of 1930. He attempted to strengthen the League of Nations by protesting firmly against Japan's establishment in 1931 of the puppet state of Manchukuo, instituting the U.S. policy of nonrecognition that endured throughout the 1930s. He left office in 1933 upon the advent of the Franklin D. Roosevelt administration.

In the later 1930s, Stimson was among the strongest advocates of firm American opposition to the fascist states' demands for territory and international influence. When World War II began in 1939, Stimson, a convinced believer in an Anglo-American alliance, outspokenly demanded extensive American assistance to the Allies and a massive U.S. rearmament effort.

Seeking bipartisan support for his foreign policies, in June 1940 the Democratic president Franklin D. Roosevelt recruited Stimson as secretary of war, a position Stimson held throughout the conflict. He quickly attracted an able

Henry L. Stimson (right), secretary of war, and George C. Marshall, chief of staff, confer over a map in the War Department. Stimson served in the cabinets of two Republican and two Democratic presidents. As secretary of war under Franklin D. Roosevelt and Harry S. Truman from 1940 to 1945, he recommended the use of the atomic bomb against Japan. (Library of Congress)

group of younger lawyers and business-men, including Robert A. Lovett, Robert P. Patterson, and John J. McCloy. Along with army chief of staff General George C. Marshall, they not only built and oversaw the massive manpower recruit-ment and industrial mobilization pro-grams the war effort demanded but also carried forward the forceful internation-alist tradition their revered chief embod-ied. Stimson directed the development of atomic weapons in the top-secret Manhattan Project, and in April 1945 he informed new president Harry S. Tru-man of the bomb's existence. In summer 1945, Stimson suggested that the Allies publicly warn the Japanese government that, unless Japan surrendered, it faced attack by unspecified but devastating new weaponry. This advice led the United States, Britain, and the Soviet Union to issue the July 1945 Potsdam Declaration to this effect. Shortly after-ward, Stimson argued to Truman that in the interests of bringing this new scien-tific discovery under international con-trol, the Allies should—with appropriate safeguards—share the secrets of nuclear power with the Soviet Union.

After retiring in 1945, Stimson endorsed a greatly enhanced American international role. He died at Huntington, New York, on October 20, 1950.

Priscilla Roberts

References

Hodgson, Godfrey. *The Colonel: The Life and Wars of Henry Stimson, 1867–1950.* New York: Alfred A. Knopf, 1990.

Isaacson, Walter, and Evan Thomas. *The Wise Men: Six Friends and the World They Made.* New York: Simon and Schuster, 1986.

Schmitz, David F. *Henry L. Stimson: The First Wise Man.* Wilmington, DE: Scholarly Resources, 2000.

Stimson, Henry L., and McGeorge Bundy. *On Active Service in Peace and War.* New York: Harper and Brothers, 1948.

Taylor, Maxwell Davenport (1901–1987)

U.S. Army general. Born in Keytesville, Missouri, on August 26, 1901, Maxwell Davenport Taylor graduated fourth in his class from the United States Military Academy, West Point, in 1922 and was commissioned in the engineers. He attended the Engineer School, Fort Belvoir, Virginia, before being transferred to the field artillery. A talented linguist, he taught French and Spanish for five years at West Point, graduated from the Command and General Staff School, Fort Leavenworth, Kansas, in 1935, and then was an assistant military attaché in Japan.

In 1937, Taylor was assigned to Colonel Joseph W. Stilwell's staff. Following graduation from the Army War College in 1940, he was appointed to the staff of army chief of staff General George C. Marshall and promoted to lieutenant colonel. In July 1942, he became chief of staff of the 82nd Airborne Division as a colonel, and in December, he was promoted to brigadier general as the divisional artillery commander.

Taylor joined the division in Sicily after the Allied invasion, and on September 7, 1943, he volunteered for a secret mission behind enemy lines, going to Rome to determine if an airborne drop there was feasible. Meeting with Italian officials, he determined that the Germans had quickly secured both Rome and the facilities that would have been necessary for such an operation to succeed. On his recommendation, the mission was scrapped just as the first troop-laden aircraft became airborne. Taylor was then senior representative on the commission that convinced the new Italian government to declare war on Germany.

Taylor returned to the 82nd Airborne, and in March 1944 in the United Kingdom, he took command of the 101st Airborne Division (the Screaming Eagles). Promoted to major general in the same month, he jumped with the division behind Utah Beach during the June 1944 Normandy Invasion. After rotating back to Britain following more than a month of combat, Taylor and his division next participated in Operation MARKET-GARDEN. On September 17, the division seized Vechel, captured and held the Zon Bridge, and then took Saint Oedenrode and Eindhoven. Taylor was subsequently wounded and was out of action for two weeks. He was in Washington on temporary assignment when the Battle of the Ardennes (Battle of the Bulge) began, and thus Brigadier General Anthony McAuliffe commanded the 101st Airborne when it was sent to defend Bastogne. Taylor rejoined his division on December 25 and fought with it in the remainder of the battle. The division then helped mop up pockets of resistance in the Ruhr, before resuming the advance east. At the end of the war in Europe, the 101st Airborne helped seize Berchtesgaden.

In September 1945, Taylor became superintendent of West Point, where he initiated various curriculum changes.

Between 1949 and 1951, he headed the Berlin Command. In 1951, he was promoted to lieutenant general and became U.S. Army deputy chief of staff for operations and training. In February 1953, Taylor took command of Eighth Army in Korea as a full general, at a time when an armistice was imminent. He was then commanding general, Army Forces Far East, in 1954 and commander in chief, Far East Command, in 1955.

Taylor was the army chief of staff between 1955 and 1959. He differed sharply with President Dwight D. Eisenhower's strategy of "massive retaliation," advocating instead greater emphasis on conventional forces and the ability to fight limited wars, which became known as "flexible response." Retiring in 1959, Taylor expressed his views publicly in his book *The Uncertain Trumpet*, which caught the attention of John F. Kennedy. In 1960, Taylor became president of the Lincoln Center for the Performing Arts.

President Kennedy brought Taylor out of retirement to serve as his military adviser during 1961 and 1962; thereafter, he was appointed chairman of the Joint Chiefs of Staff, serving in that post from 1962 to 1964. Taylor opposed the commitment of U.S. ground troops to Vietnam but urged an escalation of the war through the bombing of North Vietnam. During 1964 and 1965, he was ambassador to the Republic of Vietnam (South Vietnam). For the remainder of his life, he defended U.S. policies in Vietnam and blamed his country's defeat on the media. Taylor was president of the Institute for Defense Analysis between 1966 and 1969 and president of the Foreign Intelligence Advisory Board from 1965 to 1970. He died in Washington, D.C., on April 19, 1987.

Uzal W. Ent and Spencer C. Tucker

References

Blair, Clay. *Ridgway's Paratroopers: The American Airborne in World War II*. Garden City, NY: Dial Press, 1985.

Taylor, John M. *General Maxwell Taylor: The Sword and the Pen*. New York: Doubleday, 1989.

Taylor, Maxwell D. *The Uncertain Trumpet*. New York: Harper, 1960.

Truman, Harry S. (1884–1972)

U.S. political leader and president (1945–1953). Born in Lamar, Missouri, on May 8, 1884, Harry S. Truman grew up on the family farm in Grandview. Truman never formally attended college, but he read for the bar at night at the Kansas City School of Law. He enlisted in the National Guard as a young man and served in combat in France during World War I as a field artillery battery commander. Following the war, he transferred to the Organized Reserve Corps and reached the rank of full colonel in June 1932. He retained his reserve commission until he entered the White House in 1945.

Truman entered politics in the 1920s and was elected a judge in the court of Jackson County, Missouri. He served in that post from 1926 to 1934, when he was elected to the U.S. Senate from Missouri. He was reelected to the Senate in 1940, but he remained relatively obscure until his service as chairman of the Committee to Investigate the National Defense Program, when he helped eliminate millions of dollars of waste in defense contracting.

President Franklin D. Roosevelt selected Truman as his running mate in 1944, and Truman was sworn in as vice president in January 1945. Roosevelt did not share with Truman his thinking on many significant war-related issues, and Truman was thus poorly prepared to

Harry S. Truman became president of the United States on April 12, 1945, following the death of Franklin Roosevelt. As president, Truman oversaw the end of World War II and made the decision to drop the atomic bomb. He then led the nation in the tumultuous early years of the Cold War that included the Berlin Airlift and the Korean War. (Library of Congress)

become president when Roosevelt died suddenly on April 12, 1945. Yet despite his almost blind start, Truman made some bold moves virtually immediately. He supported the San Francisco Conference of Nations that established the United Nations, and he mustered popular and bipartisan support for that fledgling organization, with the intention of nurturing a postwar internationalist foreign policy.

When the Germans surrendered only 26 days after he assumed office, Truman appointed General Dwight D. Eisenhower to head the American Occupation Zone in Germany, and he supported a vigorous program of de-Nazification and war crimes prosecution. Attending the July 1945 Potsdam Conference, Truman

worked with Soviet dictator Joseph Stalin and new British prime minister Clement Attlee to build on the agreements that had been reached by Stalin, Roosevelt, and British prime minister Winston L. S. Churchill at Yalta. Truman also decided to use the atomic bomb against Japan, a decision he later said he never regretted.

As it became increasing clear that the Soviet Union was acting contrary to the Yalta and Potsdam agreements, Truman concluded that a strong Anglo-American stand was the only means of preventing a total Soviet domination of Europe. But rapid American demobilization had reduced U.S. military strength in Europe to 391,000 men by 1946, whereas the Soviets still had 2.8 million troops under arms. Truman used U.S. economic power and the country's momentary nuclear monopoly to blunt the Soviet aspirations in postwar Europe. He also effectively blocked the Soviets from assuming any role in the occupation of Japan.

Truman was wary of Soviet conventional military power in Europe, but he also tried to maintain the wartime alliance that he considered essential to the viability of the United Nations. When Soviet intentions finally became crystal clear—first with the 1948 communist coup in Czechoslovakia and then with the 1948 Berlin Blockade—the defining Cold War American policy of containment solidified with three landmark decisions: the Truman Doctrine, the Marshall Plan, and the establishment of the North Atlantic Treaty Organization (NATO).

Truman laid down the principles of the Truman Doctrine in a speech before Congress on March 12, 1947, when he stated that the United States had to adopt a policy to support free peoples resisting subjugation by armed minorities or by outside influences. The $12 billion Marshall Plan was the engine of economic recovery in Europe, and it effectively prevented Moscow from stoking and exploiting economic chaos. Truman decided on an airlift as the answer to the Soviet blockade of Berlin, demonstrating U.S. resolve to block the spread of communism in Western Europe. In April 1949, the United States entered into its first standing military alliance since 1800 with the establishment of NATO.

In what he described as his most difficult decision in office, Truman authorized the commitment of U.S. forces in Korea in June 1950, within a week of the North Korean invasion of South Korea. He also supervised the reorganization of U.S. defense and intelligence establishments along the lines that remain familiar at the start of the 21st century. His administration established the National Security Council, the Department of Defense, the U.S. Air Force, and the Central Intelligence Agency, and it formally established the Joint Chiefs of Staff and the global network of joint military commands.

His decision to remove General Douglas MacArthur as U.S. and United Nations commander in Korea and the negative American public reaction to this, together with the stalemate in the war, led Truman not to run for reelection in 1952. Leaving office in January 1953, Truman retired to Independence, Missouri, wrote his memoirs, and supervised his presidential library. Truman died in Kansas City, Missouri, on December 26, 1972.

David T. Zabecki

References

Hamby, Alonzo S. *Man of the People: A Life of Harry S. Truman.* New York: Oxford University Press, 1995.

McCoy, Donald R. *The Presidency of Harry S. Truman.* Lawrence: University Press of Kansas, 1984.

McCullough, David. *Truman.* New York: Simon and Schuster, 1992.

Truman, Harry S. *Memoirs.* 2 vols. Garden City, NY: Doubleday, 1955–1956.

Wedemeyer, Albert Coady (1897–1989)

U.S. Army general who succeeded General Joseph Stilwell as chief of staff to Chiang Kai-shek (Jiang Jieshi) in China in 1944. Born in Omaha, Nebraska, on July 9, 1897, Albert Coady Wedemeyer graduated from the United States Military Academy, West Point, in 1918 and was commissioned in the infantry. He then served in the United States, the Philippines, and China and attended the Command and General Staff School, making captain in 1936. Wedemeyer's father-in-law and mentor, Colonel Stanley Embick, cultivated in him a lifelong interest in strategic questions and economic issues in warfare.

From 1936 to 1938, Wedemeyer attended the German War College (Kriegsakademie), producing a lengthy final report on the German military. This document strongly impressed Major General George C. Marshall, then assistant chief of staff in the War Department General Staff War Plans Division. In 1941, after he became chief of staff, Marshall placed Wedemeyer, a major at the time, in the same division. Wedemeyer contributed heavily to the development of the War Department's "Victory Plan," which guided overall planning for the wartime mobilization of American manpower and industrial resources. Promoted to brigadier general, Wedemeyer in 1942 and 1943 served in the War Department Operations Division, where he vigorously advocated an early cross-Channel invasion of western

Europe and opposed British prime minister Winston L. S. Churchill's alternative proposals for Mediterranean operations.

In the fall of 1943, Wedemeyer, now a major general, became deputy chief of staff to Lord Louis Mountbatten's South East Asia Command. Wedemeyer helped to develop plans for future operations and unsuccessfully attempted to resolve differences between China's Chiang Kai-shek, president of the Nationalist Party—the Kuomintang (KMT)—and General Joseph W. Stilwell, commander of American military forces in the China-Burma-India Theater and Chiang's chief of staff. In October 1944, Wedemeyer replaced Stilwell and soon developed a far less antagonistic working relationship with Chiang. Although critical of corruption and ineptitude within the KMT government and military, Wedemeyer, who was promoted to lieutenant general in early 1945, energetically helped to reorganize the Chinese Army and enhance its fighting abilities, drafting never implemented plans to retake south China's coast from Japanese forces. He urged greater levels of U.S. aid for Chiang's government and the denial of such assistance to Chinese Communist leaders.

Following the Japanese surrender in August 1945, Wedemeyer supervised the demobilization of Japanese troops in China and their replacement by Chiang's forces. Despite his continuing criticism of the corruption and inefficiencies within the Nationalist government, he believed that the United States should give it staunch backing and much-expanded economic and military aid. Wedemeyer also expressed misgivings over Marshall's year-long 1946 effort to establish a coalition Chinese government that would include Communist leaders. In April 1946, Wedemeyer left China. After Marshall sent him on a two-month fact-finding mission to China and Korea the following year, he repeated these recommendations, while also forcefully urging the Chinese government to institute major reforms. The Harry S. Truman administration ignored Wedemeyer's advice and considered his report too politically sensitive, suppressing it for two years.

After serving on the War Department General Staff and commanding the Sixth Army, Wedemeyer retired in 1951 to become a business executive. In 1954, he was promoted to full general on the retired list. He was active in conservative Republican politics, and in his memoirs he openly condemned the Truman administration's failure to provide greater assistance to China. Wedemeyer died at Fort Belvoir, Virginia, on December 17, 1989.

Priscilla Roberts

References

Cline, Ray S. *Washington Command Post: The Operations Division.* Washington, DC: Department of the Army, 1951.

Kirkpatrick, Charles E. *An Unknown Future and a Doubtful Present: Writing the Victory Plan of 1941.* Washington, DC: Center of Military History, U.S. Army, 1990.

Romanus, Charles F., and Riley Sunderland. *United States Army in World War II: China–Burma–India Theater–Time Runs Out in CBI.* Washington, DC: Office of the Chief of Military History, Department of the Army, 1959.

Further Reading
in World War II

Adams, Henry H. *Witness to Power: The Life of Fleet Admiral William D. Leahy.* Annapolis, MD: Naval Institute Press, 1985.

Adleman, Robert H., and George Walton. *The Devil's Brigade.* Philadelphia: Chilton Company, 1966.

Ambrose, Stephen. *Citizen Soldiers.* New York: Simon and Schuster, 1997.

———. *Eisenhower and Berlin, 1945: The Decision to Halt at the Elbe.* New York: W. W. Norton & Company, Inc. 1967.

———. *Supreme Commander: The War Years of General Dwight D. Eisenhower.* New York: Doubleday and Co., 1971.

Appleman, Roy E., James M. Burns, Russell A. Gugeler, and John Stevens. *Okinawa: The Last Battle.* United States Army in World War II. Washington, DC: U.S. Army Center of Military History, 1948.

Arnold, Henry H. *Global Mission.* New York: Harper and Brothers, 1949.

Atkinson, Rick. *An Army at Dawn.* New York: Henry Holt and Company, 2002.

———. *The Day of Battle.* New York: Henry Holt and Company, 2007.

Beasley, Norman. *Knudsen: A Biography.* New York: McGraw-Hill, 1947.

Bedell Smith, Walter. *Eisenhower's Six Great Decisions.* New York: Longmans, Green, 1956.

Blair, Clay, Jr. *Ridgway's Paratroopers: The American Airborne in World War II.* New York: Simon and Schuster, 1985.

———. *Silent Victory: The U.S. Submarine War Against Japan.* Philadelphia: J. B. Lippincott, 1975.

Blumenson, Martin. *Breakout and Pursuit.* United States Army in World War II. Washington, DC: U.S. Army Center of Military History, 1961.

———. *Mark Clark.* New York: Congdon and Weed, 1984.

———. *Patton: The Man Behind the Legend, 1885–1945.* New York: William Morrow and Company, 1985.

———. *Salerno to Casino.* United States Army in World War II. Washington, DC: U.S. Army Center of Military History, 1969.

Booth, T. Michael, and Duncan Spencer. *Paratrooper: The Life of Gen. James M. Gavin.* New York: Simon and Schuster, 1994.

Bradley, James. *Flags of Our Fathers.* New York: Bantam Books, 2000.

Bradley, Omar M. *A Soldier's Story.* New York: Henry Holt, 1951.

Bradley, Omar M., and Clay Blair. *A General's Life.* New York: Simon and Schuster, 1983.

Brink, Randall. *Nimitz: The Man and His Wars.* New York: Penguin, 2000.

Brokaw, Tom. *The Greatest Generation.* New York: Random House, 1998.

Buell, Thomas B. *Master of Sea Power: A Biography of Fleet Admiral Ernest J. King*. Boston: Little, Brown, and Company, 1980.

———. *The Quiet Warrior: A Biography of Admiral Raymond A. Spruance*. Boston: Little, Brown and Company, 1974.

Butcher, Harry C. *My Three Years With Eisenhower*. New York: Simon and Schuster, 1946.

Byrnes, James F. *Speaking Frankly*. New York: Harper and Brothers, 1947.

Cannon, M. Hamlin. *Leyte: The Return to the Philippines*. United States Army in World War II. Washington, DC: U.S. Army Center of Military History, 1954.

Chennault, Claire L. *Way of a Fighter*. New York: G. P. Putnam's Sons, 1949.

Clark, Mark. *Calculated Risk*. New York: Harper and Brothers, 1950.

Clarke, Jeffrey J., and Robert R. Smith. *Riviera to the Rhine*. United States Army in World War II. Washington, DC: U.S. Army Center of Military History, 1993.

Clayton, James D. *The Years of MacArthur*. 3 vols. Boston: Houghton Mifflin, 1970–1985.

Cline, Ray S. *Washington Command Post: The Operations Division*. United States Army in World War II. Washington, DC: U.S. Army Center of Military History, 1951.

Codman, Charles R. *Drive*. Boston: Little Brown and Company, 1957.

Coffey, Thomas E. *Hap: The Story of the U.S. Air Force and the Man Who Built It: General Henry "Hap" Arnold*. New York: Viking, 1982.

Cole, Hugh M. *The Ardennes: The Battle of the Bulge*. United States Army in World War II. Washington, DC: U.S. Army Center of Military History, 1965.

———. *The Lorraine Campaign*. United States Army in World War II. Washington, DC: U.S. Army Center of Military History, 1950.

Cooper, Norman V. *A Fighting General: The Biography of General Holland M. "Howlin Mad" Smith*. Quantico: Marine Corps Association, 1986.

Copp, Dewitt S. *A Few Great Captains: The Men and Events That Shaped the Development of U.S. Air Power*. Garden City, NY: Doubleday, 1980.

Craven, Wesley F., and Lames L. Cate, eds. *The Army Air Forces in World War II*. 7 vols. Chicago: University of Chicago Press, 1948–1958.

Crosswell, D. K. R. *The Chief of Staff: The Military Career of General Walter Bedell Smith*. Westport, CT: Greenwood Press, 1991.

Crowl, Philip A. *Campaign in the Marianas*. United States Army in World War II. Washington, DC: U.S. Army Center of Military History, 1960.

Crowl, Philip A., and Edmund G. Love. *Seizure of the Gilberts and Marshalls*. United States Army in World War II. Washington, DC: U.S. Army Center of Military History, 1955.

Davis, Kenneth S. *FDR: Into the Storm, 1937–1940*. New York: Random House, 1993.

———. *FDR: The War President, 1940–1943*. New York: Random House, 2000.

de Guingand, Francis. *Generals at War*. London: Hodder and Stoughton, 1964.

D'Este, Carlo. *Decision in Normandy*. New York: Dutton, 1983.

———. *Patton: A Genius for War*. New York: HarperCollins, 1995.

Doolittle, James H., and Carroll V. Glines. *I Could Never Be So Lucky Again*. New York: Bantam Books, 1991.

Eisenhower, Dwight D. *Crusade in Europe*. New York: Doubleday, 1948.

Eisenhower, John S. D. *The Bitter Woods*. New York: G. P. Putnam's Sons, 1969.

Falk, Stanley L. *Bataan: The March of Death*. New York: Curtis Books, 1962.

———. *Decision at Leyte*. New York: Berkeley Publishing Corporation, 1966.

Fisher, Ernest F., Jr. *Cassino to the Alps*. United States Army in World War II. Washington, DC: U.S. Army Center of Military History, 1977.

Fletcher, Marvin E. *America's First Black General: Benjamin O. Davis, Sr., 1880–1970*. Lawrence: University Press of Kansas, 1989.

Ford, Corey. *Donovan of OSS: The Untold Story of William J. Donovan*. Boston: Little, Brown and Co., 1970.

Ford, Daniel. *Flying Tigers: Claire Chennault and the American Volunteer Group*. Washington, DC: Smithsonian Institute Press, 1991.

Foster, Mark S. *Henry J. Kaiser: Builder in the Modern American West*. Austin: University of Texas Press, 1989.

Fuchida, Mitsou, and Masatake Okumiya. *Midway: The Battle that Doomed Japan*. Annapolis, MD: Naval Institute Press, 1955.

Garland, Albert N., Howard M. Smyth, and Martin Blumenson. *Sicily and the Surrender of Italy*. United States Army in World War II. Washington, DC: U.S. Army Center of Military History, 1965.

Gavin, James M. *On to Berlin: Battles of an Airborne Commander, 1943–1946*. New York: Viking Press, 1978.

Giles, Janice H. *The Damned Engineers*. Boston: Houghton Mifflin Company, 1970.

Glines, Carroll V. *Jimmy Doolittle, Master of the Calculated Risk*. New York: Van Nostrand Reinhold Co., 1980.

Greenfield, Kent R., ed. *Command Decisions*. Washington, DC: United States Army in World War II. Washington, DC: U.S. Army Center of Military History, 1960.

Greenfield, Kent R., Robert R. Palmer, and Bell I. Wiley. *The Organization of Ground Combat Troops*. United States Army in World War II. Washington, DC: U.S. Army Center of Military History, 1947.

Gregg, Charles T. *Tarawa*. New York: Stein and Day, 1984.

Griffith, Thomas E., Jr. *MacArthur's Airman: General George C. Kenney and the War in the South Pacific*. Lawrence: University of Kansas Press, 1998.

Groves, Leslie R. *Now It Can Be Told: The Story of the Manhattan Project*. New York: Harper Brothers, 1962.

Halsey, William F., and J. Bryan III. *Admiral Halsey's Story*. New York: McGraw-Hill, 1947.

Harrison, Gordon A. *Cross-Channel Attack*. United States Army in World War II. Washington, DC: U.S. Army Center of Military History, 1951.

Hastings, Max. *Overlord: D-Day and the Battle for Normandy*. New York: Simon and Schuster, 1984.

Hayes, Grace P. *The History of the Joint Chiefs of Staff in World War II: The War Against Japan*. Annapolis, MD: Naval Institute Press, 1982.

Hodgson, Godfrey. *The Colonel: The Life and Wars of Henry Stimson, 1867–1950*. New York: Alfred A. Knopf, 1990.

Howe, George F. *Northwest Africa: Seizing the Initiative in the West*. United States Army in World War II. Washington, DC: U.S. Army Center of Military History, 1957.

Hull, Cordell. *The Memoirs of Cordell Hull*. 2 vols. New York: Macmillan, 1948.

Jeffers, H. Paul. *Theodore Roosevelt, Jr., The Life of a War Hero.* Novato, CA: Presidio, 2002.

Kahn, E. J., Jr. *McNair: Educator of an Army.* Washington, DC: Infantry Journal Press, 1945.

Keegan, John. *Six Armies in Normandy: From D-Day to the Liberation of Paris.* New York: Viking Press, 1982.

Kenney, George C. *General Kenney Reports: A Personal History of the Pacific War.* New York: Duell, 1949.

King, Ernest J., and Walter Muir Whitehall. *Fleet Admiral King: A Naval Record.* New York: Norton, 1952.

Kirkpatrick, Charles E. *An Unknown Future and a Doubtful Present: Writing the Victory Plan of 1941.* Washington, DC: U.S. Army Center of Military History, 1990.

Krueger, Walter. *From Down Under to Nippon: The Story of the Sixth Army in World War II.* Washington, DC: Combat Forces Press, 1953.

Larrabee, Eric. *Commander in Chief: Franklin Delano Roosevelt, His Lieutenants, and Their War.* New York: Simon and Schuster, 1987.

Lawson, Ted. *Thirty Seconds Over Tokyo.* New York: Random House, 1943.

Leahey, William D. *I Was There.* New York: McGraw-Hill, 1950.

LeMay, Curtis E. *Mission with LeMay.* Garden City, NY: Doubleday, 1965.

Levine, Alan J. *The Strategic Bombing of Germany, 1940–1945.* Westport, CT: Praeger, 1992.

Lewin, Ronald. *Ultra Goes to War.* London: Hutchinson and Company, 1978.

Liddell Hart, Basil H. *History of the Second World War.* New York: Putnam's Sons, 1971.

Luvass, Jay, ed. *Dear Miss Em: General Eichelberger's War in the Pacific, 1942–1945.* Westport, CT: Greenwood Press, 1972.

MacArthur, Douglas. *Reminiscences.* New York: McGraw-Hill, 1964.

MacDonald, Charles B. *Company Commander.* Washington, DC: Infantry Journal Press, 1947.

———. *The Last Offensive.* United States Army in World War II. Washington, DC: U.S. Army Center of Military History, 1973.

———. *The Mighty Endeavor.* Oxford, England: Oxford University Press, 1969.

———. *The Siegfried Line Campaign.* United States Army in World War II. Washington, DC: U.S. Army Center of Military History, 1963.

———. *A Time For Trumpets: The Untold Story of the Battle of the Bulge.* New York: William Morrow and Company, 1985.

MacDonald, Charles B., and Sidney T. Mathews. *Three Battles: Arnaville, Altuzzo, and Schmidt.* United States Army in World War II. Washington, DC: U.S. Army Center of Military History, 1952.

Manchester, William. *American Caesar: Douglas MacArthur, 1880–1964.* Boston: Little, Brown, and Company, 1978.

———. *Goodbye Darkness: A Memoir of the Pacific War.* Boston: Little, Brown, and Company, 1979.

Marshall, S. L. A. *Men Against Fire.* New York: William Morrow, 1947.

———. *Night Drop: The American Airborne Invasion of Normandy.* Boston: Little, Brown and Company, 1962.

Matloff, Maurice, and Edward M. Snell. *Strategic Planning for Coalition Warfare, 1941–1942.* United States Army in World War II. Washington, DC: U.S. Army Center of Military History, 1952.

————. *Strategic Planning for Coalition Warfare, 1943–1944.* United States Army in World War II. Washington, DC: U.S. Army Center of Military History, 1953.

Mauldin, Bill. *Up Front.* New York: Henry Holt and Company, 1945.

McCullough, David. *Truman.* New York: Simon and Schuster, 1992.

Mets, David R. *Master of Air Power: General Carl A. Spaatz.* Novato, CA: Presidio Press, 1988.

Middlebrook, Martin. *Convoy.* New York: William Morrow, 1977.

Miller, Edward G. *A Dark and Bloody Ground: The Hürtgen Forest and the Roer River Dams, 1944–1945.* College Station: Texas A&M University Press, 1995.

————. *Nothing Less Than Full Victory: Americans at War in Europe, 1944–1945.* Annapolis, MD: Naval Institute Press, 2007.

Miller, John Jr. *Cartwheel: The Reduction of Rabaul.* United States Army in World War II. Washington, DC: U.S. Army Center of Military History, 1959.

————. *Guadalcanal: The First Offensive.* United States Army in World War II. Washington, DC: U.S. Army Center of Military History, 1949.

Miller, Robert A. *Division Commander: A Biography of Major General Norman D. Cota.* Spartanburg, SC: Reprint Company, 1989.

Millet, Alan, and Williamson Murray, eds. *Military Effectiveness.* Vol. IIII, *The Second World War.* London: Routledge, 1988.

Milner, Samuel. *Victory in Papua.* United States Army in World War II. Washington, DC: U.S. Army Center of Military History, 1957.

Morelock, Jerry D. *Generals of the Ardennes: American Leadership in the Battle of the Bulge.* Washington, DC: National Defense University Press, 1993.

Morison, Samuel Elliot. *History of United States Naval Operations In World War II.* 15 vols. Boston: Little, Brown and Company, 1947–1958.

————. *The Two-Ocean War.* Boston: Little, Brown, and Company, 1963.

Morton, Louis. *The Fall of the Philippines.* United States Army in World War II. Washington, DC: U.S. Army Center of Military History, 1953.

————. *Strategy and Command: The First Two Years.* United States Army in World War II. Washington, DC: U.S. Army Center of Military History, 1962.

Motter, T. H. Vail. *The Persian Corridor and Aid to Russia.* United States Army in World War II. Washington, DC: U.S. Army Center of Military History, 1952.

Murphy, Audie L. *To Hell and Back.* New York: Henry Holt and Company, 1949.

Murphy, Thomas D. *Ambassadors in Arms: The Story of Hawaii's 100th Infantry Battalion.* Honolulu: University of Hawaii Press, 1954.

Murray, Williamson, and Allan R. Millet. *A War to be Won: Fighting the Second World War.* Cambridge, MA: Harvard University Press. 2000.

Neillands, Robin. *The Bomber War: The Allied Air Offensive Against Nazi Germany.* New York: The Overlook Press, 2001.

Nelson, Donald M. *Arsenal of Democracy: The Story of American War Production.* New York: Harcourt Brace, 1946.

Norris, Robert S. *Racing for the Bomb, General Leslie R. Groves, The Manhattan Project's Indispensable Man.* South Royalton, VT: Steerforth Press, 2002.

Palmer, Robert R., Bell I. Wiley, and William R. Keast. *The Procurement and Training of Ground Combat Forces*. United States Army in World War II. Washington, DC: U.S. Army Center of Military History, 1948.

Patton, George S. *War as I Knew It*. Boston: Houghton Mifflin, 1947.

Pfeffer, Paula A. *A. Philip Randolph: Pioneer of the Civil Rights Movement*. Baton Rouge: Louisiana State University Press, 1990.

Pogue, Forrest C. *George C. Marshall*. 4 vols. New York: Viking, 1963–1987.

———. *The Supreme Command*. United States Army in World War II. Washington, DC: U.S. Army Center of Military History, 1954.

Potter, E. B. *Bull Halsey*. Annapolis, MD: Naval Institute Press, 1985.

———. *Nimitz*. Annapolis, MD: Naval Institute Press, 1976.

Prange, Gordon. *At Dawn We Slept*. New York: McGraw-Hill, 1981.

Prange, Gordon, with Donald M. Goldstein and Katherine V. Dillon. *Miracle at Midway*. New York: McGraw-Hill, 1981.

Pratt, Fletcher. *Eleven Generals: Studies in American Command*. New York: William Sloane, 1949.

Pratt, Julius. *Cordell Hull, 1933–1934*. 2 vols. New York: Cooper Square, 1964.

Pyle, Ernie. *Brave Men*. New York: Crossett and Dunlap, 1944.

Regan, Stephen. *In Bitter Tempest: The Biography of Frank Jack Fletcher*. Ames: Iowa State Press, 1994.

Renehan, Edward J. *The Lion's Pride: Theodore Roosevelt and His Family in Peace and War*. New York: Oxford University Press, 1998.

Rickard, John N. *Patton at Bay: The Lorraine Campaign, 1944*. Washington, DC: Brassey's, 2004.

Ridgway, Matthew B. *Soldier: The Memoirs of Matthew B. Ridgway*. New York: Harper Brothers, 1956.

Romanus, Charles F., and Riley Sunderland. *Stilwell's Command Problems*. United States Army in World War II. Washington, DC: U.S. Army Center of Military History, 1956.

———. *Stilwell's Mission to China*. United States Army in World War II. Washington, DC: U.S. Army Center of Military History, 1956.

———. *Stilwell's Time Runs Out in CBI*. United States Army in World War II. Washington, DC: U.S. Army Center of Military History, 1959.

Roscoe, Theodore. *On the Seas and in the Skies: A History of the U.S. Navy's Air Power*. New York: Hawthorne Books, 1970.

Ryan, Cornelius. *A Bridge Too Far*. New York: Simon and Schuster, 1974.

———. *The Longest Day*. New York: Simon and Schuster, 1959.

Sawyer, L. A., and W. W. Mitchell. *The Liberty Ships*. London: Lloyd's of London Press, 1985.

Scott, Robert L. *God is My Co-pilot*. New York: Scribner, 1943.

Smith, Bradley F. *The Shadow Warriors: OSS and the Origins of the CIA*. New York: Basic Books, 1983.

Smith, Holland M., and Percy Finch. *Coral and Brass*. New York: Scribner, 1949.

Smith, Robert R. *The Approach to the Philippines*. United States Army in World War II. Washington, DC: U.S. Army Center of Military History, 1953.

———. *Triumph in the Philippines*. United States Army in World War II. Washington, DC: U.S. Army Center of Military History, 1963.

Smith, Stanley E., ed. *United States Marine Corps in World War II*. 3 vols. New York: Random House, 1969.

Spector, Ronald. *Eagle Against the Sun: The American War With Japan.* New York: Free Press, 1985.

Stimson, Henry L., and McGeorge Bundy. *On Active Service in Peace and War.* New York: Harper and Brothers, 1948.

Taylor, John M. *General Maxwell Taylor: The Sword and the Pen.* New York: Doubleday, 1989.

Toland, John. *The Last 100 Days.* New York: Random House, 1965.

———. *The Rising Sun.* New York: Random House, 1970.

Tregaskis, Richard. *Guadalcanal Diary.* New York: Random House, 1943.

Truman, Harry S. *Memoirs.* 2 vols. Garden City, NY: Doubleday, 1955–1956.

Tuchman, Barbara. *Stillwell and the American Experience in China, 1911–1945.* New York: Macmillan, 1970.

Tucker, Spencer C. *The Second World War.* New York: Palgrave Macmillan, 2004.

Van der Vat, Dan. *The Atlantic Campaign: World War II's Greatest Strug-gle at Sea.* New York: Harper and Row, 1988.

Watson, Mark S. *Chief of Staff: Prewar Plans and Preparations.* The United States Army in World War II. Washington, DC: U.S. Army Center of Military History, 1950.

Wedemeyer, Albert. *Wedemeyer Reports.* New York: Henry Holt, 1958.

Weigley, Russell. *Eisenhower's Lieutenants.* 2 vols. Bloomington: Indiana University Press, 1981.

White, Theodore H., ed. *The Stilwell Papers.* New York: William Sloane, 1948.

Zabecki, David T., ed. *Chief of Staff: The Principal Officers Behind History's Great Commanders.* Vol. 2, *WWII to Korea and Vietnam.* Annapolis, MD: Naval Institute Press, 2008.

———., ed. *World War II in Europe: An Encyclopedia.* New York: Garland, 1999.

Zabecki, David T., and Bruce Condell, eds. and trans. *On the German Art of War: Truppenführung.* Boulder, CO: Lynne Riener Publishers, 2001.

KOREAN WAR

Leadership in the Korean War

World War II established two primary axioms in U.S. foreign relations that would guide American civilian and military leaders in making decisions regarding Korea both before and after forces of the Democratic People's Republic of Korea (DPRK, North Korea) attacked the Republic of Korea (ROK, South Korea) on June 25, 1950. First, American isolationism had combined with European appeasement during the 1930s to encourage Axis aggression leading to World War II, convincing U.S. leaders that the United States had to play an active role in world affairs to foster and preserve stability and peace. Second, the U.S. atomic bomb attacks on Japan in August 1945, along with ending the Pacific War, taught the profound lesson that future wars had to be limited in firepower and scope to avoid a nuclear holocaust. Lingering from the pre-war era, one additional assumption would influence U.S. decision making prior to outbreak of the conventional phase of the Korean War. American civilian leaders believed it was critical for the United States to practice a restrained involvement in postwar international affairs, fearing that an unlimited commitment of U.S. resources would bankrupt the nation. Although other factors assisted in shaping events, these three motivating forces had the most decisive impact on American military and civilian leadership in the Korean War, resulting in decisions ranging from brilliant to disastrous. Most historians now agree that how U.S. leaders acted and reacted during this conflict dramatically altered the course of the Cold War, escalating its intensity and expanding its reach.

Early accounts of the Korean War almost without exception focused on events beginning with North Korean forces invading South Korea. This was because few people doubted that the Soviet Union had ordered the attack as part of its plan for global conquest. President Harry S. Truman provided support for this assumption just two days after the start of hostilities. On June 27, 1950, he told the American people that North Korea's attack demonstrated that world "communism has passed beyond the use of subversion to conquer independent nations and will now use armed invasion and war." This assessment reflected Truman's firm belief that North Korea was a puppet of the Soviet Union and its leader Kim Il Sung was acting on instructions from Moscow. In his memoirs, Truman equated Joseph Stalin's actions with Adolf Hitler's during the 1930s, arguing that military intervention to defend the Republic of Korea was vital because appeasement had not prevented but ensured the outbreak of World War II. Top administration officials, as well as the general public, fully shared these assumptions. This traditional interpretation cast American military and civilian leaders in a reactive

A Korean People's Army (North Korean army) tank regiment equipped with Soviet-made T-34 tanks shown during the Korean War 1950–1953. (AFP/Getty Images)

role, portraying their actions as defensive in responding to circumstances that were a surprise and not of their own creation.

A consensus now prevails among historians, however, that U.S. leaders, far from being passive actors in the events leading to the outbreak of the Korean War, played a determinative role in the origins of a conflict dating from at least World War II. Also, rather than characterizing the war as the product of external aggression, scholars acknowledge the centrality of domestic factors. In fact, more than a decade ago, it became fashionable to portray the Korean War as a civil conflict, rejecting not only the argument that it was a textbook example of Soviet-inspired, external aggression but even denying Moscow's involvement. Advocates of this interpretation insisted that a conventional war would start in Korea in June 1950 because the U.S. military, acting on orders from civilian leaders in Washington, prevented a leftist revolution on the peninsula in 1945 and imposed a reactionary regime in the south during the years immediately following World War II. But the release of previously classified Soviet and Chinese documents during the 1990s abruptly ended the emerging consensus that Korea was a classic civil war. The archival record made clear that Soviet leaders were partners with U.S. officials in extending their Cold War political competition to Korea, establishing competing governments on the peninsula each determined to achieve reunification.

Japan bears ultimate responsibility for the Korean War as a consequence of its annexation of Korea in 1910 in combination with its attack on Pearl Harbor in December 1941. Entry into the Pacific war compelled U.S. leaders to plan for Korea's future because the United States was committed after achieving victory to dismantling the Japanese Empire. Critics of President Franklin D. Roosevelt at first blamed him for the division of Korea at the 38th parallel in August 1945, alleging that this was part of the price he paid at the Yalta Conference for Soviet entrance into the Pacific war. But in fact, President Harry S. Truman proposed partitioning Korea on the eve of Japan's surrender to prevent the Soviets from occupying the entire peninsula. When he became president after Roosevelt's death in April 1945, Soviet expansion into Eastern Europe had begun to alarm U.S. leaders. Almost from the outset, the new president expected Soviet actions in Korea to parallel Stalin's policies in Poland, although evidence suggested that most Koreans would have welcomed rather than resisted a postwar communist government. Within a week after assuming office, Truman began to search for some way to eliminate any opportunity for a repetition of Soviet expansion.

Meanwhile, U.S. military leaders were planning for an invasion of the Japanese home islands that they predicted would carry an exorbitant cost in lives and resources. Since the Soviet Union had not yet declared war on Japan, they hoped that Stalin would enter the Pacific war and send troops into Korea, forcing Japan to divide its forces or perhaps surrender. During the Potsdam Conference in July 1945, however, news of the successful testing of the atomic bomb gave Truman an alternative. Japan's prompt surrender after an atomic attack not only would save American lives, but also preempt Soviet entry into the Pacific war, thereby permitting the United States to occupy Korea alone and removing any possibility for "Sovietization." But Truman's gamble failed. When Stalin declared war on Japan and sent the Red Army into Korea prematurely on August 12, 1945, the United States proposed Korea's division into Soviet and U.S. zones of military occupation at the 38th parallel. Only Stalin's acceptance of Truman's desperate 11th-hour plan saved the peninsula from unification under communist rule. Accepting Korea's division into spheres of influence, the Soviet leader probably also hoped to trade this concession for an occupation zone in Japan.

On September 8, 1945, the U.S. XXIV Corps arrived in southern Korea after redeployment from Okinawa nearly a month after Soviet troops had entered the north. Lieutenant General John R. Hodge commanded XXIV Corps. He had earned a reputation as a highly effective combat officer in military engagements against the Japanese, but he lacked diplomatic or administrative experience. More important, the U.S. occupation commander had no knowledge of Korean history or culture. Hodge quickly turned for information and advice to those Koreans who spoke English and had ties to American missionaries. Of greater significance was his reliance on rich and conservative Korean landlords and businessmen, including some Japanese collaborators. Mass protests demanding immediate economic, social, and political reform frightened Hodge because of his personal preference for orderly change and his visceral hostility toward communism. Equating events in Korea with those in Eastern Europe, he spurned representatives of the Korean People's Republic (KPR), an existing indigenous government that had won mass support among the Korean people, because it advocated a sweeping reform program and had created a network of local

British prime minister Clement Attlee, U.S. president Harry Truman, and Soviet leader Joseph Stalin, shown at the Potsdam Conference on August 1, 1945. (Library of Congress)

people's committees. Hodge viewed the KPR as a transparent Soviet catspaw and ordered it to disband.

Hodge's numerous mistakes encouraged the emergence of a civil war in Korea following Soviet-American division of the nation. U.S. military leaders in Washington share responsibility for this outcome because they failed to provide detailed guidelines for the occupation for nine months. By then, Hodge had established a centralized and autocratic military government modeled after Japan's colonial organization that symbolized in Korea economic exploitation, political repression, and psychological intimidation. But it was Hodge's close ties with Korea's extreme conservatives that concerned State Department officials, who saw political polarization as fueling civil strife. Acting on instructions, Hodge promoted a coalition of moderate Korean politicians whom he targeted as leaders of an interim government. His mismanagement of this admirable effort, however, would alienate Koreans of every political persuasion. Late in 1946, Hodge began urging immediate withdrawal from Korea. His superiors had been recommending this course of action for months, arguing that declining postwar defense spending meant continued commitment of U.S. resources in Korea which undermined the ability to preserve American security interests in more vital areas, such as Japan.

By early 1947, Korea found itself a captive of the Cold War. As Soviet-American relations in Europe deteriorated, neither side was willing to acquiesce to an agreement strengthening its adversary. American civilian leaders opposed pressure from the U.S. military for prompt withdrawal, arguing successfully that abandoning Korea to communist rule would damage U.S. credibility and create a threat to Japan. But by September 1947, 18 months of Soviet-American negotiations had not resolved the Korean impasse. That same month, the newly created Joint Chiefs of Staff (JCS) recommended swift military withdrawal from Korea, concluding that the peninsula was of no strategic value for U.S. security. When a parsimonious Congress refused to authorize an aid package for Korea, the State Department gained Truman's approval for referral of the dispute to the United Nations, where the Soviets prevented international action to end Korea's division. Washington and Moscow then moved toward the formation of separate regimes, resulting in the creation in August 1948 of the ROK in the south and the following month the DPRK in the north. Reunification was the highest priority for both Koreas, even if achieving this goal required military action. Border clashes the prior summer at the parallel between Korean troops suggested that a Korean war already was underway.

North Korea's attack two years later caused critics to charge the United States with abandoning the ROK and thereby encouraging the invasion. In fact, U.S. civilian leaders maintained a strong commitment to the ROK's survival. For example, they persuaded Truman to postpone military withdrawal until June 29, 1949—six months after Soviet troops left the north—over the objections of U.S. military leaders. More important, Truman and his civilian advisers believed that South Korea could survive and even prosper without protection from U.S. troops despite the existence of a powerful army in the north. This was because before U.S. troops left, the administration had assumed a commitment to train, equip, and supply a security force in the south that was capable of preserving internal order and deterring an attack from North Korea. Also, it had asked Congress to approve a three-year program of technical and economic assistance. To build political support for the Korean assistance package, Secretary of State Dean G. Acheson offered an optimistic assessment of South Korea's future in a speech before the National Press Club on January 12, 1950. Later, critics claimed that Acheson's exclusion of the ROK from the U.S. "defensive perimeter" gave Stalin a "green light" to order an attack. But declassified Soviet documents show that Acheson's words had little impact on Communist planning for the invasion.

Guiding Truman's Korea policy was the correct assumption that Moscow was reluctant to allow the North Koreans to practice open aggression. This belief allowed the administration to pursue containment through economic means and during the weeks after Acheson's address the policy seemed to be succeeding in South Korea. President Syngman Rhee's government had acted vigorously to end spiraling inflation, while elections in May had given Rhee's critics control of the legislature. Finally, the South Korean army nearly had eliminated guerrilla activities threatening internal order, prompting approval of a large increase in U.S. military aid. But while the United States was willing to be patient, awaiting the collapse of what it saw as Moscow's artificial client state in the north, Rhee was obsessed with accomplishing early reunification. The fear of U.S. civilian and military leaders that Rhee would launch an invasion prompted the United States to limit South Korea's military capabilities, refusing to provide tanks, heavy artillery, and combat planes. Moreover, the United States did not make explicit a commitment to defend the ROK if North Korea attacked. This did not stop the South Koreans from initiating most of the border clashes with North Korean forces at the parallel that reached a high level of intensity in the summer of 1949.

Korean nationalist Syngman Rhee was the first president of the Republic of Korea (South Korea), beginning in 1948. Much criticized for his authoritarian methods, the conservative Rhee was driven from power in 1960. (Corbis)

Despite the ROK's provocations, however, Stalin consistently refused to approve DPRK leader Kim Il Sung's persistent requests to approve an invasion of South Korea. This was because the Soviet leader believed that North Korea had not achieved either military superiority in the north or political strength in the south. His main concern was the threat that South Korea posed to North Korea's survival, for example, fearing an invasion northward after U.S. military withdrawal in June 1949. Although Stalin was not ready to risk war with the United States in 1949, the Communist victory in China that autumn placed pressure on him to show his support for the same outcome in Korea. In January 1950, Stalin met with Kim in Moscow. At that time, he approved a major expansion of the DPRK's military capabilities. When they met again in April, Kim persuaded Stalin that a military victory would be quick and easy, especially because of support from southern guerrillas and an expected popular uprising against Rhee. But Stalin still feared U.S. military intervention, advising Kim that he could stage an offensive only if China's Mao Zedong approved. Traveling to Beijing in May, Kim Il Sung learned that Mao shared Stalin's concerns, but still secured his reluctant consent as well.

Kim knew that time was running out and manipulated his patrons into supporting his desperate bid for reunification before Rhee could beat him to the punch. Few Americans on June 25, 1950, doubted for a moment that North Korea attacked South Korea on orders from Moscow. Early accounts on the Korean conflict also confirmed the widespread belief that Truman acted with swiftness and courage to prevent conquest of the entire peninsula. But in fact, he did not send U.S. ground troops to Korea for almost a week, referring the matter instead to the United Nations and banking on South Korea's ability to defend itself. This was consistent with Truman's containment policy in Asia that sought to prevent communist expansion without relying on U.S. military power. It also reflected his determination to limit U.S. commitments in world affairs, a preference with roots in the interwar period. At a press conference on June 29, he was still optimistic that military intervention was avoidable, agreeing with a newsman's description of the war as a "police action," rather than coining the phrase himself. The next morning, however, General Douglas MacArthur, U.S. occupation commander in Japan, advised after surveying the battlefield that without U.S. combat forces, Communist conquest of South Korea was certain. Even then Truman hesitated when Secretary of the Army Frank Pace phoned before dawn asking for approval of MacArthur's request. Told that a decision could not wait, the president sent U.S. soldiers to prevent Communist forces from reuniting Korea.

American civilian and military leaders were certain that U.S. troops would halt the North Korean offensive. But on July 5, at the Battle of Osan, Communist forces routed Task Force Smith in their first engagement with U.S. soldiers. Two days later, the United Nations Security Council passed a resolution providing for the creation of the United Nations Command (UNC) and calling upon Truman to appoint the UNC commander. The administration stymied direct UN access to the UNC, adopting instead a procedure whereby MacArthur, Truman's choice as commander, received instructions from and reported to the JCS. Very quickly, U.S. military leaders faced a crisis. By July 20, the Korean People's Army (KPA) had shattered 5 U.S. battalions and moved 100 miles south of Seoul, the ROK's capital just south of the parallel. North Korean occupation of Taejon was a devastating psychological blow for U.S. soldiers, many of whom abandoned arms and equipment in disorganized flight southward. On July 26, MacArthur traveled to South Korea and informed Lieutenant General Walton H. Walker, commander of the U.S. Eighth Army, that he would not tolerate further retreat. Walker issued a "stand or die" order, but the KPA continued to advance. Then and later, Walker would receive blame for this series of battlefield defeats. During the first week of August, UN forces finally stabilized battle lines along the Pusan Perimeter, a rectangular area in the southeast corner of the Korean peninsula.

Truman and his advisers quickly attributed U.S. military reverses in Korea to inadequate U.S. military preparedness. Spending on U.S. defense after World War II had declined steadily from about $84 billion to $13.5 billion for fiscal 1950 (July 1, 1949, to June 30, 1950). Truman was a fiscal conservative who opposed excessive government spending. But after Soviet detonation of an atomic bomb and the establishment of the People's Republic of China (PRC) in the fall of 1949, his military and civilian advisers had prepared National Security Council (NSC) Paper 68, which urged a major defense buildup to meet this perceived increase in the threat to the nation's security. Truman instead approved a final proposal for fiscal 1951 of $13.394 billion to fund overall military strength at 1.5 million men. North Korea's attack reversed this pattern. On September 6, Congress approved the original fiscal 1951 budget, but at that time, the administration already had exceeded its force limitations. In an address to Congress of July 19, Truman had announced that a supplementary appropriation was needed. On September 27, Congress authorized $11.729 billion in additional funds to support a force level of 2.1 million men. Simultaneously, the administration was developing a five-year plan for an increase in U.S. military capabilities to the levels outlined in NSC-68. That same month, Congress also passed the Defense Production Act, giving the president sweeping powers to place the U.S. economy on a wartime footing.

North Korea might have forced a humiliating U.S. evacuation had it not sent two of its best divisions into the southwestern provinces, where communist support was strongest, to recruit troops after sustaining staggering losses. On August 7, Walker's army launched its first counterattack. Soon, the United States was superior in numbers and equipment and held air control. By then, MacArthur had developed plans for an amphibious landing behind enemy lines at the port of Inchon on the northwest coast, roughly 20 miles west of Seoul. U.S. military leaders in Washington raised strong objections, not least because this would require redeployment of troops from Japan. Dangerous conditions at the landing site included shifting tides, mud flats, and seawalls, creating the great risk for a military debacle. But in late August, MacArthur, at a meeting in Tokyo, managed to persuade skeptical representatives of the JCS that surprise alone guaranteed success. Further controversy swirled around the operation following MacArthur's appointment of Major General Edward M. Almond, his chief of staff, to command the newly formed X Corps that would land at Inchon. Not only would this unit operate separately from Walker's Eighth Army, but along with the 7th U.S. Army Division, Almond would command the 1st U.S. Marines. But the JCS deferred to MacArthur, setting a pattern that soon would have disastrous consequences.

MacArthur's Inchon landing on September 15 was a spectacular success that reversed the course of the Korean War. It allowed Walker's forces to break out of the Pusan Perimeter and move north to join with the X Corps in liberating Seoul. Meanwhile, Truman's civilian advisers, certain about eventual battlefield victory despite retreat, had been debating whether to pursue forcible reunification once the KPA had retreated into the north. Initially, Acheson opposed crossing the parallel, declaring publicly on June 29 that U.S. military action sought only to restore the prewar status quo. However, State Department officials worked to change Acheson's mind, arguing that the United States should destroy the KPA and then sponsor free elections for a government to rule a united Korea. U.S. military leaders were reluctant to endorse this drastic change in war aims until, in late July, Walker's army began to establish and hold lines of defense. Roughly two weeks later, Truman decided to approve military action to achieve forcible reunification. His plan for conquering North Korea, approved on September 1, included precautions to minimize the risks of Chinese intervention. For example, no U.S. forces were to enter the provinces along the Yalu River. Seeking to register a victory in the Cold War, Truman and his civilian advisers, not MacArthur, were responsible for the ill-advised decision to pursue conquest of North Korea.

For the PRC, the UNC advance into the DPRK constituted a grave threat to China's national security and a direct challenge to its credibility and prestige in Asia. Chinese Communist leaders had not welcomed the Korean War because in response Truman had deployed U.S. naval vessels to protect the Nationalist redoubt on Taiwan. In late July, MacArthur had visited the island and announced plans to strengthen the military capabilities of Chiang Kai-shek's (Jiang Jieshi) regime. Then, much to Truman's chagrin, the militantly anticommunist general sent a message to the Veterans of Foreign Wars, which seemed to threaten the PRC. Nevertheless, Foreign Minister Zhou Enlai tried to avoid war, informing the Indian ambassador on October 2 that China would intervene militarily if American forces crossed the parallel. U.S. military and civilian leaders thought the Chinese were bluffing, but also naively believed public statements of U.S. benign intentions would reassure Beijing. MacArthur, during a personal meeting with Truman at Wake Island on October 15, predicted that "if the Chinese tried to get down to Pyongyang [North Korea's capital] there would be the greatest slaughter" (James 1985). Even after the first clash between UNC troops and Chinese "volunteers" later that month, the general remained supremely confident, despite Washington's refusal on November 8 to approve bombing in Manchuria because of British objections.

Following Inchon, U.S. military leaders did not intrude on MacArthur's conduct of the war, allowing the general to interpret his ambiguous instructions as he saw fit. For example, they did not object when MacArthur maintained a divided command. His naval redeployment of the X Corps to Wonsan on the northeast coast of Korea required nearly a month to complete. Meanwhile, the Eighth Army continued its slow advance north after occupying Pyongyang on October 19. Finally, on November 24, MacArthur launched his "Home by Christmas Offensive" with U.S. troops in the vanguard. High mountains prevented contact between the two UNC armies as they conducted separate operations against the enemy before linking to engulf the KPA. Initially, there was little resistance, but two days later, the Chinese People's Volunteers Army counterattacked in force, sending the Eighth Army into a chaotic retreat and nearly crushing the X Corps at the Changgin Reservoir. MacArthur declared publicly that his "reconnaissance in force" had exposed a Chinese trap, while blaming the UNC retreat on restrictions preventing retaliation against mainland China. An atmosphere of supreme crisis now gripped Washington as Truman declared a state of national emergency on December 16. His comment at a press conference about possible use of atomic weapons to halt the Chinese offensive caused foreign leaders to fear another world war was near.

In late November, MacArthur submitted a "Plan for Victory" in the Korean War that proposed four specific steps. First, the general called for a blockade of China's coast. Second, he wanted authorization to bomb military installations in Manchuria. Third, MacArthur advocated deploying Chinese Nationalist forces in Korea. Finally, he recommended that Chiang launch an attack from Taiwan against the mainland. The JCS, despite later denials, seriously considered endorsing implementation of these actions prior to receiving favorable reports from the battlefront late in December. By spring 1951, Truman had approved the first two proposals if UNC forces faced annihilation or China expanded the war beyond Korea. In fact, the president even was prepared to use atomic weapons, an option that he had been considering since the early days of the fighting. But by early in 1951, the UNC halted the Chinese Communist advance southward, making it possible for the administration to implement its preference for fighting a limited war in Korea. Restoration of a unified command with the Eighth Army's absorption of the X Corps contributed to this success. More important was the leadership of Lieutenant General Matthew B. Ridgway, who had replaced Walker the previous December after a freak jeep accident had killed his predecessor.

By March 1951, UNC counterattacks had forced the Chinese to retreat to defensive positions just north of the parallel. MacArthur pressed Washington to expand the war through attacking China, but the administration had decided to seek an armistice and rejected his pleas. In March, the general's demand for an immediate Communist surrender sabotaged a planned ceasefire initiative. But for various reasons, many of them political, Truman reprimanded, but did not recall, the general. By early April, a combination of factors forced the president to act. The JCS worried about a Chinese and Soviet military buildup in East Asia and thought the UNC commander should have standing authority to retaliate against any Communist escalation, even recommending deployment of atomic weapons to forward Pacific bases. U.S. military and civilian

United Nations Command (UNC) troops fighting in the Republic of Korea capital of Seoul, September 20, 1950. (National Archives)

leaders, as well as U.S. allies in Europe, rightly mistrusted MacArthur and feared he might provoke an incident to widen the war. While the general's letter to the House Republican minority leader on April 5 again criticizing the administration's efforts to limit the war was, as Truman later argued, "rank insubordination" and the "last straw," he already had decided to relieve MacArthur, with unanimous support from his top advisers, for a more compelling reason related to military strategy. At first, most Americans were furious, but during Senate hearings on MacArthur's firing, the testimony of the JCS effectively defended the need to limit the war to Korea.

During the month following MacArthur's recall, UNC forces repulsed two massive Chinese Communist offensives. A battlefield stalemate then emerged that persuaded the belligerents to open at Kaesong negotiations for an armistice during July. U.S. leaders insisted on confining discussions to military matters, thus preventing the PRC from exploiting the talks to gain admission to the UN or control over Taiwan. As a consequence, both sides appointed military officers, rather than diplomats, as main negotiators, reducing prospects for flexibility and compromise. North Korea and China created an acrimonious atmosphere at the outset with efforts to score propaganda points, but the United States raised the first major roadblock when it proposed a demilitarized zone deep in North Korea. More important, after the talks moved to Panmunjom late in October there was rapid progress in resolving all but one of the agenda items. The delegates agreed that the demilitarized zone would follow the line of battle, while adopting inspection procedures to enforce the truce. After approving a postwar political conference to discuss withdrawal of foreign troops and reunification, a trade-off settled disputes on airfield rehabilitation and members of a neutral supervisory commission. Ten months after the talks began negotiators would have signed an armistice had they not deadlocked over disposition of the prisoners of war (POWs).

Truman insisted that humanitarian motivation was behind the firm refusal of the United States to return Communist POWs to China and North Korea against their will. U.S. civilian leaders, ignoring opposition from U.S. military leaders, endorsed Truman's policy in pursuit of a propaganda victory in the Cold War, although this required misrepresenting the facts. For example, the U.S. stand on the principle of nonforcible repatriation may have seemed moral, but it contradicted the Geneva Convention, which required, as the Communists demanded, the return of all POWs. Far worse was the Truman administration's purposeful decision to allow the perception that those POWs refusing repatriation were Communists defecting to the "Free World." A vast majority of North Korean POWs were actually South Koreans who either had joined voluntarily or were impressed into the Communist army. And thousands of Chinese POWs were Nationalist soldiers trapped in China at the end of the civil war who now had the chance to escape to Taiwan. Moreover, Chinese Nationalist guards at UN POW camps had used terrorist "reeducation" tactics to compel prisoners to refuse repatriation. Those prisoners who resisted risked beatings or death. Truman's stand on voluntary repatriation not only had little to do with moral considerations, but it prolonged the Korean War for more than a year.

Events at the truce talks influenced how U.S. civilian and military leaders made decisions about conduct of the war. For example, B-29 bombers carried out mock atomic bombing test runs over North Korea in September and October 1951 to intimidate Communist negotiators. The following month, the UNC adopted a strategy of "active defense" after negotiators set the existing line of battle as the final demarcation line for a demilitarized zone on the condition that there would be an armistice within 30 days. Ridgway, having replaced MacArthur as UNC commander, sent a new directive to Lieutenant General James A. Van Fleet, now commander of the Eighth Army, instructing him for one month to limit the size of operations to no more than one division and their scope to capturing outposts in terrain suitable for temporary instead of permanent defense. When the 30-day time limit expired, the UNC had not formulated plans for offensive operations and in essence active defense became the UNC's strategy for the balance of the war. As the wartime priority shifted to pursuit of an early ceasefire, the Korean War soon resembled World War I, with a static battlefield and armies depending on barbed wire, trenches, artillery, and mortars. Van Fleet strongly opposed fighting a military stalemate and proposed many plans for offensive action, but Ridgway and the JCS rejected all of them. Critics charged that active defense allowed the Communists to build permanent defenses and needlessly lengthened the war.

In November 1952, angry American voters elected Dwight D. Eisenhower president primarily because they expected him to end what had become the very unpopular "Truman's War." The retired U.S. Army general entered office thinking seriously about using expanded conventional bombing and the threat of nuclear attack to force concessions from the Communist side. Secretary of State John Foster Dulles and JCS chairman Admiral Arthur W. Radford both endorsed this more aggressive approach, as did General Mark W. Clark, who had become the UNC commander in May 1952. A truce agreement came on July 27, 1953, after an accelerated bombing campaign in North Korea and bellicose rhetoric about expanding the war. But there is no substantive evidence to verify Eisenhower's claim that the PRC was responding to his threat of an expanded war employing atomic weapons. Available documents more strongly suggest that the Chinese, facing domestic economic problems and wanting peaceful coexistence with the West, already had decided to make peace once Truman left office. And Stalin's death in March 1953 only added to China's sense of political vulnerability,

First Lieutenant Alvin Anderson, one of the many repatriated prisoners of war, embraces his mother and sister as other members of his family watch on September 14, 1953. (National Archives)

persuading the Communist delegation to break the logjam at Panmunjom later that month before Dulles conveyed his vague atomic threat to India for delivery to Beijing.

By January 1953, both sides in fact wanted an armistice. Washington and Beijing had grown tired of the economic burdens, military losses, political and military constraints, worries about an expanded war, and pressure from allies and the world community to end the stalemated war. Food shortages in North Korea, coupled with an understanding that forcible reunification was no longer possible, caused Pyongyang to favor an armistice even earlier. Moscow's new leaders had been concerned even before Stalin's death about economic problems in Eastern Europe. A more conciliatory approach in the Cold War, they believed, not only would reduce the risk of general war, but also might create tensions in the Western alliance if the United States acted provocatively in Korea. Several weeks before Eisenhower's threats of an expanded war using nuclear weapons and the bombing of North Korea's dams and irrigation system in May, Chinese negotiators signaled a change in policy when they accepted the UNC's proposal for an exchange of sick and wounded prisoners and then recommended turning nonrepatriates over to a neutral state. Also, in late May and early June 1953, Chinese forces launched powerful attacks against positions that South Korean units were defending along the front line. Far from being intimidated, Beijing thus showed its continuing resolve, relying on military means to persuade U.S. civilian and military leaders to compromise on the final terms of the armistice.

War in Korea militarized U.S. foreign policy in the Cold War. Beginning with the budget for fiscal 1951, the United States would build an immense military establishment. Chinese intervention ended Truman's hesitation after Inchon to implement NSC-68. On January 6, 1951, Congress passed a second supplement for fiscal 1951 providing for $16.795 billion in additional defense spending to fund a force level of 2.9 million men. A final supplement of $6.38 billion came in May. In one year, the Korean War justified an expansion of the U.S. military to nearly 3.5 million men, while raising defense spending to $48.2 billion, a figure equaling all military appropriations for the prior 4 fiscal years. This expansion was not entirely for Korea; much of the money funded a buildup of U.S. forces in Europe and expanded military assistance to Indochina, the Philippines, and Taiwan. In February 1951, the JCS proposed $73 billion for fiscal 1952 to reach the levels projected in NSC-68, but Truman requested $56.3 billion. Reacting to the start of the truce talks, Congress would approve $55.5 billion in October. Supplementary appropriations raised defense spending for fiscal 1952 to $60.4 billion. Hoping for peace in an election year, Congress in July 1952 approved a reduction to $44.3 billion in military expenditures for fiscal 1953. Preliminary plans for fiscal 1954 provided for a slight decrease, but, despite the return to peace, the pattern of large peacetime defense budgets would continue for the next four decades.

Judgments about the quality of U.S. military and civilian leadership during the postwar conflict in Korea have changed over time. For years, critics blamed them for weakness in confronting the communist challenge in East Asia, thereby inviting Soviet-inspired aggression. U.S. military intervention won praise, but not fighting a limited war resulting in a prolonged stalemate and an armistice, rather than victory. More recent writers reach opposite conclusions. The impact of U.S. leadership in the Korean War is less contested. In response, American leaders, in addition to vastly increasing defense spending, strengthened the North Atlantic Treaty Organization militarily and pressed for West German rearmament. While they spoke about upholding collective security, the Korean War severely strained relations between the United States and its allies. U.S. relations with China were poisoned for 20 years, especially because Washington persuaded the UN in February 1951 to condemn the PRC for aggression in Korea. Moreover, the war left the United States closely wedded to odious regimes in South Korea and on Taiwan. Despite 33,000 dead and 105,000 wounded, the United States greatly expanded its commitment to block communist seizures of power everywhere in the world. Korea's main legacy was that U.S. civilian and military leaders joined thereafter in pursuing a foreign policy of global military intervention, for which the nation paid an enormous price in death, destruction, and damaged reputation.

James I. Matray

Reference

James, D. Clayton. *The Years of MacArthur*. Vol. III, *Triumph & Disaster, 1945–1964*. Boston: Houghton Mifflin, 1985.

About the Author

Dr. James I. Matray is professor and chair in the History Department at California State University, Chico. He earned a doctoral degree from the University of Virginia in August 1977 in U.S. history, specializing in American diplomacy. Dr. Matray is the author of *The Reluctant Crusade: American Foreign Policy in Korea, 1941–1950*, winner of the Phi Alpha Theta Book Prize in 1986, and *Japan's Emergence as a Global Power*. His most recent books are *Korea Divided: The 38th Parallel and the Demilitarized Zone*, and *East Asia and the United States: An Encyclopedia of Relations Since 1784*. Dr. Matray's other books are the *Historical Dictionary of the Korean War*, winner in 1992 of both *Choice*'s "Outstanding Academic Book Award" and a "Best Reference Book Award" from the *Library Journal*; and *Korea and the Cold War: Division, Destruction, and Disarmament*. He also has written numerous book chapters and articles in professional journals. Dr. Matray has won a number of teaching awards and has served on the board of editors for *Diplomatic History* and the *Pacific Historical Review*.

Korean War Battles

Osan, Battle of (July 5, 1950)

First battle of the Korean War involving U.S. troops, specifically Task Force Smith. Named for its commander, Lieutenant Colonel Charles B. ("Brad") Smith, Task Force Smith comprised 406 officers and enlisted men from the 1st Battalion of the 21st Infantry Regiment and 134 officers and men from the 52nd Field Artillery Battery (Battery A plus small contingents from the Headquarters and Service Batteries). It was the first U.S. Army combat unit to enter Korea after the invasion of the South by the Korean People's Army (KPA, North Korea).

Task Force Smith arrived in South Korea by air near Pusan and moved north to Taejon by train, arriving there on the morning of July 2, 1950. Smith ordered his men to rest while he and his staff officers drove north to reconnoiter. Some 3 miles north of Osan, Smith found an ideal blocking position, a line of low rolling hills about 300 feet above the level ground. This position commanded the main railroad line to the east and afforded a clear view to Suwon, about 8 miles north. On July 4, the task force was joined at Pyongtaek by part of the 52nd Field Artillery Battalion: some of the Headquarters and Service Batteries and all of A Battery with 5 105mm howitzers (1 howitzer was left behind at Pyongtaek), 73 vehicles, and 134 men under the command of Lieutenant Colonel Miller O. Perry.

On the late afternoon of July 4, Smith, Perry, and others made a reconnaissance of the position Smith had selected. The combined infantry and artillery then moved out of Pyongtaek by truck, arriving at the position about 3:00 a.m. The U.S. line was about 1 mile in length and was bisected by the Suwon–Osan road.

In cold, rainy weather the men dug foxholes and laid telephone lines to four of the howitzers, placed in a concealed position a little over a mile to the south. One howitzer was positioned halfway between the battery and the infantry to enfilade the road and serve as an antitank gun. Artillery volunteers formed 4 .50-caliber machine gun and 4 2.36-inch bazooka teams and joined the infantry position to the north. The infantry vehicles were located just to the south of their position, and the artillerymen concealed their trucks just north of Osan. The Americans were, however, vulnerable to flanking attacks, lacked the means to stop tanks, and had no reserves.

At dawn on July 5, Smith ordered his artillery, mortars, and machine guns to conduct registration fire. Steady rain precluded air support. Shortly after 7:00 a.m. the Americans detected movement to the north. Within half an hour a column of eight KPA T-34 tanks, part of the

Troops of Task Force Smith, named for its commander Lieutenant Colonel Charles B. Smith, arrive at Taejon railroad station in South Korea on July 2, 1950. Task Force Smith was the first U.S. Army unit to enter combat in Korea. (AP/Wide World Photos)

107th Tank Regiment of the 105th Armored Division, approached across the open plain from Suwon.

At 8:00 a.m. the artillery received a request for a fire mission and at 8:16 it opened fire against the tanks about 2,000 yards in front of the infantry position. The high-explosive (HE) rounds had no effect on the tanks, which had their hatches closed, but they did kill many KPA infantrymen riding on them. The battery had only six armor-piercing high-explosive antitank (HEAT) rounds available (one-third of the total in stocks on hand when the 52nd was loading at Sasebo, Japan), all of which were given to the single howitzer forward. Antitank mines would have stopped the KPA advance, but there were none in Korea.

Smith ordered 75mm recoilless rifle fire withheld until the column of tanks reached 700 yards' range. The recoilless rifle crews then scored direct hits, again without apparent effect. The tanks stopped and opened fire with their 85mm main guns and 7.62mm machine guns.

Second Lieutenant Ollie Connor engaged the tanks as they entered the infantry position, firing 22 2.36-inch bazooka rounds at the enemy armor as it passed through and out of the position. All rounds were fired from close range, and a number were fired at the more vulnerable rear ends of the T-34s. The 2.36-

inch rounds could not penetrate the T-34 armor, but Conner is credited with disabling 2 of the KPA tanks. The 3.5-inch bazooka round would have been effective, but there were none in the country.

As they approached the lone 105mm gun forward, the two lead tanks were hit and damaged, probably by HEAT rounds. One caught fire and two of its crew members came out of the turret with their hands up; a third came out with a burp gun and fired it against a U.S. machine gun position beside the road, killing an assistant gunner, possibly the first U.S. ground soldier fatality of the Korean War. The third tank through the pass, however, knocked out the forward 105mm howitzer with cannon fire. The other tanks then swept on south past the U.S. artillery battery, which fired HE rounds against them. One tank was disabled and ultimately abandoned.

Additional KPA tanks soon swept past the U.S. position, causing some of the battery crewmen to run from their guns. Officers and noncommissioned officers continued to service the guns, and the men returned. One other tank was disabled by a hit in the track. By 10:15 a.m., the last of 33 North Korean tanks had driven through the U.S. position, killing or wounding some 20 Americans by machine-gun and artillery fire. Most of the vehicles parked immediately behind the infantry position were destroyed. The tanks also severed the wire communications link with Battery A.

Fortunately for the Americans, there were no accompanying infantrymen; the KPA tankers were unable to locate the artillery battery firing on them, and the T-34s rumbled on toward Osan. A lull of about an hour followed. The steady rain continued and the defenders used the time to improve their position. At about

11:00 a.m., three more tanks were sighted advancing from the north. Behind them was a column of trucks, followed by long columns of infantry on foot, the 16th and 18th Regiments of the North Korean 4th Division. The column was apparently not in communication with the tanks that had preceded it.

It took about an hour for the head of the column to reach a point about 1,000 yards from the U.S. position, when Smith ordered fire opened. U.S. mortars and machine guns swept the KPA column but did not stop the three tanks. They advanced to within 300 yards and raked the ridge with shell and machine-gun fire. Smith had no communication with the artillery battery, which he believed had been destroyed.

Smith held his position as long as he dared, but casualties among his men rapidly mounted. The Americans were down to fewer than 20 rounds of ammunition apiece and the North Koreans threatened to cut off their position. With KPA tanks to the rear of the American position, Smith consolidated his force in a circular perimeter on the highest ground east of the road. The North Koreans were by now employing mortar and artillery fire. About 4:30 p.m. Smith ordered a withdrawal, remarking, "This is a decision I'll probably regret the rest of my days." He planned an orderly leapfrogging withdrawal, with one platoon covering another, but under heavy KPA fire many weapons and much equipment was simply abandoned. Many men had not received word of the withdrawal, including three of the eight platoon leaders present. It was at this point that the Americans suffered most of their casualties.

The infantry withdrawal was disorganized from the start. The men came out for the most part in small groups. Some went south toward Osan but west of the road; others headed west for a short distance, then south to the road leading east from Osan. Most of the infantry passed through or near the battery position.

Shortly after ordering the infantry to withdraw, Smith set out to find Perry. He discovered the artillery still in position east of the road. Smith was surprised to find the battery position intact with only Perry and one other man wounded. The artillerymen disabled their five howitzers by removing sights and breechblocks. The men then withdrew into Osan, when they discovered KPA tanks near the southern edge of the town. They then turned back and drove east out of Osan. Fortunately, there was no KPA pursuit. The infantry element split into many groups, which scattered. Some men headed east, while others went south and around Osan.

At Chonan, only 185 men of the task force could be accounted for. Subsequently, C Company commander Captain Richard Dashner came in with 65 more, bringing the total to near 250. More men trickled back to U.S. positions during the following week. One survivor even made it from the west coast by sampan to Pusan. In the battle approximately 150 U.S. infantrymen were killed, wounded, or missing. All 5 officers and 10 enlisted men of the forward observer liaison, machine gun, and bazooka group were lost. KPA casualties in the battle before Osan were approximately 42 dead and 85 wounded. The KPA also had 4 tanks destroyed and 2 or 3 damaged but repairable. In the Battle of Osan, Task Force Smith had held up the KPA advance for perhaps 7 hours.

The North Koreans continued their offensive south against more and more units of the 24th Division. On July 6, they forced a U.S. withdrawal from the next blocking position at Pyongtaek, held by the 34th Regiment. The 21st Regiment imposed another slight delay on the KPA in front of Chochiwon, but both regiments suffered heavily in these actions. These and other battles during the period until July 21 did purchase time for the 1st Cavalry and 25th Infantry divisions to arrive from Japan.

Spencer C. Tucker

References

Appleman, Roy E. *South to the Naktong, North to the Yalu.* Washington, DC: Office of the Chief of Military History, 1961.

Collins, J. Lawton. *War in Peacetime: The History and Lessons of Korea.* Boston: Houghton Mifflin, 1969.

Gugeler, Russell A. *Combat Actions in Korea.* Washington, DC: U.S. Army Center of Military History, 1954.

Rees, David. *Korea: The Limited War.* New York: St. Martin's, 1964.

Naktong Bulge, First Battle of (August 6–19, 1950)

Key battle during August 6–19, 1950, involving U.S. and Republic of Korea Army (ROKA, South Korean) forces against Korean People's Army (KPA, North Korean) troops along the Naktong River. In early August, Major General John H. Church's 24th Infantry Division numbered 9,882 men (half its authorized strength). An attachment of 486 soldiers and operational control of the 2,000-man ROKA 17th Infantry Regiment brought its aggregate strength to 12,368 men. Rated combat efficiency was 53 percent.

The division manned a 34-mile front, although doctrine called for division fronts to be only 9 miles in length. The northern 30,000-yard sector was held by the ROKA 17th Infantry; the next 12,000 yards by the U.S. 21st Infantry with the

14th Engineer Combat Battalion. The Heavy Mortar Company was on line south of the 21st. Next, in the bulge of the Naktong, was the 34th Infantry on a 16,000-yard front. Everywhere the division front was held by isolated squad and platoon enclaves, with huge gaps between them. The 3rd Battalion, 34th Infantry manned the regimental front with Companies I, L, and K, from north to south. The 1st Battalion, 34th Infantry was the regimental reserve, while the 19th Infantry was the division reserve.

At one minute after midnight on August 6, 1950, 800 members of the KPA 4th Division quietly crossed the Naktong and drove deep into the gap between Companies I and L, 34th Infantry. A counterattack by the 1st Battalion of the 34th Infantry saw its Company A reach the front line, but in effect, the counterattack failed. A subsequent attack by the 19th Infantry and 24th Recon Company relieved some pressure but failed to stay the KPA's advance.

The ROKA 17th Infantry thwarted a KPA river crossing attempt on the night of August 6–7. The next morning the Eighth Army withdrew the 17th, its place taken by Task Force Hyzer, named for Lieutenant Colonel Peter C. Hyzer, commanding officer of the 3rd Engineer Combat Battalion. Task Force Hyzer consisted of Hyzer's battalion, a light tank company (less its tanks), and the 24th Recon Company. At the same time, Eighth Army commander Lieutenant General Walton H. Walker reduced the 24th Infantry Division's front by 20,000 yards, assigning this to the 1st Cavalry Division on the 24th's right flank.

Counterattacks and fighting on August 7–10 proved fruitless, although the newly arrived 9th Infantry Regiment of the U.S. 2nd Division was thrown into

Battery B, 61st Field Artillery, of the 1st Cavalry Division fires across the Naktong River at Korean People's Army (North Korean army) positions on August 7, 1950, during the First Battle of the Naktong Bulge. (U.S. Army Center of Military History)

the battle. KPA troops now approached the town of Yongsan in the 24th Division rear area, and the 2nd Battalion, 27th Infantry Regiment of the 25th Division was committed to the southern flank of the 24th Division, attacking successfully northeast toward the town.

On August 10, Church formed Task Force Hill, named for Colonel John G. Hill, commander of the 9th Infantry. It included the 9th Infantry (less its 3rd Battalion), the 19th and 34th Infantry Regiments, and the 1st Battalion, 21st Infantry. But the force was inadequate.

KPA forces now cut the main supply route east of Yongsan. A series of ad hoc defensive positions were formed along this route by headquarters, military police, reconnaissance, and engineer troops, but most soon fell to enemy attack. On August 12, elements of the KPA 10th Division crossed the Naktong and seized a large terrain mass on the division's northern flank (Hill 409) but never moved beyond that point.

On August 13, the 2nd Battalion of the 27th Infantry, joined by the 3rd Battalion, attacked again, driving closer to Yongsan and making contact with 1st Battalion of the 21st Infantry and the freshly arrived 1st Battalion of the 23rd Infantry of the U.S. 2nd Division. This meeting opened the supply route.

Task Force Hill was not strong enough to continue attacking on August 14 and 15. The KPA attacked the 1st Battalion of the 21st shortly after midnight on the 15th, and then attacked all across the front, penetrating the 2nd Battalion of the 9th Regiment, 2nd Division's lines. Continuing on August 16, the KPA pushed the 2nd Battalion of the 19th back some 600 yards and forced the 1st Battalion of the 34th Infantry to give ground.

On August 17, Task Force Hill was disbanded, its components reverting to division control. That day the 1st Marine Provisional Brigade (5th Marine Regiment, artillery battalion, and tank company) was committed to the fray, attached to the 24th Division.

The Marine 2nd Battalion attacked the KPA on Obong-ni Ridge. The army's 9th Infantry, on the marines' right, was to attack at the same time. The commanders of the 5th Marines and 9th Infantry decided to have the marines attack first, and then support the army attack. This proved to be a mistake, for KPA troops in the army's zone poured deadly fire into the flanks and rear of the attackers. This, coupled with very stubborn resistance, limited the marines to the seizure of a single knob on the ridge. Then the 9th attacked and eliminated the threat to the marines from that quarter.

The Marine 1st Battalion continued the assault on Obong-ni, taking two-thirds of the ridge. The marines defeated a KPA counterattack that night, and the next morning seized the remainder of Obong-ni and a promontory across the valley from it. Army units also continued attacking north of the marines on August 18, some of its units taking heavy casualties. But KPA troops were dislodged and began fleeing toward and across the Naktong, hastened by heavy, accurate air, artillery, and mortar fire.

By August 19, the United Nations Command had restored the river line, but at the high cost of more than 1,800 casualties. The KPA 4th Division, which had numbered about 8,000 men, was reduced to some 3,500 men and had lost all of its artillery and heavy equipment.

Uzal W. Ent

References

Appleman, Roy E. *South to the Naktong, North to the Yalu.* Washington, DC: Office of the Chief of Military History, Department of the Army, 1961.

Blair, Clay. *The Forgotten War: America in Korea, 1950–1953.* New York: Times Books, 1987.

Ent, Uzal W. *Fighting on the Brink: Defense of the Pusan Perimeter.* Paducah, KY: Turner Publishing Co., 1996.

Montross, Lynn, and Nicholas A. Canzona. *U.S. Marine Operations in Korea 1950–53.* Vol. 1, *The Pusan Perimeter.* Washington, DC: Historical Branch, G-3, Headquarters, United States Marine Corps, 1955.

Inchon Landing: Operation CHROMITE (September 15, 1950)

Amphibious assault that turned the tide of the Korean War. By mid-July 1950, Republic of Korea Army (ROKA, South Korean) and U.S. troops were restricted to the Pusan Perimeter. Even as the U.S.

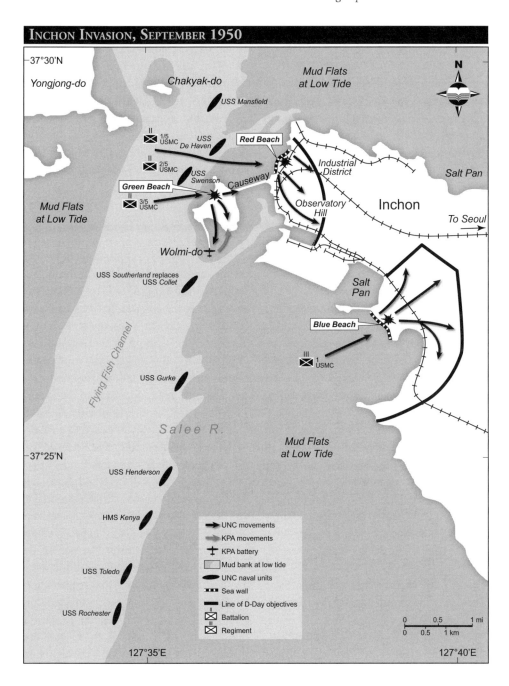

INCHON INVASION, SEPTEMBER 1950

forces endeavored to blunt the Korean People's Army (KPA, North Korean) offensive and secure the vital port of Pusan, United Nations commander General Douglas MacArthur prepared to open a second front, believing that it was preferable to a frontal assault on the Pusan Perimeter. An attack elsewhere would present the North Koreans with a two-front war. Confident that Eighth Army could hold the perimeter, MacArthur began diverting resources for an invasion force.

Inchon was the point selected. Korea's second largest port, Inchon was some 20 miles west of the ROK capital of Seoul. This area was the most important road and rail hub in Korea and a vital link in the main KPA supply line to their forces on the Pusan Perimeter. Cutting the line here would starve KPA forces facing Eighth Army. Kimpo Airfield, located on the northwest edge of Seoul, was one of the few hard-surface airfields in Korea. Further, the capture of Seoul would be a serious psychological and political blow for the North Koreans, the sort of grand gesture that so appealed to MacArthur.

MacArthur initially planned to put the 1st Cavalry Division ashore at Inchon as early as July 22. Events overtook this, and the operation was abandoned on July 10. That same day MacArthur met in Tokyo with Lieutenant General Lemuel Shepherd, commander of the Pacific Fleet Marine Force. With Joint Chiefs of Staff (JCS) approval, Shepherd said the whole 1st Marine Division could be in Korea within six weeks and in action by September 15. MacArthur immediately requested the two remaining regiments of the division. Its 5th Regiment, about to sail from San Diego, was already earmarked for action along the Pusan Perimeter, where it would be redesignated the 1st Provisional Marine Brigade. At first the JCS agreed to send only the 1st Regiment, but on August 10 it allowed MacArthur the 7th as well; however, only the 1st and 5th were at Inchon on D-Day.

Planning for the Inchon invasion, code named Operation CHROMITE, began on August 12 and was completed in only one month. It was carried out by the interservice Joint Strategic Plans and Operations Group (JSPOG), under con-

trol of the Operations Division of the Far East Command. The Special Planning Staff of JSPOG emerged as the nucleus of the staff of X Corps. The corps was activated on August 26, the same day that MacArthur appointed his chief of staff, Major General Edward M. Almond, to command it. Low morale in Eighth Army may have led MacArthur to divide military authority in Korea; X Corps was entirely separate from Eighth Army, a decision that would have unfortunate repercussions.

Objectives of Operation CHROMITE were neutralization of Wolmi-do, the island controlling access to Inchon harbor (the marines regarded this as essential to protect the subsequent assault at Inchon); the landing at Inchon and capture of the city; seizure of Kimpo Airfield; and, finally, capture of Seoul.

The only real opposition to the idea of a second front came from Eighth Army. Its staff was strongly opposed to weakening the Pusan Perimeter and believed that if reinforcements intended for X Corps were sent to them they could defeat the North Koreans without what appeared to be a risky grandstand play. Apart from Eighth Army, there was general agreement on a second front, but not on the place; only MacArthur favored Inchon.

The JCS and most of MacArthur's subordinate commanders, including all key navy and marine commanders in the Far East, opposed Inchon. Both the tide and terrain made the operation extremely hazardous. Tidal shifts there were sudden and extreme; the range of spring tides was from an average of 23 feet to a maximum of 33. At ebb tide the harbor turned into mud flats, extending as far as 3 miles from the shoreline. Although most landing craft drew 23 feet, the tank landing ships (LSTs)—considered vital in getting heavy equipment to the shore quickly—drew 29 feet. The navy estimated that there was a narrow range around two dates, September 15 and October 11, when the tides would be high enough to let the LSTs gain Inchon. Even then, the landing forces would have only a 3-hour period on each tide in which to enter or leave the port. This meant that supplies could be landed during only 6 hours in each 24-hour period.

Flying Fish channel was narrow, winding, and studded with reefs and shoals; its five-knot current was also a problem. One sunken ship there would block all traffic. There were no beaches, only 12-foot-high seawalls that would have to be scaled. Also, the marines would have to take Wolmi-do 11 hours in advance of the assault on Inchon. At the landing site at Inchon itself there were few cargo-handling facilities. Undamaged, the port had a capacity of 6,000 tons a day, only 10 percent that of Pusan. Also, steep hills from the beaches would allow the defenders to fire down on the attackers. All of these conditions precluded a night assembly of the invasion force; the main landing would have to take place in the evening with only two hours of daylight to secure a perimeter ashore.

Suggestions were made for landing at either Kunsan to the south or Chinnampo to the north, but Kunsan was too close to the Pusan Perimeter and Chinnampo, Pyongyang's port, was too far north. Posung-myon, 30 miles south of Inchon, was ruled out because of an inadequate road network from its beaches.

On August 23, MacArthur met with his critics in a final dramatic meeting in the Dai-Ichi building in Tokyo. His commanders, Lieutenant General George E. Stratemeyer, Vice Admiral C. Turner Joy, and General Almond were there. Army chief of staff General J. Lawton Collins

and chief of naval operations Admiral Forrest P. Sherman were on hand from Washington to express JCS "grave reservations" over the operation. The U.S. Navy and Marine Corps contingent included commander in chief Pacific Admiral Arthur Radford, Vice Admiral A. D. Struble, and Rear Admiral James H. Doyle; generals Shepherd and Oliver P. Smith represented the Marine Corps.

Doyle, an expert on amphibious operations, began the meeting by listing navy objections. He concluded his remarks with, "The best I can say is that Inchon is not impossible." General Collins expressed reservations about withdrawing the Marine Brigade from the Pusan Perimeter and the possibility that, once ashore, X Corps might be pinned down at Inchon. He preferred Kunsan.

Finally, MacArthur spoke for some 45 minutes. He said he recognized the hazards but expressed confidence in the navy and marines to overcome them. To inject reinforcements on the Pusan Perimeter might risk stalemate. An envelopment from a landing at Kunsan would be too narrow. That the North Koreans did not anticipate an assault at Inchon would help ensure its success.

Although some senior officers at the briefing remained unconvinced, MacArthur's remarks were the turning point in the debate. General Shepherd made one subsequent futile effort to persuade MacArthur to choose Posung-myon, where navy divers had landed and found beach conditions suitable. On August 28, MacArthur received formal approval from the JCS for the Inchon landing. The chiefs took the unusual precaution of securing the written approval of President Harry S. Truman for the operation; this undoubtedly reflected fears that, if the operation were unsuccessful, they

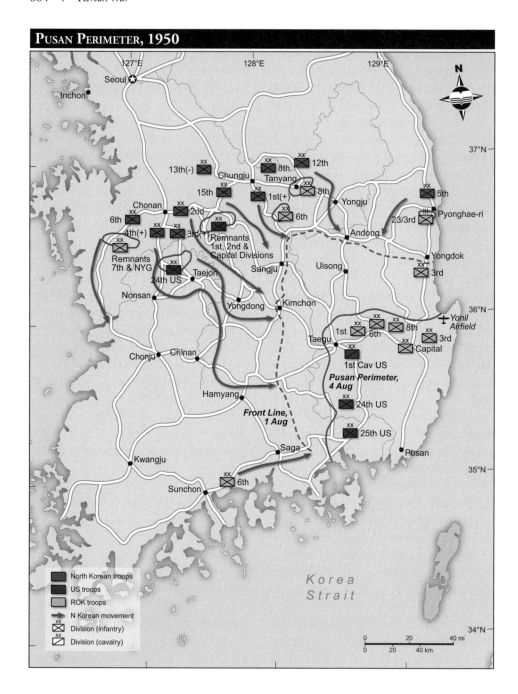

PUSAN PERIMETER, 1950

Legend:
- North Korean troops
- US troops
- ROK troops
- N Korean movement
- Division (infantry)
- Division (cavalry)

would be held responsible. There is no indication that Truman ever believed it might fail.

The major units of X Corps were the 7th Army and 1st Marine Divisions. Sup-

port units were the 92nd and 96th Field Artillery Battalions (155mm howitzers); the 50th Antiaircraft Artillery Battalion; the 19th Engineer Combat Group; and the 2nd Engineer Special Brigade.

The 7th was the one remaining division of Eighth Army not sent to Korea from Japan. Commanded by Major General David G. Barr, it was seriously under-strength and was augmented by all available reinforcements, including Koreans. More than 8,600 Korean recruits arrived in Japan before the division embarked for Inchon and approximately 100 of them were assigned to each rifle company and artillery battery. Division strength on embarkation was 24,815 men, including Koreans.

The 1st Marine Division, commanded by Major General Oliver P. Smith, was made a heavy division with the addition of the Marine Brigade, redesignated the 5th Marines. On invasion day, the 1st Marine Division numbered 25,040 men, including 2,760 army troops and 2,786 Korean marines attached; with the addition of the 7th Marine Regiment, organic marine strength increased by 4,000 men. Lieutenant General Walton Walker, commander of Eighth Army, was upset that the brigade would be withdrawn from the line with the North Koreans planning a new assault against the Pusan Perimeter in early September. He secured agreement that it would be released only at the last possible moment and that a regiment of the 7th Army Division would be kept in Pusan Harbor as long as possible to act as a floating reserve.

The Marine Corps had considerable interest in the success of the Inchon operation. Many influential figures were questioning the Marine Corps' viability. A year before, chairman of the Joint Chiefs of Staff General Omar Bradley had observed that large-scale amphibious landings were a thing of the past. As General Shepherd put it, "The Marine Corps was fighting for its very existence."

More than 200 agents inserted into the Inchon area reported approximately 500 North Korean army troops on Wolmi-do, 1,500 around Inchon, and another 500 at Kimpo Airfield. There were, however, major reinforcements only a few hours away, in the southeast.

On D-Day the tides would be at approximately 6:30 a.m. and 7:15 p.m. with a maximum of 31 feet of water in the evening. A battalion landing team of 5th Marines was to be put ashore on the morning tide at Green Beach on Wolmi-do at 6:30 a.m. The major landings would be at 5:30 p.m., at Red Beach, Inchon's sea front, and at Blue Beach, three miles to the southeast, in order to command rail and road lines from Seoul. Eight LSTs would follow the assault force with heavy equipment and landing teams.

Deception to confuse the North Koreans as to the intended landing site included bombarding Chinnampo by a British naval task force and unloading a landing party at Kunsan from a British frigate. Miraculously, although the destination of Inchon was not closely held, no word of it got to the KPA command.

Admiral Struble in the *Rochester* commanded Joint Task Force 7, the naval force organized for the Inchon landings. Rear Admiral Doyle, second-in-command, was on the *Mount McKinley*. Each of seven subordinate task forces was assigned specific objectives.

More than 230 ships took part in the operation.

The armada of vessels carrying nearly 70,000 men was a makeshift affair. It included ships from Australia, Canada, New Zealand, France, Holland, and Great Britain. Marine aircraft from two escort carriers, naval aircraft from the *Boxer,* and British aircraft from a light British carrier provided air support over the landing area. Thirty-seven of 47 LSTs in the invasion were hastily recalled from Japanese merchant service and were run by Japanese crews.

Loading was delayed for 36 hours by the 110-mph winds of Typhoon Jane on September 3. There was some damage from the storm but deadlines were met. On September 13, the task force, now at sea, was assaulted by Typhoon Kezia with 60-mph winds, although no serious damage resulted.

The convoy reached the Inchon Narrows just before dawn on September 15, the fifth day of air and naval bombardment of Wolmi-do. The naval Gunfire Support Group was made up of four cruisers and six destroyers. At approximately 6:30 a.m., the 5th Marines went ashore at Wolmi-do, MacArthur observing it from the bridge of the *Mount McKinley*. Resis-

tance was light, and Wolmi-do and nearby Sowolmi-do were both secured by noon. A total of 108 North Koreans were killed and 136 were captured. Approximately 100 more who refused to surrender were sealed in caves by tank dozers. Marine casualties were 17 wounded.

The marines requested permission to continue their advance across the 400-yard causeway to Inchon but were refused. The invaders were now cut off from the fleet by a vast sea of mud. There was little KPA fire from Inchon, and covering aircraft could detect no reinforcements en route.

At 2:30 p.m., the cruisers and destroyers in the invasion force began a shore bombardment of Inchon. KPA return fire was sporadic and light. At approximately 4:30 p.m. the first wave of landing craft left the transports for Inchon, and at 5:30

In one of the best known photographs of the Korean War, 1st Division marines use scaling ladders to climb over the sea wall in the September 15, 1950, Inchon invasion. (National Archives)

p.m. the first Americans climbed up ladders onto the seawall. As on Wolmi-do, most of the defenders were still in a state of shock from the bombardment.

The sun was setting and visibility was further inhibited by smoke and drizzle. Careful plans went awry or were forgotten as the landing craft made for the waterfront. Some in the second wave grounded and the men were forced to wade ashore, but within six hours the marines were firmly lodged in Inchon. Eight specially loaded LSTs also made it to the seawall, where they disgorged jeeps, trucks, tanks, and supplies. The marine landing force sustained casualties on D-Day of 20 killed in action, 1 missing, and 174 wounded.

On the morning of September 16, the 1st and 5th Regiments linked up ashore and began the drive east to Seoul; the ROK marines were left behind to mop up Inchon. Early on September 17, the 5th Marines ambushed a column of 6 KPA T-34 tanks and 200 infantry. By the night of the 17th, much of Kimpo Airfield had been taken; it was completely in Marine hands on September 18. That same day, the 7th Infantry Division started landing at Inchon; and on September 21 the remaining Marine regiment, the 7th, disembarked. By the end of September 19, 5th Marines had cleared the entire south bank of the Han River on their front; they crossed the river a day later, but were soon slowed by determined KPA resistance. The 1st Regiment encountered difficult fighting with a regiment of the KPA 18th Division on the 22nd, before it too reached the Han.

On September 16, a day after the Inchon invasion, General Walker's Eighth Army began its breakout along the Pusan Perimeter and drove north. The Inchon and Pusan forces made contact on September 26 at Osan.

MacArthur and Almond were determined to capture Seoul on September 25, three months to the day after the North Korean invasion. Almond had made it clear to General Smith that the city must fall by that date. But the U.S. flag, soon to be replaced by that of the United Nations, was not raised at the Capitol Building, by the 5th Marines, until the afternoon of September 27, although Almond announced just before midnight on September 25 that the city had fallen. On September 29, MacArthur presided over an emotional ceremony in the Capitol Building marking the liberation of Seoul and the return of the Syngman Rhee government.

The victory of the Inchon–Seoul Campaign greatly increased MacArthur's self-confidence, so much that he now tended to dismiss reservations from Washington about his plans. The KPA was so badly beaten that MacArthur was certain the war for Korea had been won and that it was just a matter of mopping up. He did not anticipate a massive Chinese intervention.

Spencer C. Tucker

References

Appleman, Roy E. *South to the Naktong, North to the Yalu*. Washington, DC: Office of the Chief of Military History, 1961.

Field, James A., Jr. *History of United States Naval Operations: Korea*. Washington, DC: U.S. Government Printing Office, 1962.

Gugeler, Russell A. *Combat Actions in Korea*. Washington, DC: U.S. Army Center of Military History, 1954.

Heinl, Robert D. *Victory at High Tide: The Inchon–Seoul Campaign*. Philadelphia: Lippincott, 1968.

Montross, Lynn, and Nicholas A. Canzona. *U.S. Marine Operations in Korea*. Vol. 2, *The Inchon–Seoul Operation*. Washington, DC: U.S. Marine Corps Historical Branch, 1954–1957.

Chipyong-ni, Battle of (February 13–15, 1951)

Mid-February 1951 perimeter defense engagement involving the 23rd Infantry Regimental Combat Team (RCT) of the 2nd Infantry Division and the Chinese People's Volunteer Army (CPVA, Chinese Communists) in and around the small village of Chipyong-ni, about 50 miles east of Seoul. This engagement, together with another at Wonju to the east, is described by some historians as the high water mark for the CPVA in Korea. The battle was a major turning point in the Korean War in that it marked the end of the CPVA's strategic initiative.

In the weeks after the late November 1950 entrance of Chinese forces into the fighting, there was considerable uncertainty over CPVA capabilities and intentions. United Nations (UN) forces had pulled back below the 38th parallel and given up the South Korean capital of Seoul. Large stocks of supplies had been destroyed to prevent their capture, and the UN command had even prepared plans for the total evacuation of the peninsula.

Fighting at Chipyong-ni by the 23rd RCT and at Wonju by the 2nd Division's other two regiments—the 9th and 38th—settled the question of whether U.S. and UN forces could prevail against the CPVA. Completely surrounded and cut off from friendly forces during February 13–15 in almost constant fighting from a perimeter defense formation, the 23rd RCT held off a numerically superior enemy force, and inflicted staggering casualties on it while incurring only slight casualties itself, save in the counterattacking reserve company.

The Chipyong-ni fighting also signaled a change in U.S. battlefield tactics in Korea. Before it and the Wonju engagements, United Nations Command (UNC) forces had followed the practice of "rolling with the punch" when attacked. Instead of "standing and fighting," units would withdraw to avoid anticipated encirclement.

Commanded by Colonel Paul L. Freeman, the 23rd RCT included the regiment's three infantry battalions, the French Infantry Battalion, a Ranger Company, and attached artillery, tank, and engineer elements. In early February, the 23rd RCT was in position in and around the transportation hub village of Chipyong-ni, the juncture of several roads and crossed by a railroad line. On February 11–12, two Chinese armies and a Korean People's Army (KPA, North Korean) corps struck the central UN front, scattered three Republic of Korea Army (ROKA) divisions, and forced other UN troops in the sector to withdraw southward. The Communists aimed their attack at the communication centers of Wonju and Chipyong-ni.

Colonel Freeman soon received word of the withdrawal of friendly units on his flanks and noted the ominous buildup of several divisions of enemy forces to his front. Knowing that he was greatly outnumbered, he asked Division Commander Major General Nick Ruffner when he too could begin a withdrawal. To Freeman's surprise, Ruffner refused permission. Instead, he informed Freeman that new Eighth Army commander, Lieutenant General Matthew B. Ridgway, wanted a test of strengths; Chipyong-ni and Wonju were to be defended and held. Freeman was ordered to form a tight perimeter defense pocket, to dig in deeply, and to lay in supplies of food, ammunition, and other items. He was told that if he were attacked and surrounded, he would be resupplied by air drops and a relief column by the 5th Cavalry Regiment of the 1st Cavalry Division driving up from Yoju to the south.

Freemen promptly began to comply with those instructions, while at the same time carrying out vigorous patrols for up to three miles in front of all forward positions. His battalions were displaced as follows: 1st Battalion to the north sector of the perimeter, 3rd to the east, 2nd to the south, and the French Battalion to the south and southwest. Freeman held his B Company and the Ranger Company in reserve in the center of the perimeter near his regimental command post (CP).

Shortly after dusk on February 13, Communist forces began to shell the perimeter center and some forward positions with artillery and mortar fire. Whistles, bugles, and other noise-making devices could be heard in the darkness in front of most perimeter positions. Around midnight, companies of the 1st Battalion came under attack. This spread until by daylight the entire perimeter was under assault, which continued unabated for most of the next three days. Freeman's forward companies held off the Chinese efforts to overrun the town and killed thousands of the attackers. Freeman himself was lightly wounded in the leg by a shell fragment but refused to be evacuated while fighting continued.

Around 3:15 a.m. on February 14, a large number of Communist troops forced most of F and G Companies of the 2nd Battalion from their positions on the southern rim of the perimeter, and occupied high ground there. This was a serious threat to the very existence of the perimeter. It exposed the flank of the remainder of the 2nd Battalion to the east and the French Battalion to the west, and it gave Communist forces full and unobstructed observation of, and allowed direct fire on, the entire center of the

perimeter. The CPVA also held a pathway through which forces could be channeled into the perimeter.

Freeman recognized that the gap in his perimeter must be closed at all costs if his command was to survive. He immediately ordered a counterattack by the Ranger Company and surviving elements of F and G Companies. This commenced at daylight on February 14 but was repulsed with heavy losses.

Freeman then ordered B Company, his regimental reserve, to retake the ground lost and restore the integrity of the perimeter. B Company launched its attack around noon on February 15. The attack occurred across open ground on a sunny day, in full view of Communist forces. The company advanced under intense Communist fire. Mortar and machine-gun fire rained on the attacking troops and men fell on all sides. By 4:00 p.m., with help from a napalm air strike and Communist forces apparently aware that an armored relief column was approaching from the south, B Company finally routed the enemy and closed the breach in the perimeter. Fighting ended when the perimeter was secured. In its attack, B Company had suffered more than 50 percent casualties and all of its platoon sergeants had been killed or wounded. These casualties are in sharp contrast with the half dozen or so casualties incurred by other on-line companies of the regiment, which had the advantage of being in skillfully prepared, well-protected, and deep positions.

By late afternoon on February 15, elements of the 5th Cavalry Regiment could be seen to the south approaching the perimeter. By dusk, its leading elements entered the perimeter through the road from Yoju that passed between and marked the boundaries of the 2nd and French Battalion positions.

Depiction of the Battle of Chipyong-ni on February 13–15, 1951. The 23rd Infantry Regimental Combat Team of the 2nd Infantry Division, with attached French and Dutch units, moving forward to attack in advance of the Eighth Army, was cut off and surrounded by Chinese forces in the narrow Korean valley of Chipyong-ni north of Seoul. (U.S. Army Center of Military History)

UN casualties in the fighting at Chipyong-ni were 51 killed in action, 250 wounded in action, and 42 missing in action. Confirmed Communist casualties came to 2,000 killed and 3,000 wounded, although their actual losses were assumed to be much higher. The fighting at Chipyong-ni established that UN and U.S. forces could withstand anything that the Communists could throw at them. The CPVA never again held the clear strategic initiative in the war.

Sherman W. Pratt

References

Blair, Clay. *The Forgotten War: America in Korea, 1950–1953.* New York: Times Books, 1987.

Hamburger, Kenneth E. *Leadership in the Crucible: The Korean War Battles of Twin Tunnels & Chipyong-ni.* College Station: Texas A&M University Press, 2003.

Munroe, Clark C. *The Second U. S. Division in Korea, 1950–1951.* Tokyo: Toppan Printing, n.d.

Pratt, Sherman W. *Decisive Battles of the Korean War. An Infantry Company Commander's View of the War's Most Critical Engagements.* New York: Vantage Press, 1992.

U.S. Marine Corps and ROKA officers under his command. His handling of the still-segregated black and Puerto Rican units under his command has resulted in military historian Clay Blair branding him a blatant racist. Yet Almond could also be a skillful and brave battlefield commander.

In July 1951, Almond returned to the United States to head the U.S. Army War College. He retired from the army in January 1953 and moved to Anniston, Alabama. He joined an insurance company in Alabama and served as the president of the Virginia Military Institute's Board of Visitors. Almond died on June 11, 1979.

David T. Zabecki

References

Blair, Clay. *The Forgotten War: America in Korea, 1950–1953.* New York: Times Books, 1987.

Mossman, Billy C. *U.S. Army in the Korean War: Ebb and Flow, November 1950–July 1951.* Washington, DC: U.S. Army Center of Military History, 1990.

Stanton, Shelby. *America's Tenth Legion: X Corps in Korea.* Novato, CA: Presidio Press, 1989.

Austin, Warren N. (1877–1962)

Attorney, diplomat, and U.S. representative to the United Nations (UN) (1946–1953). Born on November 12, 1877, in Highgate Center, Vermont, Warren N. Austin graduated from the University of Vermont, after which he joined his father's legal practice in St. Albans, Vermont, and took an active role in state Republican politics. From 1916 to 1917, he represented the National City Bank's American International Corporation in Beijing (Peking). He returned to practice law in Burlington, Vermont, in mid-1917, and in 1931 he won a special election to the U.S. Senate, where he served for the next 15 years.

Austin distinguished himself by belonging to the small group of internationalist Republicans who opposed the neutrality legislation of the 1930s, advocated increases in military budgets, and believed that Washington should adopt a more active foreign policy. After the United States entered World War II, Austin called for immediate planning for the postwar world.

In 1942, the Franklin D. Roosevelt administration, anxious to ensure bipartisan support for its foreign policy, invited Austin to join the State Department's congressional foreign policy advisory group. In this position, Austin played a major role in persuading the Republican Party leadership in its 1944 platform to endorse the creation of an international organization, together with international financial institutions and the UN Relief and Rehabilitation Administration. In 1942 Austin's internationalist stance led to his dismissal as informal Republican minority leader in the Senate, but in 1946 he won his reward when President Harry S. Truman appointed him the first U.S. ambassador to the UN.

Austin often found himself and his mission bypassed by more hard-line members of the Truman administration. He was in fact forced to defend positions that seemed to conflict with his personal predilections. An eloquent speaker for the highest U.S. and international ideals, Austin was not a close adviser to any of the secretaries of state under whom he served, and he exercised little influence on policy formulation. Austin's own outlook hardened as the Cold War intensified, a process reinforced by the outbreak of the Korean War.

U.S. representative to the United Nations Warren Austin holding a Russian-made submachine gun captured by U.S. forces in July 1950. Austin charged the Soviet Union was sending arms to North Korea. (National Archives)

Austin returned early from vacation to push through the June 27, 1950, UN Resolution that authorized military intervention in Korea. In July, Austin pressed strongly for a unified command in Korea under U.S. leadership, a stance that irritated his colleagues in some of the allied and neutral delegations. They were also bothered by his tendency to regard the war as a moral crusade in which U.S. and UN interests were indistinguishable.

In August 1950, when the Soviet delegation returned to the UN Security Council after its boycott, Austin resisted Soviet attempts to switch the focus from the Korean situation to the question of UN recognition of the People's Republic of China (PRC). He also hinted that the ulti-mate aim of UN intervention should not be restricted to a restoration of the antebellum status quo, but should include the reunification of the Korean peninsula.

Although less prominent in the General Assembly meetings of November 1950, which were dominated by Secretary of State Dean Acheson and State Department consultant John Foster Dulles, Austin, after the Chinese intervention of late 1950, expressed his country's outrage in the Security Council and rebutted Soviet and Chinese Communist charges of U.S. aggression. Early in 1951, Austin was also prominent in resisting attempts by U.S. allies and Arab and Asian powers to end the war by concessions to the PRC over Taiwan and its representation in the UN.

He was also influential in obtaining passage of the February 1, 1951, UN resolution that condemned the Chinese crossing of the 38th parallel. Austin fully supported President Truman's decisions to replace General Douglas MacArthur as commander in chief of UN forces and keep the war a limited conflict. Later in 1951 and 1952, his own poor health and the secretary of state's personal involvement in dealing with the UN limited Austin's activities on Korea.

In 1953, Austin retired to Burlington. Now a hard-line anticommunist, he became honorary chairman of the Committee of One Million, designed to exclude the PRC from the UN. He died on December 25, 1962, in Burlington, Vermont.

Priscilla Roberts

References

Foot, Rosemary J. *The Wrong War: American Policy and the Dimensions of the Korean Conflict, 1950–1953*. Ithaca, NY: Cornell University Press, 1985.

Mazuzan, George T. *Warren R. Austin at the U.N., 1946–1953*. Kent, OH: Kent State University Press, 1977.

Stueck, William W., Jr. *The Korean War: An International History*. Princeton, NJ: Princeton University Press, 1995.

Barr, David Goodwin (1895–1970)

U.S. Army general. Born on June 16, 1895, in Nanafalia, Alabama, David Goodwin Barr attended Alabama Presbyterian College for three years and was commissioned a 2nd lieutenant of infantry in the Officer Reserve Corps in November 1917. During World War I, he served with the 1st Division in France and in the occupation of Germany until September 1919, when he returned to the United States. A year later he was promoted to 1st lieutenant.

In the interwar years Barr served as an instructor with the New York National Guard; with the 16th Tank Battalion at Camp Meade, Pennsylvania; and with the 22nd Infantry Regiment at Camp McClellan, Alabama. During 1926–1927, he was assigned to the office of the U.S. military attaché in Paris and attended the French tank school at Versailles. He subsequently served with tank units at Fort Benning, Georgia, and in October 1930 he became adjutant of the newly formed Mechanized Force at Fort Eustis, Virginia. Barr graduated from the Army Command and Staff School at Fort Leavenworth, Kansas, in June 1936.

After graduation from the Army War College in June 1939, Barr was assigned briefly in Washington, D.C., before joining the I Armored Corps at Fort Knox, Kentucky. In May 1941 he became corps G-4 and in June 1942 was advanced to brigadier general and reassigned as chief of staff of the Armored Force, in which position he served until July 1943, when

U.S. Army major general David G. Barr, commander of the 7th Infantry Division, shown aboard ship on December 21, 1950, during the Hungnam evacuation. (Naval Historical Society)

he was sent to London to serve as chief of staff of the European Theater. In January 1944, Barr was named chief of staff, Headquarters, North African Theater of Operations. He was promoted to major general in February 1944, and that September became chief of staff of the U.S. Sixth Army Group in France.

Barr returned to the United States in July 1945 and served as a personnel officer at Headquarters, Army Ground Forces, until January 1948, when he became chief of the Army Advisory Group in Nanjing (Nanking), China. In that position he advised Secretary of Defense James Forrestal in January 1949 to discontinue arms shipments to Chiang Kai-shek (Jiang Jieshi) because they were being intercepted by Mao Zedong's communist forces.

In May 1949, General Barr assumed command of the 7th Infantry Division in Japan. With the beginning of the Korean War in June 1950, Barr took the division to Korea in September and commanded it in the hard fighting during the Inchon campaign and recapture of Seoul operations, in the X Corps amphibious landing at Wonsan (which he opposed), on the march to the Yalu River and the subsequent withdrawal, and in fighting around the Changjin (Chosin) Reservoir. Barr was an excellent staff officer and well liked by his troops but lacked the drive of the best combat commanders. He was frequently at odds with imperious X Corps commander Lieutenant General Edward M. Almond and Almond's staff. In accordance with the army policy of reassigning senior commanders with recent combat experience to training commands, Barr left Korea in January 1951 to become commandant of The Armor School at Fort Knox, Kentucky. He retired from active duty in February 1952

and died on September 26, 1970, in Falls Church, Virginia.

Charles R. Shrader

References

Blair, Clay. *The Forgotten War: America in Korea, 1950–1953.* New York: Times Books, 1987.

Heinl, Robert D. *Victory at High Tide: The Inchon–Seoul Campaign.* Philadelphia: Lippincott, 1968.

Stanton, Shelby. *America's Tenth Legion: X Corps in Korea.* Novato, CA: Presidio Press, 1989.

Bradley, Omar Nelson (1893–1981)

U.S. Army general and first chairman of the Joint Chiefs of Staff (JCS) from 1949 to 1953. Born on February 12, 1893, at Clark, Missouri, Omar Bradley graduated from the United States Military Academy, West Point, in the Class of 1915 and was commissioned a 2nd lieutenant of infantry. He served in several posts in the United States and was promoted to major in 1918.

Bradley taught at West Point and in 1925 graduated from the Infantry School at Fort Benning, Georgia. He then served in Hawaii before graduating from the Command and General Staff School at Fort Leavenworth, Kansas. He served as an instructor at the Infantry School before graduating from the Army War College in 1934. He returned to West Point and in 1936 was promoted to lieutenant colonel. He served on the army general staff from 1938 to 1941 and was promoted to brigadier general in February 1941. He then commanded the Infantry School before taking command of the 82nd Division.

During World War II, Bradley served briefly as aide to General Dwight D. Eisenhower and then commanded II Corps at the end of the Tunisian Campaign and during the Sicily Campaign. He commanded the First Army in the June 1944 invasion of France. In August, he received command of the Twelfth Army Group and directed the southern wing of the Allied drive across northern France. At its peak, Twelfth Army Group included 1.3 million men, the largest force ever commanded by a U.S. general. Modest, unassuming, and always concerned about the welfare of his men, Bradley was regarded as a "soldier's general" and one of the most successful commanders of World War II. He was widely respected for his excellent administrative skills and his calmness when under stress.

Promoted to full general in March 1945, Bradley continued in command of Twelfth Army Group until the end of the war. From 1945 to 1947, he headed the Veterans Administration. In February 1948 he succeeded Eisenhower as army chief of staff, and in August 1949 he became the first chairman of the Joint Chiefs of Staff, a post he held throughout the Korean War until August 1953. In September 1950, Bradley was promoted to general of the army. Bradley disagreed with Secretary of State Dean Acheson's January 1950 definition of a U.S. defensive perimeter that excluded Korea.

During the Korean War, Bradley participated in President Harry S. Truman's decision to commit U.S. military forces in the defense of the Republic of Korea. A proponent of U.S. military action, Bradley saw this as a chance to draw a line against communist expansion, although he initially hoped to avoid the commitment of

ground forces. During the war, Bradley regularly briefed President Truman on the military situation and he accompanied Truman when he went to Wake Island to meet with General Douglas MacArthur, commander of the United Nations Command in Korea. Bradley twice visited Korea during the conflict. Throughout the war, Bradley remained the president's most trusted military adviser.

Bradley sought to limit the conflict and avoid direct conflict with the People's Republic of China. For that reason he opposed using Chinese Nationalist troops in Korea; he also believed that they were needed in the defense of Taiwan. Bradley fought to keep Europe as the top U.S. military priority, something that MacArthur could not appreciate. But Bradley also believed in the domino principle and supported U.S. military aid for the French in Indochina in the belief that if this was not done the other states of Southeast Asia would become communist. A realist, he believed that, based on "past performances" by the French, there could be no predications regarding the effects of increased U.S. assistance.

Bradley fully supported Truman in his policies, including the president's dismissal of MacArthur in April 1951. During the U.S. Senate Foreign Relations and Armed Services Committees hearings to inquire into MacArthur's removal from command, Bradley testified against MacArthur's recommendations. Bradley's attitude toward a widened war in Asia is exemplified in his well-known remark that it would be the "wrong war, in the wrong place, at the wrong time, and with the wrong enemy." Bradley's identification with the Truman administration made him the target of some Republican criticism, but he continued as JCS chairman under President Dwight Eisenhower until the expiration of his term in August 1953, when he also retired from the army.

In 1968, Bradley advised President Lyndon B. Johnson against a U.S. withdrawal from Vietnam. Bradley died in Washington, D.C., on April 8, 1981.

Spencer C. Tucker

References

Bradley, Omar N. *A Soldier's Story*. New York: Henry Holt, 1951.

Reeder, Red. *Omar Nelson Bradley: The Soldier's General*. Champaign, IL: Garrard Publishing Company, 1969.

Stueck, William W. *Rethinking the Korean War: A New Diplomatic and Strategic History*. Princeton, NJ: Princeton University Press, 1994.

Church, John Huston (1892–1953)

U.S. Army general who headed the initial survey party dispatched to Korea immediately after the June 25, 1950, Korean People's Army (KPA, North Korean) invasion of South Korea and then commander of the 24th Infantry Division (1950–1951). Born in Glen Iron, Pennsylvania, on June 28, 1892, John Huston Church attended New York University during 1915–1917. Entering the U.S. Army during World War I, he was commissioned a 2nd lieutenant and was twice wounded while leading infantry units in combat.

Following the war, Church served in a variety of assignments. He was an instructor for the National Guard and he had a tour of duty in the Philippines. During World War II, Church was first the assistant commander of the 45th and then the 84th Infantry Divisions. In 1942, he became chief of staff of the 45th Infantry Division and participated with the division in landings at Sicily, Salerno, Anzio,

and Southern France. In August 1944 he was advanced to brigadier general, and in September 1944 he became assistant division commander of the 84th Infantry Division during fighting in Germany. His unit was one of the first to reach the Elbe River.

In June 1946, Church commanded the Infantry Replacement Training Center. Later he served in a similar post at Fort Jackson, South Carolina, where he also commanded the 5th Division. During 1948–1949, he was stationed at Fort Monroe, Virginia, as deputy chief of Army Field Forces. At the start of the Korean War, Church was serving in the general headquarters, Far East Command, Tokyo.

On June 26, 1950, commander of U.S. Forces in the Far East General Douglas MacArthur, acting on instructions from Washington, named Church to head a survey team to assess the situation in the Republic of Korea (ROK, South Korea), which had been invaded the day before by the Korean People's Army (KPA), the armed forces of the Democratic People's Republic of Korea (DPRK, North Korea). When the team arrived on the evening of June 27, 1950, they found chaos. Church took charge, corralling stragglers in an attempt to form a defensive line at the Han River just south of Seoul. The capital fell late on June 28. In a radio message to MacArthur, Church advised that only U.S. troops could contain the invasion. After a personal trip to Korea the next day, MacArthur, after some hesitation, concurred in this assessment.

On July 22, 1950, Church received command of the 24th Infantry Division. Its previous commander, Major General William F. Dean, had been captured by KPA forces when they overran Taejon. When Church took command, the 24th Division was exhausted and no longer

U.S. Army brigadier general John Church (left), heading a survey team sent to assess the situation in Korea, welcomes General Douglas MacArthur to South Korea on July 2, 1950. Three weeks later, Church assumed command of the 24th Infantry Division. (Bettmann/Corbis)

combat effective. The first U.S. division to arrive in Korea (its Task Force Smith had engaged the enemy on July 5 at Osan), it had fought delaying actions for two and a half weeks but had found itself continually outnumbered, outgunned, and outflanked. It lost almost 50 percent of its strength, almost all of its artillery, and some 60 to 70 percent of its other equipment. The toll on senior officers was high.

On July 22, the 1st Cavalry Division relieved the 24th, which was to be given a period to rest, receive replacements, and reequip. Two days later, however, Eighth Army commander General Walton H. Walker, with his entire left flank exposed, was forced to order the 24th

back into the line. The division deployed around Chinju in the southwest.

The fresh KPA 6th Division steadily forced back Church's weakened 24th. Reinforced by another regiment, however, Church was able to contain the KPA advance just west of Masan, the back door to Pusan. By August 6, an entire KPA division crossed the Naktong River into the area known as the "Naktong Bulge," which Church's division was defending. Although the 24th attacked by day, at night the KPA took back the ground gained. Church's division held for 11 days but was not strong enough to eject the KPA penetration. However, the addition of the 1st Marine Provisional

Brigade to his command enabled Church to push the KPA back across the river, destroying the crack KPA 4th Division in the process.

Reassigned to the Pohang area to the east, Church's reinforced 24th Division then contained and defeated a series of furious KPA attacks. Church continued in command of the 24th during the Pusan Perimeter breakout and the invasion of North Korea.

Church left Korea in January 1951 and became commanding general of the Infantry School, Fort Benning, Georgia. He retired from the army the next year as a major general, and died on November 3, 1953, in Washington, D.C.

Jack D. Walker

References

Appleman, Roy E. *South to the Naktong, North to the Yalu*. Washington, DC: Office of the Chief of Military History, 1992.

Blair, Clay. *The Forgotten War: America in Korea, 1950–1953*. New York: Times Books, 1987.

Ent, Uzal W. *Fighting on the Brink: Defense of the Pusan Perimeter.* Paducah, KY: Turner, 1996.

Clark, Mark Wayne (1896–1984)

U.S. Army officer and commander of United Nations forces in the Korean War. Born at Sackets Harbor, New York, on May 1, 1896, Mark Wayne Clark graduated from the United States Military Academy at West Point in 1917. He served as an infantry officer in World War I and was wounded. Following recovery, he participated in both the Saint-Mihiel and Meuse-Argonne offensives.

Clark returned to the United States in 1919, was promoted to captain, and served in a variety of posts. He graduated from the Infantry School in 1925. Pro-moted to major in 1933, he graduated from the Command and General Staff School in 1935 and from the Army War College in 1937. He served on the staff of the 3rd Infantry Division before returning to the Army War College in 1940 as an instructor. Clark was promoted to brigadier general in August 1941 and to major general in April 1942.

In May 1942, Clark became chief of staff of Army Ground Forces and, a month later, commanding general of II Corps. In October, shortly before the Allied invasion of North Africa, Clark led a covert mission to Vichy-held North Africa to meet with French leaders. Promoted to lieutenant general in November 1942, Clark commanded land forces in North Africa. Beginning in September 1943, he led the U.S. Fifth Army during its protracted march up the Italian peninsula. In early December 1944, Clark became commander of the Fifteenth Army Group, which consisted of all Allied forces fighting in the Mediterranean theater. The campaign concluded with the surrender of German troops in April–May 1945.

Clark's leadership during the Italian offensive remains controversial. He has been criticized for the Anzio landing, the bombing of Monte Casino, his determination to receive credit for liberating Rome at the expense of bagging retreating German forces, and "careless" tactics that critics claim cost thousands of lives. Clark's supporters have argued that difficult terrain, poor weather, and a fanatical German defense caused the casualties.

Following the war, Clark commanded the Allied occupation of Austria. In 1949, he became commander of Army Field Forces, Fort Monroe, Virginia, supervising troop training. When the Korean War began, Clark was concerned that this

U.S. Army general Mark W. Clark, commander of the Far East Command, signs the Korean Armistice agreement at Panmunjom, Korea, July 27, 1953. To the right are Vice Admiral Robert P. Briscoe, commander Naval Forces Far East, and Vice Admiral Joseph J. Clark, commander Seventh Fleet. (Naval Historical Center)

training be realistic. In February 1951, he traveled to Korea to inspect conditions and analyze tactics for use in training.

Clark returned to Korea on May 12, 1952, to replace General Matthew B. Ridgway as U.S. commander in chief (CINC) Far East and United Nations' CINC. He arrived to find the ground war in stalemate. The most significant combat occurred between F-86 and MiG-15 jet aircraft in the skies over an area of northwestern Korea, known as MiG Alley.

Concurrently, armistice negotiations at Panmunjom appeared hopelessly deadlocked over the repatriation of prisoners of war (POWs). The Communist side wanted all prisoners forcibly repatri-

ated, whereas the UN Command, on the insistence of President Harry S. Truman, demanded that only those wishing to return should do so.

In addition to dealing with Communist POW unrest on Koje-do, Clark had to confront the tactics of Republic of Korea (ROK, South Korean) president Syngman Rhee, who continually tried to sabotage the truce talks. While Clark agreed with Rhee's staunch anticommunist position, he was angered by Rhee's dictatorial methods and lack of understanding of military tactics. Clark even ordered the drafting of a secret contingency plan, known as Operation EVERREADY, to replace Rhee as president, but concerns about negative consequences on the battlefront caused him to consistently recommend against its implementation.

Ultimately, Clark, although obedient to President Truman's desire to limit the war, agreed with former UN commander General of the Army Douglas MacArthur's insistence on total victory. Clark also believed that the Communists would relent only if the UNC kept up military pressure. Ground action was a potential problem because it could cause significant casualties. Thus, Clark used his air assets to cut Communist communications and supply lines, hit airfields, and destroy dams and reservoirs. Some historians believe his air campaign was successful.

Throughout his tenure, Clark, like MacArthur, chafed at restrictions that prevented him from ordering direct attacks on Communist airfields and industrial centers in Manchuria. Clark had hoped that General of the Army Dwight D. Eisenhower's election as president in November 1952 would allow him to take the offensive. After Eisenhower's trip to Korea in December 1952, Clark realized that the new president, like Truman, was anxious to end the war quickly through negotiations. On July 27, 1953, a reluctant Clark signed the armistice agreement ending the Korean War. Clark returned to the United States in October 1953.

Clark retired from the U.S Army in 1954 and then became the president of the Citadel (1954–1966). He wrote two volumes of memoirs in which he made no secret of his bitterness over what he classified as a loss in Korea. He also decried what he viewed as communist sympathizers at home. Clark generally sided with conservative causes. He also publicly argued that the events in Vietnam were the result of "appeasement" in

Korea. Clark died in Charleston, South Carolina, on April 17, 1984.

William Head and Dean Corey

References

Blumenson, Martin. *Mark Clark*. New York: Congdon and Weed, 1985.

Clark, Mark W. *From the Danube to the Yalu.* New York: Harper and Row, 1954.

Toland, John R. *In Mortal Combat: Korea, 1950–1953*. New York: William Morrow, 1991.

Collins, Joseph Lawton (1896–1987)

U.S. Army general and chief of staff (1949–1953). Born in New Orleans, Louisiana, on May 1, 1896, Joseph Lawton Collins graduated from the United States Military Academy, West Point, in 1917 and served with U.S. occupation forces in Germany in 1919. He then attended and served as instructor at various service schools before being assigned to the Philippines (1933–1936). Collins later graduated from both the Industrial War College and the Army War College.

Following the Japanese attack on Pearl Harbor on December 7, 1941, Collins was assigned to the Hawaiian Department as chief of staff. He was advanced to brigadier general in February 1942 and to major general in May. Collins was appointed temporary lieutenant general in 1945. During World War II, Collins served with distinction in the Pacific and European theaters, earning the nickname "Lightning Joe." He commanded VII Army Corps in the June 1944 Normandy Invasion and during the December 1944 Ardennes Offensive.

In 1947, Collins became deputy chief of staff of the U.S. Army under General

General Joseph L. Collins served as chief of staff of the U.S. Army during the Korean War. (Corbis)

Dwight D. Eisenhower. In 1948, he was promoted to full general; during 1949–1953, he was army chief of staff. After the 1949 formation of the North Atlantic Treaty Organization (NATO), Collins became the Joint Chiefs of Staff (JCS) liaison with NATO.

Before the Korean War, Collins concurred with other members of the JCS that Korea lacked the strategic importance to be included in the U.S. defensive perimeter in Asia. In the first few days of the Korean War, Collins communicated directly with U.S. commander in the Far East General Douglas MacArthur, relaying information to President Harry S. Truman. Collins then recommended, without consulting other members of the JCS, the immediate deployment of a regimental combat team to Korea.

In early July 1950, Collins flew to Korea with U.S. Air Force Chief of Staff General Hoyt S. Vandenberg to discuss means by which the North Korean advance might be slowed and to assess MacArthur's requirements. After a second visit with MacArthur in late August, this time accompanied by chief of U.S. naval operations Admiral Forrest P. Sherman, Collins expressed to Truman "serious misgivings" about MacArthur's planned amphibious landing at Inchon. He did, however, support MacArthur's position that the Korean People's Army (KPA, North Korean) had to be completely defeated by the crossing of the 38th parallel.

Ultimately, the JCS approved the Inchon operation. Its great success made it difficult for Collins and the remainder of the JCS to challenge MacArthur's subsequent operational plans. For example, the JCS accepted MacArthur's explanation for his violation of their order not to allow non-Korean forces to approach the Manchurian border. MacArthur claimed that Republic of Korea Army (ROKA, South Korean) forces lacked the strength and "experienced leadership" to seize and hold critical border areas. Collins later admitted that the JCS should have given MacArthur greater direction and less discretion in sensitive areas.

Following the withdrawal of United Nations forces from North Korea after the massive People's Republic of China military intervention, in January 1951 Collins and Vandenberg flew to Tokyo and also visited the battlefront. Collins found the situation serious, but his report upon his return did much to lessen pressure for consideration of a hasty withdrawal and diminished the impact of MacArthur's pessimistic appraisals in order to secure support for a wider war. Collins supported Truman's decision to relieve MacArthur in April 1951.

Collins was, by the spring of 1953, sufficiently frustrated by the war's high cost and stalemate to support the use of atomic weapons, if need be, to end the war. He worked hard to meet the manpower needs of the war and to ensure that the troops were adequately trained and supplied. Less than three weeks after the signing of the armistice, in August 1953, Collins stepped down as chief of staff. A major achievement by Collins was his effort to racially integrate U.S. Army units.

At President Dwight D. Eisenhower's request, Collins remained on active duty as U.S. representative on the Military Committee and Standing Group of NATO. Eisenhower also sent Collins to Vietnam in November 1954 to assess the situation there and make recommendations as to how the government of Ngo Dinh Diem might be strengthened. His report expressed deep pessimism about the prospects for the survival of the Diem regime, but his recommendations failed to alter the thrust of U.S. policy in Vietnam. Collins retired from the U.S. Army in March 1956 at four-star rank, and the following year went to work for the pharmaceutical firm of Chas. Pfizer & Co., retiring in 1969. He died in Washington, D.C., on September 12, 1987.

Claude R. Sasso

References

Blair, Clay. *The Forgotten War: America in Korea, 1950–1953.* New York: Times Books, 1987.

Collins, J. Lawton. *Lightning Joe: An Autobiography.* Baton Rouge: Louisiana State University Press, 1979.

Pogue, Forrest C. *George C. Marshall, Statesman, 1945–1959.* New York: Viking Press, 1987.

Coulter, John Breitling (1891–1983)

U.S. Army general who served in Korea before, during, and after the Korean War. Born on April 27, 1891, in San Antonio, Texas, John Breitling Coulter graduated from the West Texas Military Academy in San Antonio in 1911 and was commissioned a 2nd lieutenant in 1912. He participated in the 1916 U.S. Punitive Expedition into Mexico. Following the U.S. entry into World War I, he saw service in France as an aide to the commander of the 42nd "Rainbow" Division and later served as a battalion commander in the Saint-Mihiel Offensive.

Returning to the United States after the war, Coulter graduated from the Cavalry School in 1922 and the Command and General Staff School in 1927. He graduated from the Army War College in 1933 and Naval War College in 1934 and was assigned to the U.S. Army military intelligence division headquarters in Washington, D.C., before becoming executive officer of the 4th Cavalry Regiment in 1935.

Promoted to brigadier general in October 1941, Coulter commanded the 3rd Cavalry Brigade when the United States entered World War II. In July 1942, he was assistant division commander (later its commander) of the 85th Infantry Division, the first all-draftee division to fight in Italy. Coulter became a major general in March 1943. After training his division in the United States and North Africa, he led it in extensive fighting in Italy. Coulter's Italian experiences resulted in his being considered an expert on mountain warfare, which would prove useful in the Korean War.

Coulter commanded the Infantry Replacement Training Center at Fort McClellan, Alabama, in 1945. In January

1948 he commanded the 7th Infantry Division in occupation of southern Korea, and by August 1948 he was deputy to Lieutenant General John R. Hodge, commanding officer of the U.S. Army Forces in Korea (USAFIK). Coulter became USAFIK commander upon Hodge's departure from Korea in August 1945 following repeated disagreements with Republic of Korea (ROK, South Korean) president Syngman Rhee about policies. Coulter stayed in Korea until January 1949.

After one year as commander of I Corps in Japan, Coulter returned to the United States as deputy commander of Fifth Army headquarters. When forces of the Democratic People's Republic of Korea (DPRK, North Korea) invaded the ROK, General Douglas MacArthur, the commander of United Nations (UN) forces in Korea, asked Coulter to command I Corps. Coulter arrived in Korea with his command staff on August 13, 1950. Eighth Army commander Lieutenant General Walton H. Walker then transferred Coulter to IX Corps.

Coulter commanded a weak portion of the South Korean front on the east coast. In charge of Task Force Jackson, consisting of ROK Army (ROKA) I Corps and other U.S. forces, Coulter removed the commander of ROKA I Corps and an ROKA division commander to bring order to what he considered a "hysterical" ROKA command. Coulter also asked Walker for additional U.S. units to halt the North Korean advance.

Although Walker admired Coulter's ability to motivate ROKA troops, he was unhappy with his overall military leadership. Walker was also antagonized by Coulter's "insistent and frequent" pleas for help when he himself was desperately seeking troops to fill gaps in the Pusan Perimeter. Walker also did not believe that Coulter was the right man to lead the breakout from the perimeter, and on September 11 he gave command of I Corps to Major General Frank W. Milburn.

Walker then gave Coulter command of IX Corps, which was not operational until a week after I Corps had begun the perimeter breakout. In mid-September, Coulter's forces focused principally on securing supply lines and eliminating pockets of bypassed Korean People's Army (KPA, North Korean) troops isolated to the rear of the UN Command advance. IX Corps continued this activity into October, when Eighth Army crossed the 38th parallel into North Korea. At the November 25–30 Battle of the Chongchon River, Coulter's IX Corps and the ROKA II Corps bore the brunt of Chinese attacks against Eighth Army by Chinese People's Volunteer Army (CPVA) forces.

Coulter initially underestimated the Chinese threat and believed that the Turkish Brigade would be able to protect Eighth Army's right flank if ROKA forces gave way. On November 30, when the U.S. 2nd Infantry Division was forced to abandon its positions, Coulter had already moved his headquarters and was in the rear at Pyongyang. Poorly informed of the dangerous situation at the front, he failed to send reserves to assist in 2nd Division's withdrawal; nor did he order a less-dangerous withdrawal route from Kunu-ri. As a result, 2nd Division suffered disaster.

Despite his reputation for poor strategic leadership, in February 1951 Coulter was promoted to lieutenant general and became deputy commander of Eighth Army by Walker's replacement, Lieutenant General Matthew B. Ridgway. Later, Ridgway named Coulter as his liaison officer to the UN Commission for the

Unification and Rehabilitation of Korea. This proved a wise choice as Coulter got along well with ROKA generals and President Rhee, whom he had known during his prewar service in Korea.

In late 1951, Coulter returned to the United States. He retired from the army in January 1952. His experiences in Korea led UN secretary-general Dag Hammarskjöld to appoint him as director of the UN Korean Reconstruction Agency (UNKRA) in May 1953. Coulter served in this post for two years and helped reconstruct war-torn South Korea. Coulter also served as Hammarskjöld's adviser after the 1956 Suez Crisis. Coulter died in Washington, D.C., on March 6, 1983.

Elizabeth D. Schafer

References

Appleman, Roy E. *Disaster in Korea: The Chinese Confront MacArthur.* College Station: Texas A&M University Press, 1989.

———. *South to the Naktong, North to the Yalu.* Washington, DC: Office of the Chief of Military History, 1961.

Blair, Clay. *The Forgotten War: America in Korea, 1950–1953.* New York: Times Books, 1987.

Dean, William Frishe (1899–1981)

U.S. Army general and commander of the 24th Infantry Division during the Korean War. William Frishe Dean was born in Carlyle, Illinois, on August 1, 1899, and graduated from the University of California at Berkeley in 1922. Dean had secured a reserve commission in May 1921, but in October 1923 he was granted a regular army commission as a 2nd lieutenant of infantry.

Dean served with the 38th Infantry Regiment at Fort Douglas, Utah, during 1923–1926. He then saw service in Panama with the 42nd and 33rd Infantry Regiments. In 1929 he rejoined the 38th Infantry, and in 1934 he was assigned to the 30th Infantry Regiment. During 1935–1936, Dean attended the Army Command and General Staff School. After a tour with the 19th Infantry Regiment, he returned to the United States and attended the U.S. Army Industrial College, graduating in June 1939. He served briefly at the Chemical Warfare School before returning to Washington that September to attend the U.S. Army War College, from which he graduated in June 1940. He then served in the Operations and Training Division of the War Department general staff and was appointed assistant to the secretary of the general staff in January 1941.

In March 1942, Dean was reassigned to Headquarters, Army Ground Forces, where he served as assistant chief, then chief, of the Requirements Section. He was promoted to brigadier general in December 1942, and in February 1944 he became assistant commander of the 44th Infantry Division in Louisiana. He moved with the division to Camp Phillips, Kansas, and from there to Southern France in August 1944. He remained with the 44th Infantry Division throughout its campaigns in Southern France and Germany. Named to command the division in December 1944, he was promoted to major general in March 1945, and in July 1945 he redeployed the division to the United States in preparation for its reassignment to the Pacific Theater.

In September 1945, Dean joined the faculty of the U.S. Army Command and General Staff School; he became assistant commandant of the school in June 1946. In October 1947, he was reassigned as military governor of U.S.-occupied southern Korea. He supervised elections there in May 1948 and then in August the inauguration of the Republic of Korea (ROK). Dean then assumed command of the 7th Infantry Division in Korea and took it to Japan in January 1949. The following June he became chief of staff of the Eighth U.S. Army in Japan. In October 1949, he was reassigned to command the 24th Infantry Division, which subsequently became the first U.S. ground combat unit to respond to the North Korean invasion of South Korea on June 25, 1950. Dean arrived at Taejon Airfield on July 3, 1950, and immediately assumed command of all U.S. forces in Korea.

Striving to stem the North Korean advance, Dean personally led his division in the bitter defense of Taejon on July 19–20, on one occasion attacking a Korean People's Army (KPA, North Korean) tank with only a hand grenade and his .45-caliber pistol. Given the near total disintegration of his division under heavy KPA attack and the lack of communications, Dean's actions can only be characterized as leading by example in desperate circumstances.

Separated from the rest of his command in the confused withdrawal from Taejon, Dean wandered alone and injured in the hills until he was betrayed by two South Koreans on August 25, 1950. He thus became the highest-ranking United Nations Command officer taken prisoner by the Communists. Dean's courageous conduct in captivity was equal to his bravery at Taejon, for which he was awarded the Medal of Honor in February 1951. He was released from captivity on September 3, 1953, and returned to the United States a hero, although he was criticized later for his defense of those U.S. prisoners of war who had cooperated with the Communists.

In December 1953, Dean became deputy commander of the Sixth U.S. Army. When he retired from active duty in October 1955, he was awarded the coveted Combat Infantryman's Badge, thus becoming only the second general officer, after General Joseph W. Stilwell, to be so honored. Dean died in Berkeley, California, on August 26, 1981.

Charles R. Shrader

References

Appleman, Roy E. *South to the Naktong, North to the Yalu.* Washington, DC: Office of the Chief of Military History, 1961.

Dean, William F., with William L. Worden. *General Dean's Story.* New York: Viking Press, 1954.

Dulles, John Foster (1888–1959)

Attorney, diplomat, and U.S. secretary of state (1953–1959). Born on February 25, 1888, in Watertown, New York, John Foster Dulles was the son of a Presbyterian minister and was raised in a conservative home. His grandfather, John Watson Foster, was President Benjamin Harrison's secretary of state and his uncle Robert Lansing would serve as President Woodrow Wilson's secretary of state. The influence of his forbears was great and opened many doors for him throughout his life.

Dulles graduated from Princeton University in 1908 and then entered law school at George Washington University. Although he never completed his law degree, he passed the New York State Bar in 1911. He then took a position as a lawyer with Sullivan and Cromwell in New York City.

When World War I began, Robert Lansing, then secretary of state, sent Dulles on a tour of Latin America to

John Foster Dulles was secretary of state in the Eisenhower administration during 1953–1959 and well known for his strong anticommunist views. (Library of Congress)

lobby support for the United States. Dulles spent the remainder of the war as a lawyer for the War Industries Board before Lansing invited him as a member of the U.S. delegation to the 1919 Paris Peace Conference.

During the 1920s and 1930s, Dulles rose to senior partner with Sullivan and Cromwell while maintaining an active interest in foreign affairs. Dulles also became associated with the moderate wing of the Republican Party. Throughout the 1940s Dulles continued to be viewed with suspicion by the Republican right wing, especially as he served on the Truman administration's delegation to the United Nations from 1946 until 1948. His own turn at office came in 1949 when then New York governor Thomas E. Dewey appointed him to serve out the remainder of Robert Wagner's U.S. Senate term.

Although Dulles was now viewed as a foreign policy expert by both parties, Republican suspicions were again raised in 1950 when President Harry S. Truman named him to be his special ambassador to Japan for negotiations on a Japanese peace treaty. By this time, Dulles had grown increasingly worried over Soviet intentions in the Cold War, and the Korean War confirmed his fears.

Dulles believed that the Soviet Union was behind the Democratic People's Republic of Korea's (DPRK, North Korean) invasion of the Republic of Korea (ROK, South Korea). Convinced that Beijing and Moscow were preparing for conflict on a world scale, he urged immediate commitment of U.S. ground troops to halt the Communist invasion. Later he came to view the Truman administration as too cautious and unwilling to fully confront communism. As soon as Senate ratification of the Japanese peace treaty was complete in 1951, Dulles resigned from his position in the State Department to begin working on the foreign policy platform of the Republican Party.

In 1952, Dwight D. Eisenhower had been a reluctant candidate for the presidency, but, once committed, he became a formidable challenger. Campaigning on the slogan known as K1C2 (Korea, Communism, and Corruption), he exploited the public perception that the Democrats were soft on Cold War issues. Perhaps even more damaging to the Democrats was the growing unpopularity of the prolonged and stalemated Korean War. Eisenhower capitalized on his image as a war hero when he made his pledge that if elected, he would "go to Korea." Although he offered few specifics, the promise that he would go to Korea gave hope that his intervention would end the conflict.

Dulles's role in the Eisenhower presidential campaign was to act as chief foreign policy adviser. His involvement in the campaign began in May 1952, when he and Eisenhower met in Paris to begin a dialogue over foreign policy. He continued this after Eisenhower's victory when the new president named him his secretary of state in 1953.

Eisenhower, who was concerned over the growing costs of the Cold War, was impressed with Dulles's views. Together they fashioned a policy that was popularly known as "massive retaliation" and later as the "New Look," which posited that the United States would scale back costly, conventional armaments through reliance on nuclear weapons as deterrents. Dulles frequently implied publicly that, if U.S. interests were threatened, the use of nuclear weapons would be considered. Massive retaliation was first tested when Eisenhower set about trying to resolve the Korean impasse almost immediately after taking office.

Eisenhower did in fact go to Korea to confer with United Nations commander Lieutenant General Mark Clark and ROK president Syngman Rhee. Upon returning home to consider his options, in mid-May 1953 Eisenhower instructed Dulles to let it be known that the United States was prepared to employ nuclear weapons to break the deadlocked peace talks. Although there is still debate over the impact of Dulles's threat, the armistice agreement was signed in July 1953. Dulles remained secretary of state until his death from cancer in Washington, D.C., on May 24, 1959.

Phillip A. Cantrell II

References

Guhin, Michael A. *John Foster Dulles: A Statesman and His Times.* New York: Columbia University Press, 1972.

Hoopes, Townsend. *The Devil and John Foster Dulles.* Boston: Little, Brown, 1973.

Pruessen, Ronald W. *John Foster Dulles: The Road to Power.* New York: Macmillan, 1982.

Eisenhower, Dwight David (1890–1969)

U.S. Army general and president of the United States (1953–1961). Born in Denison, Texas, on October 14, 1890, Dwight David Eisenhower grew up in Abilene, Kansas. In 1915, he graduated from the United States Military Academy at West Point. He served in a variety of training assignments until 1918, when he joined the U.S. Expeditionary Force in France, but World War I ended before his arrival. Postings during the 1920s to the Panama Canal Zone and Paris and staff courses at Fort Leavenworth and the Army War College led to five years in Washington (1930–1935), where Eisenhower served in the War Department.

As the United States prepared for World War II, Eisenhower initially served as chief of staff to the new Third Army. Transferred to the War Department in Washington following Japan's attack on Pearl Harbor, he held increasingly responsible staff jobs, where he helped to elaborate the Europe-first strategy. Promoted to major general in April 1942, Eisenhower that June transferred to London as commander of the European Theater of Operations and commander of U.S. forces in Europe. In November 1942 he commanded the Allied invasion of North Africa, and in 1943 he launched the invasions of Sicily and then Italy. In December 1943, Eisenhower became commander of the Allied Expeditionary Force for the

Dwight D. Eisenhower was president of the United States from 1953 to 1961. Eisenhower was determined to bring the Korean War to an end, which occurred early in his presidency. In an effort to help balance the budget, he placed greater reliance on nuclear weapons. (Library of Congress)

invasion of Western Europe. Eisenhower commanded this force through the end of the war. In December 1944, he was promoted to general of the army, and by the end of the war he was a national hero.

From May to November 1945, Eisenhower commanded Allied occupation forces in Germany. He then returned to Washington to serve as chief of staff of the U.S. Army, until his retirement in February 1948. Eisenhower then became president of Columbia University. He strongly endorsed the Truman administration's developing Cold War policies, including military intervention in Korea. In January 1951, Eisenhower was appointed the first Supreme Allied Commander Europe (SACEUR) and organized the North

Atlantic Treaty Organization (NATO) headquarters in Paris.

In 1952, the Republican Party turned to Eisenhower as its presidential candidate. Resigning his NATO post, Eisenhower campaigned hard, although he tended to leave his running mate, Sen. Richard M. Nixon, and Sen. Joseph R. McCarthy to mount the more aggressive attacks on the Truman administration. In a campaign marked by vicious rhetoric and accusations, Republicans criticized the administration for mishandling the war in Korea. They also assailed the Democrats' mobilization efforts at home.

McCarthy in particular blasted the top echelon of the Truman administration for its "communist" outlook. Many senior Republican politicians found McCarthy's tactics distasteful, but tolerated them in the interests of electoral victory. Although Eisenhower initially intended to refute McCarthy's charges, political considerations persuaded him to remain silent, a decision that many regard as a lasting stain on his reputation.

During the campaign, Eisenhower promised that, if elected, he would visit Korea personally, which he secretly did in early December 1952. The trip confirmed his suspicions that the United States should seek to bring the lengthy and deadlocked armistice negotiations to a speedy conclusion. This was reinforced by his personal desire to reduce military spending and balance the federal budget.

After meeting with Truman administration officials in November 1952, Eisenhower endorsed the administration's stance that prisoners of war should undergo only voluntary repatriation. In December 1952, he also rejected recommendations from General Douglas MacArthur that the ground war be expanded. Eisenhower demurred as well from suggestions that the

United States should follow an Asia-first policy. Eisenhower emphasized that NATO must remain the linchpin of U.S. global strategy.

Once inaugurated, Eisenhower moved quickly to end the war. He did so in part through a strategy of calculated escalation. In an effort to pressure the People's Republic of China (PRC) to resume stalled armistice talks, in February 1953 the president announced that the United States would permit Taiwan's Kuomintang leader Chiang Kai-shek (Jiang Jieshi) to attack the Chinese mainland. The same month, the National Security Council decided that, if an armistice were not soon concluded, UN forces should bomb Chinese bases in Manchuria, impose a blockade on the mainland, and possibly employ nuclear weapons. These decisions were deliberately conveyed to PRC leaders.

In early 1953, China announced its readiness to resume serious armistice talks, an offer that Eisenhower quickly accepted. Some historians attribute this break in the stalemate to the death of Soviet leader Joseph Stalin, rather than the Eisenhower administration's threats to expand the war. By June 1953, a compromise settlement had been reached on all points, including the vexing issue of the repatriation of prisoners of war. On July 27, 1953, the armistice went into effect. In the United States, there was a prevailing sense of relief that the war was finally over. Even though a final peace treaty has yet to be signed, the United States has maintained a substantial military presence in South Korea.

Eisenhower's defense policies included massive retaliation, which promised a swift and overwhelming nuclear response to any Communist advance, be it nuclear or conventional. Dubbed the "New Look," the new defense strategy was designed to eschew large, conventional armies in favor of more cost-effective nuclear deterrence. Critics charged that the policy was dangerous and gave the United States few options in case of war. Eisenhower was easily reelected president in 1956 and remained in office until 1961. In retirement Eisenhower lived on his farm in Gettysburg, Pennsylvania, but was occasionally consulted by presidents John F. Kennedy and Lyndon B. Johnson. Eisenhower died in Washington, D.C., on March 28, 1969.

Priscilla Roberts

References

Ambrose, Stephen E. *Eisenhower*. 2 vols. New York: Simon and Schuster, 1983–1984.

Chandler, Alfred D., Jr., and Louis Galambos, eds. *The Papers of Dwight D. Eisenhower*. 17 vols. to date. Baltimore: Johns Hopkins University Press, 1970–.

Eisenhower, Dwight D. *Mandate for Change, 1953–1956*. Garden City, NY: Doubleday, 1963.

Hodge, John Reed (1893–1963)

U.S. Army general who headed the military government in southern Korea after the Japanese surrender in 1945. John Reed Hodge was born on June 12, 1893, in Golconda, Illinois. In May 1917, he began army officer training at Fort Sheridan, Illinois, and was commissioned a 2nd lieutenant in October. During World War I, he served with the 61st Infantry in France and took part in the Saint-Mihiel and Meuse-Argonne offensives.

During 1921–1925, Hodge was an assistant professor of military science and tactics in the ROTC Department at the Mississippi Agricultural and Mechanical College, rising to the rank of captain.

From 1925 to 1926, he attended the Infantry School. In 1926, he was assigned to the 27th Infantry at Schofield Barracks, Hawaii. Between 1927 and 1931, he served with the 22nd Infantry Brigade, later serving with the 18th Infantry at Fort Hamilton, New York. Between 1932 and 1936, Hodge in turn completed training at the Chemical Warfare School, a two-year course of study at the Command and Staff School, another two-year course at the Army War College, and his formal military training at the Air Corps Tactical School.

In 1936, having been promoted to major, Hodge was assigned to the 23rd Infantry, Fort Sam Houston, Texas. Late that same year he returned to Washington, D.C., where he was assigned to the Operations and Training Division (G-3) of the War Department general staff. Besides being promoted to lieutenant colonel during his five years on the G-3 staff, Hodge helped prepare plans that were used when the United States entered World War II.

In 1941, Hodge was assigned to the Army's VII Corps as its organization and training officer. Shortly after the Japanese attack on Pearl Harbor, he became chief of staff, VII Corps, and was transferred to San Jose, California. In 1942, he was appointed assistant division commander of the 25th Division and participated in the Guadalcanal Campaign.

In June 1943, Hodge took command of the Americal Division, a composite division of U.S. and New Caledonian forces. A month later he assumed temporary command of the 43rd Division. Before his arrival, 30 days of continuous fighting had failed to remove the Japanese from New Georgia Island. His leadership helped bring about their rapid defeat. During his tour in the Solomon Islands, Hodge was wounded during fighting on Bougainville. He soon recovered and in April 1944 received command of the forming XXIV Corps, which he led during its assault on Japanese-held islands, including Leyte and Okinawa.

Following Japan's surrender, U.S. Far Eastern commander General Douglas MacArthur selected Lieutenant General Hodge to command U.S. Army Forces in Korea (USAFIK). These were responsible for civil control and daily operations in Korea south of the 38th parallel. This included such basic functions as running utilities and forming a security force. Occupation tasks were often difficult because few Koreans had any experience in self-government, Korea having been annexed by Japan in 1910. Moreover, Hodge and his subordinates in the USAFIK had very little knowledge of Korean history or culture.

During this period, opposition from the local populace arose when Hodge announced a plan to retain some Japanese officials in their former positions. Subsequently, the USAFIK appointed a board of U.S. officers to examine political and military conditions to determine if a national defense program was needed. Hodge approved the board's plan for creation of a South Korean army, but MacArthur disagreed. In the fall and winter 1947–1948, MacArthur's belief that the Koreans needed only a constabulary force eventually won out. In the spring of 1948, U.S. Army officials ordered Hodge to develop plans to withdraw U.S. forces by the end of the year.

In May 1948, South Korean citizens elected the Republic of Korea's (ROK, South Korea) first national assembly, which chose Syngman Rhee to be the first president. On August 15 he was inaugurated, and on August 24 Hodge and Rhee signed an agreement to transfer control of the nation's security forces to the new government. Three days later, Hodge returned to the United States.

Hodge served in various posts until 1952, when President Harry S. Truman appointed him chief of Army Field Forces, which position he held until his retirement in 1953. Hodge died on November 12, 1963, in Washington, D.C.

Dean Corey and William Head

References

Matray, James I. "Hodge Podge: U.S. Occupation Policy in Korea, 1945–1948." *Korean Studies* 19 (1995): 17–38.

Millett, Allan R. *The War for Korea, 1945–1950: A House Burning.* Lawrence: University Press of Kansas, 2005.

Sawyer, Robert K. *KMAG in War and Peace.* Washington, DC: Office of the Chief of Military History, U.S. Army, 1962.

Johnson, Louis Arthur
(1891–1966)

U.S. secretary of defense (1949–1950) who received blame for the lack of U.S. military preparedness after the outbreak of the Korean War. Born on January 10, 1891, in Roanoke, Virginia, Louis Arthur Johnson graduated from the University of Virginia in 1912. He then moved to Clarksburg, West Virginia, where he practiced law and served in the West Virginia House of Delegates as a Democrat. He saw combat during World War I as a captain in the 80th Infantry Division.

Active in Democratic Party politics and the American Legion, Johnson had ample opportunities to learn about national defense topics and meet influen-

tial people, such as future president Harry S. Truman. Johnson assisted President Franklin D. Roosevelt in assuaging veterans' groups that protested cuts in pensions. To reward him, Roosevelt appointed Johnson assistant secretary of war in 1937.

Aggressive and hardworking, Johnson often was at odds with Secretary of War Harry H. Woodring about the management of the War Department. Johnson wanted to modernize and increase the size of the U.S. Army, and he is credited for helping prepare it for mobilization in World War II. In 1941, Johnson resigned his post when incoming Secretary of War Henry L. Stimson named his own assistant. Johnson then became the president of the General Dyestuff Corporation. After Truman won the 1948 election, he appointed Johnson as secretary of defense in March 1949. When he was sworn into office, Johnson promised to continue unification of the armed forces and to maintain military strength, while reducing spending. Johnson soon closed military installations and cut back on training in an effort to cut costs.

Johnson's most immediate problem was interservice strife. He considered his most crucial decision to be delineating air force and navy roles in air warfare. He promoted land-based strategic air power, sparking the "Revolt of the Admirals" and deeply angering naval officials. Many thought Johnson's political posturing was an effort to secure the 1952 Democratic presidential nomination. While Johnson's enemies thought him arrogant and unqualified, his supporters believed him to be dynamic and capable. Johnson indeed cut wasteful expenditures in the Department of Defense, but later his detractors would blame him for the lack of U.S. military preparedness for the Korean War.

Because of congressional pressure to freeze spending and the Truman administration's economizing, the U.S. military found itself with depleted supplies and unprepared to wage war. Nevertheless, as late as mid-June 1950, Johnson believed that things were going well in the Pacific. That all changed with the beginning of the Korean War on June 25.

Meeting with Truman and the service secretaries at Blair House on the evening of June 25, Johnson opposed sending troops to Korea but agreed to send military supplies to support United Nations (UN) efforts in halting the Korean People's Army (KPA, North Korean) invasion. When the KPA invasion intensified the next day, Johnson supported the State Department's recommendation that U.S. air and naval assets be committed. By June 29, Johnson agreed with the Joint Chiefs of Staff (JCS) recommendation that ground troops be sent to defend South Korea.

Following U.S. entry into the war, Johnson's duties included overseeing the procurement of vital supplies, securing more appropriations, increasing troop strength, establishing North Atlantic Treaty Organization (NATO) forces, and overseeing public relations. New duties included creating the UN military command and securing Allied support for UN operations. Ironically, Johnson spent the summer of 1950 building up the very military forces he had assiduously downsized. He also secured $12 billion in supplemental appropriations.

During the war, Johnson met with Truman daily to share his opinions and the viewpoints of the JCS. At times Johnson supported actions like the Inchon Landing, which the JCS initially opposed. Realizing that he was not a military thinker, Johnson usually accepted JCS views and then communicated them to Truman.

On the other hand, Johnson waged a personal war with Secretary of State Dean Acheson, attacking his Asian policies, specifically regarding Taiwan. Johnson often manipulated situations to discredit Acheson and the State Department while emphasizing his own strengths. This feud with Acheson hurt important policy decisions.

As the Korean War expanded in July and August 1950, criticism increased concerning poor U.S. military performance and high casualties. Congress and the press made Johnson a scapegoat and demanded that Truman fire him. During his last months in office, Johnson became irrational and began making major public relations blunders. Acheson came to believe that Johnson was mentally unbalanced and should not influence international policy. Finally on September 12, Truman demanded Johnson's resignation, which was tendered on September 19. George C. Marshall, former army chief of staff and secretary of state, succeeded Johnson as secretary of defense.

Following his resignation, Johnson worked as a senior partner in the Washington law firm of Steptoe and Johnson. He died on April 24, 1966, in Washington, D.C.

Elizabeth D. Schafer

References

Acheson, Dean G. *Present at the Creation: My Years at the State Department.* New York: W. W. Norton, 1969.

Kinnard, Douglas. *The Secretaries of Defense.* Lexington: University of Kentucky Press, 1980.

McFarland, Keith D., and David L. Roll. *Louis Johnson and the Arming of America: The Roosevelt and Truman Years.* Bloomington: Indiana University Press, 2005.

Joy, Charles Turner (1895–1956)

U.S. Navy officer, senior United Nations Command (UNC) delegate to the Korean Armistice Conference at Kaesong and later Panmunjom (July 1951–May 1952), and commander U.S. Naval Forces, Far East (COMNAVFE) (1949–1952). Born on February 17, 1895, in St. Louis, Missouri, Charles Turner Joy attended private schools in Missouri, New York, and Pennsylvania before accepting an appointment to the United States Naval Academy, Annapolis, in 1912.

Upon graduation and commissioning as an officer in the U.S. Navy in 1916, Joy served on the battleship *Pennsylvania*, flagship of the Atlantic Fleet. After World War I he was chosen for postgraduate education in ordnance engineering and in 1923 earned a master of science degree from the University of Michigan. Over the next 19 years Joy served in the U.S. Navy's Yangtze Patrol in China, with commander destroyers, battle force, and on the destroyer *Pope* and battleship *California*. In May 1933, he took command of the destroyer *Litchfield*. Shore duty included ordnance and gunnery-related billets in the Bureau of Ordnance in Washington, D.C., the Naval Mine Depot at Yorktown, Virginia, and the U.S. Naval Academy.

During the first two years of World War II in the Pacific, while serving as a staff officer on board the cruiser *Indianapolis* and then the carrier *Lexington*,

Admiral C. Turner Joy, commander of U.S. Naval Forces, Far East, and chief United Nations Command (UNC) delegate to the Korean Armistice Talks, seen in his quarters at the UNC base camp at Musan-ni. (National Archives)

Joy helped plan successful naval operations against Japanese forces in the Solomon and Aleutian islands. He capped that tour with command of cruiser *Louisville*. After heading the Pacific Plans Division in the navy's Washington headquarters from August 1943 to May 1944, now Rear Admiral Joy rejoined the U.S. Pacific Fleet. Cruiser and amphibious commands under his leadership performed with skill and valor in the Marianas, Philippines, Iwo Jima, and Okinawa campaigns.

During the immediate postwar period, Joy led U.S. naval forces operating on the Yangtze River and along China's coast. He also oversaw the politically sensitive task of transporting troops of Nationalist Chinese leader Chiang Kai-shek (Jiang Jieshi) from south to north China and Manchuria, then invested by communist forces under Mao Zedong. Joy then had a three-year tour as commander of the Naval Proving Ground at Dahlgren, Virginia.

In August 1949, Joy was promoted to vice admiral and selected as COMNAVFE. From his headquarters in Tokyo, Vice Admiral Joy organized and directed U.S. and allied naval forces that fought desperately to stop and then turn back the Korean People's Army (KPA, North Korean) offensive that swept south into the Republic of Korea (ROK, South Korea) during the summer of 1950. Surface and air units under his command bombed and shelled advancing KPA troops, road and railway bridges, and supply depots. His combat fleet quickly established its presence in the Yellow Sea and the East Sea (Sea of Japan) to discourage Soviet and Chinese military action and to protect the seagoing reinforcement and resupply of UN forces holding the vital port of Pusan.

Naval forces, Far East carriers, cruisers, destroyers, and amphibious ships, along with allied warships, carried out the bold amphibious assault at Inchon on September 15, 1950, which deployed strong U.S. and South Korean ground units ashore in the rear of the KPA.

Joy's naval forces then successfully evacuated U.S. Marine, U.S. Army, and South Korean troops, refugees, and equipment from the port of Hungnam in December 1950, when Chinese armies swept down from the hills of North Korea and threatened to destroy the UNC. Allied naval units under Joy helped stop the spring 1951 Communist offensives.

Joy's obvious leadership qualities, ability to function well under pressure, and understanding of U.S. goals in East Asia led to his selection in June 1951 as the senior UNC delegate to the newly convened Korean Armistice Conference. Many observers noted that during the ceasefire negotiations with his Chinese and North Korean adversaries, who seemed unconcerned with the lack of progress, Joy usually exuded self-confidence, firmness, and patience. On a few occasions, however, the admiral publicly criticized the rigid negotiating posture and uncooperative manner of the Communist side. The Chinese and North Korean delegates, however, only carried out the dictates of the political leaders in Moscow, Beijing, and Pyongyang, who were not inclined to compromise on key issues. Joy also bemoaned the periodic changes in the UN's basic policy positions. Exasperated by the lack of progress in the negotiations, he asked to be replaced.

In May 1952, Joy was called home and named superintendent of the U.S. Naval Academy. Even though diagnosed with leukemia soon afterward, Joy did not retire from active service until July

1954, at the end of his tour. Joy died of cancer in San Diego, California, on June 6, 1956.

Edward J. Marolda

References

Field, James A., Jr. *History of United States Naval Operations: Korea.* Washington, DC: U.S. Government Printing Office, 1962.

Goodman, Allan E., ed. *Negotiating While Fighting: The Diary of Admiral C. Turner Joy at the Korean Armistice Conference.* Stanford, CA: Stanford University Press, 1978.

Joy, C. Turner. *How Communists Negotiate.* New York: Macmillan, 1955.

MacArthur, Douglas (1880–1964)

U.S. Army general, Philippine field marshal, and first commander of United Nations forces during the Korean War. Born on January 26, 1880, in Little Rock, Arkansas, the son of Lieutenant General Arthur MacArthur, Douglas MacArthur graduated from the United States Military Academy, West Point, in 1903 with highest honors and as 1st captain. Following service in the Philippines and Japan, he became an aide to President Theodore Roosevelt during 1906–1907. He took part in the 1914 occupation of Veracruz, Mexico, and served on the general staff (1913–1917).

After the United States entered World War I in April 1917, MacArthur went to France as chief of staff of the 42nd Infantry Division. Promoted to temporary brigadier general, he took part in the Second Battle of the Marne. MacArthur then led the 8th Infantry Brigade in the Saint-Mihiel and Meuse-Argonne offensives and, at the end of the war, commanded the 42nd Division.

Following occupation duty in Germany, MacArthur returned to the United States as superintendent of West Point (1919–1922), carrying out much-needed reforms. He again served in the Philippines. MacArthur was then chief of staff of the army (1930–1935), his reputation suffering from the 1932 Bonus Army Incident when he employed force to oust a protest by World War I veterans in Washington. In 1935, MacArthur returned to the Philippines as adviser to the Philippine government in establishing an army capable of resisting a Japanese invasion. In August 1936, he accepted the post of field marshal of Philippine forces, retiring from the U.S. Army in December 1937.

Recalled to active service with the U.S. Army in July 1941, MacArthur received command of all U.S. forces in the Far East. Believing his forces could defend the Philippine Islands, he scrapped the original sound plan to withdraw into the Bataan Peninsula in favor of a forward defense. His refusal to permit an immediate retaliatory strike against the Japanese on Taiwan after the attack on Pearl Harbor meant that most of his aircraft, including B-17 strategic bombers, were caught and destroyed on the ground.

Although the Japanese force invading the Philippines was only 57,000 men, half that of his own numbers, many of MacArthur's men were poorly trained and they were, in any case, thinly spread. The Japanese had little difficulty taking Manila and much of Luzon. MacArthur then ordered his forces to implement the original plan of withdrawing into the Bataan Peninsula. The bases there were not ready and the retreating troops had to abandon stocks of supplies and ammunition in the process. Rather than see him become a prisoner of the Japanese, on

Commander of the United Nations Command (UNC) General Douglas MacArthur observing the Inchon landing from the command ship *Mount McKinley*, September 15, 1950. From left to right are Brigadier General Courtney Whitney, Major General Edwin K. Wright, MacArthur, and Major General Edmond Almond. Disputes with President Harry S. Truman over the conduct of the war brought MacArthur's relief in April 1951. (National Archives)

February 22, 1942, President Franklin D. Roosevelt ordered MacArthur to Australia, where he became supreme commander of Allied forces in the Southwest Pacific. MacArthur also was awarded the Medal of Honor, which many defenders of Bataan and Corregidor believed was entirely undeserved. Officials in Washington were also miffed by MacArthur's acceptance of a $500,000 payment from his friend, Philippine president Manuel Quezon.

From Australia, MacArthur developed a deliberate strategy to return to the Philippines. The slow pace of the Allied advance led Washington to insist on a leapfrogging approach that would bypass strongly held Japanese islands and positions. In the spring of 1944 MacArthur's troops invaded New Guinea and isolated Rabaul. By September, they had taken New Guinea. Then, in October 1944, U.S. troops landed on Leyte. They then secured Luzon during January–March 1945, followed by the southern Philippines.

An invasion of Japan proved unnecessary and MacArthur, promoted to the new rank of general of the army in December 1944, presided over the formal Japanese surrender ceremony in Tokyo Bay on September 2, 1945, in his capacity of supreme commander, Allied

Powers. President Harry S. Truman then named MacArthur commander of Allied occupation forces in Japan. In this position he in effect governed Japan as a benevolent despot, presiding over the institution of a new democratic constitution and domestic reforms, until a "reverse course" in U.S. policy shifted the focus to transforming Japan into an anticommunist bastion of containment in East Asia. U.S. occupation forces there under his command were understrength and inadequately equipped, as well as poorly trained.

On the beginning of the Korean War in June 1950, Truman appointed MacArthur commander of United Nations forces sent to South Korea to prevent a North Korean victory there. During the perilous UN withdrawal into the Pusan Perimeter, MacArthur husbanded his resources and secured permission for a risky amphibious operation, opposed by many senior officers, behind North Korean enemy lines at Seoul's port of Inchon that would coincide with a breakout of Eighth Army along the Pusan Perimeter. The Inchon landing of September 15, 1950, was a brilliant (but lucky) invasion operation that cut North Korean supply lines to the south. Unfortunately, MacArthur held X Corps, the landing force at Inchon, separate from Eighth Army administratively thereafter.

MacArthur then oversaw the UNC invasion of North Korea, but faulty troop dispositions, including sending X Corps around South Korea by sea to land at the port of Wonsan, and his complete disdain for the possibility and consequences of a possible Chinese entry into the war nearly led to disaster. MacArthur's increasingly public disagreement with Truman over the course of the war following Chinese military intervention, to include his advocacy of bombing of China and employment of Nationalist Chinese troops in an attack on mainland China, ran counter to the desire of leaders in Washington to limit the war and continue emphasis on a Europe-first strategy. MacArthur's posturing and insubordination finally led Truman to remove him from his posts on April 11, 1951, although a more important reason was the president's desire to make atomic weapons available to the UN commander for use in Korea if U.S. forces faced the prospect of annihilation.

MacArthur returned to the United States a national hero, receiving tumultuous ticker-tape parades across the country. He addressed both houses of Congress during which he defended his performance and sharply rebuked the president's policies in Korea and Asia. He then retired from the military, accepting the position of chairman of the board of Remington Rand Corporation. His attempt to run for the presidency as a Republican in 1952 quickly collapsed, and the nomination and office went to another general whom MacArthur held in great disdain, Dwight D. Eisenhower. The increasingly shrill and intemperate speeches he gave on a national speaking tour turned many against him, even heretofore supporters. MacArthur died in Washington, D.C., on April 5, 1964. Arrogant, vain, and flamboyant, MacArthur had a nearly insatiable appetite for publicity. His staffs tended to consist of sycophants known for their loyalty rather than brilliance or independence of thought. Although he had significant failures as a commander, most notably the loss of the Philippines in 1942, MacArthur was bold and daring in his planning.

Spencer C. Tucker

References

James, D. Clayton. *The Years of MacArthur.* 3 vols. Boston: Houghton Mifflin, 1970–1985.

Perret, Geoffrey. *Old Soldiers Never Die: The Life of Douglas MacArthur.* Holbrook, MA: Adams Media Corporation, 1996.

Schaller, Michael. *Douglas MacArthur: The Far Eastern General.* New York: Oxford University Press, 1989.

Marshall, George Catlett (1880–1959)

U.S. Army general, chief of staff of the army, secretary of state, and, during the Korean War, secretary of defense. Born in Uniontown, Pennsylvania, on December 31, 1880, George Marshall graduated from the Virginia Military Institute in 1901. Commissioned in the infantry in 1902, he then held a variety of assignments, including in the Philippines. He attended the Infantry and Cavalry School, Fort Leavenworth, in 1906 and was an instructor in the Army School of the Line and Staff during 1907–1908.

After the United States entered World War I, Marshall went to France in June 1917 with the American Expeditionary Forces as training officer to the 1st Division. Promoted to lieutenant colonel in 1918, he became chief of operations of the U.S. First Army in August and was the principal planner of the highly successful Saint-Mihiel Offensive (September 12–16). He won admiration for his logistical skills in directing the repositioning of hundreds of thousands of men quickly across the battlefront immediately thereafter for the Meuse-Argonne Offensive (September 26–November 11). After working on occupation plans for Germany, Marshall reverted to his perma-

nent rank of captain and during 1919–1924 served as aide to General John J. Pershing, chief of staff of the army from 1921 to 1924. Marshall was promoted to major in 1920 and to lieutenant colonel in 1923.

Marshall then served in Tianjin (Tientsin), China, with the 15th Infantry Regiment during 1924–1927. He was assistant commandant in charge of instruction at the Infantry School, Fort Benning, Georgia (1927–1932), where he helped to train numerous future U.S. generals. Promoted to colonel in 1932, he held assorted command posts in the continental United States, including instructor with the Illinois National Guard (1933–1936). He advanced to brigadier general in 1936.

Marshall became head of the War Plans Division in Washington with promotion to major general in July 1938, then deputy chief of staff that October. President Franklin D. Roosevelt advanced Marshall over many more senior officers to appoint him chief of staff of the U.S. Army with the rank of temporary general on September 1, 1939, the day that German armies invaded Poland. Marshall then worked to revitalize the U.S. defense establishment.

Marshall instituted and lobbied for programs to recruit and train new troops; expedite munitions production; assist the Allies in resisting the Axis powers; and coordinate British and American strategy. After the United States entered the war on December 7, 1941, Marshall presided over an increase in U.S. Army strength from 200,000 to a wartime maximum of 8.1 million men and women. For his great accomplishments in the war, Marshall became known as the "Organizer of Victory."

Marshall was a strong supporter of opening a second front in Europe, a campaign ultimately deferred until June 1944. Between 1941 and 1945, he attended all the major wartime strategic conferences, including those at Placentia Bay, Washington, Quebec, Cairo, Tehran, Malta, Yalta, and Potsdam. Marshall was the first to be promoted to the newly authorized five-star rank of general of the army in December 1944.

On the urging of President Harry S. Truman, Marshall agreed to serve as special envoy to China during 1945–1947. He was then secretary of state, in which position he advanced the Marshall Plan to rebuild Europe, for which he was awarded the 1953 Nobel Prize for Peace, the first soldier so honored. Marshall next served as president of the American Red Cross from 1949 to 1950.

Marshall was called back to public service when Truman persuaded him to replace Defense Secretary Louis Johnson, who was forced to resign in September 1950. As defense secretary, Marshall increased the size and improved the readiness of the U.S. armed forces so as to be able to meet the demands of both Korea and Europe while at the same time maintaining an adequate reserve. He also restored harmony between the Defense and State departments, frayed under his predecessor, and he established a good working relationship with the members of the Joint Chiefs of Staff (JCS).

Marshall concurred with the decision to allow United Nations commander General Douglas MacArthur in Korea to conduct operations north of the 38th parallel, but he agreed with Truman and the JCS that all-out war with China must be avoided, stressing the paramount importance of Western Europe. He urged caution in discussion of whether to fire MacArthur but, after reviewing all correspondence with the general over the pre-

vious five years, declared that he should have been dismissed earlier.

In June 1951, when Sen. Joseph McCarthy demanded the resignations of Secretary of State Dean Acheson and Marshall and threatened Truman with impeachment, he all but called Marshall a Communist. The unjust attacks against him may well have confirmed Marshall's decision to step down, although at Truman's request he stayed on until September 1951. For Marshall it was the end of 50 years of dedicated government service.

Marshall died in Washington, D.C., on October 16, 1959. If not America's greatest soldier, Marshall was one of the nation's most capable military leaders and statesmen and certainly one of the most influential figures of the 20th century.

Spencer C. Tucker

References

Cray, Ed. *General of the Army: George C. Marshall, Soldier and Statesman.* New York: W. W. Norton, 1990.

Pogue, Forrest C. *George C. Marshall.* 4 vols. New York: Viking, 1963–1987.

Stoler, Mark A. *George C. Marshall: Soldier-Statesman of the American Century.* Boston: Twayne, 1989.

Muccio, John Joseph (1900–1989)

U.S. diplomat and first U.S. ambassador to the Republic of Korea (ROK) (1949–1952). Born on March 19, 1900, in Valle Agricola, Italy, John Joseph Muccio saw service in World War I in the U.S. Army. He acquired U.S. citizenship and in 1921 graduated from Brown University. Securing a U.S. Foreign Service appointment two years later, Muccio held posts in Europe, Asia, and Latin America. In August 1948, he became President Harry S. Truman's special representative to the ROK and then, on March 21, 1949, the first U.S. ambassador.

Muccio presided over the U.S. embassy, Korea Military Advisory Group (KMAG), an Economic Cooperation Administration branch, and the Joint Administrative Services, the mission's supply office. Despite disagreements with ROK president Syngman Rhee, Muccio developed a working relationship with him as well as an admiration for Rhee's intelligence and historical insight. Nevertheless, he recognized Rhee's reverence for General Douglas MacArthur and feared his suspicious nature. Characterizing the ROK leader an "egomaniac," Muccio feared that Rhee might launch an attack against the Democratic People's Republic of Korea (DPRK, North Korea).

Muccio endorsed Rhee's wish for a permanent U.S. military role in Korea and his government's request for $10 million in additional aid for 1950. A few weeks before the DPRK invasion of the ROK, Muccio informed the U.S. Congress of Seoul's military inferiority, an assessment that many did not hold. Muccio worried that the DPRK's military advantage would give it the winning edge in case of an all-out assault on the South. He cited DPRK advantages in artillery, armor, and planes, all supplied by the Soviet Union.

It was Ambassador Muccio who officially notified Washington of the outbreak of the Korean War on June 25, 1950. In a dispatch sent almost six and a half hours after the beginning of the invasion, he announced that the DPRK had mounted a full-scale, unprovoked attack. At a meeting of the United Nations Commission on Korea, Muccio expressed confidence in the capability of ROK Army (ROKA) troops, but he also pressed the Department of State to back a

KMAG plea to General MacArthur for more ammunition for the ROKA. When Rhee considered a sudden evacuation of Seoul, Muccio warned that this could demoralize ROKA troops. Muccio's own decision to stay braced Rhee, at least temporarily. Under pressure of advancing Korean People's Army (KPA, North Korean) forces, Muccio elected to evacuate U.S. civilians from Seoul via Inchon and Kimpo Airfield but delayed this step for a time in hopes of preserving South Korean morale despite the misgivings of some military personnel. Once Rhee left Seoul, however, the State Department ordered Muccio to follow, and he joined Rhee in Taejon.

Muccio conferred with MacArthur on several occasions after the war's outbreak, and he traveled with the general to meet President Truman at Wake Island in October 1950. He and MacArthur were the only participants in the general's party to take prominent roles in the discussions. Muccio later described MacArthur as irritated and uncomfortable and complaining of being "summoned for political reasons" and suggesting that the president was "not aware that I am still fighting a war." In his remarks, Muccio spoke about Korean political and economic conditions. Both he and MacArthur endorsed a reconstruction aid package and expressed fear of President Rhee's weakened political status. Before their departure, Truman awarded Muccio the Medal of Merit.

In 1952, Muccio pressed Rhee to comply with a pending ceasefire and found the ROK president uncooperative. Despite his reputation of being Rhee's "best and most patient friend in the American community," Muccio urged the State Department to ponder United Nations intervention to remove Rhee through the ROKA. On June 25, 1952, the State

Department directed Muccio and Lieutenant General Mark W. Clark to begin contingency planning in case action was required to stop Rhee's meddling.

In November 1952, Muccio was succeeded by Ellis O. Briggs and returned to the United States. Muccio retired from the Foreign Service in 1961 and died in Washington, D.C., on May 19, 1989.

Rodney J. Ross

References

Goulden, Joseph C. *Korea: The Untold Story of the War.* New York: Times Books, 1982.

James, D. Clayton. *The Years of MacArthur.* Vol. 3, *Triumph and Disaster, 1945–1964.* Boston: Houghton Mifflin, 1985.

Paige, Glenn D. *The Korean Decision, June 24–30, 1950.* New York: Free Press, 1968.

Admiral Arthur W. Radford was commander in chief, Pacific, and commander in chief of the U.S. Pacific Fleet during April 1949–August 1953. During 1953–1957, Radford was chairman of the Joint Chiefs of Staff. (Corbis)

Radford, Arthur William (1896–1973)

U.S. admiral, commander in chief, Pacific, and commander in chief, U.S. Pacific Fleet (April 1949–August 1953), then when the Korean War ended, chairman of the Joint Chiefs of Staff (1953–1957). Born in Chicago, Illinois, on February 27, 1896, Arthur William Radford graduated from the United States Naval Academy, Annapolis, in 1916 and saw action aboard the battleship *South Carolina* during World War I. During the interwar period, Radford became a naval aviator, spent three years with the Bureau of Aeronautics, and served with aviation units attached to the *Colorado, Pennsylvania,* and *Wright.* He eventually commanded a fighter squadron on the carrier *Saratoga.*

When World War II began in Europe, Radford was commander of the Naval Air Station, Seattle, Washington. He returned to sea duty in 1940 aboard the aircraft carrier *Yorktown,* then with the U.S. Pacific Fleet, and was aboard it at the time of the December 7, 1941, Japanese attack on Pearl Harbor, Hawaii. Shortly thereafter, Radford was chosen as the director of the navy's aviation training program, which was then undergoing a major expansion. In April 1943, he was promoted to rear admiral and was again assigned to the Pacific Fleet, where he commanded a carrier division that participated in numerous amphibious operations, including the November 1943 landings at Tarawa in the Gilbert Islands. In May 1944, Radford became assistant deputy chief of naval operations for air at the Navy Department in Washington. He was promoted to vice admiral in 1945.

Radford then held a number of posts, including vice chief of naval operations.

He was a primary leader in the "Revolt of the Admirals" that erupted in 1949 over the navy's opposition to the Truman administration's emphasis on creating a sizable U.S. Air Force strategic bomber capability, at the expense of sea power.

Appointed commander in chief, Pacific, and commander in chief of the U.S. Pacific Fleet in April 1949, Radford was a staunch anticommunist and a firm believer that the greatest threat to U.S. national security was in Asia rather than in Europe. He did not, however, have any direct responsibility for U.S. forces in the Korean War, because after its start one of Radford's subordinate commands, the newly formed U.S. Seventh Fleet, was placed under control of General Douglas MacArthur, commander of the United Nations Command (UNC). An advocate of an Asia-first strategy and an admirer of MacArthur, Radford supported the September 1950 Inchon Landing plan and approved of the long-range UN goal of a military reunification of the Korea peninsula. He was present at the October 1950 Wake Island Conference between President Harry S. Truman and MacArthur, later recalling that he had interpreted MacArthur's assurance that UN forces could handle Chinese forces should they intervene to mean that the Communists would not pose a problem so long as U.S. aircraft could strike their bases in Manchuria. As with MacArthur, Radford was frustrated by restrictions placed on UN forces after the intervention of the Chinese People's Volunteer Army (CPVA, Chinese Communist). When in April 1951 Truman relieved MacArthur of his command, Radford gave the returning general a hero's welcome in Hawaii.

In December 1952, Radford joined president-elect Dwight D. Eisenhower on his trip to Korea. The admiral, then commander of the Philippine-Formosa area, made a favorable impression on Eisenhower, who the following summer nominated him as chairman of the Joint Chiefs of Staff, a position he held from 1953 until 1957. As Eisenhower considered alternatives for ending the stalemated Korean War, Radford reportedly recommended threatening the People's Republic of China with attacks on their Manchurian bases and the use of atomic weapons. Radford suggested similarly aggressive measures to the president in the spring of 1954 following France's pleas for U.S. military intervention in aid of its beleaguered garrison at Dien Bien Phu in Indochina.

Retiring from the navy in 1957, Radford entered the business world, yet he also served as a military adviser in the presidential campaigns of Republican vice president Richard M. Nixon in 1960 and Republican senator Barry Goldwater in 1964. He died in Washington, D.C., on August 17, 1973.

Clayton D. Laurie

References

Jurika, Stephen, Jr., ed. *From Pearl Harbor to Vietnam: The Memoirs of Admiral Arthur W. Radford.* Stanford, CA: Hoover Institution Press, 1980.

Marolda, Edward J. ed. *The U.S. Navy in the Korean War.* Annapolis, MD: Naval Institute Press, 2007.

Ridgway, Matthew Bunker (1895–1993)

U.S. Army general, commander of the Eighth U.S. Army in Korea, and later commander in chief of all United Nations forces in Korea. Matthew Bunker Ridgway was born at Fort Monroe, Virginia, on March 3, 1895, and graduated from the United States Military Academy, West Point, in 1917. During World War I, Ridgway was stationed on the Mexican border. A capable linguist, he returned to West Point in 1918 to teach Romance languages. As one of only a handful of regular army officers fluent in Spanish, he served in several high-level postings in Latin America during the 1920s. In the 1930s, he was selected to attend the Infantry School, the Command and General Staff School, and the Army War College. He became a protégé of General George C. Marshall, who secured his advancement to brigadier general at the beginning of World War II.

Ridgway enjoyed regular promotion as a commander of airborne forces and had a distinguished record in the war, commanding first the 82nd Airborne Division and then the XVIII Airborne Corps in hard fighting in Sicily, Italy, the Normandy Invasion, and the campaign into Germany. Ridgway was advanced to lieutenant general in June 1945. From 1946 to 1948 he was U.S. representative to the United Nations Military Staff Committee, and during 1948–1949 he headed the Caribbean Defense Command. In August 1949, Ridgway became army deputy chief of staff for administration.

When U.S. Eighth Army commander Lieutenant General Walton H. Walker was killed in a jeep accident on December 23, 1950, Ridgway was named to replace him. It was a very difficult period for the U.S. forces and the United Nations Command (UNC) in Korea. Chinese forces had pushed UNC troops back below the 38th parallel, and morale in the Eighth Army was at a nadir.

Ridgway quickly employed his legendary motivational talents. He ordered the supply services to provide better and more food, served hot, and he secured

General Matthew Bunker Ridgway distinguished himself in Europe in World War II. Taking command of the Eighth U.S. Army in Korea in December 1950, he restored its morale. In April 1951, following the relief of General Douglas MacArthur, Ridgway assumed command of all United Nations Command (UNC) forces in Korea. (Library of Congress)

warmer clothing for the winter. He improved the Mobile Army Surgical Hospitals (MASHs), knowing that the troops would fight better if they knew that they would receive proper medical care if wounded. He also removed incompetent or defeatist officers, and he improved reconnaissance and intelligence-gathering capacities. Although Ridgway was forced to withdraw his forces from Seoul in early January 1951 in the face of a Communist Chinese offensive, he restored their fighting spirit and, in February, launched a major offensive, Operation KILLER. In it, Eighth Army retook Seoul and drove the Chinese back above the 38th parallel, where the battle lines began to stabilize.

When President Harry S. Truman relieved General Douglas MacArthur of his command on April 11, 1951, Ridgway was elevated to four-star rank and appointed to all of MacArthur's former positions as UNC commanding general, commander in chief of U.S. armed forces in the Far East, and supreme commander of the Allied occupation forces in Japan. Ridgway moved from the field to headquarters in Tokyo, where he oversaw the war for the next 13 months. Ridgway's accessibility and articulation made him popular with the press, and he was elevated to national prominence.

Having suffered devastating defeats in several failed offensives, the Chinese and North Koreans in July 1951 signaled their willingness to begin negotiations at Kaesong, on the 38th parallel. Official talks began on July 10 with the Communists proposing an immediate ceasefire. Ridgway and the Joint Chiefs of Staff (JCS) rejected the proposal until a satisfactory peace was negotiated. Lieutenant General James A. Van Fleet, new commander of the Eighth Army, proposed driving the Communists far back into North Korea. Ridgway believed that it would be a mistake to push deep into enemy territory, however. He wished to concentrate on punishing Communist forces along the 38th parallel and employing air power to strike the Communists' supply lines. Some of the worst fighting of the war occurred over the next two years.

In late August 1951, the Communists suspended negotiations and did not return to the table until October. Ridgway ordered a new series of attacks east of the Iron Triangle to pressure peace negotiations and to gain territory prior to an armistice agreement. These savage battles during the suspension of peace talks resulted in huge UN casualties. Ridgway emphasized that the UNC would not return to Kaesong, which was in Communist territory, and on October 25 the talks resumed at Panmunjom, five miles east of Kaesong. Shortly thereafter, the Communists offered to accept the existing battle lines as the permanent demarcation between North and South Korea if a ceasefire were promulgated within 30 days. Over Ridgway's objections, Washington instructed the UNC delegation to accept this proposal. Meanwhile, Ridgway in November 1951 launched Operation RATKILLER, which eliminated 20,000 Communist guerrillas and bandits in the mountains of South Korea near the border. The 30-day deadline passed, but Ridgway instructed Van Fleet to continue the strategy of "active defense" and the war settled into a stalemate. As 1952 began, repatriation of prisoners of war became the divisive issue that would dominate the remainder of the war.

On May 12, 1952, Ridgway replaced General Dwight D. Eisenhower as supreme commander of Allied powers in Europe. In October 1953, he became U.S. army chief of staff. After disagreement with the Eisenhower administration over its emphasis on nuclear weapons (the New Look defense policy) at the expense of conventional forces, Ridgway retired from active duty in June 1955. During the 1960s, he advocated limiting U.S. involvement in Vietnam. In 1968, President Lyndon Johnson named him to the Senior Advisory Group, known as the "Wise Men," that recommended U.S. extrication from that conflict. Ridgway died on July 26, 1993, at Fox Chapel, Pennsylvania.

Joe P. Dunn

References

Appleman, Roy. *Ridgway Duels for Korea.* College Station: Texas A&M University Press, 1990.

Ridgway, Matthew B. *The Korean War.* Garden City, NY: Doubleday, 1967.

Soffer, Jonathan M. *General Matthew B. Ridgway: From Progressivism to Reaganism, 1895–1993.* Westport, CT: Praeger, 1998.

Robertson, Walter Spencer (1893–1970)

U.S. diplomat and when the Korean War ended, assistant secretary of state for Far Eastern affairs (1953–1959). Born on December 7, 1893, in Nottoway County, Virginia, Walter Spencer Robertson studied at the College of William and Mary and Davidson College, but left school in 1912 for a career in banking. During World War I, he joined the U.S. Army Air Service and was a pursuit pilot. Following the war, he resumed his career in banking and finance.

Robertson entered government service in 1943 during World War II as Lend-Lease administrator in Australia. The next year U.S. Ambassador to China Patrick J. Hurley invited him to the embassy in Chongqing (Chungking) as counselor for economic affairs; he later became chargé d'affaires. He supervised U.S. economic activities in China until mid-1946, when he left government service to resume his business career.

Robertson was a great admirer and friend of Generalissimo Chiang Kai-shek (Jiang Jieshi). He was also one of the chief architects of U.S. pro–Nationalist China policy. Because of his conviction that U.S. policy before 1949 had helped Mao Zedong and the Communist Party come to power, he urged that the United States not extend diplomatic recognition to the People's Republic of China (PRC). He believed that the Nationalists on Taiwan constituted the legitimate Chinese government.

Robertson joined Democrats for Dwight D. Eisenhower during the 1952 election campaign, and in January 1953 president-elect Eisenhower appointed him assistant secretary of state for Far Eastern affairs in the Department of State. In this post, Robertson had a reputation for fervor and stubbornness in his beliefs. He was regarded as even more anticommunist than Secretary of State John Foster Dulles.

In late June 1953, President Eisenhower sent Robertson to the Republic of Korea (ROK, South Korea) in hopes of persuading President Syngman Rhee to accept the proposed armistice terms. Rhee had proclaimed these terms to be unsatisfactory, insisting that a U.S.-ROK joint defense pact be followed by the reciprocal removal of United Nations Command and Communist military forces from Korea. He also opposed the employment of foreign troops on South Korean soil as guardians of prisoners of war (POWs) and protested any contact between Communist officials and the captives. Rhee threatened a continuation of the war with the ultimate goal of reunification. Then, with Communist military action intensifying, on June 17, 1953, Rhee breached the armistice terms by ordering ROK guards to release Communist POWs who were refusing repatriation.

President Rhee turned down a request by Secretary of State John Foster Dulles to visit Washington for resolution of the impasse. Instead, he suggested that Dulles travel to Seoul. The secretary of state, considering such a journey ill-advised before ROK agreement to the armistice, elected to dispatch Robertson instead. Robertson lacked Korean expertise, but his staunch anticommunism led him to identify with Rhee.

Robertson arrived in South Korea amidst popular demonstrations after a tirade by Rhee against the armistice accord. On June 26, 1953, Robertson began conversations with Rhee. While Robertson admired Rhee, he proved to be skillful in negotiating and was persuasive. He informed the ROK president that the United States was not prepared to continue the war until Korea was reunified. Threatened with a withdrawal of the United Nations Command and given concessions regarding U.S. military assistance for an expanded ROK Army as well as the promise that the U.S. and the ROK would resume the war should the armistice fail, Rhee yielded. On July 9, Robertson received a pledge from Rhee that his government would not block the proposed armistice.

Three years later, President Dwight D. Eisenhower sent Robertson to Taiwan for talks with Chiang Kai-shek (Jiang Jieshi) concerning the defense of Quemoy and Matsu. After his resignation from the State Department in 1959, Robertson returned to the finance industry. He died on January 19, 1970, in Richmond, Virginia.

Rodney J. Ross

U.S. admiral Forrest Sherman, shown here in November 1949, was chief of naval operations during 1949–1951. (Naval Historical Center)

References

Alexander, Bevin. *Korea: The First War We Lost*. New York: Hippocrene Books, 1986.

Goulden, Joseph C. *Korea: The Untold Story of the War*. New York: Times Books, 1982.

Stueck, William W., Jr. *The Korean War: An International History*. Princeton, NJ: Princeton University Press, 1995.

Sherman, Forrest Percival (1896–1951)

U.S. Navy admiral and chief of naval operations (1949–1951) when the Korean War began. Born on October 30, 1896, in Merrimack, New Hampshire, Forrest Percival Sherman attended the Massachusetts Institute of Technology during 1913–1914 and then the United States Naval Academy, Annapolis, from which he graduated in 1917. Sherman served on the cruiser *Nashville* in European waters during World War I. In 1922, he completed flight training in Pensacola, Florida. After subsequent assignments in naval aviation, he graduated from the Naval War College in 1927. A variety of other postings both afloat and ashore followed.

When the United States entered World War II, Sherman was serving in the War Plans Division of the Office of the Chief of Naval Operations. He then took command of the carrier *Wasp*, and after its loss in September 1942, he became chief of staff of the commander of the Pacific Fleet Air Force. In November 1943, he was appointed deputy chief of staff to commander of the Pacific Fleet Admiral Chester Nimitz.

In October 1945, Sherman assumed command of Carrier Division I. Promoted to vice admiral, he became deputy chief of naval operations that December. In January 1948, he became chief of U.S. naval forces in the Mediterranean. In November 1949, he became chief of naval operations with the rank of admiral. Sherman forcefully defended the navy in a time of shrinking defense budgets. He secured funding for the navy's first nuclear submarine and the modernization of ships, and he was a strong advocate of naval aviation.

Once the Korean War began, Sherman participated in the series of high-level meetings involving President Harry S. Truman, the service secretaries, presidential advisers, and congressional leaders. Truman endorsed Sherman's recommendation for a naval blockade of the Democratic People's Republic of Korea (DPRK, North Korea). Sherman supported General Douglas MacArthur's call for the use of ground forces, and he oversaw the mobilization of U.S. Navy assets, including expansion of its capabilities.

Sherman and the other chiefs expressed reservations about Operation CHROMITE, MacArthur's proposed landing behind Korean People's Army (KPA, North Korean) lines at Inchon. Sherman opposed depriving the Atlantic Fleet Marine Force of the 1st Marine Division, since it might be needed elsewhere, and he disagreed with the site, suggesting a landing farther south at Kunsan. Yet Sherman did assure Truman that MacArthur would wisely employ units given him.

The Joint Chiefs of Staff (JCS) dispatched Sherman and General J. Lawton Collins to East Asia for more information before granting approval for Operation CHROMITE. MacArthur received them in Tokyo on August 21. The next day the two visited Korea for talks with Eighth Army commander Lieutenant General Walton H. Walker before flying back to Japan for MacArthur's Inchon briefing on the 23rd. At that time Sherman and Collins again pressed for the Kunsan site, and, subsequent to conversations with U.S. Navy and U.S. Marine officers, wanted MacArthur to consider Posung-myon, nearly 50 miles below Inchon, as a second alternative. But even before the briefing Sherman had decided to back MacArthur's proposal. All expected the general's forces to advance beyond the 38th parallel and occupy North Korea once KPA resistance was eliminated. On August 28, the JCS gave its qualified endorsement to Operation CHROMITE.

As United Nations Command (UNC) troops drove northward, Sherman met Defense and State Department officials on November 21, 1950, to consider changing MacArthur's mission out of concern for intervention by the People's Republic of China (PRC, Communist China). Although no alteration of MacArthur's orders ensued, Sherman thought that the general was too scornful of JCS anxiety about offending China's interests.

Later, Sherman urged retaliation if Chinese air forces attacked from Manchuria. He disapproved of seeking a ceasefire. Apparently ready to wage war to defeat the PRC, Sherman emerged as a cautious supporter of MacArthur's proposals to pressure China through a naval blockade, Republic of China military operations, guerrilla activities, and naval as well as air strikes if Chinese assaults against UNC forces carried beyond Korea.

Sherman and the other service chiefs conferred on April 5, 1951, after being informed of President Truman's displeasure at MacArthur's public defiance of policies. After considering the matter, they recommended that MacArthur be relieved from command. Sherman believed that dismissal was justified because MacArthur had violated a presidential prohibition on public statements, opposed the idea of a limited war, and endangered civilian control of the military. Later Sherman defended the decision at the MacArthur congressional hearings. Sherman also believed in the primacy of Europe in U.S. defense planning. In July 1951, he left for Europe and died of a heart attack on July 22, 1951, in Naples, Italy.

Rodney J. Ross

References

Alexander, Bevin. *Korea: The First War We Lost.* New York: Hippocrene Books, 1986.

Goulden, Joseph C. *Korea: The Untold Story of the War.* New York: Times Books, 1982.

Hastings, Max. *The Korean War.* New York: Simon and Schuster, 1987.

Smith, Oliver Prince (1893–1977)

U.S. Marine Corps general and commander of the 1st Marine Division during the Korean War. Born in Menard, Texas, on October 26, 1893, Oliver Prince Smith worked his way through the University of California, Berkeley, where he was a member of the Reserve Officers Training Corps and graduated in 1916. Smith was a Christian Scientist all his life and remained a deeply religious person who neither drank nor swore. After graduating, he worked for Standard Oil Company.

When the United States entered World War I, Smith received a Marine Corps reserve commission in May 1917; he was then assigned to Guam and soon received

a regular commission. Smith commanded a U.S. Marine detachment on board the battleship *Texas* from 1921 to 1924, and during 1924–1928 he was assigned to U.S. Marine Corps headquarters. After three years in Haiti, Smith graduated from the U.S. Army Infantry School in 1932; he was then an instructor at the U.S. Marine Corps Schools at Quantico, Virginia, before serving on the staff of the naval attaché at the Paris embassy during 1934–1936. He was then an instructor at Quantico during 1936–1939.

Following a year with the Fleet Marine Force, Pacific, in 1940 Smith commanded a battalion of the 6th Marine Regiment and, from May 1941 until March 1942, he was with that battalion in Iceland. After two years with headquarters staff, in Janu-

Major General Oliver P. Smith was the best-known Marine Corps general of the Korean War. The withdrawal of his 1st Marine Division from the Changjin (Chosin) Reservoir is considered one of the greatest accomplishments in U.S. military history. (Department of Defense)

ary 1944 he received command of the 5th Marine Regiment of the 1st Marine Division, leading it through the New Britain Campaign. Promoted to brigadier general, in April he became assistant commander of the 1st Division. He saw action on Peleliu in September and October, and in November became deputy chief of staff to the Tenth Army. After combat on Okinawa during April and June 1945, Smith was named commandant of the U.S. Marine Corps Schools.

In April 1948, Smith became assistant commandant and chief of staff of the U.S. Marine Corps. Promoted to major general, in June 1950 Smith assumed command of the 1st Marine Division at Camp Pendleton, California. He had only 20 days to prepare the division for Korea; and on September 15, 1950, Smith led the division in the Inchon landing. Smith and X Corps commander Lieutenant General Edward M. Almond did not get along, primarily because Almond insisted on depreciating him and failed to understand U.S. Marine requirements.

Following the liberation of Seoul, Smith and the 1st Marine Division shifted by sea to the port of Wonsan on the east coast of Korea, and at the end of October the division began an advance north as part of the campaign to end the war and unite Korea. Smith had serious misgivings about MacArthur's troop dispositions for the final push to the Yalu River, enough so that he communicated these to U.S. Marine commandant general Clifton B. Cates in Washington. Smith also expressed concern about the gap between his division and the U.S. Eighth Army on his left. For a U.S. Marine general in the field to counsel caution in carrying out the orders of a commander took some courage. But Smith slowed the U.S. Marine advance to about a mile a day, took care not to string out his units any more than was absolutely necessary, and hurried the establishment of a base at Hagaru-ri. In all probability this saved his division from annihilation in the next few weeks.

When troops of the Chinese People's Volunteer Army (CPVA, Communist Chinese) resumed their offensive at the end of November, Smith's division was trapped with its main elements 78 miles north of the port of Hungnam at the Changjin (Chosin) Reservoir. On the night of November 27–28, the Chinese attacked the U.S. Marines in zero-degree weather. Ultimately, the Chinese fed 12 divisions (3 armies) into the battle. The U.S. Marines then began an epic 13-day retreat, in which they brought out their wounded and their equipment with them in one of the most masterful withdrawals in military history. By December 11, what remained of the command reached the Hamhung-Hungnam area.

Following evacuation from Hungnam at the end of December, Smith's division was incorporated into the Eighth Army as part of IX Corps. During the February 1951 counteroffensive when U.S. Army major general Bryant E. Moore suddenly died, Eighth Army commander Lieutenant General Matthew B. Ridgway named Smith to command IX Corps, one of the rare instances in which a U.S. Marine general has commanded U.S. Army troops at the division or corps level. He continued in that capacity until March.

In April 1951, Smith returned to the United States as commander of Camp Pendleton, California. Promoted to lieutenant general in 1953, he commanded the Fleet Marine Force, Atlantic, from July 1953 until September 1955. Smith retired on September 1, 1955, when he was promoted to general. Smith died in Los Altos, California, on December 25, 1977.

Spencer C. Tucker

References

Blair, Clay. *The Forgotten War: America in Korea, 1950–1953.* New York: Times Books, 1987.

Heinl, Robert D. *Victory at High Tide: The Inchon–Seoul Campaign.* Philadelphia: J. B. Lippincott, 1968.

Montross, Lynn, et al. *U.S. Marine Operations in Korea, 1950–1953.* 5 vols. Washington, DC: U.S. Marine Corps Historical Branch, 1954–1972.

Stratemeyer, George Edward (1890–1969)

U.S. Air Force general and commander of the Far East Air Force (FEAF) at the start of the Korean War. Born on November 24, 1890, in Cincinnati, Ohio, George Edward Stratemeyer grew up in Peru, Indiana, and graduated from the United States Military Academy, West Point, in 1915. Stratemeyer completed flight training in 1917 at Rockwell Field in San Diego, California, and was commander at the School of Military Aeronautics at Ohio State University during World War I. He was then chief test pilot at Kelly Air Force Base, Texas, and Chanute Field, Illinois, and transferred to the U.S. Army Air Corps in 1920. He next spent three years in Hawaii and taught at West Point from 1924 to 1929. Stratemeyer was promoted to lieutenant colonel and commanded the 7th Bombardment Group at Hamilton Field, California, from 1936 to 1938. He was promoted to brigadier general in August 1941 and to major general in February 1942.

During World War II, Stratemeyer directed air operations in the China-Burma-India Theater. He was promoted to lieutenant general in May 1945, and from April 1944 to March 1946 he commanded the U.S. Army Air Forces in the China Theater. In March 1946, Stratemeyer returned to the United States to supervise the new U.S. Air Defense Command. He actively promoted autonomy for the U.S. Air Force, which came in 1947. Known for his ability to convince subordinates to do what he wanted, Stratemeyer was also considered a skilled military air tactician.

In April 1949, Stratemeyer moved to Tokyo as commanding general of the Far East Air Force (FEAF). He was flying to Tokyo when the Korean War began in June 1950. When he landed in Seoul, Republic of Korea Army (ROKA, South Korean) troops were in retreat and Americans were evacuating.

After first ordering U.S. air attacks on the North Korean attackers, President Harry S. Truman sent U.S. ground forces into action south of the 38th parallel but continued to believe that air power was the best way to stop the invasion. Stratemeyer agreed and helped organize direct air support during the crucial early days of the war. He ordered air attacks on advancing Korean People's Army (KPA, North Korean) forces and air cover for the evacuation of U.S. civilians from Seoul, and he personally flew reconnaissance missions and planned how to use available combat aircraft to defend South Korea.

When General Douglas MacArthur visited Korea on June 29, Stratemeyer asked that he approve air operations to gain control of the air and to identify targets for future air attacks in North Korea. Without securing approval from Washington, MacArthur authorized the bombing of North Korea, and Stratemeyer cabled Fifth Air Force commander Major General Earle E. Partridge and ordered him to destroy North Korean airfields, communications, and industry.

The United States quickly gained air superiority over Korea and proceeded to bomb supply lines and provide tactical support to ground forces. Some 100 heavy bombers in Stratemeyer's command struck a 27-mile area along the upper Naktong River in August 1950. One thousand tons of bombs were dropped within 26 minutes to rout KPA troops.

Following the massive intervention by the Chinese People's Volunteer Army (CPVA, Communist Chinese) in late November 1950, Chinese and Soviet jet aircraft posed a threat to United Nations operations in far North Korea along and south of the Yalu River, an area known as MiG Alley. With United Nations Command (UNC) aircraft too far away to escort bombing missions to the north, Stratemeyer devised new tactics to meet this situation. Allied airpower, however, was unable to prevent Chinese resupply overland.

Stratemeyer opposed MacArthur's flouting of directives, such as ordering without prior approval the bombing of bridges across the Yalu in early November 1950. Stratemeyer did upset Secretary of Defense George C. Marshall when he suggested that the air force should be allowed to pursue unlimited military operations against China. When UNC troops halted the Chinese offensive, Stratemeyer encouraged strategic bombing of industries and supply centers in North Korea instead of supporting Allied ground forces. This heightened the army–air force close-support controversy. Although generally loyal to MacArthur, Stratemeyer did not question the presidential decision to remove him from command in April 1951.

Stratemeyer suffered a heart attack in May 1951, relinquished his command, and retired from active duty on January 31, 1952. Stratemeyer then focused his attention on anticommunist activities. In 1954, he attempted to convince the U.S. Senate not to censure Sen. Joseph R. McCarthy. In his retirement years, he repeatedly voiced his anger about restrictions placed on the U.S. military during the Korean War. Stratemeyer died in Orlando, Florida, on August 9, 1969.

Elizabeth D. Schafer

References

Appleman, Roy E. *South to the Naktong, North to the Yalu.* Washington, DC: Office of the Chief of Military History, 1961.

Blair, Clay. *The Forgotten War: America in Korea, 1950–1953.* New York: Times Books, 1987.

Stratemeyer, George E. *The Three Wars of Lieutenant General George E. Stratemeyer: His Korean War Diary.* San Francisco: University Press of the Pacific, 2005.

Truman, Harry S. (1884–1972)

President of the United States (1945–1953) during the first two and one half years of the Korean War. Born in Lamar, Missouri, on May 8, 1884, Harry S. Truman spent most of his formative years on his family's farm near Grandview. He hoped for a college education and tried to secure appointments to the United States Military Academy and to the United States Naval Academy, but was turned down because of poor eyesight. In World War I he served as an artillery officer as a captain.

After the war, Truman studied at night at Kansas City School of Law and won election to a judgeship on the Jackson County (Missouri) court. He served from 1926 to 1934. In 1934, he was elected to the U.S. Senate and was reelected in 1940, achieving prominence as the chair

Harry S. Truman succeeded to the presidency on the death of Franklin D. Roosevelt on April 12, 1945. Truman's presidency was marked by important foreign policy initiatives, including the Truman Doctrine, the Marshall Plan, the North Atlantic Treaty Organization, and the U.S. military intervention in Korea, which Truman described as the most difficult decision of his presidency. (Harry S. Truman Presidential Library)

of the Senate committee to investigate the national defense program.

President Franklin D. Roosevelt included Truman on the 1944 Democratic Party ticket as a compromise candidate, replacing Henry Wallace, who was regarded as being too liberal. When Roosevelt died on April 12, 1945, Truman became president. Although he had little experience in foreign policy and had not been included in many major policy decisions, Truman did not shrink from difficult decisions, especially that of employing the atomic bomb against Japan to bring an end to World War II.

Less willing than Roosevelt to work with the Soviets, Truman provided firm leadership in the Cold War. He implemented the policy of containing Communist expansion, known as the Truman Doctrine, by coming to the aid of Greece and Turkey in 1947. His administration also undertook to strengthen Europe against Communist subversion with the Marshall Plan that same year and with the cofounding of the North Atlantic Treaty Organization (NATO) in 1949.

Meanwhile, the 1949 Communist victory in China and the Soviet Union's successful test of an atomic bomb intensified attitudes in the United States toward the Cold War. Although the U.S. military government in Korea ended with elections and the proclamation of the Republic of Korea (ROK, South Korea) in August 1948, the U.S. National Security Council recommended extensive military and economic aid for South Korea, and a defense agreement was signed with that country on January 26, 1950. Unfortunately, in a speech two weeks earlier, Secretary of State Dean Acheson had excluded the ROK from the U.S. defense perimeter. Fearful that ROK president Syngman Rhee might use them for offensive purposes, the Truman administration had opposed providing tanks or medium or heavy artillery to the ROK.

President Truman reacted decisively to the June 25, 1950, invasion of the ROK by the Democratic People's Republic of Korea (DPRK, North Korea). He compared the attack to Nazi Germany's aggression in the late 1930s. Truman also saw Moscow's hand in the invasion and believed that the Soviets were trying to secure South Korea "by default" on the assumption that the United States would not intervene. Truman adroitly handled the Korean issue in the United Nations and also sent the Seventh Fleet to protect Taiwan, strengthened U.S. forces in the

Philippines, and increased aid to French forces fighting in Indochina.

Truman appointed General Douglas MacArthur as commander of United Nations (UN) forces in Korea and supported his requests for more troops. The conflict led to the calling of four National Guard divisions to active duty, an increase in the size of the regular army, and an emergency appropriation of $12 billion for defense purposes. The United States was unprepared militarily for the war and, by summer's end, Truman announced plans to significantly strengthen U.S. military forces and to double the armed forces to 3 million men, warning that the nation's defense burden would become greater still.

Truman was not fond of MacArthur but approved his Inchon Landing plan, despite reasonable concerns raised by chairman of the Joint Chiefs of Staff (JCS) general Omar N. Bradley and others. Having decided to pursue forcible reunification of Korea before the success at Inchon, he then allowed MacArthur great freedom to pursue the North Koreans across the 38th parallel with the proviso that he not carry the war into Chinese territory.

Truman sought a personal meeting with MacArthur, which took place on Wake Island on October 15, 1950. There they discussed the possibility of Chinese or Soviet intervention almost as an afterthought. MacArthur dismissed the possibility of Chinese intervention but was proved wrong when the People's Republic of China (PRC) made good on its threat to enter the conflict. Truman reluctantly approved MacArthur's plea to bomb bridges over the Yalu, with the proviso that the bombing not involve Manchuria. As UN forces reeled from the massive PRC intervention, which began in late November, Truman declared a national emergency on December 15, although he and his military advisers believed that Korea was not the place to fight a major war.

Although relieving MacArthur from his command had already been suggested, Truman preferred standing by his commander in the field. Nonetheless, Truman was angered by an interview with MacArthur wherein he sought to lay the blame for the UN retreat on the administration's limited war policy. To curb MacArthur, the administration issued a series of directives that required prior State Department or White House clearance before the release of any statements of a political nature. This did not keep MacArthur from announcing his own ultimatum to the Chinese, demanding their surrender and scuttling any possibility of an early ceasefire. Frustrated by MacArthur's repeated challenges to his administration's policy in Korea, Truman now began to consult his advisers about removing the general from command. Truman was, however, concerned over the political impact of removing his field commander and wanted the unanimous concurrence of the JCS before taking such a momentous step.

Then, on April 5, 1951, Republican House Minority Leader Joseph Martin released a letter by MacArthur, which revealed the general's disagreements with the administration on war policy. After midnight on April 11, the president announced that he was relieving MacArthur from his commands. MacArthur had forced this decision, which did, however, serve to preserve the vital principle of civilian control of the military and the president's policy of fighting a limited war in Korea. It also allowed Truman, with allied approval, to implement his plan to provide authorization for the new UNC commander, Lieutenant General Matthew B. Ridgway, to utilize atomic weapons against the enemy if his forces confronted possible annihilation or the PRC widened the war beyond Korea.

MacArthur's successors carried out the Truman administration policy of doing nothing to broaden the conflict. The war became a strategic stalemate for the remainder of Truman's term, but casualties on both sides continued to mount. Although peace talks did get underway in July 1951 and made steady progress in resolving all but one issue by early 1952, Truman's insistence that no prisoners of war be repatriated against their will stalled negotiations for more than a year.

Now highly unpopular, Truman chose not to stand for reelection in 1952. Dwight D. Eisenhower, who made the war effort a major part of his campaign as the Republican Party standard-bearer, vowed to go to Korea if elected. Following his election in November 1952, in December, although the war would not end until July 1953, and only after the death of Soviet leader Joseph Stalin in March and the Eisenhower administration in May conveyed to Beijing a threat to employ nuclear weapons if the Communists did not agree to an armistice.

After leaving office, Truman wrote his memoirs and supervised construction of his presidential library. Harry S. Truman died in Kansas City, Missouri, on December 26, 1972.

Claude R. Sasso

References

Kaufman, Burton I. *The Korean War: Challenges in Crisis, Credibility, and Command.* 2nd ed. New York: McGraw-Hill, 1997.

McCullough, David. *Truman.* New York: Simon and Schuster, 1992.

Pemberton, William E. *Harry S. Truman: Fair Dealer and Cold Warrior.* Boston: Twayne, 1989.

Vandenberg, Hoyt Sanford (1899–1954)

Chief of staff of the U.S. Air Force during the Korean War. Born in Milwaukee, Wisconscin, on January 24, 1899, Hoyt Sanford Vandenberg graduated from the United States Military Academy, West Point, in 1923. In 1925, Vandenberg earned his pilot's wings. In the 1930s, Vandenberg attended the Command and General Staff School and the U.S. Army War College. Following the Japanese attack on Pearl Harbor, Vandenberg supervised the buildup program for the U.S. Army Air Forces (USAAF), and in the summer of 1942 he was assigned to Lieutenant General Dwight D. Eisenhower's staff to develop air plans for the Allied invasion of North Africa. He was then assigned as chief of staff for the Twelfth Air Force under Brigadier General James H. Doolittle.

In early 1943, Brigadier General Vandenberg became chief of strategic forces under Lieutenant General Carl Spaatz. In August 1944, Eisenhower promoted Vandenberg from vice commander of the tactical Ninth Air Force to its commander, replacing Lieutenant General Lewis Brereton. The Ninth Air Force covered the advance of Allied forces across France into Germany. Vandenberg's superiors all agreed that the Ninth performed a vital role in helping win World War II in Europe.

In July 1945, Lieutenant General Vandenberg became assistant chief of staff for operations of USAAF. At the end of the war, many younger army officers

U.S. Air Force general Hoyt S. Vandenberg was chief of staff of the air force during 1948–1953. He oversaw the growth of that service into the linchpin of U.S. defense strategy during the early years of the Cold War. (Department of Defense)

such as Vandenberg underwent reduction to their permanent rank, in his case brigadier general. Instead, President Harry S. Truman nominated Vandenberg to remain a lieutenant general. In 1946, Vandenberg spent six months as chief of the intelligence division of the War Department's general staff. He next served as director of the Central Intelligence Group (later Central Intelligence Agency, CIA). After 15 months, he rejoined USAAF commander General Spaatz as his deputy.

Vandenberg played an important role in helping Truman and Spaatz make the air force a separate service in September 1947. Spaatz became the first chief of staff of the air force (CSAF), with Vandenberg as his vice chief. When Spaatz retired in April 1948, Vandenberg succeeded him as

CSAF. His first task was to reorganize the U.S. Air Force (USAF), which was still partially tied to the U.S. Army.

When the Korean War began in June 1950, it was a difficult time for the U.S. Air Force. Development of the B-36 bomber had been slowed by monetary restrictions and political controversy. This meant the USAF would have to go to war with the B-29 as its primary strategic bomber. Worst of all, weapons and resources needed by airmen were at first simply not available. Vandenberg refused to accept the situation, and by 1953 he had resurrected the USAF as a linchpin of U.S. military policy.

Despite having available only a few mostly World War II–vintage bombers and fighters, the USAF played a decisive role in securing the Pusan Perimeter and in the subsequent United Nations Command (UNC) sweep north. When the Chinese intervened in October and November 1950, USAF aircraft helped prevent disaster. At Vandenberg's insistence, the deployment of more F-86 jet aircraft helped check Communist MiG-15s and allowed Lieutenant General Matthew B. Ridgway's forces to counterattack and restore the balance of power on the ground.

When President Truman relieved General of the Army Douglas MacArthur of his command, Vandenberg helped deflect congressional criticism of the president and U.S. military leadership. Vandenberg's level-headed testimony and measured counsel convinced Congress of the ultimate folly of using nuclear weapons in Korea, although the Truman administration had this option under serious consideration since the beginning of the war.

As the 1952 and 1953 stalemate unfolded, Vandenberg urged many of his fellow air force leaders to suspend close air support and focus on aerial interdiction. Vandenberg realized that the success of interdiction depended on ground attacks and constant and consistent bombing to force Communist consumption of supplies to rise faster than they could be replenished. Even so, he saw no alternative to at least attempting to knock out MiG bases and utilities. Thus, despite limits against attacking enemy sanctuaries in Manchuria, these targets were attacked repeatedly. Between mid-1950 and mid-1953, USAF sorties grew from 100 per day to 1,000 per day. But in 1953 losses to ground fire and MiG-15s rose to alarming levels that caused even veteran pilots to question the viability of USAF tactics. To solve these problems, Vandenberg restricted B-29s to night bombing, increased the deployment of F-86s, and had new electronic gunsights installed on the Sabres.

By the time President Dwight D. Eisenhower took office in 1953, public opinion and military policy had tilted toward strategic nuclear weapons aimed at the Soviet threat in Europe. It was the beginning of massive retaliation and the bomber days of the Strategic Air Command (SAC). In the face of this new posture, Vandenberg fell into a policy disagreement with new Secretary of Defense Charles E. Wilson, who sought to make drastic cuts in air power. In the ensuing public debate, Vandenberg vigorously defended the need for a flexible and technologically advanced conventional and nuclear U.S. Air Force capable of strategic and tactical missions. He did not agree with reliance on nuclear weapons alone for strategic defense, and worried openly that a lack of conventional military preparedness would lead the nation into more Koreas, not fewer, as Wilson believed.

Following retirement in June 1953, Vandenberg, who was suffering from cancer, died in Washington, D.C., on April 2, 1954.

William Head

References

Meilinger, Phillip S. *Hoyt S. Vandenberg: The Life of a General.* Bloomington: Indiana University Press, 1989.

Parrish, Noel F. "Hoyt S. Vandenberg: Building the New Air Force." In *Makers of the United States Air Force.* Edited by John L. Frisbee. Washington, DC: Office of Air Force History, 1987.

Van Fleet, James Alward (1892–1992)

U.S. Army general and commander of the Eighth Army during the last two years of the Korean War. Born on March 19, 1892, in Coytesville, New Jersey, and raised in Florida, James Alward Van Fleet graduated from the United States Military Academy, West Point, in 1915. He then served along the Mexican border. After the United States entered World War I, he led a machine-gun battalion and saw combat in the Meuse-Argonne Offensive. From 1918 to 1939, Van Fleet taught military science in Reserve Officers Training Corps programs in Kansas, South Dakota, and Florida; studied and taught at the Infantry School at Fort Benning, Georgia; and eventually, as a colonel, in February 1941 became commander of the 8th Infantry Regiment.

Although he remained a colonel and retained command of the 8th Infantry until 1944, Van Fleet's rise to general officer's rank began with the Normandy Invasion, when the 8th Infantry landed at Utah Beach. By the time the division participated in the capture of Cherbourg,

Van Fleet had earned recognition as a forceful, courageous, and competent commander. By March 1945, he was a major general and commanded III Corps.

In the postwar years Van Fleet gained valuable experience in the exigencies of Cold War generalship. After a tour of duty in the United States, he served in occupied Germany in 1947. In 1948, he was named head of the U.S. Military Advisory and Planning Group in civil war–torn Greece. Promoted to lieutenant general and appointed to the Greek National Defense Council, Van Fleet participated in one of the first confrontations between East and West in the Cold War. He helped mold the Greek Army into an effective fighting force, and by 1949 that army had defeated a communist-inspired insurgency. Van Fleet next received command of the U.S. Second Army.

In the wake of General Douglas MacArthur's removal by President Harry S. Truman in April 1951 and his replacement as commander of the United Nations Command (UNC) by Lieutenant General Matthew B. Ridgway, Van Fleet took over Ridgway's former position as commander of the U.S. Eighth Army. Upon his arrival in Korea, Van Fleet received orders to place his forces on the defensive while inflicting the heaviest possible losses on the enemy. Van Fleet repositioned the Eighth Army along and to the south of the 38th parallel, where a rough stalemate had by then developed. Here his troops defeated two massive spring offensives by the Chinese People's Volunteer Army. Van Fleet then launched a counterattack, and by June the Eighth Army had inflicted some 270,000 casualties on the Chinese and North Koreans.

Van Fleet chafed under the politically driven necessities of limited warfare. Although fighting in Korea was certainly hot enough, larger considerations of international politics often determined action on the ground. Thus, through the fall and winter of 1951–1952, the Eighth Army fought a continuous series of defensive actions, some of them quite bloody, which Van Fleet saw as threatening morale and discipline, and which ran counter to his predilections as a leader. On the other hand, his directives for the very defensive he was ordered to implement were perceived in the press as insufficiently aggressive. He found himself thereby caught in what would become a classic Cold War bind for U.S. battlefield commanders.

Consequently, friction sometimes arose between Van Fleet and higher echelons over questions of tactics and ultimate goals. This atmosphere forced him to make extensive use of close air support along Lines Kansas and Wyoming to avoid useless losses to U.S. ground troops. It also created for him the impression that the U.S. Eighth Army was intentionally being deprived of artillery ammunition in retaliation for his being politically troublesome, a charge he made after his retirement.

Van Fleet, nonetheless, kept the U.S. Eighth Army in fighting trim during the bitter and bloody stalemate of the war's last two years. At Heartbreak Ridge and Bloody Ridge in eastern Korea in late summer 1951, in central Korea that October, and in the Iron Triangle in summer and fall 1952, Van Fleet showed himself as a pugnacious and usually successful commander. Because of the nature of the Korean War, his troops sometimes suffered heavy casualties even in small-scale actions, but they almost always inflicted even greater losses on the enemy. Van Fleet inspired the Republic of Korea's political and military leadership as well.

Van Fleet relinquished his command in Korea in February 1953 and retired from the U.S. Army two months later as a full general. Whatever political difficulties he may have had, he went on to serve as President Dwight D. Eisenhower's special ambassador to East Asia in 1954 and as a consultant to the secretary of the army on guerrilla warfare in 1961–1962. Van Fleet died at Polk City, Florida, on September 23, 1992.

D. R. Dorondo

References

Braim, Paul F. *The Will to Win: The Life of General James A. Van Fleet.* Annapolis, MD: Naval Institute Press, 2001.

Hermes, Walter G. *United States Army in the Korean War: Truce Tent and Fighting Front.* Washington, DC: Office of the Chief of Military History, 1966.

Walker, Walton Harris (1889–1950)

U.S. Army general and commander of the U.S. Eighth Army during the first six months of the Korean War. Born on December 3, 1889, in Belton, Texas, Walton Harris Walker graduated from the United States Military Academy, West Point, in 1912. Following U.S. entry into World War I, he saw action in France in the Saint-Mihiel and Meuse-Argonne offensives. In the interwar years Walker attended the Field Artillery School, the Command and General Staff College, and the U.S. Army War College. He served with the 15th Infantry Regiment in Tianjin (Tientsin), China, and he taught at the Infantry School, the Coast Artillery School, and West Point. Just before United States entry into World War II, Walker commanded the 36th Infantry Regiment and the 3rd Armored Brigade.

U.S. Army lieutenant general Walton Walker commanded the U.S. Eighth Army during the first six months of the Korean War. His defense of the Pusan Perimeter is considered one of the masterly mobile defense operations in military history. Walker died in a vehicular accident on December 23, 1950. (Hulton-Deutsch Collection/Corbis)

Promoted to major general in February 1942, Walker took command of the 3rd Armored Division. Seven months later he assumed command of the IV Armored Corps at Camp Young, California. There he established the Desert Training Center, responsible for training armored units for desert warfare in North Africa. Walker's corps was committed in Normandy in July 1944 and became part of Lieutenant General George S. Patton's Third Army. Walker participated in the Ardennes Offensive and was promoted to lieutenant general in May 1945.

Walker finished World War II as commander of the Eighth Service Command in Dallas, Texas. In June 1948, he took command of the U.S. Fifth Army. In September 1948, he went to Japan to assume command of the U.S. Eighth Army, the army ground force element of General Douglas MacArthur's Far East Command.

When the Korean War began, Walker became the primary United Nations Command (UNC) ground forces commander. On July 13, 1950, he established the U.S. Eighth Army forward headquarters at Taegu. Four days later, Walker also received operational control of the units of the Republic of Korea Army (ROKA, South Korea), and eventually of the rest of UN ground forces in Korea.

Despite being almost equal in numbers to the invading Korean People's Army (KPA, North Korea), Walker's poorly trained and equipped field army was no match for them. KPA forces steadily pushed the UNC forces southward down the Korean peninsula until Walker finally managed to stabilize a defensive perimeter around the major port of Pusan. With his back to the sea, but with the advantage of operating on interior lines, on July 29 Walker issued his famous "Stand or Die" order.

During the next six weeks, Walker conducted one of the most skillful mobile defense operations in military history. Walker continually shifted his mobile reserves to parry every KPA thrust. The North Koreans often broke through the UN defensive lines, but Walker always managed to stop them. Throughout the entire campaign, Walker spent a great deal of time at the front lines, personally appraising the situation and issuing orders to commanders.

At the operational and strategic levels, Walker's primary objectives were to maintain the UNC foothold on the Korean peninsula and buy time for the landings at Inchon, deep in the KPA rear. Walker succeeded, and X Corps landed at

Inchon on September 15. The result was a turning movement, with some 100,000 KPA troops cut off from their lines of communication. Despite an initial rough start, Walker's forces counterattacked across the Naktong on September 16 and drove north. The U.S. Eighth Army linked up with X Corps on September 26.

Walker protested General Douglas MacArthur's decision to separate the U.S. Eighth Army and X Corps in the drive into North Korea. On October 25, Chinese troops first intervened in the war. Walker believed this was no minor counterattack. Walker now wisely brought the bulk of his forces back behind the Chongchon River. MacArthur wanted an immediate resumption of the offensive, but Walker disagreed. X Corps was dependent logistically on the U.S. Eighth Army, rather than being supplied from Japan, and this meant that both were critically short of supplies. MacArthur pushed for an attack on November 15, but Walker resisted. Not until November 20 were supply elements able to deliver the supplies required for offensive operations. Finally, Walker agreed to resume the offensive on November 24.

On the night of November 25–26, the Chinese intervened on a massive scale, threatening the very survival of the U.S. Eighth Army, and drove it back down the Korean peninsula. Facing great odds, Walker conducted a series of delaying actions as he pulled his army south. His withdrawal was a mixed success. Although the 24th and 25th Infantry Divisions escaped largely intact, the rearguard 2nd Infantry Division was almost annihilated. On December 15, Walker established a new defensive line along the 38th parallel.

On the morning of December 23, 1950, Walker left Seoul to visit units in the vicinity of Uijongbu. Along the way his jeep was hit by a Korean civilian truck. He suffered multiple head injuries and was pronounced dead at his arrival at a field hospital. Walker was promoted posthumously to (four-star) general on January 2, 1951.

Walker's performance in Korea remains a subject of debate among historians. One of his nicknames was "Bulldog," and he looked like one. His other nickname was "Johnnie Walker," because of his reputation for being able to consume large quantities of his favorite brand of Scotch. He had a flamboyant manner reminiscent of his mentor, George Patton.

Although Walker's handling of the Pusan Perimeter defense had been masterful, the U.S. Eighth Army suffered a number of serious setbacks after it moved north of the 38th parallel. Walker, however, was continually handicapped by serious command problems beyond his control. He started the war with understrength, underequipped, and untrained units. In addition to the U.S. units, Walker was also responsible for the disorganized and demoralized ROKA divisions. Never one of MacArthur's favorites, Walker had an uneasy relationship with his theater commander. MacArthur compounded Walker's problems by keeping X Corps independent of the U.S. Eighth Army, making it impossible for a single commander to synchronize all ground operations in Korea. Walker did not get along with X Corps commander Major General Edward Almond, MacArthur's chief of staff. Walker's concern over the indicators of a large-scale Chinese intervention during his advance to the Yalu River had earned him more animosity from MacArthur's staff in Tokyo. At the time Walker died, MacArthur was considering relieving him.

Walker was not a good organizer, and he probably was not a great tactician; but he was a brave and tenacious warrior who believed in leading from the front. Whether his success at the Pusan Perimeter was the result of effective tactics, excellent intelligence, or just sheer determination, what remains most important is that he held out. Had he not done so, the Korean War could have been lost almost as soon as it had started.

David T. Zabecki

References

Appleman, Roy E. *South to the Naktong, North to the Yalu.* Washington, DC: Office of the Chief of Military History, 1961.

Blair, Clay. *The Forgotten War: America in Korea, 1950–1953.* New York: Times Books, 1987.

Mossman, Billy C. *U.S. Army in the Korean War: Ebb and Flow, November 1950–July 1951.* Washington, DC: U.S. Army Center of Military History, 1990.

Whitney, Courtney (1897–1969)

U.S. Army general and key adviser to General Douglas MacArthur, and commander of the United Nations Command (UNC), when the Korean War began. Courtney Whitney was born in Takoma Park, Maryland, on May 20, 1897. Whitney enlisted as a private in the Maryland National Guard in 1917. The following year he transferred to the aviation section of the fledgling U.S. Army Signal Corps Reserve, where he was commissioned a 2nd lieutenant in March 1918. He received a commission in the regular U.S. Army in 1920. After attending the aviation school, Whitney was named assistant adjutant and then adjutant at Payne Field in Mississippi. Three years later, he earned a law degree from National University and then went to the Philippines as adjutant for the 66th Service Squadron. From 1926 to 1927, Whitney was chief of the Publications Section of the Information Division in the Office of the Chief of the U.S. Army Air Corps.

Whitney resigned his commission in 1927 and spent the next 13 years practicing corporate law in Manila. There he forged ties with many influential Filipinos and with General Douglas MacArthur, whom he had first met in Washington in the early 1920s and who from 1936 was field marshal of the Philippine armed forces. In 1941, MacArthur became commander of U.S. Army Forces Far East.

In 1940, Whitney was commissioned a major in the U.S. Organized Reserve Corps and became assistant chief of the legal division of the U.S. Army Air Forces. Still assigned to that branch after the United States entered World War II, he became a member of MacArthur's "Bataan Gang" and accompanied the general to Australia in March 1942. The following February Whitney became assistant judge advocate of the U.S. Army Air Forces before MacArthur secured his transfer to his Southwest Pacific area general headquarters to lead the Philippine Regional Section. After U.S. forces returned to the Philippines in the fall of 1944, Whitney became chief of the civil affairs section of MacArthur's headquarters, and into 1945 he assisted Filipino officials in restoring civil government.

Whitney's capacity for hard work and his loyalty impressed MacArthur, and by the end of the war he had emerged as one of the general's closest advisers and confidants. Whitney had many critics among his staff colleagues and in the media, however, because they saw him as little more than an arrogant sycophant.

Early in 1946, Brigadier General Whitney joined MacArthur's occupation headquarters (supreme commander, Allied powers) in Tokyo as chief of the government section. Putting together an able civilian and military staff, he purged militarists and ultranationalists from Japanese public life, advised the Japanese on the revision of their statutes and the writing of a new constitution, and implemented a host of administrative, civil service, and police reforms. Although criticized by some as being heavy-handed in his methods and treatment of the Japanese, Whitney ably completed the job MacArthur wanted accomplished.

Following the outbreak of the Korean War in June 1950, Whitney was appointed military secretary of the UNC. When Truman relieved MacArthur from command in April 1951, Whitney returned to the United States and served as the general's counsel and adviser during the Senate's inquiry into MacArthur's relief and Truman's East Asian policies.

At the end of May 1951, Whitney retired from the U.S. Army with the permanent rank of major general to serve as MacArthur's personal secretary. Following MacArthur even into civilian life, he joined the Remington Rand Corporation as MacArthur's assistant when the general became chairman of the board. The two men remained inseparable until MacArthur's death in 1964. Whitney spent the remainder of his life defending his former boss. Courtney Whitney died in Washington, D.C., on May 21, 1969.

Clayton D. Laurie

References

Blair, Clay. *The Forgotten War: America in Korea, 1950–1953.* New York: Times Books, 1987.

James, D. Clayton. *The Years of MacArthur.* Vol. 3, *Triumph and Disaster, 1945–1964.* Boston: Houghton Mifflin, 1985.

Whitney, Courtney. *MacArthur: His Rendezvous with History.* New York: Alfred A. Knopf, 1956.

Wilson, Charles Edward (1886–1972)

President of General Electric Company and the first director of the Office of Defense Mobilization (ODM) during the Korean War from 1950 to 1952. Born in New York City on November 18, 1886, Charles Edward Wilson grew up in poverty. Raised in the infamous Hell's Kitchen neighborhood of New York City, Wilson left school at age 12 to work as an office boy at General Electric. Despite his curtailed education, Wilson—often known as "Electric" Charlie to distinguish him from his namesake Charles E. "Engine" Wilson, the president of General Motors and later secretary of defense under President Dwight E. Eisenhower when the Korean War ended—rose from the bottom and served successively in the departments of accounting, production, engineering, manufacturing, and marketing to become president of General Electric in 1939.

In September 1942, Wilson joined the War Production Board, facilitating the manufacture of 93,369 military airplanes in 1944. Differences with board chairman Donald Nelson, however, led to his resignation in August 1944 and his return to the presidency of General Electric. Despite Wilson's political affiliation as a registered Republican, President Harry S. Truman regularly appointed him to serve on advisory panels, including the National Security Resources Board, the National Labor-Management Panel, the University Military Training Commission, and the Taft-Hartley Advisory Board, assignments that culminated in Wilson's chairmanship of the President's Commission on Civil Rights in 1946.

In December 1950, after the People's Republic of China (PRC) intervened in the Korean War, with consequent adverse impact on U.S. military operations, Truman appointed Wilson as director of the newly created ODM, an indication that the administration anticipated a lengthy and difficult conflict. Truman charged Wilson with mobilizing American industry and the economy for the accelerated war effort in Korea. Wilson accepted the post on condition that he have complete authority over all aspects of mobilization and be answerable only to the president. As ODM director, Wilson held statutory powers that exceeded those of any other civilian mobilization chief. At the time, the nation's press likened Wilson's position to a copresidency.

Wilson oversaw and facilitated a massive defense buildup, essentially that envisaged in the National Security Council's 1950 report NSC-68, which rearmed the nation for a potential global conflict even as it simultaneously waged a limited war in Korea. Beginning in 1951, military expenditures quadrupled from $15 billion to $60 billion by 1953.

One of Wilson's first priorities was to stabilize the nation's overheating economy, mainly by implementing wage and price controls through the Wage Stabilization Board and the Office of Price Stabilization. This he did in late January 1951. Wilson also began to assemble industrial advisory committees from diverse sectors of the economy that aided in developing and implementing mobilization and production priorities. Although Wilson's job was never easy, he proved to be an able administrator, negotiating the political minefields of wage and price controls, raw materials controls, and industrial expansion with much skill and success. During his tenure, U.S. military and industrial output soared, inflationary price increases and economic dislocations remained modest, and raw materials shortages eased considerably.

Wilson's methods were uncompromising. A staunch supporter of wage and price controls to prevent inflation and facilitate mobilization, he was also a long-standing opponent of labor unions. In February 1951, when a national railroad strike jeopardized rearmament, Wilson went on the radio to appeal to the patriotism of American workers to end labor strikes and defeat communism abroad. In March 1952, Wilson, infuriated by Truman's decision to veto price increases for steel while accepting a Wage Stabilization Board recommendation to increase steelworkers' pay and benefits, resigned his position and moved to W. R. Grace and Company. When management refused to acquiesce in the president's decision, a strike ensued, and in April Truman used his emergency powers to take over the steel plants, a move that the Supreme Court declared unconstitutional. A second strike followed, and ultimately the steel makers obtained price increases, about half of what they had originally requested.

Perhaps Wilson's greatest contribution to the Korean mobilization effort was his management technique. An early pioneer in centralized/decentralized corporate structures, Wilson sought to keep the ODM and its constituent agencies lean and compact, yet powerful. He accomplished this by combining centralized management and policymaking with decentralized policy implementation and operations. This management style kept administrative costs down and bureaucracies small. It also resembled the multidivisional management forms that Wilson had implemented at General Electric. Wilson died on January 3, 1972, in Scarsdale, New York.

Paul G. Pierpaoli Jr.
and Priscilla Roberts

References

Hogan, Michael J. *A Cross of Iron: Harry S. Truman and the Origins of the National Security State, 1945–1954.* New York: Cambridge University Press, 1998.

McCullough, David. *Truman.* New York: Simon and Schuster, 1992.

Pierpaoli, Paul G., Jr. *Truman and Korea: The Political Culture of the Early Cold War.* Columbia: University of Missouri Press, 1999.

Further Reading
in the Korean War

Acheson, Dean G. *Present at the Creation: My Years in the State Department.* New York: Norton, 1969.

Alexander, Bevin. *Korea: The First War We Lost.* New York: Hippocrene, 1986.

Appleman, Roy E. *South to the Naktong, North to the Yalu (June–November 1950).* Washington, DC: U.S. Government Printing Office, 1961.

Bailey, Sydney D. *The Korean Armistice.* New York: St. Martin's, 1992.

Blair, Clay. *The Forgotten War: America in Korea, 1950–1953.* New York: Times Books, 1987.

Chen Jian. *China's Road to the Korean War: The Making of the Sino-American Confrontation.* New York: Columbia University Press, 1994.

Cho Soon-sung. *Korea in World Politics, 1940–1950: An Evaluation of American Responsibility.* Berkeley: University of California Press, 1967.

Clark, Mark W. *From the Danube to the Yalu.* New York: Harper, 1954.

Collins, J. Lawton. *War in Peacetime: The History and Lessons of Korea.* Boston: Houghton Mifflin, 1969.

Condit, Doris M. *History of the Office of the Secretary of Defense.* Vol. 2, *The Test of War, 1950–1953.* Washington, DC: U.S. Government Printing Office, 1988.

Cumings, Bruce. *The Origins of the Korean War.* 2 vols. Princeton, NJ: Princeton University Press, 1981, 1990.

Dingman, Roger. "Atomic Diplomacy during the Korean War." *International Security* 13, no. 3 (Winter 1988–1989): 61–89.

Dobbs, Charles M. *The Unwanted Symbol: American Foreign Policy, the Cold War, and Korea, 1945–1950.* Kent, OH: Kent State University Press, 1981.

Eisenhower, Dwight D. *The White House Years.* Vol. 2, *Mandate for Change, 1953–1956.* Garden City, NY: Doubleday, 1963.

Endicott, Stephen L., and Edward Hagerman. *The United States and Biological Warfare: Secrets from the Early Cold War and Korea.* Bloomington: Indiana University Press, 1997.

Fehrenbach, T. R. *This Kind of War: A Study in Unpreparedness.* New York: Macmillan, 1963.

Foot, Rosemary. *A Substitute for Victory: The Politics of Peacemaking at the Korean Armistice Talks.* Ithaca, NY: Cornell University Press, 1990.

———. *The Wrong War: American Policy and the Dimensions of the Korean Conflict, 1950–1953.* Ithaca, NY: Cornell University Press, 1985.

Friedman, Edward. "Nuclear Blackmail and the End of the Korean War." *Modern China* 1, no. 1 (January 1975): 75–91.

Goncharov, Sergei N., John W. Lewis, and Xue Litai. *Uncertain Partners: Stalin, Mao, and the Korean War*. Stanford, CA: Stanford University Press, 1993.

Goodman, Allan E., ed. *Negotiating While Fighting: The Diary of Admiral C. Turner Joy at the Korean Armistice Conference*. Stanford, CA: Hoover Institution Press, 1978.

Goulden, Joseph C. *Korea: The Untold Story of the War*. New York: Times Books, 1982.

Hastings, Max. *The Korean War*. New York: Simon and Schuster, 1987.

Hermes, Walter G. *Truce Tent and Fighting Front*. Washington, DC: U.S. Government Printing Office, 1966.

Higgins, Trumbull. *Truman and the Fall of MacArthur: A Précis on Limited War*. New York: Oxford University Press, 1960.

Joy, C. Turner. *How Communists Negotiate*. New York: Macmillan, 1955.

Kaufman, Burton I. *The Korean War: Challenges in Crises, Credibility, and Command*. Philadelphia: Temple University Press, 1986.

Keefer, Edward C. "President Dwight D. Eisenhower and the End of the Korean War." *Diplomatic History* 10, no. 3 (Summer 1986): 267–289.

Kennan, George F. *Memoirs 1925–1950*. Boston: Little, Brown, 1967.

MacArthur, Douglas. *Reminiscences*. New York: McGraw Hill, 1964.

MacDonald, Callum A. *Korea: The War Before Vietnam*. New York: Free Press, 1986.

Matray, James I. "Dean Acheson's National Press Club Speech Reexamined." *Journal of Conflict Studies* 22, no. 1 (Spring 2002): 28–55.

———. "Hodge Podge: U.S. Occupation Policy in Korea, 1945–1948." *Korean Studies* 19 (1995): 17–38.

———. *The Reluctant Crusade: American Foreign Policy in Korea, 1941–1950*. Honolulu: University of Hawaii Press, 1985.

———. "Truman's Plan for Victory: National Self-Determination and the Thirty-Eighth Parallel Decision in Korea." *Journal of American History* 66, no. 2 (September 1979): 314–333.

May, Ernest R. *"Lessons of the Past": The Use and Misuse of History in American Foreign Policy*. New York: Oxford University Press, 1973.

McCormack, Gavan. *Cold War/Hot War*. Sydney: Hale and Iremonger, 1983.

McCune, George M., and Arthur L. Grey Jr. *Korea Today*. Cambridge, MA: Harvard University Press, 1950.

Meade, E. Grant. *American Military Government in Korea*. New York: King's Crown Press, 1951.

Merrill, John. *Korea: The Peninsular Origins of the War*. Newark: University of Delaware Press, 1985.

Millett, Allan R. *The War for Korea, 1945–1950: A House Burning*. Lawrence: University of Kansas Press, 2005.

Mossman, Billy. *Ebb and Flow: November 1950–July 1951*. Washington, DC: Center of Military History, 1990.

Paige, Glenn D. *The Korean Decision: June 24–30, 1950*. New York: Free Press, 1968.

Rees, David. *Korea: The Limited War*. New York: St. Martin's Press, 1964.

Ridgway, Matthew B. *The Korean War*. Garden City, NY: Doubleday, 1967.

Rovere, Richard, and Arthur M. Schlesinger Jr. *The General and the President and the Future of American Foreign Policy*. New York: Farrar, Straus, and Giroux, 1951.

Sandusky, Michael C. *America's Parallel*. Alexandria, VA: Old Dominion Press, 1983.

Sawyer, Robert K., and Walter G. Hermes. *Military Advisors in Korea: KMAG in Peace and War.* Washington, DC: U.S. Government Printing Office, 1979.

Schaller, Michael. *Douglas MacArthur: The Far Eastern General.* New York: Oxford University Press, 1989.

Schnabel, James F. *Policy and Direction: The First Year.* Washington, DC: U.S. Government Printing Office, 1972.

Schnabel, James F., and Robert J. Watson. *History of the Joint Chiefs of Staff.* Vol. III, *The Korean War.* Washington, DC: U.S. Government Printing Office, 1988.

Spanier, John W. *The Truman–MacArthur Controversy and the Korean War.* New York: Norton, 1959.

Stone, I. F. *The Hidden History of the Korean War.* New York: Monthly Review, 1952.

Stueck, William W. *The Korean War: An International History.* Princeton, NJ: Princeton University Press, 1995.

———. *The Road to Confrontation: American Foreign Policy toward China and Korea, 1947–1950.* Chapel Hill: University of North Carolina Press, 1981.

Truman, Harry S. *Memoirs.* Vol. 2, *Years of Trial and Hope.* Garden City, NY: Doubleday, 1956.

Vatcher, William H. *Panmunjom: The Story of the Korean Military Armistice Negotiations.* New York: Praeger, 1958.

Weintraub, Stanley. *MacArthur's War: Korea and the Undoing of an American Hero.* New York: Free Press, 2000.

Whiting, Allen S. *China Crosses the Yalu: The Decision to Enter the Korean War.* Stanford, CA: Stanford University Press, 1970.

VIETNAM WAR

Leadership in the Vietnam War

American involvement in Vietnam grew out of the Indochina War. The French had controlled Vietnam, Cambodia, and Laos since the latter part of the 19th century. However, when World War II broke out, the Vichy government of France had no choice but to accede to Japanese demands for bases in Indochina, although it suited Japanese interests to allow the French to continue administering Vietnam. In 1941, Ho Chi Minh, one of the founders of the Indochinese Communist Party, formed the Viet Nam Doc Lap Dong Minh (League for the Independence of Vietnam). The Viet Minh, as it became more popularly known, portrayed itself as a broad nationalist organization, but was dominated by the Communists. During the war, the Viet Minh resisted the Japanese occupation and aided the Allies.

In 1945, with an Allied victory imminent, the French plotted to overthrow the Japanese in Indochina. The Japanese learned of this and moved first, imprisoning French troops and civil servants and ultimately declaring Vietnam "independent" under Emperor Bao Dai as the head of state. When Japan surrendered in August 1945, the Chinese Army took the surrender in northern Vietnam and the British forces in the south. With the French still imprisoned, Ho and the Viet Minh sought to move into the power vacuum. The Viet Minh seized power in the north and Bao Dai abdicated. On September 2, 1945, Ho declared the independence of the Democratic Republic of Vietnam. This set up a confrontation between Ho and the French, who wished to reestablish colonial control in Vietnam. The French refusal to recognize the end of the colonial era resulted in the Indochina War beginning in late 1946.

This conflict did not attract significant American attention in its early years. However, with the victory of the Communists in China in 1949 and when Ho Chi Minh turned to Mao Zedong for assistance, Vietnam became a Cold War battlefield and the war was instantly transformed into a war against communism in the larger context of the confrontation between East and West. This was abetted by the Korean War, when U.S. forces fought with those of the United Nations against North Korea and China.

The seeming interrelation of the two fronts of Korea and Vietnam led President Harry S. Truman, two days after the start of the Korean War, to order a doubling of military aid to the French in Indochina. He decided to support France in Indochina not only in an attempt to contain the spread of communism in Asia but also to ensure that France remained a staunch ally against the Soviets in Europe (West Germany was then disarmed).

Subsequently, the U.S. Military Assistance and Advisory Group Indochina (MAAG-I) was established in Saigon to oversee the distribution of U.S. military aid to the French

A French Foreign Legionnaire in 1954 during the Indochina War. The French effort to maintain their control in the region effectively ended with their defeat in the Battle of Dien Bien Phu that same year. (National Archives)

to assist them in their fight against the Viet Minh. Between 1950 and 1954, the United States provided France more than $2.6 billion in military aid. From the beginning, U.S. policy supported the development of an independent Vietnamese army and a U.S. role in its organization and training. The French raised indigenous Vietnamese units commanded and led by French officers and noncommissioned officers, but refused any U.S. role in their training and accepted only minimal American advice on the conduct of operations. Ultimately, in one of the decisive battles of the 20th century, in the spring of 1954, Viet Minh commander General Vo Nguyen Giap surrounded the French troops at Dien Bien Phu, a remote outpost in northwestern Vietnam on the supply route into Laos. President Dwight D. Eisenhower decided against intervening to rescue the French, and in May 1954 Giap's forces overran the last French positions and took possession of the fortress. The French public had long since tired of the war and this decisive defeat enabled the politicians to shift the blame on the French military and bring the war to an end in the 1954 Geneva Conference.

The Geneva Accords temporarily partitioned Vietnam at the 17th parallel, pending national elections in 1956. This action, however, essentially established two Vietnams, leaving Ho and the Communists in charge of the Democratic Republic of Vietnam (DRV) in the north and a noncommunist State of Vietnam in the south under Emperor Bao Dai.

In September 1954, President Eisenhower, who had first espoused the "domino theory" in April 1954, determined that Vietnam was a vital link in the global U.S. strategy of containment. Wanting to establish a counterweight to the Communists in the north, he promised Prime Minister Ngo Dinh Diem of the noncommunist southern state U.S. support. Direct U.S. aid to the State of Vietnam began in January 1955, and American advisers began arriving the following month to train South Vietnamese Army troops. Diem, meanwhile, had ousted Bao Dai and become president of a new Republic of Vietnam (RVN).

Eisenhower, worried that a reunited Vietnam would succumb to the Communists, supported Diem when he announced that he would not hold the elections called for in 1956 by the Geneva Accords. Diem simultaneously launched a military campaign against the former Viet Minh cadres left in the south and permitted there under the Geneva Accords. The DRV leadership, meanwhile, focused on rebuilding the war-torn north and initially favored maintaining a political emphasis over military action in the south, hoped to cause the collapse of the Diem regime in the south by increasing internal political pressure. Nevertheless, fighting broke out in 1957 when Diem sent his troops into the Communist strongholds. Throughout the rest of 1957 and into 1958, Diem's forces enjoyed some success, killing or capturing a large number of suspected Communists.

Faced with the failure of purely political means to bring down the Diem government, the Central Party Committee in Hanoi made a momentous decision. At the Fifteenth Party Plenum in January 1959, a secret resolution was signed, authorizing the use of revolutionary violence to complement the political struggle, both focused on the overthrow of the government in the south. Hanoi began to send equipment and personnel southward along what would become the Ho Chi Minh Trail to join in the fight. Scattered and sporadic acts of terror evolved into a sustained campaign fostered in part by northerners who had infiltrated back into South Vietnam to take leading positions in the growing insurgency. To direct this effort, the National Front for the Liberation of South Vietnam (NLF) was formed on December 20, 1960. The NLF was a classic united-front organization, which included participation by noncommunist nationalists who joined the NLF to defeat the U.S.-backed Diem government in Saigon; despite protestations to the contrary during the war, Hanoi later admitted that it had controlled the NLF and directed virtually every aspect of the war in the south.

When President John F. Kennedy assumed office in 1961, he was determined to take the initiative in the global contest with the Communists for influence, wherever that conflict might be joined. In response to the rapid growth of the insurgency in Vietnam, Kennedy, urged on by his advisers, including Robert NcNamara and Walt Rostow, decided to increase U.S. support for the Diem regime, signing a military and economic aid treaty with the Republic of Vietnam. Some $65 million in military equipment and $136 million in economic aid were delivered that year. By the end of 1961, the number of U.S. military advisers had increased to more than 3,200. These advisers, who had previously been involved only in training and high-level staff work, were now advising South Vietnamese ground combat units in the field at the battalion and regimental levels. To coordinate this effort, the U.S. Military Assistance Command, Vietnam (MACV), was formed under the command of General Paul D. Harkins in Saigon in February 1962.

The insurgency continued to grow and mature. All communist armed units in the south had been unified into a single People's Liberation Armed Force (PLAF) in 1961. This force, which became popularly known as Viet Cong (VC), a derogatory slang expression for "Vietnamese communists," numbered about 15,000 and would grow rapidly as the NLF increased its recruiting effort in the south while more and more North Vietnamese soldiers flowed down the Ho Chi Minh Trail to join the fight. By the end of 1962, the NLF and its active supporters had grown to an estimated 300,000 members.

The Army of the Republic of Vietnam (ARVN), meanwhile, continued to experience severe internal problems and proved increasingly ineffective in combating the rapidly growing insurgency. This was demonstrated only too clearly at the Battle of Ap Bac on January 2, 1963. Although the battle was reported as a great victory for the ARVN because the VC quit the battlefield after the fighting, it had been just the opposite: a small VC force had soundly defeated a much larger South Vietnamese force before withdrawing from the area in good order.

While his military forces struggled to combat the insurgents in the field, Diem and his regime became more estranged from the people and less and less popular. Kennedy had provided the increased levels of military and economic aid contingent on Diem enacting democratic reforms. However, Diem steadfastly resisted American pressure to enact those reforms. Moreover, he turned to more repressive measures in an attempt to curtail dissident elements within South Vietnam.

Diem's brother, Ngo Dinh Nhu, head of the secret police, identified militant Buddhists as a source of trouble for the regime. Charging them with harboring Communists and supporting anti-Diem forces, Nhu launched a campaign against the Buddhists to bring them under control. The situation came to a head in May 1963, when ARVN troops fired into a crowd of Buddhist demonstrators in Hue who had taken to the streets to protest Diem's discriminatory policies. This was followed in June by the self-immolation of a Buddhist bonze who set himself on fire in protest at a Saigon intersection, an act that made bold headlines around the world and caused maximum consternation in Washington. When Nhu sent his special forces into a number of Buddhist monasteries, resulting in the killing of several priests and the arrest of many others, this set off a wave of student protests in which 4,000 students were rounded up and arrested by government troops. The Communists seized the opportunity to fuel anti-Diem sentiment to create further political instability.

Alarmed at the deteriorating situation in Vietnam, the Kennedy administration urged Diem to take corrective measures to modify his policies. However, Diem remained steadfast, retained Nhu, and made no conciliatory gestures toward the Buddhists. Although there was substantial disagreement within the administration about how to proceed, Kennedy and his closest advisers realized that the Diem government was on the verge of political collapse and they had become resigned since early August 1963 to the necessity of Diem's removal.

Therefore, when a group of South Vietnamese generals approached U.S. ambassador Henry Cabot Lodge Jr. to discuss the U.S. reaction to a coup against Diem, the Kennedy administration told them that the U.S. government would not openly support a coup, but would continue to provide economic and military aid to a new government in Saigon if it appeared capable of prosecuting the war against the insurgents. The generals reconsidered and did not launch the coup then. However, the situation continued to worsen and they made their move on November 1, seizing key military installations in Saigon. Diem and his brother fled the presidential palace, but they were captured and subsequently executed, something those in the Kennedy administration who had encouraged the coup had not anticipated.

Three weeks later, on November 22, 1963, President Kennedy was assassinated in Dallas. Kennedy had told close advisers that he intended to begin withdrawing from Vietnam after the 1964 elections, but what would actually have happened had he lived is a matter of speculation.

Kennedy's successor, Lyndon Johnson, inherited the worsening situation in Vietnam, where the war was going badly for the South Vietnamese and their 16,000 American advisers. In Saigon, the coup, which resulted in General Duong Van Minh taking control of the government, ushered in a tumultuous year that was marked by successive coups and increasing instability caused by the revolving door governments.

Johnson assumed office, vowing to continue the policies of the fallen president. In Vietnam, Johnson, a firm believer in the domino theory, was caught in a quandary; he could not afford to be seen as "soft on communism," but he also did not want to widen the war and risk bringing the Chinese into the conflict, as had happened in Korea. He was also concerned that a larger war effort would result in a domestic backlash that would threaten his Great Society welfare programs. Nevertheless, Johnson's strategic outlook had been molded by World War II; he had seen the effects of appeasement and he believed that the United States had to stand up to communist aggression. Therefore, America would stand firm in Vietnam. Accordingly, Johnson signed a policy statement stating that the central U.S. objective in Southeast Asia was to assist South Vietnam "to win their contest against the externally directed and supported communist conspiracy." The Kennedy administration had managed to run the war from Washington without large-scale introduction of combat troops, but the continuing problems in Saigon would convince the new president that more aggressive action was needed.

In light of America's clearly stated intention to continue U.S. support to the regime in Saigon, the leadership of the Vietnam Workers' Party in Hanoi determined that the armed struggle in the south would have to be stepped up; accordingly, they directed a forceful escalation in pursuit of a protracted war meant to exhaust the South Vietnamese and their American supporters. By mid-1964, the PLAF forces in the south, now including 35,000 guerrillas and 80,000 irregulars, were routinely defeating the ARVN in battle.

Johnson, hoping to keep the war limited, wanted to send a message to Ho Chi Minh and the other leaders in Hanoi as a warning not to escalate the war in the south. He got that opportunity on August 2, 1964, when North Vietnamese patrol boats fired on the U.S. destroyer *Maddox* in the Gulf of Tonkin. After Johnson asserted that there had been a second attack on August 4—a claim later proved to be false although Johnson believed it to be true—he sought a congressional resolution authorizing him to respond. The Tonkin Gulf Resolution passed both the House and the Senate with only two dissenting votes, authorizing the president to take "all necessary measures to repel attacks . . . and prevent further aggression." This resolution effectively gave the president complete authority for full-scale U.S. intervention in the Vietnam War. Johnson retaliated for the Tonkin Gulf incident by ordering air strikes against North Vietnamese coastal targets.

Concurrently, Hanoi began to send regular North Vietnamese Army (NVA,

President Lyndon Johnson signs the August 1964 Tonkin Gulf Resolution that gave him for all practical purposes a free hand to commit U.S. military resources in Vietnam. (Lyndon B. Johnson Presidential Library)

as the People's Army of Vietnam or PAVN were more popularly known) units down the Ho Chi Minh Trail through Laos to join the insurgents fighting in the south. Heretofore, North Vietnamese troops had gone south as fillers for the Viet Cong; the arrival of NVA main force units on the battlefield in the south represented a sea change in the nature of the war. The ARVN had been unable to stem the tide of the insurgency and now they were also faced with an invasion of regular troops from the north.

In the latter months of 1964, the Communists stepped up their attacks, hitting Bien Hoa air base, bombing an American officers' quarters in Saigon, and attacking the ARVN in Tay Ninh province on the Cambodian border. Additionally, they had occupied most of Binh Dinh province on the north-central coast.

In January 1965, when the VC struck the U.S. base at Pleiku, Johnson again ordered retaliatory air strikes against North Vietnam. By this time, the president and his advisers had come to the conclusion that American intervention was necessary to keep the Saigon government from collapsing. Several of the president's key advisers, including McNamara and other civilians in the Pentagon, convinced Johnson that limited and graduated application of military power in concert with economic and political pressure would convince North Vietnam to abandon its support of the insurgency in the south. Not everyone agreed with the utility of bombing; Under Secretary of State George Ball dissenting strongly, arguing that bombing would not achieve the desired results and might even stiffen the resolve of the North Vietnamese people. Nevertheless, Johnson ordered a sustained bombing campaign against targets in North Vietnam in what became known as Operation ROLLING THUNDER. This operation, designed to signal U.S. resolve and bolster South Vietnamese morale, began in February 1965 and would continue in fits and starts for the next three years. The air campaign would be directed from the White House through a complicated command and control arrangement.

The U.S. military and civilian leadership was deeply divided over the conduct of the campaign. The chairman of the Joint Chiefs of Staff, General Earle Wheeler, and Admiral Grant Sharp, the commander of U.S. forces in the Pacific, called for an all-out bombing campaign against key targets in the north, including the port at Haiphong. Johnson sided with his civilian advisers, who wanted to limit the war's violence and give North Vietnam an opportunity to respond as the war was gradually escalated. The result was that target lists were approved in the White House and the pilots were left to contend with a series of prohibited and restricted areas that could not be bombed. In the end, this strategy did not work; North Vietnam saw the measured bombing campaign as a sign of weakness and responded with military escalation of their own.

Meanwhile on the ground, the ARVN continued to reel under the Communist onslaught. In addition to its combat ineffectiveness, the South Vietnamese forces were also beset by widespread corruption and desertion. Indeed, 113,000 ARVN soldiers would desert their units by the end of 1965.

With ARVN apparently on the verge of collapse and following Communist attacks against American bases, U.S. involvement escalated when Johnson authorized the dispatch of first U.S. Marine Corps units and then army ground combat troops to Vietnam. General William Westmoreland, MACV commander, had requested U.S. ground troops to protect American airfields in South Vietnam. Although Johnson was counseled by several of his civilian advisers not to commit U.S. ground troops, he chose to

U.S. marines coming ashore at Da Nang on March 8, 1965. The marines were dispatched to the Republic of Vietnam to protect U.S. air bases and were the vanguard of U.S. ground troops in the country. (UPI-Bettmann/Corbis)

support Westmoreland's request. The first two U.S. Marine battalions landed in March 1965 near Da Nang and began conducting defensive operations around the huge U.S. base there.

Johnson made a conscious decision not to publicize the escalation. He was afraid that a major debate on Vietnam would have a negative impact on his domestic social agenda. At the same time, he wanted to keep the war "limited" in order not to antagonize the Soviets or the Chinese. For these reasons, he instructed Westmoreland to manage the buildup "at lowest key possible." This lack of candor with Congress, the press, and the American people would, over time, lead to a disastrous credibility gap and forfeit public support. Johnson failed to realize that his efforts to conduct the war in the shadows undermined the very support that he needed to fight the war.

The president also made another fateful decision when he decided against calling up the reserves. For many of the same reasons that he chose to be less than candid on U.S. escalation in Vietnam, he resisted the urging of the senior military leadership to mobilize the reserves and National Guard and instead instituted a draft to provide the manpower for the war.

The manpower demands increased rapidly. General Westmoreland, believing that the VC were making preparations for a major offensive and convinced that the South Vietnamese could not handle the new level of fighting, requested additional U.S. troops. Urged on by McNamara and the Joint Chiefs of Staff, Johnson began to send more troops; the plan was that the American units would guard U.S. military enclaves.

Under this plan, the U.S. troops were to be limited to operations within a 50-mile radius of their bases. However, as more American units arrived, they soon transitioned, with White House approval, from defensive to offensive operations. The first U.S. Marine battalions would ultimately be followed by seven U.S. Army divisions, two U.S. Marine divisions, and four separate U.S. Army brigade-sized units. U.S. ground troops in South Vietnam numbered 180,000 by the end of 1965; by mid-1966, the number increased to 350,000 and would grow to over 543,000 soldiers, sailors, airmen, and marines serving in Vietnam by April 1969.

As these forces flowed into Vietnam, Westmoreland directed that they seek out and destroy the enemy forces. The ARVN had tried this approach and failed, but the American general did not see the lack of success with the ARVN in this approach as a failed strategy but rather as a failure of execution on the part of the South Vietnamese troops. He had little doubt that U.S. forces would make relatively short work of the Communists. An early battle between U.S. ground troops and the North Vietnamese Army in the Battle of the Ia Drang Valley in November 1965 convinced Westmoreland that his forces could leverage firepower and air mobility to kill large numbers of enemy soldiers. Although U.S. casualties in this battle were heavy, the kill ratio was reported as 12 to 1 in their favor. Westmoreland concluded that if the enemy could be made to suffer such heavy casualties on a repetitive basis, eventually a threshold, or "crossover" point, could be reached that would force Hanoi to call off their campaign to reunite the two Vietnams under Communist control.

Westmoreland directed his army and marine commanders to focus on large-scale offensive operations to seek out and destroy the enemy main force units, while South Vietnamese forces were relegated mainly to counterinsurgency operations in and around the villages and hamlets of South Vietnam. U.S. operations during the period 1965–1967 included MASHER, WHITE WING, ATTLEBORO, CEDAR FALLS, and JUNCTION CITY, as Westmoreland's forces mounted ever larger search and destroy operations in the effort to raise the enemy body count. The strategy was fatally flawed; at the very best, it would take a long time and, even at that, it was questionable whether it could prevail, especially if the flow of fresh enemy troops from the north could not be cut off. This would never happen because President Johnson forbade his commander from crossing the border to strike at the Ho Chi Minh Trail and enemy base areas in Laos and Cambodia. Therefore, the other side could continually replenish its forces largely unimpeded. The result was a bloody war of attrition that greatly increased the casualties for both sides as heavy fighting raged from the Demilitarized Zone (DMZ) to the Mekong Delta.

The DRV leadership, meanwhile, fully understood the political nature of the war and continued to prosecute a protracted war strategy. Understanding that Johnson and Westmoreland had no real strategy for victory, the Communists hoped to get the United States bogged down in a war they could not win militarily with the hopes that the Americans would eventually tire of the war and agree to a negotiated settlement favorable to Hanoi. With these objectives in mind, the Communists were prepared to sustain as many casualties as necessary toward the desired end state.

By late 1967, the president was under mounting pressure from a growing antiwar movement as the war continued to grind on with no end in sight. In an attempt to put the best face on his conduct of the war, Johnson ordered a "success campaign" meant to convince the media and the American public that progress was being made in the fighting. Westmoreland was brought home and paraded before the media to make the administration's case; he asserted that the situation in Vietnam was getting better every day and promised that there was a "light at the end of the tunnel."

Just a few weeks after Westmoreland's return to Vietnam, on January 21, 1968, the North Vietnamese attacked and lay siege to the remote Marine base at Khe Sanh near the Laotian border in western Quang Tri province. Ten days later, with all eyes on Khe Sanh, which appeared hauntingly similar to Dien Bien Phu in 1954, the North Vietnamese and Viet Cong launched a massive surprise offensive during the Tet (Lunar New Year) holiday, with over 80,000 troops attacking 36 major South Vietnamese cities and towns ranging from the DMZ to the Mekong Delta. The scope and ferocity of the attack in the wake of Westmoreland's earlier positive assessment of the battlefield situation convinced a large number of Americans that, contrary to their government's claims, the enemy in South Vietnam had not been crushed and thus the war would go on with no foreseeable end in sight. Despite lurid and often slanted reporting from the battlefront, the Tet Offensive was actually a tactical military defeat for the Communist forces. The allied forces recovered quickly from the initial surprise and inflicted heavy casualties on the VC and North Vietnamese attackers, killing an estimated 40,000, or half of the attacking force, during the bitter fighting. However, when Westmoreland was maneuvered in the wake of the offensive into requesting an additional 206,000 troops by General Wheeler, chairman of the Joint Chiefs of Staff (who wanted to use the better part of those troops to reconstitute the strategic reserve, not in Vietnam), it gave the impression that the allied forces had sustained a devastating loss and more troops were needed to stave off defeat.

In the end, the Tet Offensive proved to be a great psychological victory for the enemy that had a tremendous impact on Johnson, the media, and the American public, who by now had lost all confidence in Johnson's ability to handle the war. On March 31, 1968, a demoralized president went on national television and announced a halt to the bombing of North Vietnam, called for peace negotiations, and, dropping a bombshell, stated that he would not run for reelection.

In the subsequent tumultuous presidential election, Richard Nixon narrowly defeated Vice President Hubert Humphrey, who suffered as the standard-bearer for Johnson's failed Vietnam policies until he publicly broke with those policies in September 1968, too late to save the Democrats from defeat in the election. Nixon had campaigned on a platform promising to end the war in Vietnam, implying that he had a secret plan to do so. He did not, so the first order of business for his administration was to come up with an exit strategy for Vietnam. After several months of study and debate within his administration, Nixon announced at the Midway Conference in June 1969 that he would order the gradual withdrawal of U.S. forces from Vietnam and the transfer of responsibility for the war to the South Vietnamese—Vietnamization, as the policy became known. Actually this had already begun under the Johnson administration.

From that point on, the U.S. objective shifted from winning the war to pursuing a face-saving way to disengage, while hopefully leaving the South Vietnamese with at least some chance for survival once U.S. forces had all departed. Nixon wanted to

Demonstrators fleeing tear gas at Kent State University on May 4, 1970. Members of the Ohio National Guard fired upon student demonstrators, killing four people. The protests at Kent State were part of a widespread reaction to President Richard Nixon having ordered U.S. ground forces into Cambodia. (Bettmann-UPI/Corbis)

extricate the United States from Vietnam while avoiding any appearance of military or political defeat that would have a damaging effect on continued American credibility on the world stage.

General Creighton Abrams, who had succeeded Westmoreland when he left Saigon to become the army chief of staff, was given the difficult mission of improving the South Vietnamese armed forces while withdrawing U.S. troops, and at the same time, continuing to hold off the North Vietnamese Army. As the troop withdrawals gained momentum, the fighting continued. In the summer of 1969, the bloody Battle of Hamburger Hill caused a controversy at home; Nixon had promised an end to the war, but the casualties continued to mount.

With no apparent end to the war in sight, there was a resurgence of the antiwar movement and congressional criticism directed against Nixon and his handling of the war. On November 3, 1969, Nixon countered with a televised speech in which he appealed for support from the "silent majority." The speech was well received by many Americans, but it was clear that the country was divided and weary of the war.

Meanwhile in Vietnam, General Abrams was having his own problems. Having to contend with the North Vietnamese in the field, Abrams protested the drawdown of troops, but Nixon ordered the continuation of the withdrawals. However, the president also made plans to expand the war into Cambodia and Laos to destroy Communist sanctuaries and supply routes.

Initially, Nixon resorted to a gradual escalation of the air war in Cambodia but then tried to conceal the bombing from the American public. When this escalation failed to achieve the desired results, Nixon took another fateful step. In April 1970, in a move designed to provide breathing room for the Vietnamization effort, he ordered a U.S.–South Vietnamese invasion of Cambodia directed against eliminating Communist sanctuaries and base areas. This resulted in a firestorm of anti-Nixon protests on college campuses all across America. At Kent State in Ohio, National Guardsmen, who had been called out to preserve order on campus, fired into a crowd of demonstrators, killing four students and bystanders. This incident and a similar occurrence at Jackson State, where two students were killed by Mississippi police, enraged and invigorated the antiwar movement. Meanwhile, the seemingly unending fighting in Vietnam, mounting U.S. casualties, and revelations about the My Lai Massacre and the secret bombing in Cambodia helped to turn more Americans against the war.

As more U.S. troops were withdrawn, the pacification effort continued while the remaining American advisers struggled to increase the combat capability of the South Vietnamese armed forces. As a test of Vietnamization, Nixon authorized a South Vietnamese invasion of Laos in early 1971 to strike enemy base areas. This operation, LAM SON 719, which started well enough, degenerated into a debacle for the South Vietnamese, who had attacked without their American advisers or accompanying U.S. ground forces. The ARVN performance in Laos raised serious questions about the success of Vietnamization.

In light of the setback suffered by the South Vietnamese forces in Laos, Nixon tried another tact. On July 15, he announced that he would visit China in early 1972; on October 12, he announced that he would travel to the Soviet Union following his return from China. Nixon and Kissinger believed that they could use the offer of détente to both China and the Soviets to get them to put pressure on the North Vietnamese. In early 1972, seeking to counter domestic criticism, Nixon revealed for the first time publicly that Kissinger had been conducting secret talks with North Vietnamese representatives in Paris.

These diplomatic moves would eventually bear fruit, but not before the North Vietnamese escalated the fighting. With most of the U.S. combat forces gone from South Vietnam and emboldened by the outcome of the failed ARVN foray into Laos, Hanoi decided to launch a new offensive against the seemingly vulnerable South Vietnamese forces. On March 30, 1972, the Nguyen Hue Campaign, or the Easter Offensive as it became known, began with a massive, three-pronged invasion of South Vietnam. In some of the bitterest fighting of the war, North Vietnamese forces, totaling more than 130,000 regulars, equipped with tanks and heavy artillery, attacked Quang Tri in the north and besieged Kontum in the Highlands and An Loc, just 65 miles from Saigon. Nixon responded by increasing the U.S. air assets in the theater to support the ARVN in South Vietnam and expanded U.S. bombing north of the 17th parallel in North Vietnam.

On May 2, Quang Tri fell to the North Vietnamese troops, a major defeat for the ARVN. Six days later, Nixon announced that he had ordered a massive bombing campaign against North Vietnam, called Operation LINEBACKER, and a naval blockade that included the mining of Haiphong Harbor. On May 22, Nixon arrived in Moscow for the scheduled summit. He urged the Soviets to rein in the North Vietnamese, linking progress in détente to progress in the negotiations in Paris. He also asked the Soviets to convey a message to Hanoi that the United States was prepared to discuss certain concessions in Paris, to include the consideration of a tripartite commission to govern South Vietnam after a ceasefire.

The North Vietnamese invasion was eventually blunted largely due to the extensive use of U.S. airpower in support of the beleaguered South Vietnamese defenders and the air interdiction campaign against North Vietnamese supply lines, ammunition storage sites, and fuel facilities. In September, South Vietnamese forces counterattacked and recaptured Quang Tri.

During the desperate fighting, the North sustained 100,000 deaths while the South Vietnamese lost 25,000 killed. Nixon proclaimed Vietnamization a great success. The truth was that the outcome had been a very near thing and the real difference had been the massive and responsive American support that enabled the South Vietnamese to hold on in the face of the Communist onslaught. Additionally, the offensive further destabilized the Saigon government and revealed many of the ARVN's continuing weaknesses. Nevertheless, the blunting of the NVA offensive provided an opportunity for Nixon to get the United States out of Vietnam once and for all.

While the offensive ran its course, Henry Kissinger continued to meet with Le Duc Tho, his North Vietnamese counterpart, in the secret talks that had been going on since 1969. With the ARVN having turned back the North Vietnamese invasion, the North Vietnamese became more accommodating in the negotiations; Kissinger and Tho worked out a preliminary peace agreement in November 1972, whereby the North Vietnamese and NLF agreed to recognize the Thieu government in exchange for the removal of U.S. forces. However, there would be no corresponding removal of North Vietnamese forces from the south, one of the earlier American demands. Thieu, not surprisingly, balked at this and demanded a number of amendments to the draft agreement.

The North Vietnamese rejected Saigon's changes and withdrew previous concessions while also introducing new revisions of their own. With the talks at an impasse, Kissinger recommended a recess on December 14 and he and Tho departed to consult with their governments. Enraged at the breakdown in negotiations, Nixon ordered Operation LINEBACKER II, the bombing of Hanoi and Haiphong. This operation, which became known as the Christmas bombings, was widely condemned by the international community, but after 11 days of bombing, the North Vietnamese agreed to resume the negotiations in Paris. Kissinger and Tho met again on January 2, 1973, and worked out a draft agreement. After several revisions, the Agreement on Ending the War and Restoring the Peace in Vietnam was signed on January 27, 1973. Thieu's protestations about the North Vietnamese troops left in the south were ignored and the agreement was essentially the same one that had been agreed to by the United States and North Vietnam before the Christmas bombing.

In accordance with the provisions of the peace accords, 60 days later North Vietnam released the American prisoners of war held in its jails. On March 29, 1973, MACV furled its colors and the last American combat personnel departed South Vietnam. The most divisive war in American history was over, at least for the United States.

However, in South Vietnam, the Paris Peace Accords provided only the briefest respite before the fighting began again in earnest as North and South Vietnamese troops fought for control of the countryside. During the bitter fighting that ensued, the South

Vietnamese held their own throughout 1973, but in mid-1974 the tide began to turn against them. Nixon, now embroiled in the Watergate scandal, was preoccupied and could not provide the support he had promised Thieu as an enticement to get him to acquiesce to the Paris accords. Meanwhile, the U.S. Congress, locked in a battle with the president over Watergate, began to cut back U.S. aid to Saigon. The final blow fell on August 9, 1974, when Nixon resigned the presidency in disgrace. The South Vietnamese were effectively abandoned. By this time, they had been relegated to fighting what Thieu described as a "poor man's war." The North Vietnamese, on the other hand, no longer inhibited by U.S. bombing, had refurbished their forces in the south by stepping up the flow of supplies and equipment along the much improved Ho Chi Minh Trail.

Gerald Ford, who had been appointed vice president when Spiro Agnew had resigned, succeeded Nixon. When he took office, the U.S.-backed governments in South Vietnam and Cambodia stood on the brink of disaster. However, Ford's pressing problems involved other international challenges, including increasing energy dependency, instability in the Middle East, and nuclear arms control negotiations. Additionally, as an unelected president tainted by his unstinting support of Nixon's Vietnam policies, Ford would be at the mercy of a belligerent Congress. He would try to make good on Nixon's promises of support to Thieu, but in the end, he would be powerless to do so.

In late December 1974, the North Vietnamese launched a major corps-level attack against Phuoc Long province, north of Saigon along the Cambodian border, as a "test case" to determine how the Vietnamese would handle a large-scale attack and what would be the response of the United States. The ARVN defenses were quickly overrun and Ford, now prohibited from direct intervention by law, could only redouble efforts to secure additional aid for the South Vietnamese. Encouraged by the rapid collapse of the South Vietnamese forces and stunned by the lack of a meaningful response from Washington, Hanoi directed a new campaign designed to set the conditions for a final victory to be achieved by follow-on operations in 1976. Campaign 275 was launched in March 1975 with Ban Me Thuot in the Central Highlands as the primary objective.

Once again, the South Vietnamese forces collapsed and once again, the United States did nothing in response. Thieu, convinced by his generals to shorten his lines and consolidate his forces, ordered an evacuation of Pleiku and Kontum to the coast to prepare for a counterattack to retake Ban Me Thuot. However, the strategic withdrawal rapidly degenerated into a chaotic rout when North Vietnamese forces cut the main roads to the coast and fleeing civilians clogged the secondary roads. The ARVN forces in the Central Highlands disintegrated, abandoning the region to the Communists with very little resistance. The same thing happened in Military Region I as the North Vietnamese attacked down Highway 1 toward Hue and Da Nang. Chaos reigned as the South Vietnamese forces and hundreds of thousands of civilians fled in panic first for the port of Da Nang and then south down Highway 1. By the end of March, eight northern provinces had fallen into Communist hands; along with the earlier fall of the Central Highlands, this meant that the South Vietnamese had abandoned the northern half of the country.

As the action unfolded in Vietnam, President Ford attempted a last-ditch effort to obtain an emergency supplemental appropriation for military aid for Saigon. At the same time, Ford tried to deflect blame for the impending disaster on Congress. Not surprisingly, this only added to congressional ire and the aid request failed.

During April 29–30, 1975, as the city of Saigon fell to Communist forces, in Operation FREQUENT WIND, U.S. helicopters evacuated the remaining Americans and some Vietnamese from the city. (UPI-Bettmann/Corbis)

Emboldened by their unexpected success with the new offensive and realizing that the United States would do nothing to rescue the South Vietnamese, Hanoi ordered an all-out final assault with Saigon as the objective. The North Vietnamese forces drove down the coast and turned for Saigon, while additional communist forces closed on the capital city from the south and west.

Although the ARVN 18th Division put up a steadfast defense for 10 days at Xuan Loc east of Saigon, it eventually succumbed to a coordinated attack by three North Vietnamese divisions, clearing the way for the final assault on the capital. On April 21, 1975, as the North Vietnamese tightened the ring around the city, Thieu resigned the presidency and was replaced by Vice President Tan Van Huong. Duong Van Minh, thought to be more acceptable to the Communists, took over the presidency on April 28. The Communists, riding the high tide of victory, refused to negotiate and began their attack on the city. In the early morning hours of April 30, the final American personnel were evacuated from the U.S. Embassy in Saigon. Around noon, when North Vietnamese tanks crashed through the gates of the Presidential Palace, Duong Van Minh tendered South Vietnam's unconditional surrender and the Republic of Vietnam ceased to exist as a sovereign nation.

It had been a bloody war for all the belligerents. The Communists admit to 1.1 million deaths from 1954 to 1975. They claim 2 million civilian casualties, but this has not been confirmed and U.S. figures estimate 30,000 killed by U.S. bombing of the north. The South Vietnamese lost more than 110,000 military personnel killed with nearly a half-million wounded. Civilian casualties in the south are estimated at more than 400,000.

The Republic of Vietnam fell two years after the departure of the United States from Vietnam and although U.S. forces had not been defeated in the field, the nation had effectively lost the first war in its history. It was lost because the military and civilian leadership of the United States did not understand the nature of the war they faced in Vietnam. Within the Cold War context, the conflict was perceived as part of the global confrontation between East and West. Based on that perception, five successive American presidents committed ever-increasing U.S. support that eventually saw the deployment of over half a million troops to Vietnam. Those troops were employed in a strategy of attrition that inflicted heavy casualties on the enemy, but achieved no lasting result and squandered the support of the American people in the process. In the end, more than 58,000 Americans died and more than 300,000 U.S. servicemen were wounded, many maimed for life. The total cost of the war exceeded $130 billion. The war almost rent American society and forever destroyed the concept of American consensus. It scarred the American psyche, caused many Americans to question America's place in the world, and resulted in a national malaise that took many years to overcome.

James Willbanks

About the Author

Dr. James H. Willbanks earned a BA degree from Texas A&M University in 1969. He then served on active duty as a U.S. Army infantry officer, seeing duty in the United States, Germany, Vietnam, Japan, and Panama. He retired from the army as a lieutenant colonel in 1992. Among military schools he attended were the School for Advanced Military Studies and the U.S. Army Command and General Staff College. Dr. Willbanks earned his PhD from the University of Kansas, and he also holds an MMAS from the U.S. Army School of Advanced Military Studies and an MS from the University of Central Texas.

Dr. Willbanks has held numerous teaching positions within the army. From 2004 he has been the director of the Department of Military History, U.S. Army Command and General Staff College, Fort Leavenworth. He is the author of seven books: *Thiet Giap! The Battle of An Loc, April 1972* (1993); *Machine Guns: An Illustrated History* (2004); *Abandoning Vietnam: How America Left and South Vietnam Lost Its War* (2004); *The Battle of An Loc* (2005, a featured selection of the Military History Book Club); *The International Library of Essays on Military History: The Vietnam War* (editor, 2006); *The Tet Offensive: A Concise History* (2006); and *Vietnam Almanac* (2008).

Vietnam War Battles

Ap Bac, Battle of (January 2, 1963)

A fierce Vietnamese War battle, fought on January 2, 1963, at the small village of Bac (*Ap* means *hamlet* in Vietnamese), located approximately 40 miles southwest of Saigon. Stung by the October 1962 loss of a South Vietnamese Ranger platoon and concerned about the ease with which the Viet Cong were recruiting support in the important Mekong Delta region, Lieutenant Colonel John Vann, senior adviser to the 7th Division of the Army of the Republic of Vietnam (ARVN), hoped for a quick victory at Ap Bac and its sister hamlet, Ap Tan Thoi, situated 1 mile to the north.

Aware that an ARVN attack was imminent, the Communist 261st Main Force Battalion of 320 men, augmented by about 30 regional guerrillas, assumed strong defensive positions in tree lines and along canals. Dedicated fighters, they demonstrated superior weapons discipline throughout the day.

Conversely, the 7th Division exhibited cowardice, confusion, and incompetence. Despite Vann's well-conceived plan calling for a three-pronged attack from the north, south, and east, the mission quickly disintegrated as ARVN soldiers refused to advance under fire, despite exhortations of the few U.S. advisers on the scene. By noon, five U.S. helicopters carrying ARVN soldiers had been downed.

Intermediate ARVN commanders refused to act. Finally, hoping to contain the Communist forces, ARVN paratroopers dropped into the battle zone, but they landed on the west, not the east, side of Ap Bac. As in the October 1962 battle, the greatly outnumbered Communist troops outfought ARVN forces and, when nighttime covered their movements, escaped.

Miscommunication, perhaps intended, compounded the negative consequences of the battle. General Paul Harkins, then the senior-ranking U.S. military officer in South Vietnam, stated that the mission was successful because Ap Bac had been secured, although he neglected to mention that this had occurred after the communist forces had escaped the ARVN's blunder-filled attack. However, reporters David Halberstam, Neil Sheehan, and Malcolm Brown, covering the battle at the site, revealed what they observed to be a debacle. Even with the assistance of American technology and planning, the ARVN was still an inferior fighting force. Although Communist forces lost 18 men killed and 39 wounded that day, ARVN suffered about 80 dead and more than 100 wounded in action.

Rather than demonstrating a strengthening South Vietnamese Army, as officials

Army of the Republic of Vietnam (ARVN) paratroopers running to board CH-21 Shawnee helicopters during the Battle of Ap Bac with Communist Viet Cong (VC) forces in January 1963. (Time & Life Pictures/Getty Images)

had hoped, the Battle of Ap Bac became symbolic of that army's difficulties. Furthermore, in mishandling communications about this event, the U.S. military damaged its credibility with the press corps, a problem that increased as the war continued.

Charles J. Gasper

References

Halberstam, David. *The Making of a Quagmire.* Rev. ed. New York: Alfred A. Knopf, 1987.

Karnow, Stanley. *Vietnam: A History.* Rev. ed. New York: Penguin Books, 1991.

Sheehan, Neil. *A Bright Shining Lie: John Paul Vann and America in Vietnam.* New York: Random House, 1988.

Toczek, David M. *The Battle of Ap Bac, Vietnam: They Did Everything But Learn From It.* Annapolis, MD: Naval Institute Press, 2001.

Ia Drang, Battle of (October 19–November 26, 1965)

Vietnam War battle between U.S. and People's Army of Vietnam (PAVN) forces, significant because it prevented the PAVN from seizing control of the Central Highlands and cutting South Vietnam in two. The battle also demonstrated the effectiveness of air mobility against conventional enemy units.

On October 19, 1965, PAVN troops attacked the Plei Me Special Forces camp southwest of Pleiku. Initially, the 1st Cavalry Division (Airmobile) helped Army of the Republic of Vietnam (ARVN) troops relieve Plei Me. On October 27, General William Westmoreland, Military Assistance Command, Vietnam (MACV), commander, ordered

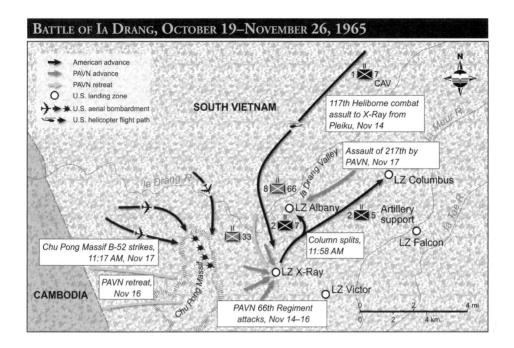

BATTLE OF IA DRANG, OCTOBER 19–NOVEMBER 26, 1965

the 1st Cavalry to seek out and destroy the 32nd, 33rd, and 66th PAVN regiments commanded by Brigadier General Chu Huy Man. General Man also sought battle to learn how to fight the 1st Cavalry, whose base at An Khe blocked his route of advance to the coast.

The location of PAVN units was unclear until November 1, when the 1st Squadron of the 9th Cavalry (1/9th), commanded by Lieutenant Colonel John B. Stockton, located and captured a hospital area 5 miles west of Plei Me, killing or capturing 135 PAVN troops. Further reconnaissance indicated a PAVN presence in the Ia Drang Valley and on the Chu Pong Massif. The 1/9th Cavalry sprang a night ambush and developed contacts that were turned over to the infantry.

The heaviest contact developed on November 14 as Lieutenant Colonel Harold G. Moore's 1st Battalion, 7th Cavalry (1/7th), assaulted landing zone (LZ) X-Ray on Chu Pong. Elephant grass, scrub trees, and tall anthills obstructed fields of fire. Moore made heavy contact before his whole under-strength battalion could be landed. PAVN lieutenant colonel La Ngoc Chau's 66th Regiment, under intense artillery fire and bombardment by the U.S. Air Force, tried to outflank LZ X-Ray to the south, but Moore was able to get his companies in line just in time. One of Moore's platoons advanced too far and was cut off and almost destroyed, but it delayed Chau in locating the main American line. His line fully extended to the south, Moore called for help and received Company B of the 2nd Battalion, 7th Cavalry, which he used as a reserve during the night.

At first light on November 15, Chau resumed the attack, and Lieutenant Colonel Robert Tully's 2nd Battalion, 5th Cavalry (2/5th), marched in to give much needed support. Chau's vicious attacks were all repulsed. The lost platoon's survivors were taken to safety, and

American B-52 bombers began the first of six days of air strikes on Chu Pong. Two more batteries of artillery arrived at LZ Columbus to provide a total of 24 pieces in support. During the night the 66th PAVN regiment withdrew.

Early on November 16, Chau launched a final attack, which was easily repulsed. Lieutenant Colonel Robert McDade's 2nd Battalion, 7th Cavalry (2/7th), arrived, and the 1st Cavalry Division troops retrieved their dead and counted the dead of the 66th. By body count, PAVN losses were 634, but U.S. estimates placed the number at 1,215 killed, over 10 times the losses of the 1st Cavalry. During the day Moore's battalion was lifted to Camp Holloway at Pleiku, but Tully's 2/5th Cavalry and McDade's 2/7th Cavalry remained to secure LZ X-Ray.

On November 17, because of continued B-52 raids on Chu Pong, McDade's 2/7th Cavalry with Company A of the 1/7th Cavalry attached was ordered to march toward LZ Albany two miles away to try to resume contact with PAVN units. Tully's unit was ordered to march to the firebase at LZ Columbus.

Having little combat experience and not yet working together as a cohesive unit, McDade's men, who were strung out in a 500-yard column in high elephant grass and jungle, blundered into a PAVN ambush, and a savage battle ensued. The head of the column had just reached LZ Albany when McDade halted it and assembled his company commanders for a council. At the same time Chau, who was on his way to attack the artillery firebase, employed one battalion of his 66th Regiment and one battalion of the 33nd to ambush McDade. He ordered his men to chop the American column into many pieces and to hug it as closely as

Second Lieutenant C. R. Rescorla of the 1st Cavalry Division (Airmobile) moves against People's Army of Vietnam (PAVN, North Vietnamese Army) snipers on November 17, 1965, during the Battle of the Ia Drang Valley. (AP/Wide World Photos)

possible in order to avoid U.S. artillery fire and air bombardment.

Bunched up at rest, McDade's men were easy targets for PAVN mortars and grenades. All unit cohesion was lost as the commanders were separated from their companies and the battle devolved into many individual combats. PAVN troops moved about killing the wounded. No artillery fire or air support was possible until McDade's men could mark their positions. After two hours of close combat, the survivors threw smoke grenades, and artillery fire and napalm rained down on the 66th and 33nd.

By late afternoon, Company B of the 1st Battalion, 5th Cavalry (1/5th), was ordered to help McDade's men. Marching from LZ Columbus, it fought its way into LZ Albany and collected the wounded into one of two perimeters for evacuation by helicopter. At dusk Company B of the 2/7th Cavalry also reinforced McDade. Chau withdrew his men during the predawn hours of November 18. His losses were unknown, but McDade's unit lost 151 men killed.

When the Ia Drang campaign battle ended on November 26, the 1st Cavalry Division had successfully spoiled the PAVN attack along Route 19 to the sea. It also demonstrated the effectiveness of a new kind of warfare, that of air mobility. In the entire campaign U.S. losses were 305 killed, while PAVN killed were estimated at 3,561.

John L. Bell

References

Moore, Harold G., and Joseph Galloway. *We Were Soldiers Once . . . and Young: Ia Drang, The Battle That Changed the War in Vietnam.* New York: Random House, 1992.

Stanton, Shelby. *The Anatomy of a Division: 1st Cav in Vietnam.* Novato, CA: Presidio Press, 1987.

Tolson, John J. *Airmobility, 1961–1971.* Washington, DC: Department of the Army, 1973.

Khe Sanh, Battles of (April–October 1967; January–April 1968)

There were two battles at Khe Sanh. The first battle occurred in 1967, evolving from U.S.-Communist engagements in northern South Vietnam. As part of his overall military strategy, U.S. commander in Vietnam General William Westmoreland ordered the construction of interconnected bases along the Demilitarized Zone (DMZ). These outposts were not meant to stop infiltration by People's Army of Vietnam (PAVN) units but to funnel it to areas where bombers could strike troop concentrations.

Khe Sanh was one such outpost. Located on high ground surrounded by dense tree-canopied heights of up to 3,000 feet, it was 6 miles from Laos and 14 miles from the DMZ. Westmoreland hoped that Khe Sanh could serve as a base for long-range patrols and aircraft gathering intelligence on Communist infiltration down the Ho Chi Minh Trail in Laos; and, hopefully, as an eventual jumping-off point for ground operations to cut the Ho Chi Minh Trail.

In October 1966, a single U.S. Marine Corps battalion occupied the base. By spring 1967, it had been reinforced to regimental strength. Soon afterward observers noted a marked increase in traffic along the Ho Chi Minh Trail. Westmoreland believed the Communists were planning an operation against Khe Sanh reminiscent of that against the French base of Dien Bien Phu in 1954. In September, he directed Seabees to upgrade the Khe Sanh

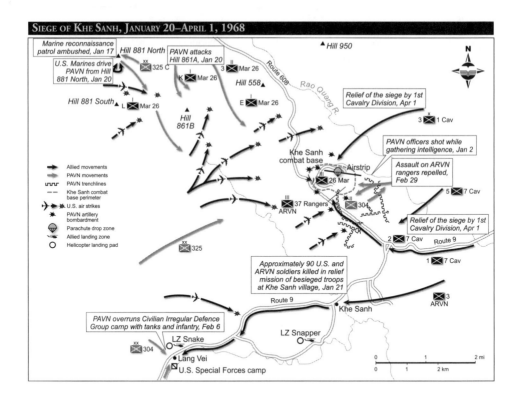

SIEGE OF KHE SANH, JANUARY 20–APRIL 1, 1968

landing strip to accommodate C-130 transport aircraft, and placed 175mm guns with a 20-mile range at Camp Carroll, 12 miles away.

In April 1967, a marine patrol was ambushed near one of the surrounding hills west of Khe Sanh, and a large rescue patrol suffered heavy casualties. During April 24–May 12, 1967, the 3rd Marines initiated several major assaults on three Communist-occupied hills surrounding Khe Sanh. These produced fierce hand-to-hand fighting that left 160 marines dead and 700 wounded, but the Americans destroyed an entire People's Army of Vietnam (PAVN) regiment and a large artillery emplacement in progress. At the end of this period the 3rd Marines were replaced by the 26th Marines, which left its 1st Battalion at Khe Sanh. The above operations were part of Operations CROCKETT

(April–July 1967) and ARDMORE (July–October 1967). Both were supported by a massive bombing campaign (SLAM) planned by U.S. Air Force general William Momyer. The 1967 engagements convinced Westmoreland that with adequate bombing and aerial resupply, U.S. outposts could survive even when outnumbered.

Between October and December 1967, the Communists greatly built up their forces near Khe Sanh. The marines, reluctant to garrison the base in the first place, were ordered to fortify their positions. In the evening of January 2, 1968, a marine reconnaissance patrol killed five of six PAVN officers near the base's outer defenses. This incident convinced Westmoreland that several thousand enemy soldiers were nearby and that Democratic Republic of Vietnam defense minister General Vo Nguyen Giap hoped to reprise his Dien Bien Phu victory. Westmoreland, who was clearly using the marines as bait to draw out the PAVN units, saw this as an opportunity for a decisive engagement.

Indeed, two regiments of the PAVN 325C Division had crossed into South Vietnam from Laos and were assembling northwest of Khe Sanh, while two regiments of the 320th Division had crossed the DMZ and were to the northeast of the marine base. They were supported by an armored regiment, two artillery regiments, and the 304th Division in Laos. PAVN forces thus totaled between 20,000 and 30,000 men, many of them support or reserve forces.

Route 9, the only road to Khe Sanh, had been cut by the Communists months earlier, so Westmoreland sent in supplies and reinforcements via air. By mid-January, 6,000 marines defended the main plateau and four surrounding hills named for their

elevation: 950, 881, 861, and 558. Some 3,000 marines defended the base itself and an equal number were split among the hill positions. Mortars and 105mm howitzers supported each position.

At 5:30 a.m. on January 20, Captain William Dabney and 185 men of his Company I launched a patrol from Hill 881 South to Hill 881 North. Dabney sensed he would make contact that day and requested additional support. Colonel David Lownds, commander of the 26th Marines, deployed 200 additional men to support the patrol. Dabney divided his company, sending one platoon up one ridge and another two platoons up the other. As they ascended, the marines were preceded by a rolling artillery barrage. Dabney hoped the Communist troops would respond and give away their positions. Instead, the PAVN veterans waited until the leading platoon came within close range and

Marine Corps artillery firing in defense of Khe Sanh. (National Archives)

opened up with automatic rifles, machine guns, and rocket-propelled grenades. Dabney sent a second platoon to flank the PAVN position, but it too was hit as it advanced. A massive firefight followed in which, with the aid of fighter-bombers dropping napalm, the marines charged and took the PAVN position.

Lownds concluded early the same morning that a larger PAVN attack would ensue, and he ordered Dabney to withdraw. Already the marines had lost 7 killed and 35 wounded. By nightfall, Dabney's men were back on Hill 881S and the Khe Sanh combat base was on maximum alert.

That night the marines received information from a deserter that a major attack was planned on 881S and 861 at 12:30 a.m. on January 21. The marines brought up additional weaponry and prepared as best they could. PAVN forces struck Hill 861 on schedule using bangalore torpedoes to break through marine defenses. At 5:00 a.m., however, the marines successfully counterattacked. At 5:30 the PAVN began an intense rocket and artillery attack against Khe Sanh combat base. The main ammunition dump took a direct hit, resulting in a succession of explosions. Despite heavy damage to the landing strip, that afternoon six C-130 planes arrived. Their 24 tons of cargo was mostly artillery ammunition, but Colonel Lownds estimated he would need 160 tons of supplies per day to hold out.

At 6:30 the PAVN attacked the village of Khe Sanh. Allied troops utilized air and artillery support to repel the attack, but thousands of local villagers fled to seek refuge with the marines. The marines did not allow them into their lines for fear of sabotage, and nearly 3,000 tried to escape down Route 9 to Dong Ha but fewer than half reached there.

Despite setbacks, the marine defenses remained strong. President Lyndon Johnson became so concerned, however, that he had hourly reports sent to him and a map room set up in the White House basement with a large replica of Khe Sanh.

Air support was vital. By March 31, B-52 bombers had dropped between 60,000 and 75,000 tons of bombs in defense of Khe Sanh. In addition, U.S. fighter-bombers flew an average of 300 sorties daily. B-52s also struck PAVN command centers in Laos. At times they dropped bombs within 1,000 yards of the Khe Sanh perimeter. Still, regular PAVN rocket attacks continued. Sniper duels were commonplace. Despite terrible conditions, morale at Khe Sanh remained high throughout the siege. Between January 21 and mid-February, PAVN forces mounted a number of attacks against the marine hill positions, with a number of fierce engagements, some hand-to-hand.

On March 6, PAVN forces began a withdrawal. By March 9, only a few thousand rear guard units remained. Operation SCOTLAND, the final part of the siege at Khe Sanh, ended on April 1, officially terminating the battle. The same day allied units began Operation PEGASUS to reopen Route 9, and on April 9 they linked up with Khe Sanh. Two months later, on June 26, 1968, U.S. forces abandoned Khe Sanh base altogether.

The official casualty count for the second Battle of Khe Sanh was 205 marines killed in action and more than 1,600 wounded, but base chaplain Ray W. Stubbe placed the death toll closer to 475. This does not include Americans killed in collateral actions, Army of the Republic of Vietnam (ARVN) Ranger casualties on the southwest perimeter, the 1,000 to 1,500 Montagnards who died during the fighting, or the 97 U.S. and 33 ARVN troops killed in relief efforts. MACV estimated PAVN losses at 10,000 to 15,000 men, most of those lost to B-52 strikes and other aerial and artillery support. The official PAVN body count was 1,602.

The siege of Khe Sanh in particular and the concurrent communist Tet Offensive in general disheartened the American public, who began to question the cost and worth of the war to America. Khe Sanh and Tet marked the beginning of the end for America's involvement in Southeast Asia.

Controversy still surrounds the battle. Some believe that Giap actually intended to replicate Dien Bien Phu, while others contend that the attack at Khe Sanh was simply part of his "peripheral strategy" to draw American forces away from the cities before the Tet Offensive. For whatever it is worth, Giap claimed the Communists never intended to overrun the base. If the siege of Khe Sanh was meant to be only a Communist ruse, then it was a success, for significant U.S. military assets were diverted there; however, PAVN forces paid a high price for this.

William Head and Peter Brush

References

Head, William, and Lawrence Grinter, eds. *Looking Back on the Vietnam War: A 1990s Perspective on the Decisions, Combat, and Legacies.* Westport, CT: Greenwood Press, 1993.

Momyer, William. *Air Power in Three Wars.* Washington, DC: U.S. Government Printing Office, 1978.

Nalty, Bernard C. *Air Power and the Fight for Khe Sanh.* Washington, DC: U.S. Government Printing Office, 1973.

Pisor, Robert. *The End of the Line: The Siege of Khe Sanh.* New York: W. W. Norton, 1982.

Prados, John, and Ray W. Stubbe. *Valley of Decision.* Boston: Houghton Mifflin, 1991.

Tet Offensive (January 1968)

Decisive turning point of the Vietnam War. In July 1967, the top leadership of the Democratic Republic of Vietnam (DRV, North Vietnam) planned to bring the Vietnam War to a speedy and successful conclusion. Militarily, the war had not been going well for the Viet Cong (VC) and People's Army of Vietnam (PAVN). The DRV leadership instructed Defense Minister General Vo Nguyen Giap to develop plans for an offensive that would end the war in one stroke. Giap was opposed, believing such an offensive to be premature, but he had his orders and proceeded with planning.

As developed, Giap's plan was based on the concept of the General Offensive. Following the General Offensive—in something of a one-two punch—would come the General Uprising, during which the people of South Vietnam were expected to rally to the Communist cause and overthrow the Saigon government. The General Uprising was a distinctly Vietnamese element of communist revolutionary dogma.

The success of the plan depended on three key assumptions: the Army of the Republic of Vietnam (ARVN) would not fight and indeed would collapse under the impact of the General Offensive; the people of South Vietnam would follow through with the General Uprising; and the Americans' will to continue would crack in the face of the overwhelming shock.

The General Offensive was set for Tet 1968, the beginning of the Lunar New Year (January) and the most important holiday in the Vietnamese year. The plans, however, were a tightly held secret, and the exact timing and objectives of the attack were withheld from field commanders until the last possible moment. Giap's buildup and staging for the Tet Offensive was a masterpiece of deception. Starting in the fall of 1967, VC and PAVN forces staged a series of bloody but seemingly pointless battles in the border regions and the northern part of South Vietnam near the Demilitarized Zone (DMZ).

The battles at Loc Ninh and Dak To were part of Giap's "peripheral campaign" intended to draw U.S. combat units out of the urban areas and toward the borders. The operations also were designed to give Communist forces experience in larger-scale conventional attack formations. In January 1968, several PAVN divisions began to converge on the isolated U.S. Marine outpost at Khe Sanh in northern I Corps, near the DMZ.

Khe Sanh may well have been a classic deception, and Giap depended on the Americans misreading history and seeing another Dien Bien Phu in the making. It worked. From January 21, 1968, until the point when the countrywide attacks erupted at Tet, the attention of most of the U.S. military and the national command structure was riveted there.

Meanwhile, the Communists used the Christmas 1967 ceasefire to move their forces into position, while senior commanders gathered reconnaissance on their assigned objectives. In November 1967, troops of the 101st Airborne Division had captured a Communist document calling for the General Offensive/General Uprising, but U.S. intelligence analysts dismissed it as mere propaganda. Such a bold stroke seemed too fantastic, because U.S. intelligence did not believe the Communists had the capability to attempt it or would want to expose their forces to open warfare in which American firepower would have a distinct advantage.

One senior U.S. commander was not thrown off by the peripheral campaign.

Lieutenant General Frederick C. Weyand, commander of U.S. II Field Forces headquartered in Long Binh near Saigon, did not like the pattern of increased Communist radio traffic around the capital, combined with a strangely low number of contacts made by his units in the border regions. On January 10, 1968, Weyand convinced U.S. commander General William Westmoreland to let him pull more U.S. combat battalions back in around Saigon. As a result, there were 27 battalions (instead of the planned 14) in the Saigon area when the communist attack came. Weyand's foresight would be critical for the allies.

The countrywide Communist attacks were set to commence on January 31, but the secrecy of Giap's buildup cost him in terms of coordination. At 12:15 a.m. on January 30, Da Nang, Pleiku, Nha Trang, and nine other cities in the center of South Vietnam came under Communist attack. Commanders in Viet Cong Region 5 had started 24 hours too early, however.

As a result of these premature attacks, the Tet holiday ceasefire was canceled, ARVN troops were called back to their units, and U.S. forces went on alert and moved to blocking positions in key areas. Giap had lost the element of total surprise, but the coming attacks would still stun the allies.

At 1:30 a.m. on January 31, the Presidential Palace in Saigon was attacked. At 2:45 a.m., in one of the most spectacular attacks of the offensive, a 19-man sapper team blasted a hole in the wall and poured into the grounds of the recently completed U.S. Embassy. By 3:40 a.m. the city of Hue, far to the north of Saigon, was under attack and the Tet Offensive was in full swing. Before the day was over, 5 of 6 autonomous cities, 36 of 44

Smoke from fires in Saigon during the 1968 Tet Offensive. While it was a military defeat for Communist forces, the Tet Offensive had a tremendous psychological effect and helped to turn American public opinion against the war. (National Archives)

provincial capitals, and 64 of 245 district capitals were under attack.

With the exception of Khe Sanh, the ancient capital of Hue, and Saigon and the area around it, the fighting was over in a few days. Hue was retaken on February 25, and the Cholon area of Saigon was finally cleared on March 7. By March 20, PAVN units around Khe Sanh began to melt away in the face of overwhelming American firepower.

Militarily, the Tet Offensive was a tactical disaster for the Communists. By the end of March 1968, they had not achieved a single one of their objectives. More than 58,000 VC and PAVN troops died in the offensive, with the Americans suffering 3,895 dead and the ARVN losing 4,954. More than 14,300 South Vietnamese civilians also died.

Giap had achieved great surprise, but he was unable to exploit it. By attacking everywhere he had superior strength nowhere. Across the country the offensive had been launched piecemeal, and it was repulsed piecemeal. Giap also had been wrong in two of his three key assumptions. The people of South Vietnam did not rally to the Communist cause, and the General Uprising never took place. Nor did the ARVN fold. Indeed, on the whole it fought and fought well.

The biggest losers in the Tet Offensive were the Viet Cong. Although a large portion of the PAVN conducted the feint at Khe Sanh, VC guerrilla forces had led the major attacks in the south, and they suffered the heaviest casualties. The guerrilla infrastructure developed over so many years was wiped out. After Tet the war was run entirely by the North, and the VC was never again a significant force on the battlefield.

Giap, however, had been absolutely correct in his third major assumption. His primary enemy did not have the will. With one hand the United States delivered the Communists a crushing tactical defeat—and then proceeded to give them a strategic victory with the other. Thus, the Tet Offensive is one of the most paradoxical of history's decisive battles.

The Americans and the South Vietnamese had been caught by surprise by the Communist offensive but had still won overwhelmingly. As a follow-up, U.S. military planners immediately began to formulate plans to finish off the Communist forces in the south. Westmoreland and Joint Chiefs of Staff chairman General Earle Wheeler submitted a request for an additional 206,000 troops to exploit the situation, when a disgruntled staff member in the Johnson White House leaked the plan to the press. The story broke in the *New York Times* on March 10, 1968. With the fresh images of the besieged U.S. Embassy in Saigon still in their minds, the press and the public immediately concluded that the extra troops were needed to recover from a massive defeat.

The Tet Offensive was the psychological turning point of the war. Military historian S. L. A. Marshall summed up the Tet Offensive well when he called it a potential major victory that became a disastrous defeat as a result of incorrect estimates, lack of nerve, and defeatism.

David T. Zabecki

References

Oberdorfer, Don. *Tet!* New York: Doubleday, 1971.

Palmer, Bruce, Jr. *The 25-Year War: America's Military Role in Vietnam.* Lexington: University Press of Kentucky, 1984.

Summers, Harry G. *On Strategy: The Vietnam War in Context.* Carlisle Barracks, PA: U.S. Army War College, Strategic Studies Institute, 1981.

Willbanks, James H. *The Tet Offensive—A Concise History.* New York: Columbia University Press, 2007.

Zabecki, David T. "Battle for Saigon." *Vietnam* (Summer 1989): 19–25.

Ap Bia Mountain, Battle of (Hamburger Hill; May 11–20, 1969)

One of the bloodiest battles of the Vietnam War. "Hamburger Hill," or the Battle of Ap Bia Mountain, occurred during May 11–20, 1969, as part of Operation APACHE SNOW (May 10–June 7, 1969). Ap Bia Mountain is located in rugged, mountainous terrain covered with dense jungle growth in western Thua Thien Province near the Laotian border. The battle was fought against People's Army of Vietnam (PAVN) regulars who were entrenched and who, as they seldom did during the war, decided to stand against repetitive U.S. frontal assaults. This created the bloody

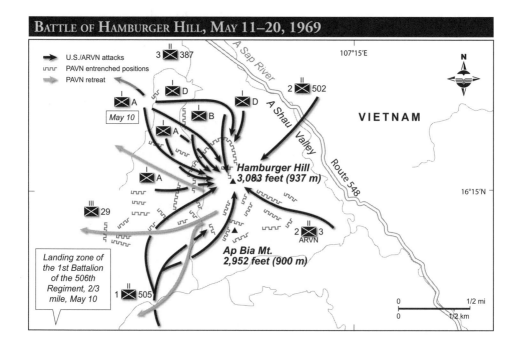

BATTLE OF HAMBURGER HILL, MAY 11–20, 1969

A wounded U.S. soldier is rushed to an evacuation helicopter amid fierce fighting against North Vietnamese forces during the Battle of Ap Bia Mountain on May 18, 1969. Known as the Battle of "Hamburger Hill," it was one of the bloodiest engagements of the Vietnam War. (UPI-Bettmann/Corbis)

"meat-grinder" battle that led U.S. participants to call it "Hamburger Hill." Coming near the time when the first American troop withdrawals were announced, it kindled controversy and a public debate over military objectives and tactics.

Dong Ap Bia, or Ap Bia Mountain, is located in the A Shau Valley southwest of the city of Hue, in what was then western I Corps. It was known to the local Montagnards as "the mountain of the crouching beast." Not part of a larger chain as are most other mountains on the western side of the A Shau Valley, Ap Bia stands alone some 3,200 feet above sea level and sends several large ridges, fingers, and ravines out in all directions covered by thick double-and-triple-canopy jungle. Hills 937 on the north and 916 on the southeast are formed from these ridges.

Operation APACHE SNOW was designed to keep pressure on PAVN units and base camps in the A Shau Valley, which was itself a base area and terminus for replacements and supplies sent south by the Democratic Republic of Vietnam (DRV) along the Ho Chi Minh Trail. The operation involved units from the 3rd Brigade, U.S. 101st Airborne Division (Airmobile), the U.S. 9th Marine Regiment, and the Army of the Republic of Vietnam (ARVN) 1st Infantry Division's 3rd Regiment.

On the second day of the operation, Company B of the 3rd Battalion, 187th Infantry (3/187th), "Rakassans," came under concentrated PAVN machine-gun and rocket-propelled grenade fire on Hill 937. The units they engaged were the 7th and 8th Battalions of the 29th

PAVN Regiment, dug into heavily fortified bunker positions on the hill. After several assaults conducted over three days, the 3/187th was reinforced with two more 101st Airborne Division battalions (1/506th Infantry and 2/501st Infantry) and a battalion of the 3rd ARVN Regiment. On May 18, with the ARVN battalion posted to seal off the hill, a two-battalion assault nearly took the summit before a torrential rainstorm forced a withdrawal. Finally, on May 20, after 10 previous tries, a 4-battalion assault drove the PAVN from their mountain fortress and into their Laotian sanctuaries.

Because the allied objective was to kill PAVN soldiers and disrupt operations in the valley, once the PAVN withdrew from the mountain, U.S. and ARVN forces abandoned it as well. And, as in previous operations, as soon as U.S. and ARVN forces withdrew, PAVN troops moved right back into the area. Official U.S. casualty figures for the whole of Operation APACHE SNOW were 56 American and 5 South Vietnamese killed in action; enemy losses were estimated at 630. Samuel Zaffiri, in his book *Hamburger Hill* (1988), however, claims American casualties as 70 dead and 372 wounded.

Massachusetts senator Edward Kennedy, no doubt speaking for many Americans, condemned the battle as "senseless and irresponsible." Fanned by media attention to the battle, which seemed to symbolize the frustration of winning battles without ever consummating the strategic victory, the debate questioned the cost in American lives of taking the hill only to abandon it for the Communists to reoccupy. The controversy led to the limiting of American military operations in the face of U.S. troop withdrawals and Vietnamization, the Richard M. Nixon administration's plan to gradually turn the war over to the South Vietnamese.

Arthur T. Frame

References

Stanton, Shelby L. *The Rise and Fall of an American Army: U.S. Ground Forces in Vietnam, 1965–1973.* New York: Dell, 1985.

Zaffiri, Samuel. *Hamburger Hill.* New York: Pocket Books, 1988.

Cambodian Incursion (May–June 1970)

Combined U.S. Army–Army of the Republic of Vietnam (ARVN) invasion of Cambodia. What became known as the Cambodian Incursion actually began in early April, when Republic of Vietnam (RVN, South Vietnam) forces, ostensibly with the consent of Cambodian prime minister Lon Nol and unaccompanied by American advisers, mounted multibattalion raids against Communist bases in the "Parrot's Beak" area. Caught by surprise, People's Army of Vietnam (PAVN) and Viet Cong (VC) communist forces withdrew deeper into the Cambodian jungles. By April 20, ARVN claimed 637 Communist dead, compared to only 34 of their own.

American leaders viewed these raids with alarm, emphasizing to Republic of Vietnam president Nguyen Van Thieu the need to maintain Cambodian neutrality. But when Communist forces seriously threatened the new Lon Nol government in Cambodia, U.S. Military Assistance Command, Vietnam (MACV), commander General Creighton Abrams argued for a full ARVN intervention with U.S. combat support. On April 25, President Richard Nixon ordered both ARVN and U.S. ground forces into Cambodia to relieve pressure on the National Khmer

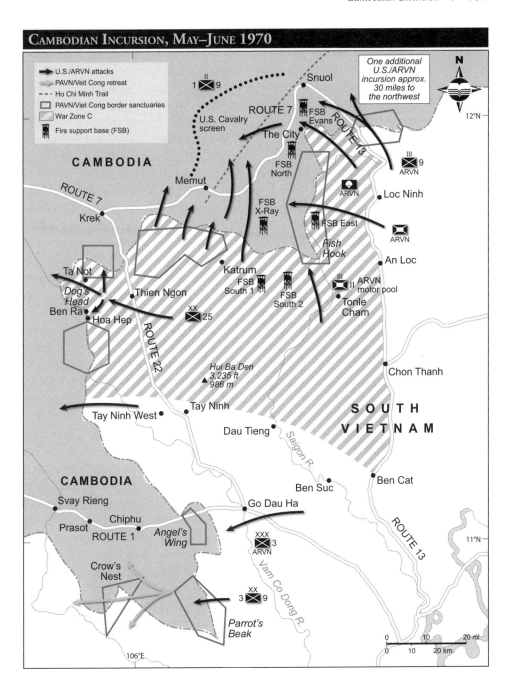

CAMBODIAN INCURSION, MAY–JUNE 1970

Armed Forces (FANK, or Forces Armées Nationale Khmer), to destroy Communist sanctuaries, and to capture the elusive headquarters of the Central Office for South Vietnam (COSVN), assumed to be in the "Fishhook" area. Broader goals included demonstrating the progress of Vietnamization, buying time for additional U.S. troop withdrawals, and breaking the peace talks stalemate.

The Cambodian Incursion involved some 50,000 ARVN and 30,000 U.S. troops and was the largest series of allied operations since 1967. The troops were divided among three groups. The ARVN would operate more than 35 miles inside Cambodia, while U.S. forces would penetrate only 18 miles. ARVN forces began the invasion on April 29 with Operation TOAN THANG 42 aimed at clearing Communist base areas in the Parrot's Beak. During the first 2 days, an 8,000-man ARVN III Corps task force reportedly killed 84 Communist soldiers while suffering 16 dead and 157 wounded. Phase II began on May 2 with ARVN III Corps forces attacking south of Route 1 into the Parrot's Beak, while a task force of the ARVN IV Corps pushed north. The Communists broke contact after losing a reported 1,043 killed and 238 captured; ARVN casualties were given as 66 killed and 402 wounded. The ARVN captured hundreds of weapons and tons of ammunition. In Phase III, which began on May 7, ARVN forces killed 182 retreating Communist soldiers near Prasot.

The allies also rushed large quantities of small arms and ammunition to Lon Nol's army, which although it expanded to more than 100,000 men soon retreated into urban areas and never launched a real offensive. When the ARVN linked up with FANK forces, it learned of the murder of hundreds of ethnic Vietnamese by Khmer soldiers. ARVN troops avenged these acts by looting several Cambodian towns. In Phase IV, ARVN forces began clearing Route 1 as far as Kompong Trabek 30 miles inside Cambodia, as RVN president Thieu began assembling an armed flotilla to move up the Mekong to repatriate as many as 50,000 ethnic Vietnamese.

While the ARVN was concerned with rescuing ethnic Vietnamese, the Cambodians asked them to relieve a FANK garrison under siege at Kompong Cham, northeast of Phnom Penh. In Phase V, General Tri dispatched a column of 10,000 men to accomplish this mission, but ARVN forces suffered significant losses in June in retaking Kompong Cham. When the Communists overran Kompong Speu southwest of Phnom Penh on June 13, a 4,000-man ARVN mechanized force quickly advanced to retake that town. ARVN and FANK troops then cleared Route 4 from Phnom Penh to Sihanoukville, which had been blockaded by the RVN Navy.

TOAN THANG 42 had upset Communist plans to overthrow the Lon Nol regime and accounted for a reported 3,588 Communist soldiers killed or captured and the seizure of more than 2,000 weapons, 308 tons of ammunition, and 100 tons of rice.

The second stage of the Cambodian Incursion, called TOAN THANG 43–46, was a series of joint U.S.-ARVN operations aimed at clearing Communist sanctuaries located in the densely vegetated Fishhook area. Commanded by Brigadier General Robert H. Shoemaker, it began early on May 1. Following extensive preparatory support by aerial and artillery bombardment, an armada of U.S. helicopters inserted the ARVN Airborne troops into three landing zones to block escape routes. The 1st Cavalry's 3rd Brigade and the 11th Armored Cavalry Regiment (ACR) then advanced across the border. On the first day, allied forces accounted for 259 killed and 7 captured from the PAVN 7th Division.

The 11th ACR then moved north to capture the Communist-occupied town of Snoul. When sporadic fire greeted the

U.S. troops in armored personnel carriers halt in a jungle clearing three miles inside Cambodia, on May 2, 1970. (AP/Wide World Photos)

armored column, the town was leveled in two days of incessant bombardment. As the expectation of open-battlefield victories faded, the mission largely became one of seizing and destroying supply depots. After entering the Fishhook on May 2, the 1st Cavalry's 2nd Brigade literally stumbled into a massive but lightly defended supply base dubbed "The City." Though not the COSVN, it contained large weapons and ammunition caches and a training base with 18 buildings. There the allies took more than 2,000 weapons, 2 million rounds of ammunition, and nearly 40 tons of foodstuffs. By mid-June, allied forces in the Fishhook also captured or destroyed more than 300 trucks and other vehicles. TOAN THANG 43 accounted for 3,190 Communist soldiers killed or captured.

TOAN THANG 44 began on May 6 as the U.S. 25th Division's 1st Brigade drove across the Cambodian border west of Tay Ninh to search for Enemy Base Area 354.

By May 14, in engagements south of the Rach Ben Go, American forces had accounted for 302 Communists killed or captured and more than 300 weapons, 4 tons of ammunition, and 217 tons of rice seized.

On May 6, the 1st Cavalry's 2nd Brigade initiated TOAN THANG 45, aimed at Enemy Base Area 351 north of Phuoc Long Province. Facing only sporadic contact, the brigade uncovered the largest depot captured during the war, so huge that it was dubbed "Rock Island East." The tonnage of supplies was so great that a road had to be constructed to remove them. By June, the entire 1st Cavalry Division was inside Cambodia. It uncovered many more weapons and supply caches, as well as a vehicle maintenance depot and an abandoned communications depot. Altogether TOAN THANG 45 accounted for 1,527 Communist troops killed or captured, as well as 3,500 weapons, 791 tons of ammunition, and

1,600 tons of rice seized. The last 1st Cavalry fire base was dismantled by June 27, with all troops back inside South Vietnam by June 29.

Simultaneously with TOAN THANG 45, an ARVN 5th Division regiment and a squadron of the ARVN 1st Armored Cavalry Regiment launched TOAN THANG 46 against Enemy Base Area 350, north of Binh Long Province. There ARVN forces discovered a surgical hospital and several major caches of supplies and ammunition. By June 20, increased Communist activity forced the termination of TOAN THANG 46, but not before it had accounted for 79 Communist soldiers killed or captured and 350 weapons, 20 tons of ammunition, and 80 tons of rice seized.

ARVN IV Corps troops initiated Operation CUU LONG I on May 9, designed to open the Mekong River. Within two days the ARVN 9th and 21st Divisions, augmented by 5 armored cavalry squadrons, cleared both banks of the river, allowing a 100-ship convoy (including 30 U.S. ships) to reach Phnom Penh and proceed north to Kompong Cham. By May 18, the ships had repatriated nearly 20,000 Vietnamese held in refugee camps. Simultaneously, ARVN III Corps forces cleared Route 1 as far as Neak Luong. In CUU LONG II, from May 16 to 24, ARVN IV Corps troops joined FANK forces in recapturing Takeo, 25 miles south of Phnom Penh, and cleared routes 2 and 3, killing 613 Communist troops, while suffering only 36 killed and 112 wounded. IV Corps forces then launched CUU LONG III, again joining with FANK forces to reestablish control over towns south of Phnom Penh and to evacuate more ethnic Vietnamese.

Two days after the Parrot's Beak and Fishhook incursions began, the allies decided to expand operations to attack Communist base areas in northeastern Cambodia facing II Corps. Allied forces in this operation, designated Operations BINH TAY I–IV, included the ARVN 22nd and 23rd Infantry Divisions, the 2nd Ranger Group, the 2nd Armor Brigade, and two brigades of the U.S. 4th Infantry Division. The 4th Division troops uncovered an abandoned PAVN training camp that included a 30-bed hospital and tons of supplies. All 4th Division troops had departed Cambodia by May 16. When terminated on May 25, BINH TAY I had accounted for 212 Communist dead and the seizure of more than 1,000 weapons and 50 tons of rice. Allied casualties were 43 killed and 18 wounded.

In BINH TAY II, from May 14 to 27, battalions of the 22nd ARVN Division swept across the border from Darlac Province, searching for Enemy Base Area 701. Contact was limited, but ARVN forces uncovered several more caches of weapons and supplies. In BINH TAY III, from May 20 to June 12, the 23rd ARVN Division searched for Enemy Base Area 740, located west of Ban Me Thuot. The most dramatic event was the destruction of a 10-truck Communist convoy. In BINH TAY II and III, ARVN forces killed 171 while losing 30 dead and 77 wounded. In BINH TAY IV, from June 23 to 27, an ARVN 22nd Division task force of military and civilian vehicles, supported by U.S. artillery and helicopter gunships, moved deep into Cambodia along Route 19 to reach a beleaguered FANK garrison at Labang Siek and managed to evacuate more than 7,000 Khmer soldiers and dependents across the border to Pleiku Province. All II Corps ARVN troops left Cambodia by June 27.

Although all American ground forces had left Cambodia by June 30, President Thieu considered the survival of Lon Nol's regime vital and would not be bound by the deadline. ARVN units continued operating up to 35 miles inside Cambodia into 1971, supported by U.S. long-range artillery, tactical air support, and B-52 bombings.

During the Cambodian Incursion the amount of supplies uncovered was 10 times more than that captured inside Vietnam during the previous year: 25,401 weapons; nearly 17 million rounds of small-arms, 200,000 rounds of antiaircraft and 70,000 rounds of mortar ammunition; 62,022 hand grenades; 43,160 B-40 and 2,123 107mm or 122mm rockets; 435 vehicles; 6 tons of medical supplies; and 700 tons of rice. The total was sufficient to supply 54 Communist main force battalions for as much as a year. The human cost also was great. According to the allies, the incursion claimed 11,349 Communist, 638 ARVN, and 338 U.S. killed; 4,009 ARVN and 1,525 U.S. wounded; and 35 ARVN and 13 U.S. missing. In addition, 2,328 Communist soldiers rallied or were captured.

The short-term gains from the Cambodian Incursion actually may have boomeranged, however. Knowing that American intervention would be limited, the Communists sought to avoid open confrontation, then quickly returned to reclaim their sanctuaries and reestablish complete control in eastern Cambodia. The PAVN compensated for their temporary losses in Cambodia by seizing towns in southern Laos and expanding the Ho Chi Minh Trail into an all-weather network capable of handling tanks and heavy equipment. Furthermore, the continuing withdrawal of U.S. combat units from III Corps forced the ARVN to deploy an excess of troops there, thus reducing their strength in the north where the Communist threat grew incessantly. In the long run, the Cambodian Incursion posed only a temporary disruption of the march of Communist forces toward the domination of all of Indochina.

An unanticipated result of the incursion was to give the antiwar movement in the United States a new rallying point. Dissent was not limited to campus confrontations such as the tragedies at Kent State University in early May and at Jackson State later that month, but also led to a series of congressional resolutions and legislative initiatives that would severely limit the executive power of the president. By the end of 1970, Congress had prohibited expenditures for U.S. forces operating outside of South Vietnam.

Finally, the widening of the battlefield in 1970 eventually left Cambodia the most devastated nation in Indochina. The Cambodian invasion had turned the war into one for all of Indochina, and the departure of U.S. troops left a void too great for the ARVN or the FANK to fill.

John D. Root

References

Coleman, J. D. *Incursion: From America's Chokehold on the NVA Lifelines to the Sacking of the Cambodian Sanctuaries.* New York: St. Martin's Press, 1991.

Nolan, Keith William. *Into Cambodia: Spring Campaign, Summer Offensive, 1970.* Novato, CA: Presidio Press, 1990.

Shaw, John M. *The Cambodian Campaign: The 1970 Offensive and America's Vietnam War.* Lawrence: University Press of Kansas, 2005.

Stanton, Shelby L. *The Rise and Fall of an American Army: U.S. Ground Forces in Vietnam, 1965–1975.* Novato, CA: Presidio Press, 1985.

Tran Dinh Tho. *The Cambodian Incursion.* Washington, DC: U.S. Army Center of Military History, 1983.

Vietnam War Leaders

Abrams, Creighton (1914–1974)

U.S. Army officer and commander, U.S. Military Assistance Command, Vietnam (1968–1972), then chief of staff of the army (1972–1974). Born on September 15, 1914, in Springfield, Massachusetts, Creighton Abrams grew up in nearby Agawam. Graduating from the United States Military Academy, West Point, in 1936, he was posted to the 7th Cavalry Regiment. When World War II loomed, he volunteered for armored service, finding there a mode of warfare entirely congenial to his hard-driving and imaginative leadership. He first rose to prominence as commander of a tank battalion in Third Army during World War II.

After World War II, Abrams served as director of tactics at the Armor School (1946–1948), graduated from the Command and General Staff College (1949), and was a corps chief of staff at the end of the Korean War (1953–1954). He graduated from the Army War College (1953), and then was advanced to brigadier general in 1956 and major general in 1960. He held a variety of staff assignments during this period, and in 1963 Abrams was appointed lieutenant general and made commander of V Corps in Germany.

When American involvement in Vietnam intensified, in 1964 Abrams was recalled from Germany, advanced to full

U.S. Army general Creighton Abrams commanded the Military Assistance Command, Vietnam (MACV), during 1968–1972. As chief of staff of the army during 1972–1974, Abrams helped rebuild the U.S. military establishment. (Herbert Elmer Abrams/Center for Military History)

general (four-star) rank, and made the army's vice chief of staff. In that assignment during 1964–1967 he was involved in the army's troop buildup, a task made infinitely more difficult by President Lyndon Johnson's refusal to call up reserve forces. In tandem with army chief of staff General Harold K. Johnson,

Abrams proved to be an effective steward of the army's affairs.

In May 1967, Abrams was assigned to Vietnam as deputy commander. He devoted himself primarily to the improvement of South Vietnamese forces. During the 1968 Tet Offensive, when the Army of the Republic of Vietnam (ARVN) forces gave a far better account of themselves than was expected, Abrams received much of the credit.

Soon after Tet, Abrams was sent north to Phu Bai to take command of I Corps (Military Assistance Command, Vietnam [MACV], Forward). Abrams concentrated chiefly on the battle to retake Hue, forming in the process a close relationship with ARVN general Ngo Quang Truong, commander of the 1st ARVN Division. Abrams coordinated the efforts of U.S. Army and Marine elements and ARVN forces while working to improve the logistical system. After a month of hard fighting, Truong's forces cleared and occupied Hue.

As commander of MACV, Abrams changed the conduct of the war in fundamental ways. His predecessor's attrition strategy, search-and-destroy tactics, and reliance on body count as the measure of success were discarded. Instead, Abrams stressed population security as the key to success. He directed a "one-war" approach, pulling together combat operations, pacification, and upgrading South Vietnamese forces into a coherent whole.

Abrams urged his commanders to reduce so-called harassment and interdiction fires (unobserved artillery fire), which he thought did little damage to the enemy and a good deal to innocent villagers. He also cut back on the multibattalion sweeps that gave Communist forces the choice of terrain, time, and duration of engagement, replacing these with multiple small-unit patrols and ambushes that blocked the Communists' access to the people.

Abrams's analysis of the enemy "system" was key to this approach. He had observed that in order to function effectively, the enemy needed to prepare the battlefield extensively, pushing forward a logistics "nose" instead of being sustained by a logistics "tail," as in common military practice. This meant that many Communist attacks could be preempted if their supply caches could be discovered and destroyed. Abrams also discerned that Communist main forces depended heavily on guerrillas and the Viet Cong infrastructure in the hamlets and villages, and that digging out that infrastructure could deprive the main forces of the wherewithal they needed to function effectively. These insights were key to revising the tactics of the war.

Abrams's force of personality and strength of character were, during his years in command, at the heart of the American effort in Vietnam. Over the course of the years, his army was progressively taken away from him, withdrawn chunk by chunk until he was in a symbolic sense almost the last man left. Still, Abrams did what he could to inspire, encourage, and support the remaining forces, American and South Vietnamese alike.

Abrams left Vietnam in June 1972 to become army chief of staff. There he grappled with the myriad problems of an army that had been through a devastating ordeal. He concentrated on readiness and on the well-being of the soldier, always the touchstones of his professional concern. Abrams died on September 4, 1974, in Washington, D.C.

Lewis Sorley

References

Colby, William, with James McCargar. *Lost Victory: A Firsthand Account of America's*

Sixteen-Year Involvement in Vietnam. Chicago: Contemporary Books, 1989.

Sorley, Lewis. *A Better War: The Unexamined Victories and Final Tragedy of America's Last Years in Vietnam.* New York: Simon and Schuster, 1992.

———. *Thunderbolt: General Creighton Abrams and the Army of His Times.* New York: Simon and Schuster, 1992.

Ball, George Wildman
(1909–1994)

Lawyer, diplomat, presidential adviser, and steadfast opponent of the Vietnam War. Born in Des Moines, Iowa, on December 21, 1909, George Wildman Ball was educated at Northwestern University, where he earned a bachelor's degree in 1930 and a law degree in 1933. Admitted to the Illinois Bar in 1934, he pursued a successful career as a lawyer both with federal government agencies and with private firms.

From 1933 to 1935, Ball served in the U.S. Treasury Department's Office of General Counsel. During World War II, he served with the Lend-Lease Administration (1940–1942) and as director of the U.S. Strategic Bombing Survey in London from 1944 to 1945. For a few months in 1945–1946, Ball also served as general counsel of the French Supply Council in Washington, D.C.

Later in 1946, he returned to his legal practice and became involved in Democratic presidential politics, first on behalf of Adlai Stevenson, who ran for the presidency in 1952 and 1956, and then John F. Kennedy. After Kennedy received the 1960 Democratic presidential nomination, Ball drew up a memorandum that urged the Kennedy campaign to begin a comprehensive review of U.S. foreign policy for the new decade. Kennedy liked the idea,

and Ball ultimately bore the responsibility for drafting the report, which was well received. When Kennedy assumed office in January 1961, Kennedy named Ball undersecretary of state for economic affairs, and, later, undersecretary of state, a post he held until 1966.

A close adviser to President Kennedy, Ball became an early opponent of American military involvement in Vietnam. In November 1961, he privately warned Kennedy that committing troops there would prove a tragic error and predicted that within five years the United States would have some 300,000 men in Vietnam. Kennedy replied, "George, you are just crazier than hell. That isn't going to happen," (Ball 1982). Although he was best known for his antipathy to U.S. military involvement in Vietnam, Ball also participated in the secret meetings of the Executive Committee (EXCOM) during the 1962 Cuban Missile Crisis, brokered a wheat deal with the Soviet Union, and served as a mediator for crises in Cyprus, Pakistan, the Congo, and the Dominican Republic.

Following Kennedy's November 1963 assassination, Ball continued in his role as devil's advocate in the Lyndon B. Johnson administration, arguing against escalation of the war in Vietnam. He opposed the conflict on the grounds that Southeast Asia was diverting attention from more important European affairs. Instead, Ball sought deescalation and a political settlement with Hanoi. Realizing that his position with the administration was increasingly untenable, he resigned in 1966 and returned to private legal practice.

Ball's public service days were not over, for in 1968 he was called upon to chair a committee investigating the *Pueblo* Incident. Later that same year, Johnson nominated him to become the permanent U.S. representative to the United Nations, a post he was reluctant to take. Nevertheless, Johnson pressured him, and he took up the post in June 1968. In September, however, he resigned, fearing that Republican presidential nominee Richard M. Nixon was poised to win the November 1968 election. He subsequently campaigned hard for Vice President Hubert H. Humphrey, who lost the contest to Nixon by a narrow margin. Had Humphrey won, Ball would undoubtedly have been named secretary of state.

After Nixon took office in 1969, Ball continued to openly criticize the U.S. government's Vietnam policies until the conflict finally ended with an American withdrawal in 1973. Ball remained active in diplomatic and Democratic political circles, serving as an ad hoc adviser to President Jimmy Carter in the 1970s and the early Bill Clinton administration in the 1990s. He wrote five books after he left office in 1968, and was working on a sixth when he died of cancer in New York City on May 26, 1994.

James Friguglietti
and Paul G. Pierpaoli Jr.

References

Ball, George W. *The Past Has Another Pattern: Memoirs*. New York: W. W. Norton, 1982.

Karnow, Stanley. *Vietnam: A History*. Rev. ed. New York: Penguin Books, 1991.

Bundy, McGeorge (1919–1996)

Special assistant to the president for national security affairs (1961–1966) and a key figure in the development of U.S. Vietnam policy. Born on March 30, 1919, in Boston, Massachusetts, McGeorge

McGeorge Bundy was special assistant to the president for national security affairs and one of President Lyndon B. Johnson's key advisers in the development of U.S. policy toward Vietnam. (Yoichi R. Okamoto/Lyndon B. Johnson Presidential Library)

Bundy graduated from Yale University in 1940. As a young man he assisted former secretary of war Henry Stimson in writing his memoirs. He served as dean of the faculty of arts and sciences at Harvard University (1953–1961) before joining the John F. Kennedy administration as national security adviser in 1961.

Bundy continued in this post under President Lyndon B. Johnson before resigning in February 1966. Robert Komer, one of Bundy's deputies, handled Bundy's job on an interim basis until Walt W. Rostow permanently assumed the position.

Bundy was known for his intelligence, although some thought him smug, even arrogant. He was, however, one of the most powerful and influential advisers in both the Kennedy and Johnson administrations, and as such he held the respect and confidence of both presidents.

During his five years as special assistant, Bundy was intimately involved in critical decisions on the Vietnam War. He was part of Kennedy's inner circle during the Buddhist Crisis of 1963 and the coup against President Ngo Dien Diem that November. He sought to ensure the survival of a democratic, independent South Vietnam, but he did not want the United States to take over the fight against the Communist insurgents.

After the assassinations of both President Diem and President Kennedy in November 1963 and the passage of the Tonkin Gulf Resolution in August 1964, Bundy changed his views. By the end of that year, he favored an enlarged U.S. role in Vietnam, including a graduated bombing campaign against North Vietnam and the buildup of U.S. troops in South Vietnam. He was in Vietnam when the Viet Cong attacked the U.S. barracks and helicopter base at Pleiku in February 1965, killing nine Americans and destroying five aircraft, an event that helped to confirm his belief that the American military had to intervene in greater force. He supported retaliatory air raids on North Vietnam and believed that a strong U.S. military presence in South Vietnam would strengthen the United States and the Republic of Vietnam governments in peace negotiations.

Yet even in the midst of the 1965 troop buildup, Bundy feared that the Americanization of the war would overwhelm civil reform programs and pacification efforts in South Vietnam. During 1965, he urged Johnson to enhance the pacification effort by allocating more resources and improving its management. By that year, he also began to question the continuing military escalation. Bundy resigned from government service in 1966 because he had already served more than five years and he questioned the continuing escalation in Vietnam. He had played an influential role in centralizing American management of pacification programs in Washington under Robert Komer and in Saigon under Ambassador William Porter.

Even after he left his post, as one of Johnson's "Wise Men," Bundy continued to advise the president. During the critical post–Tet Offensive meeting with Johnson that March 1968, he supported deescalation and a new approach to the war. That same month, on March 31, Johnson announced that he would not seek reelection; shortly thereafter he announced an end to the bombardment of North Vietnam.

After leaving government, Bundy served as president of the Ford Foundation until 1979, at which time he left to become a professor of history at New York University for 10 years. In 1990, he joined the Carnegie Corporation of New York as the chairman of its committee on reducing the danger of nuclear war. He was its scholar-in-residence at the time of his death of a heart attack in Boston on September 16, 1996.

Richard A. Hunt

References

Barrett, David M. *Uncertain Warriors: Lyndon Johnson and His Vietnam Advisers.* Lawrence: University Press of Kansas, 1993.

Halberstam, David. *The Best and the Brightest.* New York: Random House, 1972.

Hunt, Richard A. *Pacification: The American Struggle for Vietnam's Hearts and Minds.* Boulder, CO: Westview Press, 1995.

Bunker, Ellsworth (1894–1984)

Businessman, diplomat, and U.S. ambassador to the Republic of Vietnam (1967–1973). Born on May 11, 1894, in Yonkers, New York, Ellsworth Bunker graduated from Yale University in 1916 and entered the family sugar business. Not until midlife, after an extremely successful international business career, did he become a diplomat.

Named first as U.S. ambassador to Argentina (1951–1952), Bunker later held the same post in Italy (1952–1953), then India, where he stayed from 1956 to 1961. He was U.S. representative to the Organization of American States (OAS) at the time of the 1965 U.S. intervention in the Dominican Republic. Bunker played a key role in promoting a moderate civilian government there and worked closely with Lieutenant General Bruce Palmer Jr., American commander of the OAS forces.

Ellsworth Bunker was U.S. ambassador to the Republic of Vietnam (RVN) for six years, during 1967–1973. He developed a high regard for RVN president Nguyen Van Thieu. (Lyndon B. Johnson Presidential Library)

Arriving in Saigon as U.S. ambassador in April 1967, Bunker established the practice of sending periodic reporting cables to the president. These constitute an impressive record of sound judgment and wise counsel, including his insight into military matters. Bunker praised the military efforts of General Creighton Abrams. On political matters, Bunker's reporting was both practical and timely. In May 1968, he cabled that most Vietnamese regarded peace negotiations with great trepidation. He consistently urged that the United States not cease bombing North Vietnam until Hanoi agreed to stop activity in the south. The wisdom of this approach was demonstrated when, on the representations of W. Averell Harriman, the United States accepted vague assurances that reciprocity would be demonstrated, only to see the Democratic Republic of Vietnam (DRV) leadership subsequently deny that there had been any agreements while simultaneously violating their supposed terms.

Bunker developed great regard for the South Vietnamese during his years in their country. He also appreciated and stressed how the Vietnamese were taking on a growing share of the financial burden of prosecuting the war. Bunker's regard for President Nguyen Van Thieu also grew year by year. Bunker in turn enjoyed the wide respect of Republic of Vietnam (RVN) government leaders. However, he did draw criticism from some quarters for his open support for Thieu in the 1967 and 1971 RVN elections. During the early years of the Richard M. Nixon administration, Bunker supported U.S. incursions into Laos and Cambodia.

When he stepped down in 1973, Bunker had served as ambassador to the Republic of Vietnam for six years, a longer time than any other senior American official, military or civilian, had been in continuous service there. He continued to believe, as he said in an oral history interview, that America's effort to help the Vietnamese was in keeping with its commitments to individual liberty and national self-determination.

Between 1973 and 1978, Bunker performed an important last public service as chief negotiator of the Panama Canal Treaty. He died in Brattleboro, Vermont, on September 27, 1984.

Lewis Sorley

References

Bunker, Ellsworth. *The Bunker Papers: Reports to the President from Vietnam, 1967–1973.* Edited by Douglas Pike. 3 vols. Berkeley: University of California Institute for East Asian Studies, 1990.

Johnson, Lyndon Baines. *The Vantage Point.* New York: Holt, Rinehart and Winston, 1971.

Nixon, Richard M. *RN: The Memoirs of Richard Nixon.* New York: Grosset and Dunlap, 1978.

Clifford, Clark McAdams (1906–1998)

U.S. secretary of defense (1968–1969). Clark McAdams Clifford was born on December 25, 1906, at Fort Scott, Kansas. He earned an LLB from Washington University in 1928. After spending some years in St. Louis as a lawyer, in 1944 he joined the U.S. Navy and undertook various administrative assignments. A posting to the White House in 1945 as assistant naval aide soon led to his appointment as naval aide, then assistant counsel, and finally counsel, to President Harry S. Truman, a position he held until late 1949. Clifford then practiced law in Washington, D.C.

By 1960, Clifford was widely regarded as the most influential and well-connected Democratic lawyer in Washington. After handling several delicate legal matters for then-senator John F. Kennedy, in late 1960 he headed the president-elect's transition team but refused any formal office for himself. Both Kennedy and his successor, Lyndon B. Johnson, however, called upon Clifford for advice.

In the early 1960s, Clifford did not oppose the incremental increases in U.S. economic and military aid to Vietnam. In May 1965, though, Johnson consulted

Clark Clifford served as U.S. secretary of defense during 1968–1969. In early March 1968, Clifford recommended to President Lyndon Johnson that the United States commit only those forces necessary to meet immediate needs in Vietnam and not embark on another major buildup. (Yoichi R. Okamoto/Lyndon B. Johnson Presidential Library)

Clifford as to the proposed major escalation of American ground forces in Vietnam by 100,000 men, with further increases to follow. Together with George W. Ball, Clifford argued forcefully but unsuccessfully against this, urging that Washington should seek a negotiated settlement at that time, even if it was unsatisfactory, rather than entering into a potentially dangerous open-ended commitment.

After losing this argument, Clifford believed that the United States should prosecute the war strongly, without being diverted from its aims. Until 1967, therefore, he opposed bombing halts and pauses and recommended that the United States make an intensive effort to win the war. On a mission to Vietnam in late 1965, Clifford was impressed by the evidence of American progress, even as he noted the signs of North Vietnamese counterescalation. At a meeting of the "Wise Men," Johnson's senior policy advisers, in November 1967, which Clifford attended, he joined the rest in urging Johnson to stand firm in Vietnam.

On January 19, 1968, Clifford took office as secretary of defense, replacing the now-dovish Robert McNamara. Almost immediately, the Tet Offensive occurred, after which U.S. commander in Vietnam General William C. Westmoreland requested an additional 206,000 U.S. troops. Clifford set up a Vietnam Task Force to reassess the situation in Vietnam and learned that U.S. military leaders could offer no plan for victory or assurance of success. In early March, therefore, he recommended to the president that the United States commit only the forces necessary to meet immediate needs in Vietnam and not embark on another major buildup.

Fearing that victory was impossible, Clifford summoned another meeting of the "Wise Men." After extensive briefings from State and Defense Department officials, most of the group concluded that the United States could not attain its ends in Vietnam and should begin peace negotiations. Throughout 1968, Clifford battled the hawks in the administration, most notably National Security Adviser Walt W. Rostow and Secretary of State Dean Rusk, in pushing for a bombing halt and peace negotiations and in publicly putting pressure on the Republic of Vietnam (RVN) to join in peace talks. He left office on January 20, 1969, when Johnson left office.

In the early months of the Richard Nixon administration, Clifford approved of the new president's intention to withdraw American troops. But Clifford alienated both Nixon and Johnson when he published an article in the summer 1969 issue of *Foreign Affairs* in which he called for the withdrawal of 100,000 American troops by December 1969 and all U.S. ground forces by December 1970. He believed that only this prospect would impel the Democratic Republic of Vietnam to enter into serious negotiations. Clifford repeated these suggestions in an article in *Life* magazine the following summer, in which he also condemned the United States' May 1970 Cambodian Incursion.

Clifford continued to practice law in Washington and to play the role of elder statesman for the Democratic Party. In the late 1980s and early 1990s, Clifford's involvement with the Bank of Credit and Commerce International, which lost billions of dollars in fraudulent circumstances, proved highly embarrassing to him, although he pleaded ignorance of any knowledge of its criminal activities. His age, poor health, and marginal role saved him from prosecution, but his image was tarnished and his influence in Democratic circles greatly diminished. Clifford died in Bethesda, Maryland, on October 10, 1998.

Priscilla Roberts

References

Barrett, David. *Uncertain Warriors: Lyndon Johnson and His Vietnam Advisers.* Lawrence: University Press of Kansas, 1994.

Clifford, Clark. *Counsel to the President: A Memoir.* New York: Random House, 1991.

Frantz, Douglas, and David MacKean. *Friends in High Places. The Rise and Fall of Clark Clifford.* Boston: Little, Brown, 1995.

Colby, William Egan
(1920–1996)

U.S. ambassador, Central Intelligence Agency (CIA) station chief in Saigon, and deputy to the commander of U.S. Military Assistance Command, Vietnam (COMUSMACV). Born on January 4, 1920, in St. Paul, Minnesota, William Egan Colby graduated from Princeton University in 1940. He obtained a commission in the U.S. Army and in 1943 began working with the Office of Strategic Services (OSS). Colby's involvement with this organization led to a 33-year intelligence career.

In 1947 Colby earned a law degree from Columbia University, and in 1950 he joined the CIA. In 1959, he became CIA station chief in Saigon. For the next three years, Colby experimented with various forms of security and rural development programs for the Republic of Vietnam (RVN). From their endeavors, the Citizens' (later Civilian) Irregular Defense Groups (CIDGs), the Mountain Scout program, and the Strategic Hamlet project emerged in 1961. The following year

Colby became chief of the CIA's Far East Division, a position he held until 1968. This new appointment forced him to concentrate not only on Southeast Asia but also on China and other areas, such as the Philippines. In this new office he began to stress pacification as the key to overcoming communist aggression in Vietnam.

In 1965, indirectly connected with Colby's emphasis on the people's war along with other factors, CIA analysts established the Hamlet Evaluation System (HES) to measure certain factors in the villages in South Vietnam. These elements contributed to identifying the progress of pacification in the countryside. Despite this, however, an aggressive pacification strategy did not emerge until 1968.

In 1968, Colby returned to Vietnam and, with ambassadorial rank, became deputy to COMUSMACV for Civil Operations and Revolutionary (later changed to Rural) Development Support (CORDS). While serving in this post, Colby oversaw the accelerated pacification campaign (APC), initiated in November 1968, which focused on enhanced security and development within South Vietnam's villages and included such components as the Phoenix program and the People's Self-Defense Force.

From 1969 to 1970, planning for the pacification and development shifted from the Americans to the South Vietnamese in accordance with the Richard Nixon administration's policy of Vietnamization. Then, in 1971, the program shifted to a more self-oriented role for the villages of South Vietnam. In 1972, Colby returned to Washington, D.C., to become executive director of the CIA and, from May 1973 until his retirement in November 1976, director.

Colby assumed leadership of the CIA during the worst crisis in its history, triggered by that agency's assistance of E. Howard Hunt in his illegal break-ins. Colby's predecessor, James R. Schlesinger, had ordered the compilation of a list of CIA actions that might have violated its charter. Colby inherited that list and revealed to Congress the agency's involvement in domestic surveillance, plots to kill foreign leaders, use of humans as guinea pigs in mind-control experiments, and other nefarious deeds. He believed that revealing to Congress the agency's unsavory side helped to save it from congressional abolition. This action earned Colby admiration from many in Congress and the public, but angered many Cold War warriors, which brought an end to his tenure as director in 1976.

In retirement Colby maintained that the United States and the Republic of Vietnam might have won the war if only they had fought the CIA's kind of war and countered Communist guerrilla tactics. He claimed that in the early 1970s Vietnamization was succeeding and pacification was building the base for an RVN victory. He believed this chance for victory was thrown away when the United States sharply reduced its military and logistical support and then sold out the RVN government during negotiations in Paris. The final straw came when Congress dramatically cut aid to the RVN, making inevitable the 1975 Communist victory.

Colby also spoke out against the nuclear arms race and, in 1992, for cutting the defense budget by 50 percent and spending the money on social programs. William Colby died in a canoeing accident off Rock Park, Maryland, on April 27, 1996.

R. Blake Dunnavent

References

Andrade, Dale. *Ashes to Ashes: The Phoenix Program and the Vietnam War.* Lexington, MA: Lexington Books, 1990.

Colby, William, with James McCargar. *Lost Victory: A Firsthand Account of America's Sixteen-Year Involvement in Vietnam.* Chicago: Contemporary Books, 1989.

Collins, Joseph Lawton (1896–1987)

U.S. Army general and special representative of President Dwight D. Eisenhower sent to Vietnam in 1954 to assess the situation following the French defeat at Dien Bien Phu and the Geneva Accords and to determine the size and scope of future U.S. assistance. Born in New Orleans, Louisiana, on May 1, 1896, Joseph Lawton Collins graduated from the United States Military Academy at West Point in 1917 and was commissioned a 2nd lieutenant. He rose steadily through the ranks and commanded a division and a corps in World War II. In 1947, he became deputy chief of staff of the army under General Dwight D. Eisenhower. Promoted to full general in January 1948, Collins became chief of staff of the army in 1949, a post he held until 1953.

Collins was intricately involved in the Korean War and was the first commander to recommend that U.S. ground troops be sent to the Republic of Korea (ROK) to repel the June 25, 1950, invasion by forces of the Democratic People's Republic of Korea. By 1953, Collins had grown sufficiently weary of the costly and stalemated Korean War to support the use of nuclear weapons to force the Communists back to the negotiating table. He stepped down as chief of staff in August 1953, only weeks after the July armistice agreement had been signed. Collins is credited with fully integrating army units during the Korean War, per President Harry S. Truman's 1948 executive order calling for the racial integration of American armed forces.

When sending Collins to Vietnam in November 1954, President Eisenhower gave him the rank of ambassador and, in his letter of introduction, "broad authority to direct, utilize and control all agencies and resources of the U.S. government with respect to Vietnam." Upon his arrival in Saigon, Collins found the government under challenge from the Cao Dai and Hoa Hao religious sects and from the Binh Xuyen gangsters, as well as a threatened coup by Vietnamese Armed Forces chief of staff General Nguyen Van Hinh. After Collins reached agreement with the French authorities in Vietnam, combined French and U.S. pressure induced General Hinh to go to France for "consultations" with State of Vietnam titular head of state Bao Dai. Although Collins personally agreed with the French that Ngo Dinh Diem was not capable of leading the State of Vietnam, his instructions were to support the Diem government by helping it establish a military training program and agrarian reforms, which he did. The observations and reports that Collins relayed to Washington solidified the American commitment in Vietnam and served as a blueprint for U.S. policy there until the early 1960s.

Collins retired from the army in March 1956 at four-star rank and worked for the pharmaceutical firm of Chas. Pfizer & Co. from 1957 to 1969. He died in Washington, D.C., on September 12, 1987.

Arthur T. Frame

References

Collins, General J. Lawton. *Lightning Joe: An Autobiography.* Baton Rouge: Louisiana State University Press, 1979.

Spector, Ronald H. *Advice and Support: The Early Years, 1941–1960.* Washington, DC: U.S. Army Center of Military History, 1983.

Cronkite, Walter Leland (1916–)

Influential and iconic CBS television news reporter and anchorman. Born on November 4, 1916, in St. Joseph, Missouri, Walter Cronkite moved to Texas as a young boy. After two years at the University of Texas–Austin, he left school and began his journalism career at the Houston *Post* in 1933. He then entered the world of radio broadcasting, taking his first job as a radio journalist/announcer in Oklahoma City in the 1930s.

During World War II, Cronkite worked for United Press International (UPI), and in 1945–1946 he served as chief UPI correspondent at the Nuremberg War Crimes Tribunals. Cronkite spent two years as the chief UPI correspondent from the Moscow desk before joining CBS News in 1950. He was personally recruited by the venerable journalist Edward R. Murrow, who admired Cronkite's work during World War II. Besides working as a reporter, Cronkite also narrated several popular series, which earned him wide public recognition.

In 1962, Cronkite became the anchor and editor of the CBS Evening News. A year later, Cronkite convinced CBS management to extend the evening news from a 15-minute to half-hour format, which became the industry standard for years thereafter. He also anchored CBS space launches and national political conventions. From 1953 to 1957, Cronkite also hosted *You are There,* a popular television program dedicated to reenacting significant historical events.

With his reputation for hard work, accuracy, competitiveness, gravitas, and impartiality, Cronkite achieved great believability, often ranking in polls as the "most trusted man in America." As such, his rarely seen emotions carried great significance to his viewing public. His

CBS News anchor Walter Cronkite (left), widely regarded as the most trusted public figure in America, interviewing President John F. Kennedy about U.S. involvement in Vietnam at the president's summer home in Hyannis Port, Massachusetts, September 2, 1963. When Cronkite concluded in 1968 that the war could not be won, it had major repercussions on public opinion. (Library of Congress)

emotional coverage of the John F. Kennedy assassination in November 1963 mirrored the feelings of the American public.

In 1968, Cronkite, upon returning from a trip to Vietnam, from which he reported extensively, stated publicly that he believed American policy there would not win the war. This statement came shortly after the Tet Offensive and, coupled with the public's growing doubts about the war, seemed to confirm that Americans wanted out of the Vietnam War. President Lyndon B. Johnson allegedly lamented that "If I've lost Cronkite, I've lost America." Although Cronkite was not—by a long shot—the only American journalist to proclaim the Vietnam War to be unwinnable, he was certainly the most influential and well-respected reporter to do so.

During his career, Cronkite received two Peabody awards and an Emmy award; after retiring in 1981 he was honored with the Presidential Medal of Freedom. Since his retirement, Cronkite has contributed to numerous special television projects and has been active in philanthropic and political causes.

Laura Matysek Wood

References

Fensch, Thomas, ed. *Television News Anchors*. Jefferson, NC: McFarland, 1993.

Hallin, Daniel C. *Uncensored War: The Media and Vietnam.* New York: Oxford University Press, 1986.

James, Doug. *Cronkite: His Life and Times.* Brentwood, TN: JM Press, 1991.

Dulles, John Foster (1888–1959)

Lawyer, diplomat, and secretary of state (1953–1959). Born in Washington, D.C., on February 25, 1888, the son of a Presbyterian minister, John Foster Dulles graduated from Princeton in 1908. He also spent a year at the Sorbonne and then enrolled in the George Washington University law school, from which he graduated in 1911. In 1913, he joined the law firm of Sullivan and Cromwell.

Dulles's extensive family connections contributed to his wealth of experience in diplomacy. In 1907, he served as secretary to his grandfather, Secretary of State John W. Foster, who was a delegate to the second Hague Peace Conference. During World War I, Dulles served in army intelligence and on the War Board of Trade. As a member of the U.S. delegation at the Paris Peace Conference in 1919, where he dealt with the issue of German reparations, he disapproved of the harsh terms of the treaty and later wrote that the treaty contributed to the rise of totalitarianism in Europe.

Dulles was an internationalist. He believed that, as the world's leading creditor nation in the 1920s, the United States had to assume a leading role in world affairs. In the 1930s Dulles attended church councils on world peace, and in 1940 chaired the Commission on a Just and Durable Peace, sponsored by the Federal Council of Churches, which led to a call for a United Nations. Dulles served as foreign policy adviser to Republican presidential candidate Thomas E. Dewey in the 1944 and 1948 campaigns.

Following World War II, Dulles supported a bipartisan approach to foreign policy for the Cold War. During the Harry S. Truman administration, from 1945 to 1952, he was the U.S. delegate to the United Nations. In 1949, New York governor Thomas E. Dewey named him to fill New York's vacant seat in the U.S. Senate, where Dulles supported the Marshall Plan and the North Atlantic Treaty Organization (NATO). During 1950–1951, he negotiated the U.S. peace treaty with Japan and a Japan–United States security pact.

Dulles became secretary of state in the Dwight D. Eisenhower administration in 1953. Although he had earlier espoused bipartisanship in foreign relations, Dulles, who had drafted the Republican Party's foreign policy statement during the 1952 presidential campaign, criticized the Truman administration's policy of containment as "negative, futile, and immoral." Republican rhetoric promised the "rollback of the Iron Curtain" and the liberation of Eastern Europe from communism plus the prospect of massive retaliation with nuclear weapons against any attacks by America's enemies. Dulles hoped to create a European Defense Community (EDC) that combined military forces from France, Germany, Belgium, the Netherlands, and Luxembourg, linked with the North Atlantic Treaty Organization (NATO).

Dulles's ideas were tested in Southeast Asia in the spring of 1954. With French military forces under attack by the Viet Minh at Dien Bien Phu, the Joseph Laniel government requested U.S. military intervention. American officials debated a plan for intervention—Operation VULTURE—which Dulles favored, but President Eisenhower refused to accede to it unless the plan was supported by the "united action" of Britain, France, Australia, and New Zealand and by support from the U.S. Congress, both of which proved unobtainable. After Dien Bien Phu fell, a conference on Far Eastern problems met at Geneva in April 1954. The United States did not sign the final declaration. Subsequently, Dulles helped establish the Southeast Asia Treaty Organization (SEATO) to resist communist expansion in the region and undertook a program of increased military and economic aid to South Vietnam. John Foster Dulles died in Washington, D.C., on May 24, 1959.

Kenneth R. Stevens

References

Guhin, Michael. *John Foster Dulles: A Statesman and His Times.* New York: Columbia University Press, 1972.

Hoopes, Townsend. *The Devil and John Foster Dulles.* Boston: Little, Brown, 1973.

Marks, Frederick W., III. *Power and Peace: The Diplomacy of John Foster Dulles.* Westport, CT: Praeger, 1993.

Eisenhower, Dwight David (1890–1969)

General of the army and U.S. president (1953–1961). Born in Denison, Texas, on October 14, 1890, Dwight David ("Ike") Eisenhower was raised in Kansas. In 1915, he graduated from the United States Military Academy, West Point. During World War I, he held various training duties. In the interwar years, Eisenhower attended the Command and General Staff School (1926) and Army War College (1928) and established himself as a promising staff officer. During World War II, Eisenhower rose rapidly in rank and responsibility. General George C. Mar-

shall tapped him to command Operation TORCH, the 1942 Allied invasion of North Africa. Later he commanded the cross-Channel invasion of France and became supreme Allied commander in Europe.

Advanced to general of the army, after the war, Eisenhower returned to the United States to serve as U.S. Army chief of staff (1945–1948), president of Columbia University (1948–1950), and first commander of North Atlantic Treaty Organization (NATO) military forces (1950–1952). In 1952, he ran as a Republican against Democrat Adlai Stevenson for the presidency and was easily elected that November. He served two terms (1953–1961).

As president, Eisenhower sought to limit the growth of domestic programs while at the same time retaining the bulk of the New Deal reforms. In his defense policies, he placed emphasis on nuclear weapons (massive retaliation) at the expense of conventional forces. But at the end of his tenure in office, Eisenhower also warned the nation about the growth of a "military-industrial complex."

In international affairs Eisenhower endeavored to calm Cold War tensions. In July 1953, an armistice was achieved in Korea, in part by his pledge to "go to Korea" and by threatening the possible employment of nuclear weapons. The latter so impressed Vice President Richard Nixon that early in his own presidency he tried the same ("Mad Man") technique against the Democratic Republic of Vietnam (DRV), without success. Eisenhower proclaimed a new U.S. policy (Eisenhower Doctrine) for the Middle East, but his efforts to reduce international tensions with the Soviet Union's Nikita Khrushchev were stymied.

Eisenhower's policies in Indochina were cautious and measured. He fol-

United States president Dwight D. Eisenhower welcomes President of the Republic of Vietnam Ngo Dinh Diem, at Washington National Airport in 1957. Eisenhower strongly supported U.S. financial and military aid to the Diem government. (National Archives)

lowed the containment doctrine begun by his predecessor, and his administration subscribed to the domino theory that held that a Viet Minh victory in Vietnam would soon bring communists to power throughout Southeast Asia. His policies included increasing weapons and logistical support for the French in their war with the Viet Minh, and by 1954 the United States was paying as much as 80 percent of the cost of the war there. It was under Eisenhower that a Military Assistance Advisory Group (MAAG) was created for Indochina, although the French insisted that all military aid be channeled through them. Publicly the Eisenhower administration supported the French line that they had turned over political control

in Vietnam to the Vietnamese and that the war was a Cold War struggle between democracy and communism rather than a colonial war for independence. Privately, it was another matter; as late as 1953, Eisenhower was pushing U.S. ambassador to France C. Douglas Dillon to insist that the French grant independence to Vietnam.

In the spring of 1954, Eisenhower debated active U.S. military intervention, including the possible use of nuclear weapons, to help rescue the French garrison at Dien Bien Phu. He resisted intervention because army chief of staff General Matthew B. Ridgway was firmly opposed and because the British government refused to participate. Eisenhower was, in any case, thinking only in terms of air strikes and material support, rather than ground troops.

The State Department participated in the 1954 Geneva talks only as an observer, and the Eisenhower administration came to distance itself from the resulting Geneva Accords. The Eisenhower administration led the way in the creation of the Southeast Asia Treaty Organization (SEATO), which, however, did not prove supportive of U.S. plans to create a separate state in southern Vietnam and, if need be, fight collectively to maintain it. The Eisenhower administration did give unqualified and substantial economic and political support to the government of Republic of Vietnam president Ngo Dinh Diem, and it supported Diem in his refusal to hold the elections called for in the Geneva Accords.

After leaving office in 1961, Eisenhower retired. As a private citizen, he continued to support U.S. involvement in Vietnam. He reportedly warned his successor, John F. Kennedy, to stand firm there, but disapproved of President Lyndon B. Johnson's failure to use sufficient military force to bring the war to a successful conclusion. Nevertheless, he insisted that the Vietnamese would have to do the bulk of the fighting themselves. In 1968, he enthusiastically supported Nixon's run for the presidency. Eisenhower died in Washington, D.C., on March 28, 1969.

Spencer C. Tucker

References

Ambrose, Stephen E. *Eisenhower*. Vol. 2, *President and Elder Statesman*. New York: Simon and Schuster, 1984.

Anderson, David L., ed. *Shadow on the White House: Presidents and the Vietnam War, 1945–1975*. Lawrence: University Press of Kansas, 1993.

Billings-Yun, Melanie. *Decision against War: Eisenhower and Dien Bien Phu*. New York: Columbia University Press, 1988.

Ford, Gerald Rudolph (1913–2006)

U.S. congressman (1949–1973), vice president (December 1973–August 1974), and president (August 1974–January 1977). Born in Omaha, Nebraska, on July 14, 1913, as Leslie Lynch King Jr., Gerald Rudolph Ford adopted his stepfather's name as a youth. He received his bachelor's degree from the University of Michigan and his law degree from Yale University in 1941. Ford served as an ensign in the U.S. Navy during World War II and was elected to the first of 12 consecutive terms in the House of Representatives in 1948.

Throughout his years in Congress, a tenure that was highlighted by service as his party's minority leader (1965–1973), Ford developed an expertise in the area of defense appropriations. He was a consistent supporter of the U.S. commitment in Vietnam, differing with the Lyndon Johnson administration only in that he believed that more money and resources should be allocated there.

As vice president—a position to which he was appointed by President Richard Nixon in October 1973 after the resignation of Spiro T. Agnew—Ford publicly defended the Nixon administration's record on Vietnam. It was left to Ford, who became president upon Nixon's resignation on August 9, 1974, over the Watergate scandal, to preside over the final stage of the Vietnam War. He also had the unenviable job of pulling the nation together after the agony of Watergate and dealing with an economy that

Gerald R. Ford was president of the United States during 1974–1977. The final victory of Communist forces in Vietnam and Cambodia occurred during his time in office. Congress opposed further involvement in Indochina and refused Ford's requests for special aid appropriations. (Gerald R. Ford Presidential Library)

was wracked by inflation, high unemployment, and anemic growth.

As president, Ford moderated his earlier, more hawkish views on the Vietnam War. Only two weeks into his presidency, Ford ignored the advice of those—including Secretary of State Henry Kissinger—who counseled a harsh policy against "draft dodgers" and combat personnel who were absent without leave (AWOL). Ford formed the Presidential Clemency Board (PCB), which reviewed individual cases and assigned specific sanctions or acquittal.

In January 1975, Ford faced the final offensives of the Cambodian Khmer Rouge and the North Vietnamese People's Army of Vietnam (PAVN). Rather than risk political opposition to an American recommitment in Vietnam, the Ford administration took no serious steps to counter either attack. Having no treaty commitment to Cambodia, it was relatively easy for Ford to order Operation EAGLE PULL, the abandonment of the U.S. Embassy in Phnom Penh on April 11, 1975. But in a secret correspondence delivered before his resignation, President Nixon had promised RVN president Nguyen Van Thieu that, if the Democratic Republic of Vietnam (DRV) violated the 1973 truce, the United States would recommit troops to South Vietnam. Nevertheless, despite the advice of Kissinger and Ambassador Graham Martin, Ford refused to honor that pledge. Instead, after the North Vietnamese began their 1975 Spring Offensive (the Ho Chi Minh Campaign), Ford made only a half-hearted attempt to cajole Congress into appropriating money for the RVN's defense. When it refused, Ford ordered the evacuation of all remaining U.S. military and embassy personnel. The April 28 evacuation of Saigon (Operation FREQUENT WIND) removed some 1,400 Americans and 5,600 Vietnamese from the city.

The evacuations from Saigon and Phnom Penh, as well as the May 1975 *Mayaguez* Incident—America's final military engagements of the Vietnam War—were used against Ford in the 1976 presidential election. The evacuations were cited as evidence that the Ford administration did not adequately support U.S. allies, while the *Mayaguez* Incident was cited to show that, by choosing force over diplomacy in a crisis, Republican administrations had learned nothing from Vietnam. Because of his handling of the end of the Vietnam War, and, equally important, his inability to solve the nation's economic woes, Ford was defeated in the 1976 election by Georgia governor Jimmy Carter.

Ford then retired to private life. A member of many corporate boards, Ford lived in both Rancho Mirage, California, and Vail, Colorado. Ford died at his home in Rancho Mirage on December 26, 2006.

John Robert Greene

References

Ford, Gerald R. *A Time to Heal: The Autobiography of Gerald R. Ford.* New York: Harper and Row, 1979.

Greene, John Robert. *The Presidency of Gerald R. Ford.* Lawrence: University Press of Kansas, 1995.

Fulbright, James William (1905–1995)

U.S. senator and outspoken Vietnam War critic. Born in Sumner, Missouri, on April 9, 1905, James William Fulbright received his BA in history from the University of Arkansas in 1925 and an MA from Oxford University in 1928 before earning a law degree from George Washington University in 1934. He then became an attorney in the antitrust division of the Department of Justice and taught law at the University of Arkansas. In 1939, he was appointed president of the university, a post he held until 1941.

An ardent and lifelong Democrat, during 1943–1945 Fulbright represented Arkansas in the U.S. House of Representatives, authoring the Fulbright-Connally Resolution that ultimately facilitated the creation of the United Nations. He then served in the U.S. Senate from 1945 to 1974. In 1945, convinced that education brought out the good in the young and cultivated a desire to preserve the American republic, the senator, himself a Rhodes Scholar, took the lead in the establishment of Fulbright Fellowships, an international exchange program.

Independent by nature, Fulbright disagreed with aspects of foreign policy of every U.S. president from Harry S. Truman to Richard M. Nixon, but especially attacked the Lyndon B. Johnson administration on its Vietnam policies. In the early 1950s, he also took a sharp, public stand against Sen. Joseph R. McCarthy and the excesses of McCarthyism, certainly a risky move at the time.

Although he helped shepherd the 1964 Gulf of Tonkin Resolution through the Senate, by 1966 Fulbright had concluded that the Vietnam War was primarily an insurgency against a corrupt and repressive Saigon government that did not deserve the backing of the United States. He believed that Vietnam had no bearing on the vital interests of the United States and that American involvement was undermining democracy and individual liberty at home as well as overseas. That same year, televised hearings held by Fulbright's Senate Foreign Relations Committee helped turn popular opinion against the war and endeared him to antiwar activists. Johnson was furious at Fulbright's scathing criticism, but the senator kept up the pressure until the last American troops left Saigon in 1975.

Fulbright was defeated in his 1974 reelection bid and resigned from the Senate in December 1974. After leaving office, Fulbright joined the law firm of Hogan & Hartson in Washington, D.C. He also remained active in international affairs and national politics. Fulbright's greatest legacies during his long public service career are certainly his anti–Vietnam War stance and the Fulbright Fellowship, which to date has sponsored more than 250,000 individuals. In 1993, President William Clinton awarded Fulbright the Presidential Medal of Freedom. Fulbright died in Washington, D.C., on February 9, 1995.

Brenda J. Taylor

References

Berman, William C. *William Fulbright and the Vietnam War: The Dissent of a Political Realist.* Kent, OH: Kent State University Press, 1988.

Fry, Joseph A. *Debating Vietnam: Fulbright, Stennis and their Senate Hearings.* Lanham, MD: Rowman and Littlefield Publishers, 2006.

Woods, Randall Bennett. *J. William Fulbright, Vietnam, and the Search for a Cold War Foreign Policy.* New York: Cambridge University Press, 1998.

Sen. Barry Goldwater was the leader of the conservative wing of the Republican Party in the 1960s. He won his party's nomination for president in 1964 but lost the general election in a landslide to Democraric Party candidate and sitting president Lyndon B. Johnson. (Library of Congress)

Goldwater, Barry Morris (1909–1998)

U.S. senator from Arizona (1952–1965; 1969–1984), Republican candidate for president in 1964, and considered the father of modern American political conservatism. Born in Phoenix in the territory of Arizona, on January 1, 1909, Barry Goldwater graduated from the Staunton Military Academy in Virginia in 1928. He then attended the University of Arizona for one year, leaving to run the family's department store upon the death of his father in 1930. During World War II, Goldwater served in the Army Air Corps, attaining the rank of lieutenant colonel (later he rose to the rank of major general in the reserves).

Following the war, Goldwater was elected to the Phoenix City Council, and in 1952 he was elected U.S. senator. Among his varied committee assignments, he served as chair of the Armed Services Committee and the Senate Select Committee on Intelligence.

In 1964, Goldwater ran for the presidency as the Republican nominee. He had an uphill climb, for at the time President Lyndon Baines Johnson was enormously popular and was seen as the political heir to the martyred John F. Kennedy. During the campaign, Goldwater advocated a strong military establishment with a heavy reliance on air power. He was also steadfast in his commitment to halting the spread of communism, and on more than one occasion he referred to communist leaders as "captors of enslaved peoples." Goldwater was also very hawkish on the issue of the war in Vietnam. He thought the United States should do whatever it took, short of employing nuclear weapons, to support U.S. troops in the field. He also believed that if the United States was not prepared to make a major military commitment, including "carrying the war to North Vietnam," it should withdraw completely. He talked about the possibility of using low-level atomic weapons to defoliate infiltration routes, but he never actually advocated the use of nuclear weapons in Vietnam. Nonetheless, the Democrats easily painted Goldwater as a warmonger, eager to use atomic weapons against North Vietnam. This was undoubtedly a large factor in his crushing defeat at the hands of Lyndon Johnson, who took some 61 percent of the popular vote to only 39 percent for Goldwater.

In 1965, Goldwater temporarily retired from the Senate, only to return again in 1969. In the meantime, Goldwater continued to hammer home his messages that included hawkishness on military and defense issues, responsible government that did not interfere with free commerce or personal choice, and fiscal responsibility. By the 1970s, Goldwater's message had become the clarion call for conservative Republicans, including California governor and future president Ronald Reagan, who would frequently invoke Goldwater's governing philosophy. Indeed, it was largely Goldwater's vision that propelled Reagan and modern conservatism into the mainstream in the 1980s. Still, however, Goldwater was more libertarian than orthodox conservative, and so his voting record was one of surprising width and depth. He did not believe that Christian conservatism should play a role in Republican Party policies and viewed abortion as an issue of personal choice rather than public policy.

As the Vietnam War wound to a close by the mid-1970s, Goldwater remained a consistent critic of U.S. command decisions. In 1973, he voted against the War Powers Bill, a reaction to the Vietnam War, arguing that it was improper and probably illegal. Indeed, he blamed America's defeat in Vietnam on the Washington bureaucracy and governmental officials who stood in the way of aiding the troops in the field. He also decried the precedent of allowing civilian leaders to set the strategy and scope of warfare, which he argued almost always hamstrung military commanders in the field.

Goldwater retired from politics in 1986, returning to Arizona. An accomplished photographer, he published several books of his photographs of the landscape and people of the Southwest. He also kept an eye on U.S. politics, occasionally commenting on trends or circumstances of the time. Much to the chagrin of social conservatives, in the 1990s Goldwater decried the U.S. military's ban on homosexuals and urged Republicans not to pursue Whitewater against President Bill Clinton. Goldwater died in Phoenix, Arizona, on May 30, 1998.

Lauraine Bush
and Paul G. Pierpaoli Jr.

References

Goldwater, Barry N. *The Conscience of a Conservative.* New York: Victor, 1960.

Shagegg, S. Stephen. *Whatever Happened to Goldwater?* New York: Holt, Rinehart and Winston, 1965.

Harkins, Paul Donal (1904–1984)

U.S. Army general and commander of the Military Assistance Command, Vietnam (MACV), during 1962–1964. Born in Boston, Massachusetts, on May 15, 1904, Paul Donal Harkins graduated from the United States Military Academy, West Point, in 1929. Promoted to captain in June 1939, he served during World War II in Lieutenant General George S. Patton's Third Army. He was promoted to major in

U.S. Army general Paul D. Harkins, commander of the Military Assistance Command, Vietnam (MACV) during an inspection tour of a Army of the Republic of Vietnam (ARVN) training camp in 1963. Harkins expressed great confidence about the war's course and firmly supported RVN president Ngo Dinh Diem. (National Archives)

June 1946 and to lieutenant colonel in July 1948. In March 1952 he was a colonel, and in May 1952 he was promoted to brigadier general. At the end of the Korean War in 1953, Harkins was chief of staff of Eighth Army, then in Korea. He subsequently served as commandant of cadets at the U.S. Military Academy. During 1954–1957, he was stationed at the Pentagon. Promoted to major general in April 1957 and lieutenant general that July, he was deputy commander, chief of staff of U.S. Army Forces, Pacific, between 1960 and 1962 before being appointed the initial commander of MACV. Promoted to full general, Harkins arrived in Saigon on February 13, 1962.

As part of Project Beefup in 1962, President John F. Kennedy's administration replaced the Military Assistance and Advisory Group (MAAG) with an expanded and remodeled MACV, situated in Saigon and commanded by Harkins. There he expressed confidence about the war's course and stood firmly behind President Ngo Dinh Diem. Harkins favored postponing political and social improvements until the military had subdued the Communist insurgents, the Viet Cong (VC), and secured the countryside. He endorsed the use of napalm against villages housing the VC, regardless of its political effects, and he supported the Republic of Vietnam (RVN) version of the disastrous Battle of Ap Bac in the Mekong Delta on January 2, 1963. Harkins also believed that the Strategic Hamlet program was conceptually valid and impressive in implementation. In fact, Harkins was so optimistic about an eventual victory over the insurgents that he told a group of high-level policymakers in Honolulu that the conflict might well peter out by the end of 1963.

General Harkins's tenacious support for President Diem nearly caused South Vietnamese generals to hesitate in a coup attempt against the RVN president, which nonetheless occurred in early November 1963.

Harkins approved of deposing Ngo Dinh Nhu and his wife, but at no time consented to Diem's ouster. Harkins's insistence on retaining Diem while eliminating the Nhus brought him into disagreement with U.S. ambassador Henry Cabot Lodge Jr., who supported the RVN president's removal.

From the beginning, Harkins and his aides were on bad terms with the successor junta headed by Duong Van Minh. MACV became uneasy with the new administration's endeavors to assert its independence and to restrict the U.S. advisory functions. When the junta's leadership demonstrated little initiative against the Communists, Harkins, who admired General Nguyen Khanh and was aware of his plot against Minh, promoted the former's coup, a move labeled "Harkins' Revenge" by some in the South Vietnamese military.

In March 1964, President Lyndon Baines Johnson replaced Harkins with General William C. Westmoreland. Harkins retired from the army and lived in Dallas, Texas, before his death there on August 21, 1984. In retirement he authored a book entitled *When the Third Cracked Europe: The Story of Patton's Incredible Army* (1969), a largely autobiographical work, and he served as a technical consultant to the 1970 biographical film *Patton*, which starred George C. Scott as General Patton.

Rodney J. Ross

References

Hammer, Ellen J. *A Death in November: America in Vietnam, 1963.* New York: E. P. Dutton, 1987.

Kahin, George McTurnan. *Intervention: How America Became Involved in Vietnam.* New York: Alfred A. Knopf, 1986.

Sheehan, Neil. *A Bright Shining Lie: John Paul Vann and America in Vietnam.* New York: Vintage Books, 1989.

Hilsman, Roger (1919–)

Author, political scientist, U.S. State Department official, and adviser on Vietnam policy. Born in Waco, Texas, on November 23, 1919, Roger Hilsman graduated from the United States Military Academy, West Point, in 1943 and received his doctorate in international relations from Yale University in 1951. During World War II, he served in the Pacific Theater, was wounded in Burma, and also served a tour of duty with the Office of Strategic Services (OSS).

In 1961, President John F. Kennedy appointed Hilsman director of the State Department's Bureau of Intelligence and Research. Charged with analyzing current foreign developments to allow for long-term planning, Hilsman can be considered one of the principal architects of U.S. Vietnam policy in the early 1960s.

In January 1962, Hilsman presented "A Strategic Concept for South Vietnam." This plan defined the war as a political struggle and proposed policies aimed at the rural Vietnamese as the key to victory. These policies in turn led to the Strategic Hamlets program. The report also recommended that the Army of the Republic of Vietnam (ARVN) adopt guerrilla warfare tactics.

In December 1962, Hilsman and Michael Forrestal were sent on a fact-finding mission to Vietnam. In July 1963, following attacks on Buddhist dissidents by Ngo Dinh Nhu's police, Hilsman, along with Forrestal and W. Averell Harriman, recommended that new instructions be relayed to U.S. ambassador Henry Cabot Lodge Jr. in Saigon. These led to at least tacit approval by the United States of the military coup that was carried out against Republic of Vietnam president Ngo Dinh Diem and his brother Ngo Dinh Nhu in November 1963. Increasingly at odds with President Lyndon B. Johnson and Secretary of State Dean Rusk over U.S.-Vietnam policy, Hilsman resigned in February 1964. He then joined the faculty at Columbia University.

In 1967, Hilsman wrote *To Move a Nation,* which praises the process of foreign policy formulation under President Kennedy, while criticizing President Johnson's escalation of the Vietnam War.

Among his other books are *The Politics of Policy Making in Defense and Foreign Affairs* (1971), *To Govern America* (1979), *The Politics of Policy Making* (1986), and *George Bush vs Saddam Hussein: Military Success! Political Failure* (1992). As professor emeritus of government and international relations, Hilsman is associated with the Institute for War and Peace Studies at Columbia. In 1994, President Bill Clinton named him a member of the National Security Education Board.

Robert G. Mangrum

References

Barrett, David M. *Uncertain Warriors: Lyndon Johnson and His Vietnam Advisers.* Lawrence: University Press of Kansas, 1993.

Halberstam, David. *The Best and the Brightest.* New York: Random House, 1972.

Herring, George C. *America's Longest War: The United States and Vietnam, 1950–1975.* 2nd ed. New York: Alfred A. Knopf, 1986.

Karnow, Stanley. *Vietnam: A History.* New York: Penguin Books, 1984.

U.S. vice president and Democrat Hubert H. Humphrey ran against Republican Richard M. Nixon for the presidency in 1968. Humphrey distanced himself from President Lyndon Johnson's policies late in the campaign and narrowly lost the election. (Library of Congress)

Humphrey, Hubert Horatio (1911–1978)

U.S. senator, vice president, and Democratic Party candidate for president in 1968. Born on May 27, 1911, in Wallace, South Dakota, Hubert Horatio Humphrey earned a BA degree from the University of Minnesota in 1939 and an MA from Louisiana State University in 1940. He taught for a year at the University of Minnesota, and in 1941 he began his public career as head of the Minnesota branch of the Federal War Production Administration. Humphrey became involved in politics and in 1943 was an unsuccessful candidate for mayor of Minneapolis. The following year he worked to merge the state's Democratic and Farm Labor Parties. He helped manage President Franklin Roosevelt's 1944 campaign in Minnesota and was elected mayor of Minneapolis, a post to which he was reelected in 1947.

In 1948, Humphrey attracted national attention by advocating a strong civil rights plank at the Democratic Party Convention. That fall he was elected U.S. senator from Minnesota; he was reelected in 1954 and 1960. In 1964, President Lyndon B. Johnson chose Humphrey as running mate, and he was vice president of the United States from 1965 to 1969.

It was one of the many ironies of the 1968 presidential elections that the New Left repudiated Humphrey until the closing days of the campaign. Throughout his public life, Humphrey was one of the chief voices of the liberal wing of the Democratic Party. With an unabashedly liberal record, Humphrey helped found the Americans for Democratic Action and was most proud of his success in helping pass Medicare and civil rights legislation, especially his management of the epochal 1964 Civil Rights Act.

After he became vice president, Humphrey irritated Johnson by arguing against expansion of the Vietnam War. In 1966, however, Johnson sent Humphrey on a fact-finding trip to the Republic of Vietnam. Humphrey returned full of praise for administration policies, a stance that angered many liberals and intellectuals.

The Vietnam War undid Humphrey. After Johnson announced his withdrawal from the 1968 presidential campaign, Humphrey entered the race as the establishment candidate. Humphrey's dilemma was that he needed to distance himself from Johnson's unpopular Vietnam policies while at the same time maintaining the support of the party apparatus. Humphrey called for making equal opportunity and social justice realities in American life. The June 1968 assassination of Robert Kennedy ensured Humphrey of the Democratic Party's nomination, although the August party convention was divisive and even bloody.

The public associated Humphrey with this chaos and vented on him its dissatisfaction with the war. Some observers thought that, if one factor cost Humphrey the election, it was his loyalty to President Johnson that prevented him from reasserting his own liberal identity early in the campaign.

During the campaign, Humphrey was heckled by antiwar protesters. At Salt Lake City on September 30, he finally distanced himself a bit from Johnson when he announced that he would stop the bombing of North Vietnam to jump-start peace talks. Now energized, Humphrey began picking up support as the "peace" candidate. He also attacked Republican candidate Richard M. Nixon's refusal to debate and he tore into American Independence Party candidate George Wallace for his appeals to racism, segregation, and intolerance.

On October 31, Johnson announced a halt in the bombing of North Vietnam. Undoubtedly, the bombing halt helped Humphrey, but it came too late. Momentum was on his side, and many political observers believe that with only a few more days he would have won the election. Nixon's victory margin was only 500,000 votes: 43.3 percent to 42.7 percent for Humphrey and 13.5 percent for third-party candidate George Wallace. Nixon's margin in the electoral college was much larger, however (302, 191, and 5, respectively). One thing is reasonably certain: had Humphrey been elected president, the United States would have departed Vietnam earlier than it did under Nixon.

In 1970, Humphrey returned to the Senate, winning the seat vacated by Eugene McCarthy, and was reelected in 1976. Hubert Humphrey died of cancer at Waverly, Minnesota, on January 13, 1978.

Spencer C. Tucker

References

Humphrey, Hubert H. *The Education of a Public Man: My Life and Politics.* New York: Doubleday, 1976.

Solberg, Carl. *Hubert Humphrey: A Biography.* New York: W. W. Norton, 1984.

Johnson, Harold Keith (1912–1983)

U.S. Army officer and U.S. Army chief of staff (1964–1968). Born on February

22, 1912, in Bowesmont, North Dakota, Harold Johnson graduated from the United States Military Academy at West Point in 1933. Commissioned a 2nd lieutenant in the 3rd Infantry, he was assigned to Fort Snelling, Minnesota. In 1938, he graduated from the Infantry School, Fort Benning, Georgia. On the eve of World War II, Johnson was stationed in the Philippines with a regiment of Philippine Scouts. He achieved battalion command shortly before forces there were overwhelmed by the invading Japanese. With the defeat of U.S. and Filipino forces in April 1942, Johnson was taken prisoner. Surviving the infamous Bataan Death March, he spent three and a half years in a succession of prison camps and was close to death when liberation came in 1945.

Following World War II, Johnson fought his way back to professional prominence, winning the Distinguished Service Cross as a regimental commander early in the Korean War. In 1953 he graduated from the Naval War College and in 1956 was promoted to permanent colonel and temporary brigadier general. He held a series of successively more responsible positions and in 1959 was advanced to temporary major general. The next year, he was appointed to permanent brigadier general rank. After serving as commandant of the Command and General Staff College for three years, in 1963 he rose to permanent major general and temporary lieutenant general. In 1964, Johnson was selected from far down the list of lieutenant generals for advancement to full general (four-star rank) and assignment as army chief of staff at a most critical point when American involvement in Vietnam began to accelerate. Johnson would serve in this capacity until 1968.

It fell to Johnson to manage a huge and rapid expansion of the U.S. Army for the Vietnam War. To do this without resorting to reserve forces, which President Lyndon Johnson refused to permit, proved a daunting task, but he handled with characteristic energy and conscientiousness. Publicly, Johnson supported General William Westmoreland's tactics and repeated requests for additional troops, but negative findings in a study Johnson had ordered in the spring of 1965—the Program for the Pacification and Long-Term Development of South Vietnam (PROVN)—reinforced his own misgivings about how the war was being conducted, and he worked behind the scenes to have the tactics changed, the commander replaced, or both. When General Creighton Abrams took over the top post in Vietnam, he essentially put into effect the PROVN study's findings, with results that vindicated Johnson's judgment.

Indeed, the approach followed by Abrams cast aside his predecessor's attrition strategy, search-and-destroy tactics, and reliance on body count as the measure of success. Instead, he stressed population security as the key to success. He directed a "one-war" approach, pulling together combat operations, pacification, and upgrading South Vietnamese forces into a coherent whole.

Widely admired for his dedication and ethical standards, Johnson retired from military service in 1968 and for several years headed the Freedoms Foundation at Valley Forge, Pennsylvania. He also served on the board of several corporations. Johnson died of cancer in Washington, D.C., on September 24, 1983.

Lewis Sorley

References

Johnson, Harold K. *Challenge: Compendium of Army Accomplishment: A Report by the*

Chief of Staff: July 1964–April 1968. Washington, DC: Department of the Army, July 1, 1968.

Sorley, Lewis. *Honorable Warrior: General Harold K. Johnson and the Ethics of Command.* Lawrence: University Press of Kansas, 1998.

Johnson, Lyndon Baines (1908–1973)

Congressman, senator, vice president, and president (1963–1969) of the United States. Born in Stonewall, near Austin, Texas, on August 27, 1908, Lyndon Johnson graduated from Southwest Texas State Teachers College in 1930. President Franklin D. Roosevelt appointed him Texas administrator of the National Youth Administration in 1935. Two years later, Johnson won election to the U.S. House of Representatives. He served in the navy during World War II, and in 1948 was elected to the U.S. Senate. In 1953 he became Senate minority leader and in 1955 Senate majority leader.

As minority leader during the 1954 crisis over the Battle of Dien Bien Phu, Johnson opposed unilateral U.S. intervention. Later, he was instrumental in securing passage of the Civil Rights Acts of 1957 and 1960. He sought the Democratic nomination for the 1960 presidential election, but lost to Massachusetts senator John F. Kennedy, who chose Johnson as his vice presidential running mate. Johnson became president following Kennedy's assassination in November 1963.

As president, Johnson tried to establish what he termed the "Great Society," an ambitious program of civil rights and social welfare legislation. Using his legislative skills and the reverence attached to the memory of Kennedy, Johnson won

passage of the Civil Rights Act of 1964. He declared a "War on Poverty" and also secured passage of the Economic Opportunity Act. Elected in 1964, Johnson pushed through Congress the Medicare Act of 1965, federal aid to education, increased funds for the war on poverty, and enactment of consumer and environmental protection laws. In 1965, Johnson helped pass the Voting Rights Act.

It was the war in Vietnam, however, that consumed Johnson's energy and his presidency. Johnson, who believed in both the doctrine of containment and the domino theory, saw Vietnam as a test of national resolve. Moreover, Johnson had

Lyndon B. Johnson was president of the United States during 1963–1969. His Great Society programs aimed to eradicate poverty and advance civil rights for all Americans were undermined by the costly Vietnam War, which he dramatically escalated and which led to his decision not to run for reelection in 1968. (Yoichi R. Okamoto/Lyndon B. Johnson Presidential Library)

been in Congress when China became communist, and he vividly recalled the domestic political turmoil that followed as Republicans attacked Democrats for "losing" China. He also believed he needed to please the Republicans in Congress in order to assure passage of his Great Society programs.

Soon after taking office, Johnson began escalating the war. In February 1964, he endorsed U.S. support for South Vietnamese raids against North Vietnam. In April, he appointed General William C. Westmoreland as U.S. commander in Vietnam. In June, he replaced Ambassador Henry Cabot Lodge Jr. with General Maxwell Taylor. Both men favored increased troop levels in Vietnam.

Following the 1964 Tonkin Gulf Incidents, Johnson ordered the bombing of North Vietnamese naval bases and oil depots. He also asked Congress to pass the Tonkin Gulf Resolution, authorizing him to take "all necessary measures" to repel any armed attacks against American forces. The measure was approved overwhelmingly.

In the years that followed, Johnson used the Tonkin Resolution to justify presidential war-making in Vietnam. In February 1965, Johnson ordered retaliatory bombing of North Vietnam after Communist forces attacked U.S. military posts at Pleiku and Qui Nhon. That same year Johnson commenced Operation ROLLING THUNDER, regular (rather than reprisal) air strikes on North Vietnam. Along with intensified bombing came increased troop commitments. In April 1965, Johnson approved Westmoreland's request to use U.S. forces for offensive operations anywhere in South Vietnam. An important turning point came in July 1965, when Johnson announced that U.S. forces there would be increased from 75,000 to 125,000 men, with additional troops to be provided. Before the close of Johnson's presidency in January 1969, there were more than 500,000 U.S. troops in Vietnam.

Johnson frequently expressed desire for peace and ordered several bombing pauses, but none led to a lasting settlement or peace. The war had a devastating impact on Johnson's Great Society. The cost of the war forced cutbacks in programs and fostered inflation. The federal deficit grew from $8.7 billion in 1967 to $25.2 billion in 1968. By 1968, the Johnson administration suffered from a "credibility gap" resulting from public disillusion produced by falsely optimistic statements about the war.

Opposition to the Vietnam War soon developed. In October 1967, 100,000 war protestors gathered in Washington, D.C., and others followed. Passionate debate also swirled inside the Johnson administration, and several of his advisers warned the president against escalation and further entanglement. By spring 1967, Secretary of Defense Robert S. McNamara, once a proponent of escalation, recommended restricting bombing and limiting troop levels. It was during this period, in November 1967, that Johnson arranged a meeting of elder statesmen, subsequently dubbed the "Wise Men," to advise him on Vietnam policy. In their meeting with the president on November 21, they offered divided opinions that bolstered Johnson's determination to continue the war.

The January 1968 Tet Offensive caused Johnson to reevaluate the war. When General Westmoreland requested another 205,000 troops following Tet, the president turned him down, instead agreeing to send just 20,000 troops.

Preliminaries to the 1968 presidential election demonstrated the additional political costs of the Vietnam War. In the March 1968 New Hampshire primary, Sen. Eugene McCarthy, running on an antiwar platform, won 42 percent of the Democratic vote, which was regarded as a defeat for the president (who was not officially entered in the primary). Soon afterward, Sen. Robert F. Kennedy entered the nomination race as an antiwar candidate.

In a television address to the nation on March 31, Johnson announced a halt to naval and air attacks on North Vietnam except in the area just north of the Demilitarized Zone. At the end of his speech he stunned the nation when he said that he would not seek reelection.

The Democratic Republic of Vietnam (DRV) now expressed willingness to enter peace talks, which began in May 1968 in Paris. On October 31, Johnson ordered a complete cessation of air and naval attacks on North Vietnam. The Paris talks, which quickly bogged down, proved inconclusive. In the November election, Republican Richard Nixon narrowly defeated Vice President Hubert Humphrey. Johnson retired to his Stonewall, Texas, ranch in 1969, where he died on January 22, 1973.

Spencer C. Tucker

References

Berman, Larry. *Lyndon Johnson's War: The Road to Stalemate in Vietnam*. New York: Norton, 1989.

Beschloss, Michael R., ed. *Taking Charge: The Johnson White House Tapes, 1963–1964*. New York: Simon and Schuster, 1997.

Dallek, Robert. *Flawed Giant: Lyndon Johnson and His Times, 1961–1973*. New York: Oxford University Press, 1999.

Goodwin, Doris Kearns. *Lyndon Johnson and the American Dream*. New York: Harper and Row, 1976.

Herring, George C. *LBJ and Vietnam: A Different Kind of War*. Austin: University of Texas Press, 1994.

Johnson, Lyndon B. *The Vantage Point: Perspectives on the Presidency, 1963–1969*. New York: Holt, Rinehart and Winston, 1971.

Kennedy, John Fitzgerald (1917–1963)

President of the United States (1961–1963). Born in Brookline, Massachusetts, on May 29, 1917, John Fitzgerald Kennedy graduated from Harvard University in 1940 and served in the U.S. Navy in the Pacific Theater in World War II. In 1946, he was elected to the U.S. House of Representatives from Massachusetts as a Democrat. Kennedy was a strong anticommunist, and in 1953 he was elected to the U.S. Senate, where he showed continuing interest in foreign affairs as a critic of Dwight Eisenhower administration policies. In 1960, he was elected president.

Perhaps Kennedy's greatest success as president was his handling of the 1962 Cuban Missile Crisis. In domestic affairs, he sought tax cuts to stimulate the economy and proposed modest increases to the welfare state. He also jump-started the U.S. space program. Kennedy also dealt with the challenge of Soviet pressure over Berlin, but Vietnam was a problem with which he struggled until he died in 1963.

As a result of the 1961 Bay of Pigs fiasco and increasing tensions with the Soviets, Kennedy felt compelled to take a stand in Vietnam against communist aggression. In 1961, increasing infiltration of men and arms from the Democratic Republic of Vietnam (DRV) down the Ho Chi Minh Trail into the Republic of Vietnam (RVN) led Kennedy to approve sending U.S. Special Forces personnel to

John F. Kennedy was president of the United States during 1961–1963. Kennedy escalated U.S. involvement in Vietnam but he also told confidants that he intended to remove U.S. forces after the 1964 elections. Historians have argued ever since over what might have occurred had Kennedy not been assassinated in November 1963. (John F. Kennedy Presidential Library)

Vietnam and the use of roadside defoliants and crop herbicides (Operation RANCH HAND). He also approved covert operations against the DRV. Kennedy agreed to provide funding to equip 30,000 new troops in the Army of the Republic of Vietnam (ARVN) (rather than the 100,000 men President Ngo Dinh Diem requested) and to increase the size of the U.S.-funded and -advised Meo army in Laos from 9,000 to 11,000 men. U.S. advisers were also placed at every level of the RVN government and military.

Although Diem's government announced its acceptance of military reform and adopted the Strategic Hamlets program, Diem became increasingly reluctant to accept U.S. advice on political

reform. Thus, the Kennedy administration focused on increasing efficiency in the war effort, for example providing helicopters and establishing a command-level headquarters, the Military Assistance Command, Vietnam (MACV), in 1962.

Continuing Pathet Lao offensives in Laos and North Vietnamese exploitation of the Ho Chi Minh Trail led the Kennedy administration to attempt to renegotiate the neutrality of Laos, which was supposed to have been agreed upon in the 1954 Geneva Accords. The Kremlin, which had been supplying arms to the communist Pathet Lao in Laos since 1960, assured the United States that it would cooperate in keeping the DRV from using Laos as a corridor into South Vietnam. Kennedy sent U.S. Marines to the Thai-Lao border, dispatched the U.S. Seventh Fleet to the region, and obtained the neutralization of Laos at Geneva in July 1962. But the DRV did not withdraw its troops or cease infiltration into South Vietnam.

As a result, Kennedy was more determined to prevail in Vietnam, but Diem became more resistant to U.S.-advocated reform, which he charged would only make his country a protectorate. The May 1963 Buddhist crisis, which the Diem regime handled badly, was a turning point for American support of the increasingly untenable South Vietnamese government. When in August Diem's brother Ngo Dinh Nhu orchestrated raids on Buddhist pagodas, arresting many Buddhists, it strained U.S. patience.

After the pagoda raids, Washington agreed to provide tacit support for a military coup to replace Diem. Kennedy tried to put a halt to the coup after learning that the RVN generals might not have sufficient strength to prevail. Nevertheless, the generals struck on November 1 and Diem and his brother Ngo Dinh Nhu surrendered the next day, only to be summarily executed. This news shook Kennedy, but he had little time to act, as he himself fell to an assassin's bullets just three weeks later on November 22, 1963, in Dallas, Texas. Kennedy had announced to several close advisers his intention to withdraw U.S. forces from Vietnam after the presidential elections of 1964 (he believed that any announcement of this before the election would result in a conservative backlash, possibly costing him the election). Historians have argued ever since over what Kennedy might have done in Vietnam had he lived, but the United States was intimately involved in the series of unstable military-dominated governments that followed in the wake of the coup.

Claude R. Sasso

References

Hammer, Ellen, J. *A Death in November: America in Vietnam, 1963.* New York: E. P. Dutton, 1987.

Reeves, Richard. *President Kennedy: Profile of Power.* New York: Simon and Schuster, 1993.

Thompson, Kenneth, ed. *Portraits of American Presidents.* Vol. 4, *The Kennedy Presidency: Seventeen Intimate Perspectives of John F. Kennedy.* Lanham, MD: University Press of America, 1985.

Kennedy, Robert Francis (1925–1968)

U.S. attorney general (1961–1964), U.S. senator (1965–1968), and presidential candidate (1968). Born in Brookline, Massachusetts, on November 20, 1925, Robert F. Kennedy enlisted in the Naval Reserve and attended the V-12 training program at Harvard University. After a period of active duty, during which he served in a destroyer, he received his honorable discharge in May 1946 and returned to Harvard, where he graduated in 1948. In 1951, he received a law degree from the University of Virginia and was admitted to the bar. The following year he managed his brother John F. Kennedy's successful senatorial campaign. In September 1951, he covered the proceedings surrounding the U.S.-Japan Peace Treaty in San Francisco for the *Boston Post.*

As legal counsel to several Senate committees in the 1950s, Robert Kennedy served on Republican senator Joseph McCarthy's Senate Subcommittee on Investigations. In 1957, as head counsel and staff director on the committee investigating racketeering in U.S. labor unions, he engaged in a high-profile confrontation with Teamster boss James (Jimmy) Hoffa, which earned him national notoriety. He also played a peripheral role in the famous Army-McCarthy Hearings of 1954, although he allegedly professed a continued fondness for his former mentor.

In 1960, Robert Kennedy managed his brother's successful campaign for the presidency. The president-elect soon selected his brother as attorney general of the United States. Not surprisingly, the move resulted in charges of nepotism among Kennedy's detractors. At the Justice Department Kennedy made civil rights and organized crime his top priorities. Indeed, he placed the full weight of the Justice Department behind the growing civil rights effort, while also keeping close tabs on civil rights leader Martin Luther King Jr. But his influence extended beyond the Justice Department. As his brother's closest adviser, he became increasingly involved in foreign policy and national security issues and played a significant role in the October

Robert Kennedy served first as campaign adviser and then as attorney general under his brother President John F. Kennedy. Subsequently a U.S. senator from New York, he was leading in the race for the Democratic Party nomination for president when he was cut down by an assassin on June 4, 1968. (Lyndon B. Johnson Presidential Library)

Cuban Missile Crisis. He also supported U.S. initiatives in Southeast Asia, including those in Indochina.

Following his brother's assassination in November 1963, Kennedy stayed on as attorney general under President Lyndon B. Johnson, but in 1964 he resigned to run for the U.S. Senate from New York. Indeed, Johnson and Kennedy had little in common and little use for one another. In the Senate, Kennedy continued to support U.S. efforts in Vietnam, at least initially. He did lament the toll the war took upon his brother's Alliance for Progress and Johnson's Great Society programs, and he criticized the 1965 U.S. intervention in the Dominican Republic. Despite his growing apprehension toward the Vietnam War, especially the massive bombing of North Vietnam, he refrained from openly opposing administration policy. He was also acutely aware of the appearance of opportunism and the public perception of his political motives. But as racial strife and urban violence convulsed the country along with mounting antiwar sentiment and massive protests, Kennedy found it increasingly difficult to support the war or to refrain from criticizing the Johnson administration.

The presidential campaign of 1968 opened the door for Kennedy, but he held back, refusing at first to jump into the fray. After antiwar Sen. Eugene McCarthy's unexpectedly strong performance in the New Hampshire primary, which essentially was a repudiation of Johnson, Kennedy entered the race. In March 1968, when President Johnson announced that he would not seek reelection, Vice President Hubert Humphrey became the administration's presidential candidate.

In addition to his stated desire to end the fighting in Southeast Asia, Kennedy also sought to bridge the many rifts within American society. He quickly emerged as a serious contender for the presidency, and became the darling of many in the antiwar Left. On June 4, 1968, he won the all-important California primary, thereby becoming his party's front-runner. That night, after addressing his supporters at the Ambassador Hotel in Los Angeles, he was shot by Sirhan Sirhan. He died the following day at the age of 42. Kennedy's assassination, less than five years after that of his brother and only weeks after that of Martin Luther King Jr., devastated the nation and added sad punctuation to the divisive era.

David Coffey

References

Palermo, Joseph A. *In His Own Right: The Political Odyssey of Senator John F. Kennedy.* New York: Columbia University Press, 2001.

Schlesinger, Arthur M., Jr. *Robert Kennedy and His Times.* Boston: Houghton Mifflin, 1978.

King, Martin Luther, Jr. (1929–1968)

Protestant minister, U.S. civil rights leader, and critic of the Vietnam War. Born on January 15, 1929, in Atlanta, Georgia, Martin Luther King Jr. graduated from Morehouse College in 1948. Two years later he earned a BA in divinity from Crozer Theological Seminary, and in 1955 he received a PhD in theology from Boston University. An ordained minister since 1947, King moved to the forefront of the fledgling Civil Rights Movement in the mid-1950s. Under his direction, the 1955–1956 Montgomery, Alabama, bus boycott attracted national attention. In 1957, he founded the Southern Christian Leadership Conference (SCLC) to promote desegregation and minority voting rights. A strong advocate of nonviolent protest, King followed the example of India's Mahatma Gandhi by urging civil disobedience to effect change.

Following the spectacular success of his August 1963 March on Washington, during which he delivered his stirring "I Have a Dream" speech, King reached the pinnacle of his influence. He received the 1964 Nobel Peace Prize and an honorary doctorate from Yale University, but more important, he became a major player on the national political scene with access to the White House and Congress.

King had been a solid supporter of President Lyndon B. Johnson and his "Great Society." Johnson had produced a sweeping domestic agenda and landmark civil rights legislation that represented tangible progress. But King grew increasingly critical of U.S. involvement in Vietnam, and, as his concerns became increasingly public, his relationship with the Johnson administration deteriorated rapidly.

King viewed U.S. intervention in Southeast Asia as little more than imperialism carried out under the guise of fighting communism. He also claimed that African Americans constituted a disproportionate share of battle casualties. But chief among King's concerns was his belief that an enlarged U.S. commitment to Vietnam seriously threatened hard-won civil rights, social gains, and social welfare programs in the United States.

Civil rights activist Martin Luther King Jr. answers questions at a press conference in March 1964. King was a strong opponent of the Vietnam War. (Library of Congress)

In 1967, King began to devote entire speeches to Vietnam. He called for a cessation of bombing in North Vietnam and for meaningful negotiations—offering himself as a moderator. King's antiwar stance drew widespread criticism. Civil rights advocates implored him not to endanger the movement by linking it with the growing, but controversial, antiwar struggle. But to King the two were inseparable. Although most Americans still supported the war, King resolved to make it a major issue in the 1968 presidential election. By this time, the rift between King and the Johnson administration had reached open hostility, and King and his followers were subjected to FBI surveillance and government smear tactics.

Racial tensions, rioting, and concerted opposition threatened to thwart much of what had been achieved, but, despite serious challenges from both black and white critics, King elevated his campaign against the war, poverty, and inequality to new heights. In the midst of this, his most ambitious campaign to date, King was assassinated on April 4, 1968, in Memphis, Tennessee.

David Coffey

Henry Kissinger was national security adviser (1969–1973) and secretary of state (1973–1977) under presidents Richard Nixon and Gerald Ford. He and Nixon sought "peace with honor" in Vietnam but, during the period of their efforts to extract U.S. forces, there were more American casualties than during the administration of President Lyndon Johnson. (Marion S. Trikosko/Library of Congress)

References

Dyson, Michael Eric. *I May Not Get There with You: The True Martin Luther King, Jr.* New York: Free Press, 2000.

Oates, Stephen B. *Let the Trumpet Sound: The Life of Martin Luther King, Jr.* New York: Harper and Row, 1982.

Kissinger, Henry Alfred (1923–)

Foreign policy expert, national security adviser (1969–1973), and secretary of state (1973–1977). Henry Alfred Kissinger was born in Fuerth, Germany, on May 27, 1923. His family immigrated to New York in 1938, and he graduated from Harvard University in 1950. He completed a PhD in government there in 1954. In 1957, Kissinger accepted an appointment as a lecturer at Harvard and as associate director of the university's Center for International Affairs. He continued at Harvard until 1968.

President-elect Richard Nixon named Kissinger his national security adviser in late 1968. Nixon intended to keep control of foreign relations in the White House, with Kissinger as a more important adviser than Secretary of State William P. Rogers. Nixon and Kissinger agreed that foreign policy should be based on realism rather than idealism or moralism.

In developing their realist policies, Kissinger and Nixon perceived a shift from the bipolar balance of power between the United States and the Soviet Union to a triangular order that also included the People's Republic of China. Working together Nixon and Kissinger eventually brought an end to U.S. participation in the Vietnam War, reached détente with the Soviets, established diplomatic relations with China, and helped achieve an armistice in the Middle East following the 1973 Yom Kippur (Ramadan) War.

The war in Vietnam was the most difficult issue Kissinger faced, and peace talks between the United States and the Democratic Republic of Vietnam (DRV) had stalled by the time Nixon took office in 1969. Before his inauguration Nixon sent a message to the DRV indicating the new administration's desire for serious discussions. The North Vietnamese reply insisted on two points: unilateral withdrawal of U.S. forces and removal of the government of the Republic of Vietnam (RVN). These demands, which Nixon and Kissinger rejected, remained constant until nearly the end of negotiations in 1973.

Negotiations were further hindered by events in Cambodia. In March 1969, Nixon ordered the secret bombing of Cambodia (Operation MENU), which continued until May 1970. News of this was leaked to the press in May 1969.

In May 1969, Nixon had unveiled his Vietnam policy, proposing simultaneous mutual withdrawal of U.S. and North Vietnamese forces, supervised free elections in South Vietnam, and a ceasefire. The following month, Nixon announced U.S. troop withdrawals. Kissinger questioned this policy of "Vietnamization,"

arguing that unilateral troop withdrawals would only encourage DRV intransigence, demoralize troops, and bring further demands for troop reductions in the United States. Kissinger began intermittent secret peace talks with North Vietnamese representatives in Paris in August 1969. The negotiations soon deadlocked, however.

In the aftermath of the Cambodian invasion, Nixon and Kissinger developed a proposal to restart negotiations. In October 1970, Nixon suggested a ceasefire-in-place. In May 1971, Kissinger spelled out the offer in detail. It included a unilateral withdrawal of U.S. troops, with an understanding that there would be no further infiltration of "outside forces" into Vietnam; a ceasefire-in-place; guarantees for the neutrality and territorial integrity of Laos and Cambodia; release of prisoners of war; and an agreement to leave the political future of South Vietnam up to its people. Although these provisions signaled significant concessions from the United States, the DRV rejected them.

The Nixon administration's overtures to China and the Soviet Union may have had some impact on the Vietnam negotiations. In July 1971, Kissinger secretly arranged an official presidential visit to China. The historic summit, which took place in February 1972, reversed a 25-year U.S. policy of nonrecognition. Following Nixon's trip, China moderated its protests against American action in Vietnam in response to the 1972 North Vietnamese Easter (Spring) Offensive. In August 1972, following Nixon's May summit meeting with Soviet premier Leonid Brezhnev, the Hanoi Politburo authorized a negotiated settlement with the United States.

In a meeting with Kissinger on October 8, DRV representative Le Duc Tho proposed an accord settling military questions—a cease fire, withdrawal of U.S. forces, acceptance of continuing U.S. aid to the RVN, and return of prisoners of war—while leaving the future of the South Vietnamese government to a board representing the Saigon government and South Vietnamese Communists. These terms were agreed to on October 11. On his return to the United States, Kissinger announced that "peace is at hand."

Peace was not at hand. South Vietnamese president Nguyen Van Thieu refused to accede to the terms. Discussions with the DRV then bogged down in disagreements about changes demanded by Thieu and other matters. Talks broke off on December 13, 1972.

This interruption led to one of the most controversial acts of Nixon's presidency. On December 18, the United States began the so-called Christmas Bombing of North Vietnam (Operation LINEBACKER II), for the first time using B-52s over Hanoi and Haiphong. The raids proved costly for the United States as well as the DRV. Nixon halted the bombing on December 30 after Hanoi indicated its willingness to return to negotiations. The bombing met with outrage in the United States and throughout the world.

Kissinger and Le Duc Tho reached a final agreement on January 9, 1973. The terms were substantially the same as those reached the previous October. Ending U.S. involvement in the war in Vietnam was the capstone of Kissinger's career and earned him wide acclaim. In September 1973, Kissinger replaced William P. Rogers as secretary of state, a position he retained until 1977. Kissinger remains active as a consultant, commentator, and speaker on international affairs.

Spencer C. Tucker

References

Dallek, Robert. *Nixon and Kissinger: Partners in Power*. New York: HarperCollins, 2007.

Isaacson, Walter. *Kissinger: A Biography*. New York: Simon and Schuster, 1992.

Kissinger, Henry. *Ending the Vietnam War*. New York: Simon and Schuster, 2003.

———. *White House Years*. Boston: Little, Brown and Company, 1979.

Schulzinger, Robert. *Henry Kissinger: Doctor of Diplomacy*. New York: Columbia University Press, 1989.

Komer, Robert William (1922–2000)

Deputy to the commander, U.S. Military Assistance Command, Vietnam (MACV), for Civil Operations and Revolutionary Development Support (1967–1968). Born February 23, 1922, in Chicago, Robert William Komer graduated from Harvard University in 1942 and, following army duty in World War II, received an MBA at Harvard in 1947. He worked at the Central Intelligence Agency (CIA) on the analytical side from 1947 to 1960 and then was a senior staff member at the National Security Council (NSC) between 1961 and 1965.

As a deputy special assistant to the president for national security affairs (1965–1966) and later as special assistant (1966–1967), Komer became increasingly involved with the pacification program in Vietnam. In February 1966, President Lyndon Johnson appointed him Washington coordinator for pacification activities.

Komer's office became useful to young U.S. Army officers trying to overcome institutional resistance to results of the PROVN study, which had concluded that the attrition strategy and search-and-destroy tactics being employed by

General William Westmoreland were not working. According to the study, the key to success was to concentrate on population security and pacification. Komer was sympathetic to that viewpoint and helped advance such ideas. Meanwhile, reporting on a June 1966 trip to Vietnam, Komer told President Johnson that the pacification effort was lagging.

Soon Komer proposed that responsibility for support of pacification be assigned to the U.S. military establishment in the Republic of Vietnam (RVN), with a civilian deputy running it. He had in effect written his own job description, although it took Secretary of Defense Robert McNamara's backing for the idea to gain acceptance. In March 1967, the decision was announced to put the Civil Operations and Revolutionary Development Support (CORDS) program under Westmoreland with Komer as his deputy. In May 1967, Komer, given the personal rank of ambassador, headed for Vietnam to undertake his new duties.

Ambassador Ellsworth Bunker recalled that Komer was both "very able" and "very abrasive," thereby staking out the spectrum of viewpoints on Komer's contribution. In fact, Komer maintained that it was necessary to prod people aggressively if anything was going to be accomplished. He also took pride in his own incorrigible optimism. Only two months into the job he cabled the president an assessment, stating that the United States was finally winning the war of attrition in the South.

Once on the job Komer had been given a free hand by General Westmoreland who, according to William Colby, did so with relief so that he could concentrate on the military war which he believed was his primary responsibility.

Colby credited Komer with an overdue effort to build up the territorial forces and with pulling together disparate elements of the American advisory effort at the province level.

Komer's overall influence on the pacification program remains uncertain. McNamara accords him a single mention, indeed a single sentence, in his memoirs—hardly an indication of substantial impact. The record shows that it was only after General Creighton Abrams assumed command of MACV, William Colby took over as deputy for CORDS, and President Nguyen Van Thieu personally launched and pushed the Accelerated Pacification Campaign in November 1968 that pacification really began to show results.

Komer, meanwhile, had become ambassador to Turkey, an appointment that proved short-lived when the White House changed parties soon after he was nominated. He then spent a number of years at the RAND Corporation (1969–1977). Between 1977 and 1979, Komer worked on North Atlantic Treaty Organization (NATO) affairs as a Pentagon official; from 1979 to 1981, he was undersecretary of defense for policy. On April 9, 2000, Komer died of a stroke in Arlington, Virginia.

Lewis Sorley

References

Clarke, Jeffrey J. *Advice and Support: The Final Years, 1965–1973.* Washington, DC: U.S. Army Center of Military History, 1988.

Komer, Robert W. *Bureaucracy at War: U.S. Performance in the Vietnam Conflict.* Boulder, CO: Westview Press, 1986.

Scoville, Thomas W. *Reorganizing for Pacification Support.* Washington, DC: U.S. Army Center of Military History, 1982.

Krulak, Victor H. (1913–)

U.S. Marine Corps general and commanding general, Fleet Marine Force, Pacific (March 1964–May 1968). Born in Denver, Colorado, on January 7, 1913, Victor H. Krulak graduated from the United States Naval Academy, Annapolis, in 1934. In March 1943, Lieutenant Colonel Krulak took command in the Pacific of a parachute battalion of the 1st Marine Amphibious Corps at New Caledonia. That October he commanded the diversionary landing on Choiseul to cover the Bougainville invasion. Krulak also helped plan and execute the Okinawa Campaign. At the end of the war, he helped negotiate the surrender of Japanese forces in the Qingdao, China, area. During the Korean War (1950–1953), Colonel Krulak was chief of staff of the 1st Marine Division.

In June 1956, Krulak was promoted to brigadier general and named assistant division commander, 3rd Marine Division, on Okinawa. In November 1959, he was advanced to major general, and a month later he assumed command of the Marine Corps Recruit Depot at San Diego. In February 1962, he became special assistant for counterinsurgency and activities of the Joint Staff, Joint Chiefs of Staff. Over the course of the next two years, much of his time was spent gathering information regarding the developing conflict in South Vietnam. After a fact-finding mission to Vietnam, Krulak held that the war was winnable if the John F. Kennedy administration firmly supported the Ngo Dinh Diem regime in the south. His findings contradicted those of State Department official Joseph Mendenhall, who accompanied Krulak to Vietnam. In March 1964, Krulak, promoted to lieutenant general, assumed command of Fleet Marine Force (FMF), Pacific. He served in that post until he retired from active duty in May 1968.

While he was commander of FMF, Pacific, Krulak disagreed with U.S. commander in South Vietnam General William Westmoreland on several key points. First, Krulak was strongly opposed to Westmoreland's search-and-destroy strategy. Krulak believed that attrition of forces favored the Communist enemy. He saw search-and-destroy as a complete waste of time and effort that reduced the effectiveness of air and artillery support. He believed guerrillas constituted the main threat. His three-cornered strategy included protecting the South Vietnamese people from the guerrillas; concentrating air power on rail lines, power, fuel, and heavy industry in the Democratic Republic of Vietnam (DRV); and placing maximum effort in pacification. Krulak believed that the Americans were far more efficient at civic action than the Republic of Vietnam (RVN) government. The Vietnamese people were the key to victory, he believed, and if the Communists could be denied access to them the war could be won. Thus, the first order of business had to be to protect the civilian population. Krulak constantly pointed out to his superiors that the manpower necessary to protect the villages was sapped by the requirements of a war of attrition. Krulak retired from the marines in June 1968 and in 1984 published his memoirs, *First to Fight.*

W. E. Fahey Jr.

References

Krulak, Victor H. *First to Fight.* Annapolis, MD: U.S. Naval Institute Press, 1984.

Zaffiri, Samuel. *Westmoreland: A Biography of General William C. Westmoreland.* New York: William Morrow, 1994.

Lansdale, Edward Geary (1908–1987)

U.S. intelligence expert and the father of modern American counterinsurgency doctrine. Born in Detroit, Michigan, on February 6, 1908, Edward Geary Lansdale dropped out of the University of California, Los Angeles, only a few credit hours short of graduation. Following the Japanese attack on Pearl Harbor, Lansdale entered the Office of Strategic Services (OSS). In 1943, the army reinstated his UCLA Reserve Officer Training Corps (ROTC) commission and assigned him to military intelligence.

The end of the war in the Pacific found Major Lansdale in Manila. In 1947, he transferred to the newly established U.S. Air Force. After assignments in the United States, Lansdale was sent back to the Philippines in 1951, this time on loan to a new governmental intelligence and covert action group, successor to the OSS and forerunner to the Central Intelligence Agency (CIA), known as the Office of Policy Coordination (OPC).

His next assignment, now under CIA authority, took Lieutenant Colonel Lansdale to newly divided Vietnam in June 1954. As chief of the covert-action Saigon Military Mission (SMM), Lansdale was charged with weakening Ho Chi Minh's Democratic Republic of Vietnam (DRV) while helping to strengthen Bao Dai's southern State of Vietnam as a noncommunist nation. Within weeks Lansdale became a principal adviser to Ngo Dinh Diem, who was simultaneously premier, defense minister, and commander of the military. Diem accepted many of Lansdale's ideas, including urging northerners to move south; bribing sect leaders to merge their private armies into Diem's or face battle with him; instituting service organizations and a gov-ernment bureaucracy; planning reforms; and, in October 1955, offering himself and a new constitution as an alternative to the tired administration of Bao Dai. A lopsided and manipulated vote for Diem ensued. While Lansdale worked with Diem in the south, part of his SMM team labored in the DRV, with largely mixed and insignificant results to carry out sabotage and to effect a psychological warfare campaign against the communist government there.

Lansdale was a close personal friend of Diem, and he was one of the very few men to whom Diem listened. Most Westerners found Diem aloof and unresponsive and given to lengthy lectures. Not Lansdale. Their relationship bypassed normal channels of diplomatic relations, causing many U.S. leaders to view Lansdale with distrust. Yet Lansdale's record of success in the Philippines, his early accomplishments in Vietnam, and his own network of friends and contacts in high places prevented his enemies from dismissing either him or his ideas.

His influence lessened with Diem's growing reliance on his brother, Ngo Dinh Nhu, Lansdale returned to the United States in early 1957 and served both the Dwight Eisenhower and John Kennedy administrations as deputy director of the Office of Special Operations, Office of the Secretary of Defense. He also sat as a member of the U.S. Intelligence Board (USIB). On occasional visits to Vietnam he maintained his friendship with Diem. Lansdale's views often conflicted with the findings of others who were ready to give up on Diem and were contesting vigorously on behalf of their own government agencies in Vietnam.

In the waning days of the Eisenhower administration, now Brigadier General Lansdale worked with the Operations

Coordinating Board (OCB) of the USIB that oversaw CIA efforts to overthrow Cuba's Fidel Castro. He argued against such actions. In 1961 and 1963, as assistant to the secretary of defense for special operations, Lansdale served as executive officer for the president's Special Group, Augmented (SGA), charged with overthrowing Castro, a plan known as Operation MONGOOSE. After several intelligence forays to Central and South American countries, Lansdale retired from the Air Force in October 1963 as a major general.

President Lyndon Johnson recalled Lansdale to government service between 1965 and 1968, sending him to Vietnam with the rank of minister to work on pacification problems. His influence was less than in previous years and his authority not clearly defined. He accomplished little, and those years were for Lansdale a time of great frustration. He published his memoirs in 1972. Lansdale was allegedly the inspiration for Graham Greene's 1955 novel *The Quiet American*, something that both men repeatedly denied. Plagued by ill health and living quietly in retirement, Lansdale died in McLean, Virginia, on February 23, 1987.

Cecil B. Currey

References
Currey, Cecil B. *Edward Lansdale: The Unquiet American*. Boston: Houghton Mifflin, 1988.
Lansdale, Edward G. *In the Midst of Wars: An American's Mission to Southeast Asia*. New York: Harper and Row, 1972.

Lodge, Henry Cabot, Jr. (1902–1985)

U.S. senator and ambassador to the Republic of Vietnam (1963–1964 and 1965–1967). Henry Cabot Lodge Jr. was born in Nahant, Massachusetts, on July 5, 1902. Graduating from Harvard University in 1924, he was elected to the state legislature in 1932 and to the U.S. Senate as a Republican in 1936. He served two years in the military during World War II. Reelected to the Senate in 1946, Lodge was later named envoy to the United Nations and in 1960 was nominated as the Republican vice presidential candidate.

In 1963, President John F. Kennedy appointed Lodge ambassador to the Republic of Vietnam (RVN). A firm believer in the domino theory regarding Southeast Asia, Lodge thought Vietnam could be kept free of Communist control with sufficient time purchased by the presence of U.S. troops. When he became convinced that the United States could not win with President Ngo Dinh Diem as an ally, he acted to undermine

First a U.S. senator, Henry Cabot Lodge Jr. served as U.S. ambassador to the Republic of Vietnam during 1963–1964 and 1965–1967. (Yoichi R. Okamoto/Lyndon B. Johnson Presidential Library)

that regime. Lodge saw to it that Buddhist dissidents received refuge in the U.S. embassy, and opposition South Vietnamese generals were contacted through Lucien Conein, a Central Intelligence Agency operative. Lodge circumvented the pro-Diem general Paul Harkins, head of the U.S. Military Assistance Command, Vietnam (MACV), by withholding from his purview State Department communications and by undercutting his consistently upbeat assessments.

In late August 1963, the State Department instructed Lodge to give Diem an opportunity to oust Ngo Dinh Nhu, his controversial brother. Nhu controlled Colonel Le Quang Tung's Special Forces and used them to suppress protestors in Saigon. If Diem proved unwilling, Lodge was directed to tell the dissident generals that the Kennedy administration was ready to abandon the RVN president and back a successor regime. Fearing the Ngo family's repressive rule might affect the military situation in the countryside, Lodge wanted temporarily to withhold economic and military assistance, especially to Tung's unit, hoping to exert leverage and to force a change in policy. Such actions would also demonstrate support for the conspiring officers and, by October 5, 1963, President Kennedy endorsed Lodge's proposals.

Following a number of confrontations with Diem, Lodge advocated a coup. Convinced the South Vietnamese leader was unchangeable and loyal to his family, the ambassador gave tacit support to the generals' planned overthrow of the Ngos. Operation BRAVO II, the coup against Diem, began at 1:30 p.m. on November 1, 1963. Three hours later, Diem phoned Lodge from the besieged Gia Long Palace and inquired as to the U.S. attitude about the uprising. Lodge,

feigning ignorance, pretended to be alarmed for the safety of Diem and Nhu and offered both safe conduct out of the country or sanctuary in the embassy. Diem, determined to restore order and stay in power, refused. Diem and his brother were later apprehended and assassinated by the conspirators.

Ambassador Lodge soon lost confidence in the languid military leadership of General Duong Van Minh, one of the anti-Diem coup leaders. By early 1964, he supported Minh's overthrow by Lieutenant General Nguyen Khanh. That summer Lodge resigned as ambassador and was replaced by General Maxwell Taylor. Ostensibly, Lodge returned to the United States to run against Sen. Barry Goldwater for the 1964 Republican presidential nomination. In reality, he was weary and disappointed with Saigon politics, had no fresh thoughts on policy, and was ready to advise an air campaign against the Democratic Republic of Vietnam.

Lodge succeeded General Taylor for a second tour as ambassador to the RVN in 1965. He expressed qualms about holding free elections that might result in a neutral regime, halting the war, and removing the United States. When Buddhists launched the "Struggle Movement" against the government of Nguyen Cao Ky and Nguyen Van Thieu in 1966, Lodge championed the regime in overcoming the dissidents and their ally General Nguyen Chanh Thi, who was discharged from command of I Corps. Prior to leaving his post in 1967, the ambassador drafted a pacification scheme he labeled Hop Tac, or Cooperation, which emphasized subduing the areas around Saigon.

Lodge served as one of the Lyndon Johnson administration's "Wise Men" in 1968 and advocated the termination of search-and-destroy missions. In early 1969, President Richard M. Nixon assigned him as a negotiator to the Paris peace talks, but he resigned because of a lack of progress. Lodge died in Beverly, Massachusetts, on February 27, 1985.

Rodney J. Ross

References

Blair, Anne E. *Lodge in Vietnam: A Patriot Abroad.* New Haven, CT: Yale University Press, 1995.

Catton, Philip E. *Diem's Final Failure.* Lawrence: University Press of Kansas, 2002.

Herring, George C. *America's Longest War: The United States and Vietnam, 1950–1975.* New York: McGraw-Hill, 1986.

Moyar, Mark. *Triumph Forsaken: The Vietnam War, 1954–1965.* New York: Cambridge University Press, 2006.

McCarthy, Eugene Joseph (1916–2005)

U.S. senator, Democratic candidate for president in 1968, and leading critic of American involvement in Vietnam. Convinced that many Americans shared his frustration over Vietnam, McCarthy attempted to merge the antiwar movement with politics, and his early success helped bring down President Lyndon B. Johnson's presidency. Born in Watkins, Minnesota, on March 29, 1916, Eugene McCarthy graduated from St. John's University (Minnesota) in 1935 and earned a master's degree from the University of Minnesota in 1939. He worked as a high school teacher and college professor at St. John's University and the College of St. Thomas (Minnesota) and was a civilian technical assistant in the War Department's Military Intelligence Division for a time during World War II. In 1948, he was elected to the U.S. House of Representatives as a Democrat. He was elected to the U.S. Senate in 1958.

A member of the Senate Foreign Relations Committee, McCarthy voted for the 1964 Tonkin Gulf Resolution, but he considered it a vote for a holding action rather than a vote for an open-ended war. In McCarthy's view, the Vietnam War escalated in 1966 into a war of conquest. His opposition began to be evident in that year. He believed that the Johnson administration was moving from a policy of nation building in South Vietnam to an effort to save all of Southeast Asia from communism. He was also disturbed by the U.S. bombing of North Vietnam.

On November 30, 1967, McCarthy announced his bid for the 1968 presidential nomination as a candidate committed to bringing about a negotiated settlement of the war. He believed that the American people should be given the opportunity to make a determination on the Vietnam War. Large numbers of idealistic antiwar students flocked to his campaign as they had to his earlier speaking engagements on major college campuses. McCarthy's surprisingly strong showing in the March 12, 1968, New Hampshire Democratic primary (although later shown to be primarily an anti-Johnson vote rather than a vote for McCarthy's program per se) prompted Sen. Robert F. Kennedy (Democrat of New York) to join the presidential race. By month's end, President Lyndon Johnson announced that he would not seek reelection. At the same time, Johnson announced a partial bombing halt and authorized presidential emissary W. Averell Harriman to open negotiations with the Democratic Republic of Vietnam (DRV).

Kennedy's campaign soon eclipsed that of McCarthy, although McCarthy remained in the race. Kennedy's assassination in June 1968 again changed the dynamics of the presidential race. At the violence-marred August 1968 Democratic Party National Convention in Chicago, Vice President Hubert Humphrey received the nomination, ending McCarthy's idealistic antiwar political crusade.

In 1969, McCarthy resigned from the Foreign Relations Committee, and he left the Senate on completion of his second term in 1970. After his retirement from the Senate, McCarthy's involvement in politics consisted primarily of writing and speech making. He also worked in the publishing industry and authored a syndicated newspaper column for a number of years. In 1976 and again in 1988, he made unsuccessful bids for the presidency as an independent candidate. McCarthy died on December 10, 2005, in Washington, D.C.

James E. Southerland

As secretary of defense during 1961–1968, Robert S. McNamara was one of the chief architects of U.S. policy in Vietnam under presidents John F. Kennedy and Lyndon B. Johnson. He began to have doubts about the war only late in his tenure but has spent his retirement writing about the lessons to be learned from the conflict. (Yoichi R. Okamoto/Lyndon B. Johnson Presidential Library)

References

Eisele, Albert. *Almost to the Presidency: A Biography of Two American Politicians.* Blue Earth, MN: Piper, 1972.

Herzog, Arthur. *McCarthy for President.* New York: Viking, 1969.

McCarthy, Eugene. *The Year of the People.* New York: Doubleday, 1969.

White, Theodore. *The Making of the President 1968.* New York: Atheneum, 1969.

McNamara, Robert Strange (1916–)

U.S. secretary of defense (1961–1968). Born on June 9, 1916, in San Francisco, Robert Strange McNamara studied economics at the University of California at Berkeley and graduated in 1937. Two years later, he earned a master's degree in business administration, then soon joined the faculty. During World War II, he was a U.S. Army Air Corps statistical control officer. After the war, he went to work for the Ford Motor Company, where he rose to president by 1960. He became secretary of defense in 1961.

McNamara came to the job determined to take control of the Pentagon bureaucracy. Among his early initiatives were the installation of a programming-planning-budgeting system, the introduction of systems analysis into the department's decision-making process, and the revitalization of conventional forces to complement the John F. Kennedy administration's new defense approach known as "flexible response." This was to replace the Dwight Eisenhower administration's overreliance on nuclear weapons (massive retaliation) and would enable the United States to operate efficiently in smaller local or regional conflicts, such as in Vietnam.

Within a year, McNamara had also gone on record as believing that the United States should commit itself to preventing the fall of South Vietnam to communism, although he later wrote that within days he realized that to be a bad idea. During successive increases in the U.S. commitment, including the deployment of ground combat forces, to Vietnam, McNamara advocated meeting the field commander's requirements, at the same time insisting on a "graduated response" to North Vietnamese aggression. He was especially leery of any large-scale bombing campaign in the North.

By the end of 1965, however, McNamara had begun to doubt the possibility of achieving a military solution in Vietnam, a view he expressed to President Lyndon Johnson. Nevertheless, a month later, McNamara recommended adding 200,000 men to forces in Vietnam and expanding air operations.

In the autumn of 1966 McNamara advised Johnson that he saw no way to quickly end the conflict, and, by May 1967 he had advised the president in writing that it was time to alter strategy in Vietnam. He also refused to support General William Westmoreland's recent request for 200,000 more troops. But then in July 1967, just back from a trip to Vietnam, McNamara told the president that the conflict could be won using the same, existing strategy. Faced with McNamara's pervasive inconsistency, Johnson soon decided that McNamara was no longer the best man for the job. Later McNamara would recall that his assumptions and insufficient analyses led him to fundamentally misunderstand the nature of the conflict.

McNamara brought an unprecedented degree of centralization to the management of the Defense Department, but in retrospect, McNamara himself offered the observation that he was just too busy with myriad other issues to deal with the intricacies of the Vietnam War, which in part explains his attitudes and policies toward it. Under McNamara, there were huge gaps between rhetoric and reality. Some detractors argue that he had so ineptly managed the requirements of the war in Vietnam and competing commitments elsewhere that the U.S. Army in Europe was virtually destroyed to make up Vietnam shortfalls, while reserve forces were similarly ravaged. By the time McNamara was through in 1968, much of the U.S. Army had been eviscerated.

McNamara left office at the end of February 1968, in the midst of the debate over Vietnam policy precipitated by the January Tet Offensive, to become president of the World Bank, a post he held until 1982. By the time he left Defense, McNamara had again convinced himself that the war was probably not winnable. His 1995 book, *In Retrospect: The Tragedy and Lessons of Vietnam*, reignited Vietnam passions, but did little to rebuild his tarnished reputation.

Lewis Sorley

References

McMaster, H. R. *Dereliction of Duty: Johnson, McNamara, the Joint Chiefs of Staff, and the Lies That Led to Vietnam.* New York: HarperCollins, 1997.

McNamara, Robert S. *In Retrospect: The Tragedy and Lessons of Vietnam.* New York: Times Books, 1995.

Palmer, Gregory. *The McNamara Strategy and the Vietnam War: Program Budgeting in the Pentagon, 1960–1968.* Westport, CT: Greenwood Press, 1978.

Shapley, Deborah. *Promise and Power: The Life and Times of Robert McNamara.* Boston: Little, Brown, 1993.

Nixon, Richard Milhous (1913–1994)

Republican politician, vice president (1953–1961), and president of the United States (1969–1974). Born in Yorba Linda, California, on January 9, 1913, Richard Milhous Nixon graduated from Whittier College (1934) and Duke University Law School (1937). He served in the U.S. Navy in the Pacific during World War II and in 1946 won the first of two terms in the U.S. House of Representatives.

Nixon concentrated zealously on the issue of anticommunism and won election to the U.S. Senate in 1950. In 1952, Dwight Eisenhower chose Nixon as his vice presidential running mate. He took office in 1953.

When in April 1954 the French found themselves trapped at Dien Bien Phu, Nixon vociferously argued that the United States should intervene militarily. Eisenhower rejected this course of action, which only cemented in Nixon's mind the need to halt Communist aggression in the region.

Following his loss to Democrat John F. Kennedy in the 1960 presidential election and a subsequent failure in California's 1962 gubernatorial race, Nixon appeared to be finished politically. But in 1968, he emerged as the unlikely Republican candidate for president. The Vietnam War became the major issue in the 1968 campaign. Nixon had nothing to gain from meeting the issue head-on, and he refused to do so. Concentrating his efforts on denouncing President Lyndon Johnson's record on law and order, Nixon was reported to have a "secret plan" to end the war—a plan that he later admitted never existed. The tactic worked, and Nixon won a narrow victory over Democrat Hubert Humphrey in November 1968.

Richard M. Nixon was president of the United States during 1969–1974. During the 1968 presidential campaign, Nixon was reported to have a "secret plan" to end the war—a plan that, he later admitted, never existed. (National Archives)

The entirety of the Nixon presidency must be seen through the prism of Vietnam; that is unquestionably how he saw it. Yet Nixon did not seriously entertain an escalation of the war in 1969. Indeed, he was convinced that Ho Chi Minh could win the war if the United States continued to prosecute the war as Lyndon Johnson had. As a result, Nixon drastically changed American military strategy in Vietnam. Initially refusing to order the reinstatement of the bombing of North Vietnam, Nixon instead looked to withdraw American troops from combat and protect that withdrawal with a widening of the war into Cambodia and Laos. It was this strategy that Nixon hoped would force the North Vietnamese to entertain serious negotiations.

When Hanoi launched its spring offensive in February 1969, Nixon supported the bombing of North Vietnamese supply lines in Cambodia. He believed that the key to winning the war was the destruction of the Communist logistics network of the Ho Chi Minh Trail. Nixon gave the approval for Operation MENU, a wide plan for bombing suspected Communist sanctuaries in Cambodia. He also ordered that the bombings be kept secret. The MENU bombings succeeded only in driving the North Vietnamese deeper into Cambodia. They also began the chain of events known collectively as Watergate, as the White House ordered the tapping of the phones of several White House aides in an effort to find out who leaked the story about the bombing to the *New York Times*.

Nixon combined the secret bombings with attempts to show the world that American commitment to the war was winding down. In June, he ordered an immediate withdrawal of 25,000 troops from Vietnam. He also articulated the Nixon Doctrine: Unless directly attacked, the United States would not commit troops to the defense of a Developing World country. Hoping that these moves would show good faith, Nixon secretly gave the North Vietnamese a November 1 deadline to show significant steps toward peace.

However, Nixon's moves did not satisfy the antiwar movement at home, the momentum of which only grew larger. As a result, Nixon was forced to abandon his deadline. By the end of the year, Nixon had promised a further withdrawal of 50,000 troops by April 15, 1970.

However, Nixon's response to events threatened to widen the war just as his withdrawals were becoming significant. Nixon argued that it was the Democratic Republic of Vietnam (DRV) attack on Cambodia, begun in the spring of 1970, which convinced him that he must take further military action there. Other observers note the failure of the MENU bombings as the cause. Either way, the March 26 decision to send American troops into Cambodia was consistent with Nixon's desire to support his withdrawals by cutting off North Vietnam's supply routes. This decision was the most fateful of Nixon's presidency. Nixon had tried to soften the blow by announcing on April 20 the withdrawal of 150,000 more American troops before the end of 1971. However, his April 30 announcement of the Cambodian Incursion led to a firestorm of protest on U.S. college campuses.

The Cambodian Incursion proved little, except that the Army of the Republic of Vietnam (ARVN) was not yet ready to fight on its own. In an attempt to rectify that situation, in January 1971 Nixon sanctioned an offensive into Laos using only ARVN troops. The February initiative failed, and within six weeks ARVN troops were forced to withdraw. The Laotian debacle only stiffened Nixon's resolve, and it may have contributed to the harshness of his response to the leaking of the Pentagon Papers in the *New York Times* on June 13, 1971.

For the fourth straight year, Hanoi did not bow to Nixon's tactics. The DRV rebuffed requests for further talks and, on March 30, 1972, launched what was the largest offensive of the war. Furious, Nixon ordered the resumption of the bombing of the North. On April 1, 1972, Nixon authorized Operation LINEBACKER;

two weeks later, he expanded the bombing zone up to the 20th parallel, and on May 8 he ordered the mining of Haiphong Harbor. Nixon was certain that only a massive show of force would convince the North Vietnamese to negotiate. National Security Adviser Henry Kissinger and North Vietnamese representative Le Duc Tho resumed their peace talks within a month of the start of the LINEBACKER bombings; by late fall, the talks were in earnest.

It was soon clear that the only party who could not agree to a truce was RVN president Nguyen Van Thieu. In an effort to gain his support, Nixon sent a secret correspondence to Thieu, promising that, if the North Vietnamese broke the truce, the United States would recommit troops to South Vietnam. But when the North balked at changes in a document already agreed to, Nixon had enough. On December 17, Nixon ordered renewed saturation bombing of North Vietnam. Operation LINEBACKER II, also known as the "Christmas Bombing," lasted 11 days and subjected the Hanoi area to punishing blows. On December 26, 1972, Hanoi sent signals about wanting to resume negotiations, and on January 9, 1973, Secretary of State William Rogers initialed the truce.

Nixon understood that the agreement was a particularly weak one. Thus, he never believed that the truce meant that the United States was to stop sending monies and supplies to the RVN, which it continued to do until the June 30, 1973, Cooper-Church Amendment precluded it from doing so. Nevertheless, it is clear that Nixon fully expected to uphold his secret pledge to Thieu and to push the Congress to recommit troops if the DRV violated the peace. However, the November 7, 1973, passage of the War Powers Act would have precluded Nixon from making such a move, and his resignation from the presidency on August 9, 1974, in the wake of the Watergate scandal, left such a decision to his successor, Gerald R. Ford.

Most contemporary observers believe that Nixon relegated domestic policies to a secondary role, concentrating instead on the war and his other foreign policy initiatives. This is only partially true. For example, the Nixon administration developed innovative proposals for welfare reform and for new financial relationships between state and local governments. However, these initiatives were defeated by a Congress that had become increasingly alienated from his administration.

It was in foreign affairs that Nixon made his mark, again largely because of the war in Vietnam. The success of his overtures to the Chinese and the Soviets was based largely upon Nixon's skill in playing each of these nations against the other, as well as against the DRV.

Following his resignation, Nixon wrote eight books between 1978 and 1994 and worked to polish his tarnished image. Nixon died on April 22, 1994, in New York City.

John Robert Greene

References

Ambrose, Stephen E. *Nixon*. 3 vols. New York: Simon and Schuster, 1987–1991.

Dallek, Robert. *Nixon and Kissinger: Partners in Power*. New York: Harper Collins, 2007.

Greene, John Robert. *The Limits of Power: The Nixon and Ford Administrations*. Bloomington: Indiana University Press, 1992.

Kissinger, Henry. *Ending the Vietnam War*. New York: Simon and Schuster, 2003.

Nixon, Richard. *No More Vietnams*. New York: Avon Books, 1985.

Rostow, Walt Whitman
(1916–2003)

Chairman, U.S. State Department Policy Planning Council (1961–1966), and special assistant to the president for national security affairs (1966–1969). Walt Whitman Rostow was born in New York City on October 7, 1916. An economist, he studied at Yale University and was a Rhodes Scholar at Oxford University. During World War II, Rostow served in the Office of Strategic Services (OSS), where he was one of the analysts on the Strategic Bombing Survey.

Following the war, Rostow worked briefly in the State Department and then became an assistant to the assistant secretary of the Economic Commission for Europe before returning to the academic world in 1950. For the next 10 years he taught economics at the Massachusetts Institute of Technology and was also an associate of the Institute's Central Intelligence Agency–supported Center for International Studies. Rostow's academic work centered on the possibility of providing an alternative to Marxist models and historical theories of economic development.

During the election campaign of 1960, Rostow was an informal adviser to Democratic presidential candidate Sen. John F. Kennedy, with whom he had been close since 1958. Initially, he was appointed deputy to the Special Assistant to the President for National Security Affairs McGeorge Bundy. In early February 1961, he passed on to Kennedy and enthusiastically endorsed a report by Brigadier General Edward G. Lansdale, which suggested that a serious crisis was impending in South Vietnam and recommended a major expansion of U.S. programs in that country. Rostow argued

that the options of bombing North Vietnam or occupying its southern regions be considered, an outlook that made him one of the strongest hawks in the administration, a stance he would retain throughout the Vietnam War era.

In October 1961, Rostow and General Maxwell D. Taylor undertook a mission to Vietnam to assess the situation there and the merits of potential U.S. courses of action. Their report recommended that the United States change its existing advisory role to one of "limited partnership" with the Republic of Vietnam (RVN). The report also advocated increased American economic aid and military advisory support to the country. A secret annex suggested that 8,000 American combat troops be deployed there. All except the last of these recommendations were implemented.

In late 1961, Rostow was appointed a State Department counselor and chairman of the department's Policy Planning Council. He continued to be one of the administration's strongest advocates of an assertive U.S. policy in Vietnam, constantly urging increased military pressure against the Democratic Republic of Vietnam (DRV). By late 1964, he believed that escalating U.S. military measures, including the commitment of American ground forces, a naval blockade, and bombing of North Vietnam, would convince Hanoi that victory over the RVN was impossible.

When these measures were implemented in 1965, Rostow urged their expansion, as he continued to do after his March 1966 appointment as special assistant to the president for national security affairs. In the Lyndon Johnson administration's final years, Rostow's confidence in an eventual favorable outcome of the war remained unshaken, even in light of mounting public protests and the inconclusive progress of the war. In 1967, he called for the extension of the U.S. bombing program and opposed an unconditional bombing halt, although in late 1967 he did endorse proposals by Secretary of Defense Robert McNamara to try to reduce U.S. casualties and shift more of the burden of fighting to the South Vietnamese. In an increasingly divided and demoralized administration, he remained a committed hawk, opposed to the post–Tet Offensive decision of March 1968 to open negotiations with the DRV.

Following his resignation in January 1969, Rostow joined the University of Texas at Austin as a professor of economics and history. In his voluminous writings, he always defended U.S. policy in Vietnam, arguing that U.S. involvement in the war gave other Southeast Asian nations the breathing space they required to develop strong economies and become staunch regional anticommunist bastions. Rostow died on February 13, 2003, in Austin, Texas.

Priscilla Roberts

References

Barrett, David M. *Uncertain Warriors: Lyndon Johnson and His Vietnam Advisors.* Lawrence: University Press of Kansas, 1994.

Berman, Larry. *Planning a Tragedy: The Americanization of the War in Vietnam.* New York: W. W. Norton, 1982.

Halberstam, David. *The Best and the Brightest.* New York: Random House, 1972.

Rostow, Walt W. *The Diffusion of Power, 1957–1972: An Essay in Recent History.* New York: Macmillan, 1972.

Rusk, David Dean (1909–1994)

U.S. secretary of state (1961–1969). David Dean Rusk was born in rural Cherokee County, Georgia, on February

9, 1909, and worked his way through Davidson College in North Carolina, graduating in 1931. That same year he entered Oxford University on a Rhodes Scholarship and earned a BS in 1934 and an MA the following year. Returning to the United States, he taught at Mills College in Oakland, California, and attended the University of California Law School.

In 1940, Rusk entered the Army Reserve as a captain. On active duty in Washington, D.C., he worked in military intelligence. In 1943, he was transferred to the Far East, serving in China and Burma, where he became deputy chief of staff to General Joseph Stilwell. Discharged in 1946 with the rank of colonel, Rusk joined the State Department.

Dean Rusk was secretary of state during 1961–1969 during the administrations of presidents John F. Kennedy and Lyndon B. Johnson. Rush was a strong proponent of U.S. involvement in Vietnam. (Yoichi R. Okamoto/Lydon B. Johnson Presidential Library)

In the State Department, Rusk held a variety of important posts and worked with such issues as the establishment of the State of Israel and the United Nations. In 1950, he became assistant secretary of state for Far Eastern Affairs, and as such was involved in the formulation of Korean War policy. He supported the policy of containment and encouraged the decision to remove General Douglas MacArthur from command in 1951. But in 1952, Rusk left the State Department to assume the presidency of the Rockefeller Foundation. In 1960, President-elect John F. Kennedy chose Rusk as his secretary of state over such notables as Chester Bowles and Adlai Stevenson, who became Rusk's subordinates.

Upon assuming office, Rusk immediately confronted myriad international problems, the most serious being communist threats in Cuba, Southeast Asia, and Berlin. A staunch anticommunist, he largely worked behind the scenes in the Kennedy administration, offering advice only when it was solicited. But he believed that communist aggression had to be met with determination and feared that China would intervene in Vietnam, as it had in Korea in 1950. He had little faith in Ngo Dinh Diem and urged a stronger American commitment in South Vietnam. Along with Secretary of Defense Robert S. McNamara, Rusk usually deferred to the Pentagon position on Southeast Asia.

When Lyndon B. Johnson assumed the presidency after Kennedy's 1963 assassination, Rusk continued as secretary of state. Under Johnson, he took a much more active role and quickly became one of Johnson's most trusted advisers. As antiwar sentiments intensified, many of Johnson's advisers, such as Secretaries of Defense Robert McNamara and Clark Clifford, began to mirror the public's exasperation with the Vietnam War. Rusk nevertheless steadfastly supported Johnson's position. He backed Pentagon calls for larger troop commitments to Southeast Asia and the bombing of North Vietnam. He urged Johnson to stay the course, despite mounting pressure to end U.S. involvement in the war. Rusk did not, as is often suggested, oppose negotiations with Hanoi. He constantly warned against the appearance of weakness in the face of communist aggression, but in 1967 suggested that Johnson pursue negotiations. Rusk left his post in January 1969 when the Republican administration of Richard Nixon took office.

Throughout his career, Rusk displayed marked ability and an intense loyalty to his superiors. Though admirable, his loyalty proved damaging as, with the exception of Johnson, no other political figure became more closely associated with America's failure in Vietnam than Rusk. He was also an outsider. A southerner among Ivy League easterners, Rusk also found himself an outcast. Shunned by more prestigious academic institutions, he eventually accepted a position at the University of Georgia, where he taught international law until his retirement in 1984. His memoir, *As I Saw It*, was published in 1990 to much less hoopla than Robert McNamara's subsequent effort. Rusk died at his home in Athens, Georgia, on December 20, 1994.

David Coffey

References

Halberstam, David. *The Best and the Brightest*. New York: Random House, 1972.

Isaacson, Walter, and Evan Thomas. *The Wise Men: Six Friends and the World They Made*. New York: Simon and Schuster, 1986.

Karnow, Stanley. *Vietnam: A History*. New York: Viking Press, 1983.

Taylor, Maxwell Davenport (1901–1987)

U.S. Army general; military representative of the president (1961–1962), chairman of the Joint Chiefs of Staff (1962–1964), and ambassador to the Republic of Vietnam (1964–1965). Born in Keytesville, Missouri, on August 26, 1901, Maxwell Davenport Taylor graduated from the United States Military Academy, West Point, in 1922 and during World War II participated in campaigns in Sicily, Italy, and France. Serving with the 82nd Airborne Division, Taylor was appointed brigadier general in December 1942 and advanced to major general in March 1944. He commanded the 101st Airborne Division in the invasion of Normandy, France, in June 1944.

Following the war, Taylor served as superintendent of the United States Military Academy (1945–1949) and commander of the American Military Government in Berlin in 1949. He was advanced to lieutenant general in 1951. In February 1953, as a full general, Taylor assumed command of Eighth Army and United Nations (UN) forces in Korea. He then headed the U.S. Army Far East and UN Command in 1955, and he was army chief of staff from 1955 to 1959. Taking issue with the doctrine of massive retaliation favored by the Dwight Eisenhower administration, Taylor advocated a larger military capable of flexible response. When the doctrine of massive retaliation prevailed, Taylor resigned in July 1959.

Taylor had been warning for years that brushfire wars, not nuclear conflicts, presented the greatest military challenge to the United States. In July 1961, Taylor took on the newly established post of military representative of the president. The position made him the president's senior military representative at home and abroad.

In October 1961, Kennedy sent Taylor to Vietnam. There Taylor reported a "double crisis of confidence": doubts about American determination to hold Southeast Asia and doubts that Republic of Vietnam (RVN) president Ngo Dinh Diem's methods could defeat the Communists. Taylor advocated sending additional military aid and advisers while at the same time urging RVN reforms. He also wanted intensive training of local self-defense forces and large increases in aircraft and support personnel. Kennedy approved the recommendations, with the exception of sending ground combat troops. This report, flawed by its lack of emphasis on political problems and its underestimation of the Communists, marked the zenith of Taylor's influence.

In October 1962, Kennedy recalled Taylor from retirement to serve as chairman of the Joint Chiefs of Staff (JCS). Taylor and Secretary of Defense Robert McNamara were in general agreement on strategy and shared similar management styles. The two made three trips to Vietnam together; perhaps the most important came in September 1963, when they noted significant military progress and expressed confidence that it would continue.

Taylor was critical of the November 1963 coup against Diem. In January 1964, he informed McNamara that the JCS favored the elimination of military restrictions and sought bolder actions. Taylor advocated both an intensified counterinsurgency program and selected air and naval strikes against North Vietnam. He continued to stress this two-part program in years to come.

Taylor undertook his most controversial role in July 1964, when he succeeded

Henry Cabot Lodge Jr. as U.S. ambassador to the RVN. When he arrived in Saigon, Taylor was seemingly in a powerful position. He and Military Assistance Command, Vietnam (MACV), commander General William Westmoreland began to "Americanize" the war. Taylor had little patience for the political complexities of the RVN, nor did he understand its leaders. By December, relations between the ambassador and Prime Minister Nguyen Khanh became so strained that Taylor demanded he resign, while Khanh threatened to ask Washington for Taylor's recall.

In early 1965, Taylor foresaw the probability of a major U.S. troop commitment, which unnerved him. He now embraced the notion that the United States should avoid Asian land wars. In February, Westmoreland requested two marine battalions to protect the air base at Da Nang. Taylor differed with Westmoreland over the introduction of U.S. combat troops, and in March he returned to Washington to voice his objections to what he saw as an inevitably increasing American commitment. He believed that a major U.S. commitment would turn the conflict into an American-led war. Taylor did not oppose the introduction of U.S. troops per se, but he did advocate restrictions on their use. He supported an enclave strategy that would secure major towns and U.S. military bases, mainly along the coast, by aggressive patrolling, rather than Westmoreland's search-and-destroy strategy.

In April 1965, Taylor had a brief argument on the troop issue with McNamara and Westmoreland, and there was by now a major shift in U.S. policy from counterinsurgency to large-scale ground war. It was also clear that Taylor's enclave strategy was giving way to Westmoreland's search-and-destroy strategy. Taylor's defeat on these issues ended the fiction of an all-powerful ambassador and was the last time he had a significant say in war strategy.

Returning to Washington, D.C. in July 1965, Taylor was haunted by a sense of failure. He nonetheless retained an important advisory role and joined the group of Johnson's senior policy consultants known as the "Wise Men." Taylor died in Washington, D.C. on April 19, 1987.

Paul S. Daum and Elizabeth W. Daum

References
Kinnard, Douglas. *The Certain Trumpet: Maxwell Taylor & The American Experience in Vietnam.* Washington, DC: Brassey's, 1991.
Taylor, John M. *General Maxwell Taylor: The Sword and the Pen.* New York: Doubleday, 1989.
Zaffiri, Samuel. *Westmoreland: A Biography of General William C. Westmoreland.* New York: William Morrow, 1994.

Truman, Harry S. (1884–1972)

Democratic politician, U.S. senator (1935–1945), vice president (1945), and president of the United States (1945–1953). Truman was largely responsible for initiating U.S. involvement in Vietnam. Born in Lamar, Missouri, on May 8, 1884, Harry Truman served in the U.S. Army in World War I as an artillery captain. In 1923, he entered politics under the tutelage of the Kansas City Pendergast Democratic political machine and served as a county judge until 1935. Truman was elected to the U.S. Senate in 1934 and served until sworn in as vice president in 1945. He served as vice president from January 20 to April 12, 1945, and became

President Harry S. Truman commenced U.S. involvement in Vietnam by extending military assistance to the French in the Indochina War as part of the strategy to defeat communist expansion. (Harry S. Truman Presidential Library)

president upon the death of Franklin Delano Roosevelt.

In July 1945, Truman met at Potsdam with British prime minister Winston Churchill (replaced during the conference by Clement Atlee) and Joseph Stalin to negotiate the map of Europe and discuss the end of the war in the Pacific. Truman and Churchill made a far-reaching determination concerning Southeast Asia. The Allied chiefs of staff divided French Indochina along the 16th parallel for "operational purposes," with Japanese forces to surrender to the Chinese north of that line and to the British to the south. Although Roosevelt had favored independence, postwar leaders made no provisions for Indochinese self-determination and Truman ignored the question as the

threat of communism in Europe began to eclipse all other concerns.

In 1946, reacting to the communist threat in Greece and Turkey, Truman enjoined Congress to aid in preserving democracy. Congress passed emergency funding and Truman and U.S. policy-makers articulated through the 1947 Truman Doctrine and 1947 Marshall Plan diplomat George F. Kennan's containment doctrine. This policy sought to contain Soviet hegemony and encroachment virtually anywhere in the world. Containment dominated foreign relations throughout the Cold War and was quickly extended to Southeast Asia.

Believing French collaboration to be crucial in European reconstruction, Undersecretary of State Dean G. Acheson convinced Truman in March 1950 to allocate $15 million of a pending military aid bill for Western Europe to assist the French in defeating the Viet Minh. On June 28, 1950, three days after hostilities broke out in Korea and four weeks before Truman signed the aid bill, eight C-47 cargo aircraft transported to Vietnam the first of this aid, which by 1954 grew to a total of $3 billion.

Truman's decision to assist the French in Indochina was motivated by several events: the 1949 Soviet detonation of their first atomic bomb, the communist victory in China in October 1949, and Sen. Joseph R. McCarthy's ensuing attacks on the administration for supposed "softness" on communism. Of course, the communist attack in Korea and the subsequent Chinese intervention in the war in late 1950 solidified in Truman's mind the need to resist communist aggression elsewhere in Asia, lest places like Indochina also come under attack.

Subsequent administrations escalated U.S. participation in Vietnam. President

Lyndon Johnson, believing he had inherited from presidents Truman, Dwight D. Eisenhower, and John F. Kennedy a pledge to protect Southeast Asia from communism, announced within hours of his presidential oath following Kennedy's assassination that he was not going to be known as the president who permitted Southeast Asia to go the way of China.

During the war, Johnson visited Truman several times as president, seeking a public endorsement of his policies, but Truman refused to make a public statement. Privately, he was disenchanted with Johnson's leadership and believed the war to be a mistake. Truman died in Kansas City, Missouri, on December 26, 1972.

Brenda J. Taylor

References

Anderson, David L., ed. *Shadow on the White House: Presidents and the Vietnam War, 1945–1975.* Lawrence: University Press of Kansas, 1993.

McCullough, David. *Truman.* New York: Simon and Schuster, 1992.

Williams, William Appleman, ed. *America in Vietnam: A Documentary History.* Garden City, NY: Anchor Press, 1985.

Westmoreland, William Childs (1914–2005)

U.S. Army general and commander of American forces in Vietnam from June 1964 to June 1968. William Childs Westmoreland was born in Spartanburg County, South Carolina, on March 26, 1914. He attended The Citadel for a year before entering the United States Military Academy at West Point, graduating in 1936.

Commissioned a 2nd lieutenant of artillery, Westmoreland served in various posts in the United States. In 1942, he commanded an artillery battery in Tunisia and Sicily. He then served with the 9th Infantry Division in France, where he became division chief of staff. He fought with the division in Germany and after the war commanded a regiment in occupation duties. In 1946, he commanded the 504th Parachute Infantry Regiment. From 1947 to 1964, he held a series of increasingly important commands; from 1960 to 1963, he served as superintendent at West Point. Westmoreland was promoted to brigadier general in 1952; major general in 1956; and lieutenant general in 1963, when he took command of the XVIII Airborne Corps.

Westmoreland was then ordered to Vietnam as deputy commander, U.S. Military Assistance Command, Vietnam (MACV).

U.S. Army general William Westmoreland commanded the Military Assistance Command, Vietnam (MACV), during 1964–1968. Westmoreland sought to win the war by seeking out and destroying communist ground forces in pitched battle but the general, as with most Americans, underestimated North Vietnamese resolve to win at any cost. (Department of Defense)

He arrived in Vietnam in January 1964, and in June he was named to succeed General Paul D. Harkins as commander of MACV. Westmoreland believed the South Vietnamese lacked urgency. His own approach to command in Vietnam was to be one of action, not of contemplation. In August, Westmoreland was promoted to full general; it was now Westmoreland's war.

Westmoreland's military strategy of search-and-destroy seemingly was consistent with the political character of limited war in Vietnam, where the United States and South Vietnam were partners in contesting a communist insurgency. Search-and-destroy operations were designed to deny to the Viet Cong (VC) and the People's Army of Vietnam (PAVN, North Vietnamese Army) the cover and concealment of their jungle bases and to bring their military units to battle. Allied units would enter jungle sanctuaries, search during the day, and occupy strong night defensive positions, daring the Communists to attack. MACV's approach depended on superior intelligence data and sufficient airmobile combat units to reach the decisive location in time to exploit the opportunity. Search-and-destroy operations were predicated on the assumption that combat in Vietnam had moved from insurgency/guerrilla actions to larger-unit actions.

Some strategists have since concluded that MACV's assumption that large-unit warfare had supplanted the Communists' small-unit guerrilla-style "hit-and-run" tactics after 1965 was invalid. By 1967, however, Westmoreland believed that the initiative had firmly switched to the allies, noting that the VC and the PAVN had lost control over large areas and populations.

It is not surprising that Westmoreland and the MACV staff sought a strategic solution to the growing VC/PAVN capability through the application of U.S. technology and firepower. What is surprising is that they believed that an American-style quick fix could win a protracted war. In many ways, the "other war," pacification, was the more important stepping stone to an allied victory. American strategists discovered too late that carrying the war to the Communists at the same time as they were attempting to strengthen the South Vietnamese toward self-sufficiency was like pulling on both ends of a rope simultaneously.

VC/PAVN forces were fighting the Americans and their allies fiercely. But through it all the Communists had their eyes on the objective—to frustrate and damage the Americans' will to continue the war. Westmoreland's warriors had four years in the ring with PAVN general Vo Nguyen Giap's numerous and dedicated troops. Instead of being weakened by attrition, the VC/PAVN seemed to gain in strength and audacity after suffering enormous losses in their 1968 Tet Offensive.

Explaining that American intelligence had forecast a Viet Cong attack, Westmoreland admitted that he had made a mistake and that he should have called a press conference and announced that he knew the attack was coming. After the Tet Offensive, the U.S. government, reflecting the impatience and disillusionment of the American people, began withdrawing the essential moral support and then the resources necessary for victory. It was not entirely Westmoreland's fault; it was only his misfortune to be the responsible official on the ground in Vietnam.

In July 1968, President Lyndon B. Johnson recalled Westmoreland from Vietnam and appointed him U.S. Army chief of staff. Westmoreland now set his professional skills to work on issues such as the all-volunteer force. In July 1972, Westmoreland retired from the army after more than 36 years of service.

In January 1982, the Columbia Broadcasting System (CBS) and its journalist Mike Wallace aired a television documentary that accused General Westmoreland and his staff of fudging Communist casualty figures to give the appearance of progress in Vietnam. Westmoreland brought a libel suit against CBS that resulted in a two and a half month trial and ended with an out-of-court settlement in February 1985. CBS stood by its documentary but issued a statement that it did not mean to impugn General Westmoreland's patriotism or loyalty. Following his retirement, Westmoreland made a brief, unsuccessful foray into politics in search of the Republican nomination for governor of South Carolina. He died on July 18, 2005, in Charleston, South Carolina.

John F. Votaw

References

Westmoreland, William C. Interview with the author at Cantigny, Wheaton, Illinois, December 21, 1994.

———. *A Soldier Reports*. Garden City, NY: Doubleday, 1976.

Zaffiri, Samuel. *Westmoreland: A Biography of General William C. Westmoreland*. New York: William Morrow, 1994.

Weyand, Frederick Carlton (1916–)

U.S. Army general, commander, II Field Force, Vietnam, and last commander of Military Assistance Command, Vietnam (MACV). Born in Arbuckle, California, on September 15, 1916, Frederick Carlton Weyand graduated from the University of California at Berkeley in 1939 and received a Reserve Officers' Training Corps (ROTC) commission. In 1940, he

was called to active duty and assigned to the 6th Artillery. During World War II, Weyand served as an intelligence officer in Burma. After the war he transferred to the infantry.

During 1950–1951 in the Korean War (1950–1953), he was a lieutenant colonel and battalion commander in the 7th Infantry Regiment and operations officer of the 3rd Infantry Division. During 1952–1953, he was on the faculty of the Infantry School, Fort Benning, Georgia. Military assistant in the Office of the Assistant Secretary of the Army for Financial Management until 1954, Weyand was promoted to colonel in 1955 and was military assistant to the secretary of the army during 1954–1957. Weyand graduated from the Army War College in 1958. Chief of staff for the Communications Zone, U.S. Army, Europe, during 1960–1961, he made brigadier general in 1960. During 1961–1964, Weyand was deputy chief and chief of legislative liaison for the Department of the Army.

Appointed major general in November 1962, in 1964 Weyand assumed command of the 25th Infantry Division in Hawaii. He took the division to Vietnam in 1966 and commanded it during Operations CEDAR FALLS and JUNCTION CITY. In March 1967 he became deputy commander of II Field Force and then its commander from July 1967 to August 1968.

As commander of II Field Force, Weyand controlled combat operations inside the "Saigon Circle" during the January 1968 Tet Offensive. In the months leading up to Tet, Weyand's maneuver battalions were increasingly sent to outlying border regions in response to increased Viet Cong (VC) attacks in those areas. However, Weyand and his civilian political adviser, John Paul Vann, were uncomfortable with the operational patterns they were seeing. Weyand did not like the increase in Communist radio traffic around Saigon, and his units were making too few contacts in the border regions.

On January 10, 1968, Weyand visited with General William Westmoreland and convinced him to let him pull more U.S. combat battalions back in around Saigon. As a result, there were 27 battalions (instead of the planned 14) in the Saigon area when the Tet attacks came. Weyand's shrewd analysis and subsequent actions unquestionably altered the course of the Tet fighting to the allies' advantage. During the battle itself, Weyand controlled U.S. forces from his command post at Long Binh, some 15 miles east of Saigon.

Weyand left Vietnam in 1968 and, as a lieutenant general, served as the army's chief of the Office of Reserve Components until 1969. In 1969 and 1970, he was a military adviser to the Paris peace talks. In April 1970, Weyand returned to Vietnam as deputy commander of MACV. Promoted to full general in October 1970, he succeeded General Creighton Abrams as MACV commander in July 1972. Weyand presided over the U.S. military withdrawal from Vietnam and folded MACV's flag on March 29, 1973.

After he left Vietnam, Weyand became commander in chief, U.S. Army Pacific, later becoming vice chief of staff of the army in 1973 and chief of staff in October 1974. Just before the fall of the Republic of Vietnam (RVN), President Gerald Ford sent Weyand to Saigon to assess the situation. Weyand arrived there on March 27, 1975, and delivered the message to President Nguyen Van Thieu that although the U.S. government would support the RVN to the best of its ability, America would not fight in Vietnam again. Upon his return to Washington, Weyand reported—to no avail—that the military situation could not be improved without direct U.S. intervention. As chief of staff of the army, Weyand worked to improve combat-to-support troop ratios, to achieve a 16-division army, and to enhance unit effectiveness.

Weyand retired from the U.S. Army in October 1976. During his 36-year career, he had spent almost 6 years in Vietnam and another 10 in Asia and the Pacific. He was one of America's most experienced and capable commanders of the Vietnam War.

David T. Zabecki

References

Bell, William G. *Commanding Generals and Chiefs of Staff: 1775–1983.* Washington, DC: U.S. Army Center of Military History, 1983.

Oberdorfer, Don. *Tet!* New York: Doubleday, 1971.

Palmer, Bruce, Jr. *The 25-Year War: America's Military Role in Vietnam.* Lexington: University Press of Kentucky, 1984.

Zabecki, David T. "Battle for Saigon." *Vietnam* (Summer 1989): 19–25.

Wheeler, Earle Gilmore (1908–1975)

U.S. Army general, chief of staff (1962–1964), and chairman of the Joint Chiefs of Staff (JCS) during 1964–1970. Born in Washington, D.C., on January 13, 1908, Earle "Bus" Gilmore Wheeler enlisted in the National Guard at age 16 before entering the United States Military Academy at West Point, graduating in 1932. Commissioned in the infantry, he served in Tianjin, China, from 1937 to 1938.

In 1940, Wheeler returned to West Point as a mathematics instructor. During the first half of World War II, he trained infantry units in the United States. In December 1944, he went to Europe as chief of staff of the 63rd Infantry Division.

A protégé of General Maxwell Taylor, Wheeler was a full general by 1962. That March he became deputy commander in chief of the U.S. European Command, and seven months later he was named chief of staff of the army. When Taylor retired as chairman of the JCS in June 1964, Wheeler succeeded him.

Wheeler enjoyed good relations with Congress. He was fairly close to President Lyndon Johnson, and he had a reputation as a skillful player of the Pentagon's game under Secretary of Defense Robert S. McNamara's rules. Nonetheless, as the war progressed, Wheeler was increasingly overshadowed by McNamara and his systems analysis philosophy. As chairman, Wheeler worked hard to smooth over dissenting opinions in JCS recommendations. He believed they invited interference by McNamara and his civilian assistants. Although there was a wide difference of opinion within the JCS on the air war strategy, Wheeler convinced all the chiefs to go along with it. Wheeler's approach did not work. Unanimity did not produce greater JCS influence, and McNamara increasingly made military decisions to a far greater degree than his predecessors.

As American involvement in the war grew, the JCS recognized the widening discrepancy between the total force needed to meet worldwide U.S. commitments and the manpower base the political leadership was willing to support. In August 1965, Wheeler and the chiefs proposed an overall strategy for American military operations in Vietnam that centered around three tasks: (1) forcing Hanoi to cease and desist in the south; (2)

defeating the Viet Cong; and (3) deterring China from intervening. To support the strategy and to rebuild the depleted strategic reserve at home, the JCS urged at least a limited call-up of reserve forces.

The Joint Chiefs continually pressed for the adoption of this overall strategy throughout the war, but their recommendations were never fully accepted. As the American war effort grew, seemingly without end, frustration also grew among the JCS. In the fall of 1967, the chiefs even considered resigning en masse in protest over the reserve mobilization issue. Despite their frustration, however, Wheeler and the other chiefs failed in one of their most important responsibilities. They never once directly advised the president that the ad hoc strategy being pursued was sure to fail.

The 1968 Tet Offensive and the siege of Khe Sanh brought about the psychological turning point of the war. They also marked a historical low point in the relations between America's military and civilian leaders. Johnson became obsessed with Khe Sanh. In one of the most demeaning demands ever placed on military leaders by a U.S. president, Johnson insisted that Wheeler and the chiefs sign a formal declaration of their belief in General William Westmoreland's ability to hold that base.

Immediately after Tet, Westmoreland remained confident; Wheeler, however, strongly encouraged the Military Assistance Command, Vietnam (MACV), commander to request more troops. Wheeler apparently hoped that another large commitment of forces to Vietnam would finally force Johnson to mobilize the reserves. At that point, the members of the JCS were greatly alarmed over America's worldwide strategic posture. Indeed, the chiefs believed the reserve call-up was necessary to restore the military's global strategic posture.

On February 23, 1968, Wheeler flew to Saigon to confer with Westmoreland. He informed the MACV commander of McNamara's impending departure and also overstated the likelihood that Westmoreland's long-standing requests to attack Communist sanctuaries in Laos and Cambodia would be approved. The two generals developed a request for an additional 206,000 troops. Once back in Washington, however, Wheeler presented the proposal as if Westmoreland were on the verge of defeat unless he was rapidly reinforced. When a White House staffer leaked the story to the *New York Times,* it was presented in just those terms. Unfortunately, Wheeler did little to set the record straight.

From that point on, Wheeler's influence declined even more, and his advice was virtually ignored. Oddly enough, Johnson in July 1968 requested and received congressional approval to extend Wheeler's tenure as JCS chairman for another year. When Richard Nixon became president, he too requested another one-year extension. Nixon, however, also did not heed the military advice of Wheeler and the chiefs.

Wheeler retired on July 2, 1970. He died in Frederick, Maryland, on December 18, 1975.

David T. Zabecki

References

Halberstam, David. *The Best and the Brightest.* New York: Random House, 1972.

Palmer, Bruce, Jr. *The 25-Year War: America's Military Role in Vietnam.* Lexington: University Press of Kentucky, 1984.

Webb, Willard J., and Ronald Cole. *The Chairmen of the Joint Chiefs of Staff.* Washington, DC: Historical Division, Joint Chiefs of Staff, 1989.

Further Reading
in the Vietnam War

Ambrose, Stephen E. *Nixon.* Vol. 2, *The Triumph of Politician, 1962–1972.* New York: Simon and Schuster, 1989.

———. *Nixon.* Vol. 3, *Ruin and Recovery, 1973–1990.* New York: Simon and Schuster, 1991.

Anderson, David L. *Shadow on the White House: Presidents and the Vietnam War, 1945–1975.* Lawrence: University Press of Kansas, 1993.

Barrett, David M. *Uncertain Warriors: Lyndon Johnson and His Vietnam Advisors.* Lawrence: University Press of Kansas, 1994.

Berman, Larry. *Lyndon Johnson's War: The Road to Stalemate in Vietnam.* New York: Norton, 1989.

———. *No Peace, No Honor: Nixon, Kissinger, and Betrayal.* New York: Free Press, 2001.

Beschloss, Michael R., ed. *Taking Charge: The Johnson White House Tapes, 1963–1964.* New York: Simon and Schuster, 1997.

Brands, H. W. *The Wages of Globalism: Lyndon Johnson and the Limits of American Power.* New York: Oxford University Press, 1995.

Buzzanco, Robert. *Masters of War: Military Dissent and Politics in the Vietnam Era.* New York: Cambridge University Press, 1996.

Cannon, James. *Time and Chance: Gerald Ford's Appointment with History.* New York: HarperCollins, 1994.

Catton, Philip E. *Diem's Final Failure.* Lawrence: University Press of Kansas, 2002.

Clarke, Jeffrey J. *The United States Army in Vietnam: Advice and Support: The Final Years, 1965–1973.* Washington, DC: U.S. Government Printing Office, 1988.

Clifford, Clark, with Richard C. Holbrook. *Counsel to the President: A Memoir.* New York: Random House, 1991.

Coleman, J. D. *Incursion: From America's Chokehold on the NVA Lifelines to the Sacking of the Cambodian Sanctuaries.* New York: St. Martin's Press, 1991.

Cosmas, Graham A. *MACV: The Joint Command in the Years of Escalation, 1962–1967.* Washington, DC: Center of Military History, 2006.

———. *MACV: The Joint Command in the Years of Withdrawal, 1968–1973.* Washington, DC: Center of Military History, 2007.

Currey, Cecil B. *Victory at Any Cost: The Genius of Viet Nam's Gen. Vo Nguyen Giap.* Dulles, VA: Brassey's, 1999.

Dallek, Robert. *Flawed Giant: Lyndon Johnson and His Times, 1961–1973.*

New York: Oxford University Press, 1998.

———. *Nixon and Kissinger: Partners in Power*. New York: HarperCollins, 2007.

Dawson, Joseph G., ed. *Commanders in Chief: Presidential Leadership in Modern Wars*. Lawrence: University Press of Kansas, 1993.

DiLeo, David. *George Ball, Vietnam, and the Rethinking of Containment*. Chapel Hill: University of North Carolina Press, 1991.

Duiker, William J. *Ho Chi Minh*. New York: Hyperion, 2000.

Ford, Gerald R. *A Time to Heal: The Autobiography of Gerald R. Ford*. New York: Harper and Row, 1979.

Fry, Joseph A. *Debating Vietnam: Fulbright, Stennis and their Senate Hearings*. Lanham, MD: Rowman and Littlefield Publishers, 2006.

Gardner, Lloyd C. *Pay Any Price: Lyndon Johnson and the Wars for Vietnam*. Chicago: Ivan R. Dee, 1995.

Greene, John Robert. *The Presidency of Gerald R. Ford*. Lawrence: University of Kansas Press, 1995.

Haig, Alexander M., Jr. *Inner Circles: How America Changed the World—A Memoir*. New York: Warner Books, 1992.

Halberstam, David. *The Best and the Brightest*. New York: Random House, 1972.

Hallin, Daniel C. *The "Uncensored War": The Media and Vietnam*. New York: Oxford University Press, 1986.

Hammond, William M. *Reporting Vietnam: Media and Military at War*. Lawrence: University Press of Kansas, 1998.

Herring, George C. *America's Longest War: The United States and Vietnam,* *1950–1975*. 3rd ed. New York: McGraw Hill, 1996.

———. *LBJ and Vietnam: A Different Kind of War*. Austin: University of Texas Press, 1994.

Hess, Gary R. *Vietnam and the United States: Origins and Legacy of the War*. Boston: Twayne Publishers, 1990.

Hoff, Joan. *Nixon Reconsidered*. New York: HarperCollins, 1994.

Isaacs, Arnold R. *Without Honor: Defeat in Vietnam and Cambodia*. Baltimore: Johns Hopkins University Press, 1983.

Isaacson, Walter. *Kissinger: A Biography*. New York: Simon and Schuster, 1992.

Johnson, Lyndon Baines. *The Vantage Point: Perspectives of the Presidency, 1963–1969*. New York: Holt, Rinehart, and Winston, 1971.

Kaiser, David. *American Tragedy: Kennedy, Johnson, and the Origins of the Vietnam War*. Cambridge, MA: Harvard University Press, 2000.

Karnow, Stanley. *Vietnam: A History*. New York: Viking Press, 1983.

Kimble, Jeffrey. *Nixon's Vietnam War*. Lawrence: University Press of Kansas, 1998.

Kissinger, Henry. *Ending the Vietnam War*. New York: Simon and Schuster, 2003.

———. *White House Years*. Boston: Little, Brown and Company, 1979.

———. *Years of Renewal*. New York: Simon and Schuster, 1999.

———. *Years of Upheaval*. Boston: Little, Brown, 1989.

McMaster, H. R. *Dereliction of Duty: Johnson, McNamara, the Joint Chiefs of Staff, and the Lies That Led to Vietnam*. New York: HarperCollins, 1997.

McNamara, Robert S. *In Retrospect.* New York: Times Books, 1995.

Moore, Harold G., and Joseph L. Galloway. *We Were Soldiers Once . . . And Young: Ia Drang: The Battle That Changed the War in Vietnam.* New York: Random House, 1992.

Morris, Roger. *Uncertain Greatness: Henry Kissinger and American Foreign Policy.* New York: Harper and Row, 1977.

Moyar, Mark. *Triumph Forsaken: The Vietnam War, 1954–1965.* New York: Cambridge University Press, 2006.

Newman, John M. *JFK and Vietnam: Deception, Intrigue, and the Struggle for Power.* New York: Warner Books, 1992.

Nixon, Richard M. *No More Vietnams.* New York: Touchstone, 1990.

———. *RN: The Memoirs of Richard Nixon.* New York: Warner Books, 1978.

———. *Setting the Course: Major Policy Statements by President Richard Nixon.* New York: Funk and Wagnalls, 1970.

———. *The Real War.* New York: Warner Books, 1980.

Rusk, Dean. *As I Saw It.* New York: Norton, 1990.

Safire, William. *Before the Fall: An Insider's View of the Pre-Watergate White House.* New York: Doubleday, 1975.

Schandler, Herbert Y. *The Unmaking of a President: Lyndon Johnson and Vietnam.* Princeton, NJ: Princeton University Press, 1977.

Schulzinger, Robert D. *A Time for War: The United States and Vietnam, 1941–1975.* New York: Oxford University Press, 1997.

———. *Henry Kissinger: Doctor of Diplomacy.* New York: Columbia University Press, 1989.

Shapley, Deborah. *Promise and Power: The Life and Times of Robert McNamara.* Boston: Little, Brown, 1992.

Shaw, John M. *The Cambodian Campaign: The 1970 Offensive and America's Vietnam War.* Lawrence: University Press of Kansas, 2005.

Sorley, Lewis. *A Better War: The Unexamined Victories and Final Tragedy of America's Last Years in Vietnam.* New York: Harcourt Brace and Company, 1999.

———. *Honorable Warrior: General Harold K. Johnson and the Ethics of Command.* Lawrence: University Press of Kansas, 1998.

———. *Thunderbolt: General Creighton Abrams and the Army of His Times.* New York: Simon and Schuster, 1992.

Spector, Ronald H. *The United States Army in Vietnam: Advice and Support: The Early Years, 1941–1960.* Washington, DC: U.S. Government Printing Office, 1983.

Taylor, John M. *General Maxwell Taylor: The Sword and the Pen.* New York: Doubleday, 1989.

Toczek, David M. *The Battle of Ap Bac, Vietnam: They Did Everything But Learn From It.* Annapolis, MD: Naval Institute Press, 2001.

Tucker, Spencer C. *Vietnam.* Lexington: University of Kentucky Press, 1999.

Vandiver, Frank E. *Shadows of Vietnam: Lyndon Johnson's Wars.* College Station: Texas A&M University Press, 1997.

Westmoreland, William C. *A Soldier Reports.* Garden City, NY: Doubleday, 1976.

Willbanks, James H. *The Tet Offensive—A Concise History.* New York: Columbia University Press, 2007.

Wyatt, Clarence R. *Paper Soldiers: The American Press and the Vietnam War.* New York: Norton, 1993.

Zaffiri, Samuel. *Westmoreland: A Biography of General William C. Westmoreland.* New York: William Morrow, 1994.

MIDDLE EAST WARS

Leadership in the Middle East Wars

American political leadership's "default setting" for Middle East foreign policy can best be characterized historically as benign neglect. Yet, North Africa, on the far western periphery of the Middle East region (an area roughly encompassing countries from southwest Asia to North Africa), was the scene of one of the infant United States' earliest foreign military interventions when President Thomas Jefferson dispatched navy and marine forces to deal with the Barbary Coast pirates (1801–1805). In 1816, President James Madison sent the navy back to finish the job.

Until World War I caused the final collapse of the crumbling Ottoman Empire that created a proliferation of new Arab nations, initially under British or French mandate, U.S. leaders generally ignored the region. American expertise on Middle Eastern affairs tended to be held by missionaries and businessmen, not serving diplomats, and until the post–World War II era the entire region was often written off as a British sphere of influence.

During World War II, U.S. and British forces defeated German and Italian forces in North Africa during 1942–1943, while American military support troops were dispatched in large numbers to Iraq and Persia (principally to facilitate the flow of Lend-Lease supplies to the Soviet Union). Yet, these interventions were prompted by the exigencies of defeating Axis Germany and Italy, not in response to American policy decisions deliberately formulated to address Middle Eastern political and economic issues. Benign neglect remained American leadership's Middle East default setting for a century and a half.

As British influence waned (particularly after India and Pakistan gained independence in 1947, obviating the need for Britain to maintain a secure "Arabian corridor" linking the Mediterranean to its Indian empire) and Arab nationalism waxed, American interests in the Middle East focused on maintaining stability, ensuring a steady supply of oil, and (after 1948) protecting the new nation of Israel. U.S. leaders were not overly concerned with the nature of the Middle Eastern governments that they supported. For example, the Central Intelligence Agency (CIA) backed Shah Mohammad Reza Pahlavi's overthrow of Iran's popular Mohammed Mossadegh government in 1953 and the Ronald Reagan administration supported Iraqi dictator Saddam Hussein during the Iran-Iraq War (1980–1988). A regime's stability typically was judged to be more important to American interests than its political philosophy.

Even when the half-century-long Cold War accelerated the superpowers' scramble for influence throughout the Developing World, U.S. Middle Eastern policy seemed to be "leave well enough alone" so long as Israel was relatively secure and the oil continued to flow. However, American presidents did take diplomatic, economic, and, sometimes, military action when those interests seemed at risk or when Middle East instability was perceived as threatening to disrupt the Cold War balance of power. The Suez Crisis (1956), fomented by an ill-advised scheme concocted by France and Britain to use an Israeli military attack on Gamel Abdel Nasser's Egypt in the Sinai to regain control of the recently nationalized canal, prompted President Dwight Eisenhower to end the crisis by bringing U.S. diplomatic and economic pressure to bear on Britain.

In 1958, Eisenhower intervened militarily in the Lebanese civil war by dispatching some 14,000 U.S. soldiers and marines to the religiously divided country. A later American intervention in Lebanon under President Ronald Reagan produced more tragic consequences. In October 1983, 241 U.S. military personnel (220 of them marines) died in a suicide bomber attack on the marine barracks at Beirut International Airport. Although Reagan, who had sent the marines there as part of a multinational force, claimed the "despicable act" would be avenged, the perpetrators (probably the newly formed, Iranian-backed Hezbollah) avoided any serious military retaliation. Within four months, all U.S. military forces had been withdrawn from Lebanon.

American leaders' concern for Israel's security has prompted diplomatic, logistical, and economic actions over the years, particularly during the October 1973 Yom Kippur War. The war and America's response to it presents a prime example of the problems U.S. leaders faced in the Middle East region throughout the 1970s and 1980s. President Richard Nixon, abetted by his secretary of state, Henry Kissinger, reacted to the surprise attack on Israel by Egypt and Syria by mobilizing a massive airlift of weapons, ammunition, and war matériel to the Jewish state. The scope of the effort can be gauged by noting that the U.S. Army Field Artillery Center at Fort Sill, Oklahoma, was stripped of artillery ammunition during the effort, forcing the suspension of live-fire training missions until stocks could be replenished. Nixon's support for Israel sparked diplomatic and economic repercussions that extended beyond the immediate Middle East region. Soviet support of Egypt and Syria incited an ultimatum from Soviet leader Leonid Brezhnev, threatening unilateral intervention on the Arab side unless Nixon took action to rein in Israel (which by the time of the Soviet ultimatum had gained the upper hand on the battlefield). Nixon replied with a conciliatory message to Moscow, yet raised the readiness status of U.S. forces worldwide to DEFCON 3. Unwilling and unprepared to go to war with the United States over Egypt and Syria, Soviet leaders immediately backed down, avoiding a more serious confrontation. This close call, however, spurred Kissinger's "shuttle diplomacy" that negotiated an armistice, with Israel withdrawing behind United Nations (UN) buffer zones. Eventually, fallout from the 1973 war led to Egypt and Israel signing the 1978 Camp David Accords, during President Jimmy Carter's administration.

Economically, the price of supporting Israel in 1973 finally hit Americans where it really mattered most—in their pocketbooks. Spurred on by Saudi Arabia, the Organization of the Petroleum Exporting Countries (OPEC) turned to "petro-politics," retaliating with an oil embargo that sparked a U.S. energy crisis. OPEC's embargo emphasized to American leadership two crucial facts of life regarding the too-often ignored Middle East that would have serious ramifications for U.S. decision makers:

One of the U.S. hostages, blindfolded and with his hands bound, is displayed to a crowd outside the U.S. Embassy in Tehran by the Iranian hostage-takers on November 9, 1979. (AP/Wide World Photos)

the fragile vulnerability of the region's critical oil supply; and the inextricably-linked importance of maintaining good relations with Saudi Arabia, which sat atop the world's largest oil reserves.

While American leadership courted Saudi goodwill, problems on the other side of the Persian Gulf erupted in February 1979 when Islamic fundamentalists urged on by Ayatollah Ruhollah Khomeini ousted the U.S.-backed Shah of Iran and then in November stormed the U.S. embassy in Tehran. The U.S. hostages seized then were not released until President Reagan was inaugurated on January 20, 1981. Suddenly, a back-burner region demonstrated the fallacy of maintaining a benign neglect, "leave well enough alone" policy. The Middle East began to influence American presidential politics.

American political prestige in the Middle East—particularly as embodied in the leadership of President Jimmy Carter—was seriously damaged by the humiliating, 444-day hostage spectacle, while the image of U.S. military power was shattered when an ill-fated Special Operations rescue attempt (Operation EAGLE CLAW) collapsed in confusion (and eight American deaths) at the *Desert One* landing site in the Iranian desert on April 24, 1980. The hostage crisis and EAGLE CLAW disaster likely dealt a death blow to Carter's already weakened, and perceived incompetent, administration. The lesson was not lost on Reagan, Carter's successor, and the Great Communicator's own successor, George H. W. Bush, although the administration's 1987 self-inflicted

Iran-Contra Scandal demonstrated that Reagan could exhibit at least partial amnesia regarding the lesson.

American leadership's Middle Eastern focus remained fixed on the Persian Gulf region in the 1980s, initially concerned over potential Soviet influence spreading into the area but increasingly fueled by worries about the Iran-Iraq War spilling over into Kuwait, the Gulf states and, of course, Saudi Arabia. With revolutionary Iran perceived as both a regional as well as a potential global threat, American concern manifested itself diplomatically and militarily. In 1984, the United States reestablished diplomatic relations with dictator Saddam Hussein's Iraq, reflagged Kuwaiti oil tankers and escorted them through Persian Gulf waters, and continued to provide military support (arms, advanced weapons systems, training, American advisers and contractors, engineering expertise, etc.) to Saudi Arabia. Modern military installations with extensive infrastructure and service facilities in Saudi Arabia, such as King Khalid Military City, constructed with U.S. assistance and overstocked with massive amounts of war matériel (clearly more than meager Saudi forces could ever use), were "American bases" in all but name. Although the Saudis continued to refuse to allow U.S. troops to be based in their country, it was obvious that American troops could be quickly deployed to Saudi Arabia's "forward bases" on a moment's notice. That "moment" came in August 1990.

THE GULF WAR (1990–1991)

The surprised euphoria generated by the collapse of the Iron Curtain in 1989 and the apparent end of the half-century-long Cold War was barely nine months old when events in the Middle East in August 1990 reminded American civilian and military leadership that the world was still a dangerous place. In August 1990, despite claims about "the end of history" and the imminent collapse of the Soviet Union's "Evil Empire," President George H. W. Bush and his advisers were suddenly confronted by Iraqi dictator Saddam Hussein's invasion and occupation of Kuwait. The New World Order with its presumed American global hegemony ran head-on into its first post–Cold War crisis.

Fortunately, the military instrument of power that Bush and his senior advisers could call upon in 1990 was significantly and dramatically improved from the one Jimmy Carter launched with Operation EAGLE CLAW in April 1980. The U.S. military of 1990 was a far cry from that which failed miserably in the Iranian desert only a decade before. The Goldwater-Nichols Department of Defense Reorganization Act of 1986 (PL 99–433), the most sweeping changes to America's military structure since the landmark National Security Act of 1947, profoundly and permanently changed the way the U.S. Armed Forces organized, trained, and prepared for war, and how the military's major combatant commands fought. Prior to the act's fundamental reforms, the Joint Staff in the Pentagon had more than earned its nickname, "Sleepy Hollow," a uniformed debating society in which a single service could essentially veto any action it considered harmful to its parochial interests. The chairman of the Joint Chiefs of Staff was little more than a figurehead, with real power firmly held by the individual service chiefs of staff (U.S. Army, Navy, Air Force, and the Marine Corps commandant).

Iraqi president Saddam Hussein, center, accompanied by aides, tours the front line in Iraqi-occupied Kuwait in January 1991. (AP/Wide World Photos)

Military advice to the president was often watered-down, least-common-denominator pap, shorn of any controversy and, therefore, devoid of any real meaning. The military services' "best and brightest" avoided joint assignments at all costs, considering them career-ending dead ends, and the Joint Staff had become a convenient parking place for those officers whose careers long ago had peaked.

The passage of Goldwater-Nichols changed all that. Not only did it simplify and streamline the chain of command (which descends from the National Command Authority—the president—through the secretary of defense directly to the several military combatant commanders—COCOM), the act established the JCS chairman as the president's principal military adviser. That meant that the chairman became the final decision maker for all Joint Staff actions. Although the individual services could still "nonconcur" on any action, the chairman now could override service objections and approve or disapprove it. The infamous "tank sessions," the long and acrimonious meetings of the chairman and service chiefs to reach unanimous, unobjectionable consensus on even the most trivial troublesome actions, became a thing of the past.

The real teeth of Goldwater-Nichols, however, was its requirement that mandatory joint service (and career-long, progressive joint military education) was a requirement for promotion to high rank for *any* officer. Instead of avoiding joint duty, the American military's "best and brightest" began to seek it out.

Yet, the Goldwater-Nichols reforms merely gave U.S. Armed Forces the necessary structure and organization—the potential—to maximize the military's effectiveness. Turning that military potential into battlefield victory in the sands of Kuwait and Iraq required an effective operational doctrine carried out by leaders who had mastered it. In one of those serendipitous historical coincidences, such an operational doctrine had indeed been developed (although the presumed enemy was the Soviet Union), and since 1982 had served as the basis for training army ground combat units. AirLand Battle doctrine, introduced in the U.S. Army's keystone field manual, FM 100–5 *Operations*, was a maneuver-based operational concept (along the lines of British military theorist Basil H. Liddell Hart's "indirect approach"). It stressed service interoperability and sought to synchronize the combat elements of airpower and land power by training leaders to envision the totality of the battlefield through looking deep—at the army corps level, as far as 150 kilometers (90 miles) behind enemy first echelon units. AirLand Battle training (much of it, appropriately as it turned out, conducted during battalion-sized rotations at the Army's National Training Center in the California desert throughout the 1980s) indoctrinated leaders into thinking about combat and combat support within the framework of five basic tenets: initiative, agility, depth, synchronization, and versatility.

Although the other obvious key player in AirLand Battle, the U.S. Air Force (historically interested primarily in air superiority and long-range strategic interdiction), was often more reluctant than the army to fully embrace a concept largely based upon close air support of ground troops, the doctrine's emphasis on striking deep at enemy follow-on echelons appealed to air interdiction advocates. Moreover, the army's "in house" air asset—its own attack helicopter force—gave ground commanders the ability to employ immediate, close air support while the air force cleared the skies of enemy aircraft and struck at deep targets. Furthermore, because Goldwater-Nichols reforms ensured an unprecedented degree of interservice cooperation in 1990–1991, the U.S. Central Command (CENTCOM) commander exercised operational control of all of his individual service assets. Army–air force squabbling over roles and missions (differences that dated as far back as World War II) could now be resolved at the theater commander level.

After Saddam Hussein's Iraqi Army rolled across the disputed Kuwaiti border on August 2, 1990, and occupied its much smaller neighbor, the American-led military campaign that eventually ousted his invading army would resemble, as one observer noted, "a third world country fighting World War II against a global superpower waging World War III," (Morelock 1994).

In Washington that August, however, key advisers within the Bush administration debated what form the U.S. response to the Iraqi invasion should take. Certainly, Hussein's surprise invasion pushed all the right buttons regarding the U.S.' Middle East concerns. Added to the Iraqi regime's continuing hostility to Israel and its support of terrorist groups was the invasion's destabilization of the regional status quo through its serious threat to the flow of oil with the potential danger of Iraqi forces surging through Kuwait and on into Saudi Arabia. If Saddam Hussein thought his fait accompli would preempt a strong American response, he was seriously mistaken.

The key players who emerged to advise the president during the decision-making process were Secretary of Defense Dick Cheney, chairman of the Joint Chiefs of Staff General Colin Powell, and Undersecretary of Defense for Policy Paul Wolfowitz. Other key players included Undersecretary of State for Political Affairs Robert M.

Kimmitt, a West Point graduate and a protégé of Secretary James Baker, whose mission became an absolutely crucial one: assembling the coalition of 35 European and Arab nations that formed the basis of the administration's effort to oust Hussein's army from Kuwait.

At the operational level, the coalition's war effort was led by U.S. Army general Norman H. Schwarzkopf, CENTCOM commander. Despite "Stormin' Norman's" subsequent popularity in the wake of the Gulf War, he had not been hand-picked for the job, and it was only coincidental that when Hussein's forces invaded Kuwait, Schwarzkopf happened to be leading CENTCOM (naively considered by policymakers who steadfastly ignored potential Middle East problems as a "safe" place for the terminal assignment of a senior general awaiting retirement). During the war, Schwarzkopf's relations with the Joint Staff and his own service were often rocky, as his (secret) nickname among senior army staff action officers—"lard ass"—suggests. Publicly, Schwarzkopf projected a defiant, no-nonsense, Pattonesque image that inspired confidence. Privately, those who worked closely with him claimed he could often be a demanding, stubborn, bombastic, and uncooperative bully.

The strategy sessions of Bush's key advisers, as with all human undertakings awash with competing agendas, reportedly became stormy. Allegedly, at one point an exasperated Dick Cheney snapped at Colin Powell, "I think the president has had enough *political* advice from you; how about giving him some *military* options!" Much of this internal conflict can be traced as far back as the 1984 introduction of the Weinberger Doctrine: six principles laid down by Reagan's secretary of defense to govern decision making for the committal of U.S. Armed Forces to combat operations. Meant to incorporate the lessons of Vietnam, the Weinberger Doctrine included ensuring that a military action had clear and attainable political and military objectives, was backed by a "will to win," and was supported by the public and Congress (later, when an "exit strategy" was added to these, it became popularly known as the Powell Doctrine). In the 1990 strategy sessions, Colin Powell (formerly Weinberger's military aide) became the chief supporter of applying the doctrine when developing the U.S. response to Hussein's invasion, a position at odds with Bush's civilian advisers less concerned with the impact of U.S. actions on the uniformed military personnel who must suffer the consequences.

Yet, the Bush administration went to great lengths during the crisis to project a public face of determination and resolve too often rare in U.S. Middle East affairs, and it was able to achieve strong public support and, eventually, congressional backing. Domestic American opposition, which Hussein likely counted on to impede or short-circuit a U.S. military buildup, was confined to a small, uncoordinated, and largely ineffective "anti-war" movement. Bush successfully used the rhetoric of World War II, portraying Hussein as a "new Hitler" and bashing diplomatic compromise as "appeasement."

While America's leaders hammered out U.S. plans, Hussein prepared his forces for a bloody war of attrition, packing his units into the relatively small environs of Kuwait and the adjacent Iraqi desert to achieve a high troop density behind extensive fortifications. Outside observers predicted massive coalition casualties, tens of thousands by some estimates. However, what Hussein and the less perceptive observers had not considered was that the Iraqi dictator's American opponent had no intention of accepting his challenge to fight bloody, attrition warfare. Had the Iraqi dictator heeded General

Powell's pre–ground war press conference remarks, he might have gotten a clue as to the fate awaiting his army: "We're going to cut it off, then we're going to kill it."

Skill, technology, doctrine, and resolve all played key roles in the coalition victory in the Gulf War, yet serendipity also made itself felt. In addition to the Goldwater-Nichols reforms and the unintended but well-timed maturation of AirLand Battle doctrine and training, global events and Cold War military preparation significantly helped the U.S.-led coalition's cause. The newly exposed impotence of the Soviet Union robbed Hussein of a superpower sponsor, while the collapse of the Evil Empire's threat to Western Europe freed thousands of combat-ready, forward deployed U.S. troops to be moved quickly from their bases in Germany to the Kuwaiti Theater of Operations (KTO) and into all those waiting Saudi bases. And decades of preparation for rapidly deploying massive numbers of troops with their weapons, equipment, and supplies to Western Europe or other far-flung theaters of war—just in case the Cold War ever turned hot—had provided the U.S. Armed Forces with a seasoned lift and transport capacity that no other military force in the world possessed. This "Cold War dividend" of unsurpassed intercontinental mobility made possible a monumental undertaking that not only made the military triumph of Operation DESERT STORM possible, but it became the U.S. Armed Forces' greatest achievement of the Gulf War: Operation DESERT SHIELD.

As Brigadier General Frank "Pat" Cunningham, in 1990–1991 Joint Staff deputy director of logistics (J–4), said of Operation DESERT SHIELD, "We just turned the fire hose on Saudi Arabia." That "fire hose" was an unprecedented flow of troops, weapons, ammunition, and all manner of logistical support that began to flood into Saudi Arabia and the KTO on August 7, 1990. Waiting to bring some order to this flood was U.S. Army major general William "Gus" Pagonis, director of logistics for Lieutenant General John Yeosock's U.S. Army Forces, Central Command (ARCENT). Those looking for a real military hero for the Gulf War ought to examine Pagonis's substantial logistical accomplishments. The actual "incredible desert victory" in 1990–1991 was the Herculean task of moving half a million troops and all their weapons and logistical support to Saudi Arabia, not what eventually occurred during the 100-hour ground war on the battlefield that defeated an Iraqi Army seemingly more interested in finding an American to surrender to than in fighting to the death. The old military dictum that "amateurs study tactics; professionals study logistics" was never more true than in the Gulf War.

The actual conduct of the coalition military campaign, Operation DESESRT STORM, was based upon a plan that capitalized on overwhelming airpower and on the dynamics of AirLand Battle tactics. Airpower and land power proponents still debate whether or not the Gulf War victory was won exclusively by the overwhelming air campaign led by CENTCOM air commander Lieutenant General Charles "Chuck" Horner, that began on January 17, 1991 (1,000 sorties a day were flown for over a month before ground forces attacked on February 24), or whether ousting Hussein's forces from Kuwait always depended upon putting "boots on the ground"; yet, the undeniable result was a 100-hour "desert blitzkrieg" that swept Iraqi forces from the battlefield, or left them cut off and huddling in surrounded pockets containing pitiful survivors desperate to surrender.

Members of the 82nd Airborne Division watch a CH-47 Chinook helicopter as it touches down during Operation DESERT SHIELD. (Department of Defense)

Schwarzkopf's battle plan was designed to hold Iraqi forces in place with supporting attacks and by the threat of a sea-borne invasion by Lieutenant General Walter Boomer's marines, supported by Gulf naval forces under Vice Admiral Henry Mauz, while 200,000 coalition troops executed a giant "left hook" against the western flank of Hussein's fortified line. The decisive flanking maneuver, carried out by Lieutenant General Gary Luck's XVIII Airborne Corps, was egregiously misnamed by Schwarzkopf as his "Hail Mary" play. But as football fans know, a Hail Mary pass is a last-second, long bomb thrown up in desperation with the hope that a teammate will catch it in the end zone and snatch victory from the jaws of defeat. Clearly, this was not the case. The actual plan more resembled a massive End Run (or Notre Dame's famous "student body left") play, a carefully designed maneuver to avoid the strength of the enemy defense by sweeping around his flank.

Executed by bold, aggressive division commanders such as Major General Barry McCaffrey and young, competent brigade leaders such as colonels Tom Hill, Jim Riley, Don Holder, and Montgomery Meigs, all of whom later became generals, the coalition attack effectively routed Iraqi forces, made irrelevant Hussein's intricate fixed fortifications, and prevented the Iraqis from mounting any kind of cohesive defense. Although Schwarzkopf's abrasive, bullying manner alienated key subordinates—most notably manifested in an ugly incident with U.S. VII Corps commander Lieutenant General Frederick Franks—the division and brigade commanders, generally shielded from

Schwarzkopf's worst outbursts, performed magnificently, demonstrating on the battle-field that they had internalized the tenets of AirLand Battle doctrine.

Paving the way for the ground forces phenomenal success was CENTCOM's air campaign. Horner's jets chased Hussein's aircraft from the sky, paralyzed Iraqi command and control, and attritted Iraqi ground combat units in a month-long air campaign, then continued to hammer the Iraqis during the ground war. The main failure of the air campaign, however, was its inability to locate and destroy Hussein's Scud surface-to-surface missile force, dispersed in locations throughout the Iraqi desert. Despite allocating a significant percentage of air sorties to "Scud hunts," air strikes were unable to eliminate one of Hussein's only hopes of disrupting the coalition, that of provoking Israel into an armed response through Scud attacks with the hope that the Israeli reaction would cause Arab nations to withdraw from the coalition. U.S. and British special operations units, operating on the ground behind Iraqi lines, proved the most effective way to find and destroy Scud missiles, launcher vehicles, and command and control facilities.

As DESERT STORM reached its 100th hour—a nice, round, tempting number containing irresistible sound-bite appeal—and with Iraqi forces shattered or streaming out of Kuwait in disarray, President Bush approved a ceasefire that ended the fighting. Despite the dire prewar predictions of massive U.S. casualties, the coalition lost few troops and the United States suffered only 390 killed, about half of them due to accidents. Iraqi casualties, both military and civilian, remain controversial, with wildly varying estimates ranging from as low as 1,500 to more than 100,000. No one knows the exact figure, but the surprisingly small number of Iraqi corpses found on the battlefield argues for estimates at the lower end of the range. Even on the so-called Highway of Death, the road leading out of Kuwait City on which hundreds of Iraqi vehicles were smashed by coalition air attacks and which produced such macabre news images, fewer than 150 Iraqi bodies were recovered when U.S. units reached the site (1,000 live Iraqis were collected from nearby desert hiding places, however). More than 85,000 Iraqis ended the war in coalition POW cages. Twenty-one coalition prisoners (including two women) were returned safely at the end of the war.

The coalition victory was stunning, but ended in a controversy that plagued Bush administration leaders for years and even led to speculation about President George W. Bush's motives for the 2003 Iraq War. The February 28, 1991, ceasefire ended offensive operations but, unfortunately, failed to stop the killing elsewhere in Hussein's troubled country. Encouraged by the statements of coalition political leaders at the end of the ground war, Iraqi Kurds in the north and Shia Muslims in the south revolted against Hussein's rule. Using the remnants of his military forces, including helicopters that Schwarzkopf had been duped into allowing to fly after the ceasefire for "humanitarian" purposes, Hussein ruthlessly put down these challenges, once again exterminating his opposition (and in the case of the Kurds, through the use of chemical weapons of mass destruction). The Kurdish population fled north into ethnic Kurdish regions of Turkey and Iran, where the allies, principally the United States, were forced to mount Operation PROVIDE COMFORT, a massive, years-long humanitarian assistance effort.

President Bush justified his decision to call a halt to offensive operations before Saddam Hussein had been toppled from power by stating that removing the dictator had never been the goal of the coalition and supported it by claims that Arab nation members of the coalition likely would have opposed such an action. Yet, Bush and

Yekmel, a refugee camp in northern Iraq, established as part of Operation PROVIDE COMFORT, a coalition effort to aid Kurds fleeing retribution by Iraqi government forces following the Persian Gulf War. (Department of Defense)

other administration leaders were, in one sense, prisoners of their own rhetoric. In portraying Hussein as the "new Hitler," it became difficult to justify claiming victory in a war that left "Hitler" in power.

A decade after the Gulf War, the dictator that George H. W. Bush failed to remove became a target for the president's son after the attention of American civilian and military leadership was once again drawn to the Middle East. Yet, the "attention getter" occurred at a location far removed from that troubled region; it arrived from the skies over America on September 11, 2001.

AFGHANISTAN, IRAQ, AND THE WAR ON TERRORISM (2001–PRESENT)

The devastating Al Qaeda terror attacks of September 11, 2001—9/11—masterminded by disaffected Saudi Osama bin Laden were as much due to American failures in leadership as they were to U.S. intelligence lapses. At least five crucial years were squandered when the Bill Clinton administration—failing to comprehend that Al Qaeda and associated Islamic-based terrorist groups were, in effect, waging war on the United States—persisted in treating terror attacks merely as criminal acts to be handled by law enforcement. Bin Laden's 1996 fatwa (reinforced by another issued in 1998) amounted to nothing less than a public declaration of war against America and U.S. interests worldwide. Instead of launching a sustained military campaign against the terrorists, Clinton treated the burgeoning Islamo-fascist terror cells as if they were simply organized crime entities, absurdly indicting them in U.S. courts under the Racketeer Influenced and Corrupt Organizations (RICO) statute.

The Clinton administration's reluctance to unleash a major military response against terror groups responsible for the bombings of the World Trade Center (1993), Saudi Arabia's Khobar Towers (1996), the U.S. embassies in East Africa (1998), and the attack on the USS *Cole* in Yemen (2000) was in no small measure influenced by the disastrous Battle of Mogadishu, Somalia (October 3–4, 1993). The nearly 100 American casualties (18 killed, 73 wounded, and 1 captured) suffered in this "Black Hawk Down" action sparked public criticism and raised troubling questions about how a humanitarian mission had been allowed to escalate into military operations targeting Somali warlords (and without vital, life-saving armor support that the on-scene commander had requested). Avoiding U.S. military casualties became the Clinton administration's unwritten policy, as evidenced, for example, in Operation UPHOLD DEMOCRACY, the 1994–1995 U.S. occupation of Haiti, during which American commanders isolated their combat units inside heavily protected "Kevlar zones" rather than risk any casualties by moving freely among the Haitian population.

Meanwhile, Al Qaeda ("The Base") organized, recruited terrorists, and plotted even bolder attacks on U.S. interests. The threat presented by Al Qaeda and associated terror groups is unprecedented: committed, "nonstate" actors combining a range of weapons (from low-tech suicide bombers to the latest high-tech weaponry) with the global reach and power of the Internet, but fueled by humanity's oldest motivations of blood and faith. Uncompromising religious fervor and clan loyalty has produced a steady stream of recruits eager to martyr themselves, while the Internet makes it possible for the terrorists' dispersed leadership to organize, recruit, and plan attacks "online," presenting no traditional "fixed target" for convenient military retaliation.

With roots dating back to 1988 and the "Afghan Arabs" (thousands of non-Afghani Islamic volunteers who fought with the Mujahideen resistance against the Soviet Union in Afghanistan), Al Qaeda consists of terror cells loyal to bin Laden and under his control as well as "Al Qaeda–linked" groups under decentralized leadership operating regionally in countries such as Algeria, Iraq, Pakistan, and Saudi Arabia. Protected by the Taliban regime that gained control of Afghanistan after the Marxist Afghan government collapsed, Al Qaeda found a refuge for its headquarters (bin Laden moved there after his 1996 ejection from the Sudan) and sites for its training camps. From his Afghanistan safe haven, bin Laden planned and coordinated the 9/11 attack—the most devastating terror attack in U.S. history with nearly 3,000 killed, 4 airliners destroyed, the World Trade Center towers obliterated, and the Pentagon heavily damaged.

This terror strike, however, elicited a far different response from President George W. Bush than the previous attacks had received from Bill Clinton. Instead of RICO indictments, Bush prepared to mobilize the full range of America's military power. In his September 20, 2001, address to a Joint Session of Congress, Bush recognized the 9/11 attack as "an act of war against our country," challenging the Taliban government to "hand over the terrorists, or . . . share their fate." While warning terrorists that the U.S. response "involves far more than instant retaliation and isolated strikes," Bush

Smoke clouds and debris at ground zero, site of the World Trade Center towers destroyed in the terrorist attack of September 11, 2001. (U.S. Air Force)

cautioned his countrymen that "Americans should not expect one battle, but a lengthy campaign, unlike any other we have ever seen. A long struggle." In what was likely the usually ineloquent Bush's most stirring speech, he explained, "This war will not be like the war against Iraq a decade ago. Our war on terror begins with Al Qaeda but it does not end there. It will not end until every terrorist group of global reach has been found, stopped and defeated." Finally, using words that were, perhaps in part, intended to be heard in Baghdad, Bush said, "We will pursue nations that provide aid or safe haven to terrorism. Either you are with us or you are with the terrorists . . . any nation that continues to harbor or support terrorism will be regarded by the United States as a hostile regime." Bush's speech marked the beginning of what administration officials termed the global War on Terror. Beginning in October 2001 and continuing to the present, the two main theaters of that war have been Afghanistan and Iraq.

AFGHANISTAN (OCTOBER 2001–PRESENT)

Bush's principal advisers included several who were closely involved with President George H. W. Bush's decision to use military force to oppose Saddam Hussein's invasion of Kuwait during the Gulf War: Vice President Dick Cheney, Deputy Secretary of Defense Paul Wolfowitz, and Secretary of State Colin Powell. Joining the Gulf War holdovers in the group as key advisers were Secretary of Defense Donald Rumsfeld and chairman of the Joint Chiefs of Staff Air Force general Richard Myers. Contrary to the situation that existed during the Gulf War, however, the United States had been directly attacked in 2001, making the deliberations less contentious and quickly producing an American military response in Operation ENDURING FREEDOM (OEF), launched on October 7, 2001.

Much like the 1991 Gulf War, ground operations in Afghanistan to defeat Taliban forces and root out Al Qaeda terrorists were preceded by an intensive air campaign carried out by U.S. and British aircraft that destroyed Taliban air defenses, disrupted command and control nodes, and blasted Al Qaeda training bases. Unlike the Gulf War, however, American leadership began the ground campaign by employing an entirely different operational concept. Instead of massing large numbers of American ground combat troops to fight a war of maneuver on a grand scale, the ground campaign to defeat the Taliban was prosecuted by indigenous Afghani forces, principally the anti-Taliban Northern Alliance, working with small numbers of American advisers from General Charles R. Holland's U.S. Special Operations Command. With British and American special operations personnel, notably those from Colonel John Mulholland's 5th U.S. Special Forces Group, coordinating air strikes, providing advice to Northern Alliance leaders, and serving as the vital link between the Afghani forces and OEF's American commander, CENTCOM commander General Tommy Franks, Kabul fell on November 12, 2001.

Major Taliban resistance rapidly collapsed shortly after the fighting for Kabul ceased, although bands numbering several hundred men each retreated to rugged, mountainous enclaves that proved difficult to clear. By the end of November, the Taliban controlled only 4 of Afghanistan's 30 provinces, and Kandahar seemed their last remaining stronghold. However, public pressure on the Bush administration to find bin Laden mounted, as Taliban holdouts and Al Qaeda fighters hunkered down in caves that honeycombed the mountain strongholds. To increase the pressure on the holdouts, and to locate bin Laden, the decision was made to add significant numbers of U.S. combat troops to OEF. The vanguard, 1,000 marines, arrived near Kandahar on November 25, followed over the ensuing weeks and months by army units, including the 101st Airborne Division (Air Assault) and Major General Franklin "Buster" Hagenbeck's 10th Mountain Division. In battles such as Tora Bora (December 2001) and Operation ANACONDA (March 2002), U.S., British, and Afghani forces battered but could not completely destroy Taliban and Al Qaeda fighters, who continued to hold out in Afghanistan's rugged terrain (or across the border in neighboring Pakistan).

During 2003, Taliban forces, fleshed out with new recruits, many arriving via Pakistan, renewed the fighting as an insurgency, using guerrilla war and terror attacks that continue to the present. Meanwhile, the top U.S. military leadership has changed: Tommy Franks handed over CENTCOM command to General John Abizaid in 2003, who, in turn, passed along CENTCOM leadership to Admiral William J. Fallon in 2007. In September 2008, General David Petraeus filled the CENTCOM vacancy created when Fallon, under fire for published remarks interpreted as critical of the Bush administration, made an early departure from the posting the previous March.

The "American flavor" of combat forces in Afghanistan has also changed dramatically. In December 2001, a NATO (ISAF) International Security Assistance Force (as of

2008, 37 NATO and allied countries have taken part) was established, and in 2006 it began replacing U.S. combat units throughout much of the country. Today, ISAF comprises about half of the non-Afghan forces conducting both combat operations and nation-building in President Hamid Karzai's Afghanistan. Despite the efforts of NATO and U.S. forces, however, the Taliban-led insurgency continues to defy attempts to extinguish it. Early in 2009, the new Barack Obama administration announced a planned increase of U.S. troop strength in Afghanistan, called for additional troop contributions from NATO allies, and directed that US military leaders reevaluate overall strategy.

Osama bin Laden remains at large.

IRAQ (MARCH 2003–)

Those who take the long view of history may be inclined to blame Winston Churchill as much as George W. Bush for the current situation in Iraq. British and French actions after World War I to fill the Middle Eastern void left by the collapse of the Ottoman Empire created modern Iraq and other Arab nations without regard for traditional ethnic and religious boundaries. Conditions in the European-created, artificial country of Iraq (especially the long-held animosity between the country's three major ethnic and religious populations of Kurds, Sunnis, and Shias) made it a perfect breeding ground for strong-arm dictators such as Saddam Hussein to seize and hold power over a divided population, while incubating long-smoldering ethnic and religious rivalries.

Iraq, the other major theater of combat operations for President Bush's global War on Terror, has thus far played out with mixed success in two very different campaigns: a stunning conventional assault that rapidly destroyed the Iraqi Army, captured Baghdad, ousted Saddam Hussein, and paved the way for a U.S.-led occupation of the country; and a smoldering insurgency conducted by Al Qaeda fighters and both Sunni and Shia faction Iraqi militia groups that began shortly after Hussein's defeat and continues today.

Although the two Iraq campaigns bear a superficial similarity to what had transpired in Afghanistan (large-scale conventional combat operations to defeat the enemy's main forces followed by an insurgency), the Iraq War and occupation have shown striking differences in scope, intensity, and even the justification American leaders gave for invading the country. While Operation ENDURING FREEDOM was launched to strike directly at those presumed responsible for masterminding the 9/11 terror attacks and the Afghan Taliban regime that harbored them, no such justification can be claimed for the Bush administration's decision to launch the March 2003 invasion of Iraq. Despite Saddam Hussein's track record of general support of terrorist organizations hostile to America and the West, no direct link to Al Qaeda has been proven. And while U.S. strategy regarding Afghanistan might be classified as reactive, the decision of America's leaders to invade Iraq can only be termed proactive, perceived as a surprising and controversial preemptive action.

Iraqi dictator Saddam Hussein was often vilified—with shocked surprise—for using chemical weapons on "his own people" (Iraq's Kurdish minority in the wake of the 1991 Gulf War); but Hussein's "people" always were only his Baathist Party cronies and his own tribe. The only thing that should surprise observers about his use of chemical weapons of mass destruction is that he did not use them more extensively. Therefore, when Iraq's recalcitrance in cooperating with UN inspectors failed by late 2002 to produce an adequate accounting for the disposition of the weapons of mass destruction the country was known to possess (and use) in 1991, or to provide a full and open disclosure of the status of its suspected nuclear weapons program, Bush and his key advisers chose not to take the chance that Hussein somehow had mellowed over the past decade. If, as was charged by Iraqi émigrés (such as Khidhir Hamza, self-proclaimed "Saddam's Bombmaker," who toured America's college campuses in the fall of 2002 trumpeting his "insider" knowledge of Iraq's alleged nuclear program), Iraq was adding nuclear weapons to its 1991 chemical arsenal, it would be foolish to simply hope that they would not be used or provided to terror groups. By failing to promptly, fully, and openly cooperate with United Nations weapons inspectors, Hussein had almost literally signed his own death warrant. His judgment apparently had not improved since 1990.

Opting for a preemptive strategy instead of waiting for a potential repeat of the 9/11 terror attacks—with the added specter of one employing chemical, biological, or nuclear weapons—Bush and his advisers (principally Dick Cheney and Paul Wolfowitz, described as "a major architect of Bush's Iraq policy . . . and its most passionate and compelling advocate," [Boyer 2004]) decided to act, unilaterally if necessary. Armed chiefly with what would later be exposed as an egregiously inaccurate CIA report about Iraq's possession of nuclear and other weapons of mass destruction, Bush obtained a legal justification for invading Iraq when the Senate approved the Joint Resolution to Authorize the Use of United States Armed Forces Against Iraq on October 11, 2002. Based largely on the same flawed CIA report, Secretary of State Colin Powell addressed the UN Security Council in February 2003, but action was blocked by opposition from France, Germany, and Russia. Although the three UN Security Council members (France and Russia are permanent members with veto power) cloaked their opposition with claims that military action against Iraq would threaten "international security," their real motives remain suspect (France, for example, already had made billions of dollars by illegally circumventing the UN "Oil for Food" program with Iraq). Regardless of their real motives, all three countries had a vested interest in maintaining the status quo in Iraq and little motivation to participate in an American-led preemptive strike. Although Britain joined Bush's "coalition of the willing" (from 2003 to present, 75 countries have contributed troops, matériel, or services to the U.S.-led effort), the absence of France and Germany left his administration open to strong criticism for stubbornly proceeding without broad-based European support.

Bush's proactive rather than reactive strategy was heavily criticized by administration opponents as a sea-change departure from that of past U.S. presidents and slammed for its unilateralism. Yet, as historian John Lewis Gaddis points out in *Surprise, Security and the American Experience,* it is not without historical precedent. He cites the preemptive, unilateral actions of presidents John Adams, James K. Polk, William McKinley, Woodrow Wilson, and even Franklin D. Roosevelt. Yet, with U.S. ground forces already stretched thin by Operation ENDURING FREEDOM, mounting a major, preemptive invasion of Iraq was considered by many, particularly some American military leaders, as risky. Military draw-downs during Clinton's presidency, for example, had reduced U.S. Army active duty strength from 780,000 to about 480,000.

Even in the years before the 2003 Iraq invasion, army chief of staff General Eric Shinseki had clashed with Secretary of Defense Rumsfeld over Department of Defense proposals to reduce army strength even further.

Rumsfeld had taken office in 2001, firmly convinced that technology could replace large numbers of ground combat forces, and he doggedly clung to that conviction. Moreover, Rumsfeld, who had previously served as President Gerald Ford's secretary of defense (1975–1977), often acted as if he were unaware of how profoundly the 1986 Goldwater-Nichols Act had affected America's military culture by eliminating much of the petty, interservice bickering that he had earlier witnessed. Shinseki further earned Rumsfeld's ire when he told the Senate Armed Services Committee on the eve of the Iraq invasion that an occupation of that country would require "several hundred thousand" troops, an estimate that, in hindsight, seems prescient, but which was sharply criticized in 2003 by Rumsfeld and Paul Wolfowitz as "wildly off the mark."

On March 20, 2003, U.S. and British forces (plus smaller contingents from Australia, Spain, Denmark, and Poland) invaded Iraq in Operation IRAQI FREEDOM (OIF). The 297,000-strong OIF force faced Saddam Hussein's Iraqi Army numbering approximately 375,000 men, plus an unknown number of poorly trained citizens' militia. American combat strength was about half of that deployed during the 1991 Gulf War. With CENTCOM commander General Tommy Franks in overall command, the American ground forces prosecuting the invasion were led by U.S. V Corps commander, Lieutenant General William Scott Wallace.

Preceded by a "shock and awe" air campaign reminiscent of the one that blasted Hussein's forces and Iraqi infrastructure in the 1991 Gulf War (although it was significantly shorter than the month-long effort that paved the way for Operation DESERT STORM, since Iraq air defenses had already been seriously degraded during the 1991–2002 enforcement of the No Fly Zone), ground forces (U.S. Army, U.S. Marines, and British combat units) executed another "desert blitzkrieg" that quickly smashed the Iraqi Army. Baghdad fell on April 9, Hussein went into hiding (he was captured in December 2003 and executed on December 30, 2006), and President Bush declared "mission accomplished" aboard the U.S. aircraft carrier *Abraham Lincoln,* on May 1, 2003.

Subsequent events during the post-invasion occupation of Iraq have proven Bush's dramatic statement to be premature: although only 139 U.S. personnel and 33 British soldiers died during the invasion, over 4,000 Americans have been killed (as of this writing) since the occupation began.

On May 6, 2003, Bush appointed L. Paul Bremer director of reconstruction and humanitarian assistance in Iraq and head of the Coalition Provisional Authority. Bremer's tenure (he left in June 2004 when limited Iraqi sovereignty was restored) included several controversial actions that critics point to as helping to promote the insurgency, such as alleged mismanagement of Iraq's oil revenue, failure to quickly restore vital services, the dismissal of Baathist Party officials (essentially, Iraq's only trained administrators), and the disbanding of the Iraqi Army (that, at one stroke, dumped 400,000 trained soldiers and potential insurgent recruits into the Iraqi general population).

U.S. marine artillery outside of Fallujah, Iraq, firing against an insurgent position, November 11, 2004. (Department of Defense)

The lingering Iraq insurgency, initiated by Saddam Hussein's die-hard supporters, former soldiers, and Baathist Party members, evolved into a multi-headed hydra consisting of Al Qaeda fighters, Sunni and Shia militias (conducting a religious-based civil war), and Islamic Jihadist radicals (including Chechens, Filipinos, Saudis, Iranians, and Pakistanis) who see Iraq as a convenient location for killing Americans. Combat actions have ranged from single terror attacks (suicide bombers and Improvised Explosive Devices [IEDs] striking individual targets) to full-scale battles (notably Fallujah in April and again in November 2004, described as "the heaviest urban combat since the battle of Hue City in Vietnam in 1968," [Garamone 2005]).

As with Afghanistan, U.S. civilian and military leadership has changed over the course of the insurgency: Secretary of State Colin Powell stepped down in 2005 and Condoleezza Rice took over, then was replaced in 2009 by Hillary Clinton; Robert Gates succeeded an increasingly criticized and embattled Donald Rumsfeld as secretary of defense in December 2006; Paul Wolfowitz left government service in 2005; JCS chairman General Myers was replaced in 2005 by Marine general Peter Pace, who in turn handed over to Admiral Michael Mullen in 2007; Tommy Franks left CENTCOM command in July 2003 when General John Abizaid took over, and in 2007 Admiral William Fallon replaced Pace. In September 2008, General David Petraeus took command of CENTCOM. On the ground in Iraq, General George W. Casey commanded the Multi-National Force from 2004 to February, 2007, until Petraeus became his hand-picked successor. Petraeus was succeeded in September 2008 by General Ray Odierno.

While commanding the Multi-National Force–Iraq (MNF–Iraq), Petraeus (who previously commanded the 101st Airborne Division during the invasion, then led the effort to create Iraq's new army and security forces [2004–2005]) presided over the Bush administration's "surge" strategy, the influx of thousands of additional U.S. combat troops to increase American presence throughout the country while renewed efforts to train Iraqi security forces are conducted with the goal of Iraqi government forces eventually taking over the main responsibility for protecting the country. Concurrently, MNF–Iraq instituted what it calls an "Anaconda" counterinsurgency strategy designed to choke off Al Qaeda in Iraq and warring Iraqi Sunni and Shia militia from their support base in the population and from outside sources, such as Iran. In fact, MNF–Iraq command attributes recent success more to this new "Anaconda" strategy than to the troop surge. Indications are that Odierno will continue the military policies in Iraq instituted by his predecessor, Petraeus. Although substantial progress was demonstrated during 2007–2008, both Petraeus and Odierno have admitted that the requirement to keep significant numbers of U.S. ground combat troops in Iraq "for years" will likely be the price for establishing a viable, democratic government with long-term survival expectations. As the new administration of President Barack Obama takes over, and with critics still calling for the rapid redeployment of all U.S. combat troops from Iraq (or at least the establishment of a withdrawal timetable), it remains to be seen if the path America's leaders set out on in Iraq, part of the "long struggle" Bush warned Americans of in his September 20, 2001, speech, will lead to ultimate success.

Jerry D. Morelock

References

Boyer, Peter J. "The Believer: Paul Wolfowitz Defends His War." *The New Yorker*, November 1, 2004. http://www.newyorker.com/archive/2004/11/01/041101fa_fact.

Garamone, Jim. "ScanEagle Proves Worth in Fallujah Fight." *DefenseLink*, January 11, 2005. http://www.defenselink.mil/news/newsarticle.aspx?id=24397.

Morelock, Jerry D. *The Army Times Book of Great Land Battles From the Civil War to the Gulf War*. New York: Berkley Books, 1994.

About the Author

Dr. Jerry D. Morelock graduated from the United States Military Academy in 1969, and then spent 36 years in uniform, retiring from the army as a colonel. He is a decorated combat veteran of the Vietnam War, whose assignments also included command and staff positions in the continental United States, Germany, and Korea. His last of two Pentagon assignments was as chief of the Russia Branch of the Joint Chiefs of Staff, where he helped coordinate U.S. policy regarding Russia and the 15 republics of the former Soviet Union. Colonel Morelock's final active duty tour was as director of the Combat Studies Institute, the history department of the Army's Command and General Staff College (CGSC) at Fort Leavenworth, Kansas. There Colonel Morelock regularly taught graduate-level history courses, served as a member of the secretary of the army's Military History Advisory Board, and was editor-in-chief of the CGSC Press.

Upon retirement from the military, Dr. Morelock became executive director of the Winston Churchill Memorial and Library at Westminster College in Fulton, Missouri, the site of Churchill's 1946 "Iron Curtain" speech. He received his PhD from the University of Kansas. A prize-winning military historian, his numerous publications include the books *Generals of the Ardennes: American Leadership in the Battle of the Bulge,* and *Great Land Battles From the Civil War to the Gulf War*. A Westminster College adjunct professor (history and political science), Dr. Morelock is currently editor-in-chief of *Armchair General* magazine, a *Chicago Tribune* selection as one of its "50 Best" magazines in the world.

Middle East Wars Battles

DESERT STORM, **Coalition Air Campaign (January 17– February 25, 1991)**

Operation DESERT STORM, arguably, may well be the first time in history in which a war was won from the air. As brilliant as subsequent land operations proved to be, the powerful Iraqi armed forces had been largely defeated by the air operations of the coalition forces before the ground campaign commenced. The precise execution of some of the air strikes during the campaign, presented so effectively on television, made it look too easy, almost facile. Such success was owing to long years of careful effort, superb training, and a brilliant procurement effort that had been under siege for many years.

When Iraqi president Saddam Hussein rejected demands from the world community that he withdraw his troops from Kuwait, U.S. president George H. W. Bush put together an impressive coalition of powers, including Arab states, to oust the Iraqi Army from Kuwait by force. Operation DESERT STORM, the buildup of U.S. forces, first to protect Saudi Arabia and then to allow offensive operations against Iraq, began on August 7, 1990. The most visible and immediate measure of support came in the form of airpower, when the U.S. Air Force (USAF) dispatched 48 McDonnell F-

15C/D Eagles from Langley Air Force Base, Virginia, to Dhahran, Saudi Arabia. The longest operational fighter deployment in history, this nonstop flight required about 17 hours and 7 en route in-flight refuelings. It was the first step in the largest buildup of airpower in the history of the Middle East. By September 2, more than 600 aircraft were in place, buttressed by U.S. Navy and U.S. Marine air forces and by the deployed ground forces of Great Britain, France, and the Arab coalition nations. Iraq was effectively ringed by airpower, with two carrier battle groups also operating in the Red Sea and four others in the Persian Gulf.

Despite this show of force, coalition forces did not arrive in the Persian Gulf with an air-war plan in hand. The creation of the plan is still a matter of debate. Maverick Colonel John Warden III, author of *The Air Campaign: Planning for Combat* (1988), was called upon to furnish an air-war plan to Lieutenant General Charles A. Horner, commander of both U.S. Central Command (CENTCOM) Air Forces and the Joint Force Air Component. Warden and 20 colleagues in the Pentagon put forward what they called "INSTANT THUNDER" (so named to signal its difference from the attenuated and ineffective Operation ROLLING THUNDER of the Vietnam War). Horner believed that INSTANT THUNDER

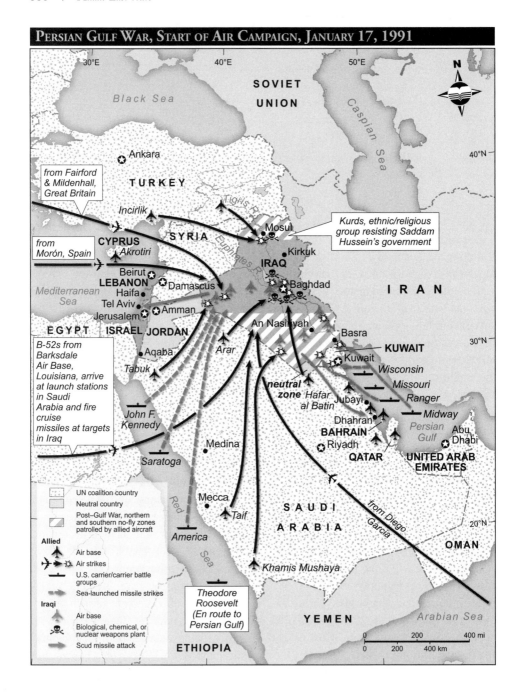

PERSIAN GULF WAR, START OF AIR CAMPAIGN, JANUARY 17, 1991

from Fairford & Mildenhall, Great Britain

from Morón, Spain

B-52s from Barksdale Air Base, Louisiana, arrive at launch stations in Saudi Arabia and fire cruise missiles at targets in Iraq

Kurds, ethnic/religious group resisting Saddam Hussein's government

Theodore Roosevelt (En route to Persian Gulf)

UN coalition country
Neutral country
Post–Gulf War, northern and southern no-fly zones patrolled by allied aircraft

Allied
Air base
Air strikes
U.S. carrier/carrier battle groups
Sea-launched missile strikes

Iraqi
Air base
Biological, chemical, or nuclear weapons plant
Scud missile attack

was insufficiently detailed and Brigadier General Buster C. Glosson was ordered to transform it into a usable document. As developed, however, the plan followed the broad brushstrokes of Warden's ideas.

From Glosson's efforts, aided by Warden's Pentagon group, a new plan emerged from which the daily Air Tasking Order (ATO) could be created. Targets were selected and apportioned to the constituent air elements of the coalition forces, along with recommendations for aircraft types, numbers, and weapons to be used. The air plan called for securing and maintaining air superiority; attacking Iraqi political and military leadership by destroying the command and control networks; severing Iraqi supply lines; destroying all Iraqi chemical, biological, and nuclear capabilities; and destroying the elite Republican Guard units. The plan required history's most intensive air battlefield preparation prior to a land offensive.

Iraq appeared to be a formidable opponent, with the typical effective Soviet-style integrated air defense system. This latter included almost 1,000 aircraft, many of them flown by pilots with combat experience gained in the war with Iran; 7,000 antiaircraft guns; 16,000 surface-to-air missiles; and a modern command, control, and communications system.

The United States and its coalition allies assembled a powerful strike force of 2,614 aircraft. The countries represented in the air war and the number of aircraft they supplied were as follows: United States, 1,990; Saudi Arabia, 339; Great Britain, 73; France, 66; Kuwait, 43; Canada, 28; Bahrain, 24; Qatar, 20; United Arab Emirates, 20; Italy, 8; and New Zealand, 3. Of the total, 1,838 were fighters, bombers, or attack aircraft and 312 were tankers.

Some crucial elements of the strike force were as yet unproven, particularly the Lockheed F-117A stealth fighter. It had been employed without notable success in Operation JUST CAUSE, the U.S. intervention in Panama. Further, there

A crew chief launches an F-16C Fighting Falcon of the 363rd Tactical Fighter Wing at Shaw Air Force Base, South Carolina, during the first wave of the air attack on Iraq in support of Operation DESERT STORM. The Falcon is armed with 2,000-pound bombs mounted under its wings. (Department of Defense)

was no way of knowing whether the Iraqis and their military suppliers had not crafted a defense against a stealth aircraft.

The military air campaign phase of Operation DESERT STORM commenced on January 17, 1991. To achieve maximum surprise, air operations actually began on the morning of January 16, when seven Boeing B-52Gs departed Barksdale Air Force Base (AFB), Louisiana, carrying AGM-86Cs, nonnuclear versions of the cruise missile. These were reinforced by some 100 TLAM Tomahawk cruise missiles launched by battleships, cruisers, and destroyers stationed in the Red Sea and the Persian Gulf. The missile combination coincided with a stealth but piloted attack force. The latter consisted first of 10 F-117As, which took off from Khamis Mushait in southern Saudi Arabia at

12:22 a.m. on January 17. Also in action were the sophisticated air force MH-53J Pave Low and army AH-64 Apache helicopters, the latter using their withering firepower in a direct attack on Iraqi early-warning radar systems. The stealth bombers dropped laser-guided bombs to cripple Iraq's air defense system, their success verified by the sudden end of Iraqi television transmissions. A lethal array of bombers, fighters, tankers, electronic warfare aircraft, and Wild Weasels (suppression of enemy air defense aircraft) were soon airborne in an attack that completely overwhelmed Iraqi defenses.

The ensuing campaign devastated Iraqi air defenses and decisively defeated its air force. The value of the F-117As was clear; they had not been detected by the Iraqi radar, nor had any succumbed to

As seen on U.S. television in footage shot by CNN, the skies over Baghdad erupt with antiaircraft fire as U.S. warplanes strike targets in the Iraqi capital on January 18, 1991, during the Persian Gulf War. (AP/Wide World Photos)

the many antiaircraft shells illuminating the night sky over Baghdad. The air campaign proceeded flawlessly. Every one of coalition commander General H. Norman Schwarzkopf's requirements and every feature of General Glosson's plan were met. The coalition forces scored 41 air-to-air victories during the war and 2 more in the following month. The United States suffered 35 losses in combat while coalition forces lost 8 aircraft, 6 of the latter being Royal Air Force (RAF) Tornados lost in low-level attacks on heavily defended airfields. Twenty-two U.S. aircraft were also lost, in noncombat accidents.

Sand storms proved to be a significant deterrent to air operations, but the single most important factor that distracted planners from executing the air-war plan as originally conceived was the emphasis that arose during the air campaign to eliminate the Iraqi Scud threat. The Scud was a Soviet-developed tactical ballistic missile widely sold abroad. Iraq possessed some 600 Scuds and these posed a strategic rather than a tactical threat. While not accurate, the Scuds could be easily dispersed, and many were on mobile missile launchers. The chief worry was an Iraqi Scud attack on Israel and a military response by the Jewish state that would unhinge the Arab-Western allied coalition.

The United States applied great pressure on Israel not to intervene in the war, but if Scuds caused significant damage to Israel it would be difficult for the Israeli government to resist public pressure for retaliation. Iraq fired its first two Scuds against Israel on January 17, followed by seven more the next day. In return for Israeli restraint, the United States supplied U.S. Army Patriot PAC-2 missiles and prepared an intensive "Scud hunt" that consumed an immense amount of time and resources. Iraq also fired Scuds against Saudi Arabia. Ultimately, the coalition flew some 2,500 sorties against the Scuds and their missile launchers, detracting from the main aerial effort. Through air operations, and significantly through ground operations conducted by U.S. and British special operations units, the Scud threat dropped to one firing or less per day.

The coalition air campaign gutted the fighting strength of the Iraqi forces. In the 43-day war, it flew some 110,000 sorties (a sortie being one flight by an individual aircraft). This effort placed an immense demand on aerial refueling capacity, with air force tankers refueling just under 46,000 aircraft (including U.S. Air Force, U.S. Navy, U.S. Marine Corps, and coalition units) and off-loading an incredible 110 million gallons of aviation fuel.

The coalition flew more than 44,000 combat sorties and dropped more than 84,000 tons of bombs. Of this amount, some 7,400 tons changed the shape of warfare, for they were precision-guided munitions (PGMs) with a much greater capability than those that had debuted in the Vietnam War.

USAF F-117s dropped more than 6,600 tons of precision-guided munitions, with the U.S. Navy and Marine Corps aircraft dropping the remainder. Although fewer than 10 percent of the total tonnage expended, PGMs accounted for more than 75 percent of the damage inflicted on key Iraqi targets. The inventory of PGMs included Paveway bombs and Maverick, Hellfire, HARMS, Tomahawk, AGM-86C, and a few other missiles.

Interestingly, the very success of the PGM may have sewn the seeds of future difficulties in the Persian Gulf. The incredible accuracy of the PGM permitted F-117As to completely dislocate Iraqi command and control capability while inflicting only minor damage on the Iraqi capital. This led to a general perception that the value of PGM lay not only in its lethality but also on its ability to avoid "collateral damage." The PGM made warfare much more refined—and much easier on the civilian populace. In the subsequent Iraq War (Operation IRAQI FREEDOM), the even more extensive use of PGMs inflicted decisive damage on Iraq's military capability but it did not convince the populace that it was—or indeed could be—defeated. The situation was unique in modern warfare. As successful as the air campaign was in destroying the Iraqi electrical grid, fuel economy, transport system, and air force, it did not have a lasting impression on Saddam Hussein.

Nevertheless, the air campaign had a catastrophic effect upon the Iraqi military's ability to resist. Schwarzkopf had stipulated the requirements for the degradation of Iraqi effectiveness that would be necessary before an attack was begun. He later reported that this had been achieved, for when he made his land attack, one-third of the Iraqi divisions were at 50 percent or lower strength, one-third at 50–75 percent, and one-third at full strength. The considerable Iraqi armored force was decimated by "tank plinking" by A-10s and helicopters. The Warthog's performance rescued it from retirement and launched an entirely new career in air force service.

On February 24, 1991, the ground campaign began, its key being a massive armor attack on the western flank of the Iraqi Army, with the goal of cutting off and destroying Iraqi Republican Guard divisions in Kuwait. The ground forces were able to accomplish this assembly and execution in complete security, for the Iraqi forces were bereft of air power, had no insight into coalition action, and were for the most part immobile. American and coalition forces were thus able to achieve a ground victory with only the most minor losses. The decimated Iraqi forces crumbled before the coalition ground offensive and a ceasefire was granted after only 100 hours of ground warfare.

The great coalition victory was achieved against an Iraqi Army that had been systematically and catastrophically attritted by overwhelming allied air power. The U.S. Air Force and Navy had put together a force of aircraft varying in age from more than 40 years (the B-52) to just a few years (F-117A). The air force had labored under funding shortages and procurement limits for decades, yet it managed to field an intricate system of satellites, airborne command and control, stealth fighters, air superiority fighters, tankers (also 40 years old), and airlift as to create a force that was unbeatable. Much was owed to the crews who operated the weapons. Satellites were "tweaked" to provide an optimum result for the combat theater. Ancient aircraft reached new reliability standards. Obsolete aircraft such as the Fairchild (later Boeing) A-10, Boeing B-52, and McDonnell Douglas F-4G Wild Weasels suddenly assumed new stature. Both stealth and precision-guided munitions had proved themselves.

Walter J. Boyne

References

Boyne, Walter J. *Operation Iraqi Freedom, What Went Right, What Went Wrong and Why.* New York: Forge Books, 2003.

Hallion, Richard P. *Storm Over Iraq: Air Power and the Gulf War.* Washington, DC: Smithsonian Institution Press, 1992.

McFarland, Stephen L. *A Concise History of the United States Air Force.* Washington, DC: Air Force History and Museum Program, 1997.

Warden, John A., III. *The Air Campaign: Planning for Combat.* Washington, DC: National Defense University Press, 1988.

DESERT STORM, Coalition Ground Campaign (February 24–28, 1991)

On August 2, 1990, Iraqi forces invaded Kuwait and speedily overran that small country. When Saddam Hussein rejected demands that he recall his troops, the George H. W. Bush administration took action. Washington feared that an unchecked Iraq would threaten Saudi Arabia, which possessed the world's largest oil reserves, and thus could control both the price and flow of oil to the West. Bush, a veteran of World War II, also saw Hussein as a new Adolf Hitler and was determined that there would be no "Munich-like appeasement" of aggression.

On paper Iraq appeared formidable. Its army numbered more than 950,000 men, and it possessed some 5,500 main battle tanks (MBTs)—of which 1,000 were modern T-2s—along with 6,000 armored personnel carriers (APCs), and about 3,500 artillery pieces. Hussein ultimately deployed 43 divisions to Kuwait, positioning most of them along the border with Saudi Arabia.

In Operation DESERT SHIELD, designed to protect Saudi Arabia and prepare for the liberation of Kuwait, the United States put together an impressive coalition that included Syria, Egypt, and Saudi Arabia, as well as Britain, France, and many other states. Altogether, coalition assets grew to 665,000 men and 3,600 tanks, as well as substantial air and naval assets.

Hussein remained intransigent but also quiescent, allowing the buildup of coalition forces in Saudi Arabia to pro-

ceed unimpeded. When the deadline for Iraq to withdraw from Kuwait passed on January 15, 1991, coalition commander U.S. CENTCOM's Army general H. Norman Schwarzkopf unleashed Operation DESERT STORM the next day. It began with a massive air offensive, striking targets in Kuwait and throughout Iraq, including Baghdad. In only a few days the coalition had established absolute air supremacy over the battlefield. The air campaign destroyed important Iraqi targets along the Saudi border. Night after night B-52s dropped massive bomb loads in classic attrition warfare; many Iraqi defenders were simply buried alive.

At the same time, Schwarzkopf mounted an elaborate deception to convince the Iraqis that the coalition was planning an amphibious assault against Kuwait. This feint pinned down a number of Iraqi divisions. In reality, Schwarzkopf had planned a return to large-scale maneuver warfare, which tested the U.S. Army's new AirLand Battle concept.

Schwarzkopf's campaign involved three thrusts. On the far left, 200 miles from the coast, XVIII Airborne Corps' 82nd Airborne Division and 101st Airborne Division (Airmobile), supplemented by the French 6th Light Armored Division and the U.S. 24th Infantry Division (Mechanized) and 3rd Armored Cavalry Regiment, were to swing wide and cut off the Iraqis on the Euphrates River, preventing resupply or retreat. The center assault, the "mailed fist" of VII Corps, was to be mounted some 100 miles inland from the coast. It consisted of the heavily armored coalition divisions: the U.S. 1st and 3rd Armored Divisions, 1st Cavalry Division, 1st Infantry (Mechanized) Division, and the British 1st Armored Division. VII Corps' mission was to thrust deep, engage, and then destroy the elite

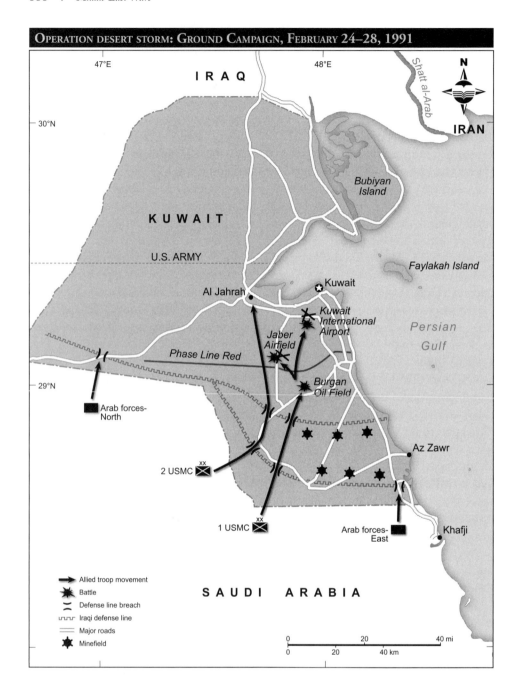

OPERATION DESERT STORM: GROUND CAMPAIGN, FEBRUARY 24–28, 1991

Iraqi Republican Guard divisions. The third and final thrust was to occur on the coast. It consisted of the U.S. 1st Marine Expeditionary force of two divisions, a brigade from the U.S. 2nd Armored Divi-

sion, and allied Arab units. It was to drive on Kuwait City.

On February 24, allied forces executed simultaneous drives along the coast, while the 101st Airborne Division established a position 50 miles behind the border. As the marines moved up the coast toward Kuwait City, they were hit in the flank by Iraqi armor. In the largest tank battle in the history of the Corps, the marines, supported by coalition air power, easily defeated the Iraqis. The battle was fought in a surrealist day-into-night atmosphere caused by the smoke of oil wells set afire by the retreating Iraqis.

As the marines prepared to enter Kuwait City, preceded by a light Arab force, Iraqi forces fled north with whatever they could steal. Thousands of vehicles and personnel were caught in the open on the highway from Kuwait City and were pummeled by air and artillery along what became known as the "Highway of Death." The allies now came up against an Iraqi rearguard of 300 tanks covering the withdrawal north toward Basra of 4 Republican Guard divisions. In perhaps the most lopsided tank battle in history, the Iraqi force was defeated at a cost of only one American death.

Lieutenant General Frederick Franks Jr., commander of VII Corps to the west, angered Schwarzkopf by insisting on halting on the night of February 24 and concentrating his forces, rather than risk an advance through a battlefield littered with debris and unexploded ordnance and the possibility of casualties from friendly fire. When VII Corps resumed the advance early on February 25, its problem was not the Iraqis but the supply of fuel; because of the speed of the advance, the M1 Abrams tanks needed to be refueled every eight to nine hours.

The afternoon of February 27 saw VII Corps engaged in some of its most intense combat. Hoping to delay the coalition, an armored brigade of the Medina Republican Guard Division established a six-mile-long skirmish line

on the reverse slope of a low hill, digging in their T-55 and T-72 tanks. The advancing 2nd Brigade of the 1st Armored Division came over a ridge, spotted the Iraqis, and took them under fire from 2,500 yards. The American tankers used sabot rounds to blow the turrets off the dug-in Iraqi tanks. This Battle of Medina Ridge was the largest single armor engagement of the war and the largest tank battle in U.S. history. In only 45 minutes, U.S. tanks and aircraft destroyed 60 T-72 and 9 T-55 tanks, as well as 38 Iraqi armored personnel carriers.

Allied tanks, especially the M1A1 Abrams and the British Challenger, proved their great superiority over their Soviet counterparts, especially in night fighting. Of 600 M1A1 Abrams that saw

Burning Kuwaiti oil wells set afire by retreating Iraqi troops form the backdrop for a knocked-out Iraqi tank during the 1991 Persian Gulf War. (Corel)

combat, not one was penetrated by an enemy round. Conversely, the M1A1's 120mm gun proved lethal to Iraqi MBTs. It could engage the Iraqi armor at 3,000 meters (1.86 miles), twice the Iraqis' effective range, and its superior fire control system could deliver a first-round hit while on the move. Overall, the coalition maneuver strategy bound up in the Air-Land Battle worked to perfection. As VII Corps closed to the sea, XVIII Corps to its left with a much larger distance to travel raced to reach the fleeing Republican Guards' divisions before they could escape to Baghdad.

In only 100 hours of ground combat, allied forces had liberated Kuwait. On February 28, President Bush stopped the war. He feared the cost of an assault on Baghdad and that Iraq might then break up into a Kurdish north, Sunni Muslim center, and Shiite Muslim south. Bush wanted to keep Iraq intact to counter a resurgent Iran.

The war was among the most lopsided in history. Iraq lost 3,700 tanks, more than 1,000 other armored vehicles, and 3,000 artillery pieces. In contrast, the coalition lost 4 tanks, 9 other combat vehicles, and 1 artillery piece. In human terms, the allies sustained 500 casualties (150 dead), many of these from accidents and "friendly fire." Iraqi casualties totaled between 25,000 and 100,000 dead, with the best estimates being around 60,000. The coalition also took 80,000 Iraqis prisoner. Perhaps an equal number simply deserted.

Following the ceasefire, Saddam Hussein reestablished his authority. In a controversial decision, Schwarzkopf had agreed in the ceasefire terms to permit the Iraqis to fly helicopters. This enabled Hussein to put down revolts against him by the Shiites in the south and the Kurds in the north, at great cost to the civilian population. Hussein also went on to defy United Nations inspection teams by failing to account for all of his biological and chemical weapons, the so-called weapons of mass destruction (WMDs). Ultimately President George W. Bush would use the alleged presence of WMDs as an excuse to send U.S. and allied forces to invade and occupy Iraq in another war in March 2003.

Spencer C. Tucker

References

Dunnigan, James F., and Austin Bay. *From Shield to Storm*. New York: William Morrow, 1992.

Romjue. John L. *American Army Doctrine for the Post–Cold War*. Washington, DC: Military History Office and U.S. Army Training and Doctrine Command, 1997.

Scales, Robert H., Jr. *Certain Victory: The U.S. Army in the Gulf War*. Washington, DC: Brassey's, 1997.

Schubert, Frank N., and Theresa L. Kraus, eds. *Whirlwind War: The United States Army in Operations Desert Shield and Desert Storm*. Washington, DC: U.S. Army Center for Military History, 1994.

Schwarzkopf, H. Norman. *It Doesn't Take a Hero*. New York: Bantam Books, 1992.

ENDURING FREEDOM, Operation (Afghanistan)

Operation ENDURING FREEDOM was the code name given to the American-led invasion of Afghanistan that began on October 7, 2001. The purpose of the invasion was to topple the Taliban government and kill or capture members of the Al Qaeda terrorist group, which had carried out the terror attacks of September 11, 2001. The Taliban had sheltered Al Qaeda and its leader, Osama bin Laden, on Afghan territory and provided the terrorists with bases, training facilities, and quite possibly financial support.

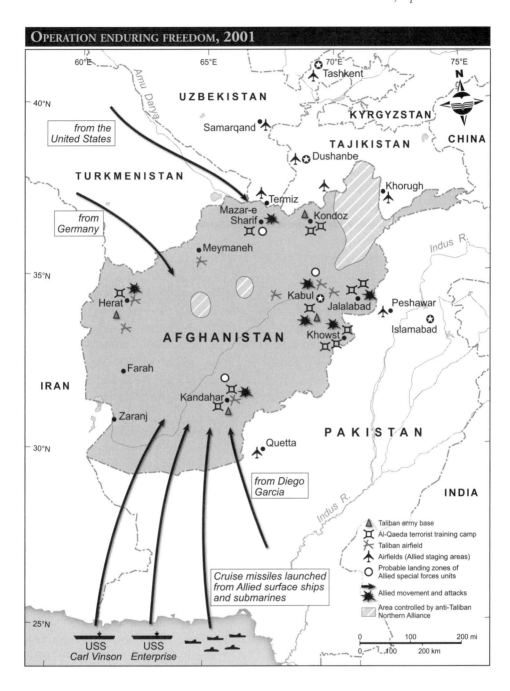

OPERATION ENDURING FREEDOM, 2001

Legend:
- △ Taliban army base
- 🏛 Al-Qaeda terrorist training camp
- ✳ Taliban airfield
- ✈ Airfields (Allied staging areas)
- ○ Probable landing zones of Allied special forces units
- ✴ Allied movement and attacks
- ▨ Area controlled by anti-Taliban Northern Alliance

from the United States

from Germany

from Diego Garcia

Cruise missiles launched from Allied surface ships and submarines

USS Carl Vinson   USS Enterprise

The United States faced major problems in planning a war against the Taliban and Al Qaeda. Prime among these were logistical concerns, for Afghanistan is a landlocked country distant from U.S. basing facilities. American planners decided that an alliance would have to be forged with the Afghan United Front (also known as the Northern Alliance), an anti-Taliban opposition force within

Afghanistan. The Northern Alliance would do the bulk of the fighting but would receive U.S. air support, along with assistance, advice, and cash from U.S. special operations forces.

The war began on October 7, 2001, with American air strikes from land-based B-52 and B-1 bombers, carrier-based F-14 Tomcat and F-18 Hornet aircraft, and Tomahawk cruise missiles. These attacks were intended to knock out the Taliban's antiaircraft defenses and communications infrastructure. However, desperately poor Afghanistan had a very limited infrastructure to bomb, and the initial air attacks had only minimal impact. Al Qaeda training camps were also targeted, although they were quickly abandoned once the bombing campaign began. U.S. special operations forces arrived in Afghanistan on October 15, at which time they made contact with the leaders of the Northern Alliance.

The first phase of the ground campaign was focused on the struggle for the northern city of Mazar-i-Sharif, which fell to the Northern Alliance forces led by Generals Abdul Dostum and Mohammed Fahim on November 10, 2001. The fighting around Mazar-i-Sharif was intense, but U.S. air strikes, directed by special operations forces on the ground, did much to break Taliban and Al Qaeda resistance.

As the fighting progressed, the Taliban and Al Qaeda improved both their tactics and combat effectiveness. Camouflage and concealment techniques were also enhanced, helping to counter American airpower. However, the Taliban's limited appeal to the population meant that the regime could not withstand the impact of a sustained assault. The repressive rule of the Taliban ensured that the regime never widened its base of support beyond the Pashtun ethnic group from which they originated.

Northern Alliance forces captured the Afghan capital of Kabul without a fight on November 13. On November 26, a besieged garrison of 5,000 Taliban and Al Qaeda soldiers surrendered at Kunduz after heavy bombardment by American B-52s. Meanwhile, an uprising by captured Taliban fighters held in the Qala-e-Gangi fortress near Mazar-i-Sharif prison was suppressed with great brutality in late November.

The scene of the fighting then shifted to the city of Kandahar in southern Afghanistan. Because the Taliban had originated in Kandahar in the early 1990s, they were expected to put up a stiff fight for the city. Kandahar was attacked by Northern Alliance forces led by Generals Hamid Karzai and Guyl Agha Shirzai, with U.S. special operations forces coordinating the offensive. The Taliban deserted Kandahar on December 6, and Taliban leader Mullah Mohammad Omar and the surviving Taliban elements went into hiding in the remote mountain regions of Afghanistan and Pakistan. The fall of Kandahar marked the end of Taliban rule in Afghanistan, only nine weeks after the beginning of the bombing campaign. On December 22, 2001, an interim administration, chaired by Hamid Karzai, took office.

Despite the rapid and efficient progress of Operation ENDURING FREEDOM, Taliban and Al Qaeda elements remained at large in Afghanistan, and the operation failed to capture or kill either bin Laden or Omar. Bin Laden was believed to be hiding in mountain dugouts and bunkers located in the White Mountains near Tora Bora. A 16-day offensive in early December 2001 failed to find him. For this offensive, the United States once again relied on Northern Alliance ground troops supported by

Afghan anti-Taliban fighters pray in front of their tank overlooking the White Mountains of Tora Bora in northeastern Afghanistan on December 10, 2001. (AP/Wide World Photos)

U.S. special operations forces and American airpower. Later, there were charges that this offensive had been mishandled and that an opportunity to take bin Laden was lost. Bin Laden escaped, probably into Pakistan through the forbidding but porous border that separates Afghanistan from Pakistan.

Despite the failure to capture or kill bin Laden, the United States could point to notable success in the so-called War on Terror by the end of 2001. The Taliban had been deposed, and Al Qaeda was on the run, with many of its members and leaders having been killed or captured. This occurred despite the fact that the United States had only deployed about 3,000 service personnel to Afghanistan by the end of the year, most of them special operations forces. The U.S. death toll had been remarkably light, with only 2 deaths attrib-

uted to enemy action. Estimates of Afghan fatalities are approximate, at best. Possibly as many as 4,000 Taliban soldiers may have been killed during the campaign. Afghan civilian deaths have been estimated at between 1,000 and 1,300, with several thousand refugees dying from disease and/or exposure. Another 500,000 Afghans were made refugees or displaced persons during the fighting.

The United States attempted a different approach in March 2002 when Al Qaeda positions were located in the Shah-i-Khot Valley near Gardez. On this occasion, U.S. ground troops from the 10th Mountain Division and the 101st Airborne Division led the way along with special operations forces from Australia, Canada, and Germany and Afghan government troops in an offensive code named Operation ANACONDA. Taliban reinforcements rushed to join the Al Qaeda fighters, but both were routed from the valley with heavy losses.

Since 2002, Taliban and Al Qaeda remnants have maintained a low-level insurgency in Afghanistan. Troops from the United States and allied countries, mainly from North Atlantic Treaty Organization (NATO) member states, remain in Afghanistan operating under the banner of Operation ENDURING FREEDOM. An upsurge of Taliban activity in 2006 and 2007, however, necessitated a series of coalition offensives. Bin Laden remains on the loose, and presumably is still alive.

Paul W. Doerr

References

Biddle, Stephen. *Afghanistan and the Future of Warfare: Implications for Army and Defense Policy*. Carlisle, PA: Strategic Studies Institute, 2002.

———. "Afghanistan and the Future of Warfare." *Foreign Affairs* 82, no. 2 (March–April 2003): 31–46.

Hanson, Victor Davis. *Between War and Peace: Lessons from Afghanistan to Iraq*. New York: Random House, 2004.

Kagan, Frederick. *Finding the Target: The Transformation of American Military Policy*. New York: Encounter, 2006.

Maley, William. *The Afghanistan Wars*. New York: Palgrave Macmillan, 2002.

Invasion of Iraq (March 20–May 1, 2003)

Following the allied victory over his forces in the 1991 Persian Gulf War, Iraqi dictator Saddam Hussein defied United Nations inspection teams seeking to account for Iraqi biological and chemical weapons programs, the so-called weapons of mass destruction (WMD). Stymied by Hussein's intransigence, the United Nations (UN) withdrew its inspectors, but it continued its economic sanctions on Iraq, while U.S. and British aircraft enforced the no-fly zones for Iraqi fixed-wing aircraft in northern and southern Iraq.

George W. Bush, elected president of the United States in November 2000, adopted an increasingly tough stance regarding Iraq following the Al Qaeda terrorist attack of September 11, 2001. President Bush asserted his intention to root out terrorism and punish states that supported it, specifically mentioning an "Axis of Evil" of Iraq, Iran, and North Korea. The U.S. government, supported chiefly by the British government of Prime Minister Tony Blair, secured a UN Security Council resolution demanding that Iraq make a full disclosure of its WMDs and threatening force unless there was full Iraqi compliance with UN inspectors.

Although Iraq claimed it had no WMD programs, UN inspectors reported frequent obstacles and only mixed success. Increasingly, the Bush administration, supported by Blair, demanded the use of force against Iraq, although a coalition of France, Germany, and Russia blocked authorization for such action in the UN. Bush and Blair then decided to proceed virtually alone. With strong U.S. public support, Bush secured congressional authorization. The Bush administration also asserted an Iraqi tie with Al Qaeda. Later its critics charged that the administration had deliberately distorted available intelligence and even knowingly lied to the American people to make the case for war. Bush now demanded not only that Hussein be disarmed but that he be removed from power and a democratic government installed.

For some time the United States had been building up forces in Kuwait. More than 300,000 personnel were deployed in the theater under U.S. Army Central Command (CENTCOM) commander

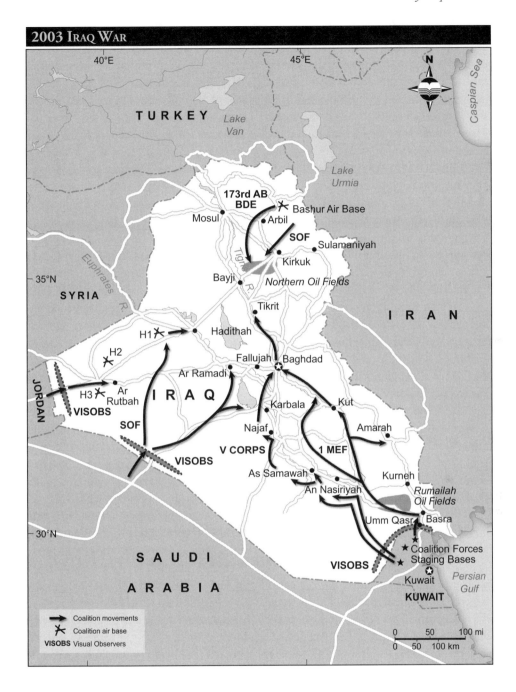

2003 IRAQ WAR

General Tommy Franks. Actual coalition combat strength on the ground numbered some 125,000 U.S., 45,000 British, 2,000 Australian, and 200 Polish troops. Unlike the 1991 Persian Gulf War, there was no broad-based coalition helping to bear the cost of the war. Although Kuwait and Qatar supported the United States, Saudi Arabia refused the use of its bases for air strikes against Iraq. Washington also experienced a major setback when the Turkish Parliament, despite promises of up to $30 billion in financial assistance, refused to allow the United States to use its territory to open up a northern front, a key component of the U.S. military plan. Three dozen ships laden with equipment for the 30,000-man U.S. 4th Infantry Division (ID) lay off Turkish ports. Only after the war began were they redirected through the Suez Canal and around the Arabian Peninsula to Kuwait. The Turkish government decision meant that the 4th ID would have to be part of the follow-on force and that Iraq could concentrate its military efforts to the south.

Although some preliminary air strikes and leaflet drops were carried out on March 19, the Iraq War officially began at 5:34 a.m. Baghdad time on March 20, 2003 (9:34 p.m., March 19 EST). Initially known as Operation IRAQI LIBERATION, it was later renamed Operation IRAQI FREEDOM (the British code name was Operation TELIC, while the Australian forces knew it as Operation FALCONER). The war commenced shortly after the expiration of President Bush's ultimatum to Saddam Hussein elapsed. Over succeeding nights, the city was repeatedly hit with cruise missile attacks and air strikes by B-1, B-2, and B-52 bombers against key headquarters and command and control targets. This "Shock and Awe" campaign did not appear to be on the massive scale that Central Command had suggested. Part of this was the use of 70 percent "smart" (guided) weapons and 30 percent "dumb" (unguided) aerial munitions, as opposed to only 10 percent "smart" weapons during the 1991 Gulf War. Also a good many of the air strikes occurred away from the capital.

The ground war began with the commencement of the air strikes. The movement north consisted of three separate routes of advance from Kuwait. British forces on the far right under 1st Armoured Divison commander Major General Robin Brims were assigned the task of securing the Shatt al Arab waterway and important Shiite city of Basra, Iraq's second largest. At the same time, Lieutenant General James Conway's 1st Marine Expeditionary Force (MEF) in the center and Lieutenant General William Scott Wallace's U.S. Army's V Corps to the west would drive on the Iraqi capital of Baghdad, 300 miles to the north. Major General Buford Blount's 3rd ID, with the 7th Armored Cavalry Regiment leading, made the most rapid progress, largely because it moved through more sparsely populated areas.

In the center part of the front, the 1st MEF, carrying out the longest march in its storied history, skirted to the west of the Euphrates River, through the cities of Nasiriya and on to Najaf and Karbala. Key factors in the allied success were coalition airpower (Iraqi aircraft and helicopters never got off the ground) including Apache helicopter gunships and the highly resilient tank-busting A-10 Thunderbolt, the rapidity of the advance, and the ability of coalition troops to fight at night.

The marines were successful in seizing by coup de main the oil fields north of Basra, some 60 percent of the nation's total with the key refineries. Having secured the Shatt al Arab, and wishing to spare the civilians and hopeful of an internal uprising, the British did not move into Basra itself. They were not actually encamped in the city until the night of April 2. In the meantime they imposed a loose blockade and carried out a series of raids into Basra to destroy symbols of the regime to demoralize the defenders and to convince them that they could move at will. At the same time, they distributed food and water in an effort to convince the inhabitants that they came as liberators rather than conquerors.

U.S. Special Forces secured airfields in western Iraq, and on the night of March 26, 1,000 members of the 173rd Airborne Brigade dropped into Kurdish-held territory in northern Iraq to work in conjunction with lightly armed Kurdish forces to open a northern front and threaten the key oil production center of Mosul. U.S. Special Forces also directed air strikes against the Islamic Ansar al-Islam camp in far northeastern Iraq on the Iranian border.

A number of Iraqi divisions, moved into position to block the coalition drive north, largely evaporated with many of their personnel deserting. Meanwhile, so-called Saddam Fedayeen, or "technicals," irregulars often wearing civilian clothes, carried out attacks with civilian vehicles mounting machine guns and rocket-propelled grenades on supply convoys along the lines of communication (LOCs) from Kuwait north, which came to be dubbed "Ambush Alley."

On March 26, U.S. 7th Cavalry regiment and 3rd ID elements defeated an Iraqi force near Najaf in the largest battle of the war thus far, killing some 450 Iraqis. On March 28, with U.S. forces some 100 miles south of Baghdad, there was an operational pause because of a fierce sand storm extending over March 25–26 and the need for some army units to resupply.

The Iraqi leadership, meanwhile, repositioned the six Republican Guard divisions around Baghdad for a defense of the capital. As some of these divisions moved to take up new positions south of the city, they came under heavy air attack

and lost much of their equipment. The coalition advance quickened again during April 1–2, following the serious degrading of the Baghdad and Medina Republican Guard Divisions.

On April 3, U.S. forces reached the outskirts of Baghdad and over the next two days secured Saddam International Airport, some 12 miles from the city center. The speed of their advance allowed U.S. forces to take the airport with minimal damage to its facilities and it soon became a staging area. By that date, too, the Iraqi people sensed the shift of momentum and an imminent coalition victory. Advancing U.S. troops reported friendly receptions from civilians and with increasing surrenders of Iraqi troops, including a reported 2,500 Republican Guards north of Kut on April 4.

By April 5, the 3rd ID was closing on Baghdad from the southwest, the marines from the southeast, and the 101st Airborne Brigade was preparing to move in from the north. Baghdad was in effect under a loose blockade, with civilians allowed to depart. On that day also, the 2nd Brigade of the 3rd ID pushed through downtown Baghdad in a 3-hour-long operation, inflicting an estimated 1,000 Iraqi casualties. This proved a powerful psychological blow to the Iraqi regime, which had claimed U.S. forces were nowhere near the city and that it still controlled the international airport. It also led to an exodus of many Baath Party officials and Iraqi military personnel.

This process was repeated on April 6 and 7. In a fierce firefight on April 6, U.S. forces killed an estimated 2,000 to 3,000 Iraqi soldiers for 1 killed of their own. On April 7, three battalions of the 3rd ID remained in the city. The next day marine elements moved into southeastern Baghdad. With the 101st Airborne closing on

U.S. marines on a foot patrol in Baghdad prepare to rush a house believed to contain a weapons cache, April 18, 2003. (Department of Defense)

the city from the northwest and the 3rd ID from the southeast, the ring around the capital was closed. On April 9, resistance collapsed in Baghdad as Iraqi civilians assisted by U.S. Marines toppled a large statue of Saddam Hussein. There was still fighting in parts of the city as diehard Baath loyalists sniped at U.S. troops, but Iraqi government central command and control had collapsed.

On April 10, following the collapse of resistance in Baghdad, a small number of Kurdish fighters, U.S. Special Forces, and the 173rd Airborne Brigade liberated Kirkuk. The next day, Iraq's third largest city of Mosul fell when the Iraqi V Corps commander surrendered some 30,000 men. Apart from some sporadic shooting in Baghdad and massive looting there and in other cities, the one remaining center of resistance was Saddam Hussein's ancestral home of Tikrit.

On April 12, the 101st Airborne relieved the marines and 3rd ID in Baghdad, allowing them to deploy northwest to Tikrit. Meanwhile, the 173rd Airborne Brigade took control of the northern oilfields from the Kurds in order to prevent any possibility of Turkish intervention. The battle for Tikrit failed to materialize. Hussein's stronghold collapsed, and on April 14 allied forces entered the city. That same day the Pentagon announced that major military operations in Iraq were at an end; all that remained was mopping up. To the end of April, the coalition had suffered 139 U.S. and 31 British dead. The coalition reported that 9,200 Iraqi military personnel had also been slain, along with 7,299 civilians, the latter figure believed by many critics of the war to be far too low.

On May 1, 2003, President Bush visited the U.S. aircraft carrier *Abraham Lin-*

coln off San Diego, the carrier having just returned from a deployment to the Persian Gulf. There the president delivered his "Mission Accomplished" speech, broadcast live to the American public. Bush's characterization that the war was won proved premature. The administration had given insufficient thought to the postwar occupation of Iraq and long-simmering tensions between Sunnis, Shiites, and Kurds erupted into sectarian violence. A series of ill-considered policy decisions, including disbanding the Iraqi Army, abetted the poor security situation, as angry Sunnis, supported by volunteers from other Arab states, took up arms and launched suicide attacks against Iraqi civilians and the U.S. occupiers. Unguarded ammunition dumps provided plentiful supplies for the improvised explosive devices (IEDs) that claimed growing numbers of allied troops.

The insurgency that began shortly after Saddam Hussein's regime fell—carried on by Al Qaeda and Al Qaeda–allied fighters, Sunni and Shiite militias, and foreign Islamic terrorist groups—continues to prevent the Iraqi government from establishing a stable, democratic regime, while U.S. forces remain unable to fully turn over the security mission to the new Iraqi Army. Although the initial invasion and defeat of Saddam Hussein's Iraqi regime accounted for few U.S. and coalition casualties, over 4,000 American personnel have been killed combating the subsequent insurgency (through 2008). The future of U.S. troop presence in Iraq—its size and duration—remains a volatile political issue in domestic American politics.

Spencer C. Tucker

References

Atkinson, Rick. *In the Company of Soldiers: A Chronicle of Combat*. New York: Little, Brown, 2004.

Murray, Williamson, and Robert H. Scales Jr. *The Iraq War*. Cambridge, MA: The Belknap Press/Harvard University, 2003.

Purdum, Todd S., and the staff of *The New York Times*. *A Time of Our Choosing: America's War in Iraq*. New York: Times Books/Henry Holt, 2003.

West, Bing, and Ray L. Smith. *The March Up: Taking Baghdad with the 1st Marine Division*. New York: Bantam, 2003.

Middle East Wars Leaders

Abizaid, John Philip (1951–)

U.S. Army officer and commander in chief of the U.S. Central Command (CENTCOM) from July 7, 2003, to March 16, 2007. John Philip Abizaid was born on April 1, 1951, in Coleville, California, into a Christian Lebanese family that had immigrated to the United States in the 1880s. He graduated from the United States Military Academy at West Point in 1973, ranked 42nd in a class of 944, and was commissioned a 2nd lieutenant. He served initially in a parachute regiment as platoon commander before moving to the Rangers as a company commander. He led a Ranger company during the U.S. invasion of Grenada in 1983.

Abizaid then won a prestigious Army Olmsted scholarship, which entitled him to study at a foreign university. After a year of training in Arabic, he enrolled in the University of Jordan (Amman) in 1978. Political tension in Jordan resulted in the shutdown of the university, however, so Abizaid used the opportunity to train with the Jordanian Army instead. In 1980, he earned a master of arts in Middle Eastern Studies from Harvard University.

Abizaid resumed his army career by taking command of the 3rd Battalion of the 325th Airborne Infantry Regiment. In 1991, the battalion was deployed in northern Iraq during Operation PROVIDE COMFORT, which immediately succeeded

U.S. Army general John P. Abizaid, commander of the U.S. Central Command (CENTCOM) during 2003–2007. (Department of Defense)

the end of Operation DESERT STORM. Abizaid subsequently studied peacekeeping at Stanford University's Hoover Institution and commanded the 504th Parachute Infantry Regiment of the 82nd Airborne Division before serving as assistant division commander of the 1st Armored Division in Bosnia-Herzegovina. Numerous staff appointments along the way included a tour as a United Nations

899

observer in Lebanon and several European staff tours.

In 1997, Abizaid became commandant of West Point as a newly promoted brigadier general. There he played a major role in suppressing the hazing of cadets. Promoted to the rank of major general in 1999, Abizaid assumed command of the 1st Infantry Division, which contributed troops to Operation JOINT GUARDIAN, the NATO campaign in Kosovo.

Abizaid's appointment as director of the Joint Staff brought with it advancement to lieutenant general. In January 2003, he became deputy commander of the U.S. Central Command, which has responsibility for covering 27 countries of the Middle East and Central Asia. During Operation IRAQI FREEDOM, which began in March 2003, Abizaid served as deputy commander (Forward), Combined Force Command. Abizaid succeeded General Tommy Franks as CENTCOM commander when the latter stepped down in July 2003. At the same time, Abizaid was appointed to full (four-star) general. When he took command of CENTCOM, insurgent violence in Iraq was escalating rapidly. Abizaid had already expressed reservations about poor planning for the postwar era in Iraq and the competence of Pentagon officials in charge of the arrangements. He believed that most Iraqis would not welcome an American occupation of their country and that widespread terrorism and guerrilla activity would likely follow an American invasion.

Abizaid used the opportunity of his first press conference to state that the United States was now fighting a classic guerrilla insurgency in Iraq, an opinion directly opposite to the views held by Secretary of Defense Donald Rumsfeld, who bristled at Abizaid's comments. The contradiction quickly made headlines and resulted in Abizaid receiving a private rebuke from Rumsfeld.

Abizaid also regretted the decision by Paul Bremer, head of the Coalition Provisional Authority, to disband the Iraqi Army, and he advocated rehiring select Sunni officers. Abizaid was also critical of Bremer's de-Baathification policy. In addition, Abizaid realized that the American intelligence apparatus in Iraq was in total disarray. On October 1, 2003, he issued orders reorganizing intelligence operations so that in the future all reports would be passed through a single intelligence fusion center. During the summer of 2004, Abizaid informed his superiors that a military victory in Iraq was unlikely. Instead of pursuing an elusive victory, Abizaid favored a policy of shifting the burden of the war to Iraqi security forces and minimizing the American presence. However, publicly and in interviews with the press Abizaid presented an optimistic version of events, despite having privately expressed doubts. In keeping with his public optimism, Abizaid appeared before the Senate Armed Services Committee on March 16, 2006, and gave another positive review of progress in Iraq. During a break in the proceedings, Abizaid approached Congressman John Murtha (D-Pa), a former marine who had been highly critical of the Iraq War, and indicated to Murtha that his views were close to his own.

Abizaid's retirement as head of CENTCOM was announced in December 2006. On March 16, 2007, he was replaced by Admiral William Fallon. Shortly thereafter, Abizaid retired from his 34-year army career to take up a post as research fellow at the Hoover Institution.

Paul W. Doerr

References

Gordon, Michael R., and General Bernard E. Trainor. *Cobra II: The Inside Story of the Invasion and Occupation of Iraq.* New York: Pantheon, 2006.

Ricks, Thomas E. *Fiasco: The American Military Adventure in Iraq.* New York: Penguin, 2006.

Woodward, Bob. *State of Denial: Bush at War, Part 3.* New York: Simon and Schuster, 2006.

Prominent Republican James Baker III served as secretary of state under President George H. W. Bush (1989–1992). In 2006 he cochaired the bipartisan Iraq Study Group. (U.S. Department of State)

Baker, James Addison, III (1930–)

U.S. politician, influential Republican adviser, secretary of the treasury (1985–1988), and secretary of state (1989–1992). Born on April 28, 1930, in Houston, Texas, to a wealthy local family, James Addison Baker III studied classics at Princeton University, graduating in 1952. After two years in the U.S. Marine Corps, he went on to earn a law degree from the University of Texas at Austin in 1957. That same year, he began his legal career with a corporate law firm in Houston, where he practiced until 1975.

Baker first entered politics in 1970, working for George H. W. Bush's unsuccessful U.S. senatorial campaign. Beginning in 1975, Baker spent a year as undersecretary of commerce in the Gerald Ford administration. He then managed Ford's unsuccessful 1976 presidential campaign. After managing Bush's unsuccessful bid for the Republican presidential nomination in 1980, Baker became a senior adviser to President Ronald Reagan's 1980 campaign after Bush withdrew from the race.

From 1981 until 1985, Baker served as White House chief of staff. In 1984, he successfully engineered Reagan's reelection campaign. Reagan subsequently appointed him secretary of the treasury in 1985. In 1988, Baker resigned from the treasury and managed Vice President George H. W. Bush's presidential campaign and was rewarded by being appointed secretary of state in 1989. In that role, Baker helped reorient U.S. foreign policy as the Cold War ended. He was involved in negotiations that led to the reunification of Germany and the dismantling of the Soviet Union. Baker also presided over negotiations before and after the successful Persian Gulf War. In 1992, Bush named Baker White House chief of staff and manager of his reelection campaign. Bush lost that election to Democrat Bill Clinton.

After leaving government service in 1993, Baker joined the Houston-based law firm of Baker Botts and became senior counselor to The Carlyle Group, a corporate banking firm in Washington, D.C. In 2000, he served as President-elect George

W. Bush's transition adviser during the controversial Florida ballot recount following the contested November election. In 2004, he served as the personal envoy of United Nations secretary-general Kofi Annan in seeking to reach a peaceful solution to the conflict over the Western Sahara. In 2003, Baker was a special presidential envoy for President George W. Bush on Iraqi debt relief.

Beginning in March 2006, Baker cochaired, along with former U.S. representative and Democrat Lee Hamilton, the 10-person bipartisan Iraq Study Group, charged with recommending changes to deal with the deteriorating situation in the Iraqi insurgency. The group presented its report to President George W. Bush and Congress in early December 2006. Among its recommendations was a strong call for a major drawdown of U.S. troops in Iraq. In January 2007, Bush did just the opposite, implementing a "troop surge" in Iraq, which began to show some signs of success late in the year. Baker continues to advise the Bush administration on an ad hoc basis.

John David Rausch Jr.

References

Baker, James A., III, with Thomas M. DeFrank. *The Politics of Diplomacy: Revolution, War, and Peace, 1989–1992.* New York: Putnam, 1995.

Gwynne, S. C. "James Baker Forever." *Texas Monthly* 31 (December 2003): 150–173.

Boomer, Walter (1938–)

U.S. Marine Corps general and commander of marine forces during Operations DESERT SHIELD and DESERT STORM. Walter Boomer was born on September 22, 1938, in Rich Square, North Carolina. He graduated from Duke University in 1960 and was commissioned a 2nd lieutenant in the Marine Corps in January 1961. His initial assignments were with the 8th and 2nd Marine Regiments at Camp Lejeune, North Carolina.

Shortly after his April 1965 promotion to captain, Boomer was ordered to South Vietnam, where he served as a company commander during the Vietnam War from 1966 to 1967. After returning from his first Vietnam tour, Boomer attended the Amphibious Warfare School. He was promoted to major in May 1968 and joined Marine Headquarters, Washington, D.C., as administrative assistant and aide-de-camp to the deputy chief of staff for plans and programs. Following that assignment, he attended the Armed Forces Staff College.

In 1971, in preparation for his second Vietnam tour, Boomer attended the short adviser course at Fort Bragg, North Carolina. In August of that year, he returned to Vietnam as adviser to a South Vietnamese marine battalion. Upon returning to the United States in September 1972, Boomer attended American University in Washington, where he earned an MA in management technology. He was promoted to lieutenant colonel in September 1976 after a three-year stint at the United States Naval Academy, where he taught management. He then joined the 3rd Marine Regiment in Hawaii, where he served as regimental executive officer and as commander of its 3rd battalion. He was promoted to colonel in November 1981 and became the director, 4th Marine District, Philadelphia, Pennsylvania, in June 1983. In February 1985, he took command of the Marine Security Battalion, Quantico. While serving in that post, he was appointed brigadier general in June 1986. Boomer earned advancement to major general in March 1989.

In August 1990, Boomer was appointed lieutenant general and ordered to Saudi Arabia as commander of Marine Forces Central Command and 1st Marine Expeditionary Force, posts he held throughout Operations DESERT SHIELD and DESERT STORM.

Throughout his military career, Boomer had staunchly advocated a separate Marine Corps combat doctrine. As with many marine officers, he had been influenced by experiences in Vietnam, where many marines believed that the army had misused them. The planning and execution of DESERT STORM gave Boomer and other Marine Corps commanders the chance to vindicate their views.

Initially, it did not appear that Boomer would get such an opportunity. Planning for the ground war, conducted in the summer and fall of 1990, did not include the active use of the marines. The original plan developed by Central Command commander General H. Norman Schwarzkopf's staff called for an attack from western Saudi Arabia in which the Marine Expeditionary Force would only breach the forward Iraqi defenses for the army's armored forces to exploit. When Boomer was finally invited to a planning meeting in early November 1990, he vigorously objected to the plan, arguing that the marines should not be used as a mere appendage to the army but that they should operate separately, although in support of army operations, and do their own planning. He wanted the marines deployed along the coast on the right flank, where their logistical base was tied to the navy. After a contentious debate, Schwarzkopf finally agreed.

Between November 1990 and the beginning of DESERT STORM in January 1991, Boomer and his marine colleagues formulated a plan that emphasized keeping the Iraqis off balance by attacking their command and control systems rather than trying to overwhelm them with superior numbers of tanks and artillery. Boomer believed, correctly, that the Iraqi statistical superiority in tanks and men in southern Kuwait was deceptive and that the Iraqi force they faced was a hollow army. Boomer's assumptions proved correct, and the marines were able to concentrate their forces south of the Wafra oil fields where the Iraqis, with their command and control centers destroyed and their intelligence apparatus blinded by concentrated air and artillery strikes, did not expect them. As a result, the marines were able to overrun most of Kuwait and capture Kuwait City within two days of the start of the ground offensive on February 24, 1991.

Boomer's success and the marine performance in the Persian Gulf War earned him considerable media attention and praise from the U.S. media, as well as from General Schwarzkopf. Upon his return from the Gulf, Boomer was appointed assistant commandant of the Marine Corps. He served in that position until his retirement in 1994. In retirement, Boomer has been surprisingly critical of the quality of American intelligence prior to the Gulf War and of the failure to move faster to cut off Iraqi forces remaining in Kuwait. Boomer has served on the boards of a number of corporations, where he has been able to apply his knowledge of management principles.

Walter F. Bell

References

Atkinson, Rick. *Crusade: The Untold Story of the Persian Gulf War*. Boston: Houghton, Mifflin Company, 1993.

Boomer, Walter. "Ten Years After." *U.S. Naval Institute Proceedings* 127, no. 1 (January 2001): 61–65.

Warren, James A. *American Spartans: The U.S. Marines: A Combat History from Iwo Jima to Iraq.* New York: Simon and Schuster, 2005.

Lewis Paul Bremer III was director of reconstruction and humanitarian assistance in postwar Iraq (2003–2004). Among his controversial decisions, accepted by the Bush administration, was disbanding the Iraqi Army. (Department of Defense)

Bremer, Lewis Paul, III (1941–)

U.S. diplomat and administrator of the Coalition Provisional Authority in Iraq (2003–2004). L. Paul "Jerry" Bremer III was born in Hartford, Connecticut, on September 30, 1941. He earned a BA from Yale University in 1963 and an MBA from Harvard University in 1966. Later that same year, he joined the Foreign Service and began a lengthy career as a diplomat.

Bremer's tenure with the State Department featured posts as an assistant to National Security Adviser and then Secretary of State Henry Kissinger (1972–1976), ambassador to the Netherlands (1983), and ambassador-at-large for counterterrorism (1986). In 1981, Secretary of State Alexander Haig named Bremer executive secretary of the State Department, where he directed the country's round-the-clock crisis management and emergency response center.

In 2002, in the aftermath of the September 11, 2001, terrorist attacks, Bremer was appointed to the Homeland Security Advisory Council. Considered an expert on terrorism, Bremer spent much of his career advocating a stronger U.S. position against states that sponsor or harbor terrorists.

Following the defeat of Iraqi forces in the March–May 2003 Iraq War (Operation IRAQI FREEDOM), on May 6, 2003, President George W. Bush named Bremer U.S. presidential envoy in Iraq. In this role, he became the top executive authority in Iraq as the administrator of the Coalition Provisional Authority. Bremer was charged with overseeing the beginning of the transition from the U.S.-led military coalition governing Iraq to Iraqi self-governance. Bremer was brought in to replace retired U.S. Army general Jay Garner, who had been installed only two weeks earlier. Bremer's job, which began just five days after President Bush declared that major combat operations were completed, was to serve as the top civilian leader of Iraq until such time that the nation was sufficiently stable to govern itself.

Garner's leadership has been generally praised but was not without its problems. Under Garner's watch, looting of commercial and government buildings was rampant, including the alleged theft of priceless archaeological treasures from Iraqi museums. Iraqi citizens also faced growing problems with failing infrastructure and burgeoning street violence.

Bremer's first move was to increase the number and visibility of U.S. military police in Baghdad, while making the reconstruction of the Iraqi police force a high priority. Bremer also pushed to speed up the rebuilding of Iraq's infrastructure and to make certain that government workers were being paid. Despite Bremer's efforts, however, violence—both sectarian and by insurgents—continued to mount and Iraqis were becoming increasingly frustrated with the U.S.-led coalition. Bremer was also forced to postpone establishing an Iraqi-led transitional government.

Bremer is credited for making some critically important decisions in his role as envoy. Among these were the removal of all restrictions against freedom of assembly, the suspension of the death penalty, and the establishment of a central criminal court. However, many were critical of some of Bremer's actions, particularly his decisions to disband the Iraqi Army and remove members of Saddam Hussein's Baath Party from critical government positions. Bremer responds to his critics that there was, in truth, no Iraqi Army left for him to dissolve, as that task had already been accomplished by the war. He also claims that his Baath Party purge was directed at only the top 3 percent of the Party leadership. During his tenure, Bremer was the target of numerous failed assassination attempts. At one point, Al Qaeda leader Osama bin Laden placed a bounty of 10,000 grams of gold on the ambassador's head.

Despite the violence and the assassination attempts, Bremer was able to achieve many of his goals. On July 13, 2003, the Iraqi Interim Governing Council, chosen from prominent Iraqis, was approved. On March 8, 2004, the interim constitution was signed after being approved by the governing council. Then, on June 28, 2004, the U.S.-led coalition formally transferred limited sovereignty to the interim government. In a move that surprised many, Bremer left Iraq the same day. After his departure, U.S. ambassador to Iraq John Negroponte became the highest-ranking U.S. civilian in Iraq.

After leaving Iraq, Bremer embarked on speaking tours and coauthored a book, *My Year in Iraq*, published in 2006. He currently serves as chairman of the advisory board for GlobalSecure Corporation, a firm that deals with homeland security issues.

Keith Murphy

References

Bremer, L. Paul, and Malcolm McConnell. *My Year in Iraq: The Struggle to Build a Future of Hope.* New York: Simon and Schuster, 2006.

Ricks, Thomas E. *Fiasco: The American Military Venture in Iraq.* New York: Penguin Press, 2006.

Bush, George Herbert Walker (1924–)

U.S. congressman, ambassador, director of the Central Intelligence Agency (CIA), vice president (1981–1989), and president (1989–1993). George Herbert Walker Bush was born on June 12, 1924, in Milton, Massachusetts, to a wealthy and patrician family. His father, Prescott Bush, was a prominent U.S. senator from Connecticut. Educated at the elite Phillips Andover Academy, on his 18th birthday Bush enlisted in the U.S. Navy, becoming the navy's youngest pilot and

George H. W. Bush, president of the United States during 1989–1993 (shown here in 1989), assembled the highly successful international coalition that drove Iraqi forces from Kuwait in 1991. An economic downturn cost him reelection in 1992. (Department of Defense)

seeing service in the Pacific Theater in World War II. Following the war, he married Barbara Pierce, graduated from Yale University with an economics degree after two and a half years, moved to Texas, and embarked on a career in the oil business.

Bush entered politics in 1964 as a Republican, winning a seat in the U.S. House of Representatives. In 1970, he ran unsuccessfully for the U.S. Senate. President Richard M. Nixon appointed Bush ambassador to the United Nations (UN) in 1971. In this post for two years, Bush fought to preserve Nationalist China's (Taiwan) seat in the UN, an effort that was ultimately unsuccessful.

From 1973 to 1976, Bush held a series of important government posts, including the directorship of the CIA. When he took over the CIA in 1975, that agency was reeling from revelations about its role in assassination plots, coups, and other covert operations conducted in the name of the Cold War. His efforts to rehabilitate the CIA during his tenure met with some success.

In 1980, Bush sought the Republican presidential nomination, but lost to former California governor Ronald Reagan, who then named Bush as his running mate. The pair went on to win an overwhelming victory in the 1980 elections. As vice president, Bush loyally backed Reagan's hard-line Cold War policies. Military spending increased dramatically during Reagan's first term, and the administration provided considerable aid to foreign governments and insurgents to combat communism

Bush bolstered these measures by traveling around the globe soliciting support for Reagan's policies, particularly in Central America. Bush met with Panamanian strongman Manuel Noriega, who had allied himself with the anticommunist Nicaraguan Contras. The Contras were fighting the Sandinista government and receiving U.S. military and financial aid. After Congress voted to cut off assistance to the Contras in 1983, the Reagan administration began covertly aiding them. Members of the National Security Agency concocted a plan by which proceeds from the sale of weapons to Iran were diverted to the Contra rebels. When the Iran-Contra story broke in 1986, Bush denied any knowledge of the illegal operation. Questions about his role in the Iran-Contra Affair surfaced when he again ran for the presidency in 1988, but he nonetheless secured a sound victory that November over Massachusetts governor Michael Dukakis.

When Bush took office in January 1989, the Cold War was winding down. During Reagan's second term, relations between the United States and the Soviet Union had improved remarkably, and Bush continued to negotiate with Soviet premier Mikhail Gorbachev in his first year as president.

In November 1989, the momentous fall of the Berlin Wall ushered in the end of the Cold War. Bush's reactions to the changes in Eastern Europe were calculatingly restrained. He and his foreign policy advisers were wary of antagonizing the Soviet leadership and were fearful that the Soviet military might be employed to stanch the prodemocracy movements. But Soviet weakness and Gorbachev's promises not to intervene led to a peaceful revolution. By January 1992, the Soviet Union had been officially dissolved, and later that year President Bush and the new Russian leader Boris Yeltsin declared an end to the Cold War.

After Iraq invaded and occupied Kuwait in August 1990, Bush successfully put together an impressive international coalition that included Arab states. Coalition troops liberated Kuwait and dealt a crippling blow to Iraqi dictator Saddam Hussein's military. The first Persian Gulf War, Operation DESERT STORM, began on January 17, 1991, with a month-long air campaign and ended in less than 100 hours of ground combat. The war liberated Kuwait and protected Saudi Arabian and Middle Eastern oil supplies but left Saddam Hussein's dictatorship in place. Bush's decision not to invade Iraq was controversial. After the war, Bush enjoyed meteoric approval ratings, but a deep economic recession combined with Bush's inability to offer solutions to the downturn resulted in his losing a presidential reelection bid in 1992 to Democrat William (Bill) Clinton.

Bush retired to Houston. He oversaw the construction of his presidential library, and he has given occasional speeches on national and international topics.

Justin P. Coffey

References
Bush, George. *All the Best, George Bush: My Life in Letters and Other Writings.* New York: Scribner, 1999.
Bush, George H. W., and Brent Scowcroft. *A World Transformed.* New York: Alfred A. Knopf, 1998.
Parmet, Herbert S. *George Bush: The Life of a Lone Star Yankee.* New York: Scribner, 1997.

Bush, George Walker (1946–)

Governor of Texas (1995–2000) and president of the United States (2001–2009). George Walker Bush was born into a wealthy and political family on July 6, 1946, in New Haven, Connecticut, the son of former president George H. W. Bush and the grandson of a U.S. senator. Bush was raised in western Texas. He graduated from Phillips Academy and then from Yale University in 1968.

Bush questioned the motives behind the Vietnam War but volunteered for the Texas Air National Guard after graduation. He became a pilot but did not have to serve in Vietnam. His motives and participation in the Air National Guard, or the lack of it, later became a campaign issue.

Bush then followed a business career. He earned an MBA from Harvard University in 1975, returned to Texas, and founded Arbusto Energy Company in 1977. Although the company failed to make money, Bush himself earned a small fortune. Personally, Bush became a

George Walker Bush was president of the United States during 2001–2009. His decisions to invade Iraq in 2003 and to undertake the war with inadequate troop resources have been widely criticized. Here Bush greets returning soldiers at Fort Campbell, Kentucky, in November 2008. (Department of Defense)

born-again Christian in 1986 and quit drinking. He served as a staffer during his father's successful 1988 presidential campaign. He also became the owner and managing partner of the Texas Rangers.

In 1994, Bush ran for the Texas governorship and won. As governor, he kept his promise to work with the Democratic-dominated legislature, while reducing state control and taxes. In 1996, he won reelection by a large margin.

By 1999, Bush was clearly preparing to run for president. Campaigning as a "compassionate conservative," he easily won the 2000 Republican nomination. Once again, he laid out a platform of specific policies designed to appeal to moderates. These included tax reductions, improved schools, Social Security reform, and increased military spending. On foreign policy, Bush downplayed his obvious lack of experience.

After one of the most contentious presidential elections in American history, and protracted vote recounts and court decisions, a deeply divided U.S. Supreme Court finally halted the recounts, virtually declaring Bush the winner. Initially, Bush concentrated on securing a large tax cut, hoping to spur the economy. His cabinet members and advisers were trusted, long-term associates (some of whom had served his father), including Colin Powell as secretary of state, Condoleezza Rice as national security adviser, and Donald Rumsfeld as secretary of defense. His vice president, Dick Cheney, had been secretary of defense for George H. W. Bush in the early 1990s.

The course of Bush's presidency was forever changed on September 11, 2001, when a group of 19 Islamic extremist hijackers seized 4 commercial airliners. Two were flown into the World Trade Center, another into the Pentagon, while the fourth went down on its way to a target in Washington, D.C. The World Trade Center twin towers were destroyed, with more than 3,000 people killed. Over the next few days, Bush visited the scenes of the attacks, reassuring the public and promising to bring those responsible to justice.

On September 20, Bush appeared before Congress, on national television, and accused the terrorist network Al Qaeda of carrying out the attacks. The president warned the American people that they faced a lengthy war against terrorism. Bush demanded that Afghanistan's Taliban government surrender the members of Al Qaeda in their country or face retribution. When the Taliban failed to comply, American and British forces began a bombing campaign on October 7 (Operation ENDURING FREEDOM). Indigenous forces, with heavy American support, defeated the Taliban by mid-November. Taliban resistance continued in the rugged parts of the country, but a multinational coalition was able to concentrate on establishing a new government and rebuilding Afghanistan.

While efforts were being made to capture Al Qaeda leaders, the Bush administration also sought to improve national security. A new Department of Homeland Security was created in 2002 to coordinate all agencies that could track and defeat terrorist attacks. The U.S. Patriot Act was passed by Congress on October 26, 2001, giving the federal government unprecedented powers to obtain intelligence about and detain those suspected

of wishing to harm the United States. Many were uncomfortable with this legislation and feared that it would do more to undermine American freedom than any terrorist attack.

During 2002, the Bush administration turned its attentions to Iraq. Intelligence reports were released indicating that Iraqi dictator Saddam Hussein was continuing to pursue a program to develop weapons of mass destruction (WMDs). When Bush demanded that Hussein comply with United Nations resolutions concerning inspection of certain facilities, Hussein refused. By the end of 2002, the Bush administration had formulated a new policy of preemptive warfare, known as the Bush Doctrine, to destroy regimes that intended to do harm to the United States before they were able to do so. In justification, Bush pointed out that it made no sense to suffer an attack by WMDs if military action could prevent it. By the beginning of 2003, a military buildup against Iraq was in place. However, Bush's efforts to create a multinational coalition failed to achieve the success of his father in Operation DESERT STORM in 1991. Although nearly 30 other countries eventually contributed troops, the vast majority of the forces were American.

On March 17, 2003, Bush demanded that Hussein and his sons leave Iraq or face the consequences. When they failed to respond, military operations began two days later (Operation IRAQI FREEDOM). Although American forces faced fierce resistance in the first days of the war, Baghdad fell by April 9. At that point, organized resistance was minimal. Iraq was plagued by social unrest over the next few weeks, however, and different religious and ethnic groups came into conflict. Although American military forces were able to overthrow the Hussein regime, they were not prepared to restore order. Opponents criticized Bush and his advisers for failing to provide enough troops to prevent the disorder and secure weapons and infrastructure.

Although efforts were soon underway to create a new Iraqi government, a vicious insurgency broke out. Far more American troops were killed trying to keep order in Iraq after May 2003 than died in the conventional fighting. The reconstruction of the country and the restoration of vital services were slowed by the fighting.

Although Bush was reelected president in 2004, critics called for the removal of American forces and for an investigation of the grounds on which he launched an invasion of Iraq. The failure to find any WMDs in Iraq undercut the stated reason for the attack.

By 2006, the main focus of the Bush administration remained the War on Terror and in Iraq. Many domestic initiatives were slowed by the lack of funds drained away by war. Although support for American soldiers remained high, public confidence in Bush's policies reached new lows. Many feared that Iraq would become another Vietnam. The Republicans lost control of Congress in the November 2006 elections largely because of Bush's dismal approval ratings and the war in Iraq. In 2007, there were several initiatives to institute benchmarks for American withdrawal from Iraq. While these did finally pass by thin margins in the House and the Senate, Bush vetoed them. While there was much talk of it, another such bill did not pass, and Bush's approval ratings remained very low, despite signs of progress in Iraq in the last months of 2007 and early 2008. He was succeeded in office by Barack Obama.

Tim Watts

References

Daalder, Ivo H., and James M. Lindsay. *America Unbound: The Bush Revolution in Foreign Policy.* Washington, DC: Brookings Institution, 2003.

Dean, John W. *Worse Than Watergate: The Secret Presidency of George W. Bush.* New York: Little, Brown and Co., 2004.

Woodward, Bob. *Bush at War.* New York: Simon and Schuster, 2002.

———. *Plan of Attack.* New York: Simon and Schuster, 2004.

———. *State of Denial: Bush at War, Part III.* New York: Simon and Schuster, 2006.

Casey, George William, Jr. (1948–)

U.S. Army general and commander of U.S. forces in Iraq (Multinational Force–Iraq; 2004–2007). George William Casey Jr. was born on July 22, 1948, in Sendai, Japan; his father, a career army officer, was serving with the army occupation forces there. He spent his early life on army posts throughout the United States and Europe and graduated from Georgetown University in 1970, where he was enrolled in the Army Reserve Officer Training Corps (ROTC).

In August 1970, Casey was commissioned a 2nd lieutenant in the army. During the next decade, he served in a variety of command and staff positions. In 1980, he earned an MA in International Relations from the University of Denver. Casey continued his military education at the Armed Forces Staff College, completing his studies there in July 1981.

Shortly thereafter, Casey was ordered to the Middle East, where he worked with the United Nations Truce Observer Supervision Organization. From February 1982 to July 1987, he was assigned to the 4th Infantry Division based at Fort Carson, Colorado. In December 1989, he became a special assistant to the army chief of staff. He was then assigned as chief of staff to the 1st Cavalry Division at Fort Hood, Texas, where he later commanded that division's 3rd brigade. In July 1996, he was promoted to brigadier general and sent to Europe, where he served as assistant division commander for the 1st Armored Division in Germany and participated in the peacekeeping missions to Bosnia and Herzegovina.

In 1999, following his advancement to major general, Casey commanded the 1st Armored until July 2001. At the end of October 2001, he was appointed lieutenant general and took control of strategic plans and policy for the Joint Chiefs of Staff. In January 2003, he became director, Joint Staff of the Joint Chiefs of Staff. That October, he became vice chief of staff of the army and was advanced to four-star rank.

Casey became a major figure in planning for the U.S. response to the terrorist attacks of September 11, 2001, and for the 2003 invasion of Iraq. As director of the Joint Staff, he had been directly involved in the allocation of units and personnel for the Iraq operation. One of his assignments was the allocation of military personnel for administration in the occupied areas. In December 2002, with planning for the invasion in full swing, Casey ordered the formation of a follow-on headquarters for the postwar occupation but gave it few resources. It was in his capacity as director of the Joint Staff that Casey first encountered conflict over troop levels for the impending invasion, which occurred between the field commanders and Secretary of Defense Donald Rumsfeld.

Conditions in Iraq in the wake of the March 2003 invasion became central to Casey's fortunes. For all of his success,

Casey had attracted little notice outside military circles. This changed when he was assigned to head the commission to investigate the abuse of prisoners by American guards at Abu Graib Prison in late 2003.

In the summer of 2004, Casey was appointed to command U.S. and coalition forces (Multinational Force–Iraq). By the time Casey took command, the Iraqi insurgency was in full swing, but the coalition response had been hampered by fundamental conflicts over strategy and tactics between the civilian commissioner in Iraq, L. Paul Bremer, and the military commander, General Ricardo Sanchez. Casey soon established a cordial working relationship with the new American ambassador to Iraq, John Negroponte.

Such a relationship was needed in the desperate situation the two men faced in 2004. Casey was shocked to discover that there was no counterinsurgency strategy. He and Negroponte thus worked to develop a coherent approach to combating the growing attacks on American forces and the threat of civil war. Casey's strategy involved securing transportation infrastructure, containing insurgent violence by aggressively attacking insurgent bases, reaching out to Iraq's Sunni Muslims, and building up Iraqi security forces. Under Casey's direction, U.S. counterinsurgency operations took on a clearer direction, but violence in Iraq continued to escalate, and the war grew increasingly unpopular in the United States.

In March 2007, Casey turned over his command to Lieutenant General David Petraeus and returned to the United States to assume the post of U.S. Army chief of staff. Casey was cautious but noncommittal in his support of the troop surge implemented by the George W. Bush administration in January 2007. He also warned that U.S. Army resources were being stretched dangerously thin.

Walter F. Bell

References

Gordon, Michael R., and General Bernard E. Trainor. *Cobra II: The Inside Story of the Invasion and Occupation of Iraq.* New York: Random House, 2006.

Ricks, Thomas E. *Fiasco: The American Military Adventure in Iraq.* New York: Penguin Press, 2006.

Woodward, Bob. *State of Denial: Bush at War, Part III.* New York: Simon and Schuster, 2006.

Cheney, Richard Bruce (1941–)

Politician, businessman, secretary of defense (1989–1993), and vice president (2001–2009). Richard Bruce (Dick) Cheney was born on January 30, 1941, in Lincoln, Nebraska. He grew up in Casper, Wyoming, and was educated at the University of Wyoming, earning a BA degree in 1965 and an MA in political science in 1966. He completed advanced graduate study there and was a PhD candidate in 1968.

Cheney acquired his first governmental position in 1969, when he became the special assistant to the director of the Office of Economic Opportunity. He served as a White House staff assistant in 1970 and 1971 and as assistant director of the Cost of Living Council from 1971 to 1973. He briefly worked in the private sector as the vice president of an investment advisory firm. In 1974, he returned to government service as President Gerald R. Ford's deputy assistant. In 1975, Ford appointed Cheney as White House chief of staff.

In 1978, Cheney was elected to the U.S. House of Representatives, serving six terms. He was elected House minority whip in December 1988. Cheney was known for his conservative votes: he opposed gun control, environmental laws, and funding for Head Start.

Cheney became secretary of defense on March 21, 1989, in the George H. W. Bush administration. In this position, Cheney significantly reduced U.S. military budgets and canceled several major weapons programs as the end of the Cold War fueled increasing pressure for a military drawdown. In addition, he was deeply involved in the politically volatile task of reducing the size of the American military force throughout the world. Cheney also recommended closing or reducing in size many U.S. military installations, despite intense criticism from elected officials whose districts would be adversely impacted by the closures.

Republican Richard Cheney served as secretary of defense during the 1991 Persian Gulf War. A highly controversial yet powerful vice president of the United States during 2001–2009, he was a prime mover behind the decision to invade Iraq in 2003. (The White House)

As secretary of defense, Cheney also provided strong leadership in several international military engagements, including the December 1989 Panama invasion and the humanitarian mission to Somalia in early 1992. It was Cheney who secured the appointment of General Colin Powell as chairman of the Joint Chiefs of Staff in 1989.

Cheney's most difficult military challenge came during the 1991 Persian Gulf War. He secured Saudi permission to begin a military buildup there that would include a United Nations (UN) international coalition of troops. The buildup proceeded in the fall of 1990 as Operation DESERT SHIELD. When economic sanctions and other measures failed to remove the Iraqis from Kuwait, the Persian Gulf War commenced with Operation DESERT STORM on January 16, 1991. A five-week air offensive was followed by the movement of ground forces into Kuwait and Iraq on February 24, 1991. Within four days, the UN coalition had liberated Kuwait. Cheney continued as secretary of defense until January 20, 1993, when Democrat Bill Clinton took office.

Upon leaving the Pentagon, Cheney joined the American Enterprise Institute as a senior fellow. He also became president and chief executive officer of the Halliburton Company in October 1995 and chairman of its board in February 2000.

Only months later, Republican presidential candidate George W. Bush chose Cheney as his vice presidential running mate. After a hard-fought campaign, the Bush-Cheney ticket won the White House in December 2000, although only after a court fight and having lost the popular vote.

Arguably one of the more powerful vice presidents in U.S. history, Cheney endured much criticism for his hawkish views (he is believed to have strongly promoted the 2003 Iraq War) and his connections to the oil and energy industry (Halliburton won several contracts for work in postwar Iraq). He also raised eyebrows by refusing to make public the records of the national energy task force he established to form the administration's energy initiatives.

Many people who knew Cheney personally have asserted that he became a changed man after the September 11 terrorist attacks. As one of the principal promoters of the U.S. invasion of Iraq (Operation IRAQI FREEDOM), which began in March 2003, Cheney was well placed to receive the burden of criticism when the war began to go badly in 2004. As the subsequent Iraqi insurgency increased in size, scope, and violence, Cheney's popularity plummeted. Following the 2006 midterm elections, which caused the Republicans to lose control of Congress principally because of the war in Iraq, Cheney took a far lower profile. When his fellow neoconservative Donald Rumsfeld, the secretary of defense, resigned in the election's aftermath, Cheney was increasingly perceived as a liability to the Bush White House, which was under intense pressure to change course in Iraq or quit it altogether.

Cheney did not help his approval ratings when he accidentally shot a friend during a hunting trip in February 2006. Even more damaging to Cheney was the indictment and conviction of his chief of staff, I. Lewis "Scooter" Libby, for his involvement in the Valerie Plame–Wilson–CIA leak case. Some alleged that it was Cheney who first leaked the classified information to Libby and perhaps others, who in turn leaked it to the press. Cheney continued to keep a remarkably low profile. Beginning in 2007, a small group of Democrats in the House attempted to introduce impeachment proceedings against Cheney, but such efforts did not make it out of committee.

Spencer C. Tucker

References

Nichols, John. *The Rise and Rise of Richard B. Cheney: Unlocking the Mysteries of the Most Powerful Vice President in American History.* New York: The New Press, 2005.

Woodward, Bob. *State of Denial: Bush at War, Part III.* New York: Simon and Schuster, 2006.

———. *Bush at War.* New York: Simon and Schuster, 2002.

———. *Plan of Attack.* New York: Simon and Schuster, 2004.

Fallon, William Joseph (1944–)

U.S. Navy officer and commander, U.S. Central Command (CENTCOM) during 2007–2008. William Joseph "Fox" Fallon was born in East Orange, New Jersey, on December 30, 1944, and grew up in Merchantville, New Jersey. He was commissioned in the U.S. Navy through the Navy Reserve Officers' Training Corps (ROTC) Program after graduating from Villanova University in 1967. That December, he completed flight training and became a naval aviator. He later graduated from the Naval War College, Newport, Rhode Island, and the National War College, Washington, D.C. Fallon also earned a master of arts degree in International Studies from Old Dominion University in 1982.

Fallon's career as a naval aviator spanned 24 years, with service in attack squadrons and carrier air wings. He logged more than 1,300 carrier-arrested landings and 4,800 flight hours. Fallon began his career in naval aviation flying an RA-5C Vigilante in Vietnam, later moving on to pilot the A-6 Intruder beginning in 1974. Fallon served in the Mediterranean and the Atlantic, Pacific, and Indian oceans on the carriers *Saratoga, Ranger, Nimitz, Dwight D. Eisenhower,* and *Theodore Roosevelt.*

Fallon's commands included Attack Squadron 65, deployed aboard the *Dwight D. Eisenhower* (May 3, 1984–September 5, 1985); Medium Attack Wing One at Naval Air Station, Oceana, Virginia; Carrier Air Wing Eight, aboard the *Theodore Roosevelt* deployed in the Persian Gulf during Operations DESERT SHIELD and DESERT STORM (Fallon led 80 strike air missions into Iraq and Kuwait) during August 1990–February 1991; Carrier Group Eight (1995); Battle Force Sixth Fleet as part of *Theodore Roosevelt* Battle Group during the North Atlantic Treaty Organization's combat Operation DELIBERATE FORCE (August 29–September 14, 1995) in Bosnia; and Second Fleet and Striking Fleet Atlantic (November 1997–September 2000).

Fallon held numerous staff assignments. He also served as deputy director for operations, Joint Task Force, Southwest Asia in Riyadh, Saudi Arabia; deputy director, aviation plans and requirements on the staff of the chief of naval operations in Washington, D.C.; assistant chief of staff, plans and policy for supreme allied commander, Atlantic (his first flag officer position); deputy and chief of staff, U.S. Atlantic Fleet; and deputy commander in chief and chief of staff, U.S. Atlantic Command.

Fallon was promoted to full (four-star) admiral and became the 31st vice chief of naval operations, which post he held from October 2000 to August 2003. While serving in that capacity, he publicly apologized to the president of Japan following a collision between the U.S. submarine *Greeneville* and the Japanese fishing training ship *Ehime Maru* off the coast of Hawaii in February 2001. In 2002, Fallon asserted before the U.S. Senate Committee on Environment and Public Works that the ability to conduct military operations superseded obedience to environmental laws. He then took command of the U.S. Fleet Forces Command (October 2003–February 2005) and the U.S. Pacific Command (February 2005–March 2007), where his approach to the People's Republic of China (PRC) was less confrontational than previous commanders and was not well received by some American policymakers who favored a tougher stance toward the PRC.

In March 2007, Fallon replaced General John P. Abizaid of the army to become the first naval officer to take command of CENTCOM. Fallon's tenure lasted only one year, from March 16, 2007, to March 28, 2008. Although the impetus for his abrupt retirement as CENTCOM commander is not disputed, its voluntary nature is. Despite the fact that Fallon was publicly lauded by President George W. Bush and Secretary of Defense Robert Gates, Gates noted that Fallon's resignation was due in part to controversy surrounding an article by Thomas P. M. Barnett entitled "The Man Between War and Peace," published in *Esquire* magazine on March 11, 2008. In it, Fallon was quoted as having disagreements with the Bush administration on the prosecution of the war in Iraq and over a potential conflict with Iran over its nuclear weapons program. The article portrayed Fallon as resisting pressure from the Bush administration for war with Iran over the latter's pursuit of a nuclear weapons program. Besides Fallon's rather open opposition to Bush's war policies, the admiral purportedly disagreed with General David Petraeus over Iranian covert exportation of weapons to Iraqi insurgents and the pace of future American troop reductions in Iraq. Many believed that Fallon was forced out principally because his superiors blamed him for the failure to halt Iranian weapons from entering Iraq.

Richard M. Edwards

References

Barnett, Thomas P. M. "The Man Between War and Peace." *Esquire* (March 11, 2008): 1–4.

Dorsey, Jack. "Navy Taps 2nd Fleet's Adm. William J. Fallon for 4-Star Pentagon Post." *The Virginian Pilot*, September 7, 2000: 1.

Lambeth, Benjamin S. *American Carrier Air Power at the Dawn of a New Century*. Santa Monica, CA: Rand Corporation, 2005.

Franks, Frederick Melvin, Jr. (1936–)

U.S. Army officer and commander of VII Corps during the 1991 Persian Gulf War (Operation DESERT STORM). Born in West Lawn, Pennsylvania, on November 1, 1936, Frederick Melvin Franks Jr. graduated from the United States Military Academy at West Point and was commissioned as an armor officer in June 1959. Following an initial assignment in Germany with the 11th Armored Cavalry Regiment, he attended the Armor Officer Advanced Course at Fort Knox, Kentucky, and then entered Columbia University, earning master's degrees in both English and philosophy before returning to West Point as an English instructor in 1966.

Rejoining the 11th Armored Cavalry Regiment, now in Vietnam, in 1969 he served as an operations officer. Seriously wounded during the Cambodian Incursion of 1970, he successfully fought to remain on active duty as an armor officer in spite of the amputation of his left leg. Following tours at the Armed Forces Staff College and the Department of the Army Staff, he took command of the 1st Squadron, 3rd Armored Cavalry Regiment at Fort Bliss, Texas, in 1975. In 1982, after an assignment with the U.S. Army Training and Doctrine Command, he returned to the 11th Cavalry, now in Europe, as its commander. Promoted to brigadier general in July 1984, Franks commanded the Seventh Army Training Center and in 1985 returned to the United States as the deputy commandant of the army's Command and General Staff College at Fort Leavenworth, Kansas. There he was instrumental in implementing small-group instructional techniques in the Regular Course and inaugurating a staff procedures course for senior captains. In addition, he oversaw the expansion and refinement of the School of Advanced Military Studies (SAMS) into one of the army's most important educational institutions.

Franks returned to the Pentagon and became the first J-7 (Plans) on the newly reorganized Joint Staff as a major general in August 1987. Returning to Europe in 1988, he assumed command of the 1st Armored Division and a year later, following his advancement to lieutenant general in August 1989, VII Corps. During the next year, he transformed the corps staff from essentially a garrison organization to a more agile, mobile command headquarters, just in time for its deployment to the Middle East in November 1990 during Operation DESERT SHIELD. While in Saudi Arabia, VII Corps grew into the largest, most powerful, tactical command ever fielded by the U.S. Army, with more than 3,000 tanks, 700 artillery pieces, and 142,000 soldiers organized into five heavy divisions, an armored cavalry regiment, an aviation brigade, and the supporting organizations needed to execute the army's AirLand Battle doctrine.

After breaking through the Iraqi defenses at the beginning of Operation DESERT STORM in February 1991, Franks maneuvered the VII Corps to confront and destroy two of the Iraqi Republican Guard Force's best units, the Tawakalna Mechanized and Medina Armored Divisions. Overall coalition commander General H. Norman Schwarzkopf, however, publicly criticized Franks for moving too slowly and allowing elements of the Republican Guard to escape destruction by withdrawing toward Basra. In his later memoirs, written with writer and novelist Tom Clancy, Franks rebutted Schwarzkopf's criticisms and gave his own version of events.

Advanced to full general (four-star rank) in August 1991, Franks headed the Training and Doctrine Command and directed the army's educational and doctrinal programs, adjusting them to meet the needs of the post–Cold War era. He retired from the service in November 1994.

Since his retirement from active duty, Franks has continued to serve as an army consultant, particularly for the Battle Command Training Program. He has served as the chairman of the VII Corps Desert Storm Veteran's Association and has traveled extensively to speak and lecture. Franks has also served on a number of boards, including the board of trustees of West Point.

Stephen A. Bourque

References

Atkinson, Rick. *Crusade: The Untold Story of the Persian Gulf War*. Boston: Houghton Mifflin Company, 1993.

Bourque, Stephen A. *Jayhawk! The VII Corps in the Persian Gulf War.* Washington, DC: U.S. Army Center of Military History, 2002.

Clancy, Tom, and Frederick M. Franks, Jr. *Into the Storm: A Study in Command.* New York: G. P. Putnam's Sons, 1997.

Gordon, Michael R., and Bernard E. Trainor. *The General's War: The Inside Story of the Conflict in the Gulf.* Boston: Little, Brown and Company, 1995.

Franks, Tommy Ray (1945–)

U.S. Army general. Tommy Ray Franks was born in Wynnewood, Oklahoma, on June 17, 1945. After studying briefly at the University of Texas, Franks joined the U.S. Army in 1965 and went into the artillery. He served in Vietnam, where he was wounded three times. He again attended the University of Texas but dropped out and rejoined the army after being placed on academic probation. Franks later earned an MA degree in public administration at Shippensburg University (1985). He also graduated from the Armed Forces Staff College in 1967 and in 1972 attended the Field Artillery School at Fort Sill, Oklahoma.

From 1976 to 1977, Franks attended the Armed Forces Staff College, Norfolk, Virginia, and in 1984–1985 he attended the U.S. Army War College at Carlisle Barracks, Pennsylvania. After advancing through the ranks, by the time of Operation DESERT STORM in 1991 he served as an assistant division commander of the 1st Calvary Division. Franks was appointed brigadier general in July 1991 and major general in April 1994. From 1994 to 1995, he was assistant chief of staff for combined forces in Korea. Franks was advanced to lieutenant general in May 1997 and to general in July 2006.

U.S. Central Command (CENTCOM) chief General Tommy Franks led the successful toppling of the Taliban in Afghanistan in 2001 and the invasion of Iraq in 2003. (Department of Defense)

After the September 11, 2001, terrorist attacks on the United States, Franks was named U.S. commander of the successful Operation ENDURING FREEDOM to topple the Taliban in Afghanistan. In early 2003, he took command of Central Command (CENTCOM) for Operation IRAQI FREEDOM, the invasion of Iraq that began in March 2003.

Franks was a principal author of the war plans for the ground element of the invasion of Iraq and was an advocate of the lighter, more rapid mechanized forces that performed so well during the ground campaign. Franks designed a plan for the 125,000 U.S., 45,000 British, 2,000 Australian, 400 Czech and Slovak, and 200

Polish troops under his command. This involved five ground thrusts into Iraq, with two main thrusts—one by the 1st Marine Expeditionary Force up the Tigris River and one through the western desert and up the Euphrates by the army's 3rd Armored Division.

The plan allowed for great flexibility, and even though CENTCOM advertised a "Shock and Awe" bombing campaign, in fact there was never any such intention. Franks's plans called for a near-simultaneous ground and air assault. When missiles struck Iraqi president Saddam Hussein's compound on March 19, 2003, ground forces moved into Iraq. Franks emphasized speed and bypassing cities and Iraqi strong points. Contrary to media reports that coalition forces were "bogged down" and had not occupied many cities, Franks maintained this was by design: CENTCOM did not want the Iraqis to see the method and tactics by which coalition forces planned to take Baghdad demonstrated in advance in Basra or Najaf.

Franks's campaign was an unqualified success, going farther, faster, and with fewer casualties than any other comparable military campaign in history. This reflected what Franks called "full-spectrum" war, in which the enemy's military forces were not only engaged, but in which there were simultaneous attacks on computer/information facilities, the banking/monetary structure, and public morale.

For the first time, American forces operated in true "joint" operations, wherein different service branches could speak directly to units in other service branches. The plans also featured true "combined arms" operations in which air, sea, and land assets were all simultaneously employed by commanders in the field to defeat the enemy.

Although sources suggest that Secretary of Defense Donald Rumsfeld offered Franks the post of army chief of staff when the ground war ended in late April 2003, Franks wanted to leave the army to pursue other interests. He retired in late May 2003 and subsequently wrote his memoirs, *American Soldier* (2004). Franks's departure was fortuitous for him, as he left Iraq prior to the start of the Iraq insurgency and thus avoided most of the criticism that it engendered. In retirement, Franks started his own consulting firm that deals in disaster recovery operations. He also sits on the boards of several large corporations.

Spencer C. Tucker

References

Cordesman, Anthony. *The Iraq War: Strategy, Tactics, and Military Lessons.* London: Center for Strategic and International Studies, 2003.

Fontenot, Gregory, E. J. Degen, and David Tohn. *On Point: The United States Army in Operation Iraqi Freedom.* Washington, DC: Office of the Chief of Staff, 2004.

Franks, Tommy. *American Soldier.* New York: Reganbooks, 2004.

Murray, Williamson, and Robert H. Scales Jr. *The Iraq War.* Boston: Belknap Press, 2003.

Woodward, Bob. *Plan of Attack.* New York: Simon and Schuster, 2004.

Gates, Robert Michael (1943–)

U.S. Air Force officer, president of Texas A&M University, director of the Central Intelligence Agency (CIA), and secretary of defense from 2006. Robert Michael Gates was born in Wichita, Kansas, on September 25, 1943. He graduated from the College of William and Mary with a BA in history in 1965, and then earned an MA in history from Indiana University in 1966 and a PhD in

Iran-Contra Affair might hamper his Senate confirmation. He then served as deputy assistant to the president for National Security Affairs (March–August 1989) and assistant to the president and deputy national security adviser from August 1989 to November 1991.

The Iran-Contra Affair erupted in 1987 when it was revealed that members of President Ronald Reagan's administration had sold weapons to Iran and illegally diverted the funds to the Nicaraguan Contras, the rightist anti-Sandinista rebels. Gates was assumed guilty by his political enemies because of his senior status at the CIA, but an exhaustive investigation by an independent counsel determined that Gates had done nothing illegal, and on September 3, 1991, the investigating committee stated that Gates's involvement in the scandal did not warrant prosecution. The independent counsel's final 1993 report came to the same conclusion. In May 1991, President George H. W. Bush renominated Gates to head the CIA, and Gates was confirmed by the Senate on November 5, 1991.

Gates retired from the CIA in 1993 and entered academia. He also served as a member of the Board of Visitors of the University of Oklahoma International Programs Center and an endowment fund trustee for The College of William and Mary. In 1999, he became the interim dean of the George Bush School of Government and Public Service at Texas A&M University before becoming president of Texas A&M University in 2002, a post he held until 2006.

Gates remained active in public service during his presidency, cochairing in January 2004 a Council on Foreign Relations task force on U.S.-Iran relations that suggested that the United States engage Iran diplomatically concerning

Former Central Intelligence Agency director Robert Gates replaced the controversial Donald Rumsfeld as U.S. secretary of defense in 2006. Gates continued in that post under President Barack Obama. (Department of Defense)

Russian and Soviet history from Georgetown University in 1974.

Gates served as an officer in the U.S. Air Force's Strategic Air Command (1967–1969) before joining the Central Intelligence Agency (CIA) in 1969 as an intelligence analyst, a post he held until 1974. He was on the staff of the National Security Council (NSC) from 1974 to 1979, before returning to the CIA as director of the Strategic Evaluation Center in 1979. Gates rose through the ranks to become director of Central Intelligence (DCI)/deputy director of Central Intelligence (DDCI) executive staff (1981), deputy director for Intelligence (DDI) (1982), and deputy director of Central Intelligence (1986–1989).

Nominated director of the CIA in 1987, he withdrew his nomination when it appeared that his connection with the that nation's pursuit of nuclear weapons. Gates was a member of the Iraq Study Group (also known as the Baker-Hamilton Commission) from March 15, 2006 to December 6, 2006, a bipartisan commission charged with studying the Iraq War when he was nominated to succeed the controversial Donald Rumsfeld as defense secretary. Gates assumed the post on December 18, 2006.

In addition to the challenges of the Iraq War, in February 2007 Gates was faced with a scandal concerning inadequate and neglectful care of returning veterans by Walter Reed Army Medical Center. In response, he removed both Secretary of the Army Francis J. Harvey and Army Surgeon General Kevin C. Kiley from their posts. Gates further tightened his control of the Pentagon when he did not recommend the renomination of U.S. Marine Corps general Peter Pace as chairman of Joint Chiefs of Staff that June. Pace would have certainly faced tough questioning by Congress. It was also Gates's job to implement the "troop surge" initiated by Bush in January 2007.

In March 2008, Gates accepted the resignation of Admiral William Joseph "Fox" Fallon, commander of the U.S. Central Command (CENTCOM), a departure that was due in part to the controversy surrounding an article by Thomas P. M. Barnett entitled "The Man Between War and Peace," published in *Esquire* magazine (March 11, 2008). The article asserted policy disagreements between Fallon and the Bush administration on the prosecution of the war in Iraq and potential conflict with Iran over that nation's nuclear arms program. Gates rejected any suggestion that Fallon's resignation indicated a U.S. willingness to attack Iran in order to stop its nuclear weapons development.

Unlike his abrasive and confrontational predecessor, Gates has brought an era of calm and focus to the Pentagon and has appeared far more willing to engage in discussion and compromise over matters of defense and military policy.

When asked by President Barack Obama, Gates agreed to stay on as head of the Defense Department. While some questioned Obama's choice, since he had been a vocal critic of the Iraq War during his campaign, others saw the choice as a smart bipartisan move because Gates had support on both sides of Congress and agreed with Obama on key matters.

Richard M. Edwards

References

Barnett, Thomas P. M. "The Man Between War and Peace." *Esquire* (March 11, 2008): 1–4.

Gates, Robert M. *From the Shadows: The Ultimate Insider's Story of Five Presidents and How They Won the Cold War.* New York: Simon and Schuster, 1996.

———. *Understanding the New U.S. Defense Policy Through the Speeches of Robert M. Gates, Secretary of Defense.* Rockville, MD: Arc Manor, 2008.

Hagenbeck, Franklin L. (1949–)

U.S. Army general and commander of Coalition Joint Task Force Mountain during Operation ENDURING FREEDOM in Afghanistan. Born in Morocco on November 25, 1942, the son of a naval officer, Franklin L. Hagenbeck attended high school in Jacksonville, Florida, and went on to graduate from the United States Military Academy at West Point in 1971, when he was commissioned a 2nd lieutenant. His subsequent military education included courses at the U.S. Army Command and General Staff College and the Army War College. Hagenbeck also earned a master's degree in exercise physiology from Florida State University and a master's of business administration from Long Island University.

Among Hagenbeck's earlier staff assignments were tours as director of the Officer Personnel Management Directorate and assistant division commander of the 101st Airborne Division. He also served abroad as an instructor in tactics at the Royal Australian Infantry Center. Having previously commanded at company, battalion, and brigade levels, Hagenbeck assumed command as a major general of the 10th Mountain Division at Fort Drum, New York, in the autumn of 2001. He entered the public spotlight in the aftermath of the September 11, 2001, terror attacks on the United States. With the commencement of Operation ENDURING FREEDOM in Afghanistan in October 2001, the 10th Mountain Division received a warning that it would provide the first conventional forces to support ongoing special operations against the Taliban regime. After initially sending a small security element, the 10th Mountain contributed a portion of the 1,200 infantrymen who took part in Operation ANACONDA in March 2002 under Hagenbeck's immediate command.

Although a tactical success, ANACONDA was not without its problems in intelligence and fire coordination. Thus, a debate over the operation and the responsibility for its shortcomings occurred in which Hagenbeck played a prominent role. In particular, in an interview published in *Field Artillery* magazine in 2002 he called into question the effectiveness of fire support provided by the air force. His analysis drew a sharp rejoinder from air force spokespersons. Whatever the problems, they almost certainly stemmed in part from a hasty planning process as well as a long-standing history of imperfect interservice coordination.

Hagenbeck next assumed the post of army deputy chief of staff, personnel. In this position, he testified several times before the Congress on the challenges facing the army in recruitment and retention resulting from waging concurrent wars in Iraq and Afghanistan. In 2006, Lieutenant General Hagenbeck became the superintendent of West Point.

Robert F. Baumann

References

"Afghanistan: Fire Support for Operation Anaconda, an interview with MG Franklin L. Hagenbeck." *Field Artillery* (September–October 2002): 5–9.

Andres, Richard, and Jeffrey Hukill. "Anaconda: A Flawed Joint Planning Process." *Joint Forces Quarterly* 47 (4th Quarter 2007): 135–140.

Lambeth, Benjamin. "Airpower Against Terror: America's Conduct of Operation Enduring Freedom." Santa Monica, CA: RAND, 2005.

Naylor, Sean. *Not a Good Day to Die: The Untold Story of Operation Anaconda.* New York: Berkley Books, 2005.

Horner, Charles (1936–)

U.S. Air Force officer responsible for U.S. and allied air operations in the 1991 Persian Gulf War. Charles Horner was born in Davenport, Iowa, on October 19, 1936, and earned a BA degree from the University of Iowa on an Reserve Officers' Training Corps (ROTC) scholarship in 1958. In November 1959, he completed pilot training and was awarded his wings. His subsequent education and training included an MBA from the College of William and Mary (1972), the Armed Forces Staff College (1972), the Industrial College of the Armed Forces (1974), and the National War College (1976).

Horner's primary distinction came as a tactical command pilot. He logged thousands of hours in a variety of fighter aircraft. He served two combat tours in Vietnam and participated in the bombing campaign against North Vietnam, Operation ROLLING THUNDER. During his second tour (May–September 1967) he flew the particularly dangerous "Wild Weasel" missions aimed at identifying and destroying North Vietnamese air defenses. Like many Vietnam veterans, Horner was embittered by the many restrictions placed on the air campaign by civilian officials. His Vietnam experience made him an outspoken critic of "absentee management" and a staunch advocate of the quick, overwhelming application of airpower.

Following the Vietnam War, Horner served in various command and staff functions, where he gained attention as a leader of the movement to reform the air force's combat doctrine and overhaul civil-military relations. Horner was advanced to brigadier general on August 1, 1982, and to major general on July 1, 1985. He established professional and personal relationships with officers in other branches of the armed forces, including U.S. Army general H. Norman Schwarzkopf, who was to become his superior as commander of U.S. Central Command (CENTCOM) with responsibility for operations in the Middle East. On May 1, 1987, Horner was appointed lieutenant general and given command of the Ninth Air Force and appointed commander, Central Command Air Forces.

In the late 1980s, CENTCOM's mission underwent numerous changes. With the winding down of the Cold War and the end of the Iran-Iraq War in 1988, senior officers in CENTCOM began examining potential threats within the Middle East region, particularly Iraq, with its large and experienced army and President Saddam Hussein's ambition to dominate the Persian Gulf. At Schwarzkopf's urging, Horner developed plans for war with Iraq before Hussein's forces invaded Kuwait on August 1, 1990. Consequently, when that crisis broke, rudimentary plans for an American response were already in place.

Within a week of the Iraqi invasion, Horner and his planners had outlined a concept for an intensive air campaign code named INSTANT THUNDER, a concept Schwarzkopf endorsed. It fell to Horner to oversee the translation of this concept into reality, including target selection, size of forces, types of ordnance to be used, and the integration of these packages into the complete air offensive. Horner selected Brigadier General Buster C. Glossen to direct the planning.

Many observers have pointed to the effectiveness of the air campaign as the most decisive factor in the quick victory by the United States and its allies in the Persian Gulf War and as a model for future conventional wars. After Schwarzkopf, Horner was perhaps the most important military leader on the coalition side in the war. Throughout both Operations DESERT SHIELD and DESERT STORM, Horner had the complete support of Schwarzkopf, who gave him a virtual free hand in the direction of the air war. Horner later observed that the close working relationships he enjoyed with Schwarzkopf and other military branch commanders were the key to victory in the 1991 Gulf War.

Horner has been increasingly critical of American military policy and diplomacy in the Middle East. He gained considerable attention when, on relinquishing his command in 1992 now at the rank of general, he declared that war is folly. Following his retirement in 1994, Horner criticized American intelligence gathering in the Middle East, particularly as it related to weapons of mass destruction (WMDs). Even before the United States invaded Iraq in March 2003, Horner took issue with the George W. Bush and Bill Clinton administrations for maintaining a military presence in the Gulf after the 1991 war. He argued that by villainizing Saddam Hussein, American policymakers were, in fact, playing into his hands. Horner also criticized the focus on WMDs in Iraq when the United States should be more concerned about nuclear proliferation in the former Soviet Union, Libya, Israel, and Iran. Horner remains active in retirement, writing and speaking extensively.

Walter F. Bell

References

Boomer, Walter E. " Ten Years After." *U.S. Naval Institute Proceedings* 127, no. 1 (January 2001): 61–65.

Hallion, Richard P. *Storm over Iraq: Air Power and the Gulf War*. Washington, DC: Smithsonian Institution Press, 1992.

Kimmitt, Robert Michael (1947–)

U.S. attorney, presidential adviser, ambassador to Germany, and deputy secretary of the Treasury. Robert Michael Kimmitt was born in Logan, Utah, on December 19, 1947, and graduated with distinction from the U.S. Military Academy at West Point in 1969. He served with the 173rd Airborne Brigade in Vietnam (April 1970–August 1971), earning three Bronze Star Medals, the Purple Heart, and the Vietnamese Cross of Gallantry. After leaving the regular army, Kimmitt remained with the reserves, retir-

ing in November 2004 as a major general. In 1977, Kimmitt earned a law degree from Georgetown University.

Kimmitt was twice a member of the National Security Council (NSC) staff, once from 1976 to 1977 and again from 1978 to 1983. During 1977–1978, he was a law clerk to Judge Edward A. Tamm of the U.S. Court of Appeals for the District of Columbia Circuit. He then served the White House as the NSC executive secretary and general counsel (1983–1985) with the rank of deputy assistant to the president for national security affairs.

From 1985 to 1987, Kimmitt served as general counsel to the U.S. Treasury Department, before leaving to become a partner in a private law firm (1987–1989). Kimmitt returned to government as undersecretary of state for political affairs (1989–1991) and then served as the ambassador to Germany (1991–1993) before returning again to the private sector.

During the 1990–1991 Gulf War, Kimmitt was instrumental in creating the U.S-led coalition of 34 Western and Arab countries that cooperated to oust Iraqi dictator Saddam Hussein's forces from Kuwait. For his accomplishments in this regard, Kimmitt was awarded the Presidential Citizen's Medal, the United States' second-highest civilian award.

During 1993–1997, Kimmitt was a managing director of Lehman Brothers. He was also a partner in the law firm of Wilmer, Cutler & Pickering (1997–2000); vice chairman and president of Commerce One, a software company (2000–2001); and executive vice president, global public policy, for Time Warner, Inc. (2001–2005). Just prior to joining the George W. Bush administration, Kimmitt again served as a partner in a law firm. Kimmitt continued his public service during his private sector tenure as a member of the National Defense Panel (1997), as a member of the director of Central Intelligence's National Security Advisory Panel (1998–2005), and as a member of the Panel of Arbitrators of the World Bank's International Center for the Settlement of Investment Disputes.

As the deputy secretary of the Treasury, a post he began in August 2005, Kimmitt appeared before the Treasury Committee House Financial Services Subcommittee on Domestic and International Monetary Policy in March 2006. At the hearing, he supported Trade and Technology DP (Dubai Ports) World's purchase of the Peninsular and Oriental Steam Navigation Company (P&O) of the United Kingdom, then the fourth-largest ports operator in the world. This would have placed numerous U.S. ports under the nominal control of Dubai, a move that elicited considerable opposition. The bid was soon dropped.

Kimmitt also served as the Bush administration's envoy to the International Compact with Iraq (ICI), an international conference at the United Nations (UN). The goal of the meeting was to help develop a framework that would transform the Iraqi economy into a self-sustaining economy within five years. The ICI was an initiative of the Iraqi government with assistance from the United States and the Assistance United Nations Mission for Iraq (UNAMI). In this capacity, Kimmitt traveled to Iraq, the United Arab Emirates, and Kuwait. He also attended the January 2008 Davos World Economic Forum and there warned against a trend toward protectionism in the United States, Europe, and Asia regarding sovereign wealth funds (SWFs) that use state wealth to invest in the assets of other sovereign nations or businesses based in

other sovereign nations. He is thought to have been a candidate for the presidency of the World Bank in May 2007.

Richard M. Edwards

References

Carter, Ralph G. *Contemporary Cases in U.S. Foreign Policy: From Terrorism to Trade.* 3rd ed. Washington, DC: CQ Press, 2007.

Coll, Steven. *Ghost Wars: The Secret History of the CIA, Afghanistan, and Bin Laden, from the Soviet Invasion to September 10, 2001.* New York: Penguin, 2004.

Oliphant, Thomas. *Utter Incompetents: Ego and Ideology in the Age of Bush.* New York: Thomas Dunne Books, 2007.

United States. *Nominations of Robert M. Kimmitt, Randal Quarles, Sandra L. Pack, and Kevin I. Fromer: Hearing Before the Committee on Finance, United States Senate.* Washington, DC: U.S. Government Printing Office, 2005.

Luck, Gary Edward (?–)

U.S. Army officer. Gary Edward Luck served in the U.S. Army from 1959 to 1994 and retired as a four-star general in 1994. A Kansas native, Luck attended Kansas State University, where he enrolled in its ROTC program. He graduated in 1959 and was commissioned a 2nd lieutenant in the army shortly thereafter. Luck fought in Vietnam as both a Special Forces officer and a cavalry troop commander.

In the years following the Vietnam War, Luck steadily moved up the military hierarchy. He commanded the 2nd Infantry Division in the mid-1980s, but his most significant assignment in that decade was as commander of Joint Special Operations Command (1989–1990), at which time he held the rank of major general. In that capacity, he had a central role in the planning for the 1989 invasion of Panama that overthrew General Manuel Noriega.

Because of Luck's considerable experience in special operations, General Colin L. Powell, then chairman of the Joint Chiefs of Staff (JSC), relied heavily on him in the planning for the Panama invasion, an operation that made much use of special operations units from all three services. Luck was particularly involved in planning for the rescue of American hostages held at Modelo Prison. On October 16, 1989, Luck and Powell briefed President George H. W. Bush on the overall invasion plan. Luck's presentation focused on the special operations capabilities for locating and rescuing American hostages, and his plans eventually formed the basis for the December 1989 invasion.

Luck also played a pivotal role in the Persian Gulf War as commander of the XVIII Airborne Corps. Luck's corps was responsible for the critical left flank and for the wide-sweeping "left-hook" designed to outflank the Iraqi Republican Guard divisions. A longtime friend of General H. Norman Schwarzkopf, Luck was not afraid to speak his mind to the theater commander during the Operation DESERT SHIELD buildup and the planning for Operation DESERT STORM. He was particularly critical of the notion of using only one corps for the flanking attack but, after a sharp rebuke from Schwarzkopf, acquiesced. Luck's approach to commanding at the corps level was highly decentralized, leaving the bulk of the operational planning for XVIII Airborne Corps assault into Iraq in the hands of his division commanders. With the commencement of the ground war, Luck's divisions advanced rapidly and completed their flanking maneuver, despite problems in coordinat-

ing their advance with VII corps. Luck saw XVIII Corps' success as a vindication of his decentralized approach to the planning and conduct of operations.

Following DESERT STORM, Luck, now advanced to full (four-star) general, served as commander in chief of United Nations Command/Combined Forces Command in Korea. He retired from the army in 1994. In retirement, he has continued to be engaged in military issues, writing a number of books and articles on the impact of new technologies on command and control. He has also remained an active consultant on current military issues—particularly the war in Iraq that began in March 2003. In the lead-up to the war, he served as a key adviser to Lieutenant General Tommy Franks. Luck has not been afraid of controversy. In late 2004 and early 2005, Luck led a study group to Iraq to analyze operations and the status of U.S. operations there. The group concluded that the security situation was worse than was being depicted, that the insurgency was gathering momentum, that progress in training Iraqi military and security forces was going slower than expected, and that U.S. intelligence operations were flawed. Needless to say, this did not endear him to the George W. Bush administration. Thanks to his activities as both an author and a consultant on military affairs, Gary E. Luck has been as influential in retirement as he was on active duty.

Walter F. Bell

References

Atkinson, Rick. *Crusade: The Untold Story of the Persian Gulf War.* Boston: Houghton, Mifflin Company, 1993.

Ricks, Thomas E. *Fiasco: The American Military Adventure in Iraq.* New York: Penguin Books, 2006.

Woodward, Bob. *The Commanders.* New York: Simon and Schuster, 1991.

Mullen, Michael Glenn (1946–)

U.S. Navy admiral and chairman of the Joint Chiefs of Staff (2007–). Born in Los Angeles, California, on October 4, 1946, Michael Glenn Mullen graduated from the U.S. Naval Academy at Annapolis and was commissioned in the navy in 1968. He first saw service in the waters off Vietnam. Additional deployments and exercises took him to the Caribbean and the Mediterranean. In 1973, Mullen assumed command of his first ship, the gasoline tanker *Noxubee*.

Mullen next served at the United States Naval Academy as a company officer and later as executive assistant to the commandant of midshipmen. He then returned to sea duty, gaining further experience aboard the guided missile cruisers *Fox* and *Sterett*. Mullen gained operational experience in the western Pacific Ocean, Indian Ocean, and Red Sea.

In 1985, Mullen graduated from the Naval Postgraduate School in Monterey, California, with a master's degree in operations research. He then assumed command of the guided missile destroyer *Goldsborough*. Deploying to the Persian Gulf, he participated in the maritime escort of Kuwaiti oil tankers during the 1980–1988 Iran-Iraq War.

Mullen next was director of the Division Officer Course at the Navy Surface Warfare Officer School and, following promotion to captain on September 1, 1989, became a staff officer in the office of the Secretary of Defense for the director, Operational Test and Evaluation Force. He then assumed command of the Ticonderoga-class cruiser *Yorktown*, conducting a broad range of missions from support of the United Nations (UN) embargo of Haiti to counterdrug operations and joint and multinational exercises in the North Atlantic. Mullen was then assigned to the

Admiral Michael Mullen was chief of U.S. Naval Operations during 2005–2007. He became chairman of the Joint Chiefs of Staff in 2007. (Department of Defense)

Bureau of Naval Personnel, where he served as the director, Surface Officer Distribution; and later as director, Surface Warfare Plans, Programs and Requirements Division. Still later, following his promotion to rear admiral on April 1, 1996, he became the bureau's deputy director.

Later in 1996, Mullen was named commander of Cruiser-Destroyer Group 2, in command of the ships, submarines, and aircraft of the *George Washington* Battle Group. He deployed with it to the Mediterranean, where the battle group served a key role in the Balkans peace process. The following year, it served as the cornerstone of the U.S. military presence in the Persian Gulf, compelling Iraq to comply with UN disarmament inspections, as well as enforcing the no-fly zone over southern Iraq.

Following advancement to rear admiral (two-star) on October 1, 1998, Mullen was chosen to serve as the director, Surface Warfare Division, Office of the Chief of Naval Operations, with responsibility for the direction of acquisition plans and programs for the navy surface force. On November 1, 2000, Mullen was appointed vice admiral (three-star) and named the combined commander, U.S. Second Fleet and NATO Striking Fleet Atlantic. Mullen soon found himself back in Washington, however, assuming responsibility for the direction and management of all navy acquisition programs as the deputy chief of Naval Operations for Resources, Requirements and Assessments. He guided the navy's resource decisions during critical reevaluations in the aftermath of the September 11, 2001, terror attacks, directing such key programs as the Next Generation Destroyer, Littoral Combat Ship, and Theater Ballistic Missile Defense. After two years as the navy resource director, Mullen was appointed full (four-star) admiral on August 28, 2003, and named the 32nd vice chief of naval operations. He served as vice chief for just over a year when he was reassigned as the combined commander of the North Atlantic Treaty Organization's (NATO) Allied Joint Force Command Naples and U.S. Naval Forces Europe. Mullen immediately established clear priorities for these diverse commands.

On July 22, 2005, Mullen became the 28th chief of naval operations. He assumed command of a service facing issues of relevance, an apparent loss of operational significance, and the profound cost of continuing war in the Middle East. In response, Mullen committed the navy to easing the strain on the nation's land forces by assigning naval personnel to serve in an unusually broad range of supporting roles. Faced with a tight fiscal environment, Mullen ensured that the navy's budget priorities were clearly aligned with the realities of the strategic environment. In regard to the navy's crisis of mission, Mullen immediately directed that a new maritime strategy be developed to guide the efforts of the nation's maritime services. After nearly two years of study and collaboration, "Cooperative Strategy for 21st Century Seapower" was released. It was the nation's first maritime strategy document developed collaboratively and signed by all three of the nation's maritime services, the U.S. Navy, Marine Corps, and Coast Guard.

On October 1, 2007, Admiral Mullen was appointed the 17th chairman of the Joint Chiefs of Staff. He assumed the post amid the most divisive and politically charged environment since the Vietnam War era. Almost immediately, Mullen demonstrated a pragmatic, long-term view of U.S. military requirements by voicing concern over the broader effects of continuing U.S. military commitments in Afghanistan and Iraq, and campaigned for a broad, strategic reassessment.

Mullen explained that a rebalancing of global strategic risks was needed and that a comprehensive, sustainable long-term Middle East security strategy was a vital priority. He also asserted the requirement for a more balanced, flexible, and ready force. Describing a future characterized by persistent conflict and irregular warfare but simultaneously uncertain and unpredictable, Mullen argued that U.S. forces must possess not only the ability to conduct counterinsurgency operations but must remain unmatched in their ability to fight a conventional war. Mullen helped secure legislation passed by Congress to increase military personnel strength by 100,000 people. He also instituted efforts to ease the tempo of operational deployments and began a measured troop redeployment from Iraq.

Kenneth A. Szmed Jr.

References

Baer, George W. *One Hundred Years of Sea Power, The U.S. Navy, 1890–1990.* Stanford, CA: Stanford University Press, 1994.

Love, Robert W. *History of the U.S. Navy, 1775–1991.* Mechanicsburg, PA: Stackpole Books, 1992.

Myers, Richard Bowman (1942–)

U.S. Air Force general and chairman of the Joint Chiefs of Staff (JCS) during 2001–2005. Born in Kansas City, Missouri, on March 1, 1942, Richard Myers graduated from Kansas State University in 1965 and entered the air force through the Reserve Officer Training Corps (ROTC) program. Myers served as a fighter pilot during the Vietnam War, accumulating 600 combat flying hours. In 1977, he earned an MA in business administration from Auburn University.

Myers was advanced to brigadier general in April 1990 while serving as deputy chief of staff for plans at Langley Air Force Base, Virginia. He then was director of Fighter, Command and Control and Weapons Programs in the Office of the Assistant Secretary of the Air Force for Acquisition in Washington, D.C. He was appointed major general in September 1992 and lieutenant general in November 1993. From July 1996 to July 1997, he was the assistant to the chairman of the JCS. Myers commanded the Pacific Air Forces, Hickham Air Force Base, Hawaii, during July 1997 to July 1998. He was appointed full (four-star) general in September 1997.

Air Force general Richard Myers was chairman of the Joint Chiefs of Staff during 2001–2005. (Department of Defense)

From August 1998 to February 2000, Myers headed the North American Aerospace Defense Command and U.S. Space Command. He also commanded the Air Force Space Command and Department and was Defense manager of the space transportation system contingency support at Peterson Air Force Base, Colorado.

Myers was vice chairman of the JCS from March 2000 to September 2001. As vice chairman, he served as chairman of the Joint Requirements Oversight Council, as vice chairman of the Defense Acquisition Board, and as a member of the National Security Council Deputies Committee and the Nuclear Weapons Council. In addition, Myers acted for the JCS chairman in most aspects of the planning, programming, and budgeting system, including participation in the Defense Resources Board.

In August 2001, President George W. Bush nominated Myers as chairman of the Joint Chiefs of Staff. Myers was thus in his new position for only a few weeks—and had not yet been confirmed by the U.S. Senate—before the terrorist attacks of September 11. After the second plane hit the World Trade Center during the attacks, Myers called the Pentagon's command center and ordered the military's alert status to defense condition (DEFCON) 3, the highest state of military readiness since the October 1973 Middle East Yom Kippur (Ramadan) War. Myers was confirmed to the chairman's position by the Senate and was sworn in on October 1, 2001.

Myers closely analyzed the status of both Afghanistan and Iraq prior to U.S. military involvement in those two countries in Operation ENDURING FREEDOM beginning in 2001 and Operation IRAQI FREEDOM beginning in 2003, respectively. While much of the blame for the debacle of the continuing insurgency erupting in the wake of the Iraq War's conventional phase of operations fell on Secretary of Defense Donald Rumsfeld, Myers has also been sharply criticized. Many argue that, among others, he underestimated the potential likelihood of a postinvasion insurgency and failed to provide enough troops to secure the country from the very beginning.

Myers retired on September 30, 2005. Two months later, he was awarded the Presidential Medal of Freedom. In 2006, he joined the board of directors of Northrup Grumman Corporation and United Technologies Corporation. He also accepted a part-time endowed professorship of military history at Kansas State University.

Charlene T. Overturf

References

Fawn, Rick, and Raymond A. Hinnebusch, eds. *The Iraq War: Causes and Conse-*
quence. Boulder, CO: Lynne Rienner Publishers, 2006.

Lifton, Robert Jay, Richard Falk, and Irene Gendzier. *Crimes of War: Iraq*. New York: Nation Books, 2006.

Pace, Peter (1945–)

U.S. Marine Corps general and chairman of the Joint Chiefs of Staff (JCS) from 2005 to 2007. Peter Pace was born on November 5, 1945, in Brooklyn, New York, to Italian American parents but was raised in Teaneck, New Jersey. He graduated from Teaneck High School in 1963. Pace secured an appointment to the United States Naval Academy at Annapolis and graduated there in 1967, taking a commission in the Marine Corps. Following officer basic training at Quantico, Virginia, in the summer of 1968 Pace was assigned as

General Peter Pace, chairman of the Joint Chiefs of Staff during 2005–2007, was the first marine to hold that position. (Department of Defense)

a rifle platoon leader in Vietnam. He returned to the United States in March 1969 and subsequently held a series of posts both in the United States and abroad, advancing steadily through the ranks.

Pace received a master's of business administration (MBA) from George Washington University in 1972 and completed advanced training at the Marine Corps Command and Staff College in Quantico, Virginia, in 1980. In 1986, he graduated from the National War College in Washington, D.C. Pace was appointed brigadier general on April 6, 1992; major general on June 21, 1994; lieutenant general on August 5, 1996; and full (four-star) general on September 8, 2000.

Pace served as president of the Marine Corps University during 1992–1994. In 1996, following advancement to lieutenant general, he took over as director for operations, Joint Staff, Washington, D.C. From 1997 to 2000, he served as commander, U.S. Marine Corps Forces, Atlantic/Europe/South. In 2000, he assumed the position of commander in chief, U.S. Southern Command, before returning to Washington to serve as vice chairman of the Joint Chiefs of Staff in 2001. He became chairman of the Joint Chiefs of Staff, the highest-ranking U.S. military post, on September 30, 2005.

As vice chairman and then chairman of the JCS, Pace was a key player in the planning and implementation of the War on Terror and the March 2003 invasion of Iraq. A loyal soldier to the end, he publicly supported the White House and his direct superiors, especially Secretary of Defense Donald H. Rumsfeld, as the invasion of Iraq was being formulated. Certainly, Rumsfeld relied heavily on Pace's support during the war planning. As the Iraq War lost public support because of the growing Iraqi insurgency,

Pace saw his direct superior, chairman of the Joint Chiefs of Staff General Richard B. Myers, come under increased pressure to step aside. Upon Myers's retirement, Pace, against the advice of many of his colleagues, accepted nomination as the 16th chairman of the Joint Chiefs of Staff on September 30, 2005. He was the first marine to hold this post.

In private Pace had questioned the planning, strategy, and implementation of many aspects of the Iraq War, although publicly he always loyally supported his superiors. Pace's position on the war was that U.S. troops were not in Iraq simply to eradicate insurgents and run up body counts. Rather, he was unwavering in his position that the military's job in Iraq was to provide a stable environment within which Iraqis could rebuild their infrastructure and society while humanitarian and development aid could flow into the war-torn nation. Remembering the consequences of such in the Vietnam War, Pace urged his superiors not to ask for or give out body counts, but rather to tout humanitarian successes and positive developments achieved by the new government in Iraq.

Pace's public position against homosexuals serving openly in the military and the fact that much of the American public continued to see the Iraq War in a negative light were key factors in the decision of newly-appointed Secretary of Defense Robert Gates not to recommend Pace for a second term as chairman of the JCS. Gates sought thereby to avoid a long, drawn-out confirmation hearing in Congress, now controlled by Democrats eager to embarrass the George W. Bush administration. In a highly unusual move, Gates asked Pace to step down, which he did on October 1, 2007, after serving only one two-year term as chairman. Pace was succeeded by Admiral Michael G. Mullen.

Following his retirement, Pace was said to be contemplating a run for the U.S. Senate, perhaps from Virginia.

Randy Taylor

References

Cloud, David S. "A Marine on Message," *New York Times*, April 23, 2005.

Keegan, John. *The Iraq War*. New York: Alfred A. Knopf, 2004.

Woodward, Bob. *State of Denial: Bush at War, Part III*. New York: Simon and Schuster, 2006.

Pagonis, William Gus (1942–)

U.S. Army general. William Gus Pagonis was born in 1942 in Charleroi, Pennsylvania, of Greek American heritage. He graduated from the Pennsylvania State University with a bachelor's degree in transportation and traffic management, and he subsequently earned a master's degree in business administration, also from Penn State. His 29-year U.S. Army career included service in Vietnam, the 1991 Gulf War, and a wide range of command and staff positions at virtually all levels.

Pagonis's most important military service occurred during Operations DESERT SHIELD and DESERT STORM, for which he earned accolades as "the logistical wizard" of the coalition war effort. Indeed, U.S. Central Command (CENTCOM) commander General H. Norman Schwarzkopf termed the Gulf War "a logistician's war," and pronounced Pagonis, who became his chief logistician, "an Einstein who could make anything happen."

As director of Logistics for Lieutenant General John Yeosock's U.S. Army Forces, Central Command (ARCENT), the major subordinate command for American ground forces during the Gulf War, then–major general Pagonis faced the Herculean task of bringing order to the flood of troops, weapons, ammunition, and supplies that began to arrive in Saudi Arabia on August 7, 1990, only days after Iraqi president Saddam Hussein's army had occupied neighboring Kuwait. Pagonis, one of the first Americans to arrive in the Kuwaiti Theater of Operations (KTO), immediately set about bringing necessary order to an otherwise chaotic situation, turning a logistician's nightmare into the vital key to the American-led coalition's victory in February 1991.

For six months (August 1990–February 1991), Pagonis's 22nd Support Command organized and supervised a methodical buildup of military might that included the gathering of 670,000 troops from 28 nations (500,000 were U.S. personnel), 150,000 wheeled vehicles, 40,000 containers, 2,000 helicopters, and 2,000 tanks in the KTO. By the time the ground war began on February 24, 1991, Pagonis had amassed over 7 million tons of supplies that had arrived from halfway around the world.

Pagonis's prodigious logistical accomplishments did not end with the completion of the troop, equipment, and supply buildup of Operation DESERT SHIELD. His further efforts largely made possible the phenomenal success of Schwarzkopf's operational plan that won the ground war, Operation DESERT STORM, during the 100-hour ground-launched blitzkrieg. The tactical battle plan, which called for a giant left hook to be delivered against the Iraqi Army by the U.S. VII and XVII Airborne Corps, relied on secretly moving 150,000 American troops 150 miles westward across the desert wasteland. Thanks to an impressive effort led by Pagonis, the combat units' progress was facilitated by prepositioned advanced supply bases placed at key locations along the route of march. Mechanized forces, including swarms of fuel-guzzling tanks and armored fighting vehicles, found much-needed supplies and all the logistical support necessary already waiting for them when they arrived at Pagonis's desert bases. Pagonis later said, "I got the idea from a fellow Greek—Alexander the Great," citing Donald W. Engels's 1977 book, *Alexander the Great and the Logistics of the Macedonian Army* as his "logistical bible." Engel's work describes the sophisticated logistical effort that made Alexander's 4,000-mile march of conquest possible, including the use of advanced logistical bases.

Equally as impressive as Pagonis's logistical efforts during the war were his no less prodigious accomplishments in moving the masses of troops and supplies back from the war zone after the fighting had stopped. Perhaps no other major American military expedition has been followed up with the level of accountability that Pagonis ensured in the wake of DESERT STORM. His Gulf War accomplishments were recognized by his promotion to lieutenant general soon after the war.

Pagonis retired from the army in 1993 and pursued a highly successful career in the business world and as a guest speaker on leadership and management topics. As executive vice president of logistics for Sears, Roebuck and Company, Pagonis was instrumental in revitalizing the giant retail chain. He retired from Sears in July 2004 and became the chairman of the board of RailAmerica, Inc., the world's largest short line railroad. He was also appointed chairman of the Defense Business Board by Secretary of Defense Donald Rumsfeld, and also serves as vice chairman of GENCO Supply Chain Solutions and CombineNet, Inc.

In addition to his successful business and a speaking career, Pagonis is an author. His book *Moving Mountains: Lessons in Leadership and Logistics from the Gulf War* was published by Harvard Business School Press in 1992.

Jerry D. Morelock

References

Pagonis, William G. *Moving Mountains: Lessons in Leadership and Logistics from the Gulf War.* Cambridge, MA: Harvard Business School Press, 1992.

Schwarzkopf, H. Norman. *It Doesn't Take a Hero.* New York: Bantam Books, 1992.

Petraeus, David Howell (1952–)

U.S. Army officer and commander of the Multinational Force–Iraq (2007–2008); commander, U.S. Central Command (CENTCOM; 2008–). Born on November 7, 1952, David Howell Petraeus grew up and graduated from high school in Cornwall, New York. Petraeus graduated 10th in his class from the United States Military Academy at West Point in 1974. Commissioned a 2nd lieutenant of infantry, he graduated from Ranger School and served as a platoon leader in the 509th Airborne Infantry Battalion in Italy. As a 1st lieutenant he served as assistant battalion operations officer, and as captain he served as company commander, battalion operations officer, and then as commanding general's aide-de-camp, all in the 24th Infantry Division (Mechanized).

From 1982 to 1995, Petraeus was largely engaged in academic pursuits. He graduated from the Army Command and General Staff College in 1983, after which he attended Princeton University's

U.S. Army general David Petraeus, commander of the U.S. Central Command (CENTCOM), confers with members of Combined Joint Task Force 101 at Combat Outpost Marghah in Afghanistan, on November 6, 2008. (Department of Defense)

Woodrow Wilson School of Public Affairs, where he earned a master's degree in public administration in 1985 and a doctorate in international relations in 1987. His doctoral dissertation dealt with the U.S. Army in Vietnam and the lessons learned there.

Petraeus returned to West Point as a professor of international relations and then was a military fellow at Georgetown University's School of Foreign Service. This latter posting ended when he was recalled to serve as chief of staff at United Nations (UN) headquarters during Operation UPHOLD DEMOCRACY in Haiti during 1994–1995.

In line service, Petraeus commanded the 3rd Battalion 187th Infantry Regiment in the 101st Airborne Division during 1991–1993 and the 1st Brigade of the

82nd Airborne Division from 1995 to 1997. He was promoted to brigadier general in 1999.

Petraeus's first combat assignment, now at the rank of major general, came as commander of the 101st Airborne Division (Air Assault) in Operation IRAQI FREEDOM in March 2003. The division engaged in the battles of Karbala and Najar, as well as the feint at Hilla. Petraeus later oversaw the administration and rebuilding of Mosul and Niveveh provinces. Subsequently, Petraeus commanded the Multinational Security Transition Command–Iraq and North Atlantic Treaty Organization (NATO) Training Mission Iraq between June 2004 and September 2005. Petraeus's next assignment was as commanding general of Fort Leavenworth, Kansas, and the U.S.

Army Combined Arms Center, where he became intimately involved in doctrinal changes to prepare the army for its continued efforts in Afghanistan and Iraq. He also coauthored *Field Manual 3–24, Counterinsurgency.*

On January 5, 2007, now a lieutenant general, Petraeus was selected by President George W. Bush and later unanimously confirmed by the U.S. Senate to command the Multinational Force–Iraq. He took formal command on February 10, 2007, replacing Lieutenant General George Casey. The Petraeus appointment was the keystone in Bush's "new" strategy in Iraq designed to bring an end to the mounting violence there and to create the conditions for the Iraqi government to establish a stable, democratic regime and take over security functions from U.S. forces.

In April 2007, Petraeus was tasked with reporting to Congress the progress of the Bush administration's surge strategy, begun that January, and met stiff and sometimes combative resistance. To his credit, however, he deftly handled the pressure and stated confidently that the strategy, given time, would show positive results. At the same time, he firmly argued against setting a timetable for the withdrawal of ground troops from Iraq. In July, he submitted his first progress report to Congress, which was positive and upbeat. It met with criticism from Democrats, however, who claimed that the situation in Iraq did not appear any more secure than it had been in January. His September 2007 report cited progress on the military and security fronts, but admitted that the political climate in Iraq remained troubled.

The September report drew sharp criticism from some Democrats and the antiwar lobby, compelling a bipartisan group of congressmen and senators to sponsor resolutions—which eventually passed—

that condemned the recent attacks on Petraeus. By early 2008, defying high odds and most critics of the war, Petraeus's surge strategy appeared to be paying off, as violence had fallen off markedly in the last quarter of 2007. Talk of troop drawdowns, however, were still subject to interpretation, as the possible numbers being cited would account mainly for the "surge," meaning that troop strength in Iraq would remain unchanged from January 2007, even after troop reductions.

On April 23, 2008, Petraeus was nominated to become CENTCOM commander. When confirmed by the Senate, Petraeus has, as CENTCOM commander, assumed responsibility for overseeing both Operation ENDURING FREEDOM in Afghanistan and Operation IRAQI FREEDOM in Iraq. His previous combat experience in both countries, as well as his involvement in creating the United States' counterinsurgency doctrine makes Petraeus well qualified for his new post.

Marcel A. Derosier

References

Atkinson, Rick. *In the Company of Soldiers: A Chronicle of Combat.* New York: Henry Holt and Company, 2005.

Day, Thomas L. *Along the Tigris: The 101st Airborne Division in Operation Iraqi Freedom: February 2003–March 2004.* Atglen, PA: Schiffer Publishing, 2007.

Fontenot, Gregory, et al. *On Point: The United States Army in Iraqi Freedom.* Annapolis, MD: Naval Institute Press, 2005.

Powell, Colin Luther (1937–)

U.S. Army officer, national security adviser (1987–1989), chairman of the Joint Chiefs of Staff (1989–1993), and secretary of state (2001–2005). Colin Luther Powell was born in New York

As chairman of the Joint Chiefs of Staff during 1989–1993, General Colin Powell played a key role in the Persian Gulf War. As secretary of state during 2001–2005 he opposed an invasion of Iraq but loyally presented the U.S. case for war before the United Nations. (U.S. Department of State)

City on April 5, 1937, the child of Jamaican immigrants. While pursuing a geology degree at the City College of New York, Powell joined the Reserve Officers' Training Corps (ROTC) and earned his commission as a 2nd lieutenant in 1958. After paratrooper and Ranger training, Powell was deployed as a military adviser to Vietnam. Even though he was wounded and received a Purple Heart during his first tour, Powell chose to volunteer for a second tour before earning a master's degree in business administration at George Washington University in 1971. He earned a White House fellowship in 1972 before returning to the military to command at the battalion and division levels.

Powell returned to duty in Washington, D.C., as an executive assistant to the Energy and Defense departments during the administration of President Jimmy Carter. Under President Ronald Reagan, Powell quickly moved up the ranks from senior military assistant to Secretary of Defense Casper Weinberger, whom Powell assisted during both the 1983 invasion of Grenada as well as the 1987 raid on Libya. That same year, Powell, now a lieutenant general, became Reagan's national security adviser. In 1989, Colin Powell became the youngest person and the first African American to serve as chairman of the Joint Chiefs of Staff.

By 1991, Powell was a four-star general, and the onus had fallen upon him to develop the strategy that would allow a coalition of nations to push Iraqi president Saddam Hussein's invasion force out of Kuwait. Powell's strategy was a simple one: when the American military is to be used, it should be used to win a conflict quickly and decisively. That was the central tenet for the coalition strategy—overwhelming force should be brought to bear against the enemy. This approach led to a rapid and decisive victory over Iraqi forces in Operation DESERT STORM. The victory came so quickly that some argued it left the job unfinished as Hussein was left in power. However, neither President George H. W. Bush nor Powell was eager to prosecute the war beyond the coalition's mandate, or to make it appear as if the West was intent on punishing the Iraqi people.

The use of overwhelming force was one of the three tenets of the Powell Doctrine, which guided U.S. military strategy in the immediate aftermath of the Cold War. The doctrine also held that the United States should use its military only when the country's vital interests were at stake, only when there was a clear goal, and a clearly defined exit strategy.

Powell served as secretary of state under President George W. Bush, beginning in 2001. It was clear from the start, however, that Powell would not play as influential a role as Vice President Richard Cheney, Secretary of Defense Donald Rumsfeld, Deputy Secretary of Defense Paul Wolfowitz, and National Security Adviser Condoleeza Rice.

Powell, who did not subscribe to the rigid ideology of neoconservativism, found himself in the difficult position of having to rally the international community around the War on Terror after the September 11 terrorist attacks. His job was not an easy one, as he walked a diplomatic tightrope between the Bush administration neoconservatives and the exigencies of the post-9/11 environment. Powell traveled less than any secretary of state in 30 years, demonstrating the demands the War on Terror and Iraq War exacted on his time.

Soon after September 11, 2001, Powell was given the responsibility for building the case for a second invasion of Iraq to topple the Hussein regime and ensure that the nation did not harbor or use weapons of mass destruction (WMDs). Powell was opposed to the forcible overthrow of Hussein, arguing that it was better to contain him. Nevertheless, he agreed to work with the administration if it sought an international coalition to effect regime change in Iraq. Powell did convince Bush to take the case for war before the United Nations; however, he had to serve as the point man for these actions.

As the United States moved toward war with Iraq, Powell addressed a plenary session of the United Nations on February 5, 2003, carefully building a case for international military action. Powell emphatically stated that the Iraqis had biological weapons in hand and that Hussein had many of the key components for the construction of a nuclear weapon. Powell's speech was immediately controversial, as many claim that Powell's statements concerning Iraqi WMDs were unsubstantiated. Powell was himself skeptical about some of the intelligence presented to him but nevertheless presented it as irrefutable. He would later refer to his UN speech as a blot on his record.

The coalition that did invade Iraq in 2003 was not nearly as large, diverse, or unified as the 1991 coalition, another disappointment for Powell. Once Hussein had been toppled, Powell had the unenviable task of building international support for the rebuilding of Iraq, which was made far more difficult when a nearly two-year search found none of the WMDs that Powell and others had claimed were in Iraq.

As the war in Iraq began to deteriorate into an insurgency, Powell became even more marginalized within the administration. Realizing that his voice had been muted, he announced his intention to resign only days after Bush's November 2004 reelection. He left office in January 2005. Powell has since joined the venture capital firm of Kleiner, Perkins, Caulfield & Byers, embarked on an extended speaking tour, and has stayed active in moderate Republican political circles. In the summer of 2007, Powell revealed that he had spent much time attempting to persuade George W. Bush not to invade Iraq. He also stated that he believed that Iraq had descended into a civil war, the outcome of which could not be determined by the United States.

B. Keith Murphy
and Paul G. Pierpaoli Jr.

References
DeYoung, Karen. *Soldier: The Life of Colin Powell.* New York: Alfred A. Knopf, 2006.

Powell, Colin, and Joseph E. Persico. *My American Journey.* New York: Ballantine, 2003.

Roth, David. *Sacred Honor: Colin Powell: The Inside Account of His Life and Triumphs.* New York: HarperCollins, 1995.

Rice, Condoleezza (1954–)

Academic, national security adviser (2001–2005), and secretary of state (2005–2009). Condoleezza Rice was born on November 14, 1954, in Birmingham, Alabama, and grew up in the segregated South in a prominent African American family. The family moved to Denver in 1967, when her father accepted a position as vice chancellor at the University of Denver. Her intellectual abilities were evident at an early age, and she graduated from the University of Denver at age 19 and went on to earn a master's degree from Notre Dame University in 1975. After working in the State Department during the Jimmy Carter administration, Rice returned to the University of Denver and received a PhD in international studies in 1981. Her area of specialty was the Soviet Union and Cold War security issues.

Condoleeza Rice, U.S. secretary of state during 2005–2009, is shown here being greeted by Saudi foreign minister Saud al-Faisal and Assistant Minister of Defense Prince Khalid bin Sultan in Jeddah, Saudi Arabia, on July 31, 2007. (Department of Defense)

Rice joined the faculty at Stanford University and became a tenured professor of political science and a fellow at the Hoover Institute. During her years in academia, Rice held a variety of government positions and posts on advisory boards. During this period, Rice became known for her intelligence and work ethic. She impressed President George H. W. Bush, who subsequently recommended her to George W. Bush when the Texas governor began to prepare for his presidential campaign.

In 1993, Rice became the provost of Stanford University; she also became a fellow at the Council on Foreign Relations and continued to serve as a government adviser during the Bill Clinton administration. In 1996, she was appointed as an adviser to the Joint Chiefs of Staff. Rice was also invited to join a number of corporate boards during the 1990s. She left her post at Stanford in 1999 to advise George W. Bush during his presidential campaign.

In 2001, Rice became the nation's first female and second African American national security adviser. Following the September 11, 2001, terrorist attacks, Rice emerged as a central figure in crafting the U.S. military and diplomatic response and in advocating war with Iraq. She also worked with then–secretary of state Colin Powell to ensure that the U.S. response to the attacks included nonmilitary actions like increased international law enforcement cooperation and the development of a comprehensive homeland security policy.

Rice helped develop the 2002 U.S. national security strategy, commonly referred to as the "Bush Doctrine," that emphasized the use of preemptive military force to prevent the use of weapons of mass destruction (WMDs). She was also instrumental in the administration's hard-line policy toward Iraq, including the effort to isolate Iraq and assemble an international coalition. She was identified as one of the main proponents of the 2003 U.S.-led invasion of Iraq, Operation IRAQI FREEDOM. In March 2004, Rice was asked to testify before the commission investigating the September 11, 2001, terrorist attacks in contravention of a long-standing informal policy that members of the White House staff did not testify before congressional committees.

During the 2004 presidential campaign, Rice became the first national security adviser to openly campaign on behalf of a candidate. She faced domestic criticism by Democrats for her hard-line national security policies and for her advocacy against affirmative action policies. Following the election, Rice was appointed secretary of state, taking office in January 2005. She handpicked her successor as national security adviser, Stephen Hadley, her former deputy. Once in office, Rice worked to repair relations with major allies such as France and Germany, who were opposed to the U.S.-led invasion of Iraq. She also endeavored to increase international support for the continuing U.S. efforts in Iraq. The sound working relationship between Rice and Hadley ensured that the State Department

and the security establishment enjoyed a high degree of cooperation.

Rice's closeness with Bush provided her with greater access to the president, and therefore more influence, than her predecessor, Colin L. Powell. One result was that in the second Bush administration, Secretary of Defense Donald Rumsfeld had less influence in broad security policy, while Rice increased, or restored, the role of the State Department in formulating such policy. Following Rumsfeld's late 2006 departure, Rice played an ever greater role in national security and foreign policy issues.

Tom Lansford

References

Felix, Antonia. *Condi: The Condoleezza Rise Story.* New York: New Market Press, 2003.

Kessler, Glenn. *The Confidante: Condoleezza Rice and the Creation of the Bush Legacy.* New York: St. Martin's Press, 2007.

Rumsfeld, Donald Henry (1932–)

Congressman, ambassador, and U.S. secretary of defense (1975–1977, 2001–2006). Born in Chicago, Illinois, on July 9, 1932, Donald Rumsfeld graduated from Princeton University in 1954. He was commissioned in the navy through the Naval Reserve Officers Training Corps (NROTC) and served during 1954–1957 as a pilot and flight instructor. Rumsfeld remained in the reserves, retiring as a navy captain in 1989.

Rumsfeld began his long association with Washington as an administrative assistant to Rep. David S. Dennison Jr. of Ohio during 1957–1959, then joined the staff of Rep. Robert Griffen of Michigan. During 1960–1962, he worked for an investment banking firm. In 1962, Rums-

Donald Rumsfeld was U.S. secretary of defense during 1975–1977 and again in 2001–2006. The confrontational Rumsfeld was one of the strongest proponents of a U.S. invasion of Iraq. (Department of Defense)

feld was elected to the U.S. House of Representatives as a Republican from Illinois and served until 1969, when he resigned to accept appointment as director of the Office of Economic Opportunity and assistant to President Richard M. Nixon (1969–1970). He was then counselor to the president and director of the Economic Stabilization Program (1971–1973). During 1973–1974, he was U.S. ambassador to the North Atlantic Treaty Organization (NATO).

When Nixon resigned and was succeeded by Gerald Ford, Rumsfeld returned to Washington in August 1974 to serve as chair of the new president's transition team. He was then Ford's chief of staff. During 1975–1977, Rumsfeld served as secretary of defense, the youngest person to hold that position. During Rumsfeld's tenure, he oversaw

the transformation of the military to an all-volunteer force and post-Vietnam reforms. He also actively campaigned for additional defense appropriations and to develop weapons systems, such as the B-1 bomber, the Trident missile system, and the MX missile.

Rumsfeld left government service when President James (Jimmy) E. Carter took office in January 1977. Following a brief period as a university lecturer, Rumsfeld entered private business. He was chief executive officer, then chairman, of G. D. Searle, the pharmaceutical company (1977–1985). From 1990 until 1993, Rumsfeld served as chairman and chief executive officer of General Instrument Corporation. During 1997–2001, Rumsfeld was chairman of Gilead Sciences, Inc. Concurrent with his work in the private sector, Rumsfeld served on numerous federal boards. He also served in the Ronald Reagan administration as special presidential envoy to the Middle East during 1983–1984.

In January 2001, newly elected President George W. Bush appointed Rumsfeld to be secretary of defense for a second time. Rumsfeld was then the oldest individual to hold the post. Bush charged him with transforming the military from its Cold War emphasis on major conventional warfare into a lighter, more efficient force capable of rapid deployment around the world. Rumsfeld worked to develop network centric warfare, an approach to military operations that relies on technological innovation and integration of weapons and information systems to produce more firepower with fewer personnel. In addition, Rumsfeld initiated the restructuring of the U.S. military presence throughout the world and the closure and consolidation of bases. Rumsfeld also refocused the strategic forces of the United States by emphasizing missile defense and space systems following the 2002 U.S. withdrawal from the Anti-Ballistic Missile Treaty.

Rumsfeld's reform efforts and his restructuring of the military were overshadowed by his role in the post September 11, 2001, War on Terror. As secretary of defense, Rumsfeld oversaw the military operation that overthrew the Taliban regime in Afghanistan (Operation ENDURING FREEDOM), although the failure to capture Osama bin Laden tarnished that otherwise successful military campaign.

Rumsfeld was one of the foremost proponents of military action against Iraq, teaming up with President Bush and Vice President Richard Cheney to overcome opposition from within the cabinet by Secretary of State Colin Powell. Rumsfeld then directed the 2003 invasion of Iraq (Operation IRAQI FREEDOM). In the campaign, Rumsfeld employed a strategy that relied on firepower and smaller numbers of troops.

While the overthrow of the Saddam Hussein regime was highly successful, the subsequent occupation of Iraq did not go well. Within the Pentagon, there were complaints of Rumsfeld running roughshod over those who disagreed with him. Certainly he was much criticized for his outspoken, combative management style, as when he pointedly referred to the French and British governments, which had opposed the war, as "Old Europe." But there was good reason to criticize his military decisions and specifically his overly optimistic assessment of the situation that would follow the overthrow of Hussein. Disbanding the Iraqi Army to rebuild it from scratch came to be seen in retrospect as a major blunder. Rumsfeld had also ignored previous recommendations that 400,000 U.S. troops would be required for any occupation of Iraq. The actual number of troops involved was only about a third that number. As a consequence, Iraqi arms depots, oil production facilities, and even the national museum were looted in the immediate aftermath of the invasion.

Occupation troops were unable to halt a growing insurgency. As U.S. casualties escalated and Iraq descended into sectarian violence, calls mounted for Rumsfeld's ouster, from Republicans as well as Democrats, and even a number of prominent retired generals. Just prior to the 2006 midterm elections, an editorial in all the *Military Times* newspapers demanded his removal.

Rumsfeld resigned on November 8, 2006. This came a week after President Bush had expressed confidence in his defense secretary and said that he would remain until the end of his term, but it was also one day after the midterm elections in which the Republican Party lost its majorities in both the House of Representatives and the Senate. The election was widely seen as a referendum on the Iraq War and, by extension, Rumsfeld's leadership in it. President Bush named former CIA director Robert Gates to succeed Rumsfeld.

Tom Lansford and Spencer C. Tucker

References

Scarborough, Rowan. *Rumsfeld's War: The Untold Story of America's Anti-Terrorist Commander*. Washington, DC: Regnery Publishing, 2004.

Woodward, Bob. *Bush at War*. New York: Simon and Schuster, 2002.

———. *Plan of Attack*. New York: Simon and Schuster, 2004.

———. *State of Denial: Bush at War, Part III*. New York: Simon and Schuster, 2006.

Schwarzkopf, H. Norman, Jr. (1934–)

U.S. Army officer, commander in chief of the U.S. Central Command (CENTCOM) (1988–1991), and commander of coalition forces during Operations DESERT SHIELD and DESERT STORM. H. Norman Schwarzkopf Jr. (sometimes referred to as "Stormin' Norman") was born on August 22, 1934, in Trenton, New Jersey. His father, Herbert Norman Schwarzkopf, disliked his first name and gave his son only its first letter. The elder Schwarzkopf had graduated from the United States Military Academy, West Point, and, following his military career, headed the New Jersey State Police. In the late 1940s, Schwarzkopf accompanied his father to Iran, where the elder Schwarzkopf helped establish and train that country's national police. This experience gave the young Schwarzkopf a lasting interest in Islamic culture and history.

Schwarzkopf followed his father in attending West Point, graduating in 1956. Schwarzkopf's first assignment was at Fort Benning, Georgia, where he received advanced infantry and airborne training. He later served with the 101st Airborne Division in Kentucky and the 6th Infantry Division in Germany. He was in Berlin during the crises there in 1960 and 1961. In 1964, Schwarzkopf earned a master's degree in mechanical engineering from the University of Southern California, and in 1965 he began a three-year teaching appointment at West Point.

The war in Vietnam intruded on his teaching career, however, and Captain Schwarzkopf served a tour as an adviser to the Republic of Vietnam Airborne Division before returning to complete his teaching assignment. Promoted to lieutenant colonel in 1968, Schwarzkopf attended the U.S. Army Command and General Staff College, and in 1969 he returned to Vietnam as a battalion commander, where he earned a Silver Star and was twice wounded. There he also acquired his reputation as a tough, nononsense commander, who was willing to risk his own life for his men. In 1970, now a colonel, Schwarzkopf returned to the United States in a body cast. On his recovery, he studied internal defense and national security issues at the Army War College. He then served in Alaska, Washington state, Hawaii, Germany, and Washington, D.C.

Schwarzkopf was advanced to brigadier general in 1978 and appointed assistant division commander of the 8th Mechanized Division stationed in the Federal Republic of Germany. Appointed major general in 1982, Schwarzkopf

As commander of the U.S. Central Command, Army general H. Norman Schwarzkopf directed the highly successful international military coalition that drove Iraqi forces from Kuwait in the Persian Gulf War in 1991. (Department of Defense)

assumed control of the 24th Mechanized Infantry Division at Fort Stewart, Georgia. A year later, he served as an adviser to the navy in Operation URGENT FURY, the U.S. invasion of Grenada. Winning the confidence of the naval commanders, he was appointed deputy commander of the joint task force. He also learned valuable lessons from the experience, especially the need for more effective coordination and control in joint operations.

In 1984, Schwarzkopf returned to the Pentagon to serve in the Office of Deputy Chief of Staff for Operations. In 1986, he was advanced to lieutenant general and appointed commander of I Corps at Fort Lewis, Washington. After serving only one year in that assignment, he returned to the Pentagon for additional service in the Office of Deputy Chief of Staff for Operations, this time as deputy chief.

Advanced to four-star general in 1988, Schwarzkopf was assigned to head the U.S. Central Command (CENTCOM). CENTCOM was tasked primarily with potential U.S. operations in the Middle East and Southwest Asia. Following the Iraqi invasion of Kuwait on August 2, 1990, Schwarzkopf moved his headquarters to Riyadh, Saudi Arabia, and played a key role in building the multinational coalition that carried out the United Nations mandate to restore the independence of Kuwait. Schwarzkopf doubted the ability of airpower alone to cause Iraqi leader Saddam Hussein to withdraw his forces from Kuwait and he insisted on a large buildup of ground forces. Operations DESERT SHIELD and DESERT STORM proved highly successful, with coalition forces winning the ground war within only 100 hours.

Reportedly, Schwarzkopf opposed the Bush administration decision to end the war without the destruction of the Iraqi Republican Guard. Yet Schwarzkopf himself made the decision in the ceasefire agreement, which very much surprised the Iraqi delegates and which allowed the Iraqis to continue to fly helicopters. This decision greatly aided the Iraqi government in crushing Kurd and Shiite insurrections against the Hussein regime.

Schwarzkopf returned to the United States a national hero, aided considerably by his ability to deal effectively with the press. He retired from the army in August 1991 and published his best-selling memoirs, *It Doesn't Take a Hero,* in 1992. He currently resides in Florida. Schwarzkopf was sharply critical of Secretary of Defense Donald Rumsfeld's management of the Iraq War. Among Schwarzkopf's many decorations are three Silver Stars and the Presidential Medal of Freedom.

Deborah Kidwell, Paul G. Pierpaoli Jr., and Spencer C. Tucker

References

Cohen, Roger, and Claudio Gatti. *In the Eye of the Storm: The Life of General H. Norman Schwarzkopf.* New York: Farrar Straus and Giroux, 1992.

Morris, M. E. *H. Norman Schwarzkopf: Road to Triumph.* New York: St. Martin's Press, 1993.

Schwarzkopf, H. Norman. *It Doesn't Take a Hero: The Autobiography: H. Norman Schwarzkopf.* New York: Diane Publishing Company, 1992.

Shalikashvili, John Malchese David (1936–)

U.S. Army officer and chairman of the Joint Chiefs of Staff (JCS) during 1993–1997. John Malchese David Shalikashvili was born on June 27, 1936, in Warsaw, Poland, to parents of Georgian descent. His father had been an army officer in the Democratic Republic of Georgia until that nation was overrun and occupied by the Soviets in 1921. During World War II, his father served in the German-raised Georgian Legion, which fought in Normandy against the Western Allies in 1944.

Shalikashvili was eight during the Warsaw Uprising of August 1944. His family survived and was evacuated to Germany, emigrating to the United States in 1952 and settling in Peoria, Illinois. Shalikashvili attended Bradley University, majoring in mechanical engineering. In May 1958, he became an American citizen, and in June he graduated from Bradley. In July 1958, he was drafted into the army. After attending officer candidate school at Fort Sill, Oklahoma, Shalikashvili was commissioned a 2nd lieutenant of artillery in 1959.

Shalikashvili rose steadily through the ranks, serving in a variety of assignments in field artillery and air defense artillery units. He served in Germany, Italy, Korea, and various places in the United States. In 1968 and 1969, he served as a senior district adviser in Vietnam. He also attended the Naval Command and Staff College (Newport, Rhode Island), the U.S. Army War College (Carlisle, Pennsylvania), and George Washington University, from which he earned a master's degree in international affairs. In 1979, he was posted to the Federal Republic of Germany (FRG, West Germany) as the divisional artillery commander of the 1st Armored Division. He later served as the assistant division commander and was promoted to brigadier general in 1982.

In 1986, Shalikashvili was promoted to major general and assigned to the Pentagon as assistant deputy chief of staff and later as deputy chief of staff of the army for operations and plans. From June 1987 to August 1989, he commanded the 9th Infantry Division (Motorized). Promoted to lieutenant general in August 1989, he became deputy commanding general of the U.S. Army, Europe, and the Seventh Army.

Shalikashvili received wide recognition for his highly effective command of Operation PROVIDE COMFORT, the major humanitarian relief effort carried out in northern Iraq in the immediate aftermath of Operation DESERT STORM. Starting in April 1991, PROVIDE COMFORT was designed to protect, feed, and house several hundred thousand Iraqi Kurds who had been forced to leave their homes. In August 1991, Shalikashvili was reassigned to Washington, D.C., as assistant to the chairman of the JCS, General Colin L. Powell.

In 1992, Shalikashvili became supreme allied commander, Europe (SACEUR), and served simultaneously as the commanding general of the U.S. European Command. After being nominated for the position of chairman of the JCS by President Bill Clinton, Shalikashvili, now a four-star general, began his four-year tour as JCS chairman on October 25, 1993.

Shalikashvili faced several thorny issues in his new role. After the flap over homosexuals serving openly in the military and the subsequent promulgation of the "don't ask, don't tell policy," Shalikashvili worked hard to bolster morale in the armed forces and smooth over the dissension in the ranks. He also presided over the scaling back of the defense budget, which led to charges by some—especially on the right—that he was complicit in the gutting of the American military establishment. The reductions in defense spending, however, were largely driven by politics, including the end of the Cold War and the so-called peace dividend, and the Clinton administration's desire to wipe out decades of budget deficits and national debt. Shalikashvili was well respected and well liked, and his steady leadership was crucial for Clinton, who did not enjoy harmonious relations with the armed services.

Shalikashvili stepped down in September 1997 at the conclusion of his second two-year term as chairman. He also retired from the army at that time, ending an impressive 38-year career. Upon his retirement he was awarded the Presidential Medal of Freedom, a rare honor for a military officer. Despite suffering a severe stroke in August 2004, he has been active in politics since retirement, having served as an adviser to Democratic senator John Kerry's failed 2004 presidential campaign and having publicly endorsed Democratic senator Hillary Rodham Clinton's 2008 presidential bid. He has served on a number of corporate boards, including that of United Defense Industries, and holds a visiting professorship at Stanford University's Center for International Security and Cooperation.

Paul G. Pierpaoli Jr.

References

Clinton, Bill. *My Life: The Presidential Years.* New York: Vintage Books, 2005.

Halberstam, David. *War in a Time of Peace: Bush, Clinton, and the Generals.* New York: Scribner, 2001.

Woodward, Bob. *The Agenda: Inside the Clinton White House.* New York: Pocket Books, 1995.

Wallace, William Scott (1946–)

U.S. Army general. Born on December 31, 1946, in Chicago, Illinois, William Scott Wallace graduated in 1969 from the United States Military Academy, West Point. He also holds a master of science degree in operations research and a master of arts degree in International Relations and National Security and Strategic Studies. On graduation from West Point, Wallace was commissioned in the armor branch.

Wallace has commanded troops at every level, from platoon to corps. He served a combat tour in Vietnam during 1972 as assistant district adviser and later operations adviser in the Bac Lieu Province. After Vietnam, he commanded a company in the 4th Battalion (Light; Airborne), 68th Armored Regiment, 82nd Airborne Division at Fort Bragg, North Carolina. Wallace attended the Naval Postgraduate School, Monterey, California (1977), and in 1986 he became commander of the 3rd Squadron, 2nd Armored Cavalry Regiment, in Germany.

As a colonel, Wallace returned to Germany in 1992 to take command of the 11th Armored Cavalry Regiment in Fulda. Following regimental command, Wallace was assigned to the National Training Center (NTC), Fort Irwin, California, and became NTC commander. As a major general, Wallace commanded the 4th Infantry Division at Fort Hood, Texas (1997–1999), after which he led the Joint Warfighting Center and was director of Joint Training, J-7, at the U.S. Joint Forces Command, Virginia, one of 10 Department of Defense combatant commands.

Wallace is perhaps best known for his command of the U.S. V Corps during the March 2003 invasion of Iraq (Operation IRAQI FREEDOM). In July 2001, Wallace, now a lieutenant general, became V Corps commander. On March 20, 2003, V Corps became the vanguard of the American-led coalition that invaded Iraq. The invasion force (combat troops and support personnel of all services) included 248,000 U.S. soldiers and marines, 45,000 British troops, and about 2,500 military personnel from Australia and Poland. Wallace's V Corps spearheaded the drive to Baghdad, defeating the Iraqi Army in three weeks, and capturing Baghdad on April 9, 2003.

Despite Wallace's prominent role in the rapid and stunning defeat of Iraqi president Saddam Hussein's army, he became the center of some controversy concerning remarks he allegedly made to reporters while still in command of V Corps in Iraq. Wallace is reported to have said that "the enemy the U.S. was facing was different from the enemy the military had planned against." Because the alleged remarks came from a top military leader personally involved with combat actions, they were immediately seized upon by opponents of President George W. Bush's invasion of Iraq as representing strong criticism of Secretary of Defense Donald Rumsfeld and the administration's handling of the war.

In the book *Cobra II* (2006) by Michael R. Gordon and Bernard Trainor, the authors claim that Wallace's superior, General Tommy Franks, U.S. Central Command (CENTCOM) commander, threatened to fire Wallace over the remarks, a claim that Franks later disputed. Wallace weathered the controversy, however. He retained command of V Corps until June 2003, when he was reassigned after serving out a typical two-year corps command tour.

After handing over command of V Corps in Iraq to Lieutenant General Ricardo S. Sanchez, Wallace took over the U.S. Army Combined Arms Center (CAC) at Fort Leavenworth, Kansas. As CAC commander, Wallace was responsible for leader development and military and civilian education, including the U.S. Army Command and General Staff College, the

Center for Army Lessons Learned, and the Battle Command Training Program. Known as the intellectual center of the Army, CAC consists of 16 major schools and centers that prepare the army's future leadership for war.

In October 2005, Wallace was promoted to full general (four-star rank) and assigned as commander, U.S. Army Training and Doctrine Command (TRADOC). TRADOC is the army's "schoolhouse," the major command responsible for recruiting and training soldiers, developing and educating leaders, supporting training in units army-wide, and developing doctrine and standards. Wallace presides over a vast system of 33 schools and centers at 16 different army installations, conducting over 2,700 courses that train annually a half million soldiers, service members from other military services, civilians, and international soldiers from around the world.

Jerry D. Morelock

References

Gordon, Michael R., and Bernard E. Trainor. *Cobra II: The Inside Story of the Invasion and Occupation of Iraq.* New York: Pantheon Books, 2006.

Keegan, John. *The Iraq War.* New York: Alfred A. Knopf, 2004.

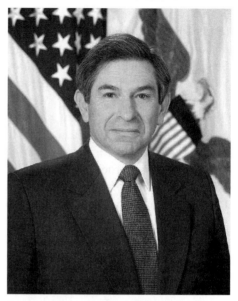

As an undersecretary of defense in the George W. Bush administration (2001–2005), Paul Wolfowitz was one of the architects of the Bush Doctrine that advocated preemptive strikes against potential threats to U.S. interests. As such, he was a strong proponent of the 2003 invasion of Iraq. (Department of Defense)

Wolfowitz, Paul Dundes (1943–)

Neoconservative academic, U.S. assistant secretary of state, and assistant and deputy secretary of defense. Born in Ithaca, New York, on December 22, 1943, Paul Dundes Wolfowitz graduated from Cornell University in 1965. He earned a doctorate in political science from the University of Chicago in 1972.

Wolfowitz taught political science at Yale University from 1970 to 1972 and became an aide in U.S. Democratic senator Henry M. "Scoop" Jackson's 1972 and 1976 presidential campaigns. He began working in the U.S. Arms Control and Disarmament Agency (ACDA) in 1972, concentrating on policies related to the strategic arms limitation talks and détente, both of which he discredited.

In 1977, Wolfowitz became deputy assistant secretary of defense for Regional Programs in the Jimmy Carter administration and continued to develop his theory that the best way to prevent nuclear war was to stop conventional war. It was also during this time that Wolfowitz became convinced that the highly petroleum-dependent West was extremely vulnerable to disruptions in Persian Gulf oil. In studying the issue, Wolfowitz envisioned the possibility that Iraq might some day threaten Kuwait and/or Saudi Arabia, a scenario realized when Iraq invaded Kuwait in August 1990. Wolfowitz determined that the United States had to be able quickly to project force into the region. His studies formed the rationale for the creation of the U.S. Central Command (CENTCOM), responsible for the U.S. Rapid Deployment Forces that proved so important to the successful prosecution of the 1991 Persian Gulf and the 2003 Iraq wars.

Wolfowitz left the Defense Department in 1980 for a visiting professorship at the Paul H. Nitze School of Advanced International Studies (SAIS) at Johns Hopkins University. He reentered public service in 1981, becoming the director of Policy Planning for the State Department, tasked with conceptualizing President Ronald Reagan's long-term foreign policy. Wolfowitz's distrust of Iraqi president Saddam Hussein resurfaced when he disagreed with the administration's policy of covertly supporting Iraq in the Iran-Iraq War (1980–1988).

U.S. secretary of state George P. Schultz appointed Wolfowitz assistant secretary for East Asian and Pacific Affairs in 1982 and, in that capacity, Wolfowitz urged the Reagan administration to support democracy in the Philippines. Wolfowitz believed that a healthy democracy was the best defense against totalitarianism, a view that would again be reflected as part of the rationale for the 2003 Iraq War. He then served as U.S. ambassador to the Republic of Indonesia (1986–1989).

President George H. W. Bush named Wolfowitz undersecretary of defense for policy in 1989, a post he held until 1993. Wolfowitz was responsible for U.S. military strategy in the post–Cold War era and

reported to then–U.S. defense secretary Richard (Dick) Cheney. Wolfowitz disagreed with the decision not to overthrow Saddam Hussein in the 1991 Persian Gulf War (Operation DESERT STORM). He saw this decision as poor strategy and believed that task would then have to be undertaken in the future. He also saw it as a betrayal of the Iraqi Shiites and Kurds, whom the United States had encouraged to revolt and then largely abandoned.

Wolfowitz again left public service in 1993, returning to Johns Hopkins as dean of SAIS until 2001. He did not forgo politics, however, and in 1997 became a charter member of the Project for a New American Century (PNAC), a neoconservative think tank. Fellow charter members included Donald Rumsfeld, Dick Cheney, and Richard Perle. In 1998, Wolfowitz signed an open PNAC letter to President Bill Clinton urging a policy shift away from containing Iraq to a preemptive attack on that country. Wolfowitz later joined a group that advised the 2000 Republican Party presidential candidate George W. Bush on foreign policy matters.

In the subsequent Bush administration, Wolfowitz became U.S. deputy secretary of defense in 2001 and served in that capacity until 2005. It was in this capacity that Wolfowitz urged Bush to mount a preemptive strike on Iraq following the September 11, 2001, terrorist attacks. This idea of preemptive strikes against potential threats, which Wolfowitz had first conceived during the Reagan era, came to be known as the Bush Doctrine.

An American- and British-led military coalition invaded Iraq in March 2003 asserting in part that Iraq's alleged weapons of mass destruction (WMDs) were an imminent threat worthy of preemptive intervention. After the stunning conventional victory over Saddam Hussein's army degenerated into a festering insurgency and no WMDs were found in Iraq, Wolfowitz and most of his neoconservative cohorts were gradually shunted aside. Bush subsequently nominated Wolfowitz to be the 10th president of the World Bank Group, and he assumed the post on June 1, 2005. In June 2007, he was forced to resign amid allegations of questionable management decisions that included nepotism.

Richard M. Edwards

References

Crane, Les, ed. *Wolfowitz on Point*. Philadelphia: Pavillion Press, 2003.

Mann, James. *Rise of the Vulcans: The History of Bush's War Cabinet*. New York: Penguin Group, 2004.

Zinni, Anthony Charles (1943–)

U.S. Marine Corps general, commander of U.S. Central Command, and special envoy for the United States to Israel and the Palestinian Authority. Anthony Charles Zinni was born to Italian immigrant parents in Philadelphia, Pennsylvania, on September 17, 1943. In 1965, he graduated from Villanova University with a degree in economics and was commissioned in the U.S. Marine Corps. In 1967, he served in Vietnam as an infantry battalion adviser to a South Vietnamese Marine unit. In 1970, he returned to Vietnam as an infantry company commander. He was seriously wounded that November and medically evacuated. Thereafter, Zinni held a variety of command, administrative, and teaching positions, including at the Marine Corps Command and Staff College at Quantico, Virginia.

In 1991, as a brigadier general, Zinni was the chief of staff and deputy commanding general of the Combined Joint Task Force (CJTF) for Operation PROVIDE COMFORT, the Kurdish relief effort in Turkey and Iraq. In 1992–1993, he was the director of operations (J-3) for Operation RESTORE HOPE in Somalia. As a lieutenant general, he commanded the I Marine Expeditionary Force (I MEF) from 1994 to 1996. In September 1996, as a full general, he became deputy commanding general of the U.S. Central Command (CENTCOM), the U.S. military combatant command responsible for most of the Middle East. He served as commanding general of CENTCOM from August 1997 until his retirement from the military in September 2000.

During 2001–2002, Zinni served as the special envoy for the United States to Israel and the Palestinian Authority. In an address Zinni gave at Harvard's Kennedy School of Government on December 8, 2004, he stressed that resuming the peace process between Israel and the Palestinians was the single most important step the United States could take to restore its stature in the world. Zinni held visiting appointments at several U.S. universities and in May 2005 became the president of international operations for M.C.I. Industries, Inc.

Although an initial supporter of the Bush administration and its foreign policy, Zinni after retiring from CENTCOM quickly became one of the highest-profile military critics of the war in Iraq. Distinguishing Afghanistan from Iraq, Zinni continued to believe that the invasion of Afghanistan to oust the Taliban regime and deprive Al Qaeda of its operating base was the right thing to do. Iraq was a totally different case. Although Saddam Hussein was a regional nuisance, Zinni believed his regime was totally contained and no real strategic threat. He also was certain that the case for the weapons of mass destruction was vastly overstated, remembering well the intelligence picture he had monitored daily while at CENTCOM.

While still at CENTCOM in early 1999, immediately following the air strikes of Operation DESERT FOX, intelligence indicators and diplomatic reporting painted a picture of Saddam's regime as badly shaken and destabilized. In anticipation of the possible requirement for CENTCOM to have to lead an occupation of Iraq should Saddam fall, Zinni ordered the preparation of a comprehensive operations plan (OPLAN). Code named DESERT CROSSING, it called for a robust civilian occupation authority with offices in each of Iraq's 18 provinces. The DESERT CROSSING plan was a dramatic contrast to what eventually played out under the anemic Coalition Provisional Authority, which for almost the first year of its existence had very little presence outside Baghdad.

During the run-up to the invasion of Iraq, Zinni became increasingly concerned about the quality of the planning, especially the posthostilities phase.

Queries to old contacts still at CENTCOM confirmed that OPLAN DESERT CROSSING had all but been forgotten. Zinni came to believe that the United States was being plunged headlong into an unnecessary war by political ideologues who had no understanding of the region. True to the promise he made to himself when he was wounded in Vietnam, Zinni became one of the first senior American figures to speak out against what he saw as "lack of planning, underestimating the task, and buying into a flawed strategy." Zinni soon found himself one of the most influential critics of the Bush administration's handling of the war in Iraq. In 2008, Zinni joined the teaching faculty at Duke University's Sanford Institute of Public Policy.

David T. Zabecki

References

Leverett, Flynt, ed. *The Road Ahead: Middle East Policy in the Bush Administration's Second Term.* Washington, DC: Brookings Institution, 2005.

Zinni, Anthony, and Tony Koltz. *Battle Ready.* New York: Putnam's, 2004.

———. *The Battle for Peace: A Frontline Vision of America's Power and Purpose.* London: Palgrave Macmillan, 2006.

Further Reading
in the Middle East Wars

Part I: Background, U.S. Defense Reform, and the Gulf War

Andrew, Christopher, and Vasili Mitrokhin. *The World Was Going Our Way: The KGB and the Battle for the Third World*. New York: Basic Books, 2005.

Atkinson, Rick. *Crusade: The Untold Story of the Persian Gulf War*. Boston: Mariner Books, 1994.

Horner, Chuck, and Tom Clancy. *Every Man a Tiger: The Gulf War Air Campaign*. New York: Berkeley, 2005.

Kissinger, Henry. *Diplomacy*. New York: Simon and Schuster, 1995.

Locher, James R., III. *Victory on the Potomac: The Goldwater–Nichols Act Unifies the Pentagon*. College Station: Texas A&M University Press, 2004.

Oren, Michael B. *Power, Faith and Fantasy: America in the Middle East, 1776 to the Present*. New York: W. W. Norton, 2007.

Powell, Colin, and Joseph E. Persico. *My American Journey*. New York: Random House, 1995.

Scales, Robert H., Jr. *Certain Victory: The U.S. Army in the Gulf War*. Washington, DC: Office of the Chief of Staff, U.S. Army, 1993.

Schubert, Frank N., and Theresa L. Kraus., eds. *Whirlwind War: The United States Army in Operations Desert Shield and Desert Storm*. Washington, DC: Chief of Military History, U.S. Army, 1995.

Schwarzkopf, Norman H. *It Doesn't Take a Hero: The Autobiography of General H. Norman Schwarzkopf*. New York: Bantam, 1992.

Swain, Richard. *Lucky War: Third Army in Desert Storm*. Fort Leavenworth, KS: U.S. Command and General Staff College Press, 1997.

Trainor, Bernard E., and Michael R. Gordon. *The Generals' War: The Inside Story of the Conflict in the Gulf*. Lebanon, IN: Back Bay Books, 1995.

Warden, John A., III. *The Air Campaign*. Rev. ed. Herndon, VA: Potomac Books, 1999.

Woodward, Bob. *The Commanders: The Pentagon and the First Gulf War, 1989–1991*. New York: Simon and Schuster, 2002.

Part II: Afghanistan, Iraq, and the War on Terrorism

Atkinson, Rick. *In the Company of Soldiers: A Chronicle of Combat*. New York: Little, Brown, 2004.

Cavaleri, David. *Easier Said Than Done: Making the Transition Between Combat Operations and Stability Operations*. Fort Leavenworth, KS: Combat Studies Institute Press, 2005.

DiMarco, Louis A. *Traditions, Changes and Challenges: Military Operations and the Middle Eastern City*. Fort Leavenworth, KS: Combat Studies Institute Press, 2004.

Franks, Tommy R. *American Soldier*. New York: HarperCollins, 2004.

Gaddis, John Lewis. *Surprise, Security and the American Experience*. Cambridge, MA: Harvard University Press, 2005.

Gebhardt, James F. *The Road to Abu Ghraib: U.S. Army Detainee Doctrine and Experience*. Fort Leavenworth, KS: Combat Studies Institute Press, 2005.

Hamza, Khidhir, and Jeff Stein. *Saddam's Bombmaker: The Daring Escape of the Man Who Built Iraq's Secret Weapon*. New York: Scribner, 2001.

Kalic, Sean N. *Combating a Modern Hydra: Al Qaeda and the Global War on Terrorism*. Fort Leavenworth, KS: Combat Studies Institute Press, 2005

Murray, Williamson, and Robert H. Scales Jr. *The Iraq War: A Military History*. Cambridge, MA: Belknap Press, 2005.

National Commission on Terrorist Attacks. *The 9/11 Commission Report: Final Report of the National Commission on Terrorist Attacks Upon the United States*. New York: W. W. Norton, 2004.

Naylor, Sean. *Not a Good Day to Die: The Untold Story of Operation Anaconda*. New York: Berkeley, 2005.

Peters, Ralph. *Never Quit the Fight*. Mechanicsburg, PA: Stackpole Books, 2006.

———. *Wars of Blood and Faith: The Conflicts That Will Shape the 21st Century*. Mechanicsburg, PA: Stackpole Books, 2007.

Ricks, Thomas E. *Fiasco: The American Military Adventure in Iraq*. New York: Penguin, 2006.

Sanchez, Ricardo S., and Donald T. Phillips. *Wiser in Battle: A Soldier's Story*. New York: Harper, 2008.

Trainor, Bernard E., and Michael R. Gordon. *Cobra II: The Inside Story of the Invasion and Occupation of Iraq*. New York: Pantheon, 2006.

Woodward, Bob. *Bush at War*. New York: Simon and Schuster, 2002.

———. *Plan of Attack*. New York: Simon and Schuster, 2004.

———. *State of Denial: Bush at War*. Vol. III. New York, Simon and Schuster, 2007.

Zinmeister, Karl. *Boots on the Ground: A Month With the 82d Airborne Division in the Battle for Iraq*. New York: St. Martin's Press, 2004.

———. *Dawn Over Baghdad: How the U.S. Military Is Using Bullets and Ballots to Remake Iraq*. New York: Encounter Books, 2004.

Index